DOCUMENTARY HISTORY OF THE FIRST FEDERAL CONGRESS OF THE UNITED STATES OF AMERICA
March 4, 1789–March 3, 1791

SPONSORED BY

THE NATIONAL HISTORICAL PUBLICATIONS AND RECORDS COMMISSION

AND

THE GEORGE WASHINGTON UNIVERSITY

VOLUME V

LEGISLATIVE

HISTORIES

FUNDING ACT [HR-63] THROUGH MILITIA BILL [HR-112]

CHARLENE BANGS BICKFORD

and

HELEN E. VEIT

Editors

The Johns Hopkins University Press

Baltimore and London

The Johns Hopkins University Press
701 West 40th Street
Baltimore, Maryland 21211
The Johns Hopkins Press Ltd., London

The paper in this book is acid-free and meets the guidelines for
permanence and durability of the Committee on Production
Guidelines for Book Longevity of the Council on Library Resources.

Library of Congress Cataloging in Publication Data
United States. Congress (1st: 1789–1791)
  Legislative histories.

  (Documentary history of the First Federal Congress of the United States of America, March 4,
1789–March 3, 1791; v. 4–6)
  Includes index.
  Contents: [1] Amendments to the Constitution through Foreign Officers Bill (HR-116)—
[2] Funding Act (HR-63) through Militia Bill (HR-112)—[3] Mitigation of Fines Bill (HR-38)
through Resolution on Unclaimed Western Lands.
    1. Bills, Legislative—United States. 2. Legislative histories—United States. I. Bickford,
Charlene Bangs. II. Veit, Helen E. III. Title. IV. Series
KF350.D63 1972 vol. 4   [KF42.2 1985]   84-15465
            328.73'09 s [348.73'1]
            328.73'09 s [347.3081]
ISBN 0-8018-3186-5 (set)

ISBN 0-8018-3163-6 (vol. 4)
ISBN 0-8018-3167-9 (vol. 5)
ISBN 0-8018-3169-5 (vol. 6)

CONTENTS

Funding Act [HR-63]

August 4, 1790

AN ACT MAKING PROVISION FOR THE DEBT OF THE UNITED STATES

WHEREAS justice and the support of public credit require, that provision should be made for fulfilling the engagements of the United States in respect to their foreign debt, and for funding their domestic debt upon equitable and satisfactory terms:

[1] BE IT ENACTED BY THE SENATE AND HOUSE OF REPRESENTATIVES OF THE UNITED STATES OF AMERICA, IN CONGRESS ASSEMBLED, that reserving out of the Monies which have arisen since the last day of December last past, and which shall hereafter arise from the duties on Goods, Wares, and Merchandize imported into the United States, and on the tonnage of ships or vessels, the yearly sum of six hundred thousand dollars, or so much thereof as may be appropriated from time to time towards the support of the government of the United States, and their common defence, the residue of the said monies or so much thereof as may be necessary, as the same shall be received in each year, next after the sum reserved as aforesaid, shall be and is hereby appropriated to the payment of the interest which shall from time to time become due on the loans heretofore made by the United States in foreign countries, and also to the payment of interest on such further loans as may be obtained for discharging the arrears of interest thereupon, and the whole or any part of the principal thereof; to continue so appropriated until the said loans, as well those already made, as those which may be made in virtue of this Act, shall be fully satisfied, pursuant to the contracts relating to the same; any law to the contrary notwithstanding. AND PROVIDED that nothing herein contained shall be construed to annul or alter any appropriation by law made prior to the passing of this Act.

[2] AND as new loans are and will be necessary for the payment of the aforesaid arrears of interest, and the instalments of the principal of the said foreign debt due and growing due, and may also be found expedient for effecting an intire alteration in the state of the same, BE IT FURTHER ENACTED, that the president of the United States be and he is hereby

authorized to cause to be borrowed on behalf of the United States a sum or sums not exceeding in the whole twelve million of Dollars, and that so much of this sum as may be necessary, to the discharge of the said Arrears and Instalments, and (if it can be effected upon terms advantageous to the United States) to the paying off the whole of the said foreign debt, be appropriated solely to those purposes, and the President is moreover further authorized to cause to be made such other contracts respecting the said debt as shall be found for the interest of the said States. PROVIDED NEVERTHELESS, that no engagement nor contract shall be entered into, which shall preclude the United States from reimbursing any sum or sums borrowed within fifteen years after the same shall have been lent or advanced.

[3] AND WHEREAS it is desirable to adapt the nature of the provision to be made for the domestic debt to the present circumstances of the United States as far as it shall be found practicable, consistently with good faith, and the rights of the creditors; which can only be done by a voluntary loan on their part: BE IT THEREFORE FURTHER ENACTED, that a loan to the full amount of the said domestic debt be, and the same is hereby proposed, and that books for receiving subscriptions to the said loan be opened at the Treasury of the United States, and by a Commissioner to be appointed in each of the said States, on the first day of October next, to continue open until the last day of September following inclusively, and that the sums which shall be subscribed thereto be payable in Certificates issued for the said debt according to their Specie value and computing the interest upon such as bear interest to the last day of December next inclusively, which said Certificates shall be of these several descriptions, TO WIT; Those issued by the Register of the Treasury: Those issued by the Commissioners of Loans in the several States including Certificates given pursuant to the Act of Congress of the second of January one thousand seven hundred and seventy nine, for bills of Credit of the several emissions of the twentieth of May one thousand seven hundred and seventy seven, and the eleventh of April one thousand seven hundred and seventy eight: Those issued by the Commissioners for the adjustment of the Accounts of the Quarter-Master, Commissary, Hospital, Clothing and Marine departments: Those issued by the Commissioners for the adjustment of accounts in the respective States: Those issued by the late and present paymaster-general or Commissioner of Army Accounts: Those issued for the payment of interest, commonly called indents of interest: And in the bills of Credit issued by the authority of the United States in Congress assembled, at the rate of one hundred dollars in the said Bills for one dollar in specie.

[4] AND BE IT FURTHER ENACTED, that for the whole or any part of any sum subscribed to the said loan, by any person or persons, or body politic which shall be paid in the principal of the said domestic debt, the subscriber or subscribers shall be entitled to a Certificate purporting that the United

States owe to the holder or holders thereof, his, her or their assigns, a sum to be expressed therein equal to two thirds of the sum so paid, bearing an interest of six per Centum per annum, payable quarter yearly, and subject to redemption by payments not exceeding in one year on account both of principal and interest the proportion of eight dollars upon a hundred of the sum mentioned in such Certificate; And to another Certificate purporting that the United States owe to the holder or holders thereof, his, her or their assigns, a sum to be expressed therein, equal to the proportion of thirty three dollars and one third of a dollar upon a hundred of the sum so paid, which after the year one thousand eight hundred shall bear an interest of six per centum per annum payable quarter yearly, and subject to redemption by payments not exceeding in one year, on account both of principal and interest, the proportion of eight dollars upon a hundred of the sum mentioned in such Certificate: PROVIDED, that it shall not be understood that the United States shall be bound or obliged to redeem in the proportion aforesaid, but it shall be understood only that they have a right so to do.

[5] AND BE IT FURTHER ENACTED, that for the whole or any part of any sum subscribed to the said loan by any person or persons, or body politic which shall be paid in the interest of the said domestic debt, computed to the said last day of december next, or in the said certificates issued in payment of interest, commonly called indents of Interest, the subscriber or subscribers shall be entitled to a Certificate, purporting that the United States owe to the holder or holders thereof, his, her or their assigns a sum to be specified therein, equal to that by him, her or them so paid, bearing an interest of three per centum per annum, payable quarter yearly, and subject to redemption by payment of the sum specified therein, whenever provision shall be made by law for that purpose.

[6] AND BE IT FURTHER ENACTED, that a Commissioner be appointed for each State to reside therein, whose duty it shall be, to superintend the subscriptions to the said Loan, to open books for the same, to receive the Certificates which shall be presented in payment thereof, to liquidate the specie-value of such of them as shall not have been before liquidated, to issue the Certificates above-mentioned in lieu thereof according to the terms of each subscription; to enter in books to be by him kept for that purpose credits to the respective subscribers to the said loan for the sums to which they shall be respectively entitled, to transfer the said Credits upon the said books from time to time, as shall be requisite, to pay the interest thereupon as the same shall become due, and generally to observe and perform such directions and regulations, as shall be prescribed to him by the Secretary of the Treasury, touching the execution of his Office.

[7] AND BE IT FURTHER ENACTED, that the Stock, which shall be created pursuant to this Act, shall be transferable only on the books of the

Treasury, or of the said Commissioners respectively, upon which the credit for the same shall exist at the time of transfer, by the proprietor or proprietors of such stock, his, her or their attorney: But it shall be lawful for the Secretary of the Treasury by special warrant under his hand and the seal of the Treasury, countersigned by the Comptroller, and registered by the register, at the request of the respective proprietors, to authorize the transfer of such Stock from the books of one Commissioner to those of another Commissioner, or to those of the Treasury, and from those of the Treasury to those of a Commissioner.

[8] AND BE IT FURTHER ENACTED, that the interest upon the said Stock, as the same shall become due, shall be payable quarter-yearly, that is to say; one fourth part thereof on the last day of March; one other fourth part thereof on the last day of June; one other fourth part thereof on the last day of September, and the remaining fourth part thereof on the last day of December in each year, beginning on the last day of March next ensuing, and payment shall be made wheresoever the credit for the said Stock shall exist at the time such interest shall become due, that is to say; at the Treasury, if the credit for the same shall then exist on the books of the Treasury, or at the office of the Commissioner upon whose books such Credit shall then exist. But if the interest for one quarter shall not be demanded before the expiration of a third quarter, the same shall be afterwards demandable only at the Treasury.

[9] AND as it may happen that some of the Creditors of the United States may not think fit to become subscribers to the said Loan, BE IT FURTHER ENACTED, that nothing in this Act contained shall be construed in any wise to alter, abridge, or impair the rights of those Creditors of the United States who shall not subscribe to the said Loan, or the Contracts upon which their respective claims are founded, but the said Contracts and Rights shall remain in full force and virtue.

[10] AND that such Creditors may not be excluded from a participation in the benefit hereby intended to the Creditors of the United States in general, while the said proposed loan shall be depending, and until it shall appear from the event thereof, what farther or other arrangements may be necessary respecting the said domestic debt; BE IT THEREFORE FURTHER ENACTED, that such of the Creditors of the United States as may not subscribe to the said Loan, shall nevertheless receive, during the year one thousand seven hundred and ninety one, a rate per centum on the respective amounts of their respective demands, including interest to the last day of December next, equal to the interest payable to subscribing Creditors, to be paid at the same times, at the same places, and by the same persons, as is herein before directed concerning the interest on the Stock which may be created in virtue of the said proposed loan. But as some of the Certificates now in circulation have not heretofore been liquidated to Specie-value, as most of them are

greatly subject to counterfeit, and counterfeits have actually taken place in numerous instances, and as embarrassment and imposition might, for these reasons, attend the payment of interest on those Certificates in their present form, it shall therefore be necessary to entitle the said Creditors to the benefit of the said payment, that those of them, who do not possess Certificates issued by the Register of the Treasury for the registered debt, should produce, previous to the first day of June next, their respective Certificates, either at the Treasury of the United States, or to some one of the Commissioners to be appointed as aforesaid, to the end that the same may be cancelled, and other Certificates issued in lieu thereof, which new Certificates shall specify the specie-amount of those, in exchange for which they are given, and shall be otherwise of the like tenor with those heretofore issued by the said Register of the Treasury for the said registered debt, and shall be transferable on the like principles with those directed to be issued on account of the subscriptions to the loan hereby proposed.

[11] AND BE IT FURTHER ENACTED, that the Commissioners, who shall be appointed pursuant to this Act, shall respectively be entitled to the following yearly salaries, that is to say; The Commissioner for the State of New-Hampshire six hundred and fifty dollars The Commissioner for the State of Massachusetts fifteen hundred dollars: The Commissioner for the State of Rhode-Island and Providence-Plantations six hundred dollars; The Commissioner for the State of Connecticut one thousand dollars; The Commissioner for the State of New York fifteen hundred dollars; The Commissioner for the State of New-Jersey seven hundred dollars; The Commissioner for the State of Pennsylvania fifteen hundred dollars; The Commissioner for the State of Delaware six hundred dollars; The Commissioner for the State of Maryland one thousand dollars; The Commissioner for the State of Virginia fifteen hundred dollars; The Commissioner for the State of North Carolina one thousand dollars; The Commissioner for the State of South Carolina one thousand dollars; The Commissioner for the State of Georgia seven hundred dollars. Which salaries shall be in full compensation for all services and expenses.

[12] AND BE IT FURTHER ENACTED, that the said Commissioners, before they enter upon the execution of their several offices, shall respectively take an oath or affirmation for the diligent and faithful execution of their trust, and shall also become bound with one or more sureties to the satisfaction of the Secretary of the Treasury, in a penalty not less five thousand, nor more than ten thousand dollars, with condition for their good behavior in their said offices respectively.

[13] AND WHEREAS a provision for the debts of the respective States by the United States would be greatly conducive to an orderly, oeconomical and effectual arrangement of the public finances BE IT THEREFORE FURTHER ENACTED, that a Loan be proposed to the amount of twenty one million and

five hundred thousand dollars, and that subscriptions to the said Loan be received at the same times and places, and by the same persons, as in respect to the loan herein before proposed concerning the domestic debt of the United States. And that the sums which shall be subscribed to the said Loan shall be payable in the principal and interest of the Certificates or Notes, which, prior to the first day of January last, were issued by the respective States, as acknowledgments or evidences of debts by them respectively owing, except Certificates issued by the Commissioners of Army-Accounts in the State of North-Carolina, in the year one thousand seven hundred and eighty six; PROVIDED, that no greater sum shall be received in the Certificates of any State, than as follows, that is to say; In those of New Hampshire, three hundred thousand dollars; In those of Massachusetts, Four million dollars; In those of Rhode-Island and Providence-Plantations two hundred thousand dollars; In those of Connecticut one million six hundred thousand dollars; In those of New-York one million two hundred thousand dollars; In those of New-Jersey, eight hundred thousand dollars; In those of Pennsylvania two million two hundred thousand dollars; In those of Delaware two hundred thousand dollars; In those of Maryland eight hundred thousand Dollars; In those of Virginia three million five hundred thousand dollars; In those of North-Carolina two million four hundred thousand dollars; In those of South Carolina four million dollars; In those of Georgia three hundred thousand dollars. AND PROVIDED, that no such Certificate shall be received, which, from the tenor thereof, or from any public record, act or document, shall appear, or can be ascertained, to have been issued for any purpose other than compensations and expenditures for services or supplies towards the prosecution of the late war, and the defence of the United States, or of some part thereof, during the same. PROVIDED ALSO, AND BE IT FURTHER ENACTED, that if the total amount of the sums which shall be subscribed to the said Loan in the debt of any State, within the time limited for receiving subscriptions thereto, shall exceed the sum by this Act allowed to be subscribed within such State, the Certificates and Credits, granted to the respective subscribers, shall bear such proportion to the sums by them respectively subscribed, as the total amount of the said sums shall bear to the whole sum so allowed to be subscribed in the debt of such State within the same. And every subscriber to the said Loan shall, at the time of subscribing, deposit with the Commissioner the Certificates or Notes to be loaned by him.

[14] AND BE IT FURTHER ENACTED, that for two thirds of any sum subscribed to the said Loan by any person or persons or body politic, which shall be paid in the principal and interest of the Certificates or notes issued as aforesaid by the respective States, the Subscriber or Subscribers shall be entitled to a Certificate, purporting that the United States owe to the holder or holders thereof, or his, her or their assigns, a sum to be expressed therein,

equal to two thirds of the aforesaid two thirds, bearing an interest of six per Centum per annum, payable quarter-yearly, and subject to redemption by payments not exceeding in one year, on account both of principal and interest, the proportion of eight dollars upon a hundred of the sum mentioned in such Certificate; and to another Certificate, purporting that the United States owe to the holder or holders thereof, his, her or their assigns, a sum to be expressed therein, equal to the proportion of thirty three dollars and one third of a dollar upon a hundred of the said two thirds of such sum so subscribed, which, after the year one thousand eight hundred, shall bear an interest of six per centum per annum, payable quarter-yearly, and subject to redemption by payments not exceeding in one year, on account both of principal and interest, the proportion of eight dollars upon a hundred of the sum mentioned in such Certificate, and that for the remaining third of any sum so subscribed, the subscriber or subscribers shall be entitled to a Certificate, purporting that the United States owe to the holder or holders thereof, his, her or their assigns, a sum to be expressed therein, equal to the said remaining third, bearing an interest of three per cent per annum, payable quarter-yearly, and subject to redemption by payment of the sum specified therein, whenever provision shall be made by law for that purpose.

[15] AND BE IT FURTHER ENACTED, that the interest upon the Certificates, which shall be received in payment of the sums subscribed towards the said Loan, shall be computed to the last day of the year one thousand seven hundred and ninety one inclusively; and the interest upon the Stock, which shall be created by virtue of the said Loan, shall commence or begin to accrue on the first day of the year one thousand seven hundred and ninety two, and shall be payable quarter-yearly, at the same time, and in like manner as the interest on the Stock to be created by virtue of the Loan above-proposed in the domestic debt of the United States.

[16] AND BE IT FURTHER ENACTED, that if the whole sum allowed to be subscribed in the debt or certificates of any State, as aforesaid, shall not be subscribed within the time for that purpose limited, such State shall be entitled to receive, and shall receive from the United States, an interest per centum per annum, upon so much of the said sum as shall not have been so subscribed, equal to that which would have accrued on the deficiency, had the same been subscribed, in trust for the non-subscribing Creditors of such State, who are holders of Certificates or Notes issued on account of services or supplies towards the prosecution of the late War, and the defence of the United States, or of some part thereof, to be paid in like manner as the interest on the stock which may be created by virtue of the said Loan, and to continue until there shall be a settlement of accounts between the United States and the individual States, and in case a balance shall then appear in favor of such State, until provision shall be made for the said balance.

[17] BUT as certain States have respectively issued their own Certificates in exchange for those of the United States, whereby it might happen that interest might be twice payable on the same sums; BE IT FURTHER EN-ACTED, that the payment of interest, whether to States or to individuals, in respect to the debt of any State, by which such exchange shall have been made, shall be suspended until it shall appear to the satisfaction of the Secretary of the Treasury, that Certificates, issued for that purpose by such State, have been re-exchanged or redeemed, or until those, which shall not have been re-exchanged or redeemed, shall be surrendered to the United States.

[18] AND BE IT FURTHER ENACTED, that so much of the debt of each State, as shall be subscribed to the said Loan, and the monies, (if any) that shall be advanced to the same, pursuant to this Act, shall be a charge against such State, in account with the United States.

[19] AND BE IT FURTHER ENACTED, that the monies arising under the Revenue-laws, which have been, or during the present Session of Congress may be passed or so much thereof as may be necessary, shall be, and are hereby pledged and appropriated for the payment of the interest on the stock which shall be created by the Loans aforesaid, pursuant to the provisions of this Act, first paying that which shall arise on the Stock created by virtue of the said first mentioned Loan, to continue so pledged and appropriated, until the final redemption of the said Stock, any Law to the contrary notwithstanding, subject nevertheless to such reservations and priorities, as may be requisite to satisfy the appropriations heretofore made, and which during the present Session of Congress may be made by law, including the sums herein before reserved and appropriated; and to the end that the said monies may be inviolably applied in conformity to this Act, and may never be diverted to any other purpose, an account shall be kept of the receipts and disposition thereof, separate and distinct from the product of any other duties, imposts, excises and taxes whatsoever, except such as may be hereafter laid to make good any deficiency, which may be found in the product thereof towards satisfying the interest aforesaid.

[20] AND BE IT FURTHER ENACTED, that the faith of the United States be, and the same is hereby pledged to provide and appropriate hereafter such additional and permanent funds, as may be requisite towards supplying any such deficiency, and making full provision for the payment of the interest which shall accrue on the Stock to be created by virtue of the loans aforesaid, in conformity to the terms thereof respectively, and according to the tenor of the Certificates to be granted for the same pursuant to this Act.

[21] AND BE IT FURTHER ENACTED, that the proceeds of the sales which shall be made of Lands in the Western Territory, now belonging, or that may hereafter belong to the United States, shall be, and are hereby

appropriated towards sinking or discharging the debts, for the payment whereof the United States now are, or by virtue of this Act may be holden, and shall be applied solely to that use, until the said debts shall be fully satisfied.

FREDERICK AUGUSTUS MUHLENBERG
Speaker of the House of Representatives
JOHN ADAMS
Vice President of the United States and
President of the Senate

Approved August
the fourth
1790

GO. WASHINGTON
President of the United States

I certify that this Act did originate
in the House of Representatives.
JOHN BECKLEY—Clerk

Enrolled Acts, RG 11, DNA.

Calendar

Date	House	Senate
1789		
Aug. 28	*Memorial of the public creditors of Pennsylvania* presented by Fitzsimons[1] and read.	
Aug. 31		Petition of the public creditors of Pennsylvania presented and read.
Sept. 2	Committed to Madison, Vining, and Boudinot.	
Sept. 10	Madison presented *committee report*, which was read.	
Sept. 21	On a motion by Vining, committee report considered and agreed to; upon a motion by Gerry, *order* agreed to.[2]	

[1] *GUS,* Aug. 29.
[2] *NYDA,* Sept. 22.

Date	House	Senate
1790		

Jan. 9   Letter received from the secretary of the treasury, stating that he was ready to submit report; motion to receive report on Jan. 14 agreed to, after agreement to a motion by Gerry that report be presented in writing rather than in person.[3]

Jan. 14   *Report of the secretary of the treasury on public credit* received; on a motion by Boudinot, 300 copies ordered printed; motion by Smith (S.C.) that the report be considered in the COWH on Feb. 2; substitute motion for Jan. 28 agreed to.[4]

Jan. 28   Postponement of report debated in COWH; motion by Ames for Feb. 8; substitute motion by Seney for Mar. 1 divided and postponement agreed to but date disagreed to by a vote of 38–14; motion by Lee for Feb. 15 ruled out of order; Ames motion agreed to.[5]

Feb. 8   Debated in COWH; motion by Livermore to debate by paragraphs; *resolutions* proposed by *Smith* (S.C.) and tabled; Boudinot read the *resolves of Congress of May and September 1779; resolutions*

---

[3] *GUS*, Jan. 13; *CR*, Jan. 9.
[4] *NYDG*, Jan. 15.
[5] *NYDA*, Jan. 29; *CR*, Jan. 28.

Date	House	Senate
1790		
	proposed by *Fitzsimons* and tabled; on motion of Page, report read.[6]	
Feb. 9	Report debated in COWH on a motion by Sherman; Smith (S.C.) resolutions withdrawn in favor of Fitzsimons', which were debated; first resolution agreed to unanimously after *amendment* by *Stone* was not seconded; motion by Jackson that the COWH should rise disagreed to; *Scott amendment* to second resolution debated.[7]	
Feb. 10	Second resolution debated in COWH; Boudinot read *resolutions of Congress of 1783 and 1784;* Scott amendment disagreed to; *amendment* proposed by *Burke.*[8]	
Feb. 11	Second resolution debated in COWH; Burke amendment withdrawn; *Livermore amendment* disagreed to; Madison proposed *substitute resolution,* seconded by Jackson, calling for discrimination between original and present holders of the debt.[9]	
Feb. 15–16	Madison substitute debated in COWH.[10]	
Feb. 17	Madison substitute debated;	

[6] *NYDG,* Feb. 9.
[7] Lloyd, Feb. 9; *GUS,* Feb. 10; *CR,* Feb. 9.
[8] *CR,* Feb. 10.
[9] *GUS,* Feb. 13, 17; *NYDG,* Feb. 19; *CR,* Feb. 11.
[10] *NYDG,* Feb. 16, 17.

Date	*House*	*Senate*
1790		

Boudinot read part of the *1783 Address to the States from Congress.* [11]

Feb. 18–19 Madison substitute debated. [12]

Feb. 22 Resolutions debated in COWH; Madison substitute disagreed to by a vote of 36–13; *White amendment* disagreed to; second resolution agreed to; third resolution debated and agreed to after *Lee motion* and *Gerry amendment* were disagreed to; fourth resolution read. [13]

Feb. 23 Fourth resolution, which called for the assumption of the state debts by the federal government, debated. [14]

Feb. 24 Assumption of state debts debated; *amendment* proposed by *Madison.* [15]

Feb. 25 Assumption of state debts debated; Madison amendment debated; *White amendment,* seconded by Livermore, to Madison amendment debated. [16]

Feb. 26 Assumption of state debts debated; White amendment debated and disagreed to, 32–15; Madison amendment

[11] *CR,* Feb. 17.
[12] *NYDG,* Feb. 19, 25.
[13] Lloyd, Feb. 22; *NYDG,* Feb. 27, Mar. 1; *CR,* Feb. 22.
[14] *NYDA, NYDG,* Feb. 24.
[15] *GUS,* Feb. 27.
[16] *GUS,* Feb. 27, Mar. 13, 17.

Date	House	Senate
1790		

debated and *proviso* proposed by *Madison*.[17]

Mar. 1   *Petition of Richard Wells and Josiah Hart* presented by Scott;[18] assumption of state debts debated; *Madison* withdrew his proviso of Feb. 26; *Ames* laid several *resolutions* on the table, to be taken up after those of Fitzsimons; Madison amendment of Feb. 24 agreed to; *substitute resolution* proposed by *Madison*.[19]

Mar. 2   *Resolution* moved by White, seconded by Carroll, debated and agreed to by a vote of 25–25, decided by the speaker after a motion by Laurance to table was disagreed to; *order* moved by Stone and agreed to; Madison resolution of Mar. 1 debated in COWH and disagreed to, 28–22, after *Smith (S.C.) motion to amend* was agreed to.[20]

Mar. 3   Motion by Carroll to discharge the COWH from considering that part of the secretary's report relating to the assumption of state debts debated and disagreed to 28–20; motion by

---

[17] *GUS*, Feb. 27; *CR*, Feb. 26. The *CR* reports the vote on White's amendment as 32–18.

[18] *GUS*, Mar. 3.

[19] *NYDA*, Mar. 2, 3; *NYDG*, Mar. 4; *CR*, Mar. 1.

[20] *GUS*, Mar. 3; *CR*, Mar. 2.

Date	House	Senate
1790		
	Madison to discharge COWH until secretary reported apparently agreed to.[21]	
Mar. 4	*Report of the secretary of the treasury,* ordered on Mar. 2, received.	
Mar. 5	Scott motion to refer petition of Wells and Hart to COWH disagreed to; motion to refer to committee agreed to and Livermore, Goodhue, Sherman, Silvester, Schureman, Scott, Seney, Brown, Burke, and Jackson appointed.[22]	
Mar. 8	Assumption of state debts debated.[23]	
Mar. 9	Fourth resolution as amended debated and agreed to by a vote of 31–26; fifth resolution agreed to; sixth resolution debated; *Boudinot substitute,* seconded by Hartley, to first alternative in resolution, debated; Tucker substitute ruled out of order; *Tucker amendment* to Boudinot substitute proposed.[24]	
Mar. 10	Boudinot substitute, including Tucker amendment, disagreed to; first alternative agreed to; second alternative debated.[25]	

[21] *NYDG,* Mar. 5; *GUS,* Mar. 6; *CR,* Mar. 3.
[22] *GUS,* Mar. 6.
[23] *NYDA,* Mar. 9.
[24] *NYDA,* Mar. 11; *NYDG,* Mar. 12.
[25] *NYDG,* Mar. 11, 13; *GUS,* Mar. 13.

Date	House	Senate
1790		

Mar. 11
Second alternative disagreed to, 32–23 or 24; *Jackson amendment* to third alternative debated.[26]

Mar. 12
Lee motion to strike out third alternative disagreed to; Jackson amendment of Mar. 11 disagreed to; *Fitzsimons* and another *amendment* to third alternative agreed to; fourth alternative debated and struck out, 23–21, on a motion by Stone; fifth alternative debated and disagreed to, 26–21.[27]

Mar. 13
Motion by Fitzsimons in COWH, for the appointment of a committee to consult with the secretary of the treasury concerning his report, disagreed to; *Gerry motion* seconded by Bland, debated and tabled after a motion by Fitzsimons that his resolutions should be disposed of before substituting others; seventh resolution debated; motion, by Vining, that a committee be appointed to consult with the secretary and that the COWH rise, disagreed to; seventh resolution agreed to; eighth resolution debated; Sherman amendment, seconded by Tucker, disagreed

---

[26] *NYDG*, Mar. 12, 13.
[27] *NYDA*, Mar. 13, 15; *GUS*, Mar. 13.

Date	House	Senate
1790		

to, 24 or 23–17; eighth resolution agreed to by about 23–17; Gerry motion taken off the table, debated and withdrawn; House debate on COWH resolutions set for Mar. 15.[28]

Mar. 23   Livermore presented *committee report* on petition of Wells and Hart.

Mar. 29   *Resolutions* reported by COWH; Williamson motion to postpone consideration of resolutions disagreed to, 27–24;[29] first, second, and third resolutions agreed to; motion by Carroll to postpone fourth resolution until secretary's plan for the ways and means was adopted; motion to recommit resolution to COWH agreed to, 29–27.[30]

Mar. 30   Motion by Laurance for debate in COWH on fourth resolution; Seney amendment, to recommit those portions of the remaining resolutions which related to assumption, disagreed to; motion by Gerry, to recommit remaining resolutions to COWH, agreed to, with 31 votes in favor; fourth resolution debated in COWH.[31]

---

[28] *NYDG*, Mar. 15; *GUS*, Apr. 3.
[29] *GUS*, Mar. 31. The *NYDG*, Mar. 30, reported the vote as 26 or 25–24.
[30] *NYDG*, Mar. 30; *GUS*, Mar. 31.
[31] *NYDG*, *GUS*, Mar. 31.

Date	House	Senate
1790		
Mar. 30– Apr. 1	Fourth resolution debated in COWH.[32]	
Apr. 2–9	Postponed as order of the day.	
Apr. 10	Laurance motion to go into COWH withdrawn.[33]	
Apr. 12	On a motion by Laurance, fourth resolution debated in COWH; Sherman read the *resolutions of Congress of November 1777 and June 1784;* several *motions* disagreed to or withdrawn; fourth resolution divided and first part disagreed to, 31–29; Gerry motion, to refer that part of the secretary's report dealing with assumption to a committee to consist of one member from each state, tabled by House.[34]	
Apr. 13	Motion, by Fitzsimons, to go into COWH disagreed to.[35]	
Apr. 14	Postponed as order of the day.	
Apr. 15	Gale motion to go into COWH agreed to by a recorded vote of 33–23; *Seney motion* on fifth resolution debated.[36]	
Apr. 16	Motion in the House, by	

---

[32] *NYDG,* Apr. 2, 3.
[33] *NYDA, NYDG,* Apr. 12.
[34] Lloyd, Apr. 12; *NYDA, NYDG,* Apr. 13.
[35] *NYDG,* Apr. 14.
[36] Lloyd, Apr. 15; *NYDG,* Apr. 16.

Date	House	Senate
1790		

Fitzsimons, to appoint a committee to report a plan for assumption and settlement of accounts between the United States and the States; Seney motion of Apr. 15 agreed to in COWH; sixth resolution debated; *Boudinot motion to amend* disagreed to.[37]

Apr. 19   Postponed as order of the day.

Apr. 20   Motion by Williamson, seconded by Wadsworth, for a committee to bring in a bill "for the purpose of expediting and settling the accounts of the individual states," agreed to; committee that presented Settlement of Accounts Bill [HR-69] appointed; motion to postpone consideration of sixth resolution in favor of a motion for assumption, disagreed to by COWH; *motion by Gerry* disagreed to; sixth resolution, through the first alternative, agreed to.[38]

Apr. 21   Sixth resolution debated in COWH; some *amendments* agreed to and other *amendments* disagreed to; sixth resolution agreed to; *Sherman* proposed *substitute* for seventh resolution.[39]

---

[37] Lloyd, Apr. 16; *GUS*, Apr. 17; *NYDG*, Apr. 19.
[38] Lloyd, Apr. 20; *NYDG*, Apr. 21, 22.
[39] *NYDG*, Apr. 22, 26.

Date	House	Senate
1790		
Apr. 22	Sherman substitute for seventh resolution debated in COWH.[40]	
Apr. 23	*Orders* agreed to by House, first one by a vote of 28–26.[41]	
Apr. 26	*Fitzsimons motion* agreed to by House by a recorded vote of 32–18; on a motion by Gerry, COWH completed debate and reported *resolutions; amendments* disagreed to by House; resolutions agreed to; motion by Stone for a committee to bring in a bill on these resolutions and on the three adopted on March 29, agreed to; Stone, White, Sherman, Clymer, and Gilman appointed to committee; motion by Gerry, for a committee consisting of one member from each state, divided equally between members favoring and opposing assumption, to report a plan of accommodation on assumption, tabled; motion by Gerry for debate in COWH on remaining resolutions on the report on the public credit.[42]	
Apr. 27	COWH agreed to additional resolutions which led to the Duties on Wines Bill	

[40] Lloyd, Apr. 22.
[41] *GUS,* Apr. 24.
[42] Lloyd, Apr. 26; *NYDG,* Apr. 27, 28, May 3.

Date	House	Senate
1790		

	[HR-64] and the Duties on Distilled Spirits Bill [HR-62].	
Apr. 30	Letter and *report of the commissioners for settling accounts* received and read.	
May 6	Stone presented *a bill making provision for the debt of the United States,* which was read twice and committed to the COWH on May 12; 100 copies ordered printed.[43]	
May 11	*Reports of the secretaries of war and treasury,* ordered on Apr. 23, received and read.	
May 17	Motion by Vining to debate bill postponed.[44]	
May 18	Motion by Stone to debate bill disagreed to.[45]	
May 19	On a motion by Vining, sections 1–3 debated and *amended* in COWH.[46]	
May 20	Committee report on the petition of Wells and Hart referred to COWH on a motion by Sedgwick; report read in COWH and section 3 of bill debated and *amended.*[47]	
May 21	Sections 3–8 debated and *amended* in COWH.[48]	

[43] *GUS,* May 8.
[44] *NYDG,* May 19.
[45] Ibid.
[46] *NYDG,* May 20.
[47] *GUS,* May 22.
[48] *NYDG, GUS,* May 22.

Date	House	Senate
1790		

May 24 Sections 9–12 debated and *amended* in COWH; *Gerry amendment* debated; motion by Lee to report the bill declared out of order; motion by Parker for COWH to rise agreed to; motion by Gale to discharge COWH withdrawn.[49]

May 25 Gerry amendment debated in COWH; motion by Sedgwick for COWH to rise; motion by Gale, seconded by Page, to amend Sedgwick motion to report "that the committee have gone through the discussion of the 12 first sections of the bill, and that they be discharged from any further consideration thereof," debated after being declared in order by Seney, chairman of COWH, and by a vote with 32 in favor; motion by Smith (S.C.), to strike out the part of the motion asking for discharge of COWH, declared out of order; Gale motion agreed to, 30–23; House adjourned before COWH could be discharged.[50]

May 26 Motion by Gale, to take up bill in House, agreed to; COWH discharged; COWH amendments agreed to and

[49] *NYDA,* May 25; *GUS,* May 26.
[50] *NYDG, GUS,* May 26.

Date	House	Senate
1790		
	further *amendments* made; motion by Seney, to add section 13, agreed to unanimously.[51]	
May 27	Bill further *amended* and third reading ordered on May 31; Boudinot resolutions for assumption tabled.[52]	
May 28	Motion by Boudinot to debate resolutions disagreed to, 25–19; motion by Gerry to refer Boudinot resolutions to COWH on May 31 superseded by a motion by Parker for the first Monday in December, which was disagreed to; motion by Livermore for June 14 disagreed to, 29–24; motion by Lee for June 7 agreed to.[53]	
May 31	Bill postponed as order of the day.	
June 1	Motion by Fitzsimons to debate bill disagreed to.[54]	
June 2	Read; *blanks filled;* agreed to as *An act making provision for the debt of the United States.*	Received and read.
June 3		Read and postponed.
June 7		Debated.
June 9		Section 4 debated; motion by Morris to strike out first two alternatives.[55]

[51] *NYDG,* May 27.
[52] *GUS,* May 29. Boudinot's resolutions were essentially the same as those moved by Gerry on May 24.
[53] *NYDG, GUS,* May 29. The COWH never considered these resolutions.
[54] *NYDG,* June 2.
[55] Maclay, June 9.

Date	House	Senate
1790		
June 10		Debated; motion by Ellsworth for assumption of state debts.[56]
June 11		Debated; Ellsworth motion disagreed to;[57] bill committed to Lee, Ellsworth, Maclay, King, and Paterson; Ellsworth gave notice of intention to bring a bill making "provision for the debts of the respective States, by the United States."
June 14		Instead of a bill, Ellsworth proposed a *resolution,* which was tabled; motion to debate it next day disagreed to.
June 15		Lee presented *committee report* on the bill, which was debated[58] and postponed.
June 16–18		Report debated and postponed.
June 21		Motion by King, seconded by Schuyler, to postpone debate, disagreed to;[59] report debated and one paragraph agreed to by a recorded vote of 13–10.
June 22		Report debated, *amended,* and agreed to.
June 23		Third reading postponed.
July 2		On a motion by Ellsworth,[60] motion of June

[56] Maclay, June 10, states that this motion was the same as that proposed by Gerry in the House on May 24 and printed.

[57] Maclay, June 11. According to this source, only nine senators voted for the motion.

[58] Maclay, June 15.

[59] Maclay, June 21, says King moved postponement because the House had disagreed to the "bill for the ways and means," the Duties on Distilled Spirits Bill [HR-62].

[60] Maclay, July 2.

Date	House	Senate
1790		
		14 committed to Carroll, Lee, Strong, Ellsworth, and Paterson.
July 12		Carroll presented *committee report* consisting of resolutions recommending the assumption of state debts, which was read and ordered printed; motion to debate bill withdrawn.[61]
July 13		Preamble of report postponed; first resolution debated and *amendments* disagreed to; motion to postpone Schuyler amendment in order "to take the opinion of the Senate, Whether the debts of the individual States shall be assumed by the United States?" disagreed to; motion to postpone report and debate bill disagreed to; motion, to apply to the report the Senate rule by which bills on their second reading are considered as if in a committee of the whole, agreed to.
July 14		Report debated; *amendments* disagreed to; report agreed to; motion to refer bill and report to a select committee disagreed to by a recorded vote of 16–10; report ordered read again.
July 15		Report read and, on a mo-

---

[61] Maclay, July 12.

Date	House	Senate
1790		
		tion by Ellsworth,[62] referred with the bill to Butler, Morris, Read, Ellsworth, King, Lee, and Strong.
July 16		Butler presented *committee report;* motion by Maclay for a one-day postponement disagreed to;[63] report agreed to and recommitted with the report of July 12 and the bill.
July 17		Butler presented *amended bill* as a report, which was ordered printed.
July 19		Report read and agreed to as an amended bill; bill read and *amended.*
July 20		Debated, *amended,* and, on a motion by King,[64] postponed.
July 21		Debated and agreed to with *amendments* by a recorded
	Senate amendments received.	vote of 14–12.
July 22	Debated and *amended.*[65]	
July 23	Debated and *amended;* motion by Jackson, to disagree to the Senate's fourteenth amendment, debated.[66]	
July 24	Debated and *amended;* Jackson motion disagreed to by a recorded vote of 32–	

---

[62] Maclay, July 15.
[63] Maclay, July 16.
[64] Maclay, July 21.
[65] *NYDG,* July 23.
[66] *GUS,* July 24.

Date	*House*	*Senate*
1790		
	29;[67] *resolution* agreed to; debate postponed.	
July 26	Debated and *amended;* fourteenth amendment agreed to by a recorded vote of 34–28;[68] *resolution* agreed to.	
July 27		House resolutions on Senate amendments received and ordered printed.
July 28		Debated; House amendments agreed to, except the third, fifth, ninth, and eleventh.
July 29	Senate action debated on a motion by Laurance; motion by Jackson, to postpone assumption until next session, disagreed to; motion by Parker to postpone debate until next session ruled out of order;[69] receded from amendments disagreed to by Senate.	
Aug. 2	Signed by speaker.	Signed by vice president.
Aug. 4	Signed by president.	

[67] *NYDG,* July 26.
[68] *NYDG,* July 27; *NYDA,* July 30.
[69] *NYDG,* July 30; *NYJ,* Aug. 3.

Memorial of the Public Creditors of Pennsylvania
August 28, 1789

TO HIS EXCELLENCY THE PRESIDENT, and the honorable The Senate and House of Representatives, of the United States,
  The Memorial & Petition of the Public Creditors who are Citizens of the

Commonwealth of Pennsylvania, by their Committee duly authorized and instructed,

MOST RESPECTFULLY SHEW

THAT your Memorialists, influenced by a faithful and uniform attachment to the Happiness and Glory of their Country, behold, with peculiar satisfaction, the establishment of a Government which is expressly constituted to promote and perpetuate Union, Order, and Justice, the great sources of National Prosperity. And when they consider the Characters that are appointed to organize and administer this System, they embrace the most flattering hope that, in its execution will be found an ample performance of the auspicious Promises which are contained in its Principles. From this anticipation, indeed, your Memorialists, whose Services and Sufferings in the public Cause cannot require a particular attestation, have derived that consolation which the imbecility of the former Union, and the political Vicissitudes of their own immediate State, would not permit them to indulge.

In the hour of extreme necessity, when complicated Want enfeebled, and impending Ruin agitated, their Country, your Memorialists avow an honorable Pride in the remembrance of the Exertions by which they then essentially contributed to her Protection and Safety. At the same Time that they partook of the Toils and Dangers of active Life, and suffered in the ruinous Depreciation of the paper Currency, at least in common with their fellow Citizens, the Wealth which had been transmitted to them by their Ancestors, or accumulated by their Industry; the Fund which Prudence had hoarded to administer Comfort to old Age, and the supply which humanity had provided for the helpless Infant, or the solitary Widow, they advanced with a liberal and patriotic Hand to relieve the exigencies of the Union. The public Faith was pledged by every solemnity of Assurance; the Honor of the States was bound by every Tie of Gratitude; to compensate so memorable a sacrafice of private Interest and personal Immunity. Yet your Memorialists, calling your attention to a melancholly Retrospect, might remind you of the ineffectual, tho' virtuous efforts of the late Congress to discharge the National Engagements; might describe the apparent disregard of the States for their Confederated Sovereignty, tho' recently purchased through a long and bloody Conflict; and, in the Language of Calamity and Complaint, might deplore the disappointment, the Poverty, the Wretchedness, and the Anguish which afflicted the first and firmest Patriots of the Union; excluding them from a participation in the Triumphs of Independence, and embittering their Love of Liberty with a painful sense of the Injuries which they sustained. Such Reflections, however, your Memorialists chearfully dismiss, in the contemplation of that Compact, which, providing for the Dignity and Honor of the Union, has made the payment of the Public Debt a fundamental Principle of the Government; and, having imposed the Obligation, has also created an adequate Power to discharge it.

But your Memorialists now humbly confess, that they have waited in anxious suspence for some evidence of the disposition of Congress upon this interesting Subject. They admit the general Importance of the Arrangements which have occupied the attention of the Federal Legislature, and they particularly rejoice in the Foundations that have been laid for the Production of an efficient Revenue. These, however, are but preliminary Steps to the attainment of the principal object of the new System; and, should Congress adjourn without any more decisive Act for the restoration of Public Credit, the mere Institution of Offices, or the Regulation of Imposts, will hardly protect the American Character from the derision of its Enemies, or the Reproaches of those who have hitherto thought that the want of Power was its only Imperfection.

Your Memorialists, with the utmost deference, beg leave to represent, that public Credit is the vital Spark of modern Policy; for the History of the World demonstrates that, whatever may be the extent of Territory, the Degree of Population, or the Fertility of Soil, unless the Faith of National Engagements is placed upon a Basis inviolable and immutable, the advantages of Nature will be lost in the uncertainty of their enjoyment, and Government will afford no encouragement to Industry, or Protection to Virtue, but, while it oppresses with its power, must Corrupt by its Example. The domestic Experience of America renders it unnecessary, indeed, to explore the Annals of Antient or Cotemporary Nations in order to collect this salutary Lesson; and there is only wanting an Exercise of that Wisdom which it inculcates, to convert her Calamity into a Blessing, and make the remembrance of what has been lost the Instrument of securing what may yet be acquired. The Decay of public Credit, engendering Licentiousness and Anarchy, has once threatned the Perversion of all that was noble in her Exertions, and the Waste of all that was valuable in her Success. To Avert a similar Danger, the most unequivocal Demonstration of an Intention to restore the Faith and Purity of her Name, is naturally expected from the Guardians of the public Interest and Honor: And your Memorialists now fervently pray them to consider that Procrastination, in a Business of so delicate a Nature, may be as fatal as a defect of Power, or a want of Disposition to be Just.

In the Resources of the Union your Memorialists discover an Ample Fund, and in the Conduct of their fellow Citizens they perceive a fair and honorable Desire, to discharge the Engagements which were incurred in the common Cause. The only Task, therefore, that seems to be imposed upon the present Government, is to adopt that mode which shall be best calculated to promote the public Welfare, at the same Time that it does Justice to the Individuals who are interested. Immediately to pay off the public Debt, principal and

Interest, if not impracticable, would be greatly inconvenient, and is certainly unnecessary; for the Example of those Nations, who enjoy the highest Commercial Reputation, has evinced that a permanent Appropriation for the punctual Payment of the Interest, will enable the public Creditor to enjoy, by the facility of a Transfer, all the advantages of the Principal, without injuring the Credit of the Country, or straining her Resources.

Your Memorialists in addition to these observations, beg leave respectfully to suggest, that it has been the deliberate opinion of some of the most enlightened Statesmen, that a Certain Amount of funded Debt (and surely the Debt of the United States would not be deemed too great) is a National Benefit. The Creation of a new Species of Money by this Means, naturally increases the Circulation of Cash, and extensively promotes every kind of useful undertaking and Enterprize, in Agriculture, Commerce and Mechanics. On this Ground alone, therefore, the advantages of a funding System would be sufficient to justify its Establishment; but there are other Arguments, arising from the political situation of America, which ought to render it, in this Country particularly, an object of Favor and Attention. It has been well maintained, that after the Revolution in England, a funding System was there encouraged as a great means of attaching the great and powerful Body of Stockholders to the Government. The Policy which prevailed in that case, is infinitely more forcible when applied to the case of the United States; for, the Credit of the Union being perfectly established, every Citizen who is not originally, will be desirous of becoming, a Proprietor in the public Funds; those Individuals who may hitherto have been inimical to the Principles of the Revolution, or averse to the Adoption of the subsisting Constitution, will be irresistably invited to partake of the Benefits, and consequently to promote the Prosperity of the Confederation; each State will find an Interest in the Welfare and punctuality of the rest; the federal Government will be zealously supported as a general Guarrantee; and, in short, a Debt originating in the Patriotism that atchieved the Independence, may thus be converted into a Cement that shall strengthen & Perpetuate, the Union, of America.

Your Memorialists conceive that it would be superfluous to prosecute a Detail of the immediate or collateral Benefits which a funding System would produce, whether by stimulating domestic Industry, or attracting foreign Capitals to the aid of the Husbandman, Merchant, and Artist of America. It is enough in this respect to urge, that Justice, Humanity and Policy require the earliest Consideration of the claim which is now respectfully submitted. Nor can it be incumbent on your Memorialists to obviate the suggestions of that pernicious Policy which aims, at once, to plunder them of their only Hope, and to undermine the foundations of an infant Government, even before the Structure is compleat. Let it not be recorded in the History of the Revolution, that, while the Monarchy of Britain generously cherished and indemnified every friend to Prerogative and Usurpation, a triumphant Republic suffered the prompt and zealous supporters of the Standard of Liberty to languish in a sad and necessitous obscurity, to lament over those vouchers of Property and Services that tend, at once, to remind them of the equality which they formerly maintained among their fellow Citizens; to mark their present lowliness and Penury, and to stigmatize the wanton Ingratitude of their Country.

When, indeed, it is considered that many of the Members of your honorable Body have also been affected by the destructive Operations and Expedients of the late War; and that all are in the actual enjoyment of that Sovereignty which has been principally purchased by the personal Exertions and voluntary Aids of such as are denominated public Creditors, it would be unjust to the Feeling, Integrity, and Gratitude of those whom they now address were your Memorialists for a Moment to admit a supposition that a Solemn Appeal, thus brought before you, in the name of so numerous a Class of meritorious Citizens, could be neglected or forgotten.

By the glorious Remembrance, therefore, of the past; by the rich Prospect of the future; by the Obligations which the Representatives of the Public owe to the surviving Orphans and Widows of those who have bravely fought the Battles of the Union, or nobly supplied its wants in the times of Peril and Distress; and by the regard which is due to the Peace and Happiness of Posterity,

Your Petitioners implore your immediate Aid and Interposition, rejoicing that their humble solicitation for Justice and Humanity necessarily includes a Prayer for the revival of public Credit, and the advancement of the national Honor.

Philadelphia Augt. 21st. 1789

Petitions and Memorials: Various subjects, SR, DNA. List of signatures will be published in the petition volume.

House Committee Report
September 10, 1789

That the object of the said memorial appears to the Committee to merit the early and particular attention of Congress; but an adjournment being speedily to take place, and as the intermediate time will be fully occupied in completing the organization of the Government, the Committee are of opinion, that it is impracticable to enter upon the subject during the present session: They are also of opinion, that it may be more advantageously considered with the aid of the additional information which may be attained by the next meeting, than it could now be: Under these impressions, the Committee submit the following resolutions:

RESOLVED, that this House consider an adequate provision for the support of the public credit, as a matter of high importance to the national honor and prosperity.

RESOLVED, that the Secretary of the Treasury be directed to prepare a plan for that purpose, and to report the same to this House, at it's next meeting.

A Record of Reports of Select Committees, Vol. 1, HR, DNA.

House Order
September 21, 1789

ORDERED, That the secretary of the treasury be directed to apply to the supreme executives of the several states, for statements of their public debts; of the funds provided for the payment, in whole or in part of the principal and interest thereof; and of the amount of the loan-office certificates, or other public securities of the United States, in the state treasuries respectively; and that he report to the House such of the said documents as he may obtain, at the next session of Congress.

HJ, p. 220.

Report of the Secretary of the Treasury on the Public Credit
January 14, 1790

TREASURY DEPARTMENT, *January* 9, 1790

THE Secretary of the Treasury, in obedience to the resolution of the House of Representatives, of the twenty-first day of September last, has, during the recess of Congress, applied himself to the consideration of a proper plan for the support of the Public Credit, with all the attention which was due to the authority of the House, and to the magnitude of the object.

In the discharge of this duty, he has felt, in no small degree, the anxieties which naturally flow from a just estimate of the difficulty of the task, from a well-founded diffidence of his own qualifications for executing it with success, and from a deep and solemn conviction of the momentous nature of the truth contained in the resolution under which his investigations have been conducted, "That an *adequate* provision for the support of the Public Credit, is a matter of high importance to the honor and prosperity of the United States."

With an ardent desire that his well-meant endeavors may be conducive to the real advantage of the nation, and with the utmost deference to the superior judgment of the House, he now respectfully submits the result of his enquiries and reflections, to their indulgent construction.

In the opinion of the Secretary, the wisdom of the House, in giving their explicit sanction to the proposition which has been stated, cannot but be applauded by all, who will seriously consider, and trace through their obvious consequences, these plain and undeniable truths.

That exigencies are to be expected to occur, in the affairs of nations, in which there will be a necessity for borrowing.

That loans in times of public danger, especially from foreign war, are found an indispensable resource, even to the wealthiest of them.

And that in a country, which, like this, is possessed of little active wealth, or in other words, little monied capital, the necessity for that resource, must, in such emergencies, be proportionably urgent.

And as on the one hand, the necessity for borrowing in particular emergencies cannot be doubted, so on the other, it is equally evident, that to be able to borrow upon *good terms,* it is essential that the credit of a nation should be well established.

For when the credit of a country is in any degree questionable, it never fails to give an extravagant premium, in one shape or another, upon all the loans it has occasion to make. Nor does the evil end here; the same disadvantage must be sustained upon whatever is to be bought on terms of future payment.

From this constant necessity of *borrowing* and *buying dear,* it is easy to conceive how immensely the expences of a nation, in a course of time, will be augmented by an unsound state of the public credit.

To attempt to enumerate the complicated variety of mischiefs in the whole system of the social oeconomy, which proceed from a neglect of the maxims that uphold public credit, and justify the solicitude manifested by the House on this point, would be an improper intrusion on their time and patience.

In so strong a light nevertheless do they appear to the Secretary, that on their due observance at the present critical juncture, materially depends, in his judgment, the individual and aggregate prosperity of the citizens of the United States; their relief from the embarrassments they now experience; their character as a People; the cause of good government.

If the maintenance of public credit, then, be truly so important, the next enquiry which suggests itself is, by what means it is to be effected? The ready answer to which question is, by good faith, by a punctual performance of contracts. States, like individuals, who observe their engagements, are respected and trusted: while the reverse is the fate of those, who pursue an opposite conduct.

Every breach of the public engagements, whether from choice or necessity, is in different degrees hurtful to public credit. When such a necessity does truly exist, the evils of it are only to be palliated by a scrupulous attention, on the part of the government, to carry the violation no farther than the necessity absolutely requires, and to manifest, if the nature of the case admits of it, a sincere disposition to make reparation, whenever circumstances shall permit. But with every possible mitigation, credit must suffer, and numerous mischiefs ensue. It is therefore highly important, when an appearance of necessity seems to press upon the public councils, that they should examine well its reality, and be perfectly assured, that there is no method of escaping from it, before they yield to its suggestions. For though it cannot safely be affirmed, that occasions have never existed, or may not exist, in which violations of the public faith, in this respect, are inevitable; yet there is great reason to believe, that they exist far less frequently than precedents indicate; and are oftenest either pretended through levity, or want of firmness, or supposed through want of knowledge. Expedients might often have been devised to effect, consistently with good faith, what has been done in contravention of it. Those who are most commonly creditors of a nation, are, generally speaking, enlightened men; and there are signal examples to warrant a conclusion, that when a candid and fair appeal is made to them, they will understand their true interest too well to refuse their concurrence in such modifications of their claims, as any real necessity may demand.

While the observance of that good faith, which is the basis of public credit, is recommended by the strongest inducements of political expediency, it is enforced by considerations of still greater authority. There are arguments for it, which rest on the immutable principles of moral obligation. And in proportion as the mind is disposed to contemplate, in the order of Providence, an intimate connection between public virtue and public happiness, will be its repugnancy to a violation of those principles.

This reflection derives additional strength from the nature of the debt of the United States. It was the price of liberty. The faith of America has been repeatedly pledged for it, and with solemnities, that give peculiar force to the obligation. There is indeed reason to regret that it has not hitherto been kept; that the necessities of the war, conspiring with inexperience in the subjects of finance, produced direct infractions; and that the subsequent period has been a continued scene of negative violation, or non-compliance. But a diminution of this regret arises from the reflection, that the last seven years have exhibited an earnest and uniform effort, on the part of the government of the union, to retrieve the national credit, by doing justice to the creditors of the nation; and that the embarrassments of a defective constitution, which defeated this laudable effort, have ceased.

From this evidence of a favorable disposition, given by the former government, the institution of a new one, cloathed with powers competent to calling forth the resources of the community, has excited correspondent expectations. A general belief, accordingly, prevails, that the credit of the United States will quickly be established on the firm foundation of an effectual provision for the existing debt. The influence, which this has had at home, is witnessed by the rapid increase, that has taken place in the market value of the public securities. From January to November, they rose thirty-three and a third per cent, and from that period to this time, they have risen fifty per cent more. And the intelligence from abroad announces effects proportionably favourable to our national credit and consequence.

It cannot but merit particular attention, that among ourselves the most enlightened friends of good government are those, whose expectations are the highest.

To justify and preserve their confidence; to promote the encreasing respectability of the American name; to answer the calls of justice; to restore landed property to its due value; to furnish new resources both to agriculture and commerce; to cement more closely the union of the states; to add to their security against foreign attack; to establish public order on the basis of an upright and liberal policy. These are the great and invaluable ends to be secured, by a proper and adequate provision, at the present period, for the support of public credit.

To this provision we are invited, not only by the general considerations, which have been noticed, but by others of a more particular nature. It will procure to every class of the community some important advantages, and remove some no less important disadvantages.

The advantage to the public creditors from the increased value of that part of their property which constitutes the public debt, needs no explanation.

But there is a consequence of this, less obvious, though not less true, in which every other citizen is interested. It is a well known fact, that in countries in which the national debt is properly funded, and an object of established confidence, it answers most of the purposes of money. Transfers of stock or public debt are there equivalent to payments in specie; or in other words, stock, in the principal transactions of business, passes current as specie. The same thing would, in all probability happen here, under the like circumstances.

The benefits of this are various and obvious.

First. Trade is extended by it; because there is a larger capital to carry it on, and the merchant can at the same time, afford to trade for smaller profits; as his stock, which, when unemployed, brings him in an interest from the government, serves him also as money, when he has a call for it in his commercial operations.

Secondly. Agriculture and manufactures are also promoted by it: For the like reason, that more capital can be commanded to be employed in both; and because the merchant, whose enterprize in foreign trade, gives to them activity an extension, has greater means for enterprize.

Thirdly. The interest of money will be lowered by it; for this is always in a ratio to the quantity of money, and to the quickness of circulation. This circumstance will enable both the public and individuals to borrow on easier and cheaper terms.

And from the combination of these effects, additional aids will be furnished to labour, to industry, and to arts of every kind.

But these good effects of a public debt are only to be looked for, when, by being well funded, it has acquired an *adequate* and *stable* value. Till then, it has rather a contrary tendency. The fluctuation and insecurity incident to it in an unfunded state, render it a mere commodity, and a precarious one. As such, being only an object of occasional and particular speculation, all the money applied to it is so much diverted from the more useful channels of circulation, for which the thing itself affords no substitute: So that, in fact, one serious inconvenience of an unfunded debt is, that it contributes to the scarcity of money.

This distinction which has been little if at all attended to, is of the greatest moment. It involves a question immediately interesting to every part of the community; which is no other than this—Whether the public debt, by a provision for it on true principles, shall be rendered a *substitute* for money; or whether, by being left as it is, or by being provided for in such a manner as will wound those principles, and destroy confidence, it shall be suffered to continue, as it is, a pernicious drain of our cash from the channels of productive industry.

The effect, which the funding of the public debt, on right principles, would have upon landed property, is one of the circumstances attending such an arrangement, which has been least adverted to, though it deserves the most particular attention. The present depreciated state of that species of property is a serious calamity. The value of cultivated lands, in most of the states, has fallen since the revolution from 25 to 50 per cent. In those farthest south, the decrease is still more considerable. Indeed, if the representations, continually received from that quarter, may be credited, lands there will command no price, which may not be deemed an almost total sacrifice.

This decrease, in the value of lands, ought, in a great measure, to be attributed to the scarcity of money. Consequently whatever produces an augmentation of the monied capital of the country, must have a proportional effect in raising that value. The beneficial tendency of a funded debt, in this respect, has been manifested by the most decisive experience in Great-Britain.

The proprietors of lands would not only feel the benefit of this increase in the value of their property, and of a more prompt and better sale, when they had occasion to sell; but the necessity of selling would be, itself, greatly diminished. As the same cause would contribute to the facility of loans, there is reason to believe, that such of them as are indebted, would be able through that resource, to satisfy their more urgent creditors.

It ought not however to be expected, that the advantages, described as likely to result from funding the public debt, would be instantaneous. It might require some time to bring the value of stock to its natural level, and to attach to it that fixed confidence, which is necessary to its quality as money. Yet the late rapid rise of the public securities encourages an expectation, that the progress of stock to the desireable point, will be much more expeditious than could have been foreseen. And as in the mean time it will be increasing in value, there is room to conclude, that it will, from the outset, answer many of the purposes in contemplation. Particularly it seems to be probable, that from creditors, who are not themselves necessitous, it will early meet with a ready reception in payment of debts, at its current price.

Having now taken a concise view of the inducements to a proper provision for the public debt, the next enquiry which presents itself is, what ought to be the nature of such a provision? This requires some preliminary discussions.

It is agreed on all hands, that that part of the debt which has been contracted abroad, and is denominated the foreign debt, ought to be provided for, according to the precise terms of the contracts relating to it. The discussions, which can arise, therefore, will have reference essentially to the domestic part of it, or to that which has been contracted at home. It is to be regretted, that there is not the same unanimity of sentiment on this part, as on the other.

The Secretary has too much deference for the opinions of every part of the community, not to have observed one, which has, more than once, made its appearance in the public prints, and which is occasionally to be met with in conversation. It involves this question, whether a discrimination ought not to be made between original holders of the public securities, and present possessors, by purchase. Those who advocate a discrimination are for making a full provision for the securities of the former, at their nominal value; but contend, that the latter ought to receive no more than the cost to them, and the interest: And the idea is sometimes suggested of making good the difference to the primitive possessor.

In favor of this scheme, it is alledged, that it would be unreasonable to pay twenty shillings in the pound, to one who had not given more for it than three or four. And it is added, that it would be hard to aggravate the misfortune of the first owner, who, probably through necessity, parted with his property at so great a loss, by obliging him to contribute to the profit of the person, who had speculated on his distresses.

The Secretary, after the most mature reflection on the force of this argument, is induced to reject the doctrine it contains, as equally unjust and impolitic, as highly injurious, even to the original holders of public securities; as ruinous to public credit.

It is inconsistent with justice, because in the first place, it is a breach of contract; in violation of the rights of a fair purchaser.

The nature of the contract in its origin, is, that the public will pay the sum expressed in the security, to the first holder, or his *assignee*. The *intent*, in making the security assignable, is, that the proprietor may be able to make use of his property, by selling it for as much as it *may be worth in the market*, and that the buyer may be *safe* in the purchase.

Every buyer therefore stands exactly in the place of the seller—has the same right with him to the identical sum expressed in the security, and having acquired that right, by fair purchase, and in conformity to the original *agreement* and *intention* of the government, his claim cannot be disputed, without manifest injustice.

That he is to be considered as a fair purchaser, results from this: Whatever necessity the seller may have been under, was occasioned by the government, in not making a proper provision for its debts. The buyer has no agency in it, and therefore ought not to suffer. He is not even chargeable with having taken an undue advantage. He paid what the commodity was worth in the market, and took the risks of reimbursement upon himself. He of course gave a fair equivalent, and ought to reap the benefit of his hazard; a hazard which was far from inconsiderable, and which, perhaps, turned on little less than a revolution in government.

That the case of those, who parted with their securities from necessity, is a hard one, cannot be denied. But whatever complaint of injury, or claim of redress, they may have, respects the government solely. They have not only nothing to object to the persons who relieved their necessities, by giving them the current price of their property, but they are even under an implied condition to contribute to the reimbursement of those persons. They knew, that by the terms of the contract with themselves, the public were bound to pay to those, to whom they should convey their title, the sums stipulated to be paid to them; and, that as citizens of the United States, they were to bear their proportion of the contribution for that purpose. This, by the act of assignment, they tacitly engage to do; and if they had an option, they could not, with integrity or good faith, refuse to do it, without the consent of those to whom they sold.

But though many of the original holders sold from necessity, it does not follow, that this was the case with all of them. It may well be supposed, that some of them did it either through want of confidence in an eventual provision, or from the allurements of some profitable speculation. How shall these different classes be discriminated from each other? How shall it be ascertained, in any case, that the money, which the original holder obtained for his security, was not more beneficial to him, than if he had held it to the present time, to avail himself of the provision which shall be made? How shall it be known, whether if the purchaser had employed his money in some other way, he would not be in a better situation, than by having applied it in the purchase of securities, though he should now receive their full amount? And if neither of these things can be known, how shall it be determined whether a discrimination, independent of the breach of contract, would not do a real injury to purchasers; and if it included a compensation to the primitive proprietors, would not give them an advantage, to which they had no equitable pretension.

It may well be imagined, also, that there are not wanting instances, in which individuals, urged by a present necessity, parted with the securities received by them from the public, and shortly after replaced them with others, as an indemnity for their first loss. Shall they be deprived of the indemnity which they have endeavoured to secure by so provident an arrangement?

Questions of this sort, on a close inspection, multiply themselves without end, and demonstrate the injustice of a discrimination, even on the most subtile calculations of equity, abstracted from the obligation of contract.

The difficulties too of regulating the details of a plan for that purpose, which would have even the semblance of equity, would be found immense. It may well be doubted whether they would not be insurmountable, and replete with such absurd, as well as inequitable consequences, as to disgust even the proposers of the measure.

As a specimen of its capricious operation, it will be sufficient to notice the effect it would have upon two persons, who may be supposed two years ago to have purchased, each, securities at three shillings in the pound, and one of them to retain those bought by him, till the discrimination should take place; the other to have parted with those bought by him, within a month past, at nine shillings. The former, who had had most confidence in the government, would in this case only receive at the rate of three shillings and the interest; while the latter, who had had less confidence would receive *for what cost him the same money* at the rate of nine shillings, and his representative, *standing in his place,* would be entitled to a like rate.

The impolicy of a discrimination results from two considerations; one, that it proceeds upon a principle destructive of that *quality* of the public debt, or the stock of the nation, which is essential to its capacity for answering the purposes of money—that is the *security* of *transfer;* the other, that as well on this account, as because it includes a breach of faith, it renders property in the funds less valuable; consequently induces lenders to demand a higher premium for what they lend, and produces every other inconvenience of a bad state of public credit.

It will be perceived at first sight, that the transferable quality of stock is essential to its operation as money, and that this depends on the idea of complete security to the transferee, and a firm persuasion, that no distinction can in any circumstances be made between him and the original proprietor.

The precedent of an invasion of this fundamental principle, would of course tend to deprive the community of an advantage, with which no temporary saving could bear the least comparison.

And it will as readily be perceived, that the same cause would operate a diminution of the value of stock in the hands of the first, as well as of every other holder. The price, which any man, who should incline to purchase, would be willing to give for it, would be in a compound ratio to the immediate profit it afforded, and to the chance of the continuance of his profit. If there was supposed to be any hazard of the latter, the risk would be taken into the calculation, and either there would be no purchase at all, or it would be at a proportionably less price.

For this diminution of the value of stock, every person, who should be about to lend to the government, would demand a compensation; and would add to the actual difference, between the nominal and the market value, an equivalent for the chance of greater decrease; which, in a precarious state of public credit, is always to be taken into the account.

Every compensation of this sort, it is evident, would be an absolute loss to the government.

In the preceding discussion of the impolicy of a discrimination, the injurious tendency of it to those, who continue to be the holders of the securities, they received from the government, has been explained. Nothing need be added, on this head, except that this is an additional and interesting light, in which the injustice of the measure may be seen. It would not only divest present proprietors by purchase, of the rights they had acquired under the sanction of public faith, but it would depreciate the property of the remaining original holders.

It is equally unnecessary to add any thing to what has been already said to demonstrate the fatal influence, which the principle of discrimination would have on the public credit.

But there is still a point in view in which it will appear perhaps even more exceptionable, than in either of the former. It would be repugnant to an express provision of the Constitution of the United States. This provision is, that "all debts contracted and engagements entered into before the adoption of that Constitution shall be as valid against the United States under it, as under the confederation," which amounts to a constitutional ratification of the contracts respecting the debt, in the state in which they existed under the confederation. And resorting to that standard, there can be no doubt, that the rights of assignees and original holders, must be considered as equal.

In exploding thus fully the principle of discrimination, the Secretary is happy in reflecting, that he is only the advocate of what has been already sanctioned by the formal and express authority of the government of the Union, in these emphatic terms—"The remaining class of creditors (say Congress in their circular address to the states, of the 26th of April 1783) is composed, partly of such of our fellow-citizens as originally lent to the public the use of their funds, or have since manifested *most confidence* in their country, by receiving transfers from the lenders; and partly of those, whose property has been either advanced or assumed for the public service. To *discriminate* the merits of these several descriptions of creditors, would be a task equally unnecessary and invidious. If the voice of humanity plead more loudly in favor of some than of others, the voice of policy, no less than of justice, pleads in favor of all. A WISE NATION will never permit those who relieve the wants of their country, or who *rely most* on its *faith,* its *firmness,* and its *resources,* when either of them is distrusted, to suffer by the event."

The Secretary concluding, that a discrimination, between the different classes of creditors of the United States, cannot with propriety be *made,* proceeds to examine whether a difference ought to be permitted to *remain* between them, and another description of public creditors—Those of the states individually.

The Secretary, after mature reflection on this point, entertains a full conviction, that an assumption of the debts of the particular states by the union, and a like provision for them, as for those of the union, will be a measure of sound policy and substantial justice.

It would, in the opinion of the Secretary, contribute, in an eminent degree, to an orderly, stable and satisfactory arrangement of the national finances.

Admitting, as ought to be the case, that a provision must be made in some way or other, for the entire debt; it will follow, that no greater revenues will be required, whether that provision be made wholly by the United States, or partly by them, and partly by the states separately.

The principal question then must be, whether such a provision cannot be more conveniently and effectually made, by one general plan issuing from one authority, than by different plans originating in different authorities.

In the first case there can be no competition for resources; in the last, there must be such a competition. The consequences of this, without the greatest caution on both sides, might be interfering regulations, and thence collision and confusion. Particular branches of industry might also be oppressed by it.

The most productive objects of revenue are not numerous. Either these must be wholly engrossed by one side, which might lessen the efficacy of the provisions by the other; or both must have recourse to the same objects in different modes, which might occasion an accumulation upon them, beyond what they could properly bear. If this should not happen, the caution requisite to avoiding it, would prevent the revenue's deriving the full benefit of each object. The danger of interference and of excess would be apt to impose restraints very unfriendly to the complete command of those resources, which are the most convenient; and to compel the having recourse to others, less eligible in themselves, and less agreeable to the community.

The difficulty of an effectual command of the public resources, in case of separate provisions for the debt, may be seen in another and perhaps more striking light. It would naturally happen that different states, from local considerations, would in some instances have recourse to different objects, in others, to the same objects, in different degrees, for procuring the funds of which they stood in need. It is easy to conceive how this diversity would affect the aggregate revenue of the country. By the supposition, articles which yielded a full supply in some states, would yield nothing, or an insufficient product, in others. And hence the public revenue would not derive the full benefit of those articles, from state regulations. Neither could the deficiencies be made good by those of the union. It is a provision of the national constitution, that "all duties, imposts and excises, shall be uniform throughout the United States." And as the general government would be under a necessity from motives of policy, of paying regard to the duty, which may have been previously imposed upon any article, though but in a single state, it would be constrained, either to refrain wholly from any further imposition, upon such article, where it had been already rated as high as was proper, or to confine itself to the difference between the existing rate, and what the article would reasonably bear. Thus the pre-occupancy of an article by a single state, would tend to arrest or abridge the impositions of the union on that article. And as it is supposeable, that a great variety of articles might be placed in this situation, by dissimilar arrangements of the particular states, it is evident, that the aggregate revenue of the country would be likely to be very materially contracted by the plan of separate provisions.

If all the public creditors receive their dues from one source, distributed with an equal hand, their interest will be the same. And having the same interests, they will unite in the support of the fiscal arrangements of the government: As these, too, can be made with more convenience, where there is no competition: These circumstances combined will ensure to the revenue laws a more ready and more satisfactory execution.

If on the contrary there are distinct provisions, there will be distinct interests, drawing different ways. That union and concert of views, among the creditors, which in every government is of great importance to their security, and to that of public credit, will not only not exist, but will be likely to give place to mutual jealousy and opposition. And from this cause, the operation of the systems which may be adopted, both by the particular states, and by the union, with relation to their respective debts, will be in danger of being counteracted.

There are several reasons, which render it probable, that the situation of the state creditors would be worse, than that of the creditors of the union, if there be not a national assumption of the state debts. Of these it will be sufficient to mention two; one, that a principal branch of revenue is exclusively vested in the union; the other, that a state must always be checked in the imposition of taxes on articles of consumption, from the want of power to extend the same regulation to the other states, and from the tendency of partial duties to injure its industry and commerce. Should the state creditors stand upon a less eligible footing than the others, it is unnatural to expect they would see with pleasure a provision for them. The influence which their dissatisfaction might have, could not but operate injuriously, both for the creditors, and the credit, of the United States.

Hence it is even the interest of the creditors of the union, that those of the individual states should be comprehended in a general provision. Any attempt to secure to the former either exclusive or peculiar advantages, would materially hazard their interests.

Neither would it be just, that one class of the public creditors should be more favoured than the other. The objects for which both descriptions of the debt were contracted, are in the main the same. Indeed a great part of the particular debts of the States has arisen from assumptions by them on account of the union. And it is most equitable, that there should be the same measure of retribution for all.

There is an objection, however, to an assumption of the state debts, which deserves particular notice. It may be supposed, that it would increase the difficulty of an equitable settlement between them and the United States.

The principles of that settlement, whenever they shall be discussed, will require all the moderation and wisdom of the government. In the opinion of the Secretary, that discussion, till further lights are obtained, would be premature.

All therefore which he would now think adviseable on the point in question, would be, that the amount of the debts assumed and provided for, should be charged to the respective states, to abide an eventual arrangement. This, the United States, as assignees to the creditors, would have an indisputable right to do.

But as it might be a satisfaction to the House to have before them some plan for the liquidation of accounts between the union and its members, which, including the assumption of the state debts, would consist with equity: The Secretary will submit in this place such thoughts on the subject, as have occurred to his own mind, or been suggested to him, most compatible, in his judgment, with the end proposed.

Let each state be charged with all the money advanced to it out of the treasury of the United States, liquidated according to the specie value, at the time of each advance, with interest at six per cent.

Let it also be charged with the amount, in specie value, of all its securities which shall be assumed, with the interest upon them to the time, when interest shall become payable by the United States.

Let it be credited for all monies paid and articles furnished to the United States, and for all other expenditures during the war, either towards general or particular defence, whether authorized or unauthorized by the United States; the whole liquidated to specie value, and bearing an interest of six per cent. from the several times at which the several payments, advances and expenditures accrued.

And let all sums of continental money now in the treasuries of the respective states, which shall be paid into the treasury of the United States, be credited at specie value.

Upon a statement of the accounts according to these principles, there can be little doubt, that balances would appear in favor of all the states, against the United States.

To equalize the contributions of the states, let each be then charged with its proportion of the aggregate of those balances, according to some equitable ratio, to be devised for that purpose.

If the contributions should be found disproportionate, the result of this adjustment would be, that some states would be creditors, some debtors to the union.

Should this be the case, as it will be attended with less inconvenience for the United States, to have to pay balances to, than to receive them from the particular states, it may perhaps, be practicable to effect the former by a second process, in the nature of a transfer of the amount of the debts of debtor states, to the credit of creditor states, observing the ratio by which the first apportionment shall have been made. This, whilst it would destroy the balances due from the former, would increase those due to the latter. These to be provided for by the United States, at a reasonable interest, but not to be transferable.

The expediency of this second process must depend on a knowledge of the result of the first. If the inequalities should be too great, the arrangement may be impracticable, without unduly increasing the debt of the United States. But it is not likely, that this would be the case. It is also to be remarked, that though this second process might not, upon the principle of apportionment, bring the thing to the point aimed at, yet it may approach so nearly to it, as to avoid essentially the embarrassment, of having considerable balances to collect from any of the states.

The whole of this arrangement to be under the superintendence of commissioners, vested with equitable discretion, and final authority.

The operation of the plan is exemplified in the schedule A.

The general principle of it seems to be equitable, for it appears difficult to conceive a good reason, why the expences for the particular defence of a part in a common war, should not be a common charge, as well as those incurred professedly for the general defence. The defence of each part is that of the whole; and unless all the expenditures are brought into a common mass, the tendency must be, to add, to the calamities suffered, by being the most exposed to the ravages of war, an increase of burthens.

This plan seems to be susceptible of no objection, which does not belong to every other, that proceeds on the idea of a final adjustment of accounts. The difficulty of settling a ratio, is common to all. This must, probably, either be sought for in the proportions of the requisitions, during the war, or in the decision of commissioners appointed with plenary power. The rule prescribed in the Constitution, with regard to representation and direct taxes, would evidently not be applicable to the situation of parties, during the period in question.

The existing debt of the United States is excluded from the computation, as it ought to be, because it will be provided for out of a general fund.

The only discussion of a preliminary kind, which remains, relates to the distinctions of the debt into principal and interest. It is well known, that the arrears of the latter bear a large proportion to the amount of the former. The immediate payment of these arrears is evidently impracticable, and a question arises, what ought be done with them?

There is good reason to conclude, that the impressions of many are more favorable to the claim of the principal than to that of the interest; at least so far, as to produce an opinion, that an inferior provision might suffice for the latter.

But to the Secretary, this opinion does not appear to be well founded. His investigations of the subject, have led him to a conclusion, that the arrears of interest have pretensions, at least equal to the principal.

The liquidated debt, traced to its origin, falls under two principal discriminations. One, relating to loans; the other to services performed and articles supplied.

The part arising from loans, was at first made payable at fixed periods, which have long since elapsed, with an early option to lenders, either to receive back their money at the expiration of those periods, or to continue it at interest, 'till the whole amount of continental bills circulating should not exceed the sum in circulation at the time of each loan. This contingency, in the sense of the contract, never happened; and the presumption is, that the creditors preferred continuing their money indefinitely at interest, to receiving it in a depreciated and depreciating state.

The other parts of it were chiefly for objects, which ought to have been paid for at the time, that is, when the services were performed or the supplies furnished; and were not accompanied with any contract for interest.

But by different acts of government and administration, concurred in by the creditors, these parts of the debt have been converted into a capital, bearing an interest of six per cent. per annum, but without any definite period of redemption. A portion of the loan-office debt has been exchanged for new securities of that import. And the whole of it seems to have acquired that character, after the expiration of the periods prefixed for re-payment.

If this view of the subject be a just one, the capital of the debt of the United States, may be considered in the light of an annuity at the rate of six per cent. per annum, redeemable at the pleasure of the government, by payment of the principal. For it seems to be a clear position, that when a public contracts a debt payable with interest, without any precise time being stipulated or understood for payment of the capital, that time is a matter of pure discretion with the government, which is at liberty to consult its own convenience respecting it, taking care to pay the interest with punctuality.

Wherefore, as long as the United States should pay the interest of their debt, as it accrued, their creditors would have no right to demand the principal.

But with regard to the arrears of interest, the case is different. These are now due, and those to whom they are due, have a right to claim immediate payment. To say, that it would be impracticable to comply, would not vary the nature of the right. Nor can this idea of impracticability be honorably carried further, than to justify the proposition of a new contract upon the basis of a commutation of that right for an equivalent. This equivalent too ought to be a real and fair one. And what other fair equivalent can be imagined for the detention of money, but a reasonable interest? Or what can be the standard of that interest, but the market rate, or the rate which the government pays in ordinary cases?

From this view of the matter, which appears to be the accurate and true one, it will follow, that the arrears of interest are entitled to an equal provision with the principal of the debt.

The result of the foregoing discussions is this—That there ought to be no discrimination between the original holders of the debt, and present possessors by purchase—That it is expedient, there should be an assumption of the state debts by the Union, and that the arrears of interest should be provided for on an equal footing with the principal.

The next enquiry, in order, towards determining the nature of a proper provision, respects the quantum of the debt, and the present rates of interest.

The debt of the union is distinguishable into foreign and domestic.

	Dollars.	Cents.

The foreign debt as stated in the schedule B.
amounts to principal
bearing an interest of four, and partly an interest of
five per cent.   10,070,307.

Arrears of interest to the last of December, 1789,   1,640,071.62

Making together, dollars   11,710,378.62

The domestic debt may be sub-divided into
liquidated and unliquidated; principal and interest.   *Dollars.   Cents.*

The principal of the liquidated part, as stated in
the schedule C, amounts to   27,383,917.74
bearing an interest of six per cent.

The arrears of interest as stated in the schedule D.
to the end of 1790, amount to   13,030,168.20

Making together, dollars   40,414,085.94

This includes all that has been paid in indents (except what has come into the treasury of the United States) which, in the opinion of the Secretary, can be considered in no other light, than as interest due.

The unliquidated part of the domestic debt, which consists chiefly of the continental bills of credit, is not ascertained, but may be estimated at 2,000,000 dollars.

These several sums constitute the whole of the debt of the United States, amounting together to 54,124,464 dollars, and 56 cents.

That of the individual states is not equally well ascertained.

The schedule E shews the extent to which it has been ascertained by returns pursuant to the order of the House of the 21st September last; but this not comprehending all the states, the residue must be estimated from less authentic information. The Secretary, however, presumes, that the total amount may be safely stated at 25 millions of dollars, principal and interest. The present rate of interest of the state debts is in general, the same with that of the domestic debt of the union.

On the supposition, that the arrears of interest ought to be provided for, on the same terms with the principal, the annual amount of the interest, which, at the existing rates, would be payable on the entire mass of the public debt, would be,

On the foreign debt, computing the interest on the
principal, as it stands, and allowing   *Dollars.   Cents.*
four per cent on the arrears of interest,   542,599.66

On the domestic debt, including that of the states,   4,044,845.15

Making together, dollars   4,587,444.81

The interesting problem now occurs. Is it in the power of the United States, consistently with those prudential considerations, which ought not to be overlooked, to make a provision equal to the purpose of funding the whole debt, at the rates of interest which it now bears, in addition to the sum which will be necessary for the current service of the government?

The Secretary will not say that such provision would exceed the abilities of the country; but he is clearly of opinion, that to make it, would require the extension of taxation to a degree, and to objects, which the true interest of the public creditors forbids. It is therefore to be hoped, and even to be expected, that they will chearfully concur in such modifications of their claims, on fair and equitable principles, as will facilitate to the government an arrangement substantial, durable and satisfactory to the community. The importance of the last characteristic will strike every discerning mind. No plan, however flattering in appearance, to which it did not belong, could be truly entitled to confidence.

It will not be forgotten, that exigencies may, ere long, arise, which would call for resources greatly beyond what is now deemed sufficient for the current service; and that, should the faculties of the country be exhausted or even *strained* to provide for the public debt, there could be less reliance on the sacredness of the provision.

But while the Secretary yields to the force of these considerations, he does not lose sight of those fundamental principles of good faith, which dictate, that every practicable exertion ought to be made, scrupulously to fulfill the engagements of the government; that no change in the rights of its creditors ought to be attempted without their voluntary consent; and that this consent ought to be voluntary in fact, as well as in name. Consequently, that every proposal of a change ought to be in the shape of an appeal to their reason and to their interest; not to their necessities. To this end, it is requisite, that a fair equivalent should be offered for what may be asked to be given up, and unquestionable security for the remainder. Without this, an alteration, consistently with the credit and honor of the nation, would be impracticable.

It remains to see what can be proposed in conformity to these views.

It has been remarked, that the capital of the debt of the union is to be viewed in the light of an annuity at the rate of six per cent. per annum, redeemable at the pleasure of the government, by payment of the principal. And it will not be required, that the arrears of interest should be considered in a more favourable light. The same character, in general, may be applied to the debts of the individual states.

This view of the subject admits, that the United States would have it in their power to avail themselves of any fall in the market rate of interest, for reducing that of the debt.

This property of the debt is favourable to the public; unfavourable to the creditor. And may facilitate an arrangement for the reduction of interest, upon the basis of a fair equivalent.

Probabilities are always a rational ground of contract. The Secretary conceives, that there is good reason to believe, if effectual measures are taken to establish public credit, that the government rate of interest in the United States, will, in a very short time, fall at least as low as five per cent. and that in a period not exceeding twenty years, it will sink still lower, probably to four.

There are two principal causes which will be likely to produce this effect; one, the low rate of interest in Europe; the other, the increase of the monied capital of the nation, by the funding of the public debt.

From three to four per cent. is deemed good interest in several parts of Europe. Even less is deemed so, in some places. And it is on the decline; the increasing plenty of money continually tending to lower it. It is presumable, that no country will be able to borrow of foreigners upon better terms, than the United States, because none can, perhaps, afford so good security. Our situation exposes us less, than that of any other nation, to those casualties, which are the chief causes of expence; our incumbrances, in proportion to our real means, are less, though these cannot immediately be brought so readily into action, and our progress in resources from the early state of the country, and the immense tracts of unsettled territory, must necessarily exceed that of any other. The advantages of this situation have already engaged the attention of the European money-lenders, particularly among the Dutch. And as they become better understood, they will have the greater influence. Hence as large a proportion of the cash of Europe as may be wanted, will be, in a certain sense, in our market, for the use of government. And this will naturally have the effect of a reduction of the rate of interest, not indeed to the level of the places, which send their money to market, but to something much nearer to it, than our present rate.

The influence, which the funding of the debt is calculated to have, in lowering interest, has been already remarked and explained. It is hardly possible, that it should not be materially affected by such an increase of the monied capital of the nation, as would result from the proper funding of seventy millions of dollars. But the probability of a decrease in the rate of interest, acquires confirmation from facts, which existed prior to the revolution. It is well known, that in some of the states, money might with facility be borrowed, on good security, at five per cent. and, not unfrequently, even at less.

The most enlightened of the public creditors will be most sensible of the justness of this view of the subject, and of the propriety of the use which will be made of it.

The Secretary, in pursuance of it, will assume, as a probability, sufficiently great to be a ground of calculation, both on the part of the government and of its creditors—That the interest of money in the United States will, in five years, fall to five per cent. and, in twenty, to four. The probability, in the mind of the Secretary, is rather that the fall may be more rapid and more considerable; but he prefers a mean, as most likely to engage the assent of the creditors, and more equitable in itself; because it is predicated on probabilities, which may err on one side, as well as on the other.

Premising these things, the Secretary submits to the House, the expediency of proposing a loan to the full amount of the debt, as well of the particular states, as of the union, upon the following terms.

First—That for every hundred dollars subscribed, payable in the debt (as well interest as principal) the subscriber be entitled, at his option, either

To have two thirds funded at an annuity, or yearly interest of six per cent, redeemable at the pleasure of the government, by payment of the principal; and to receive the other third in lands in the Western Territory, at the rate of twenty cents per acre. Or,

To have the whole sum funded at an annuity or yearly interest of four per cent. irredeemable by any payment exceeding five dollars per annum on account both of principal and interest; and to receive, as a compensation for the reduction of interest, fifteen dollars and eighty cents, payable in lands, as in the preceding case. Or

To have sixty-six dollars and two thirds of a dollar funded immediately at an annuity or yearly interest of six per cent. irredeemable by any payment exceeding four dollars and two thirds of a dollar per annum, on account both of principal and interest; and to have, at the end of ten years, twenty-six dollars and eighty-eight cents, funded at the like interest and rate of redemption. Or

To have an annuity for the remainder of life, upon the contingency of living to a given age, not less distant than ten years, computing interest at four per cent. Or

To have an annuity for the remainder of life, upon the contingency of the survivorship of the youngest of two persons, computing interest, in this case also, at four per cent.

In addition to the foregoing loan, payable wholly in the debt, the Secretary would propose, that one should be opened for ten millions of dollars, on the following plan.

That for every hundred dollars subscribed, payable one half in specie, and the other half in debt (as well principal as interest) the subscriber be entitled to an annuity or yearly interest of five per cent. irredeemable by any payment exceeding six dollars per annum, on account both of principal and interest.

The principles and operation of these different plans may now require explanation.

The first is simply a proposition for paying one third of the debt in land, and funding the other two thirds, at the existing rate of interest, and upon the same terms of redemption, to which it is at present subject.

Here is no conjecture, no calculation of probabilities. The creditor is offered the advantage of making his interest principal, and he is asked to facilitate to the government an effectual provision for his demands, by accepting a third part of them in land, at a fair valuation.

The general price, at which the western lands have been, heretofore, sold, has been a dollar per acre in public securities; but at the time the principal purchases were made, these securities were worth, in the market, less than three shillings in the pound. The nominal price, therefore, would not be the proper standard, under present circumstances, nor would the precise specie value then given, be a just rule. Because, as the payments were to be made by instalments, and the securities were, at the times of the purchases, extremely low, the probability of a moderate rise must be presumed to have been taken into the account. Twenty cents, therefore, seem to bear an equitable proportion to the two considerations of value at the time, and likelihood of increase.

It will be understood, that upon this plan, the public retains the advantage of availing itself of any fall in the market rate of interest, for reducing that upon the debt, which is perfectly just, as no present sacrifice, either in the quantum of the principal, or in the rate of interest, is required from the creditor.

The inducement to the measure is the payment of one third of the debt in land.

The second plan is grounded upon the supposition, that interest in five years, will fall to five per cent. in fifteen more, to four. As the capital remains entire, but bearing an interest of four per cent. only, compensation is to be made to the creditor, for the interest of two per cent. per annum for five years, and of one per cent. per annum, for fifteen years, to commence at the distance of five years. The present value of these two sums or annuities, computed according to the terms of the supposition, is, by strict calculation, fifteen dollars and seven hundred and ninety-two thousandth parts of a dollar; a fraction less than the sum proposed.

The inducement to the measure here is, the reduction of interest to a rate, more within the compass of a convenient provision; and the payment of the compensation in lands.

The inducements to the individual are—the accommodation afforded to the public—the high probability of a complete equivalent—the chance even of gain, should the rate of interest fall, either more speedily or in a greater degree, than the calculation supposes. Should it fall to five per cent. sooner than five years; should it fall lower than five before the additional fifteen were expired; or should it fall below four, previous to the payment of the debt, there would be, in each case, an absolute profit to the creditor. As his capital will remain entire, the value of it will increase, with every decrease of the rate of interest.

The third plan proceeds upon the like supposition of a successive fall in the rate of interest. And upon that supposition offers an equivalent to the creditor. One hundred dollars, bearing an interest of six per cent. for five years; of five per cent. for fifteen years, and thenceforth of four per cent. (these being the successive rates of interest in the market) is

equal to a capital of   122 dollars,   510,725 parts, bearing an interest of four per cent. which, converted into a capital, bearing a fixed rate of interest of six per cent, is

equal to   81 dollars,   6,738,166 parts.

The difference between sixty-six dollars and two thirds of a dollar (the sum to be funded immediately) and this last sum is   15 dollars,   0172 parts, which at six per cent per annum, amounts at the end of ten years, to

26 dollars,   8,755 parts,

the sum to be funded at the expiration of that period.

It ought, however, to be acknowledged, that this calculation does not make allowance for the principle of redemption, which the plan itself includes; upon which principle the equivalent in a capital of six per cent. would be by strict calculation,   87 dollars,   50,766 parts.

But there are two considerations which induce the Secretary to think, that the one proposed would operate more equitably than this: One is, that it may not be very early in the power of the United States to avail themselves of the right of redemption reserved in the plan: The other is, that with regard to the part to be funded at the end of ten years, the principal of redemption is suspended during that time, and the full interest at six per cent. goes on *improving* at the *same rate;* which for the *last five years,* will exceed the market rate of interest, according to the supposition.

The equivalent is regulated in this plan, by the circumstance of fixing the rate of interest higher, than it is supposed it will continue to be in the market; permitting only a gradual discharge of the debt, in an established proportion, and consequently preventing advantage being taken of any decrease of interest below the stipulated rate.

Thus the true value of eighty-one dollars and sixty-seven cents, the capital proposed, considered as a perpetuity, and bearing six per cent. interest, when the market rate of interest was five per cent. would be a small fraction more than ninety-eight dollars, when it was four per cent. would be one hundred and twenty-two dollars and fifty-one cents. But the proposed capital being subject to gradual redemption, it is evident, that its value, in each case, would be somewhat less. Yet from this may be perceived, the manner in which a less capital, at a fixed rate of interest, becomes an equivalent for a greater capital, at a rate liable to variation and diminution.

It is presumable, that those creditors, who do not entertain a favorable opinion of property in western lands, will give a preference to this last mode of modelling the debt. The Secretary is sincere in affirming, that, in his opinion, it will be likely to prove, *to the full* as beneficial to the creditors, as a provision for his debt upon its present terms.

It is not intended, in either case to oblige the government to redeem, in the proportion specified, but to secure to it, the right of doing so, to avoid the inconvenience of a perpetuity.

The fourth and fifth plans abandon the supposition which is the basis of the two preceding ones, and offer only four per cent. throughout.

The reason of this is, that the payment being deferred, there will be an accumulation of compound interest, in the intermediate period against the public, which, without a very provident administration, would turn to its detriment. And the suspension of the burthen would be too apt to beget a relaxation of efforts in the mean time. The measure therefore, its object being temporary accommodation, could only be adviseable upon a moderate rate of interest.

With regard to individuals, the inducement will be sufficient at four per cent. There is no disposition of money, in private loans, making allowance for the usual delays and casualties, which would be equally beneficial as a future provision.

A hundred dollars advanced upon the life of a person of a eleven years old, would produce an annuity*   *Dollars. Parts.*

	Dollars	Parts
If commencing at twenty-one, of	10	346
If commencing at thirty-one, of	18	803
If commencing at forty-one, of	37	286
If commencing at fifty-one, of	78	580

The same sum advanced upon the chance of the survivorship of the youngest of two lives, one of the persons being twenty-five, the other, thirty years old, would produce, if the youngest of the two, should survive, an annuity† for the remainder of life of   23 dollars, 556 parts.

From these instances may readily be discerned, the advantages, which these deferred annuities afford, for securing a comfortable provision for the evening of life, or for wives, who survive their husbands.

The sixth plan also relinquishes the supposition, which is the foundation of the second, and third, and offers a higher rate of interest upon similar terms

* *See Schedule* F.
† *Table Schedule* G.

of redemption, for the consideration of the payment of one half of the loan in specie. This is a plan highly advantageous to the creditors, who may be able to make that payment; while the specie itself could be applied in purchases of the debt, upon terms, which would fully indemnify the public for the increased interest.

It is not improbable, that foreign holders of the domestic debt, may embrace this as a desireable arrangement.

As an auxiliary expedient, and by way of experiment, the Secretary would propose a loan upon the principles of the tontine.‡

To consist of six classes, composed respectively of persons of the following ages:

> First class, of those of 20 years and under.
> Second class, of those above 20, and not exceeding 30.
> Third class, of those above 30, and not exceeding 40.
> Fourth class, of those above 40, and not exceeding 50.
> Fifth class, of those above 50, and not exceeding 60.
> Sixth class, of those above 60.

Each share to be two hundred dollars. The number of shares in each class, to be indefinite. Persons to be at liberty to subscribe on their own lives, or on those of others, nominated by them.

	Dollars.	Cents.
The annuity upon a share in the first class to be	8.	40
upon a share in the second	8.	65
upon a share in the third	9.	00
upon a share in the fourth	9.	65
upon a share in the fifth	10.	70
upon a share in the sixth	12.	80

The annuities of those who die, to be equally divided among the survivors, until four-fifths shall be dead, when the principle of survivorship shall cease, and each annuitant thenceforth enjoy his dividend as a several annuity during the life, upon which it shall depend.

These annuities are calculated on the best life in each class, and at a rate of interest of four per cent. with some deductions in favor of the public. To the advantages which these circumstances present, the cessation of the right of survivorship on the death of four-fifths of the annuitants will be no inconsiderable addition.

The inducements to individuals are, a competent interest for their money from the outset, secured for life, and the prospect of continual encrease, and even of large profit to those, whose fortune it is, to survive their associates.

It will have appeared, that in all the proposed loans, the Secretary has

‡ See Table Schedule H.

contemplated the putting the interest upon the same footing with the principal: *That* on the debt of the United States, he would have computed to the last of the present year: *That* on the debt of the particular states, to the last of the year 1791; the reason for which distinction will be seen hereafter.

In order to keep up a due circulation of money, it will be expedient, that the interest of the debt should be paid quarter-yearly. This regulation will, at the same time, conduce to the advantage of the public creditors, giving them, in fact, by the anticipation of payment, a higher rate of interest; which may, with propriety, be taken into the estimate of the compensation to be made to them. Six per cent. per annum, paid in this mode, will truly be worth six dollars, and one hundred and thirty-five thousandth parts of a dollar, computing the market interest at the same rate.

The Secretary thinks it advisable, to hold out various propositions, all of them compatible with the public interest, because it is, in his opinion, of the greatest consequence, that the debt should, with the consent of the creditors, be remoulded into such a shape, as will bring the expenditure of the nation to a level with its income. 'Till this shall be accomplished, the finances of the United States will never wear a proper countenance.

Arrears of interest, continually accruing, will be as continual a monument, either of inability, or of ill faith; and will not cease to have an evil influence on public credit. In nothing are appearances of greater moment, than in whatever regards credit. Opinion is the soul of it, and this is affected by appearances, as well as realities. By offering an option to the creditors, between a number of plans, the change meditated will be more likely to be accomplished. Different tempers will be governed by different views of the subject.

But while the Secretary would endeavour to effect a change in the form of the debt, by new loans, in order to render it more susceptible of an adequate provision; he would not think it proper to aim at procuring the concurrence of the creditors by operating upon their necessities.

Hence whatever surplus of revenue might remain, after satisfying the interest of the new loans, and the demand for the current service, ought to be divided among those creditors, if any, who may not think fit to subscribe to them. But for this purpose, under the circumstance of depending propositions, a temporary appropriation will be most adviseable, and the sum must be limited to four per cent. as the revenues will only be calculated to produce, in that proportion, to the entire debt.

The Secretary confides for the success of the propositions, to be made, on the goodness of the reasons upon which they rest; on the fairness of the equivalent to be offered in each case; on the discernment of the creditors of their true interest; and on their disposition to facilitate the arrangements of the government, and to render them satisfactory to the community.

The remaining part of the task to be performed is, to take a view of the means of providing for the debt, according to the modification of it, which is proposed.

On this point the Secretary premises, that, in his opinion, the funds to be established, ought, for the present, to be confined to the existing debt of the United States; as well, because a progressive augmentation of the revenue will be most convenient, as because the consent of the state creditors is necessary, to the assumption contemplated; and though the obtaining of that consent may be inferred with great assurance, from their obvious interest to give it; yet 'till it shall be obtained, an actual provision for the debt, would be premature. Taxes could not, with propriety, be laid for an object, which depended on such a contingency.

All that ought now to be done, respecting it, is, to put the matter in an effectual train for a future provision. For which purpose, the Secretary will, in the course of this report, submit such propositions, as appear to him adviseable.

The Secretary now proceeds to a consideration of the necessary funds.

It has been stated that the debt of the United States consists of

	Dollars.	Cents.
The foreign debt, amounting, with arrears of interest, to	11,710,378.	62
And the domestic debt amounting, with like arrears, computed to the end of the year 1790, to	42,414,085.	94
Making together; Dollars	54,124,464.	56

The interest on the domestic debt is computed to the end of this year, because the details of carrying any plan into execution, will exhaust the year.

	Dollars.	Cents.
The annual interest of the foreign debt has been stated at	542,599.	66
And the interest on the domestic debt at four per cent. would amount to	1,696,563.	43
Making together, dollars,	2,239,163.	09

Thus to pay the interest of the foreign debt, and to pay four per cent on the whole of the domestic debt, principal and interest, forming a new capital, will require a yearly income of   2,239,163 dollars, 9 cents.

The sum which, in the opinion of the Secretary, ought now to be provided in addition to what the current service will require.

For, though the rate of interest, proposed by the third plan, exceeds four per cent. on the whole debt; and the annuities on the tontine will also exceed four per cent. on the sums which may be subscribed; yet, as the actual provision for a part is, in the former case, suspended; as measures for reducing the debt, by purchases, may be advantageously pursued, and as the payment of the deferred annuities will of course be postponed, four per cent. on the whole, will be a sufficient provision.

With regard to the instalments of the foreign debt, these, in the opinion of the Secretary, ought to be paid by new loans abroad. Could funds be conveniently spared, from other exigencies, for paying them, the United States could ill bear the drain of cash, at the present juncture, which the measure would be likely to occasion.

But to the sum which has been stated for payment of the interest, must be added a provision for the current service. This the Secretary estimates at six hundred thousand dollars;* making, with the amount of the interest, two millions, eight hundred and thirty-nine thousand, one hundred and sixty-three dollars, and nine cents.

This sum may, in the opinion of the Secretary, be obtained from the present duties on imports and tonnage, with the additions, which, without any possible disadvantage either to trade, or agriculture, may be made on wines, spirits, including those distilled within the United States, teas and coffee.

The Secretary conceives, that it will be sound policy, to carry the duties upon articles of this kind, as high as will be consistent with the practicability of a safe collection. This will lessen the necessity, both of having recourse to direct taxation, and of accumulating duties where they would be more inconvenient to trade, and upon objects, which are more to be regarded as necessaries of life.

That the articles, which have been enumerated, will, better than most others, bear high duties, can hardly be a question. They are all of them, in reality—luxuries—the greatest part of them foreign luxuries; some of them, in the excess in which they are used, pernicious luxuries. And there is, perhaps, none of them, which is not consumed in so great abundance, as may, justly, denominate it, a source of national extravagance and impoverishment. The consumption of ardent spirits particularly, no doubt very much on account of their cheapness, is carried to an extreme, which is truly to be regretted, as well in regard to the health and the morals, as to the oeconomy of the community.

Should the increase of duties tend to a decrease of the consumption of those articles, the effect would be, in every respect desireable. The saving which it would occasion, would leave individuals more at their ease, and promote a more favourable balance of trade. As far as this decrease might be applicable to distilled spirits, it would encourage the substitution of cyder and malt

---

* See Schedule 1.

liquors, benefit agriculture, and open a new and productive source of revenue.

It is not however, probable, that this decrease would be in a degree, which would frustrate the expected benefit to the revenue from raising the duties. Experience has shewn, that luxuries of every kind, lay the strongest hold on the attachments of mankind, which, especially when confirmed by habit, are not easily alienated from them.

The same fact affords a security to the merchant, that he is not likely to be prejudiced by considerable duties on such articles. They will usually command a proportional price. The chief things in this view to be attended to, are, that the terms of payment be so regulated, as not to require inconvenient advances, and that the mode of collection be secure.

To other reasons, which plead for carrying the duties upon the articles which have been mentioned, to as great an extent as they will well bear, may be added these; that they are of a nature, from their extensive consumption, to be very productive, and are amongst the most difficult objects of illicit introduction.

Invited by so many motives to make the best use of the resource, which these articles afford, the essential enquiry is—in what mode can the duties upon them be most effectually collected?

With regard to such of them, as will be brought from abroad, a duty on importation recommends itself by two leading considerations; one is, that meeting the object at its first entrance into the country, the collection is drawn to a point, and so far simplified; the other is, that it avoids the possibility of interference between the regulations of the United States, and those of the particular states.

But a duty, the precautions for the collection of which should terminate with the landing of the goods, as is essentially the case in the existing system, could not, with safety, be carried to the extent, which is contemplated.

In that system, the evasion of the duties, depends as it were, on a single risk. To land the goods in defiance of the vigilance of the officers of the customs, is almost, the sole difficulty. No future pursuit, is materially, to be apprehended. And where the inducement is equivalent to the risk, there will be found too many, who are willing to run it. Consequently there will be extensive frauds of the revenue, against which the utmost rigor of penal laws, has proved, as often as it has been tried, an ineffectual guard.

The only expedient which has been discovered, for conciliating high duties with a safe collection, is, the establishment of a *second,* or interior scrutiny.

By pursuing the article, from its importation, into the hands of the dealers in it, the risk of detection is so greatly inhanced, that few, in comparison, will venture to incur it. Indeed every dealer, who is not himself the fraudulent importer, then becomes, in some sort, a centinel upon him.

The introduction of a system, founded on this principle, in some shape or other, is, in the opinion of the Secretary, essential to the efficacy of every attempt, to render the revenues of the United States equal to their exigencies, their safety, their prosperity, their honor.

Nor is it less essential to the interest of the honest and fair trader. It might even be added, that every individual citizen, besides his share in the general weal, has a particular interest in it. The practice of smuggling never fails to have one of two effects, and sometimes unites them both. Either the smuggler undersells the fair trader, as, by saving the *duty,* he can afford to do, and makes *it* a charge upon him; or he sells at the increased price occasioned by the duty, and defrauds every man, who buys of him, of his share of what the public ought to receive. For it is evident, that the loss falls ultimately upon the citizens, who must be charged with other taxes to make good the deficiency, and supply the wants of the state.

The Secretary will not presume, that the plan, which he shall submit to the consideration of the house, is the best that could be devised. But it is the one, which has appeared to him freest from objections of any, that has occurred of equal efficacy. He acknowledges too, that it is susceptible of improvement, by other precautions in favor of the revenue, which he did not think it expedient to add. The chief outlines of the plan are not original, but it is no ill recommendation of it, that it has been tried with success.

The Secretary accordingly proposes,

That the duties heretofore laid upon wines, distilled spirits, teas and coffee, should, after the last day of May next, cease, and that instead of them, the following duties be laid.

Upon every gallon of Madeira Wine, of the quality of London particular, thirty-five cents.

Upon every gallon of other Madeira Wine, thirty cents.

Upon every gallon of Sherry, twenty-five cents.

Upon every gallon of other Wine, twenty cents.

Upon every gallon of distilled Spirits, more than ten per cent. below proof according to Dicas's hydrometer, twenty cents.

Upon every gallon of those Spirits under five, and not more than ten per cent. below proof, according to the same hydrometer, twenty-one cents.

Upon every gallon of those Spirits of proof, and not more than five per cent. below proof, according to the same hydrometer, twenty-two cents.

Upon every gallon, of those Spirits above proof, but not exceeding twenty per cent. according to the same hydrometer, twenty-five cents.

Upon every gallon of those Spirits more than twenty, and not more than forty per cent. above proof, according to the same hydrometer, thirty cents.

Upon every gallon of those Spirits more than forty per cent. above proof, according to the same hydrometer, forty cents.

Upon every pound of Hyson Tea, forty cents.

Upon every pound of other Green Tea, twenty-four cents.

Upon every pound of Souchong and other black Teas, except Bohea, twenty cents.

Upon every pound of Bohea Tea, twelve cents.

Upon every pound of Coffee, five cents.

That upon Spirits distilled within the United States, from Molasses, Sugar, or other foreign materials, there be paid—

Upon every gallon of those Spirits, more than ten per cent below proof, according to Dicas's hydrometer, eleven cents.

Upon every gallon of those Spirits under five, and not more than ten per cent. below proof, according to the same hydrometer, twelve cents.

Upon every gallon of those Spirits of proof, and not more than five per cent. below proof, according to the same hydrometer, thirteen cents.

Upon every gallon of those Spirits, above proof, but not exceeding twenty per cent. according to the same hydrometer, fifteen cents.

Upon every gallon of those Spirits, more than twenty, and not more than forty per cent. above proof, according to the same hydrometer, twenty cents.

Upon every gallon of those Spirits more than forty per cent. above proof, according to the same hydrometer, thirty cents.

That upon Spirits distilled within the United States, in any city, town or village, from materials of the growth or production of the United States, there be paid—

Upon every gallon of those Spirits more than ten per cent. below proof, according to Dicas's hydrometer, nine cents.

Upon every gallon of those Spirits under five, and not more than ten per cent. below proof, according to the same hydrometer, ten cents.

Upon every gallon of those Spirits of proof, and not more than five per cent. below proof, according to the same hydrometer, eleven cents.

Upon every gallon of those Spirits above proof, but not exceeding twenty per cent. according to the same hydrometer, thirteen cents.

Upon every gallon of those Spirits more than twenty, and not more than forty per cent. above proof, according to the same hydrometer, seventeen cents.

Upon every gallon of those Spirits, more than forty per cent. above proof, according to the same hydrometer, twenty-five cents.

That upon all Stills employed in distilling spirits from materials of the growth or production of the United States, in any other place than a city, town or village, there be paid the yearly sum of sixty cents, for every gallon, English wine measure, of the capacity of each Still, including its head.

The Secretary does not distribute the duties on Teas into different classes, as has been done in the impost act of the last session; because this distribution

depends on considerations of commercial policy, not of revenue. It is sufficient, therefore, for him to remark, that the rates, above specified, are
proposed with reference to the lowest class.

The Secretary conceiving, that he could not convey an accurate idea of the
plan contemplated by him, for the collection of these duties, in any mode so
effectual as by the draft of a bill for the purpose, begs leave respectfully to
refer the House to that, which will be found annexed to this report, relatively
to the article of distilled spirits; and which, for the better explanation of some
of its parts, is accompanied with marginal remarks.

It would be the intention of the Secretary, that the duty on wines should be
collected upon precisely the same plan with that on imported spirits.

But with regard to teas and coffee, the Secretary is inclined to think, that it
will be expedient, till experience shall evince the propriety of going further,
to exclude the *ordinary* right of the officers to visit and inspect the places in
which those articles may be kept. The other precautions, without this, will
afford, though not complete, considerable security.

It will not escape the observation of the House, that the Secretary, in the
plan submitted, has taken the most scrupulous care, that those citizens upon
whom it is immediately to operate, be secured from every species of injury by
the misconduct of the officers to be employed. There are not only strong
guards against their being guilty of abuses of authority; they are not only
punishable, criminally, for any they may commit, and made answerable in
damages, to individuals, for whatever prejudice these may sustain by their
acts or neglects: But even where seizures are made with probable cause, if
there be an acquittal of the article seized, a compensation to the proprietors
for the injury their property may suffer, and even for its detention, is to be
made out of the public treasury.

So solicitous indeed has the Secretary been, to obviate every appearance of
hardship, that he has even included a compensation to the dealers, for their
agency in aid of the revenue.

With all these precautions to manifest a spirit of moderation and justice on
the part of the government: And when it is considered, that the object of the
proposed system is the firm establishment of public credit; that on this
depends the character, security and prosperity of the nation; that advantages
in every light important, may be expected to result from it; that the immediate operation of it will be upon an enlightened class of citizens, zealously
devoted to good government, and to a liberal and enlarged policy, and that it
is peculiarly the interest of the virtuous part of them to co-operate in whatever will restrain the spirit of illicit traffic; there will be perceived to exist,
the justest ground of confidence, that the plan, if eligible in itself, will
experience the chearful and prompt acquiescence of the community.

The Secretary computes the nett product of the duties proposed in this report at about one million seven hundred and three thousand four hundred dollars, according to the estimate in Schedule K, which if near the truth, will, together with the probable product of the duties on imports and tonnage, complete the sum required. But it will readily occur, that in so unexplored a field there must be a considerable degree of uncertainty in the data. And that, on this account, it will be prudent to have an auxiliary resource for the first year, in which the interest will become payable, that there may be no possibility of disappointment to the public creditors, ere there may be an opportunity of providing for any deficiency, which the experiment may discover. This will accordingly be attended to.

The proper appropriation of the funds provided, and to be provided, seems next to offer itself to consideration.

On this head, the Secretary would propose, that the duties on distilled spirits, should be applied in the first instance, to the payment of the interest of the foreign debt.

That reserving out of the residue of those duties an annual sum of six hundred thousand dollars, for the current service of the United States; the surplus, together with the product of the other duties, be applied to the payment of the interest on the new loan, by an appropriation, co-extensive with the duration of the debt.

And that if any part of the debt should remain unsubscribed, the excess of the revenue be divided among the creditors of the unsubscribed part, by a temporary disposition; with a limitation, however, to four per cent.

It will hardly have been unnoticed, that the Secretary has been thus far silent on the subject of the post-office. The reason is, that he has had in view the application of the revenue arising from that source, to the purpose of a sinking fund. The post-master-general gives it as his opinion, that the immediate product of it, upon a proper arrangement, would probably be, not less than one hundred thousand dollars. And from its nature, with good management, it must be a growing, and will be likely to become a considerable fund. The post-master-general is now engaged in preparing a plan,* which will be the foundation of a proposition for a new arrangement of the establishment. This, and some other points relative to the subject referred to the Secretary, he begs leave to reserve for a future report.

Persuaded as the Secretary is, that the proper funding of the present debt will render it a national blessing: Yet he is so far from acceding to the position, in the latitude in which it is sometimes laid down, that "public debts are public benefits," a position inviting to prodigality, and liable to dangerous abuse, that he ardently wishes to see it incorporated, as a fundamental maxim, in the system of public credit of the United States, that the

---

* *This plan, since the framing of this report, has been received, and will be, shortly, submitted.*

creation of debt should always be accompanied with the means of extinguish-
ment. This he regards as the true secret for rendering public credit immortal.
And he presumes, that it is difficult to conceive a situation, in which there
may not be an adherence to the maxim. At least he feels an unfeigned
solicitude, that this may be attempted by the United States, and that they
may commence their measures for the establishment of credit, with the
observance of it.

Under this impression, the Secretary proposes, that the nett product of the
post-office, to a sum not exceeding one million of dollars, be vested in
commissioners, to consist of the Vice-President of the United States or President of the Senate, the Speaker of the House of Representatives, the Chief
Justice, Secretary of the Treasury and Attorney-General of the United States,
for the time being, in trust, to be applied, by them, or any three of them, to
the discharge of the existing public debt, either by purchases of stock in the
market, or by payments on account of the principal, as shall appear to them
most adviseable, in conformity to the public engagements; to continue so
vested, until the whole of the debt shall be discharged.

As an additional expedient for effecting a reduction of the debt, and for
other purposes which will be mentioned, the Secretary would further propose
that the same commissioners be authorised, with the approbation of the
President of the United States, to borrow, on their credit, a sum, not exceeding twelve millions of dollars, to be applied,

First. To the payment of the interest and instalments of the foreign debt,
to the end of the present year, which will require 3,491,923 dollars, and 46
cents.

Secondly. To the payment of any deficiency which may happen in the
product of the funds provided for paying the interest of the domestic debt.

Thirdly. To the effecting a change in the form of such part of the foreign
debt, as bears an interest of five per cent. It is conceived, that, for this
purpose, a new loan, at a lower interest, may be combined with other
expedients. The remainder of this part of the debt, after paying the instalments, which will accrue in the course of 1790, will be 3,888,888 dollars,
and 81 cents.

Fourthly. To the purchase of the public debt at the price it shall bear in the
market, while it continues below its true value. This measure, which would
be, in the opinion of the Secretary, highly dishonorable to the government, if
it were to precede a provision for funding the debt, would become altogether
unexceptionable, after that had been made. Its effect would be in favor of the
public creditors, as it would tend to raise the value of stock. And all the
difference, between its true value, and the actual price, would be so much
clear gain to the public. The payment of foreign interest on the capital to be
borrowed for this purpose, should that be a necessary consequence, would

not, in the judgment of the Secretary, be a good objection to the measure. The saving by the operation would be itself, a sufficient indemnity; and the employment of that capital, in a country situated like this, would much more than compensate for it. Besides, if the government does not undertake this operation, the same inconvenience, which the objection in question supposes, would happen in another way, with a circumstance of aggravation. As long, at least, as the debt shall continue below its proper value, it will be an object of speculation to foreigners, who will not only receive the interest, upon what they purchase, and remit it abroad, as in the case of the loan, but will reap the additional profit of the difference in value. By the government's entering into competition with them, it will not only reap a part of this profit itself, but will contract the extent, and lessen the extra profit of foreign purchases. That competition will accelerate the rise of stock; and whatever greater rate this obliges foreigners to pay, for what they purchase, is so much clear saving to the nation. In the opinion of the Secretary, and contrary to an idea which is not without patrons, it ought to be the policy of the government, to raise the value of stock to its true standard as fast as possible. When it arrives to that point, foreign speculations (which, till then, must be deemed pernicious, further than as they serve to bring it to that point) will become beneficial. Their money laid out in this country, upon our agriculture, commerce and manufactures, will produce much more to us, than the income they will receive from it.

The Secretary contemplates the application of this money, through the medium of a national bank, for which, with the permission of the House, he will submit a plan in the course of the session.

The Secretary now proceeds, in the last place, to offer to the consideration of the House, his ideas, of the steps, which ought at the present session, to be taken, towards the assumption of the state debts.

These are briefly, that concurrent resolutions of the two Houses, with the approbation of the President, be entered into, declaring in substance,

That the United States do assume, and will at the first session in the year 1791, provide, on the same terms with the present debt of the United States, for all such part of the debts of the respective states, or any of them, as shall, prior to the first day of January in the said year 1791, be subscribed towards a loan to the United States, upon the principles of either of the plans, which shall have been adopted by them, for obtaining a re-loan of their present debt.

Provided that the provision to be made as aforesaid, shall be suspended, with respect to the debt, of any state, which may have exchanged the securities of the United States for others issued by itself, until the whole of the said securities shall, either be re-exchanged, or surrendered to the United States.

And provided also, that the interest upon the debt assumed, be computed to the end of the year 1791; and that the interest to be paid by the United States, commence on the first day of January, 1792.

That the amount of the debt of each state so assumed and provided for, be charged to such state in account with the United States, upon the same principles, upon which it shall be lent to the United States.

That subscriptions be opened for receiving loans of the said debts at the same times and places, and under the like regulations, as shall have been prescribed in relation to the debt of the United States.

The Secretary has now completed the objects, which he proposed to himself, to comprise in the present report. He has, for the most part, omitted details, as well to avoid fatiguing the attention of the House, as because more time would have been desirable even to digest the general principles of the plan. If these should be found right, the particular modifications will readily suggest themselves in the progress of the work.

The Secretary, in the views which have directed his pursuit of the subject, has been influenced, in the first place, by the consideration, that his duty from the very terms of the resolution of the House, obliged him to propose what appeared to him an adequate provision for the support of the public credit, adapted at the same time to the real circumstances of the United States; and in the next, by the reflection, that measures which will not bear the test of future unbiassed examination, can neither be productive of individual reputation, nor (which is of much greater consequence) public honor, or advantage.

Deeply impressed, as the Secretary is, with a full and deliberate conviction, that the establishment of public credit, upon the basis of a satisfactory provision, for the public debt, is, under the present circumstances of this country, the true desideratum towards relief from individual and national embarrassments; that without it, these embarrassments will be likely to press still more severely upon the community—He cannot but indulge an anxious wish, that an effectual plan for that purpose may, during the present session, be the result of the united wisdom of the legislature.

He is fully convinced, that it is of the greatest importance, that no further delay should attend the making of the requisite provision; not only, because it will give a better impression of the good faith of the country, and will bring earlier relief to the creditors; both which circumstances are of great moment to public credit: but, because the advantages to the community, from raising stock, as speedily as possible, to its natural value, will be incomparably greater, than any that can result from its continuance below that standard. No profit, which could be derived from purchases in the market, on account of the government, to any practicable extent, would be an equivalent for the loss, which would be sustained by the purchases of foreigners, at a low value. Not to repeat, that governmental purchases, to be honorable, ought to be preceded by a provision. Delay, by disseminating doubt, would sink the price of stock; and as the temptation to foreign speculations, from the lowness of the price, would be too great to be neglected, millions would probably be lost to the United States.

All which is humbly submitted.

ALEXANDER HAMILTON,
Secretary of the Treasury

[SCHEDULE A.]

SUPPOSITITIOUS STATEMENT OF ACCOUNTS BETWEEN THE UNITED STATES AND INDIVIDUAL STATES.

STATES.	Ratio.	Balances due to the states respectively.	Proportion of each state of the aggregate of those balances according to the ratio.	Balances against certain States.
New-Hampshire	3	57,500	60,000	2,500
Massachusetts	8	180,000	160,000	
Rhode-Island	1	20,000	20,000	
Connecticut	5	110,000	100,000	
New-York	6	135,000	120,000	
New-Jersey	4	72,500	80,000	7,500
Pennsylvania	8	170,000	160,000	
Delaware	1	30,000	20,000	
Maryland	6	110,000	120,000	10,000
Virginia	10	187,500	200,000	12,500
North-Carolina	5	90,000	100,000	10,000
South-Carolina	5	87,500	100,000	12,500
Georgia	3	50,000	60,000	10,000
	65	1,300,000	1,300,000	65,000

Balances in favor of certain states.	Proportion of each state in the aggregate of the balances against certain states.	Ultimate balances in favor of certain states upon the principle of an extinguishment of the balances owing by the debtor states, and a proportional allowance to the other states, adjusted according to the ratio given, and to be paid by the United States.
	3,000	500
20,000	8,000	28,000
	1,000	1,000
10,000	5,000	15,000
15,000	6,000	21,000
	4,000	
10,000	8,000	18,000
10,000	1,000	11,000
	6,000	
	10,000	
	5,000	
	5,000	
	3,000	
65,000	65,000	94,500

EXPLANATION

THE first column supposes a Ratio according to the present rule of representation.

The second column exhibits the balances which, on the principles of the statement suggested are supposed to be due to the several States.

The third column shews the apportionment of the aggregate of those balances according to the ratio given among the States.

The fourth column shews the balances against some States in consequence of this apportionment.

The fifth column shews the balances in favor of some States, in consequence of the same apportionment.

This completes the first process proposed.

THE second Process is illustrated by the sixth and seventh columns.

The sixth shews the share of each State, according to the ratio given in the amount of the balances against the Debtor States.

The seventh shews the ultimate balances in favor of certain States, crediting them for their proportions of the balance due from the Debtor States.

[SCHEDULE B.]

A GENERAL STATEMENT of the FOREIGN LOANS, shewing in Abstract, the Capital Sums borrowed, and the Arrearages of Interest to the 31st December, 1789.

CAPITAL SUMS Borrowed.		Livres.	Dollars. Cts.
Of the Royal French Treasury, on Interest at 5 per cent.		24,000,000	
In Holland, guaranteed by the French Court, at 4 per cent.		10,000,000	
	Livres,	34,000,000	6,296,296
Of the Royal Spanish Treasury, at 5 per cent.			174,011
Lenders in Holland,		Florins.	
First Loan,	5 per cent.	5,000,000	
Second ditto,	4 per cent.	2,000,000	
Third ditto,	5 per cent.	1,000,000	
Fourth ditto,	5 per cent.	1,000,000	
	Florins,	9,000,000	3,600,000
	Capital,		10,070,307

ARREARAGES of INTEREST to 31st December, 1789.
On the *French Loan*.

		Livres.	Dollars. Cts.
1789, Jan. 1, Five Years Interest on the	6,000,000 at 5 per cent.		277,777.77
Sept. 3, Six do.	on the 18,000,000 do.		999,999.96
Nov. 5, Four do.	on the 10,000,000 4 per cent.		296,296.

On the *Spanish Loan*.

ARREARAGES on the *Spanish Loan* of 174,011 Dollars,		
to 21st March, 1782, at 5 per cent.	5,093.27	
March 21, Seven Years Interest on do.	60,904.62	
		1,640,071.62
Total Dollars,		11,710,378.62

NOTE. There were certain parts of the Capital of the Dutch guaranteed Loan of 10,000,000 Florins, and of the French Loan of 18,000,000 Livres, which became due at the following periods, and remain unpaid, viz.

1787	Sept. 3, First Payment of the 18,000,000.	1,500,000	277,777.77
	Nov. 5, First do. of the 10,000,000.	1,000.000	185,185.19
1788	Sept. 3, Second do. of the 18,000,000.	the same.	462,962.96
	Nov. 5, Second do. of the 10,000,000.		
1789	Sept. 3, Third do. of the 18,000,000.	the same.	462,962.96
	Nov. 5, Third do. of the 10,000,000.		
	Dollars,		1,388,888.88

TREASURY DEPARTMENT, *Register's Office,* 31st Dec. 1789

JOSEPH NOURSE, Register

To the ARREARAGE of INTEREST to 31st December, 1789, above stated,

Amounting to   1,640,071.62

Add one year's Interest from 1st January, to 31st December, 1789, on 186,427, dollars, and 69 cents, being the Amount Principal Sum due to foreign officers, employed in the service of the United States, which Interest is annually payable at the House of Mons. Grand Banker at Paris, at 6 per cent.   11,185.66

ARREARAGES of INTEREST to 31st December, 1789,   Dollars,   1,651,257.28

THE above Addition was adverted to, after the conclusion of the Report; but as it makes no material difference, an alteration in consequence of it, is deemed unnecessary.

ALEXANDER HAMILTON, Secretary of the Treasury

[Schedule C.]

Abstract of the Liquidated and Loan-Office Debt of the United States, on the 3d March, 1789.

		Dollars. 90ths.
Registered Debt,		4,598,462.78
Credits given to sundries on the treasury books, by virtue of special acts of Congress, which are not yet put on the Funded Debt,		187,578.65
Certificates issued by the commissioner of army accounts, deducting those which have been cancelled and registered,		7,967,109.73
Certificates issued by the commissioners of the five departments, deducting those which have been cancelled and registered,		903,574.59
Certificates issued by the late state commissioners, deducting those which have been cancelled and registered,		3,291,156.37
Loan-office certificates issued in 1781, and expressed as specie value, deducting those which have been cancelled and registered,		112,704.15

Loan-office certificates, old emissions, reduced to specie value, agreeably to the scale made by Congress, by taking the medium of the loans made in each month, viz. 3,787,900 loaned to 1st September 1777, equal to

*3,459,000 ditto between 1st Sept. 1777 and 1st March 1778,

59,830,212 ditto between 1st March 1778, and the closure of the Loan-offices,

	Dollars. 90ths.	
	3,787,900	
	2,538,572	
	5,146,330	
	11,463,802	

Deduct specie amount cancelled and registered,

	365,983	
		11,097,818

Foreign officers, amount to their credit, the interest whereof is payable at the House of Mons. Grand Banker at Paris, and included in the estimate of foreign interest,

		186,427.69
		28,344,833.21

From which deduct this sum received into the Treasury on account of lands and other property, and cancelled,

		960,915.44
Leaves the amount of the domestic debt,	Dollars,	27,383,917.67

*On the certificates issued between the 1st September 1777 and 1st March 1778, interest is payable on the nominal sum (being 3,459,000 dollars) although the specie value of the principal is only 2,538,572 dollars.

Register's-office, March 3, 1789,

Joseph Nourse, Register

Treasury Department, *Register's-office, January 1, 1790*

The above estimate was formed to the expiration of the late government—Some variation hath since taken place in the several parts, without making any material alteration in the aggregate amount of the domestic debt: This arises from a daily exchange at the Treasury of Loan-office and Final Settlement Certificates, for Treasury Certificates given as evidences of the registered debt, whereby the increase of the latter is carried on in proportion to the cancelment of the former.

Joseph Nourse, Register

[SCHEDULE D]

An ESTIMATE of all the INTEREST which will accrue on the DOMESTIC DEBT of the United States, from its formation to the 31st December 1790, of such partial payments as have been made on account thereof, and of the balance which will remain to be provided for, to pay up the interest fully to that period.

		Dollars	Cts.
THE total amount of interest arising on the loan-office debt, from the opening of the several offices in 1776, to the 31st of December, 1790,		9,534,478	
The total amount of interest arising on the army debt, from the several periods of its drawing interest, to the 31st December, 1790,		5,105,099	
The total amount of interest arising on certificates issued by the thirteen state commissioners, estimated at		2,146,799	
The total amount of interest arising on certificates issued by the commissioners for the commissaries, quarter-masters, marine, cloathing and hospital departments, estimated at		737,338	
The total amount of interest arising on the debt registered at the treasury, estimated at		366,646	
The total amount of interest on debts entered in the treasury books, but for which certificates have not been issued by the Register, so as to become a part of the registered debt, estimated at		83,936	
	Total	17,974,296	

From this total amount of interest, the following
                    deductions are to be made, viz.   *Dollars   Cts.*

So much paid on the loan-office debt, in old emission, equal to	372,368.30	
In new emissions, as specie,	39,433.49	
In bills of exchange, as ditto,	1,663,992	
So much paid by the several states in indents, paid into the treasury on account of their quotas on the existing requisitions of the late Congress,	2,244,231.31	
So much paid by the state of New-Jersey to their own citizens, on the domestic debt, not included in the schedule of taxes,	424,442.22	
So much paid by the state of South-Carolina, being two years interest on 222,465 dollars, and 9/90ths, the amount of certificates issued to the line of that state, at 6 per cent. is	26,695.73	
Total amount of Interest paid,	4,771,163.05	
Deduct three years interest, estimated in the foregoing, on 960,915 dollars, and 42/100ths, being so much of the capital of the domestic debt received in payment for lands and other public property,	172,964.75	
Total amount of deductions		4,944,127.80

Leaves a balance of thirteen million and thirty thousand one hundred sixty-eight dollars, and twenty cents, which will accrue on the domestic debt, and for which provision is to be made to pay the interest fully up to the 31st. December 1790,   13,030,168.20

It is to be observed, that as the certificates which have been issued for the principal of a debt of more than twenty-seven millions of dollars, are in themselves exceedingly numerous; and that as those several certificates bear an interest from different periods, it has been not practicable to form a statement of arrearages, but by ascertaining in the most accurate manner, the different periods of time from which the several parts of the domestic debt bear interest, and therefrom calculating the interest to 31st. December, 1790.

TREASURY DEPARTMENT, *Register's Office*, 31st December, 1789.

JOSEPH NOURSE, Register

[Schedule E]

Abstract of the Public Debt of the States undermentioned, agreeably to statements transmitted in pursuance of the resolution of the House of Representatives of the 21st of September, 1789.

MASSACHUSETTS. *Dollars* *Cents*

Principal with interest to the 1st day of
Nov. 1789. £.1,548,040. 7. 9 Lawful.
Due to sundries for which no certificates
have yet been issued, 20,000
Total, £.1,568,040. 7. 9 at 6s. per Dol. 5,226,801.29

CONNECTICUT.
Principal bearing interest from the 1st of
Feb. 1789, 560,404
To which ought to be added for balance of
state bills emitted in the year 1780,
bearing interest at 5 per cent. to the 1st
March 1785, estimated at 24,948
Total, £. 585,352. 0. 0 at 6s. per Dol. 1,951,173.33¹/₃

NEW-YORK
Principal and interest computed to the 1st
day of January 1790, 1,032,616. 2. 0
From which ought to be deducted for
amount of principal and interest of continental securities loaned to the state in
pursuance of their act of the 18th day of
April 1786, estimated at 565,586
Leaves for state debt *proper*, £. 467,030. 2. 0 at 8s. per Dol. 1,167,575.25

NEW-JERSEY
Principal unredeemed, 295,755. 4.11 at 7/6 per Dol. 788,680.65⁵/₉

VIRGINIA
Principal of domestic debt, 1,063,396.17. 1
Ditto of foreign debt with interest to the
1st January 1790, 40,826. 1. 1
Total, £.1,104,222.18. 2 at 6s. per Dol. 3,680,743.02⁷/₉

SOUTH-CAROLINA
Principal of domestic debt, 1,069,652. 2. 4
Indents of interest on ditto in circulation, 71,325. 7. 2
Foreign debt, principal and interest, due to
the 1st of January 1789, 115,810. 0. 1
Total, £.1,256,787. 9. 7 at 4/8 per Dol. 5,386,232.05
Total dollars, 18,201,205.60⁶/₉

It will be observed, that the period to which interest is calculated on the debts abovementioned is only specified with accuracy on the statements which have been transmitted from Massachusetts, Connecticut and New-York. From the best information which the Secretary can obtain, he presumes—That in the statement made of the debt of New-Jersey, interest has been calculated to the 31st day of December 1788. That on the debt of Virginia, interest has been calculated to the 31st day of December 1788. On that of South-Carolina, to the 1st day of April 1790.

From the states of New-Hampshire, Pennsylvania, Delaware, Maryland, North-Carolina and Georgia, no accounts of their respective state debts have been forwarded.

The Secretary is however of opinion from the result of enquiries made by him—That the state debt of New-Hampshire may be estimated at about Dollars 300,000

That the state debt *proper* of Pennsylvania (that is exclusive of their assumption of the continental debt) at about Dollars 2,200,000

And that of Maryland, at Ditto 800,000

From the above statement and estimates, the amount of principal and interest of the state debts (exclusive of Delaware, North-Carolina, Georgia and Rhode-Island) appears to be about twenty-one millions and a half;

but as the debts of the four last states are not included in the above sum; and it is possible that a greater arrearage of interest may be due on the state debts than is at present ascertained, the aggregate of the principal and interest may be computed at twenty-five millions of dollars.

ALEXANDER HAMILTON, *Secretary of the Treasury*

COMMONWEALTH OF MASSACHUSETTS

A STATEMENT of the DEBT of the Commonwealth of Massachusetts, as it respects the notes issued by the several Treasurers, to the first of November, 1789

November 1, 1789, exclusive of half pay notes,	£1,403,459.16.11

Notes issued to widows and orphan children of the deceased officers of the late continental army, for the seven years half pay, agreeable to resolves of Congress,   8,246.11.10

Interest on the foregoing notes since October, 1781,	£579,660.6.4	
Of which has been paid	443,326.7.4	
Interest remaining due, November 1, 1789,		136,333.19. 0
		£1,548,040. 7. 9

Remains due on the books of the committee for settling with the late continental army, to the widows and orphan children of deceased officers of said army, and to officers and soldiers for their services, about   20,000

N. B. By an act of the legislature, one third part of the revenue of Excise is appropriated to pay the exigencies of government, and the other two third parts for the payment of interest of the notes, which pays about one quarter part of the interest; the other three quarters are unprovided for.

Treasury-Office, Boston, October 31, 1789
ALEXANDER HODGDON, Treasurer

COMPARED with the original, in the office of the Secretary of the Treasury.

WILLIAM DUER

STATE OF CONNECTICUT

A STATEMENT of the PUBLIC DEBT of the State of Connecticut, as it stood November 1, 1789.

Notes issued to the Connecticut line, payable June 1, 1782,			£2,334.13.11¹/₂
Ditto	ditto	1783,	2,339.13. 4
Ditto	ditto	1784,	3,252.12. 1
Ditto	ditto	1785,	42,309. 6. 1³/₄
Ditto	ditto	1786,	28,189. 6. 3³/₄
Ditto	ditto	1787,	28,448. 5. 6³/₄
Ditto	ditto	1788,	21,593. 0. 4¹/₄
Ditto	ditto	1789,	20,097. 5. 7¹/₄
Ditto date February 1, 1781, issued per act of Assembly, Nov. 1780,			153,229. 8. 6³/₄
Ditto of various dates,	ditto per act of ditto,	May, 1781,	33,947.11. 8¹/₂
Ditto dated June 1, 1781,	ditto ditto, for remounting dragoons,		1,932. 8. 0
Ditto of various dates,	ditto ditto,	May, 1783,	41,841. 6. 1³/₄
Ditto issued per act of May, 1789, for old notes re-loaned,			180,890. 1. 0
			560,404.18. 9¹/₄

Notes issued per particular acts of Assembly, payable out of civil list funds,   2,856.11. 4

Certificates for interest, &c. issued on the state debt, up to February 1, 1789, and remaining unpaid November 1, 1789,   19,140. 3. 9³/₄

Balance of orders unpaid, drawn by Oliver Wolcott, Esq. payable out of the 1/ tax, granted in January 1783,   692. 8.10

Balance of state bills, which were emitted in March, June and July, 1780, with the interest at 5 per cent. to the 1st of March, 1785, estimated at   24,948. 9. 1

There are a number of pay table orders drawn on former taxes, the amount, supposed not great, cannot be ascertained.

There is also out-standing, a sum of old emissions of paper, issued before the war—the amount unknown.

ACCOUNT of LOAN-OFFICE and FINAL SETTLEMENT CERTIFICATES in the treasury of the State
of CONNECTICUT

Loan-office certificates,	£442.19. 7
Final settlement certificates,	2,151.17. 1
	£ 2,594.16. 8

Amount of interest certificates that were issued upon the evidence of the United
States debt, received by the treasurer of the state of Connecticut for taxes and impost
duties, and delivered to William Imlay, Esq. continental loan-officer, from January
9, 1786, to November 1, 1789,   £33,996.15. 3

COMPARED with the original in the office of the Secretary of the Treasury.

A STATEMENT of the FUNDS provided for the payment of the principal and interest of the public debt
of the state of CONNECTICUT

BALANCES of taxes laid for the payment of interest on the state debt, and the first three classes of army
notes, as appears from the treasury books, November 1, 1789, being the balance of fifteen taxes, including
abatements, collecting fees, &c.   £40,489.14.10

Balance of excise and impost bonds payable, including collecting fees, &c.   9,070.15. 2

A tax of four pence on the pound, laid on the list, 1788, amounting to
£1,462,860.10.11 for the payment of interest on the state debt, and the balance of
the three first classes of the state notes; the nett avails estimated at   20,266.14. 4

A tax of eight pence on the pound, on the same list, laid for the payment of the
balance of state bills, orders on 2s. 6d. and 1s. taxes, and part of the principal of the
state debt; the nett avails estimated at   40,533. 8. 8

Excise for the payment of interest on the state debt, &c. estimated at   5,000. 0. 0

The first article in the above statement of funds will probably, upon settlement of those old taxes, fall
greatly short of the sum set down; to say how much, is merely conjectural. There will also be a loss upon the
excise and impost bonds. The amount of the excise for the current year is very uncertain.

Comptroller's-Office, 1st December, 1789.

RALPH POMEROY, Comptroller

STATE OF NEW-YORK
A STATEMENT of the DEBT of the State of NEW-YORK
The following species of Certificates, &c. have been issued by the State, and are still unredeemed, viz.

	Principal Sum, Spec. val.	Interest to Jan. 1, 1790.
Certificates for Money loaned, pursuant to resolutions of the		
4th day of April, 1778,	£111.13. 3	£78.14. 5
for do. pursuant to a law of the 30th of June, 1780,	741. 6. 0	422.10. 9
for horses purchased in the year 1780,	904. 5. 0	515. 8. 5
for depreciation of pay to the army dated 31st July, 1780,	54,520. 1. 7	25,669.17. 4
for pay of the year 1781, to do. dated the 1st January, 1782,	17,972. 6. 9	8,626.14. 0
for pensions to widows of military officers,	8,104.18. 2	3,647. 4. 2
for pay of levies, militia, &c. &c.	42,871. 4. 3	18,220. 5. 3
for other certificates received on loan, pursuant to a law passed the 18th April, 1786,	523,848. 5. 1	144,058. 5. 4
for four-fifths of the interest due on those received on loan,	105,669. 9. 8	
for claims on forfeited estates	25,897. 8.10	3,884.12. 3
Bills of credit, called New Emission, emitted pursuant to a law passed the 30th of June, 1780, bearing interest,	3,612.16. 0	1,174. 3. 1
Ditto, emitted pursuant to resolutions of Congress, and Convention of this State, reduced to specie value,	1,047. 0. 0	
	£785,300.14. 7	£206,297.15. 0

There are large demands against forfeited estates, unliquidated,
   and others liquidated, for which no certificates have yet
   issued, to the amount of   41,017.12. 5
   There are no funds specially provided for redeeming the aforesaid Certificates,
except the following, viz.
   The arrears of old taxes may probably produce about   £10,000. 0. 0
   Quit rents, about   20,000. 0. 0
   Fifteen townships of new lands, or 375,000 acres, ordered to be sold (by a law
passed the 25th February, 1789,) and are now surveying.

                           GERARD BANCKER, *Treasurer of the State of New-York*

   New-York, November 30, 1789

An ACCOUNT of CONTINENTAL SECURITIES now in the Treasury of the State of NEW-YORK, viz.

	Principal.	Int. 1st Jun. 1790.
Certificates issued by William Barber,	£352,471.13. 1	£105,741. 9.11
Ditto, by loan-officers in this State,	277,448.16. 4	83,234.12.11
Ditto, by John Pierce, Burrall, Denning, Bindon, and Fox,	299,614. 4. 5	89,884. 5. 4
Interest facilities,	2,502.14. 8	
	£932,037. 8. 6	£278,860. 8. 2

   OF the above-mentioned Loan-Office and Barbers's Certificates, the sum of £470,649.17.6 was received
in on loan by the State in 1786, and one fifth of the interest that was due thereon, to the 31st December,
1784, then paid, and certificates for the remaining four fifths issued, payable in one year, of which
certificates three fourths remain unredeemed, as represented in the former part of this statement.

                           GERARD BANCKER, *Treasurer of the State of New-York*

   New-York, November 30, 1789

COMPARED with the Original in the office of the Secretary of the Treasury.

An ACCOUNT of CERTIFICATES due from the UNITED STATES to the INHABITANTS of the State of
NEW-JERSEY, which draw interest at the TREASURY

	Principal.	Annual Interest.
1st. Continental loan-office certificates,	£420,511. 0.10	25,230.13. 3
2d. Certificates issued by John Pierce, commissioner, for arrears of pay, &c.	147,118.15. 2¹/₄	8,827. 2. 6
3d. Certificates by Benjamin Thompson, Commissioner,	344,237.11. 2	20,654. 5. 0
	£911,867. 7. 2¹/₄	54,712. 0. 9

                     COMMUTATION.

   4th. Certificates issued by John Pierce, Commissioner,
and given to the officers of the late Jersey line, for their
commutation,   66,899. 2. 6

                       STATE DEBT.

   1st. Certificates given to the officers and soldiers of the
late Jersey line, for the depreciation of their pay, of which
there was outstanding October 1, 1786,   99,526.11. 4

   2d. Ditto given by the Commissioners in the several
counties for militia pay, of which there was outstanding
October 1, 1786,   55,365.17. 7¹/₂

   3d. Certificates given by Silas Condict, Commissioner,   121,521. 8. 7

   4th. Ditto given by the Treasurer and Auditor for
demands against confiscated estates,   32,020. 2. 9

   5th. Ditto issued by the Auditor for militia pay,   821. 4. 7¹/₂

                           £309,255. 4.11

Paid into the Treasury since October 1786,   13,500. 0. 0
                                                      £295,755. 4.11
   Annual interest of state debt,   £ 17,745. 6. 3$^{1}/_{2}$
COMPARED with the Original in the Office of the Secretary of the Treasury.

ABSTRACT of the PUBLIC DEBTS due from the State of VIRGINIA.

ON interest at 6 per cent. { Army debt for pay and depreciation of the officers and soldiers,   £936,830. 7. 6
Loan-office debt,   119,382. 7. 4
Certificates issued for the paper money funded,   7,183. 2. 3

  Balance due to Foreign creditors, including the interest (at 6 per cent.) to the
1st. of January, 1790, on £9,415.0.2 part of the said balance, for which warrants
have not been drawn by the creditors,   40,826. 1. 1
Virginia, Auditor's Office, November 20, 1789   JOHN PENDLETON, Auditor of Public Accounts

COMPARED with the original in the office of the Secretary of the Treasury.

  The Auditor-General reports the following STATEMENT of the DEBT due by the State of
SOUTH-CAROLINA, viz.

    PRINCIPAL INDENTS.
BALANCE issued from the treasury of the state
aforesaid, and yet remaining to be issued on the 1st of
October, 1789,   £1,069,652. 2. 4$^{1}/_{2}$
     To be cancelled by
Balance of bonds for confiscated property,   £79,985.10. 0$^{1}/_{4}$
Purchases of ditto, unsettled for,   12,910. 0. 0
Balance of amercements,   7,713. 4. 6
Ditto for bonds for public property   35,065.10. 6
Ditto of lands granted to 1st November, 1789,   42,568. 1. 7$^{1}/4$ 178,242. 6. 8
    Balance still to be cancelled,   Sterling,   £891,409.15. 8$^{1}/_{2}$
    SPECIAL INDENTS.
Amount issued, and to be issued,   £440,368. 0. 0
Deduct, for so much received into the treasury,   369,042.12. 9$^{3}/4$
    Balance in circulation, and yet to be issued,   £ 71,325. 7. 2$^{1}/4$
Agreeably to a report of the committee of ways and
  means, the debts due to the State for the arrears of
taxes, &c. are sufficient to cancel the above balance.
    FOREIGN DEBT.
Amount due to sundry persons,   £93,244.17. 4
Balance of interest due 1st January, 1789,   £29,558. 4.11$^{1}/_{4}$
Deduct, for so much not paid
J. S. Cripps, agent,   £4,949. 5. 4$^{1}/_{4}$
Balance paid to such creditors as
were here or their attorneys,   2,043.16.10   6,993. 2. 2$^{1}/4$ 22,565. 2. 9
    Principal and balance due 1st January, 1789,   £115,810. 0. 1
   FUNDS appropriated by the Legislature.
Out of the taxes payable the 1st April, 1790,   £10,000.
Interest on the paper medium, to 1st May, 1791,   12,750.
Balance of bonds given for confiscated property,
payable in specie,   1,610.17. 3$^{1}/_{4}$
The sums due, and that shall become due, for
amercements, in specie,   8,371.16. 6
Balance of bonds given for duties, payable by
instalments,   6,240.14. 3
  Bonds for duties due prior to 1st Jan. 1788, not
installed,   233. 3. 4$^{1}/_{2}$

A tax of 1/4th of a dollar per head, per annum, on
all negroes, mustizoes, and mulattoes, for ten years,
from February 1791, the number computed to be about
100,000, which will amount to   58,333. 6. 8
                                Sterling,   £97,539.18. 0¹/₄

                                                    J. McCALL, Auditor

Auditor's-Office, Charleston, 30th November, 1789

COMPARED with the original in the office of the Secretary of the Treasury

(Schedule F.)

Table shewing the Annuity which a person of a given age, would be entitled to during life, from the time he should arrive at a given age, upon the present payment of a hundred dollars, computing Interest at four per cent.

Age at the time of payment.	Age when entitled.	Annuity	Age when entitled.	Annuity.	Age when entitled.	Annuity.	Age when entitled.	Annuity.
1	21	23.453	31	42.625	41	84.522	50	174.11
2	22	20.376	32	37.365	42	74.936	50	143.14
3	23	19.415	33	35.775	43	72.440	50	128.46
4	24	18.826	34	34.970	44	71.697	50	117.64
5	25	18.457	35	34.660	45	71.840	50	108.95
6	26	18.280	36	34.619	46	72.584	50	101.60
7	27	18.188	37	34.767	47	73.752	50	95.210
8	28	18.258	38	35.235	48	75.720	50	89.971
9	29	18.383	39	35.830	49	78.025	50	85.238
10	30	18.617	40	37.006	50	81.960		
11	21	10.346	31	18.803	41	37.286	50	75.500
12	22	10.414	32	19.072	42	38.162	50	73.058
13	23	10.519	33	19.382	43	39.249	50	70.246
14	24	10.608	34	19.704	44	40.493	50	66.279
15	25	10.727	35	20.088	45	41.638	50	63.151
16	26	10.818	36	20.489	46	42.957	50	60.129
17	27	10.939	37	20.911	47	44.358	50	57.258
18	28	11.065	38	21.354	48	45.888	50	54.520
19	29	11.195	39	21.821	49	47.519	50	51.907
20	30	11.352	40	22.313	50	49.415		
21	31	11.515	41	22.836	50	47.038		
22	32	11.687	42	23.386	50	44.770		
23	33	11.846	43	23.987	50	42.534		
24	34	12.028	44	24.719	50	40.460		
25	35	12.253	45	25.396	50	38.510		
26	36	12.462	46	26.128	50	36.572		
27	37	12.682	47	26.902	50	34.726		
28	38	12.913	48	27.749	50	32.967		
29	39	13.155	49	28.647	50	31.329		
30	40	13.385			50	29.643		
31	41	13.629			50	28.073		
32	42	13.884			50	26.580		
33	43	14.190			50	25.161		
34	44	14.547			50	23.812		
35	45	14.827			50	22.483		
36	46	15.157			50	21.217		
37	47	15.512			50	20.023		
38	48	15.896			50	18.886		
39	49	16.301			50	17.806		
40	50	16.783						

(Schedule G.)

Table shewing what Annuity would be enjoyed by the Survivor of any two persons of certain ages, for hundred dollars, computing Interest at four per cent. per annum,

Age of the youngest.	Age of the eldest.	Annuity of Survivor.	Age of the youngest.	Age of the eldest.	Annuity of Survivor.
	10	28.248		20	28.169
	15	26.392		25	26.041
	20	24.545		30	23.923
	25	22.716		35	21.753
	30	20.920		40	19.825
	35	19.168	20	45	17.876
10	40	17.464		50	16.018
	45	15.847		55	14.261
	50	14.263		60	12.620
	55	12.782		65	11.100
	60	11.237		70	9.707
	65	10.099			
	70	8.905		25	27.816
				30	25.556
	15	28.169		35	23.331
	20	26.198		40	21.159
	25	24.219		45	19.047
	30	22.276	25	50	17.030
	35	20.376		55	15.117
	40	18.528		60	13.331
15	45	16.750		65	11.689
	50	15.053		70	10.173
	55	12.968			
	60	11.948			
	65	10.553			
	70	9.270			

To find the Annuity upon the Survivorship of the youngest of any two lives, expressed in this table, look age of the eldest will be seen the Annuity required.

the remainder of life, after the determination of the life in expectation, upon the present payment of one and the duration of life according to Doctor Halley's Tables.

Age of the youngest.	Age of the eldest.	Annuity of Survivor.	Age of the youngest.	Age of the eldest.	Annuity of Survivor.
	30	28.555		45	30.620
	35	26.001		50	27.005
	40	23.496		55	23.375
	45	21.061	45	60	20.040
30	50	18.730		65	16.957
	55	16.529		70	14.240
	60	14.484			
	65	12.600		50	32.164
	70	10.894		55	27.731
			50	60	23.513
	35	28.993		65	19.662
	40	26.164		70	16.257
	45	23.381			
	50	20.702		55	34.286
35	55	18.172		60	28.843
	60	15.820	55	65	23.742
	65	13.666		70	19.175
	70	11.724			
				60	37.509
	40	29.673	60	65	30.423
	45	26.469		70	24.044
	50	23.337			
40	55	20.354		65	42.481
	60	17.604	65	70	32.679
	65	15.060			
	70	12.799	70	70	50.994

for the respective ages under their respective heads, and opposite the number, which corresponds with the

[Schedule H.]

Table for a Tontine of Six Classes, the number of lives in each class being indefinite, calculated on a payment of two hundred dollars by each subscriber, and at a rate of interest of four per cent. The computation on the best life in each class, and on the supposition that the subscribers to each class will not be less than the respective numbers specified in the first column.

Number of Lives in each Class.	Ages.	Annuity whilst all are in life.	Dividends at successive periods during the probable continuance of life.						
			At the expiration of 10 years.	At the expiration of 20 years.	At the expiration of 30 years.	At the expiration of 40 years.	At the expiration of 50 years.	At the expiration of 60 years.	At the expiration of 70 years.
75	1 to 20	8,426	9,722	11,490	14,042	18,054	25,278	42,130	126,390
64	21 to 30	8,676	10,272	12,606	16,314	23,110	39,618	138,666	
54	31 to 40	9,046	11,102	14,366	20,354	34,890	122,282		
44	41 to 50	9,650	12,488	17,608	30,328	106,150			
34	51 to 60	10,714	15,178	26,020	91,068				
24	61 to 70	12,802	20,518	71,802					

This Table, which is calculated on so small a number of persons, will serve to shew the greatness of the advantage to fortunate survivors, in case of a numerous subscription.

[SCHEDULE I.]

GENERAL ESTIMATE for the Services of the Current Year

Civil List, as per No. 1,	254,892.73
War department, No. 2,	155,537.72
Military Pensions, No. 3,	96,979.72
Dollars,	507,410.17

With an eye to the necessary provisions for the foreign department, and to other arrangements which may be found requisite, it appeared advisable to state in the report, to which this is annexed, a sum of six hundred thousand dollars for the current service.

Treasury Department, January 5, 1790

[No. I.]

ESTIMATE of the Expenditure for the Civil List of the United States, on the present establishment for the year 1790.

	Dollars.
For the compensation to the President of the United States,	25,000
That of the Vice-President,	5,000
Compensation to the Chief Justice,	4,000
Ditto to each of the five Associate Justices, 3,500 dollars each,	17,500
To the Judges of the following Districts, viz.	
District of Maine,	1,000
New-Hampshire,	1,000
Massachusetts,	1,200
Connecticut,	1,000
New-York,	1,500
New-Jersey,	1,000
Pennsylvania,	1,600
Delaware,	800
Maryland,	1,500
Virginia,	1,800
Kentuckey,	1,000
South-Carolina,	1,800
Georgia,	1,500
Attorney-General,	1,500

Compensation to the members of Congress, estimating the attendance of the whole number for six months, viz.

	Dols.	Cts.	Dols.	Cts.
Speaker of the House of Representatives, at twelve dollars per day,	2,190			
Eighty members, at six dollars per day,	87,600			
Travelling expences computed,	13,000		104,790	
To the Secretary of the Senate, one year's salary,	1,500			
Additional allowance estimated for six months, at two dollars per day,	365		1,865	
Principal Clerk to the Secretary of the Senate, for the same time, at three dollars per day,			547.50	
Engrossing Clerk to the Secretary of the Senate, estimated for same time, at two dollars per day,			365	
Chaplain to the Senate, estimated for six months, at five hundred dollars per annum,			250	
Compensation to the door-keeper of the Senate, for the same time, at three dollars per day,			547.50	
Messenger to the Senate, for the same time, at 2 dollars per day,			365	
Clerk of the House of Representatives, for one year's salary,	1,500			
Additional allowance calculated for six months, at two dollars per day,	365		1,865	

	Dols.	Cts.	Dols.	Cts.
Principal Clerk in the office of do. estimated for same time, at three dollars per day,	547.50			
Engrossing Clerk for same time, estimated at two dollars per day,	365			
Chaplain to the House of Representatives, estimated for same time, at five hundred dollars per annum,	250			
Serjeant at arms, estimated for same time at 4 dols. per day,	730			
Door-keeper, for same time, at 3 dollars per day,	547.50			
Assistant door-keeper for do. at 2 dollars per day,	365		183,100	
TREASURY DEPARTMENT.				
Secretary of the Treasury,	3,500			
Assistant of the Secretary of the Treasury,	1,500			
Five Clerks, at 500 dollars per annum each,	2,500			
Messenger and office keeper,	150			
Comptroller of the Treasury,	2,000			
Principal Clerk to do.	800			
Four Clerks, at 500 dollars each,	2,000			
Treasurer,	2,000			
Principal Clerk to do.	600			
Auditor of the Treasury,	1,500			
Principal Clerk to do.	600			
Twelve Clerks to do. who, besides the current business under the New Government, has the settlement of the accounts which arose under the Confederation, in the quarter-master, commissary, clothing, hospital, and marine departments, and ordnance stores; and also the accounts of the secret and commercial committees of Congress, at 500 dollars each,	6,000			
Register of the Treasury,	1,250			
One Clerk on the books of the public creditors, called Funded Debt at the Treasury, transfers, &c.	500			
One Clerk in the office of the Register, employed in keeping the accounts of interest arising on the domestic debt,	500			
One do. on the principal books of the treasury, in journalizing and posting into the ledger,	500		25,850	
One Clerk in copying fair statements of the public accounts, and other transcripts as required from the treasury books,	500			
One do. in keeping the accounts of the registers, signed and sealed, &c. for ships transmitted to the collectors of the customs at the several ports; filing duplicates of registers issued by the collectors; keeping the accounts of the transfers of vessels, and other business of record, arising from Act for registering of vessels, regulating the coasting trade, and other purposes therein mentioned,	500			
Two do. on the old accounts of the treasury, and books and accounts of the thirteen late state commissioners, at five hundred dollars each,	1,000			
Messenger and office keeper to the comptroller, auditor and register's office,	150		2,150	
DEPARTMENT OF STATE.				
Secretary of that department,	3,500			
Chief Clerk,	800			
Three Clerks at five hundred dollars each,	1,500			
Messenger and office keeper,	150		5,950	
DEPARTMENT OF WAR.				
Secretary of the department,	3,000			

	Dols.	Cts.	Dols.	Cts.
Chief Clerk,	600			
Two Clerks at five hundred dollars each,	1,000			
Messenger and office keeper,	150		4,750	

GOVERNMENT OF THE WESTERN TERRITORY.

	Dols.	Cts.	Dols.	Cts.
The Governor for his salary as such, and for discharging the duties of Superintendant of Indian affairs in the northern department,	2,000			
The Secretary of the Western Territory,	750			
The Three Judges, at eight hundred dollars each,	2,400		5,150	

OFFICERS employed to settle the accounts between the United States and individual States.

	Dols.	Cts.	Dols.	Cts.
Three Commissioners of the General Board, at two thousand two hundred and fifty dollars per annum,	6,750			
Chief Clerk,	600			
Four Clerks, at four hundred dollars each,	1,600			
Messenger and office keeper,	150			
Paymaster-General, and Commissioner of Army Accounts,	1,250			
Eight Clerks, at five hundred dollars each,	4,000			
One do. at four hundred dollars,	400			
One do. at four hundred and fifty dollars,	450		15,200	

PENSIONS granted by the late Government.

	Dols.	Cts.	Dols.	Cts.
Isaac Van Vert, } John Paulding, } David Williams, } a pension of two hundred dollars per annum to each, pursuant to an act of Congress of 3d November, 1780,	600			
Dominique L'Eglise, per act of 8th of August, 1782,	120			
Joseph Traversie, per do.	120			
Youngest Children of the late Major-General Warren, per act of 1st July, 1780,	450			
Eldest Son of do. per act of 8th April, 1777, estimated at,	600			
Youngest Son of General Mercer, per act of 8th April, 1777, estimated at,	700			
James M'Kenzie, } Joseph Brussels, } John Jordan, } per act of 10th September, 1783, entitled to a pension of forty dollars each per annum,	120			
Elizabeth Bergen, per act of 21st August, 1781,	53.33			
Joseph De Beauleau, per act 5th August, 1782,	100			
Richard Gridley, per acts of 17th November, 1775, and 26th February, 1781,	444.40			
Lieutenant-Colonel Touzard, per act of 27th October, 1778,	360		3,667.73	

For INCIDENTAL and CONTINGENT EXPENCES relative to the CIVIL LIST Establishment.

Under this head are comprehended fire wood, stationary, together with printing work, and all other contingent expences for the two Houses of Congress; rent and office expences of the three several departments, viz. Treasury, State, War, and of the General Board of Commissioners, and Paymaster-General.

			Dols.	Cts.
Congress, estimated at,			5,000	
Treasury Department, viz.				
Rent,	500			
Contingencies of the Secretary's office,	500			
Comptroller's	400			
Auditor's	200			
Register's	200			
Treasurer's	200		2,000	
Ditto War Department,			600	
Department of State,			500	

	Dols.	Cts.	Dols.	Cts.
Board of Commissioners,	500			
Paymaster, and Commissioner of Army Accounts,	425		9,025	
		Dollars,	254,892.73	

THIS estimate corresponds with the existing provisions; but it will probably receive additions from others in the course of the session: In particular it will be observed, that there is no article respecting the salaries of foreign Ministers, their allowances not having been regulated by law. Neither does the estimate include those objects which remain to be provided for, in consequence of some deficiency in the estimate for the services of last year, and also from certain demands on the Treasury, founded on acts of the late Government, which require an appropriation by Congress, previous to their being discharged—These will form an estimate by themselves under the head of Contingencies.

Register's-Office, 5th January, 1790

JOSEPH NOURSE, Register

[No. II.]

ESTIMATE of MONIES Requisite for the DEPARTMENT of WAR, for the year 1790.

INFANTRY.

		Dollars.		
1 Brigadier General with the pay of Lieutenant Colonel Commandant for 12 Months at 50 dollars,		600		
2 Majors,	45	1,080		
7 Captains,	35	2,940		
7 Lieutenants,	30	2,520		
8 Ensigns,	20	1,920		
1 Pay master,	10	120		
1 Adjutant,	10	120		
1 Quarter Master,	10	120		
1 Surgeon,	45	540		
4 Surgeon's Mates,	30	1,440		
28 Sergeants,	6	2,016		
28 Corporals,	5	1,680		
14 Musicians,	5	840		
490 Privates,	4	23,520		
			39,456	

ARTILLERY.

		Dols.	Cts.	Dols.	Cts.
1 Major 12 Months,	at 45 Dol.	540			
4 Captains,	35	1,680			
8 Lieutenants,	30	2,880			
1 Surgeon's Mate,	30	360			
16 Serjeants,	6	1,152			
16 Corporals,	5	960			
8 Musicians,	5	480			
240 Matrosses,	4	11,520			
				19,572	

SUBSISTENCE.

1 Brigadier General, 12 Months,	at 48 Dol.	576		
3 Majors,	20	720		
11 Captains,	12	1,584		
23 Subalterns,	8	2,208		
1 Surgeon,	16	192		
5 Surgeon Mates,	8	480		
			5,760	

RATIONS.

For 840 Non Commissioned Officers and Privates, one ration pr. day, each for 365 days, is 306,600 rations at 12 cents pr. ditto,	36,792	
		101,580

Clothing, 840, }		
Contingencies, 100, } 940 suits at 26 dollars each,		24,440

	Dols.	Cts.	Dols.	Cts.

QUARTER MASTER'S DEPARTMENT.

TRANSPORTATION. Including the transportation of the recruits to the frontiers, the removal of troops from one station to another, the transportation of clothing, ordnance, and military stores for the troops on the frontiers—the necessary removal of ordnance military stores—the hire of teams and pack-horses—the purchase of tents, boats, axes, camp-kettles, boards, fire-wood, company books, stationary for the troops, and all other expences in the quarter-master's department,   15,000

HOSPITAL DEPARTMENT.

For medicines, instruments, furniture and stores for an hospital for the frontiers, also for attendance when necessary at West-Point,   1,000

ORDNANCE DEPARTMENT.

For salaries for the store keepers at the several deposits, viz.

West-Point,
Virginia,   } 3 at 40 dollars pr. month,   1,440
Springfield,

Charleston, 1 Store keeper at 100 dols. pr. annum,   100
          2 Assistants, at 15 do. pr. month,   360
1 Store keeper at Philadelphia,   500
1 ditto,   Rhode-Island,   96
1 ditto,   Lancaster,   96
1 ditto,   Fort Harkemer,   120
His subsistence, 1 dollar pr. week,   52   172

RENTS of BUILDINGS for DEPOSITS.

Philadelphia,   752.66
Virginia,   350
West-Point,   400   1,502.66
Labourers at the several Deposits,   400
8 Artificers at the posts on the frontiers, including armourers, at 5 dollars pr. month,   480
Coopers, armourers, and carpenters employed occasionally at the several arsenals,   500
The expence of materials and constructing twenty new carriages for cannon and howitzers,   2,000   7,646.66
Buildings for arsenals and magazines are highly requisite in the southern and middle departments, for which particularly estimates will be formed.

CONTINGENCIES of the WAR Department, viz.

For maps, hiring expresses, allowances to officers for extra expences, printing, loss of stores of all kinds, advertising and apprehending deserters,   3,000

CONTINGENCIES of the WAR Office, viz.

Office rent, wood, stationary, desks, book cases, sweeping, &c.   600
Subsistence due the officers of Colonel Marinus Willet's regiment in 1782,   786.06
Pay due Lieutenant Joseph Wilcox, pay master to the regiment lately commanded by Col. David Humphreys,   315
Pay subsistence and forage due the officers appointed by the State of Rhode-Island, under the act of Congress of the 20th October, 1786,   1,770   2,871.06
                                                        156,137.72

Total amount as above,   156,137.72
Deduct contingencies of the War Office, office rent, wood, stationary, desks, &c. as above, the same being included with the salaries in the civil list estimate,   600

                                    Dollars   155,537.72

SUMMARY of the Foregoing.

Pay of the troops,	59,028
Subsistence of ditto,	42,552
Clothing of ditto,	24,440
Quarter masters department	15,000
Hospital department,	1,000
Contingencies of the war department,	3,000
Contingencies of the war office,	600
Arrears of pay and subsistence unprovided for,	2,871.06
Ordnance department,	7,646.66

War-Office, December 29th, 1789   Dollars,   156,137.72
                    (Signed)   HENRY KNOX, Secretary for the Department of War

[*No.* III.]
ESTIMATE of the Annual PENSIONS of the INVALIDS of the United States, viz.
Taken from returns in the War-Office, dated as follows:

		Dols. Cts.	Dols. Cts.
November 28, 1789,	New-Hampshire,	3,024	
December 14,	Massachusetts,	11,166	
December 1,	Connecticut,	7,296	
December 31,	New-York,	15,588	
February 2,	New-Jersey,	4,357.06	
December 10,	Pennsylvania,	16,506	
For 1787,	Virginia,	9,276.66	
			67,213.72

Conjectural—No returns having been received.
Suppose Rhode-Island and Delaware nearly equal to New-
Hampshire,   3,170
Maryland nearly equal to Connecticut,   7,000
North-Carolina, South-Carolina and Georgia, nearly equal to New-
Hampshire, Connecticut, and Virginia,   19,596
                                                                    29,766
                                              Dollars,   96,979.72
                    (signed.) H. KNOX, Secretary for the Department of War
War-Office, 31st December, 1789.
☞ *For Schedule K, which should have been inserted here, see the last page.*

An ACT repealing, after the last day of   next, the Duties heretofore laid upon distilled Spirits imported from abroad, and laying others in their stead, and also upon Spirits distilled within the United States, as well to discourage the excessive use of those Spirits, and promote Agriculture, as to provide for the support of the Public Credit, and for the Common Defence and General Welfare.

I. BE it enacted by the Senate and House of Representatives of the United States of America in Congress assembled,* that after the last day of   next, the duties laid on distilled spirits by the act entitled "An act for laying a duty on goods, wares and merchandizes imported into the United States," shall cease; and that upon all distilled spirits which shall be imported into the United States, after that day, from any foreign port or place, there shall be paid for their use the duties following, that is to say,

1st. For every gallon of those spirits more than ten per cent. below proof, according to Dicas's hydrometer, twenty cents.

2d. For every gallon of those spirits under five, and not more than ten per cent. below proof, according to the same hydrometer, twenty-one cents.

3d. For every gallon of those spirits of proof, and not more than five per. cent below proof, according to the same hydrometer, twenty-two cents.

4th. For every gallon of those spirits above proof, but not exceeding twenty per cent. according to the same hydrometer, twenty-five cents.

5th. For every gallon of those spirits more than twenty, and not more than forty per cent. above proof, according to the same hydrometer, thirty cents.

6th. For every gallon of those spirits, more than forty per cent. above proof, according to the same hydrometer, forty cents.

II. And be it further enacted, that the said duties shall be collected in the same manner, by the same persons, under the same regulations, and subject to the same forfeitures and other penalties, as those heretofore laid; the act concerning which shall be deemed to be in full force for the collection of the duties herein before imposed, except as to the alterations contained in this act.

III. And be it further enacted,† that the said duties, at the option of the

---

* *The four first of these classes of proof correspond with the different kinds of spirits now usually imported: The first with gin; the second with St. Croix rum; the third with Antigua rum; the fourth with Jamaica spirits; the fifth corresponds with the usual proof of high wines; the last with that of Alcohol. These distinctions are necessary, not only to proportion the duty, but to prevent evasions of it. According to the present act, high wines, or even Alcohol, which is from 30 to 40 per cent. above Jamaica proof, might be imported liable only to the duty of Jamaica proof.*

† *The extension of the time is for the accommodation of the merchants in consideration of the encreased rate. It is proposed to reduce the discount, because ten per cent. is more than either the interest of money, or the risk of non-payment seems to warrant. Generally speaking, transient persons are those who avail themselves of the advantage; and they, without it, would commonly pay down, from the inconvenience of procuring and leaving sureties.*

proprietor, importer or consignee, may either be paid immediately, or secured by bond, with one or more sureties, to the satisfaction of the collector, or person acting as such, with condition for the payment of one moiety in four months, and the other moiety in eight months: Provided that where the said duties shall not exceed fifty dollars, the same shall be immediately paid; and that where the same shall exceed fifty dollars, if the said proprietor, importer or consignee shall think fit to make present payment thereof, there shall be an abatement to him or her, at the rate of seven per cent per annum, only for such present payment, the allowance of ten per cent. in the said former act notwithstanding.

And as not only a due regard to the exigencies of the public, and to the interest and ease of the community, but justice to those virtuous citizens, who, content with the emoluments of fair and honorable trade, disdain to violate the laws of their country, and the principles of probity, requires that every possible impediment should be opposed to the fraudulent views of those who wish to profit at the expence both of the fair trader and of the community—

IV. Be it further enacted,‡ that the President of the United States of America, be authorised to appoint, with the advice and consent of the Senate, such number of officers as shall appear to him necessary, to be denominated Inspectors of the revenue; and to assign to them respectively such districts or limits for the exercise of their respective offices, as he shall judge best adapted to the due execution thereof; dividing the districts, if he shall think it adviseable, into general and particular, and placing the Inspectors of the latter under the superintendance of the former, within the limits whereof they shall be respectively comprehended; and also to make such allowances to the said Inspectors, and to the Deputies and officers by them appointed and employed for their respective services in the execution of this act, to be paid out of the product of the said duties, as shall be reasonable and proper: Provided always, that the whole amount of the said allowances shall not exceed   per cent. of the said product, computed throughout the United States; and that, being once regulated by the said President, they shall be alterable in such manner only as shall from time to time be prescribed by law.

V. And be it further enacted, that the Inspector or Inspectors of the revenue for each district, shall establish one or more offices within the same, and that there shall be one at least at each port of delivery; and in order that the said offices may be publicly known, there shall be painted or written, in large legible characters, upon some conspicuous part outside and in front of each house building or place in which any such office shall be kept, these words, "Office of Inspection;" and if any person shall paint or write, or cause

‡ *This appears to be the only practicable method of compassing the details of so complicated a business.*

to be painted or written, the said words, upon any other than such house or building, he or she shall forfeit and pay for so doing, one hundred dollars.

VI. And be it further enacted, that within forty-eight hours after any ship or vessel, having on board any distilled Spirits brought in such ship or vessel from any foreign port or place, shall arrive within any port of the United States, whether the same be the first port of arrival of such ship or vessel or not; the master or person having the command or charge thereof, shall report to the Inspector or other chief officer of Inspection of the port at which she shall so arrive, the place from which she last sailed with her name and burthen and the quantity and kinds of the said spirits on board of her, and the casks or cases containing them, with their marks and numbers on pain of forfeiting five hundred dollars.

VII. And be it further enacted, that the Collector or other officer, or person acting as Collector of any port, with whom entry shall have been made of any of the said spirits, pursuant to the said act laying a duty on goods, wares and merchandizes imported into the United States, shall forthwith after such entry certify and transmit the same, as particularly as it shall have been made with him, to the Inspector of the revenue, or other proper officer of inspection, of the port where it shall be intended to commence the delivery of the spirits so entered, or any part thereof; for which purpose, every proprietor, importer or consignee, making such entry, shall deliver two manifests or contents (upon one of which the said certificate shall be given) and shall at the time thereof declare the port at which the said delivery shall be so intended to be commenced, to the Collector or officer with whom the same shall be made. And every permit granted by such Collector for the landing of any of the said spirits, shall previous to such landing be produced to the said officer of inspection, who shall make a minute in some proper book, of the contents thereof, and shall indorse thereupon the word "Inspected," the time when, and his own name, after which he shall return it to the person by whom it shall have been produced; and then, and not otherwise, it shall be lawful to land the spirits therein specified; and if the said spirits shall be landed without such indorsement upon the permit for that purpose granted, the master or person having charge of the ship or vessel, from which the same shall have been so landed, shall for every such offence forfeit the sum of five hundred dollars.

VIII. And be it further enacted, That whenever it shall be intended that any ship or vessel shall proceed with the whole or any part of the Spirits which shall have been brought in such ship or vessel from any foreign port or place, from one port in the United States to another port in the said United States, whether in the same or in different districts, the master or person having the command or charge of such ship or vessel, shall previous to her departure, apply to the proper officer of inspection for the port from which she is about to depart, for a certificate of the quantity and particulars of such of the said spirits as shall have been certified to him to have been entered as imported in such ship or vessel, and of so much thereof as shall appear to him to have been landed out of her at such port, which certificate the said officer shall forthwith grant without fee or charge. And the master or person having the command or charge of such ship or vessel, shall, within twenty-four hours after her arrival at the port to which she shall be bound, deliver the said certificate to the proper officer of inspection of such last mentioned port. And if such ship or vessel shall proceed from one port to another within the United States, with the whole or any part of the spirits brought in her as aforesaid, without having first obtained such certificate; or if within twenty-four hours after her arrival at such other port, the said certificate shall not be delivered to the proper officer of inspection there, the master or person having the command or charge of the said ship or vessel, shall in either case forfeit five hundred dollars; and the spirits on board of her at her said arrival, shall be forfeited, and may be seized by any officer of inspection.

IX. And be it further enacted, That all spirits which shall be imported as aforesaid, shall be landed under the inspection of the officer or officers of inspection for the place where the same shall be landed, and not otherwise, on pain of forfeiture thereof, for which purpose the said officer or officers shall at all reasonable times attend: Provided that this shall not be construed to exclude the inspection of the officers of the customs as now established and practised.

X. And be it further enacted, That the officers of inspection, under whose survey any of the said spirits shall be landed, shall, upon landing thereof, and as soon as the casks and cases containing the same shall be guaged or measured, brand or otherwise mark in durable characters, the several casks or cases containing the same, with progressive numbers, and also with the name of the ship or vessel wherein the same was or were imported, and of the port of entry, and with the proof and quantity thereof, together with such other marks, if any other shall be deemed needful, as the respective inspectors of the revenue may direct. And the said officer shall keep a book, wherein he shall enter the name of each vessel in which any of the said spirits shall be so imported, and of the port of entry and of delivery, and of the master of such vessel, and of each importer, and the several casks and cases containing the same, and the marks of each, and if not an inspector or the chief officer of inspection for the place, shall as soon as may be thereafter, make an exact transcript of each entry, and deliver the same to such inspector or chief officer, who shall keep a like book for recording the said transcripts.

XI. And be it further enacted, That the inspector of the revenue or other chief officer of inspection within whose survey any of the said spirits shall be landed shall give to the proprietor, importer, or consignee thereof, or his or her agent, a certificate to remain with him or her of the whole quantity of the said spirits which shall have been so landed, which certificate besides the said quantity shall specify the name of such proprietor, importer, or consignee, and of the vessel from on board which the said spirit shall have been landed, and of the marks of each cask or case containing the same. And the said inspector or other chief officer of inspection shall deliver to the said proprietor, importer or consignee, or to his or her agent, a like certificate for each cask or case which shall accompany the same wheresoever it shall be sent as evidence of its being lawfully imported. And the officer of inspection granting the said certificates, shall make regular and exact entries in the book to be by him kept as aforesaid, of all spirits for which the same shall be granted as particularly as therein described. And the said proprietor, importer, or consignee, or his or her agent upon the sale and delivery of any of the said spirits, shall deliver to the purchaser or purchasers thereof, the certificate or certificates which ought to accompany the same, on pain of forfeiting the sum of fifty dollars for each cask or case with which such certificate shall not be delivered.

XII. And be it further enacted,* That upon all spirits which after the said last day of   next, shall be distilled within the United States, wholly or in part from molasses, sugar, or other foreign materials, there shall be paid for their use the duties following, that is to say—

1st. For every gallon of those spirits more than 10 per cent. below proof, according to Dicas's hydrometer, eleven cents.

2d. For every gallon of those spirits under five and not more than ten per cent. below proof, according to the same hydrometer, twelve cents.

3d. For every gallon of those spirits of proof, and not more than five per cent. below proof, according to the same hydrometer, thirteen cents.

4th. For every gallon of those spirits above proof, and not exceeding twenty per cent. according to the same hydrometer, fifteen cents.

5th. For every gallon of those spirits more than twenty and not more than forty per cent. above proof, according to the said hydrometer, twenty cents.

6th. For every gallon of those spirits more than forty per cent. above proof, according to the same hydrometer, thirty cents.

XIII. And be it further enacted,† That upon all spirits which after the said

---

*The first class of proof here corresponds with what is understood by common proof at our distilleries and answers to that of gin. Hence our common rum, compared with the lowest kind of imported rum, and including the duty on molasses, stands charged in the proportion of 14 to 21, which difference it is presumed will afford due encouragement. The remaining classes also correspond with those above.

† The several classes of proof here agree with those in the preceding section, but it will be observed that the rates are lower. This will operate as an encouragement to distillation from our own materials. It is evident that a higher duty being laid on spirits distilled from foreign materials, than on those made from our own, the difference is a bounty on the latter, and places it in a better situation than if there were no duty on either; in general it may be remarked, that the rates proposed on these different kinds of spirits, though considerably higher than heretofore, are much less than they bear in most other countries.

last day of   next, shall be distilled within the United States, from any article of the growth or production of the United States, in any city, town or village, there shall be paid for their use the duties following, that is to say:

1st. For every gallon of those spirits more than ten per cent. below proof, according to Dicas's hydrometer, nine cents.

2d. For every gallon of those spirits under five and not more than ten per cent. below proof, according to the same hydrometer, ten cents.

3d. For every gallon of those spirits of proof, and not more than five per cent. below proof, according to the same hydrometer, eleven cents.

4th. For every gallon of those spirits above proof, but not exceeding twenty per cent. according to the same hydrometer, thirteen cents.

5th. For every gallon of those spirits more than twenty and not more than forty per cent. above proof, according to the same hydrometer, seventeen cents.

6. For every gallon of those spirits more than forty per cent. above proof, according to the same hydrometer, twenty-five cents.

XIV. And be it further enacted, That the said duties on spirits distilled within the United States, shall be collected under the management of the inspectors of the revenue.

XV. And be it further enacted, That the said duties on spirits distilled within the United States, shall be paid or secured previous to the removal thereof from the distilleries at which they are respectively made. And it shall be at the option of the proprietor or proprietors of each distillery, or of his, her or their agent having the superintendence thereof, either to pay the said duties previous to such removal, with an abatement at the rate of two cents for every ten gallons, or to secure the payment of the same, by giving bond quarter yearly, with one or more sureties, to the satisfaction of the officer of inspection within whose survey such distillery shall be, and in such sum as the said officer shall direct, with condition for the observance of the regulations in this act contained, on his, her, or their part, and also for the payment of the duties upon all such of the said spirits as shall be removed from such distillery, within three months next ensuing the date of the bond, at the expiration of six months from the said date.

XVI. And be it further enacted,* That the inspector or inspectors of each district, shall appoint a proper officer to have the charge and survey of each distillery within his or their district, who shall attend such distillery at all reasonable times, for the execution of the duties by this act enjoined upon him.

* *This inspection is essential to a secure collection. Experience has shown that proper dependence cannot be placed on any plan which relies on the exactness of the accounts to be rendered by the individuals interested, and such a reliance not only defeats the revenue, but throws an undue proportion of the burthen on the upright and consciencious.*

XVII. And be it further enacted, That previous to the removal of any of the said spirits from any distillery, the officer of inspection within whose survey the same may be, shall brand or otherwise mark each cask containing the same in durable characters, and with progressive numbers, and with the name of the acting owner or other manager of such distillery, and of the place where the same was situate, and with the quantity therein, to be ascertained by actual guaging, and with the proof thereof, And the duties thereupon having been first paid, or secured, as above provided, the said officer shall grant a certificate for each cask of the said spirits, to accompany the same wheresoever it shall be sent, purporting that the duty thereupon hath been paid or secured, as the case may be, and describing each cask by its marks; and shall enter in a book for that purpose to be kept, all the spirits distilled at such distillery, and removed from the same; and the marks of each cask, and the persons for whose use, and the places to which removed, and the time of each removal, and the amount of the duties on the spirits so removed. And if any of the said spirits shall be removed from any such distillery without having been branded or marked as aforesaid, or without such certificate as aforesaid, the same, together with the cask or casks containing them, and the horses and waggons, with their harness and tackling, employed in removing them, shall be forfeited, and may be seized by any officer of inspection. And the superintendant or manager of such distillery shall also forfeit the full value of the spirits so removed, to be computed at the highest price of the like spirits in the market.

XVIII. And be it further enacted, That no spirits shall be removed from any such distillery except by a person or persons licensed in the manner herein after directed, nor at any other times than between the hour of   and the hour of   and between the hour of   and the hour of   of each day, from the   day of   to the   day of   in each year; and between the hour of   and the hour of   and between the hour of   and the hour of   of each day, from the   day of   to the   day of   in each year.

XIX. And be it further enacted,† That licenses to convey or carry spirits from the said distilleries, shall, in each district, be granted by the inspector or inspectors of the revenue thereof, to such discreet person or persons as shall appear to him or them proper for the trust, who shall respectively give bonds, with one or more sureties to the satisfaction of the said inspector or inspectors of the revenue, in a sum not exceeding   dollars, nor less than   dollars, with condition faithfully and diligently, to carry and deliver

---

† *This regulation would certainly add much to the safety of the collection: But it is doubtful whether it would not be exceptionable in some parts of the country. Perhaps it may be limited to the principal cities; or it may be general, and a discretion vested somewhere, to make the necessary exceptions.*

all such of the said spirits as shall be committed to their care respectively, and in so doing to observe the directions of this act: Provided always, That nothing herein contained shall in any wise infringe or interfere with any exclusive privilege which any individuals or bodies politic may have or be entitled to, by virtue of any charter, grant or act of incorporation touching the right of carrying or of licensing persons to carry goods and commodities within particular limits. But where any such privilege shall exist, the person to be licensed pursuant to this act, shall execute the trust thereby reposed in them, through and by means of the person or persons who by virtue of such privilege shall be authorised to carry within such limits; and in such manner as shall be perfectly consistent with such privilege and not otherwise.

XX. And be it further enacted,‡ That upon stills which after the last day of　　　next, shall be employed in distilling spirits from materials of the growth or production of the United States, in any other place than a city, town or village, there shall be paid for the use of the United States, the yearly duty of sixty cents for every gallon, English wine measure, of the capacity or content of each and every such still, including the head thereof: Provided that the said duty shall not extend to any still of less than　　　except where such still shall be worked at the same distillery, together with another of dimensions exceeding　　　gallons.

XXI. And be it further enacted, That the evidence of the employment of the said stills shall be, their being erected in stone, brick or some other manner whereby they shall be in a condition to be worked.

XXII. And be it further enacted, That the said duties on stills shall be collected under the management of the inspectors of the revenue, who in each district shall appoint and assign proper officers for the surveys of the said stills and the admeasurement thereof, and the collection of the duties thereupon; and the said duties shall be paid half yearly, within the first fifteen days of the months of　　　and　　　upon demand made of the proprietor or proprietors of each still at his, her or their dwelling, by the proper officer charged with the survey thereof: And in case of refusal or neglect to pay, the amount of the duties so refused or neglected to be paid, may either be recovered with costs of suit in an action of debt in the name of the inspector or inspectors of the district, within which such refusal shall happen, or may be levied by distress and sale of goods of the person or persons refusing or neglecting to pay, rendering the overplus (if any there be after payment of the said amount and the charges of distress and sale) to the said person or persons.

‡ *The duty is here laid upon the stills because it would be inconvenient, to extend the inspection of the officers in its full extent throughout the country. The rates is adjusted according to an estimate of what a still of any given dimensions, worked for the usual time is capable of producing, but lest this rule should in any instance operate injuriously, it is by a subsequent provision put in the power of the proprietor to redress himself. This provision certainly opens a door to fraud, but it is presumed to be adviseable to submit to this inconvenience rather than to those which would be apt to attend the supposition of inequality.*

And whereas the duties hereby charged upon stills, have been estimated upon a computation that a still of each of the dimensions herein before enumerated, worked for the usual time would produce in the course of a year a quantity of spirits, which at the rate of   cents per gallon, would amount to the duty charged thereon: And as from different causes it may in some instances happen, that the said computation may subject the said stills to greater duties than are intended;

XXIII. Be it therefore enacted, That if the proprietor of any such still finding himself or herself aggrieved by the said rates, shall enter or cause to be entered in a book or on a paper to be kept for that purpose, from day to day when such still shall be employed the quantity of spirits distilled therefrom, and the quantity from time to time sold or otherwise disposed of, and to whom and when, and shall produce the said book or paper to the proper officer of inspection within whose survey such still shall be, and shall make oath, or if a known Quaker, affirmation, that the same doth contain to the best of his or her knowledge and belief, true entries made at their respective dates of all the spirits distilled within the time to which such entries shall relate, from such still, and of the disposition thereof; and shall also declare upon such oath or affirmation the quantity of such spirits then remaining on hand, it shall be lawful in every such case for the said officer to whom the said book or paper shall be produced, and he is hereby required to estimate the duties upon such still, according to the quantity so stated to have been actually made therefrom at the rate of nine cents per gallon, which, and no more, shall be paid for the same: Provided, That if the said entries shall be made by any person other than the said proprietor, a like oath or affirmation shall be made by such person.

And the more effectually to prevent the evasion of the duties hereby imposed to the no less injury of the fair trader than of the revenue;

XXIV. Be it further enacted, *That every person who shall be a dealer or

---

* The provisions in this section form an essential part of the plan. They serve to bring all those who deal in the sale of spirits in considerable quantities, and the places in which they are kept, under the immediate eye of the law. It must always be very difficult to conceal any quantity of spirits in a place which is not announced and entered in the manner prescribed. Whoever sees them in any such place, or in going from it, will know that they are liable to forfeiture, and will have inducements enough to give intelligence of the fact. And when every man can, from so simple a circumstance, discern that a fraud has been committed, it will be hardly possible for it to escape detection. Besides this, the article, whenever it leaves its concealment, is liable to discovery from the want of those indications which are necessary to shew that it was lawfully imported or made. And it is not supposeable that it can continue concealed, and pass safe through all its stages, from the importation or making, to the consumption. The consumer himself, if not interested in the fraud, will detect and disclose it. The necessity of entry is limited to a distance of ten miles, to prevent inconvenience. In remote places, where little business is done, the precaution may be relaxed, and offices of inspection will be found less necessary. Articles must be carried, for sale, to places where there is considerable demand; and if at such places the requisite guards are kept up with strictness, the end will be substantially answered.

trader in distilled spirits (except as a maker or distiller thereof) in the original casks or cases in which they shall be imported, or in quantities of twenty five gallons at one sale, shall be deemed a wholesale dealer in spirits, and shall write or paint or cause to be written or painted, in large, legible and durable characters, upon some conspicuous part outside and in front of each house or other building or place, and upon the door or usual entrance of each vault, cellar or apartment within the same in which any of the said spirits shall be at any time by him or her deposited or kept or intended so to be, the words "wholesale dealer in spirits;" and shall also, within three days at least before he or she shall begin to keep or sell any of the said spirits therein, make a particular entry in writing at the nearest office of inspection of the district in which the same shall be situate, if within ten miles thereof of every such house or other building or place, and of each cellar, vault or apartment within the same in which he or she shall intend to put or keep any of the said spirits; and if any such dealer shall omit to write or paint, or cause to be written or painted the words aforesaid, and in manner aforesaid, upon any such house or other building or place, or vault, cellar or apartment thereof, in which he or she shall so have or keep any of the said spirits, or shall in case the same be situated within the said distance of ten miles of any office of inspection omit to make entry thereof as aforesaid, such dealer shall for every such omission or neglect forfeit the sum of five hundred dollars, and all the spirits which he or she shall have or keep therein, or the value thereof to be computed at the highest price of such spirits in the market.

XXV. And be it further enacted, That every person who shall be a maker or distiller of spirits shall write or paint or cause to be written or painted upon some conspicuous part outside and in front of each house or other building or place made use of or intended to be made use of by him or her for the distillation or keeping of spirituous liquors, and upon the door or usual entrance of each vault, cellar or apartment within the same in which any of the said liquors shall be at any time by him or her distilled, deposited or kept, or intended so to be, the words "Distiller of spirits;" and shall also, three days at least before he or she shall begin to distil therein, make a particular entry in writing, at the nearest office of inspection, if within ten miles thereof, of every such house, building or place, and of each vault, cellar and apartment within the same, in which he or she shall intend to carry on the business of distilling, or to keep any spirits by him or her distilled. And if any such distiller shall omit to paint or write, or cause to be painted or written the words aforesaid, in manner aforesaid, upon any such house or other building or place, or vault, cellar or apartment thereof, or shall, in case the same be situate within the said distance of ten miles of any office of inspection, omit to make entry thereof as aforesaid, such distiller shall for every such omission or neglect, forfeit the sum of five hundred dollars, and all the spirits which he or she shall have or keep therein, or the value thereof, to be computed at the highest price of such spirits in the market: Provided also, and be it further enacted, that the said entry, to be made by persons who shall be dealers in or distillers of spirits, on the last day of   next, shall be made on that day, or within three days thereafter, accompanied (except where the duties hereby imposed are charged on the still) with a true and particular account or inventory of the spirits, on that day and at the time, in every or any house, building or place by him or her entered, and of the casks, cases and vessels containing the same, with their marks and numbers, and the quantities and qualities of the spirits therein contained, on pain of forfeiting, for neglecting to make such entry, or to deliver such account, the sum of five hundred dollars, and all the spirits by him or her had or kept in any such house, building or place: And provided further, that nothing herein contained shall be construed to exempt any such distiller, who shall be, besides his dealing as a distiller, a dealer or trader in distilled spirits as described in the twenty-fourth section of this act, from the regulations therein prescribed; but every such distiller, so being also a dealer or trader in distilled spirits, shall observe and shall be subject to all the rules, regulations and penalties therein specified.

XXVI. And be it further enacted, that where any entry shall be made by any such dealer, of any such house, building or other place for keeping of any of the said spirits, no other such dealer, not being in partnership with the dealer aforesaid, making such entry, shall on any pretence make entry of the same house or building, or of any apartment, vault, cellar or place within the same house, building or tenement in which such first entry shall then be existing; but every such other dealer, making such further entry of the same house, building or place, or of any apartment, vault, cellar or place within the same, shall, notwithstanding such further entry, be deemed a dealer without entry, and shall be subject to the like penalties and forfeitures as any dealers without entry are subject to by this act.

XXVII. And be it further enacted, that the Inspector or Inspectors of the revenue for the district wherein any house, building or place shall be situate, whereof entry shall be made as last aforesaid, shall as soon as may be thereafter, visit and inspect, or cause to be visited and inspected by some proper officer or officers of inspection, every such house or other building or place within his or their district, and shall take or cause to be taken an exact account of the spirits therein respectively contained, and shall mark or cause to be marked in durable characters, the several casks, cases or vessels containing the same, with progressive numbers, and also with the name of each dealer or distiller to whom the same may belong, or in whose custody the same may be, and the quantities, kinds and proofs of spirits therein contained, and these words, "Old Stock." And the said inspector or inspectors shall keep a book wherein he or they shall enter the name of every such dealer or distiller within his or their district, and the particulars of such old stock in the possession of each, designating the several casks and cases containing the same, and their respective quantities, kinds, proofs and marks. And he or they shall also give a certificate to every such dealer or distiller, of the quantity and particulars of such old stock in his or her possession; and a separate certificate for each cask, case or vessel, describing the same, according to its marks, which certificate shall accompany the same wheresoever it shall be sent. And in case there shall be no officer of inspection within the said distance of ten miles of any such house or other building or place, then it shall be the duty of such dealer to whom the same may belong, to mark with the like durable characters the several casks containing the spirits therein, and in like manner as above directed to be done by the said Inspector or Inspectors. And the said dealer shall make entry thereof in some proper book or in some proper paper to be by him or her kept for that purpose, specifying particularly each cask, case or vessel, and its marks, and the quantity and quality of the spirits therein contained (of which entry he or she shall, upon request, deliver an exact copy to the Inspector or Inspectors of the revenue for the district) and if required by him or them, shall attest the same by oath, or, being a known Quaker, by affirmation. And the said dealer, with every such cask, case or vessel which shall be delivered out of his or her house or other building or place, shall give a certificate or permit, signed by himself or herself, of the like import of that above directed to be given by the said Inspector or Inspectors, which certificate shall in like manner accompany the same wheresoever it may be sent. And if any such dealer shall in the said case omit to mark the said several casks, cases or vessels containing the said spirits, or to make entry thereof in some proper book, or on some proper paper as aforesaid, he or she shall forfeit and pay for every such neglect two hundred dollars. And if in the same case he or she shall deliver out or send away any of the said spirits without such certificate by him or her directed to be furnished as aforesaid, the said spirits so delivered out or sent away, shall be forfeited, and may be seized by any officer of inspection, and the said dealer shall also forfeit the full value thereof.

XXVIII. And be it further enacted, that every proprietor of any still on which a duty shall be charged according to the twentieth section of this act, shall brand or otherwise mark in durable characters, every cask, barrel or keg containing any spirits distilled by him or her, previous to the sale thereof, with his or her name, and with progressive numbers, and shall grant a certificate with each cask, barrel or keg by him or her sold, describing the same by its marks, and purporting that the same was made by him or her, to accompany such cask, barrel or keg, wheresoever it shall be sent.

XXIX. And be it further enacted, that when any such wholesale dealer in spirits, shall bring in his or her entered house, building or place, any of the said spirits, if such house, building or place be within two miles of any office of inspection, he or she shall within twenty-four hours after the said spirits shall be brought into such house, building or place, send notice thereof in writing to the said office, specifying therein the quantity and kinds of the spirits so brought in, and the marks of the cask or casks, case or cases containing the same, on pain of forfeiting, for every neglect to give such notice, fifty dollars. And it shall be the duty of the officer to whom such notice shall be given, forthwith thereafter to inspect and take an account of such spirits.

XXX. And be it further enacted, that if any distilled spirits shall be found in the possession of any such dealer, without the proper certificates which ought to accompany the same, it shall be presumptive evidence that the same are liable to forfeiture, and it shall be lawful for any officer of inspection to seize them as forfeited; and if, upon the trial in consequence of such seizure, the owner or claimant of the spirits seized, shall not prove that the same were imported into the United States according to law, or were distilled as mentioned in the twelfth and thirteenth sections of this act, and the duties thereupon paid, or were distilled at one of the stills mentioned in the twentieth section of this act, they shall be adjudged to be forfeited.

XXXI. And be it further enacted, that it shall be lawful for the officers of inspection of each district, at all times in the day time, upon request, to enter into all and every the houses, storehouses, ware-houses, buildings and places, which shall have been entered by the said wholesale dealers in manner aforesaid, and by tasting, guaging or otherwise to take an account of the quantity, kinds and proofs of the said spirits therein contained, and also to take samples thereof, paying for the same the usual price.

XXXII. And be it further enacted, that every such dealer shall keep the several kinds of spirits in his or her entered warehouse, building or place, separate and apart from each other, on pain of forfeiting upon every conviction of neglect one hundred dollars; and shall also, upon request, shew to the officers of inspection of the district wherein he or she is so a dealer, or to any of them, each and every cask, vessel and case in which he or she shall keep any distilled spirits, and the certificates which ought to accompany the same, upon pain of forfeiting every such cask, vessel or case, as shall be shewn, together with the spirits therein contained.

XXXIII. And be it further enacted, that if any person or persons shall rub out or deface any of the marks set upon any cask or case pursuant to the directions of this act, such person or persons shall, for every such offence, forfeit and pay the sum of one hundred dollars.

XXXIV. And be it further enacted, that no cask, barrel, keg, vessel or case, marked as "Old stock," shall be made use of by any dealer or distiller of spirits, for putting or keeping therein any spirits other than those which were contained therein when so marked, on pain of forfeiting five hundred dollars for every cask, barrel, keg, vessel or case wherein any such other spirits shall be so put or kept: Neither shall any such dealer have or keep any distilled spirits in any such cask, barrel, keg, vessel or case, longer than for the space of one year from the said last day of   next, on pain of forfeiting the said spirits.

XXXV. And be it further enacted, that in case any of the said spirits shall be fraudulently deposited, hid or concealed in any place whatsoever, with intent to evade the duties hereby imposed upon them, they shall be forfeited. And for the better discovery of any such spirits so fraudulently deposited, hid or concealed, it shall be lawful for any Inspector of the revenue, or for any Judge of any Court of the United States, or either of them, or for any Justice of the peace, upon reasonable cause of suspicion, to be made out to the satisfaction of such Inspector, Judge or Justice, by the oath, or, in the case of a known Quaker, by the affirmation, of any person or persons, by special warrant or warrants under their respective hands and seals, to authorise any of the officers of inspection, by day or night, but if in the night time in the presence of a constable or other officer of the peace, to enter into all and every such place and places, in which any of the said spirits shall be suspected to be so fraudulently deposited, hid or concealed, and to seize and carry away any of the said spirits which shall be there found, so fraudulently deposited, hid or concealed, as forfeited.

XXXVI. And be it further enacted, That no person shall carry on the business of distilling, rectifying or compounding of spirituous liquors in any cellar, vault, or other place below the surface of the ground; or have or use any pipes, stop cocks, or other communications under ground, for the purpose of conveying spiritous liquors from one back or vessel to another, or from any such back or vessel to its still, or to any other place, on pain of forfeiting for every such place, below the surface of the ground in which the said business shall be carried on the sum of five hundred dollars, and for every such pipe, stop-cock, or other communication under ground, the sum of two hundred and fifty dollars. And in case the said person shall carry on the said business in any such place below the surface of the ground, or shall have or use any such communication under ground, it shall be lawful for any inspector of the revenue, or Judge of any court of the United States, or Judge of any court of a particular State, or Justice of the Peace, upon reasonable cause of suspicion to be made out to the satisfaction of such inspector, judge or justice, by oath or affirmation of any person or persons, by special warrant under his or either of their respective hands and seals, to authorise any of the officers of inspection, by day or night; but if in the night, in the presence of a constable or other officer of the peace, to enter into all and every such place or places after request first made, and the cause declared, therein to search and examine for the same, and for that purpose to break the ground, wall, partition or other place; and upon finding such cellar, vault, or other building, or place below the surface of the ground, or such pipe, stop-cock, or other communication under ground, to destroy the same, and to seize such spirituous liquors as may be found below the surface of the ground, or which shall have been conveyed through such pipe, stop-cock, or other communication, which warrant or warrants may be lawfully executed by such officer accordingly. Provided that nothing herein contained shall be construed to authorise any inspector of the revenue to issue any warrant to himself, or upon his own oath, to any other officer. And provided further, That if upon such search, no place below the surface of the ground, nor any such pipe, stop-cock, or other communication be found, the said officer shall make good the ground, wall, partition, or other place so broken up as aforesaid, together with such reasonable damages as shall be adjudged by two neighboring justices of the peace, or the party or parties injured may bring his, her or their action against such officer of inspection, for the damages so sustained, which damages in either case, shall be paid out of the revenue arising from this act.

XXXVII. And be it further enacted, *That after the last day of   next, no spirituous liquors, except gin in cases, shall be brought from any foreign port or place in any other way than in casks capable each of containing one hundred gallons at the least, on pain of forfeiture of the said spirits, and of the ship or vessel in which they shall be brought. Provided always, that nothing in this act contained, shall be construed to forfeit any spirits for being imported or brought into the United States, in other casks or vessels than as aforesaid, or the ship or vessel in which they shall be brought, if such spirits shall be for the use of the seamen on board such ship or vessel, and shall not exceed the quantity of   gallons for each such seaman.

XXXVIII. And be it further enacted, That in every case in which any of the said spirits shall be forfeited by virtue of this act, the casks, vessels and cases containing the same, shall also be forfeited.

XXXIX. And be it further enacted, That every dealer by wholesale, or distiller of spirits, on which the duty is hereby charged by the gallon, shall keep or cause to be kept, an exact account of all the said spirits which he or she shall sell, send out or distill, distinguishing their several kinds and proofs; and shall every day make a just and true entry in a book or on a paper,

---

* The first part of this section seems to be free from any solid objection. It will be constantly the interest of importers (except with a view to smuggling) to bring spirits in large casks. But the object of the latter part will not be without difficulty. It is however, submitted. Perhaps, if the restriction to casks of one hundred gallons, should appear improper, it may be limited to a less size, yet such an one as will be less apt to elude the vigilance of the officers, than the smaller dimensions now in use. The restriction would certainly add materially to the security of the revenue.

to be kept for that purpose, of the quantities and particulars of the said spirits by him or her sold, sent out or distilled, on the preceding day, specifying the marks of the several casks in which they shall be so sold or sent out; and the person to whom, and for whose use they shall be so sold or sent out: Which said books and papers shall be prepared for the making such entries and shall be delivered upon demand to the said dealers and distillers, by the inspectors of the revenue of the several districts, or by such person or persons as they shall respectively for that purpose appoint, and shall be severally returned or delivered at the end of each year, or when the same shall be respectively filled up, which shall first happen to the proper officers of inspection; and the truth of the entries made therein shall be verified upon the oath, or in the case of a known quaker, the affirmation of the person by whom those entries shall have been made; and as often as the said books and papers shall be so returned, other books and papers shall be furnished upon like demand by the proper officers of inspection, to the said dealers and distillers respectively. And the said books and papers shall from time to time while in the possession of the said dealers and distillers, lie open for the inspection of, and upon request shall be shewn to the proper officers of inspection, under whose survey the said dealers and distillers shall respectively be, who may take such minutes, memorandums, or transcripts therefrom as they may think fit. And if any such dealer or distiller shall neglect or refuse to keep such book or books, paper or papers, or to make such entries therein, or to shew the same upon request to the proper officer of inspection, or not return the same according to the directions of this act, he or she shall forfeit for every such refusal or neglect, the sum of one hundred dollars.

And as a compensation to the said dealers for their aid in the execution of this act:

XL. Be it further enacted, That for every quantity of the said spirits not exceeding one hundred and twenty gallons, which shall be sold by any such dealer, in one day, to one person or copartnership, in the casks or cases in which the same shall have been imported, after the said last day of ____ next, or delivered out of any distillery (in respect to which the duty hereby imposed is rated by the gallon) and distilled after the said day, and of the bringing of which into his or her entered store-house, building or other place, he or she shall have given due notice according to the directions of this act, to the proper officer of inspection, and for which he or she shall have produced to the said officer the proper certificates corresponding therewith, the said dealer shall be entitled to an allowance of one cent per gallon, which allowance shall be estimated by the inspector of the revenue of each district, according to the evidence of the entries in the books and papers kept and returned according to the next preceding section of this act, confirmed as to the production of the proper certificates, by the certificate of the officer to whom they shall have been produced, and shall also be paid by such inspector, according to such rules as shall be prescribed in that behalf, by the Secretary of the Treasury, which said inspector shall be furnished with money for such payment out of the product of the duties imposed by this act. Provided always, That if more than one delivery shall be entered as made to one person or copartnership in one day, the same shall be deemed but one delivery and one quantity.

XLI. And be it further enacted, That the several kinds of proof herein before specified, shall in marking the casks, vessels and cases containing any distilled spirits be designated, corresponding with the order in which they are mentioned by the words—First Proof—Second Proof—Third Proof— Fourth Proof—Fifth Proof—Sixth Proof: which words may be expressed by their respective initials. And that it be the duty of the Secretary of the Treasury, to provide and furnish to the officers of Inspection and of the Customs, proper instruments for ascertaining the said several proofs.

And to the end that wanton and oppressive seizures may be effectually restrained, and that the owners and importers of spirits, may suffer no improper damage or burthen;

XLII. Be it further enacted, That in any prosecution or action which may be brought against any Inspector or other officer of Inspection for any seizure by him made, it shall be necessary for such Inspector or Officer to justify himself by making it appear, that there was probable cause for making the said seizure, upon which, and not otherwise, a verdict shall pass in his favor. And in every such action or prosecution, or in any action or prosecution which may be brought against such inspector or other officer, for irregular or improper conduct in the execution of his duty, the trial shall be by jury. And in any action for a seizure, in which a verdict shall pass for such inspector, the jury shall nevertheless assess reasonable damages for any prejudice or waste (according to the true amount in value thereof) which shall be shewn by good proof to have happened to the spirits seized, in consequence of such seizure, and also for the detention of the same, at the rate of six per cent. per annum, on the true value of the said spirits, at the time of such seizure, from that time to the time of restoration thereof, which shall be paid out of the treasury of the United States; provided that no damages shall be assessed when the seizure was made for want of the proper certificate or certificates or by reason of a *refusal* to shew any officer of inspection upon his request the spirits in any entered house, or other building or place.

XLIII. And be it further enacted, That if any inspector or other officer of inspection in any criminal prosecution against him shall be convicted of oppression or extortion in the execution of his office, he shall be fined or imprisoned or both at the discretion of the court, and shall also forfeit his office, unless the judge who shall try the cause shall certify that he was dissatisfied with the verdict.

XLIV. And be it further enacted, That no fee shall be taken for any certificate to be issued or granted pursuant to this act.

XLV. And be it further enacted, That if any of the said inspectors or other officers of inspection, shall neglect to perform any of the duties hereby enjoined upon them respectively according to the true intent and meaning of this act, whereby any person or persons shall be injured or suffer damage, such person or persons shall, and may have an action founded upon this act against such inspector or other officers, and shall recover full damages for the same, together with costs of suit.

To the intent nevertheless, that the officers to be appointed by virtue of this act who may have undesignedly erred in the execution of their respective offices, may be enabled by offering timely and sufficient amends to the party aggrieved, thereby to avoid unnecessary expence and trouble;

XLVI. Be it further enacted, That it shall be lawful for any inspector or officer of inspection or other person acting in aid of the one or the other, at any time before an action shall be commenced against him or them to tender amends to the person or persons aggrieved, or to his her or their agent or attorney, and in case such amends are not accepted, to plead such tender in bar to any action which may be brought against him or them, together with the plea of *not guilty,* and any other plea or pleas with leave of the court in which such action shall be depending. And if upon issue joined thereon the jury shall find the amends so tendered to have been sufficient, then they shall give a verdict for the defendant or defendants. And in such case, or in case the plaintiff or plaintiffs shall become nonsuited, or shall discontinue such action, or in case judgment shall be given for the defendant or defendants upon demurrer, then the defendant or defendants shall be intitled to, and shall recover costs of suit: But if upon issue so joined, the jury shall find that no, or insufficient amends were tendered, then they shall find a verdict for the plaintiff or plaintiffs and such damages as shall be reasonable.

XLVII. And be it further enacted, That any action or suit to be brought against any person or persons for any thing by him or them done, as in pursuance of this act, shall be commenced within three months next after the matter or thing done, *and shall be laid in the proper county* in which the cause of action shall have arisen, and the defendant or defendants in any such action or suit may plead the general issue, and on the trial thereof give this act, and the special matter in evidence. And if a verdict shall pass for the defendant or defendants, or the plaintiff or plaintiffs become nonsuited, or discontinue his, her or their action or prosecution, or judgment shall be given against such plaintiff or plaintiffs upon demurrer or otherwise, then such defendant or defendants shall have costs awarded to him, her or them, against such plaintiff or plaintiffs.

And in order that persons who may have incurred any of the penalties of this act without wilful negligence or intention of fraud, may be relieved from such penalties;

XLVIII. Be it further enacted, *That it shall be lawful for the judge of the district court, of the district within which such penalty or forfeiture shall have been incurred, upon petition of the party who shall have incurred the same to inquire in a summary manner into the circumstances of the case, first causing reasonable notice to be given to the person or persons claiming such penalty or forfeiture, and to the Attorney-General of such district, to the end that each may have an opportunity of shewing cause against the mitigation or remission thereof; and if upon such enquiry it shall appear to the said judge that such penalty or forfeiture was incurred without willful negligence, or any design or intention of fraud, it shall be lawful for him to remit the same, and to cause any spirits which may have been seized, to be restored to the proprietor or proprietors upon such terms and conditions as shall appear to him reasonable. And the decision of the judge, if the terms and conditions prescribed by him be complied with, shall be conclusive to the parties. Provided, That such penalty, or the value of the spirits forfeited, does not exceed five hundred dollars: But if the amount of such penalty or forfeiture exceed five hundred dollars, the person or persons claiming the same, may, within three days after such decision shall be pronounced, appeal from the same to the supreme court of the United States, which court shall summarily hear the parties, and either confirm or reverse the decision of the district judge, as shall appear to them proper. Provided always, That after the last day of May, in the year one thousand seven hundred and ninety, one such remission shall in no case exceed one half the penalty, or one half the spirits forfeited, or the value thereof.

XLIX. And be it further enacted, That all penalties and forfeitures incurred by virtue of this act, shall be for the benefit of the person or persons who shall make a seizure, or who shall first discover the matter or thing, whereby the same shall have been incurred, and if other than the inspector of the revenue shall give information thereof to such inspector or inspectors, reserving thereout for the United States the amount of the duties payable on the spirits, in respect to which, such penalty or forfeiture may have been incurred. And such penalty and forfeiture shall be recoverable with costs of

---

* *A discretionary power to remit or mitigate penalties in laws of this nature is indispensable. It is peculiarly so in the commencement. Heavy penalties are frequently incurred through inadvertence, misconstruction or want of information. Instances of this kind have happened under the existing system. The discretion however which is proposed to be given in the outset, is to be abridged at the expiration of a period which will allow sufficient time for persons to become acquainted with the law.*

suit by action of debt, in the name of the person or persons intitled thereto, or by information in the name of the United States of America. And it shall be the duty of the Attorney-General of the district, wherein any such penalty or forfeiture may have been incurred upon application to him, to institute or bring such information accordingly. Provided always that no officer of inspection, other than chief officer or officers of a district shall be entitled to the benefit of any forfeiture unless notice of the seizure by him made, shall be by him given within twelve hours next after such seizure to the said chief officer or officers. But in such case the United States shall have the entire benefit of such forfeiture.

L. And be it further enacted, That if any person or persons shall counterfeit, or forge, or cause to be counterfeited or forged any of the certificates herein before directed to be given, or shall knowingly or willingly accept or receive any false or untrue certificate with any of the said spirits, or shall fraudulently alter or erase any such certificate after the same shall be given, or knowingly or willingly publish or make use of such certificate so counterfeited, forged, false, untrue, altered or erased, every person or persons so offending, shall for each and every offence, severally forfeit and pay the sum of one thousand dollars.

LI. And be it further enacted, That any person or persons that shall be convicted, of wilfully taking a false oath or affirmation, in any of the cases in which oaths and affirmations are required to be taken by virtue of this act, shall be liable to the pains and penalties to which persons are liable for wilful and corrupt perjury.

LII. And be it further enacted, That if any person or persons shall give or offer to give any bribe, recompence or reward whatsoever, to any inspector or inspectors of the revenue, in order to corrupt, persuade or prevail upon such officer, either to do any act or acts contrary to his duty in the execution of this act, or to neglect or omit to do any act or thing which he ought to do in execution of this act, or to connive at, or to conceal any fraud or frauds relating to the duties hereby imposed on any of the said spirits, or not to discover the same, every such person or persons shall for such offence, whether the same offer or proposal be accepted or not, forfeit and pay the sum of one thousand dollars.

LIII. And be it further enacted, That if any person or persons shall assault, resist, oppose, molest, obstruct or hinder any inspector in the execution of this act, or of any of the powers or authorities hereby vested in him, or shall forcibly rescue or cause to be rescued any of the said spirits, after the same shall have been seized by any such inspector or officer, or shall attempt or endeavor so to do, all and every person and persons so offending, shall for every such offence, for which no other penalty is particularly provided by this act, forfeit and pay the sum of five hundred dollars.

LIV. And be it further enacted, That if any such inspector or officer, shall enter into any collusion with any person or persons for violating or evading any of the provisions of this act, or the duties hereby imposed, or shall fraudulently concur in the delivery of any of the said spirits, out of any house, building or place, wherein the same are deposited without payment, or security for the payment of the duties thereupon, or shall falsely or fraudulently mark any cask, case or vessel, contrary to any of the said provisions, such inspector or officer shall for every such offence forfeit the sum of one thousand dollars, and upon conviction of any of the said offences, shall forfeit his office and shall be disqualified for holding any other office under the United States.

LV. And be it further enacted, that it shall be lawful for the Inspectors of the revenue, and when requested by any such dealer, they are hereby required to provide blank certificates, in such form as shall be directed by the Secretary of the Treasury, and in the cases in which certificates are hereby directed to be issued or granted by the said dealers, to furnish them therewith the blanks in which certificates shall be filled up by such dealers, according to the nature and truth of each particular case, subject to the penalty heretofore declared for granting or using false or untrue certificates. And every such dealer shall from time to time, when thereunto requested, account with such Inspectors respectively, for the number of certificates received by him, and for the disposition of such of them as may have been disposed of, and shall produce and shew the residue thereof to the said Inspector, and shall pay for every certificate for which he cannot satisfactorily account, the sum of fifty cents.

LVI. And be it further enacted, that in every case in which an oath or affirmation is required by virtue of this act, it shall be lawful for the Inspectors of the revenue, or any of them, or their lawful deputy, or the lawful deputy of one of them where not more than one in a district, to administer and take such oath or affirmation. And that wherever there are more than one Inspector for one district, a majority of them may execute all and any of the powers and authorities hereby vested in the Inspectors of the revenue: Provided, that this shall not be construed to make a majority necessary in any case in which, according to the nature of the appointment or service, and the true intent of this act, the authority is or ought to be several.

And for the encouragement of the export trade of the United States:

LVII. Be it further enacted, that if any of the said spirits (whereupon any of the duties imposed by this act shall have been paid or secured to be paid) shall after the last day of   next, be exported from the United States to any foreign port or place, there shall be an allowance to the exporter or exporters thereof, by way of drawback, equal to the duties thereupon, according to the rates in each case by this act imposed, deducting therefrom one cent per gallon, and adding to the allowance upon spirits distilled within the United

States from molasses, which shall be so exported, two cents and an half cent per gallon, as an equivalent for the duty laid upon molasses by the said act for laying a duty on goods, wares and merchandizes imported into the United States: Provided always, that the said allowance shall not be made unless the said exporter or exporters shall observe the regulations hereinafter prescribed: And provided further, that nothing herein contained shall be construed to alter the provisions in the said former act, concerning drawbacks or allowances, in nature thereof, upon spirits imported prior to the said last day of last.

LVIII. And be it further enacted, that in order to entitle the said exporter or exporters to the benefit of the said allowance, he, she or they, shall previous to putting or lading any of the said spirits on board of any ship or vessel for exportation, give twenty-four hours notice at the least, to the proper officer of inspection of the port from which the said spirits shall be intended to be exported, of his, her or their intention to export the same, and of the number of casks and cases, or either of them, containing the said spirits so intended to be exported, and of the respective marks thereof, and of the place or places where the said spirits shall be then deposited, and of the place to which, and ship or vessel in which they shall be so intended to be exported. Whereupon it shall be the duty of the said officer to inspect, by himself or deputy, the casks and cases so noticed for exportation, and the quantities, kinds and proofs of the spirits therein, together with the certificates which ought to accompany the same according to the directions of this act, which shall be produced to him for that purpose; and if he shall find that the said casks and cases have the proper marks according to the directions of this act; and that the spirits therein correspond with the said certificates, he shall thereupon brand each cask or case with the word "Exportation;" and the said spirits shall, after such inspection, be laden on board the same ship or vessel of which notice shall have been given, and in the presence of the same officer who shall have examined the same, and whose duty it shall be to attend for that purpose. And after the said spirits shall be laden on board such ship or vessel, the certificates aforesaid shall be delivered to the said officer, who shall certify to the Collector of the said port the amount and particulars of the spirits so exported, and shall also deliver the said certificates which shall have been by him received to the said collector, which shall be a voucher to him, for payment of the said allowance.

Provided nevertheless, and be it further enacted, That the said allowance shall not be made, unless the said exporter or exporters shall make oath, or if a known Quaker, affirmation, that the said spirits so noticed for exportation, and laden on board such ship or vessel, are truly intended to be exported to the place whereof notice shall have been given, and are not intended to be relanded within the United States; and that he or she doth verily believe that the duties thereupon charged by this act, have been duly paid; and shall also give bond to the collector, with two sureties, one of whom shall be the master, or other person having the command or charge of the ship or vessel in which the said spirits shall be intended to be exported; the other, such sufficient person as shall be approved by the said collector, in the full value in the judgment of such collector, of the said spirits so intended to be exported, with condition that the said spirits (the dangers of the seas and enemies excepted) shall be really and truly exported to, and landed in such ports and places without the limits of the United States, according to the late treaty of peace with Great-Britain, as shall be specified in such bond; and that the said spirits shall not be unshipped from on board of the said ship or vessel, whereupon the same shall have been laden for exportation, within the said limits, or any ports or harbors of the United States, or relanded in any other part of the same (shipwreck or other unavoidable accident excepted.)

Provided also, and be it further enacted, that the said allowance shall not be paid until six months after the said spirits shall have been so exported.

LIX. And be it further enacted, That if any of the said spirits, after the same shall have been shipped for exportation, shall be unshipped for any purpose whatever, either within the limits of any part of the United States, or within four leagues of the coast thereof, or shall be relanded within the United States, from on board the ship or vessel wherein the same shall have been laden for exportation, (unless in case of necessity or distress to save the ship and goods from perishing, which shall be immediately made known to the principal officer of the customs, residing at the port nearest to which such ship or vessel shall be at the time such necessity or distress shall arise) then not only the spirits so unshipped, together with the casks and cases containing the same, but also the ship or vessel in or on board which the same shall have been so shipped or laden, together with her guns, furniture, ammunition, tackle and apparel; and also the ship, vessel or boat into which the said spirits shall be unshipped or put, after the unshipping thereof, together with her guns, furniture, ammunition, tackle and apparel, shall be forfeited, and may be seized by any officer of the customs, or of inspection.

LX. And be it further enacted, That the said allowance shall not be made when the said spirits shall be exported in any other than a ship or vessel of the burthen of   tons and upwards, to be ascertained to the satisfaction of the collector of the port from which the same shall be intended to be exported.

LXI. And be it further enacted, That the bonds to be given as aforesaid, shall and may be discharged by producing within one year from the respective dates thereof (if the delivery of the spirits in respect to which the same shall have been given, be at any place where a consul or other agent of the United States resides) a certificate of such consul or agent, and if there be no such consul or agent, then a certificate of any two known and reputable American merchants residing at the said place, and if there be not two such merchants residing at the said place, then a certificate of any other two reputable merchants, testifying the delivery of the said spirits, at the said place, which certificate shall in each case be confirmed by the oath or affirmation of the master and mate or other like officer of the vessel in which the said spirits shall have been exported; and when such certificate shall be from any other than a consul or agent, or merchants of the United States, it shall be a part of the said oath or affirmation, that there were not upon diligent enquiry to be found two merchants of the United States at the said place. Provided always, that in the case of death, the oath or affirmation of the party dying, shall not be deemed necessary: And provided further, that the said oath or affirmation, taken before the chief civil magistrate of the place of the said delivery, and certified under his hand seal, shall be of the same validity as if taken before a person qualified to administer oaths within the United States: or such bonds shall and may be discharged upon proof that the spirits so exported, were taken by enemies or perished in the sea, or destroyed by fire; the examination and proof of the same being left to the judgment of the collector of the customs, naval officer, and chief officer of inspection, or any two of them, of the place from which such spirits shall have been exported.

LXII. And be it further enacted, That the prosecution for all fines, penalties and forfeitures incurred by force of this act, and for all duties payable in virtue thereof, and which shall not be duly paid, shall and may be had before any justice of the peace or court of any state of competent jurisdiction, or court of the United States, of or within the state or district, in which the cause of action shall arise, with an appeal as in other cases: Provided, that where the cause of action shall exceed in value fifty dollars, the same shall not be cognisable before a justice of the peace only.

LXIII. And be it further enacted, That this act shall commence and take effect as to all matters therein contained, in respect to which no special commencement is hereby provided (except as to the appointment of officers and regulation of the districts) from and immediately after the last day of next.

(SCHEDULE K.)

ESTIMATE of the probable product of the funds proposed for funding the debt and providing for the current service of the United States, including the present duties on imports and tonnage.

Dollars,

Probable product of the duties on imports and tonnage, according to the
acts of the last session,   1,800,000
Including the State of North-Carolina, this estimate may be said to
correspond with the statement made by the committee of ways and
means during the last session; which statement the Secretary is
inclined to think is as near the truth as can be now obtained.

In the preceding estimate are comprehended wines, distilled spirits, teas,
and coffee, amounting to about   600,000
Which being deducted, leaves   1,200,000
From which deducting 5 per cent for expence of collection,   60,000
                                          Leaves nett product,   1,140,000
                        Probable product of duties proposed.
                                       Imported.
1,000,000 gallons wine, at   20 cents,   200,000
4,000,000 gallons distilled spirits, at   20   800,000
  700,000 pounds bohea tea, at   12   84,000
  800,000 pounds souchong and other black teas, at   20   160,000
  100,000 pounds green tea, average at   25   25,000
1,600,000 pounds coffee, at   5   80,000
                       Made in the United States.
3,500,000 gallons distilled spirits from foreign materials, at 11 cents,   385,000
3,000,000 ditto, distilled from materials of the United States, at 9 cents,   270,000
                                                        2,004,000
         Deduct for drawbacks, and expence of collection, 15 per cent.   300,600   1,703,400
                                                          Dollars,   2,843,400

American Imprints, RBkRm, DLC.

Smith (S.C.) Resolutions
February 8, 1790

Resolved, That congress ought not to adjourn, until they have adopted such measures as will make an adequate provision for the public debt.

Resolved, That in making such provision, no discrimination shall be made, between the original holders of the evidences, and the assignees thereof.

Resolved, That such of the debts of the individual states, as have been incurred by them, during the late war, ought to be assumed by the general government, and like funds provided for them.

Resolved, That the arrearages of interest, on the continental and state debts, ought to be funded, and consolidated with the principal.

Resolved, That the interests to be paid thereon, does not exceed   per cent. per annum, for the present.

CR, Feb. 8, 1790.

Resolves of Congress of May and September, 1779
February 8, 1790

Resolved. That a comee. of three be appointed to prepare an address to the several states on the present ~~state~~ situation of affairs and particularly on the necessity of paying their respective quotas.

Journals of Congress, PCC, DNA. The resolve was agreed to on May 21, 1779.

To the Inhabitants of the United States of America
May 26, 1779

Friends and Countrymen,

The present situation of public affairs demands your most serious attention, and particularly the great and encreasing depreciation of your currency requires the immediate, strenuous, and united efforts of all true friends to their country, for preventing an extension of the mischiefs that have already flowed from that source.

America, without arms, ammunition, discipline, revenue, government, or ally, almost totally stript of commerce, and in the weakness of youth, as it were with a "staff and a sling" only, dared "in the name of the Lord of Hosts" to engage a gigantic adversary, prepared at all points, boasting of his strength, and of whom even mighty warriors "were greatly afraid."

For defraying the expences of this uncommon war, your representatives in Congress were obliged to emit paper money; an expedient that you knew to have been before generally and successfully practised on this continent.

They were very sensible of the inconveniences with which too frequent emissions would be attended, and endeavored to avoid them. For this purpose they established loan-offices so early as in October 1776, and have from that time to this repeatedly and earnestly sollicited you to lend them money on the faith of the United States. The sums received on loan have nevertheless proved inadequate to the public exigencies. Our enemies prosecuting the war by sea and land with implacable fury and with some success, taxation at home and borrowing abroad, in the midst of difficulties and dangers, were alike impracticable. Hence the continued necessity of new emissions.

But to this cause alone we do not impute the evil before mentioned. We have too much reason to believe it has been in part owing to the artifices of men who have hastened to enrich themselves by monopolizing the necessaries of life, and to the misconduct of inferior officers employed in the public service.

The variety and importance of the business entrusted to your delegates, and their constant attendance in Congress, necessarily disables them from investigating disorders of this kind. Justly apprehensive of them they by their several resolutions of the 22d of November and 20th of December 1777, and of the 3d and 9th of February 1778, recommended to the legislative and executive powers of these states a due attention to these interesting affairs. How far those recommendations have been complied with we will not undertake to determine; but we held ourselves bound in duty to you to declare that we are not convinced there has been as much diligence used in detecting and reforming abuses as there has been in committing or complaining of them.

With regard to monopolizers it is our opinion, that taxes judiciously laid on such articles as become the objects of engrossers, and those frequently collected, would operate against the pernicious tendency of such practices.

As to inferior officers employed in the public service, we ANXIOUSLY desire to call your most vigilant attention to their conduct with respect to every species of misbehaviour, whether proceeding from ignorance, negligence or fraud, and to the making of laws for inflicting exemplary punishments on all offenders of this kind.

We are sorry to hear that some persons are so slightly informed of their own interests as to suppose that it is advantageous to them to sell the produce of their farms at enormous prices, when a little reflection might convince them that it is injurious to those interests and the general welfare. If they expect thereby to purchase imported goods cheaper, they will be egregiously disappointed; for the merchants, who know they cannot obtain returns in gold, silver, or bills of exchange, but that their vessels if loaded here at all must be loaded with produce, will raise the price of what they have to sell, in proportion to the price of what they have to buy; and consequently the land holder can purchase no more foreign goods for the same quantity of his produce than he could before.

The evil, however, does not stop at this point. The land holder by acting on this mistaken calculation is only labouring to accumulate an immense debt by encreasing the public expences, for the payment of which his estate is engaged, and to embarrass every measure adopted for vindicating his liberty and securing his prosperity.

As the harvests of this year, which by the divine goodness promise to be plentiful, will soon be gathered, and some new measures relating to your foreign concerns, with some arrangements relating to your domestic, are now under consideration, from which beneficial effects are expected, we entertain hopes that your affairs will acquire a much greater degree of regularity and energy than they have hitherto had.

But we should be highly criminal if we did not plainly tell you that those hopes are not founded wholly upon our own proceedings. These must be supported by your virtue, your wisdom, and your diligence. From the advantage of those seats in the national council with which you have honored us, we have a pleasing prospect of many blessings approaching this our native land. It is your patriotism must introduce and fix them here.

In vain will it be for your delegates to form plans of oeconomy; to strive to stop a continuation of emissions of taxation or loan, if you do not zealously co-operate with them in promoting their designs and use your utmost industry to prevent the waste of money in the expenditure, which your respective situations in the several places where it is expended, may enable you to do. A discharge of this duty and a compliance with recommendations for supplying money, might enable Congress to give speedy assurances to the public that no more emissions shall take place, and thereby close that source of depreciation.

Your governments being now established, and your ability to contend with your invaders ascertained, we have on the most mature deliberation judged it indispensably necessary to call upon you for forty-five millions of dollars, in addition to the fifteen millions required by a resolution of Congress of the 2d of January last, to be paid into the continental treasury before the 1st day of January next, in the same proportion, as to the quotas of the several states, with that for the said fifteen millions.

It appeared proper to us to fix the first day of next January for the payment of the whole; but as it is probable that some states, if not all, will raise part of the sums by installments or otherwise before that time, we recommend in the strongest manner the paying as much as can be collected as soon as possible into the continental treasury.

Though it is manifest that moderate taxation in times of peace will recover the credit of your currency, yet the encouragement which your enemies derive from its depreciation, and the present exigencies demand great and speedy exertions.

We are persuaded you will use all possible care to make the promotion of the general welfare interfere as little as may be with the ease and comfort of individuals; but tho' the raising these sums should press heavily on some of our constituents, yet the obligations we feel to your venerable clergy, the truly helpless, widows and orphans, your most gallant, generous, meritorious officers and soldiers, the public faith and the common weal, so irresistably urge us to attempt the appreciation of your currency, that we cannot withold obedience to those authoritative sensations.

On this subject we will only add, that as the rules of justice are most pleasing to our infinitely good and gracious Creator, and an adherence to them most likely to obtain his favour, so they will ever be found to be the best and safest maxims of human policy.

To our constituents we submit the propriety and purity of our intentions, well knowing they will not forget, that we lay no burthens upon them, but those in which we participate with them—a happy sympathy, that pervades societies formed on the basis of equal liberty. Many cares, many labours, and may we not add, reproaches—are peculiar to us. These are the emoluments of our unsolicited stations; and with these we are content, if YOU approve our conduct. If you do not, we shall return to our private condition with no other regret, than that which will arise from our not having served you as acceptably and essentially as we wished and strove to do, though as chearfully and faithfully as we could.

Think not we despair of the commonwealth, or endeavour to shrink from opposing difficulties. No. Your cause is too good, your objects too sacred, to be relinquished. We tell you truths, because you are freemen who can bear to hear them and may profit by them; and when they reach your enemies, we fear not the consequences, because we are not ignorant of their resources or our own. Let your good sense decide upon the comparison. Let even their prejudiced understandings decide upon it, and you need not be apprehensive of the determination.

Whatever supposed advantages from plans of rapine, projects of blood, or dreams of domination, may heretofore have amused their inflamed fancies, the conduct of one monarch, the friend and protector of the rights of mankind, has turned the scale so much against them, that their visionary schemes vanish as the unwholesome vapours of night before the healthful influences of the sun.

An Alliance has been formed between his Most Christian Majesty and these States, on the basis of the most perfect equality, for the direct end of maintaining effectually their Liberty, Sovereignty and Independence, absolute and unlimited, as well in matters of government as of commerce. The conduct of our good and great Ally towards us in this instance and others, has so fully manifested his sincerity and kindness as to excite on our part correspondent sentiments of confidence and affection.

Observing the interests of his kingdom, to which duty and inclination prompted his attention, to be connected with those of *America,* and the combination of both clearly to coincide with the beneficient designs of the Author of Nature, who unquestionably intended men to partake of certain rights and portions of happiness, his Majesty perceived the attainment of these views to be founded on the single proposition of a separation between *America* and *Great-Britain.*

The resentment and confusion of our enemies will point out to you the ideas you should entertain of the magnanimity and consummate wisdom of his Most Christian Majesty on this occasion.

They perceive, that selecting this grand and just idea from all those specious ones that might have confused or misled inferior judgment or virtue, and satisfied with the advantages which must result from that event alone, he has cemented the harmony between himself and these states not only by establishing a reciprocity of benefits, but by eradicating every cause of jealousy and suspicion. They also perceive with similar emotions, that the moderation of our ally, in not desiring an acquisition of dominion on this continent, or an exclusion of other nations from a share of its commercial advantages, so useful to them, has given no alarm to those nations, but in fact has INTERESTED them in the accomplishment of his generous undertaking to dissolve the monopoly thereof by *Great-Britain,* which has already contributed to elevate her to her present power and haughtiness, and threatened if continued to raise both to a height insupportable to the rest of *Europe.*

In short, their own best informed statesmen and writers confess, that your cause is exceedingly favoured by courts and people in that quarter of the world, while that of your adversaries is equally reprobated; and from thence draw ominous and well-grounded conclusions, that the final event must prove unfortunate to the latter. Indeed, we have the BEST reason to believe that we shall soon form other Alliances, and on principles honourable and beneficial to these States.

Infatuated as your enemies have been from the beginning of this contest, do you imagine they can now flatter themselves with a hope of conquering you, unless you are false to yourselves?

When unprepared, undisciplined, and unsupported, you opposed their fleets and armies in full conjoined force, then, if at any time, was conquest to be apprehended. Yet what progress towards it have their violent and incessant efforts made? Judge from their own conduct. Having devoted you to bondage, and after vainly wasting their blood and treasure in the dishonorable enterprize, they deigned at length to offer terms of accommodation with respectful addresses to that once despised body the Congress, whose humble supplications ONLY for Peace, Liberty and Safety, they had contemptuously rejected, under pretence of its being an unconstitutional assembly. Nay more; desirous of seducing you into a deviation from the paths of rectitude, from which they had so far and so rashly wandered, they made most specious offers to tempt you into a violation of your faith given to your illustrious Ally. Their arts were as unavailing as their arms. Foiled again, and stung with rage, embittered by envy, they had no alternative, but to renounce the inglorious and ruinous controversy, or to resume their former modes of ·prosecuting it. They chose the latter. Again the savages are stimulated to horrid massacres of women and children, and domestics to the murder of their masters. Again our brave and unhappy brethren are doomed to miserable deaths in gaols and prison-ships. To complete the sanguinary system, all the "EXTREMITIES of War" are by authority denounced against you.

Piously endeavour to derive this consolation from their remorseless fury, that "the Father of Mercies" looks down with disapprobation on such audacious defiances of his holy laws; and be further comforted with recollecting, that the arms assumed by you in your righteous cause, have not been sullied by any unjustifiable severities.

Your enemies despairing however, as it seems, of the success of their united forces against our main army, have divided them, as if their design was to harrass you by predatory, desultory operations. If you are assiduous in improving opportunities, *Saratoga* may not be the only spot on this continent to give a new denomination to the baffled troops of a nation impiously priding herself in notions of her omnipotence.

Rouze yourselves therefore, that this campaign may finish the great work you have so nobly carried on for several years past. What nation ever engaged in such a contest under such a complication of disadvantages, so soon surmounted many of them, and in so short a period of time had so certain a prospect of a speedy and happy conclusion. We will venture to pronounce that so remarkable an instance exists not in the annals of mankind. We well remember what you said at the commencement of this war. You saw the immense difference between your circumstances and those of your enemies, and you knew the quarrel must decide on no less than your lives, liberties and estates. All these you greatly put to every hazard, resolving rather to die freemen than to live slaves; and justice will oblige the impartial world to confess you have uniformly acted on the same generous principle. Consider how much you have done, and how comparatively little remains to be done to crown you with success. Persevere; and you ensure Peace, Freedom, Safety, Glory, Sovereignty, and Felicity to Yourselves, your Children, and your Children's Children.

Encouraged by favours already received from infinite goodness, gratefully acknowledging them, earnestly imploring their continuance, constantly endeavouring to draw them down on your heads by an amendment of your lives and a conformity to the divine will, humbly confiding in the protection so often and wonderfully experienced, vigorously employ the means placed by Providence in your hands, for compleating your labours.

Fill up your battalions—be prepared in every part to repell the incursions of your enemies—place your several quotas in the continental treasury—lend money for public uses—sink the emissions of your respective states—provide effectually for expediting the conveyance of supplies for your armies and fleets, and for your allies—prevent the produce of the country from being monopolized—effectually superintend the behaviour of public officers—diligently promote piety, virtue, brotherly love, learning, frugality and moderation—and may you be approved before Almighty God worthy of those blessings we devoutly wish you to enjoy.

Done in CONGRESS by unanimous Consent, this twenty-sixth day of May, one thousand seven hundred and seventy-nine.

JOHN JAY, President.

Attest.

CHARLES THOMSON, Secretary.

PHILADELPHIA: Printed by DAVID C. CLAYPOOLE, Printer to the Honorable the Congress of the United States of America.

PPL. E–16636.

Resolved That the president be requested to prepare a circular letter to the several states to accompany the resolutions of Congress of the first and third instant for stopping the further emissions of bills of credit.

Journals of Congress, PCC, DNA. The resolve was agreed to on September 8, 1779.

A CIRCULAR LETTER FROM THE
CONGRESS OF THE UNITED STATES
TO THEIR CONSTITUENTS
SEPTEMBER 13, 1779

FRIENDS AND FELLOW CITIZENS!

IN governments raised on the generous principles of equal liberty, where the rulers of the state are the servants of the people, and not the masters of those from whom they derive authority; it is their duty to inform their fellow citizens of the state of their affairs, and by evincing the propriety of public measures, lead them to unite the influence of inclination to the force of legal obligation in rendering them successful. This duty ceases not, even in times of the most perfect peace, order and tranquility, when the safety of the commonwealth is neither endangered by force or seduction from abroad, or by faction, treachery, or misguided ambition from within. At this season, therefore, we find ourselves in a particular manner impressed with a sense of it, and can no longer forbear calling your attention to a subject much misrepresented, and respecting which dangerous as well as erroneous opinions have been held and propagated: we mean your finances.

The ungrateful despotism and inordinate lust of domination which marked the unnatural designs of the British King and his venal Parliament to inslave the people of America, reduced you to the necessity of either asserting your rights by arms, or ingloriously passing under the yoke. You nobly preferred war. Armies were then to be raised, paid and supplied: Money became necessary for these purposes. Of your own there was but little; and of no nation in the world could you then borrow. The little that was spread among you could be collected only by taxes, and to this end regular governments were essential; of these you were also destitute. So circumstanced, you had no other resource but the natural value and wealth of your fertile country. Bills were issued on the credit of this bank, and your faith was pledged for their redemption. After a considerable number of these had circulated, loans were solicited, and offices for the purpose established. Thus a national debt was unavoidably created, and the amount of it is as follows:

	Dollars.
Bills emitted and circulating,	159,948,880
Monies borrowed before the 1st of March 1778, the interest of which is payable in France,	7,545,196 67/90
Monies borrowed since the 1st of March 1778, the interest of which is payable here,	26,188,909
Money due abroad, not exactly known—the balances not having been transmitted, supposed to be about	4,000,000

For your further satisfaction we shall order a particular account of the several emissions, with the times limited for their redemption, and also of the several loans, the interest allowed on each, and the terms assigned for their payment, to be prepared and published.

The taxes have as yet brought into the treasury no more than 3,027,560, so that all the monies supplied to Congress by the people of America, amount to no more than 36,761,665 dollars and 67/90ths, that being the sum of the loans and taxes received. Judge then of the necessity of emissions, and learn from whom and from whence that necessity arose.

We are also to inform you, that on the first day of September instant we resolved "that we would on no account whatever emit more bills of credit than to make the whole amount of such bills two hundred millions of dollars, and as the sum emitted and in circulation amounted to 159,948,880 dollars, and the sum of 40,051,120 dollars remained to compleat the two hundred million above mentioned, we on the third day of September instant further resolved, that we would emit such part only of the said sum of 40,051,120 dollars as should be absolutely necessary for public exigencies before adequate supplies could otherwise be obtained, relying for such supplies on the exertions of the several states."

Exclusive of the great and ordinary expences incident to the war, the depreciation of the currency has so swelled the prices of every necessary article, and of consequence made such additions to the usual amount of expenditures, that very considerable supplies must be immediately provided by loans and taxes; and we unanimously declare it to be essential to the welfare of these states that the taxes already called for be paid into the continental treasury by the time recommended for that purpose. It is also highly proper that you should extend your views beyond that period, and prepare in season as well for bringing your respective quotas of troops into the field early the next campaign, as for providing the supplies necessary in the course of it. We shall take care to apprize you from time to time of the state of the treasury, and to recommend the proper measures for supplying it. To keep your battalions full, to encourage loans and to assess your taxes with prudence, collect them with firmness, and pay them with punctuality, is all that will be requisite on your part. Further ways and means of providing for the public exigencies are now under consideration, and will soon be laid before you.

Having thus given you a short and plain state of your debt, and pointed out the necessity of punctuality in furnishing the supplies already required, we shall proceed to make a few remarks on the depreciation of the currency, to which we entreat your attention.

The depreciation of bills of credit is always either natural or artificial, or both. The latter is our case. The moment the sum in circulation exceeded what was necessary as a medium in commerce, it began and continued to depreciate in proportion as the amount of the surplus encreased and that proportion would hold good until the sum emitted should become so great as nearly to equal the value of the capital or stock, on the credit of which the bills were issued. Supposing, therefore, that 30,000,000 was necessary for a circulating medium, and that 160,000,000 had issued, the natural depreciation is but little more than as five to one: But the actual depreciation exceeds that proportion, and that excess is artificial. The natural depreciation is to be removed only by lessening the quantity of money in circulation. It will regain its primitive value whenever it shall be reduced to the sum necessary for a medium of commerce. This is only to be effected by loans and taxes.

The artificial depreciation is a more serious subject, and merits minute investigation. A distrust (however occasioned) entertained by the mass of the people either in the *ability* or *inclination* of the United States to redeem their bills is the cause of it. Let us enquire how far reason will justify a distrust in the *ability* of the United States.

The ability of the United States must depend on two things: First, the success of the present revolution, and secondly, on the sufficiency of the natural wealth, value and resources of the country.

That the time has been when honest men might, without being chargeable with timidity, have doubted the success of the present revolution, we admit; but that period is passed. The independence of America is now as fixed as fate, and the petulant efforts of Britain to break it down are as vain and fruitless as the raging of the waves which beat against their clifts. Let those who are still affected with these doubts consider the character and condition of our enemies. Let them remember that we are contending against a kingdom crumbling into pieces; a nation without public virtue; and a people sold to and betrayed by their own representatives; against a Prince governed by his passions and a Ministry without confidence or wisdom; against armies half paid and generals half trusted; against a government equal only to plans of plunder, conflagration and murder—a government by the most impious violations of the rights of religion, justice, humanity and mankind, courting the vengeance of Heaven and revolting from the protection of Providence. Against the fury of these enemies you made successful resistance, when single, alone, and friendless, in the days of weakness and infancy, before your hands had been taught to war or your fingers to fight. And can there be any reason to apprehend that the Divine Disposer of human events, after having separated us from the house of bondage, and led us safe through a sea of blood, towards the land of liberty and promise, will leave the work of our political redemption unfinished, and either permit us to perish in a wilderness of difficulties, or suffer us to be carried back in chains to that country of oppression, from whose tyranny he hath mercifully delivered us with a stretched-out arm?

In close alliance with one of the most powerful nations in Europe which has generously made our cause her own, in amity with many others, and enjoying the good will of all, what danger have we to fear from Britain? Instead of acquiring accessions of territory by conquest, the limits of her empire daily contract: her fleets no longer rule the ocean, nor are her armies invincible by land. How many of her standards, wrested from the hands of her champions, are among your trophies, and have graced the triumphs of your troops? and how great is the number of those, who, sent to bind you in fetters, have become your captives, and received their lives from your hands? In short, whoever considers that these states are daily encreasing in power; that their armies have become veteran; that their governments, founded in freedom, are established; that their fertile country and their affectionate ally furnish them with ample supplies; that the Spanish monarch, well prepared for war, with fleets and armies ready for combat, and a treasury overflowing with wealth, has entered the lists against Britain; that the other European nations, often insulted by her pride, and alarmed by the strides of her ambition, have left her to her fate; that Ireland, wearied with her oppressions, is panting for liberty, and even Scotland displeased and uneasy at her edicts: Whoever consider these things, instead of doubting the issue of the war, will rejoice in the glorious, the sure and certain prospect of success.

This point being established, the next question is whether the natural wealth, value and resources of the country will be equal to the payment of the debt?

Let us suppose for the sake of argument, that at the conclusion of the war, the emissions should amount to 200,000,000, that exclusive of supplies from taxes, which will not be inconsiderable, the loans should amount to 100,000,000, then the whole national debt of the United States would be

300,000,000. There are at present 3,000,000 of inhabitants in the thirteen states: three hundred million of dollars divided among three million of people would give to each person one hundred dollars; and is there an individual in America unable in the course of eighteen or twenty years to pay it again? Suppose the whole debt assessed, as it ought to be, on the inhabitants in proportion to their respective estates, what would then be the share of the poorer people? Perhaps not ten dollars. Besides, as this debt will not be payable immediately, but probably twenty years allotted for it, the number of inhabitants by that time in America will be far more than double their present amount. It is well known that the inhabitants of this country encreased almost in the ratio of compound interest. By natural population they doubled every twenty years, and how great may be the host of emigrants from other countries cannot be ascertained. We have the highest reason to believe the number will be immense. Suppose that only ten thousand should arrive the first year after the war, what will those ten thousand with their families count in twenty years time? probably double the number. This observation applies with proportionable force to the emigrants of every successive year. Thus you see great part of your debt will be payable not merely by the present number of inhabitants, but by that number swelled and encreased by the natural population of the present inhabitants, by multitudes of emigrants daily arriving from other countries, and by the natural population of those successive emigrants, so that every person's share of the debt will be constantly diminishing by others coming in to pay a proportion of it.

These are advantages which none but young countries enjoy. The number of inhabitants in every country in Europe remains nearly the same from one century to another. No country will produce more people than it can subsist, and every country, if free and cultivated, will produce as many as it can maintain. Hence we may form some idea of the future population of these states. Extensive wildernesses, now scarcely known or explored, remain yet to be cultivated, and vast lakes and rivers, whose waters have for ages rolled in silence and obscurity to the ocean, are yet to hear the din of industry, become subservient to commerce, and boast delightful villas, gilded spires, and spacious cities rising on their banks.

Thu[s] much for the number of persons to pay the debt. The next point is their *ability*. They who enquire how many millions of acres are contained only in the settled part of North-America, and how much each acre is worth, will acquire very enlarged and yet very inadequate ideas of the value of this country. But those who will carry their enquiries further, and learn that we heretofore paid an annual tax to Britain of three millions sterling in the way of trade, and still grew rich; that our commerce was then confined to her; that we were obliged to carry our commodities to her market, and consequently to sell them at her price; that we were compelled to purchase foreign commodities at her stores, and on her terms, and were forbid to establish any manufactories incompatible with her views of gain; that in future the whole world will be open to us, and we shall be at liberty to purchase from those who will sell on the best terms, and to sell to those who will give the best prices; that as the country encreases in number of inhabitants and cultivation, the productions of the earth will be proportionably encreased, and the riches of the whole proportionably greater: Whoever examines the force of these and similar observations, must smile at the ignorance of those who doubt the ability of the United States to redeem their bills.

Let it also be remembered that paper money is the only kind of money which cannot "make unto itself wings and fly away." It remains with us, it will not forsake us, it is always ready and at hand for the purpose of commerce or taxes, and every industrious man can find it. On the contrary, should Britain like Ninevah (and for the same reason) yet find mercy, and escape the storm ready to burst upon her, she will find her national debt in a very different situation. Her territory diminished, her people wasted, her commerce ruined, her monopolies gone, she must provide for the discharge of her immense debt by taxes to be paid in specie, in gold or silver, perhaps now buried in the mines of Mexico or Peru, or still concealed in the brooks and rivulets of Africa or Indostan.

Having shewn that there is no reason to doubt the ability of the United States to pay their debt, let us next enquire whether as much can be said for their inclination.

Under this head three things are to be attended to:

1st. Whether and in what manner the faith of the United States has been pledged for the redemption of their bills.

2d. Whether they have put themselves in a political capacity to redeem them, and

3d. Whether, admitting the two former propositions, there is any reason to apprehend a wanton violation of the public faith.

1st. It must be evident to every man who reads the journals of Congress or looks at the face of one of their bills, that Congress have pledged the faith of their constituents for the redemption of them. And it must be equally evident, not only that they had authority to do so, but that their constituents have actually ratified their acts, by receiving their bills, passing laws establishing their currency, and punishing those who counterfeit them. So that it may with truth be said that the people have pledged their faith for the redemption of them not only collectively by their representatives, but individually.

2d. Whether the United States have put themselves in a political capacity to redeem their bills, is a question which calls for more full discussion.

Our enemies, as well foreign as domestic, have laboured to raise doubts on this head. They argue that the confederation of the states remains yet to be perfected; that the union may be dissolved; Congress be abolished, and each state resuming its delegated powers proceed in future to hold and exercise all the rights of sovereignty appertaining to an independent state. In such an event, say they, the continental bills of credit, created and supported by the union, would die with it. This position being assumed, they next proceed to assert this event to be probable, and in proof of it urge our divisions, our parties, our separate interests, distinct manners, former prejudices, and many other arguments equally plausible and equally fallacious. Examine this matter.

For every purpose essential to the defence of these states in the progress of the present war, and necessary to the attainment of the objects of it, these states now are as fully, legally and absolutely confederated, as it is possible for them to be. Read the credentials of the different delegates who composed the Congress in 1774, 1775, and part of 1776. You will find that they establish an union for the express purpose of opposing the oppressions of Britain and obtaining redress of grievances. On the 4th of July 1776 your representatives in Congress, perceiving that nothing less than unconditional submission would satisfy our enemies, did in the name of the people of the Thirteen United Colonies declare them to be free and independent states, and "for the SUPPORT of that declaration, with a firm reliance on the protection of Divine Providence, did mutually pledge to each other their LIVES, their FORTUNES and their SACRED HONOUR." Was ever confederation more formal, more solemn or explicit? It has been expressly assented to and ratified by every state in the union. Accordingly, for the direct SUPPORT of this declaration, that is for the support of the independence of these states, armies have been raised, and bills of credit emitted and loans made to pay and supply them. The redemption therefore of these bills, the payment of these debts, and the settlement of the accounts of the several states for expenditures or services for the common benefit and in this common cause, are among the objects of this confederation; and consequently while all or any of its objects remain unattained, it cannot, so far as it may respect such objects, be dissolved, consistent with the laws of God or Man.

But we are persuaded, and our enemies will find, that our union is not to end here. They are mistaken when they suppose us kept together only by a sense of present danger. It is a fact which they only will dispute, that the people of these states were never so cordially united as at this day. By having been obliged to mix with each other, former prejudices have worn off, and their several manners become blended. A sense of common permanent interest, mutual affection (having been brethren in affliction,) the ties of consanguinity daily extending, constant reciprocity of good offices, similarity in language, in governments, and therefore in manners, the importance, weight and splendor of the union, all conspire in forming a strong chain of connection, which must for ever bind us together. The United Provinces of the Netherlands and the United Cantons of Switzerland became free and independent under circumstances very like ours: their independence has been long established, and yet their confederacies continue in full vigor. What reason can be assigned why our union should be less lasting? or why should the people of these states be supposed less wise than the inhabitants of those? You are not uninformed that a plan for a perpetual confederation has been prepared and that twelve of the thirteen states have already acceded to it. But enough has been said to shew that for every purpose of the present war, and all things incident to it, there does at present exist a perfect solemn confederation, and therefore that the states now are and always will be in political capacity to redeem their bills, pay their debts, and settle their accounts.

3d. Whether, admitting the ability and political capacity of the United States to redeem their bills, there is any reason to apprehend a wanton violation of the public faith?

It is with great regret and reluctance that we can prevail upon ourselves to take the least notice of a question which involves in it a doubt so injurious to the honour and dignity of America.

The enemy, aware that the strength of America lay in the union of her citizens, and the wisdom and integrity of those to whom they committed the direction of their affairs, have taken unwearied pains to disunite and alarm the people, to depreciate the abilitites and virtue of their rulers, and to impair the confidence reposed in them by their constituents. To this end repeated attempts have been made to draw an absurd and fanciful line of distinction between the Congress and the People, and to create an opinion and a belief that their interests and views were different and opposed. Hence the ridiculous tales, the inviduous insinuations, and the whimsical suspicions that have been forged and propagated by disguised emissaries and traitors in the garb of patriots. Hence has proceeded the notable discovery that as the Congress made the money they also can destroy it; and that it will exist no longer than they find it convenient to permit it. It is not surprising that in a free country, where the tongues and pens of such people are and must be licensed, such political heresies should be inculcated and diffused, but it is really astonishing that the mind of a single virtuous citizen in America should be influenced by them. It certainly cannot be necessary to remind you that your representatives here are chosen from among yourselves; that you are or ought to be acquainted with their several characters; that they are sent here to speak your sentiments, and that it is constantly in your power to remove such as do not. You surely are convinced that it is no more in their power to annihilate your money than your independence, and that any act of theirs for either of those purposes would be null and void.

We should pay an ill compliment to the understanding and honour of every true American, were we to adduce many arguments to shew the baseness or bad policy of violating our national faith, or omitting to pursue the measures necessary to preserve it. A bankrupt faithless republic would be a novelty in the political world, and appear among reputable nations, like a common prostitute among chaste and respectable matrons. The pride of America revolts from the idea; her citizens know for what purposes these emissions were made, and have repeatedly plighted their faith for the redemption of them; they are to be found in every man's possession, and every man is interested in their being redeemed; they must therefore entertain a high opinion of American credulity, who suppose the people capable of believing, on due reflection, that all America will, against the faith, the honor and the interest of all America, be ever prevailed upon to countenance, support or permit so ruinous, so disgraceful a measure. We are convinced that the efforts and arts of our enemies will not be wanting to draw us into this humiliating and contemptible situation. Impelled by malice, and the suggestions of chagrin and disappointment, at not being able to bend our necks to their yoke, they will endeavour to force or seduce us to commit this unpardonable sin, in order to subject us to the punishment due to it, and that we may thenceforth be a reproach and a by-word among the nations. Apprized of these consequences, knowing the value of national character, and impressed with a due sense of the immutable laws of justice and honour, it is impossible that America should think without horror of such an execrable deed.

If then neither our ability or inclination to discharge the public debt, are justly questionable, let our conduct correspond with this confidence, and let us rescue our credit from its present imputations. Had the attention of America to this object been unremitted, had taxes been seasonably imposed and collected, had proper loans been made, had laws been passed and executed for punishing those who maliciously endeavoured to injure the public credit; had these and many other things equally necessary been done, and had our currency, notwithstanding all these efforts, declined to its present degree of depreciation, our case would indeed have been deplorable. But as these exertions have not been made, we may yet experience the good effects which naturally result from them. Our former negligences therefore should now animate us with hope, and teach us not to dispair of removing by vigilance and application the evils which supineness and inattention have produced.

It has been already observed that in order to prevent the further natural depreciation of our bills we have resolved to stop the press, and to call upon you for supplies by loans and taxes. You are in capacity to afford them, and are bound by the strongest ties to do it. Leave us not therefore without supplies, nor let in that flood of evils which would follow from such a neglect. It would be an event most grateful to our enemies, and depend upon it they will redouble their artifices and industry to compass it. Be therefore upon your guard, and examine well the policy of every measure and the evidence of every report that may be proposed or mentioned to you before you adopt the one or believe the other. Recollect that it is the price of the liberty, the peace and the safety of yourselves and posterity, that now is required; *that* peace, liberty and safety, for the attainment and security of which you have so often and so solemnly declared your readiness to sacrifice your lives and fortunes. The war, tho' drawing fast to a successful issue, still rages. Disdain to leave the whole business of your defence to your Ally. Be mindful that the brightest prospects may be clouded, and that prudence bids us be prepared for every event. Provide therefore for continuing your armies in the field till victory and peace shall lead them home, and avoid the reproach of permitting the currency to depreciate in your hands, when by yielding a part to taxes and loans, the whole might have been appreciated and preserved. Humanity as well as justice makes this demand upon you, the complaints of ruined widows, and the cries of fatherless children, whose whole support has been placed in your hands and melted away, have doubtless reached you—take care that they ascend no higher. Rouse therefore; strive who shall do most for his country; rekindle that flame of patriotism which at the mention of disgrace and slavery blazed throughout America, and animated all her citizens. Determine to finish the contest as you began it, honestly and gloriously. Let it never be said that America had no sooner become independent than she became insolvent, or that her infant glories and growing fame were obscured and tarnished by broken contracts and violated faith, in the very hour when all the nations of the earth were admiring and almost adoring the splendor of her rising.

By the unanimous Order of Congress,
JOHN JAY, PRESIDENT.

PHILADELPHIA,
September 13, 1779.

RBkRm, DLC. E-16558.

Fitzsimons Resolutions
February 8, 1790

[1] Resolved, That adequate provision ought to be made for fulfilling the engagements of the United States in respect to their foreign debt.[1]

---

[1] On February 9, Stone moved to strike out "in respect to their foreign debt" in the first resolution and "domestic" in the second resolution, but he was not seconded. (*CR*, Feb. 9) The first resolution was agreed to unanimously on February 9. (*GUS*, Feb. 10)

[2] Resolved, That permanent funds ought to be appropriated[2] for the payment of interest[3] on, and the gradual discharge of the domestic debt of the United States.[4]

[3] Resolved, That the arrears of interest, including indents issued in payment thereof, ought to be provided for on the same terms with[5] the principal of the said debt.[6]

[4]Resolved, That the debts of the respective States ought, with the consent of the creditors, to be assumed and provided for by the United States.[7]

---

[2] On February 22, the COWH disagreed to a motion by White to strike out "permanent" and substitute "provided" in place of "appropriated." (CR, Feb. 22)

[3] On February 11, the COWH disagreed to a motion by Livermore to insert "at a certain rate" at this point. (GUS, Feb. 13)

[4] A motion by Scott to insert "as soon as the same shall be ascertained, and duly liquidated" at this point was introduced on February 9 and disagreed to the next day. (GUS, Feb. 10, 13) On February 10, a motion by Tucker to substitute "as shall appear consistent with equity and agreeable to the resources of the country" for Scott's amendment was apparently not seconded. (NYDG, Feb. 12) Also on February 10, Burke proposed adding, "provided a discrimination be made between the original holders and their assignees, and that a scale of depreciation be prepared accordingly," but he withdrew his motion the next day. (GUS, Feb. 13) On February 11, Madison proposed the following as a substitute for the second resolution:

> Resolved, that adequate funds ought to be provided for paying the interest and principal of the domestic debt, as the same shall be liquidated: and that, in such liquidation, the present holders of public securities, which have been alienated, shall be settled with according to the highest market rate of such securities; and that the balance of the sums due from the public, be paid in such proportion to the original holder of such securities. (CR, Feb. 11)

On February 19, Gerry, seconded by Bland, moved to strike out that part of the Madison resolution relating to a discrimination between original and present holders of public securities, but he withdrew the motion. (GUS, Mar. 10) On February 22 the Madison substitute was disagreed to. (NYDA, NYDG, Feb. 23)

[5] On February 22, Gerry moved to strike "provided for on the same terms with" and insert "incorporated with, and made part of." (CR, Feb. 22) He then changed the amendment into the following proviso, to be inserted at the end of the resolution: "Provided the states who are in possession of these indents shall be credited for the same in the settlement of the account between the said state and the United States." This was disagreed to on the same day. (NYDG, Mar. 1)

[6] On February 22, Lee moved to add "that appropriations of the lands in the Western Territory be assigned for the purpose of discharging the interest due on the debt of the United States" to the resolution. This was not seconded. (NYDG, Feb. 23; CR, Feb. 22)

[7] On Feb. 24, Madison moved to add the following at this point:

> And that effectual provision be at the same time made for liquidating and crediting, to the States, the whole of their respective expenditures during the war, as the same have been or may be stated for the purpose; and that in such liquidation the best evidence shall be received that the nature of the case will permit. (NYDA, Feb. 25)

On February 25, White proposed to add the following proviso to Madison's motion:

> such assumption shall not exceed the sum that any state may have advanced above its just proportion of the public debt, and which shall appear on a liquidation of the accounts. (NYDA, Feb. 27)

This was disagreed to on February 26. Also on February 26, Madison proposed adding the following to his amendment:

[5] Resolved, that it is adviseable to endeavour to effect a new modification of the domestic debt, including that of the particular States, with the voluntary consent of the creditors, by a loan, upon terms mutually beneficial to them and to the United States.

[6] Resolved, that for the purpose expressed in the last preceding resolution, subscriptions towards a loan ought to be opened, to the amount of the said domestic debt; including that of the respective States, upon the terms following, to wit:

That for every hundred dollars subscribed, payable in the said debt (as well interest as principal) the subscriber be entitled, at his option, either

To have two thirds funded at an annuity, or yearly interest of six per cent. redeemable at the pleasure of the government, by payment of the principal; and to receive the other third in lands in the Western Territory, at the rate of twenty cents per acre.[8] Or,

To have the whole sum funded at an annuity or yearly interest of four per cent. irredeemable by any payment exceeding five dollars per annum on account both of principal and interest; and to receive, as a compensation for the reduction of interest, fifteen dollars and eighty cents, payable in lands, as in the preceding case.[9] Or

To have sixty-six dollars and two-thirds of a dollar funded immediately, at an annuity, or yearly interest of six per cent. irredeemable by any payment

---

Provided, that in case a final liquidation and adjustment of the whole of such expenditures, and provision for the payment of the balances due from Debtor States to Creditor States, shall not be made before the   day of   the debts assumed shall be liquidated and adjusted, among the States, according to the ratio of representation, and effectual provision be henceforth made for paying the ballances to the Creditor States, at the expence of the Debtor States. (*GUS,* Feb. 27)
This was withdrawn on March 1 and Madison's original amendment of February 24 was agreed to. (*NYDA,* Mar. 2, 3) Madison then proposed the following substitute resolution:
Resolved, That the amount of the debts actually paid by any state to its creditors, since the   day of   shall be credited and paid to such state, on the same terms as shall be provided in the case of individuals. (*CR,* Mar. 1)
On March 2, Smith (S.C.) moved to insert "as well principal as interest" after "actually paid" in Madison's resolution of March 1. Smith's amendment was agreed to, but Madison's proposal was defeated. (*NYDA,* Mar. 3)
8 On March 9 Boudinot, seconded by Hartley, moved to strike out "and to receive" through "per acre" and to replace it with "that 4 per cent. be funded, and the remaining 2 per cent. be paid by a certificate, payable in 10 years, and bearing an interest of six per cent." Tucker then moved to add the words "that such certificates be received as specie in all payments of western lands" to the Boudinot substitute. This was agreed to. On March 10 the amended substitute was disagreed to. (*NYDG,* Mar. 11)
9 On March 11 the COWH struck out this alternative by a vote of 32–33 or 24. (*NYDG,* Mar. 12)

exceeding four dollars and two-thirds[10] of a dollar per annum, on account both of principal and interest; and to have, at the end of ten years, twenty-six dollars and eighty eight cents,[11] funded at the like interest and rate of redemption.[12] Or,

To have an annuity for the remainder of life, upon the contingency of living to a given age, not less distant than ten years, computing interest at four per cent.[13]

Or, To have an annuity for the remainder of life, upon the contingency of the survivorship of the youngest of two persons, computing interest, in this case also, at four per cent.[14]

[7] Resolved, that immediate provision ought to be made for the present debt of the United States; and that the faith of government ought to be pledged to make provision, at the next session, for so much of the debts of the respective States, as shall have been subscribed upon any of the terms expressed in the last resolution.

[8] Resolved, that the funds which shall be appropriated according to the second of the foregoing resolutions, be applied, in the first place, to the payment of interest on the sums subscribed towards the proposed loan; and that if any part of the said domestic debt shall remain unsubscribed, the surplus of the said funds be applied, by a temporary appropriation, to the payment of interest on the unsubscribed part, so as not to exceed, for the present, four per cent. per annum; but this limitation shall not be understood to impair the right of the non-subscribing creditors to the residue of the interest on their respective debts: And in case the aforesaid surplus should prove insufficient to pay the non-subscribing creditors, at the aforesaid rate of

---

10 On March 11 Jackson moved to strike out "irredeemable by any payment exceeding four dollars and two-thirds." This was disagreed to on March 12 by a vote of 29–22. On the same day the COWH agreed to a motion by Fitzsimons to strike "four dollars and two thirds of a dollar" and to leave a blank to be filled. (NYDG, Mar. 13)

11 On March 12 the COWH agreed to a motion to strike out "ten" and "twenty-six dollars and eighty-eight cents" and to leave blanks to be filled. (NYDA, Mar. 13)

12 On March 12 a motion by Lee to strike out this alternative was disagreed to. (NYDG, Mar. 13)

13 On March 12 a motion by Stone to strike out this alternative was agreed to by a vote of 23–21. (NYDG, Mar. 13)

14 On March 12 this alternative was struck out by a vote of 26–21. (NYDG, Mar. 13) On March 13 Gerry moved to add the following alternative but then withdrew the motion:

> Or to have sixty-six dollars and two-thirds of a dollar funded immediately, at a yearly interest of 6 per cent.; and thirty-three dollars and one-third of a dollar in an unfunded certificate, bearing an annual interest of 6 per cent. payable at the option of the holder, annually, in a funded certificate at a yearly interest of 6 per cent. or, as soon as funds can be provided, in specie; and that the faith of Congress be pledged to fund, as soon as possible, the unfunded certificates. (NYDG, Mar. 15)

four per cent. that the faith of government to be pledged to make good such deficiency.

NYDA, Feb. 9.

Resolution of Congress, May 16, 1783
February 10, 1790

Resolved That the commutation in leiu of half pay ~~shall be calculated by what they are entitled~~ as well to chaplains as to the Officers of the hospital department and medical staff shall be calculated by what they are respectively entitled to agreeably to the resolutions of the 17 Jany. & 8 May 1781.

Journals of Congress, PCC, DNA.

Resolution of Congress, April 22, 1784
February 10, 1790

Resolved That the paymaster general be and he hereby is directed to govern himself in settling the accounts of the army since the year 1779 by the payments made by the respective States to their lines so that when the pay has been secured by any state the same shall not be again secured by the United States.

Journals of Congress, PCC, DNA.

Resolution of Congress, June 1, 1784
February 10, 1790

Resolved That the several States shall be credited in their accounts with the United States for the specie value of all sums by them paid to their Officers & soldiers in the continental army due from the United States, provided such payment shall have been notified to the paymaster general & by him charged to such officers and soldiers in settling their accounts with the United States And said States shall be allowed interest on the sums so paid from the time of payment.

   That the superintendant of finance be directed to render to Congress, a particular Statement of the Articles comprized under the head of Contingencies in his Accounts already rendered: and that when the said Statement, and also his Accounts showing the expenditure of 2,486,511.71, of the 8 millions of dollars, required by a resolve of the 30th of October 1781, shall be rendered, the Committee of the States shall transmit a Copy of the said Statement, and also of such expenditures, specifying Contingencies, to any State whose Delegates may require the same.

That 190,000 Dollars, and 687,828 Dollars, contained in the estimate of the 18th of April 1783, being comprized in the requisition of the present year, under the Article of Interest of the domestic debt to the 31st of December 1782, are when paid agreeably to the said requisition, to be deducted from the estimate first mentioned.

Journals of Congress, PCC, DNA.

Address and Recommendations to the States
from Congress, April 26, 1783
February 17, 1790

First: The present creditors, or rather the domestic part of them, having either made their loans for a period which has expired, or having become creditors in the first instance involuntarily, are entitled, on the clear principles of justice and good faith, to demand the principal of their credits, instead of accepting the annual interest. It is necessary, therefore, as the principal cannot be paid to them on demand, that the interest should be so effectually and satisfactorily secured, as to enable them if they incline, to transfer their stock at its full value. Secondly: if the funds be so firmly constituted as to inspire a thorough and universal confidence, may it not be hoped, that the capital of the domestic debt, which bears the high interest of six per cent. may be cancelled by other loans obtained at a more moderate interest? The saving by such an operation, would be a clear one, and might be a considerable one. As a proof of the necessity of substantial funds for a support of our credit abroad, we refer to paper No. 4.

Thus much for the interest of the national debt: for the discharge of the principal, within the term limited, we rely on the natural encrease of the revenue from commerce, on requisitions to be made from time to time for that purpose, as circumstances may dictate, and on the prospect of vacant territory. If these resources should prove inadequate, it will be necessary, at the expiration of twenty-five years, to continue the funds now recommended, or to establish such others as may then be found more convenient.

With a view to the resource last mentioned, as well as to obviate disagreeable controversies and confusions, Congress have included in their present recommendations, a renewal of those of the 6th day of September, and of the 10th day of October, 1780. In both those respects, a liberal and final accommodation of all interfering claims of vacant territory, is an object which cannot be pressed with too much solicitude.

The last object recommended is a constitutional change of the rule, by which a partition of the common burdens is to be made. The expediency and even necessity of such a change has been sufficiently inforced by the local injustice and discontents which have proceeded from valuations of the soil in every state where the experiment has been made. But how infinitely must these evils be increased, on a comparison of such valuations among the states themselves! On whatever side indeed this rule be surveyed, the execution of it must be attended with the most serious difficulties. If the valuations be referred to the authorities of the several states, a general satisfaction is not to be hoped for: If they be executed by officers of the United States traversing the country for that purpose, besides the inequalities against which this mode would be no security, the expence would be both enormous and obnoxious: If the mode taken in the act of the 17th day of February last, which was deemed on the whole least objectionable, be adhered to, still the insufficiency of the data to the purpose to which they are to be applied, must greatly impair, if not utterly destroy all confidence in the accuracy of the result; not to mention that as far as the result can be at all a just one, it will be indebted for the advantage to the principle on which the rule proposed to be substituted is founded. This rule, altho' not free from objections, is liable to fewer than any other that could be devised. The only material difficulty which attended it in the deliberations of Congress was, to fix the proper difference between the labour and industry of free inhabitants, and of all other inhabitants. The ratio ultimately agreed on was the effect of mutual concessions; and if it should be supposed not to correspond precisely with the fact, no doubt ought to be entertained that an equal spirit of accommodation among the several legislatures, will prevail against little inequalities which may be calculated on one side or on the other. But notwithstanding the confidence of Congress, as to the success of this proposition, it is their duty to recollect that the event may possibly disappoint them, and to request that measures may still be pursued for obtaining and transmitting the information called for in the act of the 17th of February last, which in such event will be essential.

The plan, thus communicated and explained by Congress, must now receive its fate from their constituents. All the objects comprised in it are conceived to be of great importance to the happiness of this confederated republic; are necessary to render the fruits of the revolution, a full reward for the blood, the toils, the cares and the calamities which have purchased it. But the object, of which the necessity will be peculiarly felt, and which it is peculiarly the duty of Congress to inculcate, is the provision recommended for the national debt. Although this debt is greater than could have been wished, it is still less on the whole than could have been expected; and when referred to the cause in which it has been incurred, and compared with the burdens which wars of ambition and of vain glory have entailed on other nations, ought to be borne not only with cheerfulness but with pride. But the magnitude of the debt makes no part of the question. It is sufficient that the debt has been fairly contracted, and that justice and good faith demand that it should be fully discharged. Congress had no option but between different modes of discharging it. The same option is the only one that can exist with the states. The mode which has, after long and elaborate discussion, been preferred, is, we are persuaded, the least objectionable of any that would have been equal to the purpose. Under this persuasion, we call upon the justice and plighted faith of the several states to give it its proper effect, to reflect on the consequences of rejecting it, and to remember that Congress will not be answerable for them.

If other motives than that of justice could be requisite on this occasion, no nation could ever feel stronger; for to whom are the debts to be paid?

To AN ALLY, in the first place, who to the exertion of his arms in support of our cause, has added the succours of his treasure; who, to his important loans, had added liberal donations; and whose loans themselves carry the impression of his magnanimity and friendship. For more exact information on this point we refer to paper No. 5.

To *individuals in a foreign country,* in the next place, who were the first to give so precious a token of their confidence in our justice, and of their friendship for our cause, and who are members of a republic which was second in espousing our rank among nations. For the claims and expectations of this class of creditors, we refer to paper No. 6.

Another class of creditors is, *that illustrious and patriotic band of fellow citizens,* whose blood and whose bravery have defended the liberties of their country, who have patiently borne, among other distresses, the privation of their stipends, whilst the distresses of their country disabled it from bestowing them; and who, even now, ask for no more than such a portion of their dues as will enable them to retire from the field of victory and glory into the bosom of peace and private citizenship, and for such effectual security for the residue of their claims, as their country is now unquestionably able to provide. For a full view of their sentiments and wishes on this subject, we transmit the paper No. 7: and as a fresh and lively instance of their superiority to every species of seduction from the paths of virtue and of honour, we add the paper No. 8.

The remaining class of creditors is composed partly of such of our fellow citizens as originally lent to the public the use of their funds, or have since manifested most confidence in their country, by receiving transfers from the lenders, and partly of those whose property has been either advanced or assumed for the public service. To discriminate the merits of these several descriptions of creditors, would be a task equally unnecessary and invidious.

If the voice of humanity plead more loudly in favour of some than of others, the voice of policy, no less than of justice, pleads in favour of all. A wise nation will never permit those who relieve the wants of their country, or who rely most on its faith, its firmness and its resources, when either of them is distrusted, to suffer by the event.

Let it be remembered finally, that it has ever been the pride and boast of America, that the rights for which she contended, were the rights of human nature. By the blessing of the author of these rights, on the means exerted for their defence, they have prevailed against all opposition and form the basis of thirteen independent states. No instance has heretofore occurred, nor can any instance be expected hereafter to occur, in which the unadulterated forms of republican government can pretend to so fair an opportunity of justifying themselves by their fruits. In this view the citizens of the United States are responsible for the greatest trust ever confided to a political society. If justice, good faith, honour, gratitude and all the other qualities which enoble the character of a nation, and fulfil the ends of government, be the fruits of our establishments, the cause of liberty will acquire a dignity and lustre which it has never yet e[njoyed]; and an example will be set which cannot but have [the m]ost favourable influence on the rights of mankind. If on the other side, our governments should be unfortunately blotted with the reverse of these cardinal and essential virtues, the great cause which we have engaged to vindicate, will be dishonoured and betrayed; the last and fairest experiment in favour of the rights of human nature will be turned against them, and their patrons and friends exposed to be insulted and silenced by the votaries of tyranny and usurpation.

RBkRm, DLC. E–18224. The first half of the Address was not read and so is not printed here. Madison was the author of the address, and an annotated text appears in Robert Rutland, ed., *The Papers of James Madison,* 6: 487–98.

Petition of Richard Wells and Josiah Hart
March 1, 1790

To the House of Representatives of the United States of America,
The petition of the Subscribers, inhabitants of the State of Pennsylvania. *Respectfully sheweth,*
THAT by virtue of divers acts of the assembly of Pennsylvania for giving currency to continental bills emitted by congress, your petitioners became possessed of sundry sums of the said continental money: That the faith and honor of the United States stand pledged to them on the face of the said bills, ensuring full and unequivocal payment, in Spanish milled dollars, or the value thereof in gold and silver; which bills your petitioners received under the sanction and operation of positive laws, and which they conceive ought to

be faithfully discharged, agreeably to the express tenor thereof. In support of this their claim, your petitioners beg leave to quote some passages from the solemn declaration, or circular letter of congress, dated in September, 1779; wherein, after reciting the situation of America, and the causes of the war, they say,

"So circumstanced, you had no other resource but the natural value and wealth of your fertile country: Bills were issued on the credit of this bank, and your faith was pledged for their redemption; after a considerable number of these had circulated, loans were solicited, and offices for the purpose was established.

Thus a *national debt* was unavoidably created, and *the amount of it is as follows:*

	Dollars.
Bills emitted and circulating	159,948,880
Monies borrowed before the 1st of March, 1778, the interest of which is payable in France,	7,545,196 67/90
Monies borrowed since the 1st of March, 1778, the interest of which is payable here,	26,188,909
Money due abroad, not exactly known, the balances not having been transmitted, supposed to be about	4,000,000."

Here your petitioners observe, that the continental bills rank as part of the debt of the United States, and are united with the domestic and foreign loans, *as of equal validity.*

The congress then proceed to consider the state of their continental money in three points of view:

1st. Whether, and in what manner, the faith of the United States has been pledged for the redemption of their bills.

2d. Whether they have put themselves in a political capacity to redeem them: And,

3d. Whether, admitting the two former propositions, there is reason to apprehend a wanton violation of the public faith.

On the first head, they say, "It must be evident to every man who reads the journals of congress, or *looks at the face of one of their bills,* that congress have pledged the faith of their constituents *for the redemption of them.* And it must be equally evident, not only that they have authority to do so, but that their constituents have *actually ratified their acts,* by receiving their bills, *passing laws establishing their currency,* and punishing those who counterfeited them."

After shewing the indissolubleness of the confederacy, they say, "The *redemption, therefore, of these bills,* the payment of these debts, and the settlement of the accounts of the several states, for expenditures, or services for the common benefit, and in the common cause, are among the objects of *this confederation;* and consequently, while all, *or any* of its objects remain unattained, it cannot, so far as it may respect such objects, be dissolved consistently with the *laws of God or man.*"

Speaking on the third proposition, after shewing the fallacy of those rumors which supposed that, "as the congress made the money, they also can destroy it;" they add, "It is not surprising, that in a free country, where the tongues and pens of such people are, and must be licensed, such *political heresies* should be inculcated and diffused; but it is really astonishing that the mind of a single virtuous citizen should be influenced by them!"

Then adverting to their own representative situation, they proceed, "You surely are convinced that it is *no more in their power to annihilate your paper money than your independence;* and that any act of theirs, for either of these purposes, *would be null and void.* We should pay an ill compliment to the understanding and honor of every true American, were we to adduce many arguments to shew the baseness or bad policy of violating our national faith, or omitting to pursue the measures necessary to preserve it.

A bankrupt, faithless republic, would be a novelty in the political world, and appear among reputable nations like a common prostitute among chaste and respectable matrons. The pride of America revolts from the idea; her citizens know for what purposes these emissions were made, and *have repeatedly plighted their faith* for the redemption of them, &c.

We are convinced that the efforts and arts of our enemies will not be wanting to draw us into this humiliating and contemptible situation. Impelled by malice, and the suggestions of chagrin and disappointment, at not being able to bend our necks to their yoke, they will endeavor to force or seduce us to commit this *unpardonable sin,* in order to subject us to the punishment due to it, and that we may be thenceforth a reproach and a bye-word among the nations. Apprised of these consequences, knowing the value of national character, and impressed with a due sense of the *immutable laws of justice and honor,* it is impossible that America should think, without horror, of the execrable deed."

In the conclusion of this *faith-plighting letter,* they add—

"Let it never be said that America had no sooner become independent than she became insolvent; or that her infant glories and growing fame were obscured and tarnished by broken contracts and violated faith, in the very hour when all the nations of the earth were admiring and almost adoring the splendor of her rising."

Your petitioners view this declaration of congress as amounting to the most solemn contract that a nation could enter into; and they conceive that their claims stand upon equal ground with the other creditors of the United States. They received the money they now hold, under the early sanction of congress, which, on the first emission, resolved as follows: "That the twelve confederated colonies be pledged for the redemption of the bills of credit now directed to be emitted;" and the same pledge is implied in every subsequent emission.

Your petitioners fully subscribe to the principles laid down in the *Secretary's Report,* viz. "While the observance of that good faith, which is the basis of public credit, is recommended by the strongest inducements of political expediency, it is enforced by considerations of still greater authority. There are arguments for it which rest on the immutable principles of moral obligation; and in proportion as the mind is disposed to contemplate in the order of Providence, an intimate connection between public virtue and public happiness, will be its repugnancy to a violation of those principles."

But these immutable principles of moral obligation, your petitioners apprehend, can never be monopolized by one set of creditors, whilst another set, equally relying on the great order of Providence, which connects public happiness with public virtue, present their honest claims to the congress of the United States of America.

Your petitioners cannot be induced to believe that *the evidences* of their debts are of less validity for having originated under the former congress; because the constitution provides, "that all debts contracted, and engagements entered into before the adoption of that constitution, shall be as valid against the United States under it, as under the confederation."

Your petitioners are convinced, that not a single argument can be advanced in favor of the holders of public securities, which will not apply with equal force in favor of the holders of continental bills, who have one solemn assurance after another, and one law after another, to hold up as their guarantees: They have the plighted faith of America, couched in the strongest language which the pen of man could convey; and depending on that plighted faith, they beg leave to present a copy of one of the evidences of their claims, viz. a thirty dollar bill, emitted, prior to the circular letter just quoted:
"THIRTY DOLLARS.

This bill entitles the bearer to receive thirty Spanish milled dollars, or the value thereof in gold and silver, according to a resolution of congress, passed at Philadelphia July 22d, 1776."

This is expressed in the most plain and unequivocal language, and connecting itself with the deliberate protestations made in the circular letter, becomes an undeniably sure pledge of payment from the United States. No sophistry can explain it away, or draw a line of distinction between the fair holder of this bill, and the holder of an alienated certificate; no veil can cover, no art can dissipate the deeply imprinted words of national faith, given forth by congress; nor can the magnitude of the sum which may come forward under similar claims with your petitioners, lessen the public obligation.

Before you, as the representatives of that public, as guardians of their honor and plighted faith, we now lay our claim, and pray that in considering the ways and means to discharge the debts of the United States, and to ascertain the demands of individuals, you will be pleased to make equal and just provision for satisfying those early and just creditors, *the holders of continental bills*, received by them as *bona fide equivalents* for gold and silver to them justly due, and by them still retained as evidences of their just demands against the United States of America.

(Signed)

RICHARD WELLS
J. HART

Philadelphia, February 23, 1790

CR, Mar. 1.

Ames Resolutions
March 1, 1790

Resolved, That effectual provision be made for the settlement of accounts between the United States and the individual states.

Resolved, That in the said settlement, the states respectively be charged with the advances to them severally made by the United States, liquidated to specie value, with interest thereon at the rate of six per cent. per annum, and that they be also charged with the amount of their respective debts (which with the consent of the creditors shall have been assumed by the United States) with the interest thereon to the time from which interest shall be payable by the United States.

Resolved, That in the said settlement the said states respectively be credited with all monies paid and supplies furnished to or for, and debts incurred on account of the United States, and in general with all expenditures whatsoever towards general or particular defence during the late war between the United States and Great Britain, with interest thereon at the rate of six per cent. per annum.

Resolved, That the said settlement be made under the direction of commissioners whose authority shall continue until the said settlement shall be effected, and whose decisions shall be final and conclusive upon the United States, and upon the several states.

Resolved, That in case a ratio for adjusting the contributions of the respective states shall not be prescribed by Congress during the present session the said commissioners shall have full power to settle such ratio, and shall also have power to determine in all other respects the principles of the said settlement in conformity to these resolutions.

Resolved, That the several states may exhibit their claims against the United States until the   day of   next, but not afterwards; and that the said commissioners shall, as soon as may be after the said day, proceed to a final adjustment of the said accounts, whether the whole of the claims of the respective states shall have been then exhibited or not.

NYDA, Mar. 2.

House Resolution
March 2, 1790

RESOLVED, That the Secretary of the Treasury be instructed to report to this House, such funds as in his opinion may be raised and applied towards the payment of the interest of the debts of individual States, should they be assumed by Congress.

HJ, p. 312.

House Order
March 2, 1790

ORDERED, That the Secretary of the Treasury lay before this House the amount of the duties on goods, wares and merchandize, and on tonnage, in the several States, from the time that the collection of those revenues commenced to the thirty-first of December last.

HJ, p. 312.

Report of the Secretary of the Treasury
March 4, 1790

Treasury Department, March 4th. 1790
In obedience to the Order of the House of
Representatives, of the second Instant,
The Secretary of the Treasury

Respectfully Reports,

THAT in his opinion, the funds, in the first instance requisite towards the payment of interest on the debts of the individual States, according to the modifications proposed by him in his report of the ninth of January past, may be obtained from the following objects:

An increase of the general product of the duties on goods imported, by abolishing the discount of ten per Cent allowed by the fifth Section of the Act for laying a duty on goods, wares and merchandizes imported into the United States, in respect to goods imported in American bottoms, and adding ten per Cent to the rates specified, in respect to goods imported in foreign bottoms, with certain exceptions and qualifications: This change, without impairing the commercial policy of the regulation, or making an inconvenient addition to the general rates of the duties, will occasion an augmentation of the revenue little short of two hundred thousand dollars.

An additional duty on imported Sugars. Sugars are an object of general consumption, and yet constitute a small proportion of the expense of families. A moderate addition to the present rates would not be felt. From the bulkiness of the article, such an addition may be made with due regard to the safety of Collection. The quantity of brown and other inferior kinds of Sugar imported, appears to exceed twenty two millions of pounds, which, at a half cent per pound, would produce one hundred and ten thousand dollars. Proportional impositions on foreign refined sugar, and proper drawbacks on exportation, ought of course to indemnify the manufacturers of this article among ourselves.

MOLASSES, being in some of the States a substitute for Sugar, a small addition to the duty on that article ought to accompany an increase of the duty on Sugar. This, however, ought to be regulated with proper attention to the circumstance, that the same article will contribute largely in the shape of distilled spirits. Half a Cent per Gallon on Molasses would yield an annual sum of thirty thousand dollars. Our distillers of Spirits, from this material, may be compensated by a proportional extension of the duty on imported spirits.

SNUFF, and other manufactured tobacco, made within the United States: Ten Cents per pound on the Snuff, and six Cents on other kinds of manufactured tobacco, would be likely to produce annually, from ninety to one hundred thousand dollars. From as good evidence as the nature of the case will admit, the quantity of these articles, manufactured in the United States, may be computed to exceed a million and a half of pounds. The imposition of this duty would require an increase of the duty on importation, and a drawback on exportation, in favor of the manufacture. This, being an absolute superfluity, is the fairest object of revenue that can be imagined, and may be so regulated, as, in no degree, to injure either the growth or manufacture of the Commodity.

PEPPER, Pimento, Spices in general, and various other kinds of groceries. These articles will bear such additional rates, as may be estimated to yield a sum of not less than thirty thousand dollars. Computing, according to the entries in the State of New York, in 1788, the yearly quantity of pepper, and pimento brought into the United States, is not less than eight hundred thousand pounds, of which about a third is pepper. Six Cents on pepper, and four cents on pimento (with drawbacks on exportation) may, without inconvenience be laid.

SALT. An additional duty of six cents per bushel, may, in the judgment of the Secretary, with propriety be laid on this Article. It is one of those objects, which, being consumed by all, will be most productive, and yet, from the smallness of the quantity in which it is consumed by any, and of the price, will be least burthensome, if confined within reasonable limits. If a government does not avail itself, to a proper extent, of resources like these, it must of necessity overcharge others, and particularly, give greater scope to direct taxation. The quantity of this article annually imported, being at least, a million and a half of bushels, the annual product of an additional duty of six Cents may be computed at ninety thousand dollars.

CARRIAGES, such as Coaches, Chariots &c. These articles may certainly be the subject of a considerable duty. How productive it would be, is not easy to be estimated. But it is imagined, that it would yield not less than fifty thousand dollars per annum.

Licences to practisers of the law. Certain law-writings, and various kinds of writings. The extent of this resource can only be determined upon trial; but the Secretary feels a strong assurance, that there may be drawn from it, yearly, not less than two hundred thousand dollars. The system for collecting a duty of this kind, would embrace playing-cards, and some other objects of luxury, which do not fall under the above descriptions, but which are estimated in the supposed product.

Sales at Auction (exclusive of houses or lands, or of those made in consequence of legal process, or of acknowledged insolvency). One per Cent on such Sales would, probably, produce a yearly sum of forty or fifty thousand dollars.

Wines and Spirits sold at retail. These articles are, in the opinion of the Secretary, capable of being rendered far more productive, than has been generally contemplated; and they are certainly, among the most unexceptionable objects of Revenue. It is presumed, that two hundred thousand dollars per annum may, with facility, be collected from the Retail vent of these Articles.

The foregoing objects are those, which appear to the Secretary, preferable towards a provision for the debts of the individual States. There are others, which have occurred to him as supplementary, in case the experiment should discover a deficiency in the expected product; but which, he conceives it unnecessary now to detail. He will only add, that he entertains no doubt of it's being practicable to accomplish the end, on the principles of his former report, without the necessity of taxing, either houses or lands, or the stock or the produce of farms.

The Secretary, conceiving the design of the House to have been to obtain from him a general delineation only of the funds, competent in his judgment to the provision in question, has refrained from those details, which would be indispensible, if that provision were immediately to be made; and to have furnished which, would have occasioned greater delay, than would, probably, have suited with the present state of the business, or the Convenience of the

House. He, with great deference, trusts, that what is now offered will be deemed a satisfactory compliance with their Order.

The Statement required respecting the product of the duties on imports and tonnage to the last of December, as far as returns have come to hand, is contained in the Schedule herewith.

All which is humbly submitted
ALEXANDER HAMILTON
Secretary of The Treasury

ABSTRACT of the nett PROCEEDS of the DUTIES on IMPORTS and TONNAGE

STATES	From what period 1789	Nett Product of the Duties Dollars. Cents	Remarks
New-Hampshire	11th. Aug. to 31st Dec.	7,789.21 $^1/_2$	The
Massachusetts	10th ditto, to 31st. ditto	113,439.54 $^1/_2$	Product
Connecticut	11th. ditto, to 31st. ditto	20,352.87 $^1/_2$	of the
New-York	5th. ditto, to 31st. ditto	152,198.97	Duties of
New-Jersey	1st. ditto, to 31st. ditto	1,971.51	Boston
Pennsylvania	10th. ditto, to 31st. ditto	188,497.94	are only
Delaware	1st. ditto, to 31st. ditto	6,573.98 $^1/_2$	ascer-
Maryland	10th. ditto, to 31st. ditto	87,751.06 $^1/_2$	tained,
Virginia	17th. ditto, to 31st. ditto	142,028.62	up to
South Carolina	31st. ditto, to 1st. ditto	55,032.61 $^1/_2$	the
Georgia	22d. ditto, to 1st. ditto	8,850.80 $^3/_4$	19th. of
	Dollars,	748.487.14 $^3/_4$	Decem-
Deduct for Drawbacks 2 per Cent		15,689.74	ber.
	Dollars,	768,797.40 $^3/_4$	

Treasury Department, March 4th. 1790

ALEXANDER HAMILTON
Secretary of the Treasury

A Record of the Reports of the Secretary of the Treasury, Vol. I, HR, DNA.

House Committee Report on the Petition of Richard Wells and Josiah Hart
March 23, 1790

That the possessors of the Continental bills of credit emitted by the authority of Congress before the 18th. day of March, 1780, on bringing the same into the Treasury of the United States, shall receive certificates for the same, at the rate of one dollar specie value for one hundred dollars of the said bills.

And the same shall be funded on interest in the same manner as the other debts of the United States. The interest to commence on the day the said bills shall be lodged in the said Treasury. And all such bills in the Treasury of any State, exceeding its' quota required by the acts of Congress of the seventh of October, 1779, and the eighteenth day of March 1780, on being brought into the Treasury of the United States, shall be credited to the account of such State, at the rate aforesaid, on interest of six per cent, per annum, from the time it was received into the Treasury of the respective States.

A Record of the Reports of Select Committees, HR, DNA.

COWH Resolutions
March 29, 1790

1. RESOLVED, That adequate provision ought to be made for fulfilling the engagements of the United States, in respect to their foreign debt.

2. RESOLVED, That permanent funds ought to be appropriated for the payment of interest on, and the gradual discharge of the domestic debt of the United States.

3. RESOLVED, That the arrears of interest, including indents issued in payment thereof, ought to be provided for on the same terms with the principal of the said debt.

4. RESOLVED, That the debts of the respective States, ought, with the consent of the creditors, to be assumed and provided for by the United States. And that effectual provision be at the same time made for liquidating and crediting to the States, the whole of their respective expenditures during the war, as the same have been or may be stated for the purpose; and that in such liquidation the best evidence shall be received that the nature of the case will permit. [1]

5. RESOLVED, That it is adviseable to endeavour to effect a new modifica-

---

[1] On April 12 Sherman moved to strike out "And that effectual" through "case will permit," and insert "and that any further provision that may be necessary for the speedy, just, and final settlement of the accounts with the several states and the United States ought at the same time to be made." A motion by Bland to insert "and that effectual provision be made &c." in Sherman's motion was probably meant as a substitute for "and that any" through "be necessary." Sherman then withdrew his motion in favor of one by Gerry to strike out "during the war as the same have been or may be stated for the purpose" and insert "for the common defence and general welfare of the United States." After Gerry's motion failed by a vote of 31–29, Benson moved to strike out from "And that effectual" through "case will permit" and insert the following:
> that the President of the United States by and with the advice and consent of the Senate, appoint five commissioners with plenary powers for apportioning among the several states the whole expenses of the war.

This motion was seconded by Ames but then withdrawn. (Lloyd, Apr. 12; *NYDA, NYDG,* Apr. 13)

tion of the domestic debt, including that of the particular States,[2] with the voluntary consent of the creditors, by a loan, upon terms mutually beneficial to them and to the United States.

6. RESOLVED, That for the purpose expressed in the last preceding resolution, subscriptions towards a loan ought to be opened, to the amount of the said domestic debt, including that of the respective States,[3] upon the terms following, to wit:

That for every hundred dollars subscribed, payable in the said debt (as well interest as principal) the subscriber be entitled, at his option, either

To have two-thirds funded at an annuity, or yearly interest of six[4] per cent. redeemable at the pleasure of the government, by payment of the principal; and to receive the other third in lands in the Western Territory, at the rate of twenty cents per acre.[5] Or,[6]

To have sixty-six dollars and two-thirds of a dollar funded immediately, at an annuity, or yearly interest of six per cent. irredeemable by any payment exceeding   [7] per annum, on account both of principal and interest; and to have, at the end of   years,   ,[8] funded at the like interest and rate of redemption.

---

[2] On April 15, Seney, seconded by Parker, moved to strike out "including that of the particular States." This was agreed to on April 16. (*GUS*, Apr. 17)

[3] On April 20, the COWH adopted the sixth resolution, with the exception of the words "including that of the respective States." (*NYDG*, Apr. 21)

[4] On April 20, the COWH disagreed to a motion by Gerry to strike out "six" and leave a blank. (*NYDG*, Apr. 21)

[5] On April 16, Boudinot, seconded by Williamson, moved to strike out "to receive" through "per acre" and substitute the following:
that the third to be paid in a certificate, payable with interest in ten years, which shall be taken at all times as specie for lands in the Western Territory, and those lands shall be pledged for the payment of the said certificate.
Boudinot accepted an amendment from Tucker to add, "that the said certificate, with the interest which may have accrued thereon, shall be taken in payment of lands." Boudinot's motion was divided and the motion to strike was disagreed to, 32–23. (*NYDG*, Apr. 19)

[6] On April 21, Laurance moved to insert at this point the second alternative, which had been disagreed to by the COWH on March 11, as follows:
To have the whole sum funded at an annuity or yearly interest of four per cent. irredeemable by any payment exceeding five dollars per annum, on account both of principal and interest; and to receive, as a compensation for the reduction of interest, fifteen dollars and eighty cents, payable in lands, as in the preceding case.
After a motion by Fitzsimons (*NYDG*) or Sherman (*NYDA*) to strike "five" and insert "six" dollars in the alternative was agreed to, the COWH adopted Laurance's motion by a vote of 26–21. (*NYDG*, Apr. 22, 26; *NYDA*, Apr. 23)

[7] On April 21, Fitzsimons moved to insert "six dollars" in place of "four and two-thirds of a dollar," indicating that the COWH was acting as if the blank were filled with the original wording of the February 8 resolutions, despite the action of March 12. Tucker, seconded by Page, moved to insert "eight dollars," but this was disagreed to. The Fitzsimons motion was adopted. (*NYDG*, Apr. 26)

[8] On April 21, Fitzsimons moved to fill these blanks with "seven" and "thirty-three dollars and one-third of a dollar." Both figures were agreed to, the first unanimously. (Lloyd, Apr. 21; *NYDG*, Apr. 26)

7. RESOLVED, That immediate provision ought to be made for the present debt of the United States; and that the faith of government ought to be pledged to make provision, at their next session, for so much of the debts of the respective States, as shall have been subscribed upon any of the terms expressed in the last resolution.[9]

8. RESOLVED, That the funds which shall be appropriated according to the second of the foregoing resolutions, be applied, in the first place, to the payment of interest on the sums subscribed towards the proposed loan; and that if any part of the said domestic debt shall remain unsubscribed, the

---

[9] On April 21, Sherman moved to transpose the words "immediate" and "present" and to substitute the following for the seventh resolution:

Resolved, That the debts contracted by the several states for the common defence and benefit of the union, ought to be considered as a part of the domestic debt of the United States: that present provision ought to be made for the immediate debt of the United States; and that the faith of government ought to be pledged to make provision, at the next session, for so much of the debts of the respective states as shall have been subscribed upon any of the terms expressed in the last resolution; provided that subscriptions shall not be received for a greater amount than the following sums viz.

[Here the names of the states are inserted, without any sums prefixed, as Mr. Sherman afterwards explained the proportion.]

That the remainder ought to be left to the respective states to provide for, until a final settlement of their accounts with the United States, for which settlement effectual provision ought now to be made.

Provided also, that no debts be assumed but such as have been liquidated in specie value, and evidenced by notes or certificates issued by authority of the respective states, before the   day of   , 1790.

And if the creditors of any state shall not subscribe to the amount of the debt of such state to be assumed as aforesaid, such state shall receive interest at the rate of four per cent. per annum, on the remainder of said sum, until a final settlement of its accounts with the United States, to be applied to the payment of interest to its non-subscribing creditors, for which, and for the sums that may be assumed, the respective states shall be accountable to the United States.

When called upon, Sherman gave the following to explain his motion:

Assumption of the States Debts, not exceeding the sums in the last column

	Due as per Sec'ry's Report	Sums to be assumed
		Dollars
New-Hampshire	300,000	300,000
Massachusetts	5,226,801	4,000,000
Connecticut	1,951,173	1,600,000
New-York	1,167,575	1,000,000
New-Jersey	788,680	750,000
Pennsylvania	2,200,000	2,000,000
Delaware		100,000
Maryland	600,000	750,000
Virginia	3,680,743	3,000,000
North-Carolina		1,600,000
South-Carolina	5,386,234	4,000,000
Georgia		200,000
		19,300,000

The remaining sums will be left for the states to provide for, until a final settlement of their accounts.

This motion was debated, but the COWH rose without taking action on it. (*NYDG*, Apr. 22)

surplus of the said funds be applied, by a temporary appropriation, to the payment of interest on the unsubscribed part, so as not to exceed, for the present, four per cent. per annum; but this limitation shall not be understood to impair the right of the non-subscribing creditors to the residue of the interest on their respective debts: And in case the aforesaid surplus should prove insufficient to pay the non-subscribing creditors, at the aforesaid rate of four per cent. that the faith of government be pledged to make good such deficiency.

HJ, pp. 347–48.

Resolution of Congress, November 22, 1777
April 12, 1790

That the sums so assessed and to be raised shall not be considered as the proportion of any state, but being paid into the treasury shall be placed to their respective credit bearing an interest of six per cent per annum from the time of payment, until the quotas shall be finally ascertained and adjusted by the Congress of the united States agreeable to the Confederation hereafter to be adopted and ratified by the several states. And if it shall then appear, that any state is assessed more than its just quota of the said tax, it shall continue to receive interest on the surplus, & if less it shall be charged with interest on the deficiency, until by a future tax such surplus or deficiency shall be properly adjusted.

Journals of Congress, PCC, DNA.

Resolution of Congress, June 3, 1784
April 12, 1790

RESOLVED That all monies or Articles supplied by the United States to any particular State, shall be charged to such State at their just value in specie, with an interest of six per cent per annum, from the date of such supplies until the final adjustment and payment of the Account; but the former requisitions of Congress for supplies from the States, not being considered as their real quotas of the common expence, are not to be charged.

Journals of Congress, PCC, DNA.

House Orders
April 23, 1790

ORDERED, That the Secretary of the department of War, be directed to lay before the House an account of the troops, (including the militia) and also of the ordnance stores furnished from time to time by the several States, towards the support of the late war:[1] And that the commissioners for settling the accounts of the United States with the respective States, be directed to lay before the House an abstract of the claims of the several States against the United States, specifying the principles on which the claims are founded.[2]

ORDERED, That the Secretary of the Treasury be directed to report the sums of money, including indents and paper money of every kind reduced to specie value, which have been received from or paid to the several States by Congress, from the commencement of the revolution to the present period.[3]

ORDERED, That the commissioners for settling accounts between the United States and individual States, report the amount of such claims of the States as have been offered to them since the time expired for receiving claims, specifying the principles on which the claims are founded, and distinguishing them from other claims.[4]

HJ, pp. 377–78. The movers of the orders are named in the GUS, Apr. 24.

[1] This clause of the order was moved by Ames.
[2] This clause of the order was moved by Bland as an amendment to the Ames motion.
[3] This order was moved by Gerry.
[4] This order was moved by Madison.

Fitzsimons Motion
April 26, 1790

That the committee of the whole House on the report of the Secretary of the Treasury, relative to a provision for the support of the public credit, be for the present discharged from proceeding on so much of the said report as relates to an assumption of the State debts.

HJ, p. 379.

COWH Resolutions
April 26, 1790

Resolved, That it is advisable to endeavor to effect a new modification of the domestic debt, with the voluntary consent of the creditors, by a loan, upon terms mutually beneficial to them and to the United States.

Resolved, That for the purpose expressed in the last preceding resolution, subscriptions towards a loan ought to be opened, to the amount of the said domestic debt, upon the terms following, to wit:

That for every hundred dollars subscribed, payable in the said debt (as well interest as principal) the subscriber be entitled at his option, either

To have two thirds funded at an annuity or yearly interest of six per cent. redeemable at the pleasure of the government, by payment of the principal, and to receive the other third in lands in the western territory, at the rate of twenty[1] cents per acre.[2] Or,

To have the whole sum funded at an annuity or yearly interest of four per cent. irredeemable by any payment exceeding six dollars per annum on account both of principal and interest, and to receive as a compensation for the reduction of interest, fifteen dollars and eighty cents payable in lands as in the preceding case: Or,

To have sixty-six dollars and two-thirds of a dollar funded immediately, at an annuity or yearly interest of six per cent. irredeemable by any payment exceeding six dollars per annum, on account both of principal and interest; and to have at the end of seven years, thirty-three dollars and one-third of a dollar, funded at the like interest and rate of redemption.

Resolved, That immediate provision ought to be made for the present debt of the United States.

Resolved, That the funds which shall be appropriated according to the second of the foregoing resolutions, be applied, in the first place, to the payment of interest on the sums subscribed towards the proposed loan; and that if any part of the said domestic debt shall remain unsubscribed, the surplus of the said funds be applied, by a temporary appropriation, to the payment of interest on the unsubscribed part, so as not to exceed, for the present, four per cent. per annum; but this limitation shall not be understood to impair the right of the non-subscribing creditors to the residue of the interest on their respective debts: And in case the aforesaid surplus should prove insufficient to pay the non-subscribing creditors, at the aforesaid rate of four per cent., that the faith of government be pledged to make good such deficiency.

HJ, p. 380–81. The motions to amend are from the *NYDG*, May 3.

---

[1] On April 26 the House disagreed to a motion by Williamson to strike out "twenty" and insert "thirty."

[2] On April 26, a motion by Smith (S.C.) to strike out this alternative was disagreed to.

	Specie Dollars	90ths	Old Emissions Dollars	90ths	Dollars	Lbs. Tobac[co] 90
Amount of Sums exhibited to John White district Commissioner by Schedule No. 18	66,878	74	4,139	71		
Amount of Sums exhibited to the Commissioner of Army Accounts by Schedule No. 19	131,787	32	128,540	09		
	198,666	16	132,679	80		
Amount of Sums liquidated and admitted to the credit of the State by John White district Commissioner by Schedule No. 20.	617,141	14	3,133,020	56		332,886
Amount of sums exhibited to said White District Commissioner for examination by Schedule No. 21	1,442,887	68	1,241,680	67		
Amount of sums exhibited to the Commissioner of Army Accounts by Schedule No. 22	314,704	02				
	2,374,732	84	4,374,701	33		332,886

THE CLAIMS OF DELAWARE

In this State the Scale of depreciation extends no farther than July 1780 & is then rated at 64 1/2 for 1.

THE CLAIMS OF MARYLAND.

THE CLAIMS OF VIRGINIA.

Many of the Claims of this State being made for specified Articles such as tobacco, Arms, military stores, clothing the army &c. without any fixed value, we cannot say what the amount of her claim really is—The paper marked M will shew their suppositious Claim which amounts to 4,000,000 Dollars Specie & 10,000,000 Dollars paper money.

The Scale of depreciation in this State is extended until May 1781, and is then rated at 280 Old Emission or 7 State Dollars for 1.

The House will please to observe that some of the claims of this State are said to be extracted from the Auditors Books—no other documents are produced in support of the charges but an account signed by the Auditor of State and said to be extracted.

On this head the Board feel themselves much at a loss to say any thing satisfactory, because they have not received from the district Commissioner any Abstract that will give a precise idea of what the state does claim, nor can they obtain from the Agents of the State of Virginia a specification of her claim in any other than general terms and those so couched as to conclude little or nothing, nor can the Commissioner of Army Accounts give any statement from the papers in his Office nor the Auditor from the papers in his Office relative to specific supplies. Thus situated the Board feel themselves compelled to go into a discussion highly disagreeable to them.

In some measure to comply with the order of the House it will be necessary to make a Statement of facts and a few observations which may enable the House to form some opinion of the Claims of this State.

It appears that numerous papers were exhibited to the district Commissioner by the Agents of Virginia, without being accompanied by any specification of their amount or purport or without being arranged or methodized as the ordinance of Congress contemplated—these the district Commissioner proceeded to arrange under a variety of heads in two folio Volumes now in this Office, in order as the Board conceive to have a more perfect idea of what the claims of the State ~~are~~ were. The time limited by the Act of Congress for receiving claims being nearly expired, a difference of opinion arose between the district Commissioner & the State Agents about the claims, the nature of which difference of opinion, as stated by the Agents of Virginia the house will see from the protest marked A which is all the evidence the board has upon the subject. The Agents then withdrew many Books & papers, & exhibited certain papers which they call the claim of the State, copies whereof accompany this report, marked B but which are stated so generally & appear to have been formed so much from conjecture, that the board cannot say what their amount is or in what kind of money they are made—The Agent of Virginia then came on to this place and on the 5th. day of May 1789 applied to the Board for their interposition so that the papers might be received, at the same time requesting that no precise time for the delivery of the papers might be fixed, or if a time was specified that it might be so long as to enable the State to send on the papers without inconvenience—thus the matter was until the month of November last, when it was represented by the Agent of Virginia, that no precise Statement of the claims of that State could be made, without having the unlimited use of the Books & papers which had been brought on by the district Commissioner—finally on a specification of certain books & papers by the agent of Virginia, it was agreed that he should have the books & papers he requested, but they together with all the books & papers which had been tendered in due time to the district Commissioner were to be returned (without the addition of any new Claim) on the 1st. of February last, & if possible with a precise statement of the claim of Virginia—when this time arrived further time was again, requested, but the board were of opinion that they were not authorized to grant the request, on which the Books & papers were delivered into this Office, but no further or other specification than those papers which have been before mentioned was made—it must also be observed that the Agent never availed himself of the books & papers which he had requested the use of, and which had been granted with a view of having an exact statement of the claim of the State exhibited.

(continued)

863

Specie Dollars	90ths.	Old Emissions Dollars	90ths.	Dollars	90

THE CLAIMS OF VIRGINIA (*continued*)

In the books mentioned before to have been opened by the district Commissioner for the arrangement of the Accounts of this State under the heads of specifics, Cavalry, State Cavalry, State Hospitals, provisions, cloathing, forage, & a great number of other heads, we find entered claims to the amount of 23,074,188 2/90 dollars in paper money & 537,435 25/90 dollars in specie; In several instances the district Commissioner has classed these claims under the heads of unsupported unascertained, irregular &c. This amount cannot be viewed as the whole claim because no part of the State's expenditure before 1780 is entered in these books.

The depreciation in this State was fixed by law in December 1781, at 1,000 for 1. It will appear from the documents herewith transmitted No. 396. 431. 445. 437. 448. 680. 685 & 741 that some articles have been charged to 600 for 1. it will also appear that the depreciation established by Act of Assembly was not so great at the time the Voucher is dated as it is charged at in these books, as for instance the depreciation in June 1781 by law is 250 for 1, Voucher No. 448 is given in that month for a sum in specie which is charged at 600 for 1. if it should be said that this is occasioned by the money not being paid when the certificates were given and that an intermediate depreciation had taken place, then it will appear necessary, that the receipt of the Individual should be produced to ascertain the precise time when the payment was made, not only to fix the value of the money but to determine the period when interest is to commence in favour of the State. The necessity of turning specie certificates into Continental money is not apparent.

The Agents of Virginia declare in their protest (page 10) "That the general accounts formed as before recited are lodged with him (the district Commissioner) and are upon every principle of justice claimed as a sufficient & under the circumstances before mentioned a proper specification on the part of the State of the general amount of her advances in behalf of the United States;" if by this is meant that the figures on those papers which are marked B represent specie sums it will then be necessary to consider from whence they arise, and if from depreciated paper, the rate by which they have been reduced into specie will claim attention, as it will materially affect the real specie value of their claim, this will more fully appear if any given sum is taken into consideration for instance Vo. No. 445, is for 400,000 dollars if the Continental scale is used in reducing this sum, (the lowest rate being 40 for 1) the value then, would appear to be 10,000 dollars whereas the actual rate of depreciation being 600 for 1 the sum ought to be no more than 666 2/3 dollars and which is the appraised value of the horse mentioned in this voucher, from this instance the house will perceive, that as the rate of depreciation by which any sum is reduced is less than the real rate

864

of depreciation, so is the claim increased beyond its real specie value and in the instance above stated (if that was the rate of reduction) the claim would be increased fifteen times the real amount in specie.

With respect to the State of the evidence in support of these claims the protest of the Agents goes so fully into that matter as to render it unnecessary to say any thing upon the subject.

THE CLAIMS OF NORTH CAROLINA

What has been observed with respect to the claims of Virginia will very generally be found to apply to the claims of this State.

The district Commissioner has made no return of the Claims of the State—he and the Agents of the State differed in opinion about them—the Agents brought on such books & papers as he would not receive and they were finally received into this Office on the 1st. of February last since which the Agents have made a specification of the Claims of the State as follows. Viz.,

	North Carolina currency Dolls.		Specie Dollars.	
Amount of sundry sums rendered to the general board for settling accounts by Schedule No. 23 estimated at	11,102,357	74	1,664,053	34
Amount of sums exhibited to the Commissioner of Army Accounts by Schedule No. 24 estimated at	24,684,035	83	5,026,707	83
	35,786,393	67	6,690,761	27

The first observation to be made is that all the sums stated as above by the Agents of North Carolina Amounts—The rate of depreciation in this State in December 1781 is 725 for 1. No New Emission was issued in this State.

In this State also the district Commissioner has filled a folio Volume in attempting to digest and methodize the papers exhibited to him, as far as he has progressed the amount is 8,185,986 dollars in paper and 328,064 dollars in specie. this arrangement seems to have come down as far as the year 1784 and it must be observed that the district Commissioner has in numerous instances classed the Claims under the heads of irregular unsupported, unascertained, doubtful and extra and unguarded.

THE CLAIMS OF SOUTH CAROLINA.

	Specie Dollars	90ths.
Amount of sums liquidated and credited the State by George Reid district Commissioner by Schedule No. 25	807,517	05
Amount of sums not liquidated by the district Commissioner included in said Schedule	697,227	78
Amount of sums exhibited to the Commissioner of Army Accounts by Schedule No. 26	1,927,271	27
Amount of specific supplies credited the State in the Books of the Treasury and not included in the above Schedules	87,927	80
	3,519,944	10

(continued)

Specie Dollars	90ths	Old Emissions Dollars	90ths
125,395	51	438,671	65
425,497	67	870,069	46
550,893	28	1,308,741	21

THE CLAIMS OF SOUTH CAROLINA (*continued*)

This State being over-run by the ~~enemy~~ enemy, few payments were made in depreciated paper money after the 18th March 1780.

New Emission was not issued in this State. The State scale of depreciation extends to May 1780 the depreciation was then 52 for 1—These accounts are regularly arranged and methodized.

The Board ~~has~~ have reason to believe that this State has many Claims which have not been exhibited in due time—The nature and supposed amounts of which will more fully appear from the paper No. 31.

THE CLAIMS OF GEORGIA

Amount of sums exhibited to George Reid district Commissioner by Schedule No. 27

Amount of sums exhibited to the Commissioner of Army Accounts by Schedule No. 28

This State was over-run by the enemy in 1779 and continued to be so during the year 1780 it is therefore supposed that few payments were made in depreciated money after the 18th. of March 1780.

No New Emission Money was issued in this State. The State Scale of depreciation extends to June 1780, the depreciation then was 80 for 1.

Exclusive of the above claims there has been lodged in this Office a paper (Copy of which is herewith transmitted No. 29) purporting to be claims of this State not received by the district Commissioner—this paper was lodged the 19th. January last—is not signed by any person, the time for exhibiting claims had expired and no satisfactory evidence has been produced to shew that these claims were exhibited to the district Commissioner in due time.

The House will please to distinguish between the claims immediately before this Board and those which are in the Office of Army Accounts because the observations which accompany the foregoing statements, are intended to apply to those claims only which are in this Office.

They will also be pleased to observe that where old Emission Money was paid after the 18th. of March 1780 on account of the Army or Militia, the Commissioner of Army Accounts has estimated it at the rate of forty for One; this may materially affect the real Specie value of the claims.

Such States as have offered Claims since the time expired for receiving them are noted under their several heads.

We have endeavored to place every matter in as proper a point of view as the time and the situation of the papers in the Office would admit of—We feel it cannot be perfectly satisfactory—because it does not shew the real amount of the claims of the States, nor can it be done until the monies claimed are reduced to specie value which will depend upon a final examination of the Accounts.

With sincere wishes that their endeavours to elucidate this subject may be conducive to the real advantage of the Union, and with the utmost defference to the judgment of the House The Board now respectfully submit this information to their indulgent construction.

Office of Accounts
April 29th. 1790

JOHN TAYLOR GILMAN } Commissioners of
JOHN KEAN   } Accounts

Note. Since closing the above the Board have received the Auditors report on the specific supplies, a copy of which is herewith transmitted marked No. 30—from this it appears that the Claims of the following States ought to have been so much more by the sums affixed to their names—being the amount credited them in the Books of the Treasury & not included in the Schedules returned to this Office by the district Commissioners.

Massachusetts   3,288 25/90 Dollars Specie
Pennsylvania   295,095 36/90 ditto

Philadelphia, 10th. February 1791
I certify the foregoing to be a true Copy of the Original report now on the files in my Office.

JOHN BECKLEY, Clerk to the
House of Representatives of
the Ud. States

John Taylor Gilman, Miscellaneous Manuscripts Collection, DLC. The first two pages of the manuscript and the enclosures are missing.

867

Funding Bill [HR-63]
May 6, 1790

A BILL *making Provision for the Debt of the United States*

WHEREAS justice and the support of public credit require, that provision should be made for fulfilling the engagements of the United States, in respect to their foreign debt, and for funding their domestic debt upon equitable and satisfactory terms,

SEC. I. *Be it enacted by the Senate and House of Representatives of the United States of America in Congress assembled,* That reserving out of the monies which have arisen since the last day of December last past, and which shall hereafter arise from the duties on goods, wares and merchandize imported into the United States, and on the tonnage of ships or vessels, the yearly sum of six hundred thousand dollars,[1] towards the support of the government of the United States, and their common defence, the residue of the said monies, or so much thereof as may be necessary, as the same shall be received in each year, next after the sum reserved as aforesaid, shall be and is hereby appropriated to the payment of the interest which shall from time to time become due on the loans heretofore made by the United States in foreign countries, and also to the payment of interest on such further loans as may be obtained for discharging the arrears of interest thereupon, and the whole or any part of the principal thereof; to continue so appropriated until the said loans, as well those already made as those which may be made in virtue of this act shall be fully satisfied, pursuant to the contracts relating to the same; any law to the contrary notwithstanding. *And provided,* That nothing herein contained shall be construed to annul or alter any appropriation by law made prior to the passing of this act.

And as new loans are and will be necessary for the payment of the aforesaid arrears of interest and the instalments of the principal of the said foreign debt due and growing due, and may also be found expedient for effecting an intire alteration in the state of the same,

SEC. 2. *Be it further enacted,* That the Secretary of the Treasury be and he is hereby authorized to borrow,[2] on the behalf of the United States, a sum or

---

[1] On May 19, on a motion by Madison, the COWH added "as the same may be appropriated" after "six hundred thousand dollars." The COWH then disagreed to a motion by Jackson to strike out "six hundred thousand dollars." (*NYDA,* May 21)

[2] On May 19, Madison, seconded by Bland, moved to strike "Secretary of the Treasury" and insert "the President of the United States," and to strike "to borrow" and insert "or cause to be borrowed such sums as may be necessary." The COWH disagreed to a motion by Steele to amend Madison's motion by inserting "by and with the advise and consent of the Senate" after "the President of the United States." Madison's motion was agreed to, 33–15. (Lloyd says 32 voted in favor.) (Lloyd, May 19; *NYDG,* May 20; *NYDA,* May 21)

sums not exceeding in the whole   3 and to apply the same[4] to the discharge of the said arrears and instalments, and (if it can be effected upon terms advantageous to the United States) to the paying off the whole of the said foreign debt,[5] and to make[6] such other contracts respecting the said debt as shall be found for the interest of the said states. *Provided nevertheless,* That no engagement nor contract shall be entered into, which shall preclude the United States from reimbursing any sum or sums borrowed within   7 years after the same shall have been lent or advanced.

And whereas it is desireable to adapt the nature of the provision to be made for the domestic debt, to the present circumstances of the United States, as far as it shall be found practicable consistently with good faith and the rights of the creditors; which can only be done by a voluntary loan on their part:

Sec. 3. *Be it therefore further enacted,* That a loan to the full amount of the said domestic debt be and the same is hereby proposed; and that books for receiving subscriptions to the said loan be opened at the Treasury of the United States, and by a commissioner to be appointed in each of the said States, on the   day of   next, to continue open until the last   of   8 following inclusively, and that the sums which shall be subscribed thereto, be payable in certificates issued for the said debt according to their specie value, and computing the interest upon such as bear interest to the said last day of December inclusively,[9] which said certificates are of these several descriptions, to wit:

Those issued by the Register of the Treasury.

Those issued by the Commissioners of Loans in the several States.

Those issued by the Commissioners for the adjustment of the accounts of the Quarter-Master, Commissary, Hospital, Cloathing and Marine Departments.

Those issued by the Commissioners for the adjustment of accounts in the respective States.

---

3 On June 2, the House filled this blank with "12,000,000 dollars." (*NYDA,* June 3)

4 On May 19, the COWH unanimously agreed to a motion by Madison to strike out "and to apply the same" in order to insert "to be applied." (*NYDG,* May 20)

5 On May 19, the COWH agreed to a motion by Gerry to change the wording from "to apply" through "foreign debt" to the following:

that so much of the same as may be necessary to the discharge of the said arrears and instalments, and if it can be effected on good terms, for the payment of the whole of the said foreign debt, be appropriated solely to that purpose. (*NYDA,* May 21)

6 On May 19, the COWH agreed to a motion to strike out "to make" and insert "that the President be further authorised, to cause [to] be made." (*NYDG,* May 20)

7 On June 2 the House filled this blank with "15." (*NYDA,* June 3)

8 On June 2 the House filled these blanks with "first," "September," "day," and "August." (*NYDA,* June 3)

9 On May 27 the House disagreed to a motion to strike out from "computing the interest" through "December inclusively." (*NYDG,* May 28)

Those issued by the late and present Paymaster-General, or Commissioner of army accounts.

Those issued for the payment of interest, commonly called indents of interest.[10]

SEC. 4. *And be it further enacted,* That for any sum which shall be subscribed to the said loan by any person or persons or body politic, the subscriber or subscribers shall be entitled at his, her or their option, either

To a certificate for a quantity of land equal to one third of the sum so subscribed, computing at the rate or price of twenty[11] cents per acre (to be located in the western territory of the United States, in such manner as shall be hereafter provided by law) and to another certificate for the remaining two thirds of the said sum, purporting that the United States owe to the holder or holders thereof, his, her or their assigns, a sum equal to the said two thirds, bearing an interest of six per centum per annum, payable quarter yearly, and subject to redemption at the pleasure of the government of the United States, by payment of the principal sum mentioned in such certificate, together with the interest which shall at any time have accrued thereupon. Or,

To a certificate purporting that the United States owe to the holder or holders thereof, his, her or their assigns, the whole of the sum by him, her or them subscribed, bearing an interest of four per centum per annum, payable

---

[10] On May 20, the COWH agreed to a motion proposed by Sedgwick on May 19 to add "the continental bills of credit at   dollars for one specie dollar," after it was amended by Madison to read:

> Those which shall be issued for the bills of credit issued by the authority of the United States in Congress assembled, at the rate of   dollars in those bills for one dollar in specie.

Hartley moved to fill the blank with 100; Scott with 500; and Partridge with 40. (*NYDG,* May 21; *GUS,* May 22) on May 21, the COWH disagreed to a motion by Hartley to postpone filling the blank. After several motions to insert various sums were disagreed to, the COWH agreed to a motion to insert "one hundred." A motion by Heister to add, "That this clause shall not be deemed to be a rule to the commissioners for settling the accounts between the United States and individual States," was disagreed to. The COWH agreed to a motion by Boudinot to add the following:

> Provided that the interest paid by any of the States on certificates of either of the above descriptions and endorsed on the same shall not be funded as aforesaid—but in such case indents of interest shall be issued from the Treasury of the United States in favor of such States. (*GUS, NYDG,* May 22)

On May 26, in the House, Sedgwick moved to strike out "one hundred dollars" in order to insert another figure, but withdrew his motion to make way for one by Gerry to strike out the same sum and insert "seventy five." Gerry's motion was agreed to by a recorded vote of 31–25. (*NYDG,* May 27)

Also on May 26, the House disagreed, by a recorded vote of 42–15, to a motion "that interest should be computed on the said bills from the   day of   ." (*GUS,* May 29)

On May 27, the House disagreed to a motion by Heister to strike out "Those issued for the payment" through "indents of interest." (Lloyd, May 27, states that twelve members supported the motion; *GUS,* May 29, says ten or eleven.)

[11] On May 21, the COWH agreed to motions by Fitzsimons to strike out "twenty" and insert "thirty" at this point and in the next alternative. (*NYDG,* May 22)

quarter yearly, and subject to redemption by payments not exceeding in one year, on account both of principal and interest, the proportion of six dollars upon a hundred of the said sum; and as a compensation for the reduction of interest, to another certificate for a quantity of land, which at the rate of twenty cents per acre shall be equal to the proportion of fifteen dollars and eighty cents upon a hundred of the said sum. Or,

To a certificate purporting that the United States owe to the holder or holders thereof, his, her or their assigns, a sum equal to two thirds of the said sum subscribed, bearing an interest of six per centum per annum, payable quarter yearly, and subject to redemption by payments not exceeding in one year, on account both of principal and interest, the proportion of eight dollars upon a hundred of the sum mentioned in such certificate, and to another certificate purporting that the United States owe to the holder or holders thereof, his, her or their assigns, a sum equal to one third of the said sum subscribed, which after the year 1797, shall bear an interest of six per cent. per annum, payable quarter yearly, and subject to redemption by payments not exceeding in one year, on account both of principal and interest, the proportion of eight dollars upon a hundred of the sum mentioned in such certificate.

SEC. 5. *Provided always,* That it shall not be understood, that the United States shall be bound or obliged to redeem in the proportions aforesaid, but it shall be understood only that they have a right so to do.

SEC. 6. *And be it further enacted,* That a Commissioner be appointed for each State to reside therein, whose duty it shall be to superintend the subscriptions to the said loan, to open books for the same, to receive the certificates which shall be presented in payment thereof, to liquidate the specie value of such of them as shall not have been before liquidated, to issue the certificates above mentioned in lieu thereof, according to the terms of each subscription, as well for land as stock, to record such as shall be issued for land, to enter in books to be by him kept for that purpose, credits to the respective subscribers to the said loan for the sums to which they shall be respectively entitled, to transfer the said credits upon the said books from time to time as shall be requisite; to pay the interest thereupon as the same shall become due, and generally to observe and perform such directions and regulations as shall be prescribed to him by the Secretary of the Treasury touching the execution of his office.

SEC. 7. *And be it further enacted,* That the stock which shall be created pursuant to this act, shall be transferable only on the books of the Treasury or of the said Commissioners respectively, upon which the credit for the same shall exist at the time of transfer, by the proprietor or proprietors of such stock, his, her or their attorney: But it shall be lawful for the Secretary of the Treasury by special warrant under his hand and the seal of the Treasury, countersigned by the Comptroller, and registered by the Register, to authorize the transfer of such stock, from the books of one Commissioner to those of another Commissioner, or to those of the Treasury, and from those of the Treasury to those of a Commissioner.

SEC. 8. *And be it further enacted,* That the interest upon the said stock as the same shall become due, shall be payable quarter yearly, that is to say, one fourth part thereof on the last day of March; one other fourth part thereof on the last day of June; one other fourth part thereof on the last day of September, and the remaining fourth part thereof on the last day of December in each year, beginning on the last day of March next ensuing, and payment shall be made wheresoever the credit for the said stock shall exist at the time such interest shall become due, that is to say, at the Treasury, if the credit for the same shall then exist on the books of the Treasury, or at the office of the Commissioner upon whose books such credit shall then exist. But if the interest for one quarter shall not be demanded before the expiration of a second quarter,[12] the same shall afterwards be demandable only at the Treasury.[13]

SEC. 9. *And be it further enacted,* That the monies arising from the duties, imposts and excises,[14] which have been, or during the present Session of Congress shall be, laid or imposed by the United States, or so much thereof as may be necessary, shall be and are hereby pledged and appropriated for the payment of interest on the stock which shall be created by the loan aforesaid, according to the terms of the respective subscriptions thereto, and pursuant to the provisions of this act, until the final redemption of the said stock; any law to the contrary notwithstanding; subject nevertheless to such reservations and priorities as may be requisite to satisfy the appropriations heretofore made, and which during the present Session of Congress may be made by law, including the sums herein before reserved and appropriated. And to the end that the said monies may be inviolably applied in conformity to this act, and may never be diverted to any other purpose, an account shall be kept of the receipts and disposition thereof, separate and distinct from the product of any other duties, imposts, excises or taxes whatsoever.

And as it may happen that some of the creditors of the United States may not think fit to become subscribers to the said loan,

SEC. 10. *Be it further enacted and declared,* That nothing in this act contained shall be construed in any wise to alter, abridge or impair the rights of those creditors of the United States, who shall not subscribe to the said loan,

---

[12] On May 21, the COWH agreed to a motion by Gilman to strike out "second quarter" and insert "third quarter." (*NYDG,* May 22)

[13] On May 21, the COWH disagreed to a motion by Heister to strike out from "But if the interest" through "at the Treasury." (*NYDG,* May 22)

[14] On May 26, in the House, Stone moved to strike "from the duties, imposts and excises," and accepted an amendment proposed by Laurance to insert "the duties which have or may be" in place of this phrase. The House agreed to a substitute motion by Tucker to insert "arising under the revenue laws which have passed or may be passed." (Lloyd, May 26)

or the contracts upon which their respective claims are founded, but the said contracts and rights shall remain in full force and virtue.

And that such creditors may not be excluded from a participation in the benefit hereby intended to the creditors of the United States in general, while the said proposed loan shall be depending, and until it shall appear from the event thereof what further or other arrangements may be necessary respecting the said domestic debt;

SEC. 11. *Be it therefore enacted,* That such of the creditors of the United States as may not subscribe to the said loan, shall nevertheless receive[15] during the year 1791, four per centum on the respective amounts of their respective demands,[16] to be paid at the same times, at the same places, and by the same persons as is herein before directed, concerning the interest on the stock which may be created in virtue of the said proposed loan. But as some of the certificates now in circulation, have not heretofore been liquidated to specie value, as most of them are greatly subject to counterfeit, and counterfeits have actually taken place in numerous instances, and as embarrassment and imposition might, for these reasons, attend the payment of interest on those certificates in their present form, it shall therefore be necessary to entitle the said creditors to the benefit of the said payment, that those of them who do not possess certificates issued by the Register of the Treasury, for the registered debt, should produce previous to the   day of   [17] next, their respective certificates either at the Treasury of the United States, or to some one of the Commissioners to be appointed as aforesaid, to the end that the same may be cancelled, and other certificates issued in lieu thereof, which new certificates shall specify the specie amount of those, in exchange for which they are given, and shall be otherwise of the like tenor with those heretofore issued by the said Register of the Treasury for the said registered debt, and shall be transferable on the like principles with those directed to be issued on account of the subscriptions to the loan hereby proposed.[18]

---

[15] On May 24, the COWH disagreed to a motion by Heister to insert "from and" at this point. (*GUS,* May 26)
[16] On May 24, the COWH disagreed to a motion by Tucker to strike from "*Be it therefore enacted*" through "respective demands" in order to insert a clause to the effect "that those who do not subscribe will receive 6 per cent in certificates of arrears of interest to which the residue of the payment of funds." (Lloyd, May 24)

On May 27, the House agreed to a motion by Fitzsimons to insert "including the interest to the last day of December next." (*GUS,* May 29)
[17] On June 2, the House filled these blanks with "first" and "June." (*NYDA,* June 3)
[18] On May 24, the COWH disagreed to a motion by Gerry to include interest for non-subscribers. Boudinot moved to clarify the bill's language by adding the word "principal" at some point in this section. Sherman moved to amend the Boudinot motion "to provide for issuing a Certificate for interest, to the end of the year 1791, to non-subscribers," but the Boudinot and Sherman motions were withdrawn. (*GUS,* May 26)

SEC. 12. *And be it further enacted,* That the Commissioners who shall be appointed pursuant to this act, shall respectively be entitled to the following yearly salaries, that is to say:

Dollars.

The Commissioner for the state of New-Hampshire,
The Commissioner for the state of Massachusetts,
The Commissioner for the state of Connecticut,
The Commissioner for the state of New-York,
The Commissioner for the state of New-Jersey,
The Commissioner for the state of Pennsylvania,
The Commissioner for the state of Delaware,
The Commissioner for the state of Maryland,
The Commissioner for the state of Virginia,
The Commissioner for the state of North-Carolina,
The Commissioner for the state of South-Carolina,
The Commissioner for the state of Georgia,[19]

Which salaries shall be in full compensation for all services and expences, except for the hire of clerks, in respect to whom it shall be in the discretion of the Secretary of the Treasury to allow so many as he shall judge requisite, to receive from the United States salaries not exceeding   dollars per annum each.[20]

---

[19] On May 24, the COWH disagreed to a motion by Steele to insert "to reside at   " after the name of each state. (*NYDG,* May 25) On June 2, the House filled in the blanks for the salaries with "650," "1,500," "1,000," "1,500," "700," "1,500," "600," "1,000," "1,500," "1,000," "1,000," and "700." (*NYDG,* June 3)

[20] On May 24, the COWH agreed to a motion by Williamson to strike "except for the hire" through "per annum each." (*GUS,* May 26)

In the COWH on May 24, Gerry moved the addition of the following sections for the purpose of assuming the state debts:

    Sec.   *And* whereas a provision for the debts of the respective States, by the United States, would be greatly conducive to an orderly, oeconomical and efficient arrangement of the public finances; would tend to an equal distribution of burthens among the citizens of the several States; would promote more general justice to the different classes of public creditors; and would serve to give additional stability to public credit: And whereas the said debts having been essentially contracted in the prosecution of the late war, it is just that such provision should be made.

    Sec.   *Be it therefore further enacted,* That a loan be also proposed to the amount of the said debts, and that subscriptions to the said loan be received at the same times and places, by the same persons, upon the same terms, and with the same options to the subscribers, as in respect to the loan above proposed, concerning the domestic debt of the United States, subject to the exceptions and qualifications hereafter declared.

    Sec.   *And be it further enacted,* That the sum which shall be subscribed to the said loan, shall be payable in the principal and interest of the certificates, which, prior to the   day of   last, were issued by the respective States, as acknowledgements or evidences of debt, by them respectively owing; and which shall appear by oath, or in regard to a known Quaker, by affirmation, to have been the property of an individual or individuals, or body politic, other than a State, on the said ⟨blank⟩ day of ⟨blank⟩ last. *Provided,* That no greater sum shall be received, in the certificates of any State, than as follows, that is to say:

In those of New-Hampshire,
In those of Massachusetts,
In those of Connecticut,
In those of New-York,
In those of New-Jersey,
In those of Pennsylvania,
In those of Delaware,
In those of Maryland,
In those of Virginia,
In those of North-Carolina,
In those of South-Carolina,
In those of Georgia,

And provided, That no such certificate shall be received, which, from the tenor thereof, or from any public record, act or document, shall appear, or can be ascertained to have been issued for any purpose, other than compensations and expenditures for services or supplies towards the prosecution of the late war, and the defence of the United States, or of some part thereof, durin[g] the same.

Sec. ⟨blank⟩ *And be it further enacted,* That the interest upon the certificate[s] which shall be received in payment of the sums subscribed towards the said loan, shall be computed to the last day of the year one thousand seven hundred and ninety-one, inclusively; and that the interest upon the stock which shall be created by virtue of the said loan, shall commence or begin to accrue upon the first day of the year one thousand seven hundred and ninety-two, and shall be payable quarter yearly, at the same times, and in like manner, as the interest on the stock to be created by virtue of the said loan, in the domestic debt of the United States. *Provided always,* That the interest on one-third of the [respective sums] which may be subscribed according to the last of the three options or alternatives upon which subscriptions may be made as aforesaid, shall not commence or begin to accrue until the first day of the year one thousand seven hundred and ninety-nine.

Sec. ⟨blank⟩ *And be it further enacted,* That if the whole of the sum allowed to be subscribed, in the debt or certificates of any State as aforesaid, shall not be subscribed within the time for that purpose limited, such State shall be entitled to receive, and shall receive from the United States, at the rate of four per centum per annum, upon so much of the said sum, as shall not have been so subscribed, in trust, for the non-subscribing creditors of such State, to be paid in like manner as the interest on the stock, which may be created by virtue of the said loan, and to continue until there shall be a settlement of accounts between the United States and the individual States; and in case a balance shall then appear in favor of such State, until provision shall be made for the said balance.

But as certain States have respectively issued their own certificates, in exchange for those of the United States, whereby it might happen, that interest might be twice payable on the same sums,

Sec. ⟨blank⟩ *Be it therefore further enacted,* That the payment of interest, whether to States or to individuals, in respect to the debt of any State, by which such exchange shall have been made, shall be suspended, until it shall appear to the satisfaction of the ⟨blank⟩ that certificates, issued for that purpose, by such State, have been re-exchanged or redeemed, or until those which shall not have been re-exchanged or redeemed, shall be surrendered to the United States.

Sec. ⟨blank⟩ *And be it further enacted,* That the faith of the United States be,

SEC. 13. *And be it further enacted,* That the said Commissioners before they enter upon the execution of their several offices, shall respectively take an oath for the diligent and faithful execution of their trust, and shall also become bound with one or more sureties to the satisfaction of   in a penalty not less than   nor more than   [21] thousand dollars, with condition for their good behavior, in their said offices respectively.[22]

PRINTED BY FRANCIS CHILDS AND JOHN SWAINE

Broadside Collection, RBkRm, DLC.

and the same is hereby pledged to make provision, before the third of March, one thousand seven hundred and ninety-one, for payment of interest on the amount of the stock, arising from subscriptions to the said loan, upon the like principles with the provision herein before expressed, touching the loan, to be made in the said domestic debt of the United States; and also for the payment of the said four per centum per annum, on so much of the said debts of the respective States, as shall remain un-subscribed to the said loan.

Sec.   *And be it further enacted,* That so much of the debt of each State as shall be subscribed to the said loan, shall be a charge against such State in account with the United States.

Sec.   *And be it further enacted,* That the commissioners to be appointed aforesaid, shall have the like powers and authorities, and shall perform the [like] services and duties in respect to the said last mentioned loan, as in respect [to] the one first above proposed, relatively to the said domestic debt of the United States. (Senate Simple Resolutions and Motions, SR, DNA)

The COWH, after debating this motion, rose without taking action on it. On May 27 Boudinot moved in the House for the addition of the same language, and on the next day the House made his resolutions the order of the day for June 7. In the meantime they were printed. The House did not take them up; instead they were proposed by Ellsworth in the Senate on June 10. (*NYDA*, May 25, 29; *NYDG*, May 28)

[21] The House filled these blanks with "the Secretary of the Treasury," "five thousand," and "ten," probably on June 2.

[22] Section 13 was not reported by the COWH, but was adopted unanimously by the House on a motion by Seney on May 26. (*NYDG*, May 27)

Report of the Secretary of War
May 11, 1790

WAR OFFICE OF THE UNITED STATES
MAY 10th. 1790

In obedience to the orders of the House of Representatives the Secretary of war submits the statement hereunto annexed of the troops and militia furnished from time to time by the several States, towards the support of the late war.

The numbers of the regular troops having been stated from the Official returns deposited in the war-Office, may be depended upon—and in all cases where the numbers of Militia are stated from the returns, the same confidence may be observed.

BUT in some years of the greatest exertions of the Southern States, there are no returns whatever of the militia employed—In this case recourse has been had to the letters of the Commanding officers, and to well informed individuals, in order to form a probable estimate of the numbers of the militia in service—and although the accuracy of the estimate cannot be relied upon, yet it is the best information which the Secretary of war can at present obtain—When the accounts of the militia service of the several States shall be adjusted, it is probable that the numbers will be better ascertained.

There are not any documents in the War-Office from which accurate returns could be made of the ordnance Stores furnished by the several States during the late war—The charges made by the several States against the United States, which have been presented by the Commissioners of Accounts, are probably the only evidence which can be obtained on the subject.

ALL which is humbly submitted to the House of Representatives.

H. KNOX
Secretary of War

A STATEMENT

of the number of non commissioned Officers and privates of the regular troops and militia furnished by the several States from time to time, for the support of the late war.

Statement of the Troops furnished by the following States, taken from actual returns of the army for the year 1775.

1775			Troops Furnished		
			Number of Men in Continental pay	Number of Militia	
New Hampshire			2,824		
Massachusetts			16,444		
Rhode-Island			1,193		
Connecticut			4,507		
New York			2,075		
Pennsylvania			400		
Total			27,443	27,443	

NB. The above troops were enlisted to serve to the last of December 1775.

Conjectural estimate of Militia employed in addition to the above.

Virginia	for 6 Months	2,000		
ditto	State Corps for 8 Months	1,180		3,180
North Carolina	for 3 Months			2,000
South Carolina	for 6 Months	2,500		
ditto	State troops	1,500		4,000
Georgia	for 9 Months			1,000
				10,180
		Grand Total		37,623

Statement of the troops furnished by the following States taken from actual returns of the army for the year 1776.

1776		Quotas required		Troops furnished			
				Number of Men in Continental pay	Number of Militia	Total of Militia and Conti-nentals	
†See New Jersey below	New Hampshire			3,019			
	Massachusetts			13,372	4,000	17,372	
	Rhode Island			798	1,102	1,900	Militia
	Connecticut			6,390	5,737	12,127	service
	New York			3,629	1,715	5,344	including
	†Pennsylvania			5,519	4,876	10,395	flying camp,
	Delaware			609	145	754	averaged at
	Maryland			637	2,592	3,229	5-Months
	Virginia			6,181			
	North Carolina			1,134			
	South Carolina			2,069			
	Georgia			351			
	New Jersey			3,193	5,893	9,086	
				46,891	26,060	72,951	

Conjectural estimate of militia employed in addition to the above

New Hampshire	averaged at 4 Months		1,000
Massachusetts	ditto		3,000
Connecticut	ditto		1,000
New York	ditto		2,750
Virginia			
North Carolina	averaged at 8 Months		3,000
South Carolina	ditto at 6 Months		4,000
Georgia		750	
ditto	State troops	1,200	1,950
			16,700
	Grand Total		89,651

Statement of the troops furnished by the following States taken from actual returns of the Army for the year 1777.

Quotas fixed by Congress September 1776 for three years or during the War	1777 Quotas required		Troops furnished		Total of Militia and Continentals
	No. Battalns. 680 Men each	Number of Men	No. of Contil. Troops	Number of Militia	
New Hampshire	3	2,040	1,172	1,111 3 Mo.	2,283
Massachusetts	15	10,200	7,816	2,775 do.	10,591
Rhode Island	2	1,360	548		548
Connecticut	8	5,440	4,563		4,563
New York	4	2,720	1,903	929 6 Mo.	2,832
New Jersey	4	2,720	1,408		1,408
Pennsylvania	12	8,160	4,983	2,481 5 do.	7,464
Delaware	1	680	299		299
Maryland	8	5,440	2,030	1,535 3 Mo.	3,565
Virginia	15	10,200	5,744	1,269 5 do.	7,013
North Carolina	9	6,120	1,281		1,281
South Carolina	6	4,080	⊕1,650		1,650
*Georgia	1	680	1,423	& State troops	1,423
Besides the above Congress authorised the Commander in chief on the 27th. day of Decem. 1776 to raise sixteen additional Regiments of Infantry.	16	10,880			
Three Regiments of Artillery	3	2,040			
Cavalry		3,000			
Total	107	75,760	34,820	10,100	44,920

*NB. By the resolve of the 5th. of July 1776 Georgia was authorized to raise in Virginia, North and South Carolina two Regiments of Infantry and also two Companies of Artillery of 50 Men each, these troops were chiefly enlisted for one year and their times expired in 1777.

⊕ Returns of May 1778

Conjectural estimate of militia employed in addition to the above

New Hampshire & Vermont	for 2 Months	2,200	
Massachusetts	for 2 Months	2,000	
+ Connecticut	for 2 Months	2,000	
New York	for 6 do.	2,500	
New Jersey	for 2 Months	1,500	
Pennsylvania	for 3 Months	2,000	
Delaware	for 2 do.	1,000	
Maryland	for 2 Months	4,000	
Virginia	for 2 Months	4,000	
South Carolina	for 8 do.	350	
Georgia	for	750	
Rhode Island	for 6 Months	1,500	23,800
	Grand Total		68,720

+ See Rhode
Island be-
low

881

Statement of the troops furnished by the following States taken from actual returns of the army for the year 1778

February 26. 1778 Congress resolved to have the following number of men furnished by each State.	1778 Quotas required		Furnished		Total of Militia and Continental troops	
	No. of Battn. of 522 Men each	Number of Men	Number of Continental troops	Number of Militia		
New Hampshire	3	1,566	1,283		1,283	
Massachusetts	15	7,830	7,010	1,927 X	8,937	X guarding Convention troops
Rhode Island	1	522	630	2,426 Ø	3,056	
Connecticut	8	4,176	4,010		4,010	
New York	5	2,610	2,194		2,194	Ø Short levies and militia for 6 Months.
New Jersey	4	2,088	1,586		1,586	
Pennsylvania	10	5,220	3,684		3,684	
Delaware	1	522	349		349	
Maryland, including the Gern. Battn.	8	4,176	3,307		3,307	
Virginia	15	7,830	5,236		5,236	
North Carolina	9	4,698	1,287		1,287	
South Carolina	6	3,132	1,650		1,650	
Georgia	1	522	673		673	
Total	86	44,892	32,899	4,353	37,252	

Conjectural estimate of the militia employed in addition to the above

New Hampshire	for 2 Months	500	
Massachusets	2 Months	4,500	
New Jersey	"	1,000	
Virginia	2 Months	2,000	
Ditto	Guarding Convention troops	600	
South Carolina	3 Months	2,000	
Georgia	2,000 Militia 6 Months & 1,200 Stae. troops	3,200	13,800
	Grand Total		51,052

883

Statement of the Troops furnished by the following States, taken from actual Returns of the Army for the year 1779

March 9th. 1779. Congress resolved that the Infantry of these States for the next Campaign be composed of 80 Battalion. Viz.	1779 Quotas required		Furnished		
	No. of Battalions 522 Men each	No. of Men	No. of Men	Militia	
New Hampshire	3	1,566	1,004	222	
Massachusetts	15	7,830	6,287	1,451	
Rhode Island	2	1,040	507	756	
Connecticut	8	4,176	3,544		
New York	5	2,610	2,256		
New Jersey	3	1,566	1,276		
Pennsylvania	11	5,742	3,476		
Delaware	1	522	317		
Maryland	8	4,176	2,849		
Virginia	11	5,742	3,973		
North Carolina	6	3,132	1,214	2,706	8 Months
South Carolina	6	3,132	909		
Georgia	1	522	87		
Total	80	41,760	27,699	5,135	Total from returns 32,834

Conjectural Estimate of Militia employed in addition to the above

New York	for 3 Months	1,500	
Virginia	for 2 Months	3,000	
Do.	for 6 Months	1,000	
Do.	Guarding Convention troops	600	
North Carolina	for 8 Months	1,000	
South Carolina	for 9 Months	4,500	
Georgia		750	
	Total Conjectural	12,350	12,350
			Grand Total 45,184

Statement of the Troops furnished by the following States taken from actual Returns of the Army for the year 1780

January 24th. 1780, Resolved that the States furnish by draughts or otherwise the deficiencies of their respective quotas of 80 Battans. apportion'd by a resolve of Congs. of 9th. March 1779.	1780 Quotas required		Furnished		
	No. of Battans. 522 Men each	No. of Men	No. of Men	Militia	
New Hampshire	3	1,566	1,017	760	
Massachusetts	15	7,830	4,453	3,436	
Rhode Island	2	1,044	915		
Connecticut	8	4,176	3,133	554	
New York	5	2,610	2,179	668	
New Jersey	3	1,566	1,105	162	
Pennsylvania	11	5,742	3,337		
Delaware	1	522	325	231	
Maryland	8	4,176	2,065		
Virginia	11	5,742	2,486		
No. Carolina	6	3,132			
So. Carolina	6	3,132			
Georgia	1	522			
Total	80	41,760	21,015	5,811	Total from Returns 26,826

Conjectural Estimate of Militia employed in addition to the above

New York 2,000	2 Months	Virginia	1,500, for 12 Mos. & 3,000 for 3 Mos.
		North Carolina	3,000, averaged for 12 Months
		South Carolina	5,000 for 4 Mos. & 1,000 for 8 Months
		Georgia	750
2,000			·10,250 4,000

Conjectural 16,000
Grand Total 42,826

Statement of the troops furnished by the following States, taken from actual Returns of the army for the year 1781

Arrangement 3d. October 1780	1781 Quotas required		Furnished			
	No. of Battns. 576 each	No. of Men	No. of Men	No. of Militia		
New Hampshire	2	1,152	700			
Massachusetts	11	6,336	3,732	1,566	4 Months Men	
Rhode Island	1	576	464			
Connecticut	6	3,456	2,420	1,501	4 Months Men	
New York	3	1,728	1,178			
New Jersey	2	1,152	823			
Pennsylvania	9	5,184	1,346			
Delaware	1	576	89			
Maryland	5	2,880	770	{ 1,337 with General Green		
Virginia	11	6,336	1,225	{ 2,894 before York Town.		
North Carolina	4	2,304	545			
South Carolina	2	1,152				
Georgia	1	576				
Total Battalions &c.	58	33,408	13,292	7,298		20,590 Total from Returns.

Conjectural estimate of Militia employed in addition to the above

Virginia		2,000	} The averag'd number employ'd during 10	
North Carolina		3,000	} Months of this year may be estimat'd at 6,000	
South Carolina		3,000		
Georgia		750		
		8,750	8,750 Total Conjectural	
			29,340 Grand Total	

Statement of the Troops furnished by the following States, taken from actual Returns of the army for the year 1782

	Quotas required		Furnished		No. of	
	No. of Battn. 576 each	No. of Men	No. of Men		Militia	
New Hampshire	2	1,152	744			
Massachusetts	11	6,336	4,423			
Rhode Island	1	576	481			
Connecticut	6	3,456	1,732			
New York	3	1,728	1,198			
New-Jersey	2	1,152	660			
Pennsylvania	9	5,184	1,265			
Delaware	1	576	164			
Maryland	5	2,880	1,280			
Virginia	11	6,336	1,204			
North Carolina	4	2,304	1,105			
South Carolina	2	1,152				
Georgia	1	576				
Total	58	33,408	14,256			14,256 Total from Returns

Conjectural estimate of Militia employed in addition to the above

Virginia		1,000		
South Carolina		2,000	for 4 Months	
Georgia		750		
		3,750		3,750 Total conjectural

18,006 Grand Total

Statement of the troops furnished by the following States, taken from actual Returns of the army for the year 1783

	1783 Quotas required		Furnished		Total Number of Continentals and Militia
	No. of Battns. 576 each	Number of Men	Number of Continentals	Number of Militia	
New Hampshire	2	1,152	733		
Massachusetts	11	6,336	4,370		
Rhode Island	1	576	372		
Connecticut	6	3,456	1,740		
New York	3	1,728	1,169		
New Jersey	2	1,152	676		
Pennsylvania	7	5,184	1,598		
Delaware	1	576	235		
Maryland	5	2,880	974		
Virginia	11	6,336	629		
North Carolina	4	2,304	697		
South Carolina	2	1,152	139		
Georgia	1	576	145		
Total	58	33,408	13,476		13,476

NB. The army in the Northern department discharged the 5 November 1783 and that in the Southern States, on the 15 of November 1783.

War Office of the United States May 10th 1790

H. KNOX
Secretary of War

Reports and Communications from the Secretary of War, Vol. I, HR, DNA.

Report of the Secretary of the Treasury on Money Received From or Paid to the States
May 11, 1790

The Secretary of the Treasury in obedience to the order of the House of Representatives of the 23rd of April respectfully submits the several statements in the Schedules herewith transmitted marked A and B and No. 1. 2 3 4 and 5.

Upon these statements the Register of the Treasury in His report to the said Secretary makes the following remarks.

"The Debits and Credits in Continental Money advanced from or received into the Treasury of the United States as Stated in the within Schedule may be relied on as the true nominal amount Stated on Record in the Treasury Books, but the reduction to specie value, is subject to the examination of the General Board of Commissioners.

The Credits for Specie and also of Indents paid into the Treasury of the United States on account of the existing requisitions of Congress are accurate and it is presumed conclusive, but with respect to the extension in Specie of the several payments into the Treasury in the emission of Continental Bills of Credit called old emissions and the Emissions of the 18th March 1780, although the nominal sums specified in the subordinate statements, are as accurate as the Treasury records will admit, yet as there is no legislative Guide on a question of so great import as [*torn*] Treasury Officers have felt themselves [*torn*] embarrassed, on the one hand they could not presume to affix a Scale not warranted by any act of the Legislature; and on the other, the order of the House required a compliance as far as possible; they have therefore on this occasion governed themselves by the only existing regulation of the late Congress, according to the Table herewith presented by a reduction to Specie all sums either paid or received from the States from the commencement of the Revolution to 18th March 1780 and from that period to the present date, all sums in Continental Money are reduced to Specie at forty for one.

The new Emissions are estimated equal to specie.

Where State paper has been received by the United States from any particular State, the State making the payment, has received a Credit at which it has been accounted for by those who have received it."

The Secretary begs leave to observe from principals which have governed the said statements, they cannot be considered as exhibiting the actual Specie value of the monies received from the respective States.

But an impression, that it might not be advisable, on his part to enter into considerations; which are relative to the duty of the Commissioners for settling accounts between the United States and the Individual States, has led him to seek in the acts of Congress and the Records of the Treasury, for the rules by which the liquidation of the paper money should be conducted, rather than to indulge a latitude of opinion as to what might be in the Abstract right.

All which is humbly submitted.

Schedule A

General Abstract of the sums of Money including Indents, and paper Money of every Kind reduced to Specie value, which have been received by or paid to the several States by Congress from the commencement of the Revolution to the present period made in pursuance of the order of House of Representatives of 23rd April 1790

States	Paid to State			Received from State		
	Dollars	90.	8	Dollars	90.	8.
New Hampshire	440,974	29	5	466,554	60	4
Massachusetts	1,245,737	25	"	3,167,020	32	4
Rhode Island	1,028,511	33	6	310,395	21	"
Connecticut	1,016,273	15	5	1,607,259	31	2
New York	822,803	6	"	1,545,889	45	"
New Jersey	366,729	63	1	512,916	23	4
Pennsylvania	2,087,276	15		2,629,410	41	3
Delaware	638,170	5		208,878	68	"
Maryland	609,617	6	5	945,537	39	
Virginia	482,[?]81	58	3	1,963,811	7	1
N. Carolina	788,031	12	6	219,835	79	
South Carolina	1,014,808	25	2	499,325	22	1
Georgia	679,412	49	3	122,744	52	2

Treasury Department
    Registers Office

Schedule [B]

Schedule of the accounts of the United States with Individual States shewing the particulars of the Debits and Credits as extended in General abstract of the sums of money including Indents and Paper Money of every Kind reduced to Specie value which have been received by or paid to the Several states by Congress from the commencement of the Revolution to the present period, made in pursuance of the order of the House of Representatives of 23rd April 1790

	Debits				
States	Continental Money advanced from the Treasury of the United States from the commencement of the War to the present period	New emissions advanced in like manner equal to Specie	Specie advanced in like manner	Debits on the Books of the qr. Master commissary Marine clothing and hospital departmts. reduced to specie	Value of Specie in Continental Money advanced
	Dollars 90. 8	Dol. 90. 8	Dol. 90. 8	Dollars 90. 8	Dollars 90. 8
New Hampshire	820,400				440,974.29.5
Massachusetts	4,272,186.15				1,245,737.25
Rhode Island	2,049,000				1,028,511.33.6
Connecticut	1,716,517.22				1,016,273.15.5
New York	1,118,500			10,082.15	812,720.81
New Jersey	556,300			34,863.45	331,866.18.1
Pennsylvania	4,454,913.30		8,325.79	5,503.30	2,073,446.86
Delaware	118,500				63,817.05
Maryland	2,292,083.30				609,6[1]7.06.5
Virginia	1,739,639.15	1,200			482,081.58.3
North Carolina	2,780,959.08	7,400			788,831.12.6
South Carolina	1,594,929.85	9,935			1,014,808.25.2
Georgia	2,290,831.30	8,166			679,412.49.3

Since the above was stated the Register has received from the Comptrollers office Acots. which entitle the State of New Hampshire to the following Credits viz.

in Specie 4,964 ⎫
in Indents 64,551 $^{35}/_{90}$ ⎬ Dollars
⎭

Schedule [B] (Continued)

States	Credits				
	Total extension, of Specie as shewn in General Abstract	Specie paid into the Treasury of the United States on Account of the Specie requisitions Vide No. 1	Indents paid in like manner Vide No. 1	New Emissions of March 1780 for so much of the $4/_{10}$ applied to the service of the U. States Vide No. 2	Amt. in specie value of Continl. emissions at 40 for 1 pd. into the Treasury in pursuance of the requisition of Congress of 18 March No. 3
	Dolls. 90. 8	Dols. 90. 8	Dols. 90. 8	Dols. 90. 8	Dols. 90. 8
New Hampshire	440,974.29.5	35,630.25	86,474.24	58,000	130,000
Massachusetts	1,245,737.25	364,533.72	767,399.83	530,048.31.4	747,500
Rhode Island	1,028,511.33.6	87,950.83.2		51,228.73.6	64,833.75
Connecticut	1,016,273.15.5	210,419.62	111,791.10		228,787.10.4
New York	822,803. .6	375,025.12	399,358.37.4	56,500.	197,633.78
New Jersey	366,729.63.1	160,442. .1		130,401.73	170,666.67.4
Pennsylvania	2,087,276.15	658,402. .5	471,548.13.4	500,979.84.7	711,366.78
Delaware	63,817. .5	67,686.31	57,330.13		55,250.
Maryland	609,617.06.5	443,691.00.5		138,440.24	[torn]
Virginia	483,281.58.3	650,542.09.4	477,252.37	126,623.30	328,[torn] .4
North Carolina	795,431.12.6	48,626.47			126,671[torn]
South Carolina	1,024,743.25.2	446,244.38			
Georgia	687,578.49.3				

Schedule [B] (*Continued*)

Credits (*Continued*)

Amount in specie value of the Taxes collected in old emissions on the several requisitions for that purpose as per Statement No. 4	Continl. money credited on the Treasury Books from the Commenct. of the War to the present period	New emissions in like manner equal to Specie	Specie in like manner	Credits on the Books of the qr. Master Commissary Marine clothing and Hospital departments as estimated in Specie value	Nominal State paper
Dols. 90. 8	Dol. 90. 8	Dol. 90. 8	Dols. 90. 8	Dol. 90. 8	Dol. 90. 8
123,948.54.4			4,089.15	28,412.32	
447,081.12	506,239.	400		284,408.81	
66,248.69	2,513.			38,377.79	
375,995.78	251,719.86			507,468.41	
98,026.15	416,020.		24,233.45		
46,256.62		5,149			
188,544.36	182,955.78	17,740	5,232.18		
41,317.	231,810.60		1,500		
[torn] 836.85	328,300.85	4,200		[torn]	
278,541.27	[torn]			[torn]	413.3
	52,040		26,641 [torn]		
	618,120.10				
	551,112.40				

(*continued*)

Schedule [B] (*Continued*)

States	Value of State paper	Value in Specie of Continental Money credited	Total Estimation in Specie as shewn in General Abstract
	Dol. 90. 8	Dollars 90. 8	Dollars 90. 8
New Hampshire		26.	461,554.60.4
Massachusetts		26,048.23	3,167,020.32.4
Rhode Island		1,755.01	310,395.21
Connecticut		172,797.04.6	1,607,259.31.2
New York		395,112.37.4	1,545,889.45
New Jersey			512,916.23.4
Pennsylvania		75,596.76	2,629,410.41.3
Delaware		5,795.24	208,878.68
Maryland		14,388.[*torn*]	94[*torn*]7.39
Virginia	[*torn*] 826.60	[*torn*]	[*torn*]
North Carolina		17,896.01	219,835[*torn*].9
South Carolina		53,080.74.1	499,325.22.1
Georgia		122,744.52.2	122,744.52.2

Treasury Department Registers Office 4th May 1790

No. 1 Schedule

Of the Requisitions on the Several States by the United States, in Congress assembled, of the 10th September 1782. 30th October 1781 and 27th and 28th April 1784 of 27th Septr. 1785 2nd August 1786 and of 11th October 1787 and 20th August 1788. Shewing the Quotas assigned to each the Amount paid thereon and the Balances due according to the Treasury Statements to the 4th. May 1790

| States | 10 Septr. 1782 | | 30 October 1781 | | 27th and 28 |
	Indents	Quota	Paid previous to the 31st Decemr. 1783 Vide Journal of Congress for 1784 Page 178	Sum required 27th and 28th April 1784. 3/4 whereof being paid in Specie 1/4 were made renewable in Indents	3/4 thereof, or Specie proportion
	Dol. 90ths	Dol. 90ths	Dol. 90ths	Dol. 90ths	Dol. 90ths
New Hampshire	48,000	186,799	3,000	183,799	137,849.22.4
Massachusetts	192,000	653,798	247,676.59	405,121.31	304,591.00.6
Rhode Island	28,000	108,342	67,847.85	40,494.05	30,370.48.6
Connecticut	133,000	373,598	131,577.75	242,020.15	181,515.11.2
New York	54,000	186,799	39,064	147,735	110,801.22.4
[New] Jersey	66,000	[torn]	[torn]4.85	14[torn].04	105,62 [torn]
Pennsylvania	180,000	560,397	346,632.88	213,764.02	160,323.01.4
Delaware	16,800	56,042.45		56,042.45	42,031.78.6
Maryland	132,000	466,998	89,302.10	377,695.80	283,271.82.4
Virginia	174,000	653,797	115,103.48	538,693.42	404,020.09
North Carolina	88,800	34,338.45		311,338.45	233,503.78.6
South Carolina	72,000	186,799	186,799		
Georgia	14,400	12,452.45		9,339.33.6	9,339.33.6
	1,200,000	4,000,000	1,329,009	2,670,991	2,003,343.22

No. 1 Schedule (*Continued*)

	Requisitions and Quotas (*continued*)			
	April 1784		27th. September 1785	
	Total in Specie Payable on this requisition	Proportion of Indents receivable on this requisition	Specie	Indents
	Dol. 90ths	Dol. 90ths	Dol. 90ths	Dol. 90ths
New Hampshire	140,849.22.4	45,947.67.4	35,138.60	70,277.30
Massachusetts	552,267.59.6	101,530.30.2	149,618	299,236
Rhode Island	98,218.43.6	10,123.46.2	21,545.30	43,090.60
Connecticut	313,092.86.2	60,505.03.6	88,060.60	176,121.30
New York	149,865.22.4	36,933.67.4	85,495.30	170.990.60
[New] Jersey	[?]07,630,77.4	55,208.57.4	[*torn*]	111.[*torn*]
Pennsylvania	506,955.89.4	53,441.00.4	136,792.06	273,585.30
Delaware	42,031.78.6	14,010.56.2	14,962	29,924
Maryland	372,574.02.4	94,423.87.4	94,344.60	188,689.30
Virginia	519,123.57	134,673.33	170,991.30	341,982.60
North Carolina	233,503.78.6	77,834.56.2	72,670.60	145,341.30
South Carolina			192,366	
Georgia	9,339.33.6	3,123.11.2	10,686.60	21,373.30
	2,332,252.22.4	667,747.67.4	1,128,244	1,871,756

No. 1 SCHEDULE (*Continued*)

Requisitions and Quotas (*continued*)					Total Amount Paid
2nd August 1786		11th Octr. 1787	20th Augt. 1788		
Specie	Indents	Indents	Indents	Specie	
Dol. 90ths	Dol. 90ths	Dol. 90ths	Dol. 90ths 8	Dol. 90ths 8	
76,268	56,452	59,684	59,258	35,630.25	
324,746	240,370	254,381	252,339.63	364,533.72	
41,764	34,613	36,558	36,326.18	87,950.83.2	
191,135	141,474	149,976	148,516.18	210,419.62	
185,567	157,434	145,535	144,185.57	375,625.12	
[*torn*]	89,279	94,372	93,728.36	160,442.01	
296,908	219,765	232,616	230,698.18	658,402.05	
32,475	24,037	25,506	25,238.72	47,686.31	
204,775	151,570	160,349	159,096.81	443,691.57	
371,136	274,707	290,770	288,391.18	650,542.09.4	
157,732	116,749	123,450	122,564.54	48,626.47	
139,0[?]7	103,015	108,996	108,160.54	446,224.38	
23,288	17,167	18,194	18,036.63		
2,170,630	1,606,632	1,700,407	1,686,541.12	3,529,194.82.6	

No. 1 SCHEDULE (*Continued*)

States	Total Amount Paid		Balances due
	Indents	Specie	Indents
	Dol. 90ths 8	Dol. 90ths 8	Dol. 90ths 8
New Hampshire	86,474.24	216,625.57.4	253,146.73.4
Massachusetts	767,399.83	662,097.77.6	572,457.10.2
Rhode Island		78,576.80.4	189,511.34.2
Connecticut	111,791.10	381,868.84.2	698,001.41.6
New York	399,358.37.4	45,902.40.4	289,740.57
[New] Jersey		223,379.76.4	[??][*torn*]3.4
Pennsylvania	471,548.13.4	282,254.54.4	[*torn*]
Delaware	57,330.13	41,782.47.6	78,186.25.2
Maryland		228,002.05.4	886,129.18.4
Virginia	477,252.37.1	410,708.77.4	1,027,271.73.7
North Carolina		415,280.01.6	674,739.50.2
South Carolina		71,937.52	329,171.54
Georgia		43,314.03.6	92,284.14.2
	2,371,154.38.1	3,100,731.29.6	6,361,929.41.3

Treasury of the United States, Registers Office 4th May 1790
JOSEPH NOURSE Register

No. 2

Schedule of the Sums in the Money of the Emission of the 18th March 1780 which have been appropriated by the United States of the four tenths, which upon the Principles of the said became subject to their orders

	Dolls.	90ths	8ths
New Hampshire	58,000.	31.	4
Massachusetts	530,048.		
Rhode Island	51,288.	73.	6
New York	56,500.		
New Jersey	130,401.	73.	
Pennsylvania	500,979.	84.	7
Maryland	138,440.	24.	
Virginia	126,623.	30.	
	1,592,222.	47.	1

In all One Million Five Hundred Ninety two Thousand Two hundred and Twenty two Dollars, forty seven Ninetieths and one eighth of one Ninetieth, For the redemption of this Emission. Funds were provided by the Legislatures of the aforesaid States respectively to the requisition of Congress. It may be proper to remark that, although Legislative Acts were thus passed, yet as Congress became security for the redemption of this emission the several States above mentioned may not be considered entitled to an absolute credit, untill it shall appear that Congress are released from their obligation, by a cancelment of the whole Emission. With respect to its extension at Specie value, if the Act of Congress of the 18 March 1780 is followed, wherein it is considered equal to Specie; and untill Congress shall otherwise direct the Treasury have no guide. The peculiar state of the Public Credit, when this money came into circulation, together with the pressing demands on the Treasury for the current service, induced the United States to submit in some cases to a depreciation of this Money, on the paying it from the Treasury— The medium of depreciation was three for one Dollar. It is likewise to be noted, that from the adequacy of the Funds, at least in some, if not all the States this Money has been brought into the State Treasuries according to the tenor of the bill, which being on Interest, both principal and Interest have been redeemed at specie value.

No. 3

Statement of the sums in the Old Continental Emission, paid by the following States into the Treasury of the United States on account of their several quotas of the Requisitions of Congress of the 18th March 1780

		Dollars
NEW HAMPSHIRE 1781. June 11th Paid		2,299,769
1782. Septr. 18 Ditto		2,900,231
		5,200,000

Being the total Amount of said States quota which at 40 for 1. is in Specie according to the extention in the Account

130,000

All whereof has been examined, counted and Burnt by the Commissioners appointed for that purpose.

MASSACHUSETTS 1781	June 11th Paid	12,984,670
	Novr. 6th. Do.	16,876,618
1782	Augt. 31st Do.	38,725
		29,900,000

Being the total Amount of said States quota, which at 40 for 1 is in Specie

747,500

Examined, counted and Burnt as above.

RHODE ISLAND   1787 August 13th. Paid   2,593,353.30/90

Being on account of her quota of 2,600,000 Dollars which at 40 for 1 is

64,833.75/90

Examined counted and Burnt as above.

CONNECTICUT	1786. December 7th Paid	802,424.75/90
	1788 August 25 Ditto	1,049,059.75/90
		9,151,484 50/90

Which at 40 for 1 is in Specie   228,787 10/90

Examined, counted and burnt in like manner and is on Account of 22,100,000 Dollars the Quota of Said State.

NEW YORK	1781	January 1st Paid	599,369
	1782	January 30 Ditto	1,373,811.45/90
	1786	June 9th Ditto	2,759,217.15/90
		July 2 Ditto	848,775.75/90
		August 2 Ditto	2,151,478.15/90
	1788	March 28th Ditto	172,676.75/90
			7,905,355.45/90

Which at 40 for 1 is in Specie   197,633.78/90

Examined counted and burnt in like manner and is on account of 9,750,000 Dollars the Quota of said State.

NEW JERSEY	1780	November 25th Paid	940,430
		December 23 Ditto	237,839.60/90

1781	March 23	Ditto		631,523
	May 30	Ditto		712,824.45/90
	August 2	Ditto		1,456,417.15/90
	October 6	Ditto		1,139,180.75/90
1782	February 23	Ditto		1,207,111
1783	" 21	Ditto		392,833.30/90
1787	August 17	Ditto		99,516.15/90
				6,826,675

which at 40 for 1 in Specie   17,666.67.4
Examined counted and burnt in like manner and is on Account of 11,700,000
Dollars the Quota of said State.

PENNSYLVANIA	1781	February	13th	Paid	1,400,527
	"	April	3	Ditto	2,599,987
	"	May	15	Ditto	1,999,995
	"	August	4th	Ditto	4,402,413
	1782	May	30th	Ditto	3,367,670
	"	June	3rd	Ditto	2,805,317.60/90
	"	July	30	Ditto	5,009,343.15/90
	"	August	7th	Ditto	1,599,758.30/90
	"	November	22nd	Ditto	2,954,918
	"	December	6th	Ditto	1,000,391
	"	"	19	Ditto	77,623.45/90
	1783	January	20	Ditto	47,535.45/90
	"	"	29th	Ditto	331,268.45/90
	1787	November	13	Ditto	857,827
					28,454,674 60/90

Which at 40 for 1 is in Specie   711,366 78/90
Examined and counted in like manner and is on Account of 29,900,000
Dollars the Quota of said State.

DELAWARE	1782	January	7th	Paid	2,210,000

which at 40 for one, is in Specie   55,250
being the full Quota of said State examined counted and burnt as above.

MARYLAND	1780	November	25th	Paid	115,116.60/90
	1786	July		Ditto	827,490.45
		August	22	Ditto	430,968.60
		"	"	Ditto	473,778.60
		September	5th	Ditto	151,417.15
		"	12th	Ditto	23,650
		"	16	Ditto	132,929
		November	9th	Ditto	62,481.30

	December	13	Ditto	40,072
		29	Ditto	21,750
1787	January	22	Ditto	89,905
1788	September	5th	Ditto	6,780,026.30

                                                    9,149,585 30/90

Which at forty for one is in Specie   228,739.57/
Examined counted and burnt as before and is on Account of 20,940,000
Dollars the Quota of said State.

VIRGINIA	1781. April		17th. Paid	802,717
	May	29	Ditto	5,785,555.45
1786	Septemr.	16.	Ditto	2,880,720.45
	November	1	Ditto	1,523,223.60
1787	July	5	Ditto	2,048,160

                                                   13,040,376.60/90

Which at forty for one is in Specie   328,509.37.4
Examined counted and burnt as before and is on Account of 32,500,000
Dollars the quota of said State.

NORTH   1789. Paid into the hands of the Treasurer a Sum
CAROLINA   said to be 5,066,061 which is ready for
                      examination counting &c. if no deficiencies
                      should appear the State will be entitled to a
                      Credit on Account of 13,000,000 Dollars
                      being the Quota of this Requisition in Con-
                      tinental Dollars. 5,066,861 at 40 for 1 is
                      126,671.65/90.

With respect to the computation of Forty for one it is made in like manner
with the foregoing subject therewith to the General exception herewith
marked A.

ABSTRACT OF WARRANTS entered in the Treasury Books to the credit of Individual States upon whose Treasuries the same were drawn to the Amount of 55,750,484.59/90 Dollars as per annexed

SCHEDULE

Date of Warrant	Date of Receipt	In whose favor	For what Department	Amount in old Emissions Dollars 90ths	Rate of Exchange	Amount in Specie Dollars
1779 Decemr. 14		New Hampshire Jeremiah Wadsworth	Commissaries	300,000	Dol. 90ths 14.69 ℔ Cent	44,300
1780 Jany. 1		Ditto	Ditto	300,000	3-36.3 8ths	10,213.45
April 15		Ditto	Ditto	500,000	40 for one	12,500
	1779 June 11th	Emissions of Bills of Credit burnt by the Commissioners		200,000	7.19.15	14,436.10
	1780 July. 1	Michael Hillegas Treasurer	Treasury	312,450	40 for one	34,688.67.4
	1783 Novr. 12th	Emissions of Bills of Credit Burnt, &c.		1,487,550	40 for one	[torn]
		Massachusetts State of Massachusets ℔ act of Congress 22nd Nov. 1778		300,000		[?]3,948[torn]
1778 July 22nd				300,000	30.5	90,166.60
1779 Decr. 14		Jeremiah Wadsworth	Commissaries	800,000	3-59.3	29,277.70
1780 Jany. 1st		Ditto	Ditto	1,000,000	3-36.3	34,041.40
20th		Ephraim Blaine	Ditto	500,000	3-13-7	15,770.75

(continued)

SCHEDULE (*Continued*)

Date of Warrant	Date of Receipt	In whose favor	For what Department	Amount in old Emissions Dollars 90ths	Rate of Exchange	Amount in Specie Dollars
April 5th		Doctor Isaac Foster	Medical	40,000		
" 11		Ephraim Blaine	Commissaries	1,800,000		
		State of Massachusetts ⅌ Act of Congress 11th April 1780 }		200,000		
" 15		Jeremiah Wadsworth	Commissaries	190,000	40 for one	269,686.15
May 10th		Joseph Carleton	Clothing	118,648		
13		William Palfrey	Pay of the Army	430,000		
	1781 July 3d	Emissions of Bills of Credit Burnt by the Commissioners }		821,152		
	1787 Septr. 18	Paid by the State to the loan offices }		3,677,646.88		
1781 Jany. 30		Commercial Committee	Total	32,553.02 — 13,420,000	40 for one	8,188.22 — 44,081.12

RHODE ISLAND

Date of Warrant	Date of Receipt	In whose favor	For what Department	Amount in old Emissions Dollars 90ths	Rate of Exchange	Amount in Specie Dollars
1778 June 26th		State of Rhode Island ⅌ Act of Congress 22nd Novemr. 1788 }		50,000	Dol. 90th 8th 33-70.2	16,890.25
1779 Novr. 12		Ditto for Ditto		300,000	4-14-4	12,483.30
Decr. 14		Jeremiah Wadsworth	Commissaries	100,000	3-59-3	3,659.65
1780 Jany. 1		Ditto	Ditto	75,000	3-36.3	2,553.11
20		Ephraim Blaine	Ditto	175,000	3-13-7	5,519.71
Feby. 28		Major General Greene	Qr. Master	80,000	2-62.6	2,157.70
April 11th		Ephraim Blaine	Commissaries	204,000	40 for one	5,100.
14		Jeremiah Wadsworth	Ditto	100,000	Ditto	2,500.

(continued)

Date		Name	Office	Amount	Rate	£ Sterling
1779 July 23d		Emissions of Bills of Credit destroyed by the Commissioners		195,018	6.28.1	12,310.45
1780 June 9th		M. Hillegas Treasurer on Acct. of Taxes		114,732	40 for one	2,868.27
1782 Feby. 23		Emissions of Bills of Credit destroyed		8,238	Ditto	205.85
		Total		1,401,988		66,248.69
		CONNECTICUT				
[?] June 26th		State of R. I[sland] ℔ act of Congress	D.P. Master General	100,000	33.70.2	33,802.70
1779 Feby. 24		Ebenezer Hancock		100,000	29.70.7	29,787.45
Octr. 20		Wm. Buchanan	Commissary	100,000	19.45.5	15,506.85
July 3rd		State of Connecticut ℔ act of Congress		200,000	6.65.5	13,458.30
Decr. 14		Jeremiah Wadsworth	Commissary	600,000	3.59.3	21,958.30
22		Major General Greene	Qr. Master	150,000	3.48.7	5,323.30
1780 Jany. 1		Jeremiah Wadsworth	Commissy.	1,500,000	3.36.3	57,062.45
19		Ephraim Blaine	Do. 1,550,000 Paid only	1,203,299	3.15.	38,104.39
April 11th		Ditto	Commissary	229,225.45		
15		Jeremiah Wadsworth	Ditto	150,000		
18		William Palfrey	P.M. General	20,000	40 for one	91,141.11
May 13		Ditto	Ditto	296,421.63		
June 17		Major General Greene	Qr. Master	600,000		
July 1		Ephraim Blaine	Commissy.	1,000,000		

SCHEDULE (*Continued*)

Date of Warrant	Date of Receipt	In whose favor	For what Department	Amount in old Emissions Dollars 90ths	Rate of Exchange	Amount in Specie Dollars
	1780 Jany. 1	Emission of Bills of Credit } destroyed		1,367,537	3.11.15	42,729.44
	" 20	Ephraim Blaine	Commissary	921,231.51	3.13.7	29,058.04
		New York	Total	9,887,714.69		375,995.78
1779 Novr. 24		Major Genl. Greene	Qr. Master Genl.	617,000	3.86.7	24,465.43
Decr. 14		Jeremiah Wadsworth	Commissary	400,000	3.59.3	14,658.80
22		Maj. Genl. Greene	Qr. Master	400,000	3.48.7	14,172.20
1780 Jany. 21		Ephraim Blaine	Commissary	183,000	2.9.3	5,680.11
March 1		Maj. Genl. Greene	Qr. Master	100,000	2.62.6	2,697.20
April 11		Ephraim Blaine	Commy.	448,750 }	40 for one	13,968.67
June 1		Major Genl. Greene	Qr. Master	110,000 }		
	1779 May 14	Emission of Bills of Credit } destroyed		183,000	7.80.4	14,446.75
	1780 July 1	Michael Hillegas } Treasr. on Acct. Taxes }		318,258	40 for one	7,956.04
		New Jersey	Total	2,760,008		98,026.15
1779 Decr. 16		Jeremh. Wadsworth	Commissary	200,000	3.59.3	7,319.80
18		Ditto	Ditto	250,000	3.54.[torn]	9,003.42

906

Date	Name	Department	Amount	40 for one	Value
1780 Apl. 11 June 20	Ephraim Blaine Major [Genl.] Greene	Ditto Qr. Master	107,333.30 } 120,000	40 for [one]	29,933.30
			1,647,333.30		[torn]256[.?].02
1778 Octobr. 17 "	PENNSYLVANIA Marine Committee Count Pulaski	Marine Army	5,000 10,000	19.72.5 19.72.5	990.31 2,971.03
1779 Decemr. 14 " 22nd	Jeremiah Wadsworth Majr. General Greene	Commissy. Qr. Master	100,000 200,000	3.59.3 3.48.7	3,659.65 7,086.10
1780 Jany. 1	Jeremh. Wadsworth	Commissy.	250,000	3.36.3	8,510.37
3	Benjamin Flowers	Military stores	1,000,000	3.34.	33,777.70
14	Majr. Genl. Greene	Qr. Master	300,000	3.20.7	6,463.80
24	Ephm. Blaine	Commy.	1,000,000	3.9.3	31,041.60
28	Willm. Henry	Clothing	100,000	3.4.7	3,054.15
Feby. 8	Majr. Genl. Greene	Qr. Master	300,000	2.8.3	8,766.60
Apl. 11	Ephm. Blaine	Commisy.	1,940,800		
18	James Wilkinson	Clothing	40,000		
20	Major Genl. Greene	Qr. Master	298,604.60		
"	William Palfrey	Army	20,000	40 for one	82,222.55
27	Majr. Genl. Greene	Qr. Master	200,000		
May 19	James Wilkinson	Clothing	300,000		
June 9	Major Genl. Greene	Qr. Master	250,000		
1782 Feby. 23	Emission of Bills of Credit destroyed		239,600		
	Total		6,454,804.60		188,544.36

(continued)

Date of Warrant	Date of Receipt	In whose favor	For what Department	Amount in old Emissions Dollars 90ths	Rate of Exchange	Amount in Specie Dollars
	1779 May 3	DELAWARE Emission of Bills destroyed		59,997	8.15.7	4,832.03
1779 Decr. 22		Major Genl. Greene	Qr. Master	50,000	3.48.7	1,771.47
1780 Jany. 1		Jeremiah Wadsworth	Commissary	75,000	3.36.3	2,553.40
20		Ephraim Blaine	Ditto	175,000	3.13.7	5,519.71
Feby. 28		Major Genl. Greene	Qr. Master	50,000	2.62.6	1,348.67
March 25		Ditto	Ditto	200,000		
Apl. 20		Ditto	Ditto	90,000	40 for one	9,750.
June 9		Ditto	Ditto	30,000		
	1780 June 30	M. Hillegas Treasr. on Acct. Taxes		72,000		
	1779 May 3	Emissions of Bills of Credit destroyed		150,000	8.15.7	12,264.34
	"	Ditto	Ditto	48,000	8.15.7	3,277.08
			Total	1,000,000		41,317.
1779 Decr. 14		MARYLAND Jeremiah Wadsworth	Commissaries	700,000	3.59.3	25,618.05
22		Major General Greene	Qr. Master	400,000	3.48.7	14,172.20
1780 Jany. 1		Jeremh. Wadsworth	Commy.	500,000	3.36.3	17,020.75
20		Ephraim Blaine	Ditto	300,000	3.17.3	9,462.45

(continued)

Date		Description		Amount	Rate	Amount
April 12	1780 July 1st	Michael Hillegas Treasurer on Account of Taxes	Ditto	1,822,533.30 } 200,000 }	40 for one	50,563.30
		VIRGINIA	Total	3,922,5[torn]		[torn]6,836.85
1779 Decemr. 16		Jeremiah Wadsworth	Commissaries	1,600,000	3.56.6	58,088.80
22		Major General Greene	Quarter Mastr.	600,000	3.48.7	21,258.30
1780 Jany. 1		Jeremh. Wadsworth	Commrs.	750,000	3.36.3	25,531.22
Feby. 28		Major Genl. Greene	Qr. Master	150,000	2.62.6	4,045.75
March 11		State of Georgia ⅌ Act of Congress Ult.		300,000	2.50.2	7,675.
" 16		Major General Greene	Quarter Master	100,000	2.46.6	2,519.40
1780 April 3		William Palfrey	Pay Master Genl.	100,000	40 for one	2,500.
April 8		Joseph Carlton Pay Master to the Board of War for expediting the Troops		533,333.30		
May 2		Ephraim Blaine	Commissaries	1,500,000		
" 10		Joseph Carleton	Clothing	123,077.45	40 for one	156,922.50
July 19		Wm. Palfrey Pay Master Genl.	Army	150,000		
Augt. 9	1780 Augt. 4	M. Hillegas Treasurer on Account of Taxes		713,326.50		
		Benjamin Flowers	Military Stores	200,000		
1781 April 26	1780 Octr. 15	Major General Greene for 5,346,438.15 paid only	Quarter Master	2,500		
		Michael Hillegas as on Acct. of Taxes		556,665.15		

SCHEDULE (*Continued*)

Date of Warrant	Date of Receipt	In whose favor	For what Department	Amount in old Emissions Dollars 90ths	Rate of Exchange	Amount in Specie Dollars
				9,876,902.3		278,541.27
		NORTH CAROLINA				
1779 Decemr. 14		Jeremh. Wadsworth	Commissris.	400,000	3.59.3	14,638.80
22		Major General Greene	Qr. Master	200,000	3.48.7	7,806.10
1780 Jany. 1		Jeremh. Wadsworth	Commissrs.	750,000	3.36.3	25,531.22
Feby. 9		Stephen Moore	Qr. Master	30,000	2.82.	873.30
March 16		William Palfrey	Pay Mastr. Genl.	900,000	2.46.6	22,675
June 14		Major General Gates	Army	100,000	40 for one	2,500
				2,380,000		73,304 52/90ths

RECAPITULATION of the Foregoing

	Dollars	90ths	Dollars	90ths
New Hampshire	94,646	10	123,984	54
Massachusetts	358,801	45	447,081	12
Rhode Island	65,149	07	66,248	69
Connecticut	357,949	58	375,995	78
New York	90,719	36	98,026	15
New Jersey	36,279	32	46,256	62
Pennsylvania	159,328	12	188,544	36
Delaware	37,941	41	41,317	
Maryland	99,761	11	116,836	85
Virginia	204,869	25	278,541	27
North Carolina	72,430	"	73,304	52

Treasury Department
Registers Office
May

Reports and Communications from the Secretary of the Treasury, HR, DNA.

Report of the Secretary of the Treasury
May 11, 1790

TREASURY-DEPARTMENT, 11th. May 1790
The Secretary of the Treasury respectfully submits an Abstract of the duties which have accrued
on the Tonnage of ships or vessels, from the
~~from the~~ first day of September to the thirty
first day of December last, pursuant to the
order of the House of Representatives of the
fifth Instant.

ABSTRACT of DUTIES which have accrued on the TONNAGE of foreign
and domestic VESSELS from the first of September to the thirty first of
December 1789.

States	Foreign Tonnage		Domestic Tonnage		Total Amount of Tonnage	
New Hampshire	469	50	339	30	808	80
Massachusetts	4,829	37¹/₂	3,855	60	8,684	97¹/₂
Connecticut	618	08	722	47¹/₂	1,340	55¹/₂
New York	8,739	87¹/₂	1,496	66¹/₂	10,236	54
New Jersey	83	50	224	31	307	81
Pennsylvania	11,587	64	1,515	06	13,102	70
Delaware	603	"	123	96	726	96
Maryland	4,994	05¹/₂	1,728	88¹/₂	6,722	94
Virginia	11,210	93¹/₂	1,423	30¹/₂	12,634	24
South Carolina	4,630	59	433	84	5,064	43
Georgia	2,600	17	126	65	2,726	82
	50,366	72	11,990	05	62,356	77

ALEXR. HAMILTON Secy. of the Treasury

A Record of the Reports of the Secretary of the Treasury, vol. I, HR, DNA.

Funding Bill [HR-63]
June 2, 1790

An ACT making Provision for the Debt of the United States

SECT. I. WHEREAS justice and the support of public credit require, that
provision should be made for fulfilling the engagements of the United States,
in respect to their foreign debt, and for funding their domestic debt upon
equitable and satisfactory terms:

Be it enacted by the Senate and House of Representatives of the United States of America, in Congress assembled, That reserving out of the monies which have arisen since the last day of December last past, and which shall hereafter arise from the duties on goods, wares and merchandize imported into the United States, and on the tonnage of ships or vessels, the yearly sum of six hundred thousand dollars, or so much thereof as may be appropriated from time to time, towards the support of the government of the United States, and their common defence, the residue of the said monies, or so much thereof as may be necessary, as the same shall be received in each year, next after the sum reserved as aforesaid, shall be and is hereby appropriated to the payment of the interest which shall from time to time become due on the loans heretofore made by the United States in foreign countries; and also to the payment of interest on such further loans as may be obtained for discharging the arrears of interest thereupon, and the whole or any part of the principal thereof; to continue so appropriated until the said loans, as well those already made as those which may be made in virtue of this act, shall be fully satisfied, pursuant to the contracts relating to the same, any law to the contrary notwithstanding. *And provided,* That nothing herein contained shall be construed to annul or alter any appropriation by law made prior to the passing of this act.

SEC. 2. And as new loans are and will be necessary for the payment of the aforesaid arrears of interest, and the instalments of the principal of the said foreign debt due and growing due, and may also be found expedient for effecting an entire alteration in the state of the same:

Be it further enacted, That the President of the United States be, and he is hereby authorized, to cause to be borrowed on behalf of the United States, a sum or sums, not exceeding in the whole twelve million of dollars; and that so much of this sum as may be necessary to the discharge of the said arrears and instalments, and (if it can be effected upon terms advantageous to the United States) to the paying off the whole of the said foreign debt be appropriated solely to those purposes: And the President is moreover further authorized to cause to be made such other contracts respecting the said debt as shall be found for the interest of the said States. *Provided nevertheless,* That no engagement nor contract shall be entered into, which shall preclude the United States from reimbursing any sum or sums borrowed within fifteen years after the same shall have been lent or advanced.

SEC. 3. And whereas it is desirable to adapt the nature of the provision to be made for the domestic debt, to the present circumstances of the United States, as far as it shall be found practicable consistently with good faith and the rights of the creditors; which can only be done by a voluntary loan on their part:

Be it therefore further enacted, That a loan to the full amount of the said domestic debt be, and the same is hereby proposed; and that books for receiving subscriptions to the said loan be opened at the Treasury of the United States, and by a commissioner to be appointed in each of the said States, on the first day of September[1] next, and to continue open until the last day of August[2] following, inclusively; and that the sums which shall be subscribed thereto, be payable in certificates issued for the said debt according to their specie value, and computing the interest upon such as bear interest to the said[3] last day of December inclusively, which said certificates shall be of these several descriptions, to wit:

Those issued by the Register of the Treasury.

Those issued by the Commissioners of Loans in the several States, including certificates given pursuant to the act of Congress of the second January, 1779, for bills of credit of the several emissions of the twentieth of May, 1777, and the eleventh of April, 1778.

Those issued by the Commissioners for the adjustment of the accounts of the Quarter-Master, Commissary, Hospital, Cloathing and Marine Departments.

Those issued by the Commissioners for the adjustment of accounts in the respective States.

Those issued by the late and present Paymaster-General, or Commissioner of Army Accounts.

Those issued for the payment of interest, commonly called indents of interest.

Those which shall be issued for[4] the bills of credit issued by the authority of the United States in Congress assembled, at the rate of 75[5] dollars in the said bills, for one dollar in specie: *Provided,* That the interest which shall have been paid on certificates of either of the above descriptions by any State, and endorsed thereon by the officers of such State, shall not be computed and funded as aforesaid. And certificates shall be issued for the amount of interest which shall appear to have been paid by such State, in the like manner as if indents had been originally given for the same.[6]

---

[1] The Senate struck out "September" and inserted "October." The House agreed to this amendment on July 24.

[2] The Senate struck out "August" and inserted "September." The House agreed to this amendment on July 24.

[3] The Senate struck out "said" and inserted "next" after "December." The House agreed to this amendment on July 24.

[4] The Senate struck out "Those which shall be issued for" and inserted "And in." This amendment was recommended by the committee report of June 15. The House agreed to it on July 24.

[5] The Senate struck out "75" and inserted "one hundred." This amendment was recommended by the committee report of June 15. The House agreed to it on July 24.

[6] The Senate struck out the proviso. This amendment was recommended by the committee report of June 15. The House agreed to it on July 24.

SEC. 4. *And be it further enacted,* That for any sum which shall be subscribed to the said loan by any person or persons or body politic, the subscriber or subscribers shall be entitled at his, her or their option, either—

To a certificate for a quantity of land equal to one third of the sum so subscribed, computing at the rate or price of thirty cents per acre (to be located in the western territory of the United States, in such manner as shall be hereafter provided by law) and to another certificate for the remaining two thirds of the said sum, purporting that the United States owe to the holder or holders thereof, his, her or their assigns, a sum equal to the said two thirds, bearing an interest of six per centum per annum, payable quarter yearly, and subject to redemption at the pleasure of the government of the United States, by payment of the principal sum mentioned in such certificate, together with the interest which shall at any time have accrued thereupon; or—

To a certificate purporting that the United States owe to the holder or holders thereof, his, her or their assigns, the whole of the sum by him, her or them subscribed, bearing an interest of four per centum per annum, payable quarter yearly, and subject to redemption by payments not exceeding in one year, on account both of principal and interest, the proportion of six dollars upon a hundred of the said sum; and as a compensation for the reduction of interest, to another certificate for a quantity of land, which, at the rate of thirty cents per acre shall be equal to the proportion of fifteen dollars and eighty cents upon a hundred of the said sum; or—

To a certificate purporting that the United States owe to the holder or holders thereof, his, her or their assigns, a sum equal to two thirds of the said sum subscribed, bearing an interest of six per centum per annum, payable quarter yearly, and subject to redemption by payments not exceeding in one year, on account both of principal and interest, the proportion of eight dollars upon a hundred of the sum mentioned in such certificate, and to another certificate purporting that the United States owe to the holder or holders thereof, his, her or their assigns, a sum equal to one third of the said sum subscribed, which after the year 1797, shall bear an interest of six per cent. per annum, payable quarter yearly, and subject to redemption by payments not exceeding in one year, on account both of principal and interest, the proportion of eight dollars upon a hundred of the sum mentioned in such certificate. *Provided always,* That it shall not be understood, that the United States shall be bound or obliged to redeem in the proportion aforesaid, but it shall be understood only that they have a right so to do.[7]

---

[7] The Senate struck out this section and inserted the following:
AND BE IT FURTHER ENACTED, that for the whole or any part of any sum subscribed to the said Loan, by any Person or Persons, or Body Politic, which shall be paid in the Principal of the said Domestic Debt, the subscriber or subscribers shall be entitled to a Certificate purporting that the United States owe to the holder or holders thereof, his, her or their Assigns, a sum to

Sec. 5. *And be it further enacted,* That a Commissioner be appointed for each State to reside therein, whose duty it shall be to superintend the subscriptions to the said loan, to open books for the same, to receive the certificates which shall be presented in payment thereof, to liquidate the specie value of such of them as shall not have been before liquidated, to issue the certificates above mentioned in lieu thereof, according to the terms of each subscription, as well for land as stock, to record such as shall be issued for land,[8] to enter in books to be by him kept for that purpose, credits to the respective subscribers to the said loan for the sums to which they shall be respectively entitled, to transfer the said credits upon the said books from time to time as shall be requisite; to pay the interest thereupon as the same shall become due, and generally to observe and perform such directions and

---

be expressed therein, equal to two thirds of the sum so paid, bearing an interest of six per Centum per Annum, payable quarter yearly, and subject to redemption by payments not exceeding in one year, on account both of Principal and Interest, the proportion of seven dollars upon a hundred of the sum mentioned in such Certificate; And to another Certificate purporting that the United States owe to the holder or holders thereof, his, her or their Assigns a sum to be expressed therein, equal to the proportion of twenty six dollars & eighty eight Cents, upon a hundred of the sum so paid, which after the year One thousand eight hundred, shall bear an interest of six per Centum per Annum, payable quarter yearly, and subject to redemption by payments not exceeding in one year on account both of principal and Interest, the proportion of seven dollars, upon a hundred of the sum mentioned in such Certificate: Provided, that it shall not be understood that the United States shall be bound or obliged to redeem in the proportion aforesaid, but it shall be understood only that they have a right so to do.

Sect. 5. AND BE IT FURTHER ENACTED, that for the whole or any part of any sum subscribed to the said Loan, by any Person or Persons, or Body Politic, which shall be paid in the interest of the said Domestic debt, computed to the said last day of December next, or in the said Certificates issued in payment of interest, commonly called Indents of interest, the subscriber or subscribers shall be entitled to a Certificate purporting, that the United States owe to the holder or holders thereof, his, her or their Assigns, a sum to be specified therein, equal to that by him, her or them so paid, bearing an interest of three Per Centum per Annum, payable quarter yearly, and subject to redemption by payment of the sum specified therein, whenever provision shall be made by Law for that purpose.

The new section 4 is an amended version of an amendment proposed by the committee report of June 15.

On July 24 the House agreed to these new sections but amended them by striking out "seven" both times it appears in section 4 and inserting "eight," striking out "twenty six dollars & eighty eight Cents" and inserting "thirty-three dollars and one third of a dollar," striking out "eight hundred" and inserting "seven hundred and ninety seven," and striking out "three" from section 5 and inserting "four." The motions for these amendments were made by Gerry (*NYDG,* July 23; *GUS,* July 24). The Senate disagreed to the last two of these amendments and the House receded from them.

[8] The Senate struck out "as well for land" through "issued for land." This amendment was recommended in the committee report of June 15. The House agreed to it on July 24.

regulations as shall be prescribed to him by the Secretary of the Treasury touching the execution of his office.

SEC. 6. *And be it further enacted,* That the stock which shall be created pursuant to this act, shall be transferrable only on the books of the Treasury, or of the said Commissioners respectively, upon which the credit for the same shall exist at the time of transfer, by the proprietor or proprietors of such stock, his, her or their attorney: But it shall be lawful for the Secretary of the Treasury, by special warrant under his hand and the seal of the Treasury, countersigned by the Comptroller, and registered by the Register, at the request of the respective proprietors, to authorize the transfer of such stock, from the books of one Commissioner to those of another Commissioner, or to those of the Treasury, and from those of the Treasury to those of a Commissioner.

SEC. 7. *And be it further enacted,* That the interest upon the said stock as the same shall become due, shall be payable quarter yearly, that is to say, one fourth part thereof on the last day of March; one other fourth part thereof on the last day of June; one other fourth part thereof on the last day of September; and the remaining fourth part thereof on the last day of December in each year, beginning on the last day of March next ensuing, and payment shall be made wheresoever the credit of[9] the said stock shall exist at the time such interest shall become due, that is to say, at the Treasury, if the credit for the same shall then exist on the books of the Treasury, or at the office of the Commissioner upon whose books such credit shall then exist. But if the interest for one quarter shall not be demanded before the expiration of a third quarter, the same shall be afterwards demandable only at the Treasury.[10]

SEC. 8. *And be it further enacted,* That the monies arising under the revenue laws, which have been, or during the present Session of Congress, may be passed, or so much thereof as may be necessary, shall be, and are hereby pledged and appropriated for the payment of interest on the stock which shall be created by the loan aforesaid, according to the terms of the respective subscriptions thereto, and pursuant to the provisions of this act, until the final redemption of the said stock; any law to the contrary notwithstanding; subject nevertheless to such reservations and priorities as may be requisite to satisfy the appropriations heretofore made, and which during the present Session of Congress may be made by law, including the sums herein before reserved and appropriated. And to the end that the said monies may be inviolably applied in conformity to this act, and may never be diverted to any other purpose, an account shall be kept of the receipts and disposition there-

---

[9] The Senate struck out "of" and inserted "for." The House agreed to this amendment on July 24.

[10] On July 19, the Senate disagreed to a motion to strike out "But if the interest" through "at the Treasury."

of, separate and distinct from the product of any other duties, imposts, excises or taxes whatsoever.[11]

SEC. 9. And as it may happen that some of the creditors of the United States may not think fit to become subscribers to the said loan,

Be it further enacted, That nothing in this act contained shall be construed in any wise to alter, abridge or impair the rights of those creditors of the United States, who shall not subscribe to the said loan, or the contracts upon which their respective claims are founded, but the said contracts and rights shall remain in full force and virtue.

SEC. 10. And that such creditors may not be excluded from a participation in the benefit hereby intended to the creditors of the United States in general, while the said proposed loan shall be depending, and until it shall appear from the event thereof what further or other arrangements may be necessary respecting the said domestic debt;

Be it therefore further enacted, That such of the creditors of the United States as may not subscribe to the said loan, shall nevertheless receive during the year 1791, four[12] per centum on the respective amounts of their respective demands, including interest to the last day of December next,[13] to be paid at the same times, at the same places, and by the same persons as is herein before directed, concerning the interest on the stock which may be created in virtue of the said proposed loan. But as some of the certificates now in circulation have not heretofore been liquidated to specie value, as most of them are greatly subject to counterfeit, and counterfeits have actually taken place in numerous instances, and as embarrassment and imposition might, for these reasons, attend the payment of interest on those certificates in their present form, it shall therefore be necessary to entitle the said creditors to the benefit of the said payment, that those of them who do not possess certificates issued by the Register of the Treasury, for the registered debt, should produce previous to the first day of June next, their respective certificates, either at the Treasury of the United States, or to some one of the Commissioners to be appointed as aforesaid, to the end that the same may be cancelled, and other certificates issued in lieu thereof; which new certificates shall specify the specie amount of those in exchange for which they are given, and shall be otherwise of the like tenor with those heretofore issued by the said Register of the Treasury for the said registered debt, and shall be transferable on the like principles with those directed to be issued on account of the subscriptions to the loan hereby proposed.

---

[11] The Senate struck out this section. The House agreed to this amendment on July 24.

[12] The Senate struck out "four" and inserted "and interest." The House agreed to this amendment on July 24.

[13] The Senate inserted "equal to the interest payable to subscribing Creditors" at this point. The House agreed to this amendment on July 24.

SEC. 11. *And be it further enacted,* That the Commissioners who shall be appointed pursuant to this act, shall respectively be entitled to the following yearly salaries; that is to say,   *Dollars*

The Commissioner for the State of New-Hampshire,	650
The Commissioner for the State of Massachusetts,	1,500[14]
The Commissioner for the State of Connecticut,	1,000
The Commissioner for the State of New-York,	1,500
The Commissioner for the State of New-Jersey,	700
The Commissioner for the State of Pennsylvania,	1,500
The Commissioner for the State of Delaware,	600
The Commissioner for the State of Maryland,	1,000
The Commissioner for the State of Virginia,	1,500
The Commissioner for the State of North-Carolina,	1,000
The Commissioner for the State of South-Carolina,	1,000
The Commissioner for the State of Georgia,	700

Which salaries shall be in full compensation for all services and expences.

SECT. 12. *And be it further enacted,* That the said Commissioners, before they enter upon the execution of their several offices, shall respectively take an oath or affirmation for the diligent and faithful execution of their trust, and shall also become bound with one or more sureties, to the satisfaction of the Secretary of the Treasury, in a penalty not less than five thousand, nor more than ten thousand dollars, with condition for their good behavior in their said offices respectively.[15]

Printed by JOHN FENNO

Broadside Collection, RBkRm, DLC. The amendments are in House Bills, SR, DNA, and are printed in the *SLJ*, 423n, 424, and 430n. All except the last were agreed to by the Senate on July 19. The Senate's actions prior to final passage of its amendments are contained in the amended bill of July 17 and the notes to that document. House actions on Senate amendments, unless otherwise mentioned, are in the *HJ*, pp. 527–28 and 530–34. Senate actions on House amendments are in the *SLJ*, pp. 448–56. Specific Senate votes are included in the notes to the House resolutions of July 24 and 26.

---

[14] The Senate inserted "The Commissioners for the State of Rhode Island and Providence Plantations, 600 Dollars" at this point. This amendment was recommended by the committee report of June 15.

[15] The Senate inserted the following additional sections at this point:

    Section 13 AND WHEREAS a provision for the debts of the respective States by the United States, would be greatly conducive to an orderly, oeconomical and effectual arrangement of the public finances.

    BE IT THEREFORE FURTHER ENACTED, That a loan be proposed, to the amount of twenty one million and five hundred thousand Dollars, and that subscriptions to the said loan be received at the same times and places, and by the same Persons, as in respect to the loan herein before proposed, concerning the domestic debt of the United States. And that the sums which shall be subscribed to the said loan, shall be payable in the Principal and interest of the Certificates or Notes, which, prior to the first day of January last, were issued by the respective States, as acknowledgements or evidences of debts by them respectively owing, except certificates issued by the Commissioners of army accounts in the State of N. Carolina in the year 1786. PROVIDED, that no greater sum shall be received in the certificates of any State, than as follows— That is to say,

	Dollars.
In those of New Hampshire,	300,000.
In those of Massachusetts,	4,000,000.
In those of Rhode Island and Providence Plantations	200,000.
In those of Connecticut,	1,600,000.
In those of New York,	1,200,000.
In those of New Jersey,	800,000.
In those of Pennsylvania,	2,200,000.
In those of Delaware,	200,000.
In those of Maryland,	800,000.
In those of Virginia,	3,500,000.
In those of North Carolina,	2,400,000.
In those of South Carolina,	4,000,000.
In those of Georgia,	300,000.
	21,500,000.

And provided that no such certificate shall be received which from the tenor thereof or from any public record, act or document, shall appear or can be ascertained to have been issued for any purpose other than compensations and expenditures for services or supplies towards the prosecution of the late war, and the defence of the United States, or of some part thereof during the same.

Sect. 14 AND BE IT FURTHER ENACTED, That for two thirds of any sum subscribed to the said loan by any Person or Persons or body-politic which shall be paid in the Principal and interest of the certificates or notes issued as aforesaid by the respective States, the subscriber or subscribers shall be entitled to a certificate purporting that the United States owe to the holder or holders thereof, or his, her or their Assigns, a sum to be expressed therein equal to two thirds of the aforesaid two thirds, bearing an interest of six per centum per Annum payable quarter yearly and subject to redemption by payments not exceeding in one year on account both of principal and interest the proportion of seven dollars upon a hundred of the sum mentioned in such certificate, and to another certificate purporting that the United States owe to the holder or holders thereof, his, her, or their Assigns, a sum to be expressed therein equal to the proportion of twenty six dollars and eighty eight cents upon a hundred of the said two thirds of such sum so subscribed, which after the year one thousand eight hundred shall bear an interest of six per centum per annum payable quarter yearly and subject to redemption by payments not exceeding in one year on account both of principal and interest the proportion of seven dollars upon a hundred of the sum mentioned in such certificate, and that for the remaining third of any sum so subscribed the subscriber or subscribers shall be entitled to a certificate purporting that the United States owe to the holder or holders thereof, his, her or their Assigns, a sum to be expressed therein equal to the said remaining third, bearing an interest of three per cent per annum payable quarter-yearly, and subject to redemption by payment of the sum specified therein whenever provision shall be made by law for that purpose.

Sect. 15 AND BE IT FURTHER ENACTED, That the interest upon the certificates which shall be received in payment of the sums subscribed towards the said loan, shall be computed to the last day of the year one thousand seven hundred and ninety-one inclusively; and the interest upon the stock which shall be created by virtue of the said loan, shall commence or begin to accrue on the first day of the year one thousand seven hundred and ninety two, and shall be payable quarter-yearly, at the same time, and in like manner as the interest on the stock to be created by virtue of the loan above proposed in the domestic debt of the United States.

Sect. 16. AND BE IT FURTHER ENACTED, That if the whole sum allowed to be subscribed in the debt or certificates of any State, as aforesaid, shall not be subscribed within the time for that purpose limited, such State shall be entitled to receive, and shall receive from the United States, an interest per centum per annum, upon so much of the said sum as shall not have been so subscribed equal to that which would have accrued on the deficiency had the same been subscribed, in trust for the non subscribing creditors of such State, who are holders of certificates or notes issued on account of services or supplies towards the prosecution of the late war and the defence of the United States or of some part thereof, to be paid in like manner as the interest on the stock which may be created by virtue of the said loan, and to continue until there shall be a settlement of accounts between the United States and the individual States; and in case a balance shall then appear in favor of such State, until provision shall be made for the said balance.

Sect. 17. But as certain States have respectively issued their own certificates, in exchange for those of the United States, whereby it might happen that interest might be twice payable on the same sums:

BE IT FURTHER ENACTED, That the payment of interest, whether to States or to individuals, in respect to the debt of any State, by which such exchange shall have been made, shall be suspended, until it shall appear to the satisfaction of the Secretary of the Treasury, that certificates issued for that purpose, by such State, have been re-exchanged or redeemed, or until those which shall not have been re-exchanged or redeemed, shall be surrendered to the United States.

Sect. 18 AND BE IT FURTHER ENACTED, That so much of the debt of each State as shall be subscribed to the said loan and the monies (if any) that shall be advanced to the same pursuant to this Act shall be a charge against such State, in account with the United States.

Sect. 19 AND BE IT FURTHER ENACTED, that the monies arising under the Revenue laws, which have been, or during the present session of Congress, may be passed for so much thereof, as may be necessary, shall be, and are hereby pledged and appropriated for the payment of the interest on the Stock which shall be created by the loans aforesaid, pursuant to the provisions of this Act, first paying that which shall arise on the stock created by virtue of the said first mentioned loan, to continue so pledged and appropriated, until the final redemption of the said stock, any law to the contrary notwithstanding, subject nevertheless to such reservations and priorities, as may be requisite to satisfy the appropriations heretofore made, and which during the present session of Congress may be made by law, including the sums herein before reserved and appropriated; and to the end, that the said monies may be inviolably applied in conformity to this act, and may never be diverted to any other purpose, an account shall be kept of the receipts and disposition thereof, separate and distinct from the product of any other duties, imposts, excises and taxes whatsoever, except such as may be hereafter laid, to make good any deficiency which may be found in the product thereof towards satisfying the interest aforesaid.

Sect. 20 AND BE IT FURTHER ENACTED, That the faith of the United States be, and the same is hereby pledged to provide and appropriate hereafter such additional and permanent funds as may be requisite towards supplying any such deficiency, and making full provision for the payment of the interest which shall accrue on the stock to be created by virtue of the loans aforesaid, in conformity to the terms thereof respectively, and according to the tenor of the certificates to be granted for the same pursuant to this act.

Sect. 21. AND BE IT FURTHER ENACTED, That the proceeds of the sales which shall be made of lands in the Western Territory, now belonging, or that may hereafter belong to the United States, shall be, and are hereby appropriated towards sinking or discharging the debts, for the payment whereof the United States now are, or by virtue of this act may be holden, and shall be applied solely to that use until the said debts shall be fully satisfied.

The sections numbered 13, 15, 16, 17, and 20 were derived from the committee report of July 12. Section 21 is an amended version of that recommended in the committee report of June 15.

On July 24, by a recorded vote of 32-29, the House disagreed to a motion to disagree to the amendment adding these sections. The *GUS,* July 24, says this motion was made by Jackson on July 23. Also on July 24, the House disagreed to a motion by Williamson to strike "2,400,000" from the new section 13 and insert "3,000,000" as the amount to be assumed for North Carolina. On July 26, on a motion by White (*NYDA,* July 30), the House inserted the following proviso after the Senate's new section 13:

> *Provided always, and be it further enacted,* That if the total amount of the sums which shall be subscribed to the said loan in the debt of any State within the time limited for receiving subscription thereto, shall exceed the sum by this act allowed to be subscribed within such State, the certificates and credits granted to their respective subscribers, shall bear such proportion to the sums by them respectively subscribed, as the total amount of the said sums shall bear to the whole sum so allowed to be subscribed in the debt of such State within the same; and every subscriber to the said loan shall, at the time of subscribing, deposit with the commissioner the certificates or notes to be loaned by him.

On the same day, by a recorded vote of 45-15, the House disagreed to a motion by Williamson (*NYDA,* July 30) to insert the following at the same point:

> *And provided,* That the original holders of certificates in the several states shall have the exclusive right of subscribing for the space of six months from the time in which the offices shall be opened in the States respectively, and that the whole of their claims shall be funded.

The House then agreed to amend the new section 14 by striking out "seven" both times it appears and inserting "eight," striking out "twenty six dollars and eighty eight cents" and inserting "thirty-three dollars and one third of a dollar," striking out "eight hundred" and inserting "seven hundred and ninety-seven," and striking out "three" and inserting "four."

The House disagreed, by a recorded vote of 25-23, to a motion by Jackson (*NYDG,* July 27) to strike out the new section 16.

By a recorded vote of 34-28, the House then agreed to the amended last Senate amendment inserting the additional sections on assumption.

The Senate disagreed to the last two House amendments and the House receded from them.

Ellsworth Resolution
June 14, 1790

Resolved, That provision shall be made the next session of Congress, for loaning to the United States a sum not exceeding twenty two millions of dollars in the certificates issued by the respective States for services or supplies towards the prosecution of the late war. The certificates which shall be loaned to stand charged to the respective States by whom they were issued, until a liquidation of their accounts with the United States can be compleated.

Senate Simple Resolutions and Motions, SR, DNA, hand of Ellsworth.

Senate Committee Report
June 15, 1790

The Committee to whom was referred the Bill entitled "An Act making provision for the debt of the U. States" beg leave to submit the following report.

That the Bill, in the opinion of your Committee, may be amended by striking out the following words from the third Section, page the 2d. lines 14. 15. & 16 to wit—"Those issued for the payment of interest, commonly called

and insert "And in"

Indents of interest"[1] Also these words "Those which shall be issued for" Also the figures "75" and insert 100—Also the whole of the provision in the last part of the 3d. Section—And then the Bill will read "And in the Bills of credit issued by the authority of the United States in Congress Assembled at the rate of an hundred dollars in the said bills for one dollar in Specie—The Object of this Amendment of your Committee is to destroy the provision in the bill for funding the Indents, and to receive the Old Continental money at an hundred

as

for one, instead of 75 proposed by the Bill.

In the 4th. Sect. third line strike out from the word "entitled" to the word "Or" at the end of the next paragraph inclusive—Also strike out from the word "Sum" in the 6th. line of the next paragraph to the proviso at the end of the Section—And then the bill will read "That for any sum which shall be subscribed to the said Loan by any person or persons, or body politic, the Subscriber or Subscribers shall be entitled To a Certificate purporting that the United States owe to the Holder, or Holders thereof, his, her or their Assigns, the whole of the sum by him, her, or them subscribed; bearing an interest of four per Centum per Annum, payable quarter yearly, and subject to redemption by payments not exceeding in one year, on account both of principal and interest, the proportion of six dollars upon a hundred of the same sum. Provided always, that it shall not be understood, that the U. States shall be bound or obliged to redeem in the proportion aforesaid, but it shall be understood only that they have a right ~~to do~~ so to do.

The design of this Amendment of your Committe is, to discharge the

domestic

Alternatives proposed in the Bill, and to fund the debt of the U. States at an interest of 4 per Cent per Annum.[2]

Sect. 5 Line 7 strike out the words "As well for Land as Stock, to record such as shall be issued for land."

---

[1] On June 21 the Senate disagreed to this amendment. (Maclay, June 21)
[2] On June 21, by a recorded vote of 13–10, the Senate agreed to the previous two paragraphs relative to the fourth section.

The design of this amendment of your Committee is, to discharge the Alternatives proposed in the Bill, and to fund the domestic debt of the U. States at an interest of per Cent per Annum — B

Sect 5 line 7 strike out the words "as well for Land as stock, to read such as shall be issued for Land" a

Sect. 8. line 5 of the same Section strike out the words "according to the terms of the respective subscriptions thereto" a

Sect. 11. Between the 5 & 6 Lines insert "The Commissioner for Rhode Island & Providence Plantations 600" a

To the end of the Bill add "And be it further enacted, that the monies or other effects which shall arise from all Sales hereafter made of the Western Lands belonging or which may belong to the United States, are hereby appropriated as a sinking fund for the debts incurred in the prosecution of the late war, for the payment of which the United States are or may be holden. And shall be applied solely to that use until the said debts shall be fully paid" a

Senate Committee Report, June 15, 1790. (Courtesy of the National Archives)

Sect. 8. Line 5 of the same Section strike out the words "According to the terms of the respective subscriptions thereto."

Sect. 11. Between the 5 & 6 Lines insert "The Commissioner for Rhode Island & Providence Plantations 600."

To the end of the Bill add "And be it further enacted, that the monies or other effects which shall arise from all Sales hereafter made of the Western Lands, belonging or which may belong to the United States, are hereby appropriated as a Sinking fund for the debts incurred in the prosecution of the late War, for the payment of which the United States are or may be holden. And shall be applied solely to that use until the said debts shall be fully paid."[3]

Various Select Committee Reports, SR, DNA, hand of Lee. The amendments agreed to were incorporated into the Senate's intermediate printing of the bill on July 17, but the wording of the amendment to section 4 was changed. Senate actions on the various clauses are indicated by annotations in the hand of Otis.

---

[3] Everything from "Sect. 5" through "fully paid" was adopted by the Senate on June 22.

Senate Committee Report
July 12, 1790

Congress   ~~In Senate July~~   ~~1790~~

Whereas a Provision for the Debt of the respective States by the United States would be greatly conducive to an orderly oeconomical and effectual Arrangement of the publick Finances, would tend to an equal Distribution of Burthens among the Citizens of the several States, would promote more general Justice to the different Classes of publick Creditors, and would serve to give Stability to publick Credit—and whereas the said Debts having been essentially contracted in the prosecution of the late War it is just that such Provision should be made.[1]

~~by the Senate & House of Representatives of the United States of America in~~

Resolved that a Loan be proposed to the Amount of twenty one million

~~Congress assembled~~

~~five hundred thousands~~ of Dollars,[2] and that Subscriptions to the said Loan be received at the same Times and places by the same Persons and upon the same Terms as in Respect to the Loan which may be proposed concerning the

---

[1] The Senate postponed consideration of the preamble on July 13 and agreed to it on July 14 by a recorded vote of 16–10. However, "would tend" through "be made" was omitted when the amended bill was reported on July 17.

[2] On July 13 the Senate disagreed to a motion to strike out "twenty one million of Dollars" and insert a blank.

domestick Debt of the United States subject to the Exceptions and Qualifications hereafter mentioned[3]—And the Sums which shall be subscribed to the said Loan shall be payable in the Principal and Interest of the Certificates or Notes which prior to the first Day of January last were issued by the respective States as acknowledgments or Evidences of Debt by them respectively owing, and which shall appear by Oath or Affirmation (as the Case may be) to have been the Property of an Individual or Individuals or Body politic, other than a State, on the said first Day of January last[4]—Provided that no greater Sum shall be received in the Certificates of any State than as follows that is to say

	Dollars
In those of New Hampshire	300,000
In those of Massachusetts	4,000,000
In those of Rhode Island & Providence Plantns.	200,000
In those of Connecticutt	1,600,000
In those of New York	1,200,000
In those of New Jersey	800,000
In those of Pennsylvania	2,200,000
In those of Delaware	200,000

[3] On July 13 the Senate disagreed to a motion by Schuyler to strike out "and upon the same" through "United States" and insert the following after "mentioned":

And the Subscribers shall receive -a- Certificates for the principal and Interest of the sum so subscribed -purporting- that the united States owe to the holder
one of which certificates shall purport
or holders thereof his her or their Assigns, a sum equal to two thirds of the said sum So subscribed bearing an Interest of Six per Centum per Annum payable quarter yearly a sum or herein after Mentioned, and Subject to redemption by payments not exceeding in one Year on Account both of principal and Interest the proportion of Eight dollars upon a hundred of the sum mentioned in Such certificate. And to another Certificate purporting that the united states owe to the holder or holders thereof his her or their Assigns a sum equal to one third
twenty Six dollars & Eighty Eight Cents.
on every hundred dollars of the sum
1800
of the said Sum so Subscribed which after the year -1797- shall bear an Interest of Six per centum per Annum payable quarter yearly and Subject to redemption by payments not exceeding in one year on account both of principal and Interest the proportion of Eight dollars upon a hundred of the sum mentioned in such certificate Provided always that It shall not be understood that the united States shall be bound or obliged to redeem in the proportion aforesaid, but It shall be understood only that they have a right so to do.
This motion, in the hand of Schuyler, is in Senate Simple Resolutions and Motions, SR, DNA.

On July 14, by a recorded vote of 14–11, the Senate agreed to this portion of the resolution.

[4] On July 14 the Senate disagreed to a motion to insert "and in bills of the new emission money due from the States respectively" at this point.

In those of Maryland	800,000
In those of Virginia	3,200,000[5]
In those of North Carolina	2,200,000[6]
In those of South Carolina	4,000,000
In those of Georgia	300,000
	21,000,000

And provided that no such Certificate shall be received which from the Tenor thereof or from any publick Record Act or Document shall appear or can be ascertained to have been issued for any purpose other than Compensations and Expenditures for Services or Supplies towards the Prosecution of the late War and the Defense of the United States or of some part thereof during the same.[7]

Resolved that the Interest upon the Certificates which shall be received in payment of the Sums subscribed toward the said Loan shall be computed to the last Day of the Year one thousand seven hundred and ninety one inclusively and the Interest upon the Stock which shall be created by Virtue of the said Loan shall commence or begin to accrue on the first Day of the Year one thousand seven hundred and ninety two and shall be payable quarter yearly at the same Time and in like Manner as the Interest on the Stock to be created by Virtue of the Loan that may be proposed in the domestick Debt of the United States.

Resolved that if the whole of the Sum allowed to be subscribed in the Debt or Certificates of any State as aforesd. shall not be subscribed within the Time for that Purpose limited, such State shall be entitled to receive, and shall receive from the United States, at the Rate of four per Centum per Annum[8] upon so much of the said Sum, as shall not have been so subscribed, in trust for the non subscribing Creditors of such State, to be paid in like manner as the Interest on the Stock which may be created by Virtue of the said Loan, and to continue untill there shall be a Settlement of Accounts between the United States and the Individual States—And in Case a Balance shall then appear in favour of such State untill Provision shall be made for the said Balance.[9]

But as certain States have respectively issued their own Certificates, in

---

[5] Strong wrote the figure "2" over another figure, probably "5."
[6] Strong wrote the figure "2" over another figure, probably "4."
[7] On July 14 the Senate disagreed to a motion to strike out this proviso.
[8] On July 14 the Senate disagreed to a motion by Schuyler to strike out "at the Rate of four per Centum per Annum" and insert "An interest per Centum per Annum at the same rate as shall be Allowed to the domestic creditors of the united States." This motion, in the hand of Schuyler, is in Senate Simple Resolutions and Motions, SR, DNA.
[9] On July 14, by a recorded vote of 15–11, the Senate agreed to this paragraph of the report. Maclay, July 14, says Morris and Langdon had moved to strike it out.

exchange for those of the United States whereby it might happen that Interest might be twice payable on the same Sums

Resolved that the payment of Interest whether to States or to individuals in Respect to the Debt of any State by which such Exchange shall have been made, shall be suspended untill it shall appear to the Satisfaction of the Secretary of the Treasury that Certificates, issued for that purpose, by such State, have been re-exchanged or redeemed or untill those which shall not have been reexchanged or redeemed shall be surrendered to the United States.

And it is further Resolved That the Faith of the United States be and the same is hereby pledged to make like Provision for the Payment of Interest on the Amount of the Stock arising from subscriptions to the said Loan,[10] with the Provision which shall be made touching the Loan that may be proposed in the domestick Debt of the United States And so much of the Debt of each State as shall be subscribed to the said Loan shall be a Charge against such State in Account with the United States.

Various Select Committee Reports, SR, DNA, hand of Strong. Senate actions on the report are indicated by annotations in the hand of Otis on a printed copy in the same location.

[10] On July 14 the Senate disagreed to a motion to strike out "from subscriptions to the said Loan" and insert "under this act."

Senate Committee Report
July 16, 1790

The Committee to whom was rifered the Funding Bill, and the Resolves for the Assumption of the States Debts—

REPORT

That having maturely Considered all Circumstances they are of Opinion that
the principal of the _∧~~Continental~~ domestic Debt shoud be funded agreeable to the third Alternative in the Report of the Secretary of the Treasury; And that the
Interest which may be due thereon_∧including Indents be Funded at the rate of three ℔ Ct. per Annum—And that whatever sum the Legislature may think proper to As-
sume ~~on Acct.~~ of the States Debts be funded at the Proportion of two thirds_∧thereof ~~of the Principal and Interest~~ [agreeable] to the 3d. Alternative [in the Secretary's report] And the other 3d. at three ℔ Ct. per Annum.[1]

Your Committee further recommend that the_∧resolution for the Assumption be Added to the funding Bill and the whole made One system.[2]

[1] The report to this point was agreed to by a vote of 20–4. (Maclay, July 16)
[2] This clause of the report was agreed to by a recorded vote of 15–11.

Various Select Committee Reports, SR, DNA, hand of Butler. Drafts of the report are in the Butler Papers, PHi. The document is torn where it was folded so that some words are missing; the bracketed words are from a clerk's copy in Senate Records. Otis noted Senate agreement with the various clauses on the report.

Amended Funding Bill [HR-63]
July 17, 1790

An ACT making Provision for the Debt of the United States

SEC. 1. WHEREAS justice and the support of public credit require, that provision should be made for fulfilling the engagements of the United States, in respect to their foreign debt, and for funding their domestic debt upon equitable and satisfactory terms:

Be it enacted by the Senate and House of Representatives of the United States of America, in Congress assembled, That reserving out of the monies which have arisen since the last day of December last past, and which shall hereafter arise from the duties on goods, wares and merchandize imported into the United States, and on the tonnage of ships or vessels, the yearly sum of six hundred thousand dollars, or so much thereof as may be appropriated from time to time, towards the support of the government of the United States, and their common defence, the residue of the said monies, or so much thereof as may be necessary, as the same shall be received in each year, next after the sum reserved as aforesaid, shall be, and is hereby appropriated to the payment of the interest which shall from time to time become due on the loans heretofore made by the United States in foreign countries; and also to the payment of interest on such further loans as may be obtained for discharging the arrears of interest thereupon, and the whole or any part of the principal thereof; to continue so appropriated until the said loans, as well those already made as those which may be made in virtue of this act, shall be fully satisfied, pursuant to the contracts relating to the same, any law to the contrary notwithstanding. *And provided,* That nothing herein contained, shall be construed to annul or alter any appropriation by law made prior to the passing of this act.

SEC. 2. And as new loans are and will be necessary for the payment of the aforesaid arrears of interest, and the instalments of the principal of the said foreign debt due and growing due, and may also be found expedient for effecting an entire alteration in the state of the same:

Be it further enacted, That the President of the United States be, and he is hereby authorized, to cause to be borrowed on behalf of the United States, a sum or sums, not exceeding in the whole twelve million of dollars; and that so much of this sum as may be necessary to the discharge of the said arrears and instalments, and (if it can be effected upon terms advantageous to the United States) to the paying off the whole of the said foreign debt be appropriated solely to those purposes: And the President is moreover further authorized to cause to be made such other contracts respecting the said debt as shall be found for the interest of the said States. *Provided nevertheless,* That no engagement nor contract shall be entered into, which shall preclude the United States from reimbursing any sum or sums borrowed within fifteen years after the same shall have been lent or advanced.

SEC. 3. And whereas it is desirable to adapt the nature of the provision to be made for the domestic debt, to the present circumstances of the United States, as far as it shall be found practicable consistently with good faith and the rights of the creditors; which can only be done by a voluntary loan on their part:

Be it therefore further enacted, That a loan to the full amount of the said domestic debt be, and the same is hereby proposed; and that books for receiving subscriptions to the said loan be opened at the Treasury of the United States, and by a commissioner to be appointed in each of the said States, on the first day of September[1] next, and to continue open until the last day of August[2] following, inclusively; and that the sums which shall be subscribed thereto, be payable in certificates issued for the said debt according to their specie value, and computing the interest upon such as bear interest to the last day of December next, inclusively; which said certificates shall be of these several descriptions, to wit:

Those issued by the Register of the Treasury.

Those issued by the Commissioners of Loans in the several States, including certificates given pursuant to the act of Congress of the second January, 1779, for bills of credit of the several emissions of the twentieth of May, 1777, and the eleventh of April, 1778.

Those issued by the Commissioners for the adjustment of the accounts of the Quarter-Master, Commissary, Hospital, Cloathing and Marine Departments.

Those issued by the Commissioners for the adjustment of accounts in the respective States.

Those issued by the late and present Paymaster-General, or Commissioner of Army Accounts.

Those issued for the payment of interest, commonly called indents of interest.

And in the bills of credit issued by the authority of the United States in

---

[1] The Senate struck out "September" and inserted "October."
[2] The Senate struck out "August" and inserted "September."

Congress assembled, at the rate of one hundred[3] dollars in the said bills, for one dollar in specie.

SEC. 4. *And be it further enacted,* That for the whole or any part of any sum subscribed to the said loan, by any person or persons, or body-politic, which shall be paid in the principal[4] of the said domestic debt, the subscriber or subscribers shall be entitled to a certificate purporting that the United States owe to the holder or holders thereof, his, her, or their assigns, a sum to be expressed therein equal to two thirds of[5] the sum so paid, bearing an interest of 6 per centum per annum, payable quarter-yearly, and subject to redemption by payments not exceeding in one year on account both of principal and interest, the proportion of seven dollars upon a hundred of the sum mentioned in such certificate; and to another certificate purporting that the United States owe to the holder or holders thereof, his, her or their assigns a sum to be expressed therein equal to the proportion of twenty-six dollars and eighty-eight cents[6] upon a hundred of the sum so paid, which after the year one thousand eight hundred shall bear an interest of six per centum per annum, payable quarter-yearly, and subject to redemption by payments not exceeding in one year on account both of principal and interest the proportion of seven dollars upon a hundred of the sum mentioned in such certificate:[7] *Provided,* That it shall not be understood that the United States shall be bound or obliged to redeem in the proportion aforesaid, but it shall be understood only that they have a right so to do.[8]

---

[3] On July 19, by a recorded vote of 16–9, the Senate disagreed to a motion to strike out "one hundred" and insert "forty." The Senate then disagreed to a motion to substitute "seventy-five" for "one hundred."

[4] On July 19, by a recorded vote of 17–8, the Senate disagreed to a motion to insert "and interest" at this point.

[5] On July 19, by a recorded vote of 19–6, the Senate disagreed to a motion to strike out "two thirds of."

[6] On July 19, by a recorded vote of 15–9, the Senate disagreed to a motion to strike out "twenty-six dollars and eighty-eight cents" and insert "thirty-three and one third dollars."

[7] On July 19, by a recorded vote of 19–6, the Senate disagreed to a motion to strike out "and to another certificate" through "such certificate."

[8] On July 19, by a recorded vote of 17–8, the Senate disagreed to a motion to amend this section to read as follows:

And be it further enacted, That for the whole or any part of any sum subscribed to the said loan by any person or persons, or body politic, which shall be paid in the principal of the said domestic debt, the subscriber or subscribers shall be entitled to a certificate purporting that the United States owe to the holder or holders thereof, his, her or their assigns, the whole of the sum by him, her or them subscribed, bearing an interest of four per centum per annum, payable quarter yearly, and subject to redemption by payments, not exceeding in one year, on account both of principal and interest, the proportion of six dollars upon a hundred of the said sum: Provided, that it shall not be understood, that the United States shall be bound or obliged to redeem in the proportion aforesaid, but it shall be understood only that they have a right so to do.

SEC. 5. *And be it further enacted,* That for the whole or any part of any sum subscribed to the said loan by any person or persons or body-politic, which shall be paid in the interest of the said domestic debt computed to the said last day of December next, or in the said certificates issued in payment of interest commonly called Indents of interest, the subscriber or subscribers shall be entitled to a certificate purporting that the United States owe to the holder or holders thereof, his, her or their assigns, a sum to be specified therein equal to that by him, her or them so paid, bearing an interest of three[9] per centum per annum, payable quarter-yearly, and subject to redemption by payment of the sum specified therein, whenever provision shall be made by law for that purpose.[10]

SEC. 6. *And be it further enacted,* That a commissioner be appointed for each State to reside therein, whose duty it shall be to superintend the subscriptions to the said loan, to open books for the same, to receive the certificates which shall be presented in payment thereof, to liquidate the specie value of such of them as shall not have been before liquidated, to issue the certificates above mentioned in lieu thereof, according to the terms of each subscription, to enter in books to be by him kept for that purpose, credits to the respective subscribers to the said loan for the sums to which they shall be respectively entitled, to transfer the said credits upon the said books from time to time as shall be requisite; to pay the interest thereupon as the same shall become due, and generally to observe and perform such directions and regulations as shall be prescribed to him by the Secretary of the Treasury touching the execution of his office.

SEC. 7. *And be it further enacted,* That the stock which shall be created pursuant to this act, shall be transferable only on the books of the Treasury, or of the said Commissioners respectively, upon which the credit for the same shall exist at the time of transfer, by the proprietor or proprietors of such stock, his, her, or their attorney: But it shall be lawful for the Secretary of the Treasury, by special warrant under his hand and the seal of the Treasury, countersigned by the Comptroller, and registered by the Register, at the request of the respective proprietors, to authorize the transfer of such stock, from the books of one Commissioner to those of another Commissioner, or to those of the Treasury, and from those of the Treasury to those of a Commissioner.

SEC. 8. *And be it further enacted,* That the interest upon the said stock as the same shall become due, shall be payable quarter-yearly, that is to say, one fourth part thereof on the last day of March; one other fourth part thereof on

---

[9] On July 19, by recorded votes of 20–5 and 17–8, the Senate disagreed to motions to strike out "three" and insert "six" and "four" respectively. The motion for "six" was made by Morris. (Maclay, July 19)

[10] The Senate agreed on July 19 to the amended sections 4 and 5.

the last day of June; one other fourth part thereof on the last day of September; and the remaining fourth part thereof on the last day of December in each year, beginning on the last day of March next ensuing, and payment shall be made wheresoever the credit for the said stock shall exist at the time such interest shall become due, that is to say, at the Treasury, if the credit for the same shall then exist on the books of the Treasury, or at the office of the Commissioner upon whose books such credit shall then exist. But if the interest for one quarter shall not be demanded before the expiration of a third quarter, the same shall be afterwards demandable only at the Treasury.

SEC. 9. And as it may happen that some of the creditors of the United States may not think fit to become subscribers to the said loan,

Be it further enacted, That nothing in this act contained shall be construed in any wise to alter, abridge or impair the rights of those creditors of the United States, who shall not subscribe to the said loan, or the contracts upon which their respective claims are founded, but the said contracts and rights shall remain in full force and virtue.

SEC. 10. And that such creditors may not be excluded from a participation in the benefit hereby intended to the creditors of the United States in general, while the said proposed loan shall be depending, and until it shall appear from the event thereof what further or other arrangements may be necessary respecting the said domestic debt:

Be it therefore further enacted, That such of the creditors of the United States as may not subscribe to the said loan, shall nevertheless receive during the year 1791, [11] per centum on the respective amounts of their respective demands, including interest to the last day of December next,[12] to be paid at the same times, at the same places, and by the same persons as is herein before directed, concerning the interest on the stock which may be created in virtue of the said proposed loan. But as some of the certificates now in circulation have not heretofore been liquidated to specie value, as most of them are greatly subject to counterfeit, and counterfeits have actually taken place in numerous instances, and as embarrassment and imposition might, for these reasons, attend the payment of interest on those certificates in their present form, it shall therefore be necessary to entitle the said creditors to the benefit of the said payment, that those of them who do not possess certificates issued by the Register of the Treasury, for the registered debt, should produce previous to the first day of June next, their respective certificates, either at the Treasury of the United States, or to some one of the Commissioners to be

---

[11] On July 20 the Senate inserted "a rate   " at this point. The *SLJ*, p. 435n, says the words "an interest" were struck out, but they do not appear in the bill, and a motion to insert them in the committee report of July 12 was disagreed to on July 14.

[12] On July 20 the Senate inserted "equal to the interest payable to subscribing Creditors" at this point.

appointed as aforesaid, to the end that the same may be cancelled, and other certificates issued in lieu thereof; which new certificates shall specify the specie amount of those in exchange for which they are given, and shall be otherwise of the like tenor with those heretofore issued by the said Register of the Treasury for the said registered debt, and shall be transferable on the like principles with those directed to be issued on account of the subscriptions to the loan hereby proposed.

SEC. 11. *And be it further enacted,* That the monies arising under the revenue laws, which have been, or during the present session of Congress, may be passed or so much thereof, as may be necessary, shall be, and are hereby pledged and appropriated for the payment of the interest on the stock which shall be created by the loans aforesaid, pursuant to the provisions of this act, first paying that which shall arise on the stock created by virtue of the said first mentioned loan, to continue so pledged and appropriated, until the final redemption of the said stock, any law to the contrary notwithstanding, subject nevertheless to such reservations and priorities, as may be requisite to satisfy the appropriations heretofore made, and which during the present session of Congress may be made by law, including the sums herein before reserved and appropriated; and to the end, that the said monies may be inviolably applied in conformity to this act, and may never be diverted to any other purpose, an account shall be kept of the receipts and disposition thereof, separate and distinct from the product of any other duties, imposts, excises and taxes whatsoever, except such as may be hereafter laid, to make good any deficiency which may be found in the product thereof towards satisfying the interest aforesaid.

SEC. 12. *And be it further enacted,* That the faith of the United States be, and the same is hereby pledged to provide and appropriate hereafter such additional and permanent funds as may be requisite towards supplying any such deficiency, and making full provision for the payment of the interest which shall accrue on the stock to be created by virtue of the loans aforesaid, in conformity to the terms thereof respectively, and according to the tenor of the certificates to be granted for the same pursuant to this act.

SEC. 13. *And be it further enacted,* That the proceeds of the sales which shall be made of lands in the Western Territory, now belonging, or that may hereafter belong to the United States, shall be, and are hereby appropriated towards sinking or discharging the debts, for the payment whereof the United States now are, or by virtue of this act may be holden, and shall be applied solely to that use until the said debts shall be fully satisfied.[13]

SEC. 14. *And be it further enacted,* That the Commissioners who shall be appointed pursuant to this act, shall respectively be entitled to the following yearly salaries; that is to say,

---

[13] On July 20 the Senate agreed to move sections 11–13 to the end of the bill and renumber them as sections 19–21.

	Dollars.
The Commissioner for the State of New-Hampshire,	650
The Commissioner for the State of Massachusetts,	1,500
The Commissioner for the State of Rhode-Island and Providence Plantations	600
The Commissioner for the State of Connecticut,	1,000
The Commissioner for the State of New-York,	1,500
The Commissioner for the State of New-Jersey,	700
The Commissioner for the State of Pennsylvania,	1,500
The Commissioner for the State of Delaware,	600
The Commissioner for the State of Maryland,	1,000
The Commissioner for the State of Virginia,	1,500
The Commissioner for the State of North-Carolina,	1,000
The Commissioner for the State of South-Carolina,	1,000
The Commissioner for the State of Georgia,	700

Which salaries shall be in full compensation for all services and expences.

SEC. 15. *And be it further enacted,* That the said Commissioners, before they enter upon the execution of their several offices, shall respectively take an oath or affirmation for the diligent and faithful execution of their trust, and shall also become bound[14] with one or more sureties, to the satisfaction of the Secretary of the Treasury, in a penalty not less than five thousand, nor more than ten thousand dollars, with condition for their good behaviour in their said offices respectively.

SEC. 16. And whereas a provision for the debts of the respective States by the United States, would be greatly conducive to an orderly, oeconomical and effectual arrangement of the public finances.

Be it therefore further enacted, That a loan be proposed, to the amount of twenty-one million and five hundred thousand dollars, and that subscriptions to the said loan be received at the same times and places, and by the same persons, as in respect to the loan herein before proposed, concerning the domestic debt of the United States. And that the sums which shall be subscribed to the said loan, shall be payable in the principal and interest of the certificates or notes, which, prior to the first day of January last, were issued by the respective States, as acknowledgements or evidences of debts by them respectively owing. Provided, that no greater sum shall be received in the certificates of any State, than as follows—That is to say,

Dollars.

In those of New-Hampshire,   300,000[15]

---

[14] According to the *SLJ*, p. 436n, on July 20 the Senate inserted "except certificates issued by the Commissioners of army accounts in the State of North Carolina in the year 1786" at this point, but the phrase actually appears in the new section 13 added by the Senate.

[15] On July 20 the Senate disagreed to a motion to strike out "300,000" and insert "400,000."

In those of Massachusetts,	4,000,000
In those of Rhode-Island and Providence Plantations,	200,000
In those of Connecticut,	1,600,000
In those of New-York,	1,200,000[16]
In those of New-Jersey,	800,000
In those of Pennsylvania,	2,200,000
In those of Delaware,	200,000
In those of Maryland,	800,000
In those of Virginia,	3,500,000
In those of North-Carolina,	2,400,000
In those of South-Carolina,	4,000,000
In those of Georgia,	300,000
	21,500,000

And provided that no such certificate shall be received which from the tenor thereof or from any public record, act or document, shall appear or can be ascertained to have been issued for any purpose other than compensations and expenditures for services or supplies towards the prosecution of the late war, and the defence of the United States, or of some part thereof during the same.

SEC. 17. *And be it further enacted,* That for two thirds of any sum subscribed to the said loan by any person or persons or body-politic which shall be paid in the principal and interest. of the certificates or notes issued as aforesaid by the respective States, the subscriber or subscribers shall be entitled to a certificate purporting that the United States owe to the holder or holders thereof, or his, her or their assigns, a sum to be expressed therein equal to two thirds of the aforesaid two thirds, bearing an interest of six per centum per annum payable quarter-yearly and subject to redemption by payments not exceeding in one year on account both of principal and interest the proportion of seven dollars upon a hundred of the sum mentioned in such certificate, and to another certificate purporting that the United States owe to the holder or holders thereof, his, her, or their assigns, a sum to be expressed therein equal to the proportion of twenty-six dollars and eighty-eight cents upon a hundred of the said two thirds of such sum so subscribed, which after the year one thousand eight hundred shall bear an interest of six per centum per annum payable quarter-yearly and subject to redemption by payments not exceeding in one year on account both of principal and interest the proportion of seven dollars upon a hundred of the sum mentioned in such certificate, and

---

[16] On July 20 the Senate disagreed to a motion to strike out "1,200,000" and insert "1,400,000."

that for the remaining third of any sum so subscribed the subscriber or subscribers shall be entitled to a certificate purporting that the United States owe to the holder or holders thereof, his, her or their assigns, a sum to be expressed therein equal to the said remaining third, bearing an interest of three per centum per annum payable quarter-yearly, and subject to redemption by payment of the sum specified therein whenever provision shall be made by law for that purpose.

SEC. 18. *And be it further enacted,* That the interest upon the certificates which shall be received in payment of the sums subscribed towards the said loan, shall be computed to the last day of the year one thousand seven hundred and ninety-one inclusively; and the interest upon the stock which shall be created by virtue of the said loan, shall commence or begin to accrue on the first day of the year one thousand seven hundred and ninety-two, and shall be payable quarter yearly, at the same time, and in like manner as the interest on the stock to be created by virtue of the loan above proposed in the domestic debt of the United States.

SEC. 19. *And be it further enacted,* That if the whole sum allowed to be subscribed in the debt or certificates of any State, as aforesaid, shall not be subscribed within the time for that purpose limited,[17] such State shall be entitled to receive, and shall receive from the United States, at the rate of   [18] per centum per annum, upon so much of the said sum as shall not have been so subscribed,[19] in trust for the non subscribing creditors of such State, who are holders of certificates or notes issued on account of services or supplies towards the prosecution of the late war and the defence of the United States or of some part thereof, to be paid in like manner as the interest on the stock which may be created by virtue of the said loan, and to continue until there shall be a settlement of accounts between the United States and the individual States; and in case a balance shall then appear in favor of such State, until provision shall be made for the said balance.[20]

SEC. 20. But as certain States have respectively issued their own certificates, in exchange for those of the United States, whereby it might happen that interest might be twice payable on the same sums:

Be it further enacted, That the payment of interest, whether to States or to

---

[17] On July 20 the Senate disagreed to a motion to insert "The Commissioner to be appointed for" at this point.

[18] On July 20 the Senate struck out "at the rate of   " and inserted "and Interest."

[19] On July 20 the Senate inserted "equal to that which would have accrued on the deficiency had the same been subscribed" at this point.

[20] On July 20 the Senate disagreed to motions to strike out this section and to insert the following at this point:

Provided always that each State which shall receive any Interest in trust as aforesaid shall report to the Secretary of the Treasury (annually) the expenditure of such Interest.

individuals, in respect to the debt of any State, by which such exchange shall have been made, shall be suspended, until it shall appear to the satisfaction of the Secretary of the Treasury, that certificates issued for that purpose, by such State, have been re-exchanged or redeemed, or until those which shall not have been re-exchanged or redeemed, shall be surrendered to the United States.

SEC. 21. *And be it further enacted,* That so much of the debt of each State as shall be subscribed to the said loan,[21] shall be a charge against such State, in account with the United States.[22]

Printed by JOHN FENNO

House Bills, SR, DNA. The amendments are printed in the *SLJ*, pp. 423n–430, 432–436n. Most of them were noted on the bill by Otis. These amendments affect the language of this intermediate Senate version of the bill. The Senate's final amendments were written to correspond to the House engrossed bill of June 2 and may be found in the notes to that document.

---

[21] On July 20 the Senate agreed to insert "and the Monies (if any) that shall be advanced to the same pursuant to this Act" at this point.

[22] On July 20, by a recorded vote of 14–12, the Senate disagreed to a motion to strike sections 16–21 from the bill.

House Resolutions
July 24 and 26, 1790

IN THE HOUSE OF REPRESENTATIVES OF THE UNITED STATES, SATURDAY, the 24th of July 1790.

RESOLVED, That this House do agree to the first, second, third, fourth, fifth, sixth, seventh, eighth, ninth, tenth, eleventh, twelfth and thirteenth amendments, with amendments to the said seventh amendment, as follow. In the clauses proposed to be inserted by the Senate, in lieu of the fourth section:

Line 12th, strike out *"seven,"* and insert "eight."[1]

Line 17th, strike out *"twenty-six dollars and eighty-eight cents,"* and insert "thirty-three dollars, and one third of a dollar."[2]

Line 19th, strike out *"eight hundred,"* and insert "seven hundred and ninety-seven."[3]

---

[1] The Senate agreed to this amendment.

[2] The Senate agreed to this amendment by a recorded vote of 12–12, decided by the vice president.

[3] The Senate agreed to this amendment by a recorded vote of 12–12, decided by the vice president, but decided to reconsider by a recorded vote of 16–8 and then disagreed to the amendment by a recorded vote of 16–8. The House receded from it by a recorded vote of 33–27, in which Laurance called for the yeas and nays (*NYJ*, Aug. 3).

Line 23d, strike out *"seven,"* and insert "eight."[4]
Line 40th, strike out *"three,"* and insert "four."[5]

MONDAY, the 26th of July 1790.

The House resumed the consideration of the amendments proposed by the Senate to the Bill, entitled, "An Act making provision for the debt of the United States:" Whereupon

RESOLVED, That this House do agree to the last amendment for adding to the end of the Bill sundry clauses, "making a provision for the debts of the respective States;" with the following amendments, to wit: to the end of the first clause or section of the said amendment, add "Provided also, and be it further enacted, That if the total amount of the sums which shall be subscribed to the said loan, in the debt of any State within the time limitted for receiving subscriptions thereto, shall exceed the sum by this Act allowed to be subscribed within such State, the certificates and credits granted to the respective subscribers, shall bear such proportion to the sums by them respec-tively subscribed, as the total amount of the said sums shall bear to the whole sum so allowed to be subscribed in the debt of such State within the same: And every subscriber to the said loan, shall, at the time of subscribing, deposit with the Commissioner, the certificates or notes to be loaned by him."[6]

To the second clause or section:

Line 13th, strike out *"seven,"* and insert "eight."[7]

Lines 18th and 19th, strike out *"twenty-six dollars and eighty eight cents,"* and insert "thirty-three dollars, and one third of a dollar."[8]

Line 21st, strike out *"eight hundred,"* and insert "seven hundred and ninety-seven."[9]

Line 25th, strike out *"seven,"* and insert "eight."[10]

Line 31st, strike out *"three,"* and insert *"four."*[11]

Printed by JOHN FENNO

Other Records: Yeas and nays, SR, DNA. Senate actions on the amendments were noted on the document by Otis. The recorded votes are printed in the *SLJ,* pp. 448–56, and the *HJ,* pp. 539–41. The House actions are keyed to legislation as printed in this volume in the notes to the June 2 bill.

---

[4] The Senate agreed to this amendment.
[5] The Senate disagreed to this amendment by a recorded vote of 16–8, and the House receded from it by a recorded vote of 33–27.
[6] The Senate agreed to this amendment.
[7] The Senate agreed to this amendment.
[8] The Senate agreed to this amendment by a recorded vote of 13–11.
[9] The Senate disagreed to this amendment by a recorded vote of 13–11, and the House receded from it.
[10] The Senate agreed to this amendment by a recorded vote of 12–12, decided by the vice president.
[11] The Senate disagreed to this amendment by a recorded vote of 16–8, and the House receded from it.

Georgia Bill [HR-94]

Calendar

Date	House	Senate
1790		
Aug. 2	Jackson gave notice of intention to present a "bill to provide for the assumption of three hundred thousand dollars State debt, on account of the State of Georgia, in addition to the sum in the Funding Bill."[1]	
Aug. 3	On a motion by Jackson,[2] committee to prepare a bill appointed (Jackson, Page, and Trumbull); Jackson presented "a bill making further provision for the debt of the United States, so far as respects the assumption of the debt of the state of Georgia," which was read.	
Aug. 4	Read; debated and amended in COWH; amendments agreed to by House; third reading disagreed to by one vote.[3]	

[1] *GUS*, Aug. 4.
[2] *NYDG, GUS*, Aug. 4.
[3] *NYDG*, Aug. 5.

Hospitals and Harbors Bill [HR-22]

Calendar

Date	House	Senate
1789		
July 20	On a motion by Smith (S.C.),[1] committee appointed (Smith, Clymer, and Carroll) to prepare a bill "providing for the establishment of Hospitals for sick and disabled seamen and for the regulation of harbours."	
Aug. 27	Smith presented a bill, which was read; bill provided "that hospitals shall be established and maintained in such sea port towns of the United States as the President shall direct, by a deduction from the wages of Seamen, which Captains and commanders of vessels shall pay to the officers of the customs at each entry of their vessels."[2]	
Aug. 28	Read; committed to COWH.	
Sept. 15	Postponed as order of the day.	
Sept. 16	Postponed until second session.	

[1] *GUS*, July 22.
[2] *NYDA*, Aug. 28.

Impost Act [HR-2]

July 4, 1789

An Act for laying a duty on Goods, Wares, and Merchandises, imported into the United States

Whereas it is necessary for the support of Government, for the discharge of the Debts of the United States, and the encouragement and protection of Manufactures, that duties be laid on Goods, Wares, and Merchandizes imported.

[1] Be it enacted by the Senate and House of Representatives of the United States of America, in Congress assembled, That from and after the first day of August next ensuing, the several duties herein after mentioned shall be laid on the following Goods, Wares, and Merchandizes imported into the United States from any foreign port or place, that is to say;

On all distilled spirits of Jamaica proof imported from any Kingdom or Country whatsoever per Gallon ten Cents; On all other distilled spirits per Gallon eight Cents; On Molasses per Gallon two and a half Cents; On Madeira Wine per Gallon eighteen Cents; On all other Wines per Gallon ten Cents; On every Gallon of Beer, Ale or Porter in Casks five Cents; On all Cyder, Beer, Ale, or Porter in bottles per dozen twenty Cents; On Malt per bushel ten Cents; On brown Sugars per pound one Cent; On loaf Sugars per pound three Cents; On all other Sugars per pound one and a half Cents; On Coffee per pound two and a half Cents; On Cocoa per pound one Cent; On all Candles of Tallow per pound two Cents; On all Candles of Wax or Spermaceti per pound six Cents; On Cheese per pound four Cents; On Soap per pound two Cents; On Boots per pair fifty Cents; On all Shoes, Slippers, or Goloshoes made of leather per pair seven Cents; On all Shoes or Slippers made of Silk or Stuff per pair ten Cents; On Cables for every one hundred and twelve pounds seventy five Cents; On tarred Cordage for every one hundred and twelve pounds seventy five Cents On untarred ditto, and Yarn for every one hundred and twelve pounds ninety Cents; On Twine or Packthread, for every one hundred and twelve pounds two hundred Cents; On all Steel unwrought for every one hundred and twelve pounds fifty six Cents; On all Nails and Spikes per pound one Cent; On Salt per bushel six Cents; On manufactured Tobacco per pound six Cents; On Snuff per pound ten Cents; On Indigo per pound sixteen Cents; On Wool and Cotton Cards per dozen fifty Cents; On Coal per bushel two Cents; On Pickled Fish per barrel seventy five Cents; On dried Fish per quintal fifty Cents; On all Teas imported from China or India in Ships built in the United States, and belonging to a Citizen or Citizens thereof, or in Ships or Vessels built in foreign Countries, and on the sixteenth day of May last wholly the property of a Citizen or Citizens of the United States, and so continuing until the time of importation, as follows; On Bohea Tea per pound six Cents; On all Souchong or other black Teas per pound ten Cents; On all hyson Teas per pound twenty Cents; On all other green Teas per pound twelve Cents; On all Teas imported from Europe in Ships or Vessels built in the United States, and belonging wholly to a Citizen or Citizens thereof, or in Ships or Vessels built in foreign Countries, and on the sixteenth day of May last wholly the property of a Citizen or Citizens of the United States, and so continuing until the time of importation, as follows; On Bohea Tea per pound eight Cents; On all Souchong and other black Teas per pound thirteen Cents; On all Hyson Teas per pound twenty-six Cents; On all other green Teas per pound sixteen Cents; On all Teas imported in any other manner than as abovementioned as follows; On Bohea Tea per pound fifteen Cents; On all Souchong or other black Teas per pound twenty two Cents; On all Hyson Teas per pound forty five Cents; On all other green Teas per pound twenty seven Cents; On all Goods, Wares, and Merchandizes other than Teas, imported from China or India in Ships not built in the United States, and not wholly the property of a Citizen or Citizens thereof, nor in Vessels built in foreign Countries, and on the sixteenth day of May last wholly the property of a Citizen or Citizens of the United States, and so continuing until the time of importation, twelve and a half per Centum ad valorem; On all looking Glasses, Window and other Glass (except black quart bottles) On all China, Stone, and Earthen ware, On Gunpowder, On all Paints ground in Oil, On Shoe and Knee buckles, On gold and Silver lace, and on gold and Silver leaf, ten per Centum ad-valorem; On all blank Books, on all writing, printing, or wrapping paper, paper hangings, and paste board, on all Cabinet Wares, on all Buttons, on all Saddles, on all gloves of leather, on all Hats of beaver, fur, wool, or mixture of either, on all millinary ready made, on all castings of iron, and upon slit and rolled iron, on all leather tanned or tawed, and all manufacture of leather, except such as shall be otherwise rated, on Canes, walking Sticks, and whips, on cloathing ready made, on all brushes, on gold, silver and plated ware, and on jewellery and paste work, On anchors, and on all wrought tin and pewter ware, seven and a half per Centum advalorem; On playing Cards per pack ten Cents; On every Coach, Chariot, or other four wheel carriage, and on every chaise, solo, or other two wheel carriage, or parts thereof, fifteen per Centum advalorem; On all other goods, Wares, and merchandize, five per Centum on the value thereof, at the time and place of importation, except as follows; Saltpetre, Tin in pigs, Tin plates, Lead, old Pewter, Brass, Iron and Brass wire, Copper in plates, Wool, Cotton, dying woods, and dying Drugs, raw hides, Beaver and all other Furrs and deer skins.

[2] AND BE IT FURTHER ENACTED BY THE AUTHORITY AFORESAID, That from and after the first day of December, which shall be in the Year One thousand seven hundred and ninety, there shall be laid a duty on every one hundred and twelve pounds weight of hemp imported as aforesaid of sixty Cents, and on Cotton per pound three Cents.

[3] AND BE IT ENACTED BY THE AUTHORITY AFORESAID, That all the duties paid or secured to be paid upon any of the goods, Wares, and Merchandizes as aforesaid, except on distilled Spirits other than Brandy and Geneva, shall be returned or discharged upon such of the said goods, Wares, or Merchandizes, as shall within twelve months after payment made, or security given, be exported to any Country, without the limits of the United States, as settled by the late treaty of peace, except one per Centum on the amount of the said duties, in consideration of the expence which shall have accrued by the entry and safe keeping thereof.

[4] AND BE IT ENACTED BY THE AUTHORITY AFORESAID That there shall be allowed and paid on every quintal of dried, and on every barrel of pickled Fish of the Fisheries of the United States, and on every barrel of salted provision of the United States exported to any Country without the limits thereof, in lieu of a drawback of the duties imposed on the importation of the Salt employed and expended therein, vizt. On every quintal of dried fish five Cents; On every barrel of pickled fish five Cents, On every barrel of salted Provision five Cents.

[5] AND BE IT FURTHER ENACTED BY THE AUTHORITY AFORESAID, That a discount of ten per Cent on all the duties imposed by this Act, shall be allowed on such goods, Wares, and Merchandizes, as shall be imported in Vessels built in the United States, and which shall be wholly the property of a Citizen or Citizens thereof, or in Vessels built in foreign Countries, and on the sixteenth day of May last, wholly the property of a Citizen or Citizens of the United States, and so continuing until the time of importation.

[6] AND BE IT FURTHER ENACTED BY THE AUTHORITY AFORESAID That this Act shall continue and be in force until the first day of June, which shall be in the Year of our Lord, One thousand seven hundred and ninety six, and from thence until the end of the next succeeding Session of Congress, which shall be held thereafter, and no longer.

FREDERICK AUGUSTUS MUHLENBERG
Speaker of the House of Representatives
JOHN ADAMS
Vice-President of the United States,
and President of the Senate

Approved
July 4th. 1789   GO. WASHINGTON
President of the United States

I certify that this Act did originate
in the House of Representatives.
JOHN BECKLEY Clerk

Enrolled Acts, RG 11, DNA.

Calendar

Date	House	Senate
1789		
Apr. 8	*Resolution* on impost and tonnage presented in COWH by *Madison* and debated; motion by Boudinot, to fill blanks in Madison resolution in accord with recommendations by Congress in 1783, which laid a 5% tax on all imported goods and an additional duty on certain enumerated articles, postponed on a motion by White, seconded by Page. [1]	
Apr. 9	*Resolution* on impost presented by *Fitzsimons,* seconded by Schureman, and debated with Madison	

[1] *NYDA,* Apr. 9; *CR,* Apr. 8, 9.

Date	House	Senate
1789		

resolution; subject was
whether to place a duty
on specific enumerated articles in order to encourage manufactures, or to
establish a temporary tax
of a set percentage on all
imports as an immediate
source of revenue; motion
by Madison, to combine
Fitzsimons and Madison
resolutions, agreed to.[2]

Apr. 11   *Petition of tradesmen, manu-*
facturers and others of Bal-
timore, Md. presented by
Smith (Md.)[3] and referred
to COWH; Madison and
Fitzsimons resolutions debated in COWH; on a
motion by *Goodhue, articles*
added to above resolu-
tions; motion by
Boudinot, for COWH to
rise and to appoint a
committee to prepare a
bill for a temporary sys-
tem of impost and ton-
nage; Bland motion,
seconded by Lee, to de-
cide whether the system
should be temporary or
permanent; Boudinot mo-
tion disagreed to; Clymer
motion to strike the word
"temporary" from the
Bland motion; Bland mo-
tion withdrawn; motion

[2] *NYDA,* Apr. 10; *CR,* Apr. 9.
[3] *NYDA,* Apr. 13.

Date	House	Senate
1789		
	by Madison, to separate the question of the level of duties from their collection by appointing a committee to bring in a Collection Bill [HR-3], agreed to; motion by Lee to consider impost and tonnage resolutions agreed to; resolutions debated.[4]	
Apr. 13	*Petition of the Shipwrights of Charleston, S.C.* presented by Burke[5] and referred to COWH.	
Apr. 14	*Motion* by *Bland* in COWH, for a vote on whether the impost system should be permanent or temporary, withdrawn; resolutions debated and *blanks filled.*[6]	
Apr. 15	Resolutions debated and *blanks filled.*[7]	
Apr. 16	Resolutions debated and *blanks filled.*[8]	
Apr. 17	Resolutions debated and *blanks filled.*[9]	
Apr. 18	*Petition of mechanics and manufacturers of New York City* presented by Laurance[10] and referred to	

---

4 Lloyd, Apr. 11; *NYDA*, Apr. 13; *CR*, Apr. 11. The Madison resolution and action on it are printed with the Collection Bill [HR-3].
5 *NYDA*, Apr. 14.
6 *NYDG*, Apr. 15; *CR*, Apr. 14.
7 Lloyd, Apr. 15; *NYDA*, *NYDG*, Apr. 16; *GUS*, Apr. 18; *CR*, Apr. 15.
8 Lloyd, Apr. 16; *NYDA*, *NYDG*, Apr. 17; *GUS*, Apr. 18; *CR*, Apr. 16.
9 Lloyd, Apr. 17; *NYDA*, *NYDG*, *GUS*, Apr. 18.
10 *NYDG*, Apr. 20.

Date	House	Senate
1789		
	COWH; resolutions debated and *blanks filled*.[11]	
Apr. 20	Resolutions debated and *amendments* agreed to.[12]	
Apr. 21	*Amendment* agreed to; *resolutions* agreed to and reported by COWH.[13]	
Apr. 24	Resolutions debated in House.	
Apr. 25	Resolutions debated and *amended*.	
Apr. 27	Resolutions debated and *amended*.	
Apr. 28	Resolution debated; resolutions on tonnage postponed on a motion by Madison;[14] impost resolutions *amended*, agreed to, and committee appointed (Clymer, White, and Baldwin) to bring in a bill pursuant to them.	
May 4	*Petition of the shipwrights of Baltimore* presented by Smith (Md.),[15] read, and committed to COWH.	
May 5	Clymer presented "a bill for laying a duty on goods, wares, and merchandizes, imported into the United States," which was read.	
May 6	Read and committed to COWH.	

[11] *NYDA, NYDG*, Apr. 20.
[12] *GUS*, Apr. 22.
[13] *CR*, Apr. 21.
[14] Lloyd, Apr. 28; *NYDA, NYDG*, Apr. 29.
[15] *NYDG*, May 5.

Date	House	Senate
1789		
May 7	Postponed as order of the day.	
May 8	Debated in COWH; motion by Tucker, to reduce duty on distilled spirits of Jamaica proof imported from allied nations, from 12¢ to 6¢.[16]	
May 9	Debated in COWH; Tucker motion of May 8 renewed and seconded by Jackson; motion by Goodhue, to insert 10¢ in lieu of 12¢; motion divided and striking out disagreed to, 26–19.[17]	
May 11	Debated in COWH; motion by Gerry to strike 6¢ duty on molasses and insert 2¢.[18]	
May 12	Debated in COWH; motion to strike out 6¢ duty on molasses agreed to by a vote of 24–22; motion by Lee to insert 5¢, by White to insert 4¢, and motions to insert 3¢ and 2¢; motion for 5¢ agreed to, 25–23; motion to insert cider agreed to; motion to substitute hyson tea for superior green tea agreed to.[19]	
May 13	*Petition of the merchants and traders of Portland, Mass.*	

---

[16] *NYDG, GUS,* May 9.
[17] Lloyd, May 9; *NYDG,* May 11; *CR,* May 9. The *NYDG* says that a motion to reduce the duties generally was disagreed to, 19–10.
[18] *NYDA,* May 12; *GUS,* May 13.
[19] Lloyd, *CR,* May 12.

Date	House	Senate
1789		

(Maine) presented by
Thatcher, read, and ta-
bled; debated in COWH;
motion by Ames to insert
imposts on china and
crockery, amended on a
motion by Fitzsimons to
replace "crockery" with
"earthen and stoneware,"
and agreed to at a rate of
7 1/2% ad valorem; mo-
tion by Ames to insert
gunpowder disagreed to
after Fitzsimons moved a
2¢ duty on it; motion to
insert looking glasses and
brushes agreed to; motion
to exempt saltpeter agreed
to; motion to strike out
hemp disagreed to; mo-
tion by Parker, seconded
by Scott, to insert a duty
of $10 each on slaves de-
bated and withdrawn.[20]

May 14   *Petition of distillers of Phil-*
adelphia presented; bill de-
bated in COWH; blanks
in clause providing for a
drawback of duties on re-
shipped goods filled with
"12" for the time allowed
and "1%" for the sum to
be retained from the im-
post paid in such cases; a
bounty of 5¢ on dried
and pickled fish and salted provisions to prevent
discouragement to fish-

---

[20] Lloyd, May 13; *NYDA,* May 14; *GUS,* May 16; *CR,* May 13.

Date	House	Senate
1789		
	eries from the duty on salt agreed to; motion by Fitzsimons for a drawback on loaf sugar made from raw sugar made and withdrawn; motion by Smith (Md.), seconded by Parker, to insert a drawback on all goods imported in American-owned ships, agreed to by a vote of 30–16; drawback set at 10%; COWH amendments agreed to by House.[21]	
May 15	Read; amendment proposed to insert the phrase "from any other country whatever" into the impost on spirits of Jamaica proof imported from countries not allied with the United States; bill recommitted to COWH and this amendment and others agreed to; COWH amendments agreed to by House; Madison motion to add a clause limiting the duration of the act debated.[22]	
May 16	Madison motion debated and withdrawn; Madison substitute motion "that the act should expire on the day of unless continued	

[21] Lloyd, May 14; *NYDA,* May 15; *GUS,* May 16, 20.
[22] *GUS,* May 16.

Date	*House*	*Senate*
1789		

by the act which should
appropriate the revenue
arising therefrom," sec-
onded by Fitzsimons;
Smith (S.C.) motion to
divide the question agreed
to; Lee motion, seconded
by Livermore, to strike
out the excepting clause,
agreed to; amended
Madison motion agreed to
by a recorded vote of 41–
8; blanks in first and last
clauses filled with "15th
of June next" and "first
of June 1796";[23] bill read
and agreed to as *An act
for laying a duty on goods,
wares, and merchandizes,
imported into the United
States.*

May 18		Received; read; 50 copies ordered printed.
May 21		Postponed.
May 25	*Petition of shipwrights of Philadelphia* presented by Fitzsimons.[24]	Debated and *amended.*[25]
May 26– June 2		Debated and *amended.*[26]
June 3		Debated and amended; Lee motion to postpone bill until June 8 debated and superseded by Morris motion for

---

[23] *NYDA*, May 18; *CR*, May 16.
[24] *NYDG*, May 26.
[25] Maclay, May 25. Maclay says the debate was in a committee of the whole in accordance with a resolution introduced on May 21 by Ellsworth.
[26] Maclay, May 26–29, June 1, 2. The *SLJ* for May 26 and 27 records no action on this subject.

Date	House	Senate
1789		
		second reading on June 4, which was agreed to.[27]
June 4		Read; debated and *amended*.
June 5	*Petition of the tradesmen and manufacturers of Boston* presented by Ames.[28]	Debated and *amended*.
June 8		Debated and amended;[29] Ellsworth, Morris, Lee, Butler, and Dalton appointed to committee to consider adding a clause "prohibiting the importation of goods from China or India, in ships or vessels, other than those belonging to the citizens of the United States."
June 9		Committee reported and report agreed to as *amendment* to the bill.
June 10		Read; debated and *amended*.
June 11		*Amended;* agreed to with amendments.
June 12	Senate amendments received.	
June 15	Senate amendments considered; some agreed to, others disagreed to.[30]	
June 16	Senate amendments considered; some agreed to, others disagreed to, one agreed to with an *amendment*.	
June 18		House action received.

---

[27] Maclay, June 3.
[28] *GUS,* June 6.
[29] Maclay, June 9.
[30] *NYDA,* June 16.

Date	House	Senate
1789		
June 19		Insisted on some amendments, receded from others.
June 23	Senate action considered on a motion by Laurance; one amendment agreed to with an *amendment*; disagreement to another insisted on 27–25.[31]	
June 24	Disagreement to two Senate amendments insisted on; Boudinot, Fitzsimons, and Madison appointed to conference committee on other Senate amendments disagreed to by House.	
June 25		House amendment agreed to; two amendments disagreed to by House adhered to and referred to conference committee; Morris, Lee, and Ellsworth appointed to committee.
June 27	Boudinot presented *conference report;* House receded from disagreement to several amendments with *amendments* to two of them.	Morris presented conference report; House amendments received and agreed to.
July 2	Signed by speaker.	Signed by vice president.
July 4	Signed by president.	

[31] *GUS,* June 24.

Madison Resolution
April 8, 1789

Resolved, as the opinion of this committee, That the following duties ought to be levied on goods wares and merchandise imported into the United States, viz.

On rum, per gallon,   of a dollar.[1]
On all other spiritous liquors   [2]
On molasses   [3]
On Madeira wine   [4]
On all other wines   [5]
On common bohea teas, per lb.
On all other teas   [6]
On pepper   [7]
On brown sugars   [8]
On loaf sugars   [9]
On all other sugars   [10]
On cocoa[11] and coffee   [12]
On all other articles   [13] per cent. on their value at the time and place
of importation.[14]

[1] On April 11 Madison moved for 15/90ths of a dollar, Sherman moved for 15¢, and Smith (S.C.?) for 10¢. On April 14, a motion by Gale to strike out "rum" and insert "all distilled spirits of Jamaica proof" was agreed to, and Laurance moved 12¢. 15¢ per gallon was agreed to.

[2] On April 14, this blank was filled with 12¢.

[3] On April 14, a motion by Madison, seconded by Parker, to fill this blank with "8¢ per gallon" was withdrawn. A motion by Madison for 7¢ was disagreed to. 6¢ was agreed to.

[4] On April 14, Sherman moved to fill this blank with "15¢ per gallon," Gilman with 20¢, and Hartley 30¢. Fitzsimons's motion for 50¢ was seconded by P. Muhlenberg and withdrawn. Another motion by Fitzsimons for 33 1/3¢ was agreed to by a vote of 21–19.

[5] On April 14, this blank was filled with "20¢ per gallon."

[6] According to the *CR*, on April 18 Fitzsimons offered the following resolutions on teas:

> On all teas imported from China or India, in ships built in the United States, and belonging wholly to a citizen or citizens thereof, as follows: On bohea tea per pound, 6 cents; on all souchong and other black teas, 10 cents; on superior green teas, 20 cents; on all other teas, 10 cents.
>
> On all teas imported from any other country or from India or China, in ships which are not the property of a citizen or citizens of the United States, as follows: on bohea tea per pound, 10 cents; souchong and other black teas, 15 cents; on superior green teas, 30 cents; on all other green teas 18 cents per pound.

The 10¢ figure on all other teas at the end of the first paragraph is apparently a *CR* error. It should have been 12¢. In debate on the second resolution, Goodhue moved for 7¢ on bohea tea. A motion by Fitzsimons for 8¢ was agreed to, as were the other duties as proposed.

[7] Debate on pepper was postponed on April 14. Pepper does not appear in the resolutions reported by the COWH on April 21.

[8] On April 14, a motion was made to fill this blank with "2¢ per pound." Boudinot's motion for 1¢ was agreed to.

[9] On April 14, this blank was filled with "3¢ per pound."

[10] On April 14, this blank was filled with "1 1/2¢ per pound."

[11] On April 15, a motion by Sherman for 1¢ per pound on cocoa was agreed to.

[12] On April 14, a duty of 2 1/2¢ per pound on coffee was agreed to.

[13] On April 20, this blank was filled with "five."

[14] On April 20, the COWH agreed to the following exceptions to the general duty:

That there ought, moreover, to be levied on all vessels in which goods, wares or merchandises, shall be imported, the duties following, viz. On all vessels built within the United States, and belonging wholly to citizens thereof, at the rate of   per ton

On all vessels belonging wholly to the subjects of powers with whom the United States have formed treaties, or partly to the subjects of such powers, or partly to citizens of the said states at the rate of

On all vessels belonging wholly or in part to the subjects of other powers, at the rate of   [15]

Fitzsimons Resolution
April 9, 1789

Resolved, as the opinion of this committee, that the following duties ought to be laid on goods, wares and merchandise imported into the United States, to wit.

Upon every gallon of beer, ale or porter,   parts of a dollar. [16]
Upon every barrel of beef
Upon every barrel of pork
And so in proportion for any greater or lesser quantity.
Upon every lb. of butter   [17]
Upon all candles of tallow per lb.   [18]
Upon all candles of wax or spermaciti per lb.   [19]
Upon cheese per lb.   [20]
Upon soap per lb.   [21]
Upon cyder per gallon   [22]

Tin in pigs, tin plates, lead, pewter, brass, . . . copper in plates, wool, dying woods, dying drugs, (other than indigo), raw hides, beaver and all other furs, and deer skins. (CR, Apr. 20)
The CR also includes "iron or brass wire," but this does not appear as an exception in the resolutions reported by the COWH on April 21.

[15] Debate on the three tonnage resolutions proposed by Madison was postponed until the end of the impost debate and may be found under the Tonnage Act [HR-5].

[16] On April 15, a motion by Fitzsimons to provide different duties on these products, depending on whether they were in bottles or casks, was agreed to. On casks, a motion for 6¢ per gallon was made by Fitzsimons and seconded by Laurance; a motion by Madison for 8¢ was agreed to. On bottles, 24¢ per dozen was agreed to.

[17] On April 15, Goodhue made a motion for $1 per barrel on beef; Tucker's motion to strike out beef, pork, and butter was agreed to.

[18] On April 15, Tucker's motion to strike out this item was disagreed to, while a motion for 2¢ by Fitzsimons, seconded by Laurance, was agreed to.

[19] On April 15, a motion by Boudinot to fill this blank with 6¢ was agreed to.

[20] On April 15, Goodhue moved to fill this blank with 3¢; Gilman's motion for 4¢ was agreed to.

[21] On April 15, Fitzsimons moved to fill this blank with 1¢. Gilman's motion for 2¢ was agreed to.

[22] This item does not appear in the resolutions reported by the COWH on April 21.

Upon boots per pair   [23]
Upon all steel unwrought for every 112 lb.   [24]
Upon cables for every C. weight   [25]
Upon tarred cordage for every 112 lb.   [26]
Upon untarred do. for every 112 lb.   [27]
Upon twine or pack thread for every 112 lb.   [28]
Upon malt for every bushel   [29]
Upon all nails, spikes, tacks or brads for every lb.   [30]
Upon salt per bushel   [31]
Upon manufacture tobacco per lb.   [32]
Upon snuff per lb.   [33]
Upon all blank books
Upon all writing, printing and wrapping paper, and upon all paste board
Upon all cabinet-ware
Upon all buttons of metal
Upon all Saddles
Upon all gloves of leather
Upon all hats of beaver, fur, wool or mixture of either

---

[23] On April 15, Gilman moved to fill this blank with $1, which he changed to 75¢. Madison's motion for 50¢ was agreed to.

[24] On April 15, a motion to strike out this item, made by Lee and seconded by Madison, was disagreed to. Fitzsimons moved 66¢ and Bland 40¢; Boudinot's motion for 56¢ was agreed to.

[25] The resolutions of April 21 include an impost of 50¢ per hundredweight on cables.

[26] On April 15, this blank was filled with 50¢.

[27] On April 15, this blank was filled with 60¢.

[28] On April 15, Partridge made a motion to strike out the duty on twine or pack thread. Fitzsimons made a motion for a duty of $1, Parker moved 56¢. $1 was agreed to. Also on April 15, a motion by Madison to insert a duty on hemp at this point was debated. On April 16, Gilman moved to strike out the duty on hemp. Motions were made by White for 75¢, and by Partridge, seconded by Laurance, for 40¢. A motion by Boudinot for 50¢ was agreed to.

[29] On April 16, Sherman made and withdrew a motion to strike out malt. Smith (?) moved 20¢. According to the CR, a motion by Fitzsimons for 10¢ was agreed to. Lloyd says Fitzsimons moved 6¢ and the motion for 10¢ was Madison's. On the same day, on a motion by Ames, duties of 6¢ per bushel on barley and $1 per hogshead on lime were inserted at this point.

[30] On April 16, a motion by Lee, seconded by Madison and Bland, to strike out these items was withdrawn. Tacks and brads were struck out. An impost of 1¢ on nails and spikes was agreed to.

[31] On April 16, Laurance moved to fill this blank with 6¢. On April 17, Burke's motion to strike out salt was seconded by Gilman and disagreed to by a vote of 19–17. (Lloyd, Apr. 17) The NYDG, April 18, reports this vote as 21–19. Smith (S.C.?) moved one shilling; Cadwalader, seconded by Smith (Md.), moved 8¢. Laurance's motion for 6¢ was agreed to. According to the CR and the GUS, Apr. 18, a motion by Goodhue for a drawback of the tax on salt used in salted provisions and fish was agreed to. This does not appear in the resolutions of April 21.

[32] On April 17, the COWH agreed to a motion by Sherman to fill this blank with 6¢.

[33] On April 17, this blank was filled with 10¢.

Upon all millinary
Upon all castings of iron, and upon slit or rolled iron
Upon all leather tanned or tawed, and upon all manufactures of leather
    (except such as are otherwise rated by this act)   34
Upon all shoes, slippers and golo-shoes,   35
For every hundred dollars value
Upon every coach, chariot and other four wheel carriages
Upon every chaise, solo or other two wheel carriage,   36
for every hundred dollars value thereof, and so in proportion for any part thereof
Upon every lb. of nutmegs
Upon every lb. of cinnamon
Upon every lb. of cloves
Upon raisins for every 112 lb.
Upon figs for every 112 lb.
Upon currants for every 112 lb.
Upon almonds for every 112 lb.   37

Goodhue Articles
April 11, 1789

Upon anchors for every 112 lb.   38
Upon every dozen of wool cards   39
Upon wrought tin ware   40
Upon every box of lemons
Upon every barrel of limes   41

CR, Apr. 8, 9, 11. The amendments are from Lloyd, Apr. 15–20; *NYDA,* Apr.
13, 16–18; *NYDG,* Apr. 15–17; *GUS,* Apr. 18; *CR,* Apr. 14–20.

---

34 On April 17, the COWH agreed to an impost of 7 1/2% ad valorem on all items
from blank books through leather.
35 On April 15, the COWH agreed to motions by Goodhue to tax leather shoes,
slippers, and goloshoes 10¢ per pair, and silk or stuff shoes and slippers also 10¢ per
pair.
36 On April 17, this blank was filled with 15% ad valorem.
37 On April 18, the COWH agreed to Sherman's motion to strike out imposts on
nutmegs, cinnamon, cloves, raisins, figs, currants, and almonds.
38 On April 18, the COWH agreed to a motion by Goodhue to fill this blank with
7 1/2% ad valorem.
39 On April 18, Laurance moved to fill this blank with 75¢. Ames's motion for
50¢ was agreed to.
40 On April 18, Lee made a motion to strike out this item. A motion for a duty of
7 1/2% was agreed to.
41 Lemons and limes were struck out on April 18.
On April 17, the COWH agreed to Carroll's motion to insert a duty on window

and other glass, except black quart bottles. Gale's motion for 10%, seconded by Carroll, was agreed to.

On April 18, the COWH inserted an impost on coal. Laurance moved 2¢ per bushel, Partridge 7 1/2% ad valorem, Hartley 1¢, Madison (Lloyd) or Bland (CR) 3¢. 3¢ was agreed to.

Also on April 18, duties of 75¢ per barrel on salted mackerel, shad, and salmon, and 50¢ per quintal on dried fish were added to the resolutions.

On the same day, a motion to insert an impost on axes, iron spades, and shovels was disagreed to.

On April 20, a motion by Fitzsimons for a drawback of 6¢ per gallon on rum distilled in the United States and then exported was disagreed to.

On the same day, Fitzsimons moved to insert the following:

> That all the duties paid or secured to be paid upon goods imported, shall be returned or discharged upon such of the said goods, as shall within   months be exported to any country without the limits of the United States, except so much as shall be necessary to defray the expence that may have accrued by the entry and safe keeping thereof. (CR, Apr. 20)

This was agreed to without debate on April 21.

Petition of the Tradesmen, Manufacturers, and Others of Baltimore
April 11, 1789

To the PRESIDENT and CONGRESS of the UNITED STATES.
The PETITION of the TRADESMEN, MANUFACTURERS, and others, of the TOWN of BALTIMORE,

Humbly Sheweth,

THAT since the Close of the late War, and the Completion of the Revolution, your Petitioners have observed, with serious Regret, the manufacturing and trading Interest of the Country rapidly declining, while the Wealth of the People hath been prodigally expended in the Purchase of those Articles from Foreigners, which our Citizens, if properly encouraged, were fully competent to furnish.

To check this growing Evil, Applications were made, by Petitions, to some of the State Legislatures: These Guardians of the People, in several of the States, interposed their Authority: Laws were by them enacted with the View of subduing, or, at least, diminishing the Rage for Foreign, and of encouraging Domestic Manufactures, but the Event hath clearly demonstrated to all Ranks of Men, that no effectual Provision could reasonably be expected, until one uniform efficient Government should pervade this wide-extended Country.

The happy Period having now arrived, when the United States are placed in a new Situation; when the Adoption of the General Government gives one Sovereign Legislature the sole and exclusive Power of laying Duties upon Imports: Your Petitioners rejoice at the Prospect this affords them, that

America, freed from the commercial Shackles which have so long bound her, will see and pursue her true Interest, becoming independent in Fact as well as in Name; and they confidently hope, that the Encouragement and Protection of American Manufactures will claim the earliest Attention of the Supreme Legislature of the Nation, as it is an universally acknowledged Truth, that the United States contain within their Limits, Resources amply sufficient to enable them to become a great manufacturing Country, and only want the Patronage and Support of a wise energetic Government.

Your Petitioners conceive it unnecessary to multiply Arguments to so enlightened a Body as the one they have now the Honour of addressing, to convince them of the Propriety and Importance of attending to Measures so obviously necessary, and, indeed, indispensable, as every Member must have observed and lamented the present melancholy State of his Country; the Number of her Poor increasing for Want of Employment; Foreign Debts accumulating; Houses and Lands depreciating in value; Trade and Manufactures languishing and expiring. This being a faint Sketch of the gloomy Picture this Country exhibits, it is to the Supreme Legislature of the United States, as the Guardians of the whole Empire, that every Eye is now directed—from their united Wisdom; their Patriotism; their ardent Love of their Country, your Petitioners expect to derive that Aid and Assistance, which alone can dissipate their just Apprehensions, and animate them with Hopes of Success in future, by imposing on all Foreign Articles, which can be made in America, such Duties as will give a just and decided Preference to their Labours, and thereby discountenancing that Trade which tends so materially to injure them, and empoverish their Country; and which may also, in their Consequences, contribute to the Discharge of the National Debt, and the due Support of Government.

Your Petitioners take the Liberty to annex a List of such Articles, as are or can be manufactured in this Place, on moderate Terms; and they humbly trust that you will fully consider their Request, and grant to them, in common with the other Mechanics and Manufacturers of the United States, that Relief which, in your Wisdom, may appear proper.

A List, of enumerated Articles, Manufactured, in Baltimore Town, & State of Maryland, which are affected by the Importation.

Ship Building	Cabinet work & all other	Beer, Ale, &
Anchors, Adzes, Axes,	Wooden household	Porter
hatchets Iron Bolts,	Furniture	
Spikes, & all kinds of		Loaf Sugar,
Nails, Scythes (dutch	Coaches, Chariots,	Chocolate
excepted) Sickles,	Chaises, & all other	

Drawing Knives Bits, for boring Pumps Carriage hoops & attire Scale Beams, Steelyards, Spades Shovels, Hoes, Mattocks, Pick Axes Andirons, Shovels & Tongs Chimney Grates, Iron Traces & Chains Thumb Latches, Plane Irons, Augers, Chissels, & Gouges Gridirons, Curry Combs, Bits & Stirrup Irons, Smiths & hand Bellows's— Guns & Pistols Gun & Pistol Locks

Copper & Tin Ware, including Worms for Stills

Brass Andirons, Candlesticks & all rough Brass Castings, under 100 lb. wt. Brass Carriage, & harness Furniture—

Cordage, Cables, & Spun Yarn White Rope, Log line & Sein Twine

Ships Blocks, of all kinds

Wrought Gold, Jewellery & all kinds of Plated Ware

Clocks, of all kinds

riding Carriages

Carpenters & Joiners planes

Spinning Wheels & all other Turners work

Buck & Sheeps Skin Breeches Buck & do. Gloves

Boots, & Shoes, of all sorts
Boot Legs, Vamps, & all kinds of Curried Leather

Hatts, of all sorts

Saddles, do. Cloths, Girth's surcingles, Cruppers, stirrup leathers Bridles, Saddle Bags, Leather Trunks, Portmanteaus, Valises, Shot Pouches, Holsters, Leather, & Velvet Caps, & Carriage Harness

Bur Mill Stones, & all kinds of wrought Stone—Earthen Ware

Brusshes of all kinds

Womens Stays

Ready made Cloaths, & wearing Apparal

Beef, Pork, Butter & Cheese,

———

Bar Iron, & Nail Rods, all kinds of Iron Castings Window Glass, & all other kinds of Glass Ware—manufactord in great quantities in other parts of the State—

Wool, & Cotton Cards

All Kinds of Snuff and
　　Manufactured Tobacco

all Kinds of Ivory and
　　Horn Combs—

Printing, Writing &
　　Wrapping Paper,
Blank Books, & all
　　kinds of Stationary

Starch, Hair Powder &
　　Fig Blue

Soap & Candles

Linseed Oyl

Mathematical Instru-
　　ments

Petitions and Memorials: Various subjects, SR, DNA. List of signatures will be printed in the petition volume.

Petition of the Shipwrights of Charleston, S.C.
April 13, 1789

STATE OF SOUTH CAROLINA
　　To the Honorable the President and the Honble. the Members of the
　　Senate in the Congress of the United States of America
THE PETITION of the Shipwrights of this State
　　HUMBLY SHEWETH
　　THAT your petitioners reflect with pleasure that the Constitution of the United States gives the exclusive right of forming treaties and regulating Commerce to the General Government of the Union which can alone equally, safely and effectually exercise the same.
　　FROM the diminished State of Ship building in America and the ruinous restrictions to which our Vessels are subject in foreign ports—from the distrest condition of our Commerce languishing under the most disgraceful inequalities—its benefits transferred from our own Citizens to Strangers who do not nor ever will feel those Attachments which can alone render a Mercantile interest useful to a Country. and above all mortified at the daily humiliating Sight of our Valuable Staples lading the Vessels and enriching the Merchants of Powers who neither have treaties with us or are friendly to our Commerce, with deference and respect your Petitioners humbly entreat the early and earnest attention of your Honorable House to these important Considerations.

ENJOYING a Country which possesses every thing to make its Commerce flourishing, and its reputation respectable—there wanted but a Supreme energetic System capable of uniting its efforts and drawing its resources to a point to render us a great and happy People This System WE trust the Wisdom of the General Convention has produced and the Virtue of the People confirmed. Under your able and upright Administration of the ample powers it contains we look forward with pleasing hopes to the period when we shall once more see public Credit firmly established—private rights Secured and our Citizens enjoying the Blessings of a mild and active Government.

No more we trust shall we lament our trade almost wholly in the Possession of Foreigners—Our Vessels excluded from the ports of some Nations and fettered with restrictions in others. OR, *Materials the produce of our Country* which should be retained for our *own use* exported and increase the Maritime consequence of other Powers.

To the Wisdom of the General Legislature we look up for a correction of these Public evils—the formation of treaties, and the regulation of Commerce are Questions which can be committed with Safety to the enlightened Councils of the Union alone. it would be as unnecessary as it would be unbecoming in us to presume to point out the Measures proper to be adopted. It is Sufficient for us to join our Northern Brethren in asserting that we have most Severely felt the want of such a Navigation Act as will place our Vessels upon an equality with other Nations. To you who are the only proper Guardians of our General rights WE resort with Confidence for redress— Assured that no means will be left unattempted to remedy these evils and to render us respectable abroad and at home.

AND your Petitioners as in Duty Bound will ever pray
Signed in the City of Charleston
this 2nd. day of April Anno Domini
1789 by Order of the Shipwrights—
PAUL PRITCHARD ⎤
JAMES GEORGE ⎬ Committee
DAVID HAMILTON ⎦

Petitions and Memorials: Various subjects, SR, DNA.

Bland Motion
April 14, 1789

Resolved as the opinion of this Committee that untill the Congress of the U.S. shall have passed Laws for the better Organization & arranging a Revenue System, so far as it respects the Collection of Duties on Articles imported from foreign Countries, & on Tonage; All offices heretofore established by the last Laws passed in the respective States, for the establishing of ports of Entry & for the Collection of duties on Articles imported from foreign Countries, & on Tonage, ought to be continued & established by Law for the aforesaid purpose—And that the Offices who shall be appointed to collect the said Revenue ought to be subject to the same pains & penalties & forfeitures which they might have incurred under the said Laws respectively—

All distilled spirits of Jamaca proof	15 Cents pr. Gal.
All other distilled ~~spirituous~~ Liquors of inferior proof	12 Do.
On Molasses—pr. Gallon	6 Do.
Every Gallon Madeira Wine	33 1/3 Do.
Do. of all other wines	20 Do.
On every pound of Brown Sugar	1 Do.
Do. Loaf Sugar	3 Do.
Do. of all other Sugars	1 1/2 Do.
Every pound of Coffee	2 1/2 Cents

Thatcher Papers, MHi, hand of Thatcher.

Petition of the Mechanics and Manufacturers of New York City
April 18, 1789

To the honorable the Congress of the United States of America The Petition of the Mechanics and Manufacturers of the City of New York, humbly sheweth

That on the fortunate issue of the late Revolution, your Petitioners relied for the enjoyment of that prosperity which attends the establishment of political and civil Freedom. They contemplated this event as the point at which a happy aera was to commence, and as the source whence a new system of blessings should spring—They entertained a hope that the independence which they had sought and acquired, would have been not merely a nominal but substantial acquisition; an Independence not only seen in speculation, but felt and realized in practice. Your Petitioners were early led to fear, that those prospects were visionary; and that their country having gained the form of liberty had left in the hands of their enemies the instruments of oppression, and the spirit to exercise it. They soon perceived with the deepest regret, that their prospects of improving wealth were blasted by a system of commercial usurpation, originating in prejudices and fostered by a feeble government—They saw the trade of these States laboring under foreign impositions and loaded with fetters forged in every quarter to discourage enterprize and defeat industry. In this situation they have been prevented from applying to those abundant resources with which nature has blessed this country. Agriculture has lost its capital stimulus, and Manufacture, the sister of Commerce, has participated in all its distresses, and has languished, notwithstanding the spirit of individuals and Societies exerted for its support. Thus in, lamenting the misfortunes of a foreign intercourse, your Petitioners do but recite their own peculiar complaints; for in its prosperity or decay, they feel themselves deeply interested.

Your Petitioners conceive that their countrymen have been deluded by an appearance of plenty—by the profusion of foreign articles, which has deluged the Country, and thus have mistaken excessive importation for a flourishing trade. To this deception they impute the continuance of that immoderate prepossession in favor of foreign commodities which has been the principal cause of their distresses and the subject of their complaint.

Wearied by their fruitless exertions, your Petitioners have long looked forward with anxiety for the establishment of a government which would have power to check the growing evil, and extend a protecting hand to the interests of commerce and the arts. Such a government is now established. On the promulgation of the Constitution just now commencing its operations, your Petitioners discovered in its principles the remedy which they had so long and so earnestly desired—They embraced it with ardor, and have supported it with persevering attachment. They view with the highest satisfaction the prospects now opening and adorning this auspicious period. To your Honorable Body the Mechanics and Manufacturers of New York look up with confidence, convinced, that, as the united voice of America has furnished you with the means, so your knowledge of our common wants has given you the spirit to unbind our fetters and rescue our country from disgrace and ruin.

Your petitioners have subjoined a list of such articles as can be manufactured in this State. And they are encouraged to commend them to your attention, by this reflection, that the countenance of your Honorable Body to the useful Arts, so far from injuring other parts of the great Political system, must eventually operate to the general benefit of the community.

In your wisdom, your justice and patriotism, we rest with an assurance only equalled by our profound respect.

Petitions and Memorials: Various subjects, HR, DNA. List of signatures will be printed in the petition volume.

COWH Resolutions
April 21, 1789

Resolved as the opinion of this committee, that the following duties ought to be laid on goods, wares and merchandises imported into the United States, to wit:

	In Cents
On all distilled spirits of Jamaica proof	15[1]
On all distilled liquors of inferior proof	12
On molasses	6[2]
On Madeira wine	33 1/3[3]
On all other wines	20[4]
On every gallon of beer, ale, or porter imported in casks	8
On all beer, ale, or porter imported in bottles, per dozen	24
On malt per bushel	10
On barley per bushel	6
On lime per hogshead	100[5]
On brown sugars per lb.	1
On loaf sugars per lb.	3
On all other sugars per lb.	1 1/2
On coffee per lb.	2 1/2
On cocoa per lb.	1
On all candles of tallow per lb.	2
On all candles of wax or spermaceti per lb.	6

[1] On April 24, a motion by Boudinot to strike out "15" and insert "12" was seconded by Jackson. Tucker moved to strike out "15" and insert "8," but did not receive a second because the motion was not in order. On April 25, Boudinot's motion was disagreed to. Smith (Md.) moved 6¢ on spirits of Jamaica proof from nations allied with the United States, in order to discriminate between these nations and those not allied with the United States. The House agreed to strike out this phrase and the one following and insert:

	In Cents
On all distilled spirits of Jamaica proof, imported from any state or kingdom in alliance with the United States, per gal.	12
On all other distilled spirits imported from any such state or kingdom, per gal.	10
On all distilled spirits of Jamaica proof, imported from any state or kingdom not in alliance with the United States, per gal.	15
On all other distilled spirits imported from any such state or kingdom, per gal.	12

(HJ, p. 35)

[2] On April 28, a motion by Thatcher to strike out all duties on molasses was disagreed to. Boudinot moved to reduce the duty from 6¢ to 3¢. A motion by Fitzsimons to insert a drawback of 6¢ per gallon on spirits distilled in the United States, using imported rum and later exported, was agreed to.

[3] On April 25, Boudinot moved to reduce this duty, and Madison's suggestion of 25¢ was agreed to.

[4] On April 25, the House struck out "20" and inserted "15."

[5] On April 25, the House agreed to a motion by Ames to strike out the imposts on barley and lime.

	In Cents
On cheese per lb.	4
On soap per lb.	2
On boots per pair	50
On all shoes, slippers or goloshoes made of leather per pair	10[6]
On all shoes or slippers made of silk or stuff per pair	10
On cables for every cwt.	50
On tarred cordage for every 112 lb.	50[7]
On untarred do. and yarn for every 112 lb.	60[8]
On twine or pack thread for every 112 lb.	100[9]
On hemp per cwt.	50[10]
On all steel unwrought for every 112 lb.	56
On all nails and spikes per lb.	1
On salt per bushel	6
On manufactured tobacco per lb.	6
On snuff per lb.	10
On every dozen wool[11] cards	50
On every bushel of coal	3
On salted mackrel, shad and salmon per barrel	75
On dried fish per quintal	50
On all teas imported from China or India in ships built in the United States, and belonging to a citizen or citizens thereof, as follows:	
On bohea tea per lb.	6
On all souchong and other black teas per lb.	10
On superior green teas per lb.	20
On all other teas per lb.	10
On all teas imported from any other country, or from India or China in ships which are not the property of a citizen or citizens of the United States, as follows:	

---

[6] On April 25, the House struck out "10" and inserted "7."

[7] On April 27, Fitzsimons's motion to strike out "50" as the duty on both cables and tarred cordage and insert "100" was seconded by Goodhue and disagreed to. Ames moved "60," but a motion by Madison for "75" was agreed to.

[8] On April 27, the House agreed to a motion by Fitzsimons to strike out "60" and insert "90."

[9] On April 27, the House agreed to strike out "100" and insert "200."

[10] On April 27, the House agreed to Hiester's motion to insert a duty of 60¢ after December 31, 1790, at this point.

[11] On April 27, the House agreed to Fitzsimons's motion to insert "and cotton" at this point.

	In Cents
On bohea tea per lb.	8[12]
On all souchong, or other black teas per lb.	15
On superior green tea per lb.	30
On all other green tea per lb.	18

On all window and other glass, ten per cent. ad
valorem.

On all blank books,

On all writing, printing, or wrapping paper,[13] and on
all pasteboard,

On all cabinet wares,

On all buttons of metal,

On all saddles,

On all gloves of leather,

On all hats of beaver, fur, wool, or a mixture of
either,

On all millinary,[14]

On all castings of iron, and upon slit, or rolled iron,

On all leather tanned or tawed, and on all manufacture
of leather, except such as shall be otherwise rated,

On canes, walking sticks and whips,

On cloathing ready made,

On gold, silver, and plated ware, and on jewellry and
paste work,

On anchors, and

On all wrought tin ware,

Seven and half per cent. ad valorem.

On every coach, chariot, or other four wheel carriage,
and on every chaise, solo, or other two wheel
carriage,[15] 15 per cent. ad valorem.

On all other articles, five per cent. on their value at
the time and place of importation, except as follows:
Tin in pigs, tin plates, lead, pewter, brass, copper
in plates, wool, dying woods, and dying drugs
(other than indigo) raw hides, beaver and all other
furs, and deer skins.

That all the duties paid or secured to be paid upon goods imported, shall
be returned or discharged upon such of the said goods as shall with-

---

[12] On April 27, the House struck out "8" and inserted "10."

[13] On April 27, the House inserted "paper hangings" at this point.

[14] The *GUS* and *NYDA* for April 28 report that on April 27 the House agreed to a
duty of 15% ad valorem on millinery. This change is not in the resolutions agreed to
by the House on April 28.

[15] On April 27, the House inserted "or parts thereof" at this point.

in   months be exported to any country without the limits of the United States, except so much as shall be necessary to defray the expence that may have accrued by the entry and safe keeping thereof.

That there ought moreover to be levied on all vessels entered or cleared in the United States, the duties following, to wit:

On all vessels built within the United States, and belonging wholly to citizens thereof, at the rate of six cents per ton.

On all vessels not built within the United States, but belonging wholly to citizens thereof, at the rate of six cents per ton.

On all vessels belonging wholly to the subjects of powers with whom the United States have formed treaties; or partly to the subjects of such powers, and partly to citizens of the said States, at the rate of thirty cents per ton.

On all vessels belonging wholly or in part to subjects of other powers, at the rate of fifty cents per ton.

Provided, That no vessel built in the United States, and belonging to a citizen or citizens thereof, whilst employed in the coasting trade, or in the fisheries, shall pay tonnage more than once in any one year; nor shall any ship or vessel built within the United States, pay tonnage on her first voyage.[16]

NYDA, Apr. 23. The amendments are in Lloyd, Apr. 24–28; CR, Apr. 24–28; NYDA, Apr. 25, 27, 28, 29; NYDG, Apr. 28, 29; GUS, Apr. 25, 29, May 2.

---

[16] The amendments to the resolutions on tonnage are printed with the Tonnage Act [HR-5].

Petition of the Shipwrights of Baltimore
May 4, 1789

To the CONGRESS of the UNITED STATES of AMERICA.

The Humble PETITION of the SHIPWRIGHTS, &c. Inhabitants of BALTIMORE TOWN.

AMONGST the advantages looked for from the national government is the increase of the shipping and maritime strength of the United States of America, by laws similar in their nature and operation to the British navigation acts; or laws differing only from these where a difference in the circumstances of the two countries may render any deviation necessary. Your petitioners on which ever side they turn their eyes, see reason to believe, that the United States may soon become as powerful in shipping as any nation in the world. Perhaps it will appear on the closest examination of the subject, that we are better prepared for a navigation act than England when she established hers. That generally called the British navigation act was passed in the year

1660, at which time the registered commercial tonnage of that kindom did not exceed 96,000. Eight years after, *Sir Josiah Child* says, "without this act, we had not now (1668) been owners of one half the shipping nor trade; nor should have employed one half the seamen we now do at present." From this period, we find their shipping rapidly augmenting till in 1774 the registered commercial tonnage alone was near 800,000, which gives an increase in little more than one hundred years of about 704,000 ton of shipping.

It is worthy of notice moreover, that when this act passed, England could neither dress nor dye her white wool cloths. The linens she used were chiefly imported from foreign countries—She was unacquainted with the weavers loom-engine—Calico printing was unknown—She had made neither white, writing nor printing paper—She had no manufactures of fine glass—There was not a single wire-mill in the kingdom, nor could she as yet tin iron-plates. About this time also the legal interest of money was eight per cent.

With respect to our manufactures, we have several valuable ones already established, and others which it is well known want only encouragement to prove of the greatest national advantage. With respect to our shipping, we cannot pretend to offer any accurate estimate of their tonnage. It appears however, from an authentic return; signed Thomas Irwin, Inspector-General of the imports and exports of North-America, and register of shipping, that the eleven States, which form the United States of America, employed in the year 1770, three hundred and nine thousand, five hundred and thirty-four ton of shipping; from which we think it reasonable to infer, that the present tonnage belonging to the United States of America, greatly exceeds the commercial tonnage of England, when she passed her navigation act.

These facts encourage us to hope that our expectations from the new government will soon be realized.

Although we joined our fellow-citizens in a general petition which embraced this object, we nevertheless have deemed it incumbent upon us, on account of its vast importance, to unite with our brethren of Charlestown and elsewhere, in bringing it before Congress disconnected with any other matter. Permit us to add, that for want of national protection and encouragement our shipping, that great source of strength and riches has fallen into decay, and involved thousands in the utmost distress.

Trusting to the wisdom of Congress for a due consideration of the premises, we as in duty bound, &c.

Baltimore-Town, April 17, 1789

NYDG, May 8.

Petition of the Merchants and Traders of Portland, Mass. (Maine)
May 13, 1789

To the most honourable the Senate, and the honourable the House of Representatives of the United States of America, in Congress assembled—
The Petition of the Merchants & Traders of the town of Portland,
Humbly sheweth—

That, in their opinion, the proposed Duty on Molasses will operate injuriously upon all the Newengland States; but more particularly on this part of the State of Massachusetts.

Your Petitioners are sensible of the present exigencies of Government—that there is an immediate necessity of a publick Revenue—and that the mode proposed of raising it by an Impost on certain articles is preferable to any other. But, with submission we would ask Whether Imposts should not be confined to Luxuries, and to such articles as are, or may be manufactured in our own country?

Molasses, on which the astonishing duty of *six cents* per gallon has been proposed, is an article which comes not within either of those descriptions. It is by no means an article of Luxury, but a real necessary of life—an article that is chiefly consumed by the poorer part of the community, and those who are unable to furnish themselves with Sugar.

As to our Manufactures—it is well known that a duty on Molasses cannot possibly opperate to the advantage of these: On the contrary, that it will be attended with the most pernicious consequences to the manufacture and exportation of Lumber, and consequently to our navigation and shipbuilding.

Although the manufacture of Newengland Rum might here with propriety be introduced, we should have remained silent, had not an honourable Gentleman from Virginia held up the pernicious effects of this article as a reason why a heavy duty should be laid on Molasses. It is true, Newengland Rum is distilled from *northern Molasses;* and is it not as true that Whiskey is distilled from *southern Grain?* When that honourable gentleman, therefore, shall consent to a duty on the latter, your Petitioners will have no objection to an impost on the former. Till then, your Petitioner humbly pray—not only that the proposed Impost on Molasses may be omitted—but also, as the importation of this article gives life to several important branches of our own manufactures—as it tends greatly to promote our navigation—and as it employs and feeds a large number of our inhabitants—that it may remain intirely free from all Imposts and Duties whatever.

And your Petitioners, as in duty bound, will ever pray.

Jos. McLellan Chairn.

Portland, May 4, 1789

At a Meeting of the Merchants and Traders of the town of Portland, held agreeably to adjournment—Capt. Joseph McLellan in the Chair—

Voted, That the above Petition be signed by the Chairman, and immediately forwarded.

True Copy of the Minutes.

Attest.

JAMES DUNN Clerk

Petitions and Memorials: Various subjects, SR, DNA.

Petition of Distillers of Philadelphia
May 14, 1789

To the Honorable the House of Representatives of the United States of America—

THE Memorial of the Subscribers, on Behalf of themselves and others, Distillers in and near the City of Philadelphia Most respectfully sheweth.

THAT your Memorialists have perceived by the public Prints that the Legislature of the United States have it in Contemplation to impose specific Duties on certain enumerated Articles of Commerce, and that an Impost of Six Cents ℔ Gallon is proposed to be laid on Molasses and from Twelve to Fifteen Cents ℔ Gallon on Westindia Rum.

As the Object of the Legislature in laying those Duties is, to cherish and promote the Agriculture, Manufactures and Commerce of the United States, as well as to raise a Revenue, we beg Leave to submit to the Consideration of of Your honorable House the following Remarks respecting the proposed Duties on Rum and Molasses.

Your Memorialists are of Opinion, that a greater Difference in the Duties on the said Articles, (either by encreasing the Duties on Rum or lessening that on Molasses) would be of Advantage to the Interests of the United States, for the following Reasons.

First, The Rum imported from the Westindia Islands, is imported in foreign Bottoms, which are freighted back with Produce of the United States, whereby the Citizens of these States are deprived of the Carriage of their own Produce, to the Prejudice of Shipbuilding, Navigation and Commerce.

Secondly The proposed Duties on the Articles aforesaid being nearly equal (according to their respective Value) will operate in Favour of the Importation of foreign Rum—as they will not leave Room for a Difference in the Prices of foreign Rum and that distilled on this Continent, sufficient to induce a Preference of the latter, whereas a greater Distinction in those Duties would admit of such Difference in the Prices as would probably occasion an Increase of Consumption of Continental and a proportionate Decrease in the Consumption of foreign Rum.

Thirdly. Thus favouring the Consumption of Continental Rum will not only encourage and protect the Manufacture thereof among ourselves, but will also encrease the Demand for Molasses; the Importation whereof will tend to encourage the important Business of Shipbuilding and extend the Navigation of the United States; The Vessels of whose Citizens are permitted to enter the Ports of His most Christian Majesty and of the United Provinces with the Produce of our Country, and to carry from thence Molasses in Return.

Your Memorialists further beg Leave to observe that in their Opinion the Molasses Trade and the manufacture of Rum would be still further encouraged by allowing, on all Rum distilled within the United States and exported to the East Indies or other foreign Parts, a Drawback of the Duty which shall be laid on Molasses.

These Remarks have occurred to Your Memorialists on the Subject of the proposed Duties on Rum and Molasses; which they respectfully submit to the Consideration of Your honorable House, in full Confidence that Your honorable House will determine in the Premises as to you in Wisdom shall seem most conducive to the true Interest and Prosperity of the United States. Philadelphia 4th. May 1789

Petitions and Memorials: Various subjects, SR, DNA. List of signatures will be printed in the petition volume.

Madison Motion
May 16, 1789

And be it farther enacted by the authority aforesaid, that this act shall continue and be in force until the   day of   [1] and from thence until the end of the next succeeding session of Congress, which shall happen thereafter.

HJ, p. 64.

---

[1] On the same day, the House filled the blanks with "first" and "June, 1796."

Impost Bill [HR-2]
May 16, 1789

An ACT for laying a DUTY on GOODS, WARES, and MERCHANDIZES, imported into the UNITED STATES

WHEREAS it is necessary for the support of Government,[1] and the encouragement and protection of Manufactures, that Duties be laid on Goods, Wares, and Merchandizes, imported:

[1] BE IT ENACTED BY THE CONGRESS OF THE UNITED STATES,[2] That from and after the fifteenth day of June[3] next ensuing, the several duties herein after mentioned, shall be laid on the following goods, wares, and merchandizes, imported into the United States, from any foreign port, or place, that is to say:

On all distilled spirits of Jamaica proof, imported from the European dominions of any state or kingdom, having a commercial treaty with the United States, per gallon,   12[4] cents.

On all other distilled spirits, imported from the European dominions of such state or kingdom, per gallon,   10 cents.[5]

On all distilled spirits of Jamaica proof, imported from any other[6] kingdom or country whatsoever, per gallon,   15[7] cents.

On all other distilled spirits,   per gallon,   12[8] cents.

---

[1] On June 4, the Senate inserted "for the discharge of the debts of the United States" at this point.

[2] On June 4, the Senate changed the phrase "CONGRESS OF THE UNITED STATES" to "Senate and Representatives of the United States in Congress assembled." The House disagreed to this on June 15. After the Senate insisted on its amendment, the House agreed, with a further amendment, proposed by Thatcher, to insert "House of" before "Representatives." (NYDA, June 16; GUS, June 24)

[3] On June 4, the Senate changed "fifteenth day of June" to "first day of July." On June 16, the House agreed, with an amendment changing "July" to "August."

[4] On May 25, the committee of the whole Senate struck out "12" and inserted "8."

[5] On May 26 and June 4, the Senate struck out "On all distilled spirits of Jamaica proof" through "10 cents." The House disagreed to this on June 15, and insisted on its disagreement on June 23 by a vote of 28–27. The conference committee was unable to agree on this amendment and the House then agreed to it. (Maclay, May 26; GUS, June 17; CR, June 23)

[6] On June 4, the Senate struck out "other." The House disagreed to this, the Senate and House both insisted on their actions, and the conference committee reached no agreement. The House then agreed to the amendment.

[7] On June 4, the Senate struck out "15" and inserted "10." The House disagreed to this on June 15, the Senate insisted, and it was referred to the conference committee. The House followed the committee's recommendation and agreed to the amendment. (GUS, June 17)

[8] On June 4, the Senate struck out "12" and inserted "8." The House disagreed to

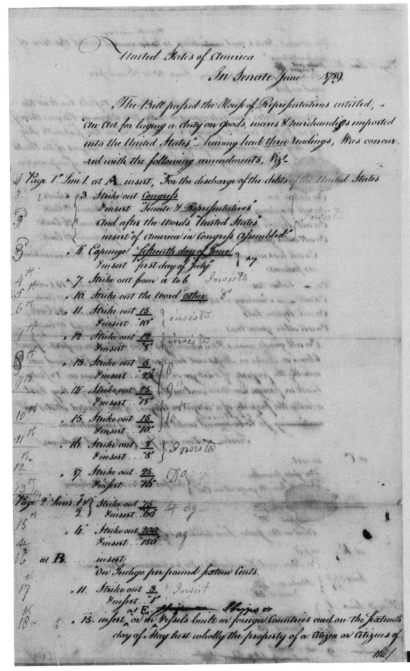

Senate Amendments, May 17, 1789. (Courtesy of the National Archives)

On molasses,	per gallon,	5[9] cents.
On Madeira wine,	per gallon,	25[10] cents.
On all other wines,	per gallon,	15[11] cents.
On every gallon of beer, ale, or porter, in casks,		8[12] cents.
On all cyder, beer, ale, or porter, in bottles,		
	per dozen,	25[13] cents.
On malt,	per bushel,	10 cents.
On brown sugars,	per pound,	1 cent.
On loaf sugars,	per pound,	3 cents.[14]
On all other sugars,	per pound,	1 1/2 cents.
On coffee,	per pound,	2 1/2 cents.
On cocoa,	per pound,	1 cent.
On all candles of tallow,	per pound,	2 cents.
On all candles of wax, or spermaceti,	per pound,	6 cents.
On cheese,	per pound,	4 cents.
On soap,	per pound,	2 cents.
On boots,	per pair,	50 cents.
On all shoes, slippers, or goloshoes, made of leather,		
	per pair,	7 cents.
On all shoes or slippers made of silk or stuff,		
	per pair,	10 cents.
On cables, for every one hundred and twelve pounds,		75[15] cents.
On tarred cordage, for every one hundred and twelve		
pounds,		75[16] cents.

this on June 15, the Senate insisted, and the subject was referred to the conference committee. The House agreed to the committee's recommendation to agree to the amendment. (*GUS*, June 17)

[9] On May 26, the Senate in committee struck out "5." Motions were made and seconded to insert "2," "3," and "4." This last motion, considered first, was agreed to. (Maclay, May 28) On June 4, the Senate agreed to 3¢, but reconsidered its action on June 8 and agreed to 2 1/2¢.

[10] On May 27 and June 5, the Senate struck out "25" and inserted "18."

[11] On June 5, the Senate struck out "15" and inserted "10."

[12] On June 5, the Senate struck out "8" and inserted "5." The House disagreed to this on June 15, but after the Senate insisted and the conference committee recommended agreement, the House approved the amendment. (*NYDA*, June 16)

[13] On June 5, the Senate struck out "25" and inserted "16." The House disagreed on June 15, the Senate insisted, and the conference committee recommended agreement. The House agreed, with an amendment striking out "16" and inserting "20," and the Senate accepted this amendment. (*NYDA*, June 16)

[14] On May 28, a motion to alter the impost on loaf sugars was agreed to by the vote of the vice president. On June 5, the duty was returned to 3¢. (Maclay, June 5)

[15] On May 28, on a motion by Morris, the Senate in committee struck out "75" and inserted "60." This was agreed to by the Senate on June 5. The House disagreed on June 15, and the Senate receded from the amendment. (*NYDA*, June 16)

[16] On May 28, on a motion by Morris, the Senate in committee struck out "75" and inserted "60." This was agreed to by the Senate on June 5. The House disagreed on June 15, and the Senate receded from the amendment. (Ibid.)

On untarred ditto, and yarn, for every one hundred and twelve pounds,		90 cents.
On twine or packthread, for every one hundred and twelve pounds,		200[17] cents.
On all steel unwrought, for every one hundred and twelve pounds,		56 cents.
On all nails and spikes,	per pound,	1 cent.
On salt,	per bushel,	6[18] cents.
On manufactured tobacco,	per pound,	6 cents.
On snuff,	per pound,	10 cents.[19]
On wool and cotton cards,	per dozen,	50 cents.
On coal,	per bushel,	3[20] cents.
On pickled fish,	per barrel,	75 cents.
On dried fish,	per quintal,	50 cents.

On all teas imported from China or India in ships built
in the United States, and belonging to a citizen or
citizens thereof,[21] as follows:

On bohea tea,	per pound,	6 cents.
On all souchong or other black teas,	per pound,	10 cents.
On all hyson teas,	per pound,	20 cents.
On all other green teas,	per pound,	10[22] cents.

On all teas imported from any country other than
China or India, in any ship or vessel whatsoever, or
from China or India in any ship or vessel, which is
not wholly the property of a citizen or citizens of the
United States, as follows:[23]

---

[17] On May 28 and June 5, the Senate struck out "200" and inserted "150." The House disagreed to this on June 15 and the Senate receded from it.

[18] On May 29, in committee of the whole Senate, a motion by Lee, seconded by Carroll, to strike out "6" and insert "12" was disagreed to by the vote of the vice president.

[19] On June 5, the Senate inserted "On Indigo per pound 16 Cents" at this point. A motion by Butler to strike out this impost was disagreed to on June 10. (Maclay, June 10)

[20] On June 5, the Senate struck out "3" and inserted "1." The House disagreed to this on June 15, the Senate insisted, and the House agreed to the conference committee's recommendation by agreeing to the amendment with an amendment striking out "1" and inserting "2." The Senate agreed to this House change. (*NYDA*, June 16)

[21] On June 10, the Senate inserted the following at this point:
   or in ships or Vessels built in foreign Countries, and on the sixteenth day of May last, wholly the property of a Citizen or Citizens of the United States, and so continuing until the time of importation.

[22] On June 5, the Senate struck out "10" and inserted "12."

[23] On June 1, by a vote of 9–8, the Senate in committee of the whole disagreed to

On bohea tea,	per pound,	10^{24} cents.
On all souchong or other black teas,	per pound,	15 cents.
On all hyson teas,	per pound,	30 cents.
On all other green teas,	per pound,	18 cents.[25]

On all looking glasses, window, and
other glass, except black quart
bottles,
} ten per centum, ad valorem.[26]

On all china, stone, and earthern
ware,   ten per centum ad valorem.

On all blank books,

On all writing, printing, or wrapping paper, paper hangings,
and pasteboard,

On all cabinet wares,

---

a motion by Ellsworth, seconded by Lee, to strike discrimination against foreign ships importing bohea tea.

[24] On June 1, by a vote of 9–8, the Senate disagreed to a motion by Lee to lower the impost on bohea tea to 8¢.

[25] On June 1 in committee of the whole, the Senate disagreed to motions by Morris to raise all duties on teas.

On June 5, a motion by Dalton to confine the India and China tea trade to American vessels was seconded by Carroll. It was disagreed to on June 8. (Maclay, June 5)

On June 5, the Senate struck out the clause from "On all teas imported from any country" through "18 cents." On June 9, on the recommendation of a committee appointed on June 8, the Senate replaced the phrases struck out with the following:
On all teas imported from Europe in Ships or Vessels built in the United States, and belonging wholly to a Citizen or Citizens thereof, or in Vessels built in foreign Countries and on the sixteenth day of May last, wholly the property of a Citizen or Citizens of the United States, and so continuing until the time of importation, as follows:

On bohea tea	per pound, 8 Cents
On all Souchong & other black teas	per pound, 13 Cents
On all hyson teas	per pound, 26 Cents
On all other green teas	per pound, 16 Cents

On all teas imported in any other manner than as above mentioned as follows:

On bohea tea	per pound, 15 Cents
On all Souchong or other black teas	per pound, 22 Cents
On all hyson teas	per pound, 45 Cents
On all other green teas	per pound, 27 Cents

On all goods, wares & merchandizes other than teas imported *from China or India in Ships not built in the United States,* and not wholly the property of a Citizen or Citizens thereof, nor in Vessels built in foreign Countries and on the sixteenth day of May last, wholly the property of a Citizen or Citizens of the United States and so continuing until the time of importation Twelve & one half per Centum ad Valorem.

The committee report, in the hands of Ellsworth and Strong, with notations of agreement by Otis, is filed with the bill.

[26] On June 5, the Senate inserted "On gunpowder, on all paints ground in oil, 10 per centum ad valorem" at this point.

On all buttons of metal,[27]
On all saddles,
On all gloves of leather,
On all hats of beaver, fur, wool, or a mixture of either,
On all millinery ready made,
On all castings of iron, and upon slit and rolled iron,[28]
On all leather tanned or tawed, and all manufacture of leather, except such as shall be otherwise rated,
On canes, walking-sticks, and whips,[29]
On cloathing ready made,
On all brushes,
On gold, silver, and plated ware, and on jewellery and paste work,[30]
On anchors,[31]
On all wrought tin and pewter ware,[32]

} Seven and a half per centum ad valorem.

On every coach, chariot, or other four wheel carriage, and on every chaise, solo, or other two wheel carriage, or parts thereof,

} fifteen per centum ad valorem.

On all other goods, wares, and merchandize, five per centum on the value thereof, at the time and place of importation, except as follows:

Salt-petre, tin in pigs, tin plates, lead, old pewter, brass, iron and brass

---

[27] On June 5, the Senate struck out "of metal" and changed the duty from 7 1/2 to 10 percent. The House disagreed to this and the Senate receded from it. The enrolled act, however, omits "of metal."

On June 10, the Senate inserted "On Shoe & Knee buckles, ten per Centum ad Valorem" at this point.

[28] On June 5, the Senate changed the duty on saddles, gloves, hats, millinery, and iron from 7 1/2 to 10 percent. The House disagreed to this and the Senate receded from it.

[29] On June 5, the Senate changed the duty on canes, walking-sticks, and whips from 7 1/2 to 10 percent. The House disagreed to this amendment and the Senate receded from it.

[30] On June 10, the Senate inserted
On gold and silver lace ⎫   ten per Centum
On gold and silver leaf ⎭   ad Valorem
at this point.

[31] On June 5, the Senate changed the imposts on gold, silver, and plated ware, jewellery, paste work, and on anchors from 7 1/2 to 10 percent. The House disagreed to this and the Senate receded from it.

[32] On June 2, the Senate disagreed to a motion by Morris to insert a duty of 10 percent on scythes, sickles, axes, spades, shovels, locks, hinges, plow-irons, etc., at this point.

On June 10, the Senate inserted "On playing cards per pack—10 cents" at this point.

On June 5, the Senate agreed "that all the Articles dutied ad Valorem be arranged together under their respective rates." The House disagreed to this and the Senate receded from it.

wire, copper in plates, wool,[33] dying woods, and dying drugs (other than indigo)[34] raw hides, beaver, and all other furs, and deer-skins.

[2] AND BE IT FARTHER ENACTED BY THE AUTHORITY AFORESAID, That from and after the first day of December, which shall be in the year one thousand seven hundred and ninety, there shall be laid a duty on every one hundred and twelve pounds weight of hemp imported as aforesaid, of sixty cents.[35]

[3] AND BE IT ENACTED BY THE AUTHORITY AFORESAID, That all the duties paid, or secured to be paid, upon any of the goods, wares, and merchandizes, as aforesaid,[36] shall be returned or discharged upon such of the said goods, wares, or merchandizes, as shall within twelve months after payment made, or security given, be exported to any country without the limits of the United States,[37] except one per centum on the amount of the said duties, in consideration of the expence which shall have accrued by the entry and safe keeping thereof.

[4] AND BE IT ENACTED BY THE AUTHORITY AFORESAID, That there shall be allowed and paid on every quintal of dried, and on every barrel of pickled fish, of the fisheries of the United States, and on every barrel of salted provision of the United States, exported to any country without the limits thereof, in lieu of a drawback of the duties imposed on the importation of the salt employed, and expended therein, viz.

On every quintal of dried fish,   5 cents.
On every barrel of pickled fish,   5 cents.
On every barrel of salted provision,   5 cents.

[5] AND BE IT FARTHER ENACTED BY THE AUTHORITY AFORESAID, That there shall be allowed and paid on every gallon of rum distilled within the United States, and exported beyond the limits of the same, in consideration of the duty on the importation of the molasses, from which the said rum shall have been distilled, 5 cents.[38]

[6] AND BE IT FARTHER ENACTED BY THE AUTHORITY AFORESAID, That a discount of ten per cent. on all the duties imposed by this act, shall be allowed on such goods, wares, and merchandizes, as shall be imported in

---

[33] On June 5, the Senate inserted "cotton" at this point. This was first agreed to on a motion by Morris on June 2. (Maclay, June 2)

[34] The Senate struck out "(other than indigo)."

[35] On June 5, the Senate inserted "And on Cotton per pound 3 cents" at this point.

[36] On June 11, the Senate inserted "except on distilled Spirits other than Brandy & Geneva" at this point.

[37] On June 11, the Senate inserted "as settled by the late treaty of peace" at this point.

[38] The Senate struck out this section. This action may have resulted from the June 4 reduction of the molasses duty. (Maclay, June 4)

vessels built in the United States, and which shall be wholly the property of a citizen or citizens thereof.[39]

[7] AND BE IT FARTHER ENACTED BY THE AUTHORITY AFORESAID, That this act shall continue and be in force until the first day of June, which shall be in the year of our Lord one thousand seven hundred and ninety-six, and from thence until the end of the next succeeding session of Congress, which shall be held thereafter, and no longer.[40]

1789, May 16.
Read the third time, and passed the House of Representatives.

JOHN BECKLEY, CLERK

House Bills, SR, DNA. Actions in the Senate committee of the whole and final amendments were noted on the bill by Otis, and a list of the amendments, annotated by Otis, is filed with the bill. They are also printed in the *SLJ*, pp. 60n–64n and 64–67. Two dates are given for many of the Senate amendments because they were first debated and agreed to in committee of the whole and then passed by the Senate out of committee. The source for the action in committee of the whole is Maclay on the date indicated, unless otherwise noted. The House agreed to all of the amendments except those indicated as disagreed to in the notes. House amendments to the Senate amendments are printed in the *HJ*, pp. 88 and 99. Sources of information not included in the *SLJ* or *HJ* are included in the respective notes.

---

[39] On June 11, the Senate inserted the following at this point:
or in Vessels built in foreign Countries, and on the sixteenth day of May last, wholly the property of a Citizen or Citizens of the United States and so continuing, until the time of importation.
[40] On June 2, the Senate disagreed to a motion by Morris to strike out the last section.

Petition of the Shipwrights of Philadelphia
May 25, 1789

To the Honorable the Representatives of the Freemen of the United States of America in General Congress assembled—
The Memorial & Petition of the Subscribers Master-Shipwrights in the Port of Philadelphia—
Most respectfully Sheweth,
That before the late Revolution the Shipwrights of the Port of Philadelphia, had acquired the reputation of building Ships of a moderate size as well & as faithfully as in any part of the World, by means whereof they obtained constant Employment for themselves, their Journeymen, & apprentices, by Building Ships to the amount of four thousand five hundred Tons Annually, besides the repairs of Old Ships—That the revolution in its Conse-

quences & effects has borne harder upon your Petitioners than upon any other Class of Mechanics (or perhaps Citizens at large) whatever, in depriving them of two thirds of their former Employment; as it appears from an average for three years past, that they have built only to the amount of fifteen hundred Tons Annually—That the British navigation Act totally prevents them from Building Ships for that Nation, but their Merchants generally repair their Vessels in America, as far as the Act allows, and often run the Risque of a forfieture by exceeding the Limitation—That although the Arret of France, of December 1787, grants, that "Vessels built in the united States and sold in France, or purchased by Frenchmen, shall be exempted from all duties, on proof that they were built in the United States," yet your Petitioners build few Vessels for That Nation—That an Edict of Spain of January 1786, lays a heavy duty on American built Ships, purchased by their subjects, and also prohibits them from Trading to their Colonies, although the duty is paid & they are owned by the Subjects of Spain, Nevertheless the Spaniards have purchased more Vessels from your Petitioners than any other Nation—That under these discourageing Circumstances they have waited with anxious Expectation for the sitting of the Honorable Congress under the new Constitution of the United States, firmly relying that every Exertion would be used to reinstate so necessary & useful a branch of Business, as nearly as possible upon it's former flourishing Establishment; to effect which your Petitioners with great Deference beg leave to suggest the following hints to your Consideration.

1st. That a Tonage duty should be laid upon all shipping built & owned by Foreigners, sufficient to give a decided Preference to the Shipping Built in the United States, but at the same time so moderate, as not to prevent the Resort of foreign Shipping to these States until by a gradual increase they shall be in a Condition to carry for themselves, Nevertheless some preference ought to be given the French for their preference to American build Vessels.

2nd That to encourage the Increase of American Shipping, there be no ~~duty~~ Tonage duty on Shipping built in the United States, Owned in part or in whole by Citizens of these States, except for the support of Bays & Lighthouses.

3rd That American built Ships purchased by Foreigners ought to be nearly on the Same footing as if owned by American Merchants.

4th. That Foreign built Ships, purchased by American Merchants after the passing of this Act, Ought to pay the same duty & under the same restrictions as foreign Built Vessels Owned by Foreigners.

5th That there be a difference in the duties payable on the Importation of foreign goods between these imported in American built shipping, Owned as aforesaid & those imported in foreign built Ships.

6th That there be also a difference in the duties payable on the Importation of foreign goods from ports or places, where they are not originally produced or Manufactured, & the same goods imported directly from the place of their Growth or Manufacture, and that this duty should be greater when the Importation from the second port in foreign Bottoms, than in American built Ships.

7th That many possible advantages may arise from Negociations with the Courts of Madrid & London on Principles of Reciprocity, respecting American built Ships.

8th That high duties laid on Materials necessary for fiting Ships, augment their price & retard the progress of Ship Building.

9th That many Inconveniences, have arisen from the different modes of Tonageing Ships in the different States in America; That your petitioners had foreseen the Inconveniences, and endeavoured to remedy the evil by adopting the inclosed nearly average mode of Measurement, which has not yet been carried into effect waiting for your Honorable Body to establish one general System for the Measurement of all ships built in America.

YOUR PETITIONERS humbly conceive that Negociations & Regulations somwhat simelar to the foregoing would tend to the Rapid Increase of American Shippen & before long enable the United States to become Carriers by Sea of all the Produce of this extensive Continent to foreign Markets.

All which is Respectfully submitted to the Consideration of your Honorable House.

Petitions and Memorials: Various subjects, SR, DNA. List of signatures will be printed in the petition volume.

Petition of the Tradesmen and Manufacturers of Boston
June 5, 1789

To the Honorable the Congress of the United States of America—
The Petition of the Tradesmen & Manufacturers of the Town of Boston
                    SHEWETH—

That the great decrease of American Manufactures, & almost total stagnation of American Ship-building, urge us to apply to the sovereign Legislature of these States for their Assistance to promote these important Branches so essential to our national Wealth and Prosperity—It is with regret we observe the resources of this Country exhausted for foreign Luxeries; our Wealth expended for various Articles which could be manufactured among ourselves, & our Navigation subject to the most severe restrictions in many foreign Ports, whereby the extensive branch of American Ship-building is essentially injured, & a numerous body of Citizens, who were formerly employed in its various departments, deprived of their support & dependence—Your Petitioners are farther induced to express their concern, that the Subjects of those Nations, who are endeavoring to annihilate our Navigation, are permitted to send their Vessels to any part of the United States for Bread Flour Tobacco & every other produce, while American Ships are totally excluded from many of their Ports.

Your Petitioners beg leave to inform Congress that previous to the War upwards of 60 Vessels from 150 to 300 Tons have been built in the Town of Boston in the course of one year & provided such restrictions were laid upon foreign Vessels as to give a decided preference to American built Ships, we apprehend (from the aforesaid number built in this Town only) that these States would be able in a short period, to supply a large proportion, if not the whole, of the Navigation necessary for the carrying Trade of these States.

Your Petitioners need not inform Congress that on the revival of our mechanical Arts & Manufactures depend the Wealth & prosperity of the Northern States, nor can we forbear mentioning to your Honors that the Citizens of these States conceive the object of their Independence but half obtained till those national purposes are established on a permanent & extensive basis by the legislative acts of the Foederal Government. Unless these important branches are supported we humbly conceive that our Agriculture must greatly decline, as the impoverished State of our Seaports will eventually lessen the demand for the produce of our Lands.

It would be tedious to your Honors should we attempt to enumerate the variety of Articles which could (with the Assistance of Government) be manufactured with advantage among ourselves—Your Petitioners however wish not to deceive Congress by boasting of Manufactures which cannot at present be carried on to a sufficient degree to answer our demands, for which reason our Applications have been wholly confined to the several branches hereafter mentioned, which are established among us, & which we humbly received by due encouragement, might be more extensively promoted.

Your Petitioners would farther mention to Congress that the Encouragement of many of our Manufactures depends on a free Importation of certain raw materials, we therefore flatter ourselves that the Duties imposed on such Articles as are absolutely necessary to forward our several branches will not operate to the injury of the American Manufacture.

Your Petitioners formerly experienced the Patronage of this State Legislature in their Act laying Duties & Prohibitions on certain Articles of Manufacture, which encourages your Petitioners to request that heavy Duties may be laid on such Articles as are manufactured by our own Citizens, humbly conceiving that the Impost is not solely considered by Congress as an Object of Revenue but in its operation, intended to exclude such Importations, & ultimately establish these several branches of Manufacture among ourselves.

Your Petitioners do not presume to dictate to your Honors the Mode to be adopted for accomplishing the purposes we have mentioned, they flatter themselves however that every necessary Assistance will be afforded by Congress to induce them to prosecute with cheerfulness & alacrity their several Occupations & that such measures will be pursued for the relief of your Petitioners in Congress as in their great Wisdom shall judge consistent with the Inter[nal] Prosperity & Happiness of this extensive Empire—And as in Duty bound shall ever pray.
Boston May 1789

Petitions and Memorials: Various subjects, SR, DNA. List of signatures will be printed in the petition volume.

Conference Committee Report
June 27, 1789

The Committee appointed to confer with a Committee of the House of Representatives, on the Subject matter of the 4th. 5th. 6th. 7th. 11th. 12th & 17th Amendments of the Senate, to the Bill entitled "An Act for laying a Duty on Goods, Wares & Merchandizes, imported into the United States" beg leave to report
That your Committee have held the sd. Conferrence with the Committee of the House of Representatives and after a full Consideration of the Subject matter of the Same,[1] in presence of several Members of both Houses, have agreed to report[2] to their Respective Houses—as follows
That the sd. Committees could not come to any Agreement on the 4th. & 5th. Amendments—
That it be recommended to the House of Representatives, to agree to the 6th. 7th. & 11th. Amendments of the Senate—
That the 12th. Amendment, be amended by the Senate—by striking out the Word *Sixteen* & inserting the Word *Twenty*—
That the 17th. Amendment be amended by the Senate—by striking out the Word *One* and inserting the Word *Two*.

Joint Committee Reports, RG 128, DNA, hand of Lee.

---

[1] The word "Same" was written over the word "Conferrence."
[2] The word "report" was written over the word "recommend."

Indian Trade Bill [HR-51]

Calendar

Date	House	Senate
1790		
Jan. 12	President's message enclosing a report of the secretary of war received and partly read. [1]	
Jan. 13	Report read and referred to Wadsworth, Brown, Boudinot, Burke, and Baldwin.	
Jan. 14	Livermore, Ames, Laurance, Scott, and Smith (Md.) added to committee.	
Jan. 20	Wadsworth presented committee report, which was read.	
Jan. 21	Read; debated in COWH on a motion by Wadsworth; report agreed to in COWH without amendments. [2]	
Mar. 30	Wadsworth presented *a bill to regulate trade and intercourse with the Indian Tribes,* which was read.	

[1] *GUS,* Jan. 13. The president's message is printed in the *SLJ,* p. 221. The Secretary's report is printed with the Military Establishment Act [HR-50a]. Although the actions of Jan. 12, 13, 20, and 21 were journalized, the newspapers reported that they took place in secret sessions. (*NYDG,* Jan. 13, 14, 21, 22)

[2] *GUS,* Jan. 23. The *HJ* reports no further action on this committee report, but it was probably the basis for [HR-50a] and [HR-51].

Date	House	Senate
1790		
Mar. 31	Read; committed to COWH.	
Apr. 7–9	Postponed as order of the day.	
Apr. 10	On a motion by Scott, debated in COWH; *amendment* debated; motion for COWH to rise agreed to; motion by Fitzsimons to recommit bill to a select committee disagreed to.[3]	
Apr. 12–27	Postponed as order of the day.	
Apr. 28	Debated in COWH and, on a motion by Jackson,[4] recommitted to the original committee on the president's message with the addition of Sumter and Steele.[5]	

[3] *NYDG,* Apr. 12; *GUS,* Apr. 14.
[4] *NYDG,* Apr. 29.
[5] On May 14 Wadsworth presented a new Indian Trade Bill [HR-65].

Indian Trade Bill [HR-51]
March 30, 1790

A BILL to regulate Trade and Intercourse with the INDIAN TRIBES

SEC. 1. BE *it enacted by the* SENATE *and* HOUSE *of* REPRESENTATIVES *of the United States of America, in Congress assembled,* That there be established so many military posts, and in such situations on the frontiers, as the President of the United States shall judge necessary, to be garrisoned by the troops of the United States. And there shall be a suitable person appointed, at such of said posts as the President of the United States shall find it necessary, being an officer in the line of said troops,[1] to superintend the trade and intercourse with the Indians contiguous thereto; and the Indian nations or tribes shall be divided into districts for that purpose. And the said Superintendants shall be, and hereby are authorized, under the direction of the President of the United States, to hold conferences with the heads of the several nations within their respective districts; thereby fully informing them of the regulations contained in this act; and making proper arrangements for trade and intercourse with the said Indians, mutually beneficial to them and to the citizens of the United States. And the said Superintendants shall also, at each and every such conference with said Indians, make them suitable presents, in the name of the United States, of such goods as are best adapted to their use, and to conciliate their friendship. Provided that the presents given at any one post, shall not exceed the value or sum of   dollars, in one year.

SEC. 2. *And be it further enacted,* That no person or persons whatsoever, shall be permitted to use any trade or commerce, or hold any intercourse with any Indian or Indians, within the United States, without a permit from the Superintendant of the district to which such Indians belong, on penalty of forfeiting all peltries, furs, or other goods that may be found upon them in the Indian Territory, and also the sum of   dollars, the one half to the use of the United States, and the other half to the use of him or them that shall prosecute for the same, in any court proper to try the same.

SEC. 3. *And be it further enacted,* That each and every of the said Superintendants shall be, and hereby is authorized and directed to licence suitable and discreet persons to use trade and commerce, and to hold intercourse with the Indians within his district, which licence shall be in writing, under the seal and signature of the said Superintendant, and shall express the time of its duration, which shall not exceed two years from the date thereof. And for each licence the said Superintendant shall receive   dollars, and no more, which shall be a full compensation for his services as Superintendant. And no Superintendant, or officer in the army of the United States, shall be permitted directly or indirectly to be concerned or interested in any trade or commerce with the said Indians, on pain of forfeiting   dollars, to be recovered as aforesaid, for the uses aforesaid. And no trader shall sell more than   gallons of spirituous liquors under one licence; and the quantity permitted shall be expressed in the licence.

SEC. 4. *And be it further enacted,* That no sale of lands made by any Indians, or any nation or tribe of Indians, within the United States, after the passing of this act, shall be valid to any person or persons, or to any State, whether having the right of pre-emption to such lands or not, unless the same shall be

---

[1] On April 10 a motion to strike out "being an officer in the line of said troops" was debated. On the same date Scott moved for a substitute clause. (*NYDG,* Apr. 12; *GUS,* Apr. 14)

made at some public treaty, under a special licence given by the President of the United States for that purpose.

SEC. 5. *And be it further enacted,* That each and every of the Superintendants aforesaid, shall make returns from time to time, as the President of the United States shall direct, of all treaties or conferences held with any Indians as aforesaid, fully stating the same, and the goods given the said Indians, with the amount thereof; and also all licences granted as aforesaid to any person or persons for trade.

PRINTED BY FRANCIS CHILDS AND JOHN SWAINE

Wingate Papers, NhD.

Indian Trade Act [HR-65]

July 22, 1790

An Act to regulate Trade and Intercourse with the Indian Tribes

[1] Be it enacted by the Senate and House of Representatives of the United States of America, in Congress assembled, That no person shall be permitted to carry on any trade or intercourse with the Indian Tribes without a licence for that purpose under the hand and seal of the Superintendant of the Department, or of such other person as the President of the United States shall appoint for that purpose; which Superintendant, or other person so appointed, shall, on application, issue such licence to any proper person who shall enter into Bond with one or more Sureties approved of by the Superintendant, or person issuing such licence, or by the President of the United States, in the penal sum of one thousand dollars, payable to the President of the United States for the time being, for the use of the United States, conditioned for the true and faithful observance of such rules, regulations and restrictions, as now are, or hereafter shall be made for the government of trade and intercourse with the Indian Tribes. The said Superintendants, and persons by them licensed as aforesaid, shall be governed in all things touching the said trade and intercourse by such rules and regulations as the President shall prescribe. And no other person shall be permitted to carry on any trade or intercourse with the Indians without such licence as aforesaid. No licence shall be granted for a longer term than two years. Provided nevertheless, that the President may make such order respecting the tribes surrounded in their settlements by the Citizens of the United States as to secure an intercourse without licence if he may deem it proper.

[2] And be it further enacted, that the Superintendant, or person issuing such licence, shall have full power and authority to recall all such licences as he may have issued, if the person so licensed shall transgress any of the regulations or restrictions provided for the government of trade and intercourse with the Indian Tribes, and shall put in suit such Bonds as he may have taken immediately on the breach of any condition in said Bond. Provided always, that if it shall appear on trial, that the person, from whom such licence shall have been recalled, has not offended against any of the

provisions of this Act, or the regulations prescribed for the trade and intercourse with the Indian Tribes, he shall be entitled to receive a new Licence.

[3] AND BE IT FURTHER ENACTED, that every person, who shall attempt to trade with the Indian Tribes, or be found in the Indian Country with such Merchandize in his possession as are usually vended to the Indians without a licence first had and obtained, as in this Act prescribed, and being thereof convicted in any Court proper to try the same, shall forfeit all the Merchandize so offered for sale to the Indian Tribes, or so found in the Indian Country, which forfeiture shall be, one half to the benefit of the person prosecuting, and the other half to the benefit of the United States.

[4] AND BE IT ENACTED AND DECLARED, that no sale of lands made by any Indians or any nation or tribe of Indians within the United States, shall be valid to any person or persons or to any State, whether having the right of pre-emption to such lands or not, unless the same shall be made and duly executed at some public Treaty held under the authority of the United States.

[5] AND BE IT FURTHER ENACTED, that if any Citizen or Inhabitant of the United States, or of either of the Territorial Districts of the United States, shall go into any town, settlement or territory belonging to any nation or tribe of Indians, and shall there commit any Crime upon, or trespass against, the person or property of any peaceable and friendly Indian or Indians, which, if committed within the Jurisdiction of any State, or within the Jurisdiction of either of the said Districts against a Citizen or white Inhabitant thereof, would be punishable by the laws of such State or District, such offender or offenders shall be subject to the same punishment, and shall be proceeded against in the same manner, as if the offence had been committed within the Jurisdiction of the State or District to which he or they may belong, against a Citizen or white inhabitant thereof.

[6] AND BE IT FURTHER ENACTED, that for any of the Crimes or Offences aforesaid, the like proceedings shall be had for apprehending, imprisoning or bailing the offender, as the case may be, and for recognizing the witnesses for their appearance to testify in the case, and, where the offender shall be committed, or the witnesses shall be in a district other than that in which the offence is to be tried, for the removal of the offender and the Witnesses or either of them, as the case may be, to the District in which the trial is to be had, as by the Act to establish the Judicial Courts of the United States are directed for any Crimes or Offences against the United States.

[7] AND BE IT FURTHER ENACTED, that this Act shall be in force for the term of two years and from thence, to the end of the next Session of Congress and no longer.

FREDERICK AUGUSTUS MUHLENBERG
Speaker of the House of Representatives

JOHN ADAMS
Vice President of the United States and
President of the Senate

Approved July ⎫
the Twenty second ⎬   GO. WASHINGTON
1790. ⎭   President of the United States

I Certify that this Act did originate
in the House of Representatives.
JOHN BECKLEY—Clerk

Enrolled Acts, RG 11, DNA.

Calendar

Date	House	Senate
1790		
May 14	Wadsworth, for the committee to which the Indian Trade Bill [HR-51] was recommitted on April 28 (Wadsworth, Brown, Boudinot, Burke, Baldwin, Livermore, Ames, Laurance, Scott, Smith [Md.], Sumter, and Steele), presented *A Bill to regulate Trade and Intercourse with the Indian tribes,* which was read.	
May 17	Read and committed to COWH.	
May 19–June 21	Postponed as order of the day.	
June 22	Debated in COWH and *amended;* House agreed to amendments.	
June 23	Read; motion by Burke, to recommit in order to	Received and read.

Date	House	Senate
1790		
	strike out section 4, disagreed to;[1] blanks filled; agreed to as *An act to regulate trade and intercourse with the Indian tribes.*	
June 24–25		Postponed.
July 2		Read; committed to Hawkins, Few, and Schuyler.
July 8		Hawkins presented *committee report,* which was agreed to.
July 9		Read; agreed to with *amendments.*
July 10	Senate amendments agreed to.	
July 12	*Letter* received from Senate notifying House of a Senate amendment that had been omitted from the original message to the House; amendment disagreed to by a vote of 33–30.[2]	Amendment insisted upon.
July 13	Disagreement to Senate amendment adhered to by a vote of 27–24;[3] Madison, Scott, and Moore appointed to conference committee.	
July 14		Schuyler, Ellsworth, and Strong appointed to conference.
July 19	Madison reported for conference that House should	

[1] *NYDG,* June 24.
[2] *NYDG,* July 13.
[3] *GUS,* July 14.

Date	House	Senate
1790		
	recede from disagreement to amendment;[4] amendment agreed to.	
July 20	Signed by speaker.	Signed by vice president.
July 22	Signed by president.	

[4] *NYDA*, July 20.

Indian Trade Bill [HR-65]
May 14, 1790

A BILL to regulate Trade and Intercourse with the Indian Tribes

SEC. 1. BE *it enacted by the* SENATE *and* HOUSE *of* REPRESENTATIVES *of the United States of America in Congress assembled,* That no person shall be permitted to carry on any trade or intercourse with the Indian tribes, without a licence for that purpose, under the hand and seal of the Superintendant of the department, or of such other person as the President of the United States shall appoint for that purpose; which Superintendant, or other person so appointed, shall, on application, issue such licence to any   [1] who shall enter into bond with one or more sureties, approved of by the Superintendant, or person issuing such licence, or by the President of the United States, in the penal sum of   [2] payable to the President of the United States, for the time being, for the use of the United States, conditioned for the true and faithful observance of such rules, regulations and restrictions, as now are, or hereafter shall be made, for the government of trade and intercourse with the Indian tribes. The said Superintendants, and persons by them licenced as aforesaid, shall be governed in all things touching the said trade and intercourse, by such rules and regulations as the President shall prescribe: And no other person shall be permitted to carry on any trade or intercourse with the Indians, without such licence as aforesaid. No licence shall be granted for a longer term than   .[3]

SEC. 2. *And be it further enacted,* That the Superintendant, or person issuing such licence, shall have full power and authority to recal all such licences as he may have issued, if the person so licensed shall transgress any of the regula-

---

[1] The House filled this blank with "proper person."
[2] The House filled this blank with "Three Thousand Dollars."
[3] The House filled this blank with "two years."

tions or restrictions provided for the government of trade and intercourse with the Indian tribes, and shall put in suit such bonds as he may have taken, immediately on the breach of any condition in said bond. *Provided always,* That if it shall appear, on trial, that the person, from whom such licence shall have been recalled, has not offended against any of the provisions of this act, or the regulations prescribed for the trade and intercourse with the Indian tribes, he shall be entitled to receive a new licence, without paying any fees therefor.[4]

SEC. 3. *And be it further enacted,* That every person who shall attempt to trade with the Indian tribes, or be found in the Indian country, with such merchandize in his possession as are usually vended to the Indians, without a licence first had and obtained, as in this act prescribed, and being thereof convicted in any court proper to try the same, shall forfeit all the merchandize so offered for sale to the Indian tribes, or so found in the Indian country, which forfeiture shall be, one half to the benefit of the person prosecuting, and the other half to the benefit of the United States.

SEC. 4. *And be it further enacted,* That a sum not exceeding   [5] thousand dollars, be appropriated out of the monies arising from duties on imports and tonnage, subject to the orders of the President of the United States, to be laid out in goods and articles of trade suitable for supplying the wants and necessities of the Indians, and to be vended and retailed to them, through the agency of the said Superintendants, and persons to be licensed by them for that purpose, in such manner, and conformably to such regulations, as the President of the United States shall establish.[6]

SEC. 5. *And be it further enacted,* That no sale of lands made by any Indians or any nation or tribe of Indians within the United States, shall be valid to any person or persons, or to any State, whether having the right of pre-emption to such lands or not, unless the same shall be made and duly executed at some public treaty, held under the lawful[7] authority of the United States.

SEC. 6. *And be it further enacted,* That if any citizen or inhabitant of the United States, or of either of the territorial districts of the United States shall go into any town, settlement or territory belonging to any nation or tribe of Indians, and shall there commit any crime upon, or trespass against the person or property of any peaceable and friendly Indian or Indians, which, if committed within the jurisdiction of any State, or within the jurisdiction of either of the said districts, against a citizen or white inhabitant thereof,

[4] The House struck out "without paying any fees therefor."
[5] The House filled this blank with "ten."
[6] On June 22, by a recorded vote of 27–26, requested by Jackson, the House disagreed to a motion by Sherman to strike out the fourth section. (*HJ*, p. 471; *NYDG, GUS,* June 23)
[7] The House struck out "lawful."

would be punishable by the laws of such State or district, such offender or offenders shall be subject to the same punishment, and shall be proceeded against in the same manner as if the offence had been committed within the jurisdiction of the State or district to which he or they may belong, against a citizen[8] thereof.

SEC. 7. *And be it further enacted,* That for any of the crimes or offences aforesaid, the like proceedings shall be had for apprehending, imprisoning or bailing the offender, as the case may be, and for recognizing the witnesses for their appearance to testify in the case, and where the offender shall be committed, or the witnesses shall be in a district other than that in which the offence is to be tried, for the removal of the offender and the witnesses, or either of them, as the case may be, to the district in which the trial is to be had, as by the act to establish the judicial courts of the United States are directed, for any crimes or offences against the United States.[9]

Wingate Papers, NhD. Unless otherwise stated, the amendments were determined by a comparison of the bill as introduced with the engrossed bill.

---

[8] The House inserted "or white inhabitant" at this point.

[9] On June 22, on a motion by Steele (*GUS,* June 23), the House added the following section at this point:

SEC. 8. *And be it further enacted,* That this Act shall be in force for the term of two years, and from thence to the end of the next session of Congress, and no longer.

Indian Trade Bill [HR-65]
June 23, 1790

An ACT to regulate Trade and Intercourse with the Indian Tribes

SEC. 1. BE *it enacted by the Senate and House of Representatives of the United States of America, in Congress assembled,* That no person shall be permitted to carry on any trade or intercourse with the Indian tribes, without a license for that purpose, under the hand and seal of the Superintendant of the department, or of such other person as the President of the United States shall appoint for that purpose; which Superintendant, or other person so appointed, shall, on application, issue such license to any proper person, who shall enter into bond with one or more sureties approved of by the Superintendant or person issuing such license, or by the President of the United States, in the penal sum of Three[1] Thousand Dollars, payable to the President of the

---

[1] The Senate struck out "Three" and inserted "One."

United States for the time being, for the use of the United States; conditioned for the true and faithful observance of such rules, regulations and restrictions as now are, or hereafter shall be made for the government of trade and intercourse with the Indian tribes: The said Superintendants, and persons by them licensed as aforesaid, shall be governed in all things touching the said trade and intercourse, by such rules and regulations as the President shall prescribe; and no other person shall be permitted to carry on any trade or intercourse with the Indians, without such license as aforesaid. No license shall be granted for a longer term than two years.[2]

SEC. 2. *And be it further enacted,* That the Superintendant, or person issuing such license, shall have full power and authority to recall all such licenses as he may have issued, if the person so licensed shall transgress any of the regulations or restrictions provided for the government of trade and intercourse with the Indian tribes, and shall put in suit such bonds as he may have taken, immediately on the breach of any condition in said bond: *Provided always,* That if it shall appear on trial, that the person from whom such license shall have been recalled, has not offended against any of the provisions of this Act, or the regulations prescribed for the trade and intercourse with the Indian tribes, he shall be entitled to receive a new license.

SEC. 3. *And be it further enacted,* That every person who shall attempt to trade with the Indian tribes, or be found in the Indian country with such merchandize in his possession as are usually vended to the Indians, without a license first had and obtained, as in this Act prescribed, and being thereof convicted in any court proper to try the same, shall forfeit all the merchandize so offered for sale to the Indian tribes, or so found in the Indian country; which forfeiture shall be one half to the benefit of the person prosecuting, and the other half to the benefit of the United States.

SEC. 4. *And be it further enacted,* That a sum not exceeding Ten Thousand Dollars, be appropriated out of the monies arising from duties on imports and tonnage, subject to the orders of the President of the United States, to be laid out in goods and articles of trade suitable for supplying the wants and necessities of the Indians, and to be vended and retailed to them through the agency of the said Superintendants, and persons to be licensed by them for that purpose, in such manner and conformably to such regulations as the President of the United States shall establish.[3]

SEC. 5. *And be it further[4] enacted,* That no sale of lands made by any Indians, or any nation or tribe of Indians within the United States, shall be

---

[2] The Senate added the following proviso at this point:
    Provided nevertheless that the President may make such order respecting the tribes surrounded in their Settlements by the Citizens of the United States as to secure an intercourse without license if he may deem it proper.
[3] The Senate struck out this section.
[4] The Senate struck out *"further"* and inserted "and declared" after "enacted."

valid to any person or persons, or to any State, whether having the right of pre-emption to such lands or not, unless the same shall be made and duly executed at some public treaty held under the authority of the United States.

SEC. 6. *And be it further enacted,* That if any citizen or inhabitant of the United States, or of either of the territorial districts of the United States, shall go into any town, settlement or territory belonging to any nation or tribe of Indians, and shall there commit any crime upon, or trespass against the person or property of any peaceable and friendly Indian or Indians, which, if committed within the jurisdiction of any State, or within the jurisdiction of either of the said districts, against a citizen or white inhabitant thereof, would be punishable by the laws of such State or district, such offender or offenders shall be subject to the same punishment, and shall be proceeded against in the same manner, as if the offence had been committed within the jurisdiction of the State or district to which he or they may belong, against a citizen or white inhabitant thereof.

SEC. 7. *And be it further enacted,* That for any of the crimes or offences aforesaid, the like proceedings shall be had for apprehending, imprisoning or bailing the offender, as the case may be, and for recognizing the witnesses for their appearance to testify in the case, and, where the offender shall be committed, or the witnesses shall be in a district other than that in which the offence is to be tried, for the removal of the offender and the witnesses, or either of them, as the case may be, to the district in which the trial is to be had, as by the Act to establish the Judicial Courts of the United States are directed for any crimes or offences against the United States.

SEC. 8. *And be it further enacted,* That this Act shall be in force for the term of two years, and from thence to the end of the next session of Congress, and no longer.

1790, June the 23d—

Read the third time, and passed the House of Representatives.

Printed by JOHN FENNO

House Bills, SR, DNA. The amendments are from the *SLJ,* pp. 404n–405n.

Senate Committee Report
July 8, 1790

The committee to whom the act to regulate trade and Intercourse with the Indian Tribes was referred reports

three & insert one
Sec. 1 Line 10 strike out *thousand*∧and insert *hundred.*[1]
at the end of ~~the~~ Section 1st. add, Provided nevertheless that the president may make such order respecting the tribes surrounded in their settle-
of the United States
ments by the Citizens∧as to secure an intercourse without license if he may deem it proper.
~~Strike out sections 4th and 5th~~[2]

Various Select Committee Reports, SR, DNA, hand of Hawkins.

---

[1] The amendment agreed to by the Senate changed the amount from three thousand to one thousand.
[2] Otis wrote "a" under "4th" and "not a" under "5th." These markings were lined out and were evidently the source of the confusion over the striking out of section 4.

Letter from the Secretary of the Senate to the Speaker of the House July 12, 1790

Office of the Secretary of the
Senate July 12th. 1790

Sir

Thro' a mistake not wholly indeed my own, one of the proposed amendments of the Senate to the Bill entitled "An Act to regulate trade and intercourse with the Indian Tribes" was omitted to wit:
"Strike out the fourth Section."
As this was in fact the vote of Senate, I rely on the indulgence of the Honorable House to permit me to correct the Certificate, which I have accordingly done.

I have the honor to be
Your most obedt. hble. Servt.
SAM. A. OTIS

The Honble. The Speaker
of the House of Representatives
of the United States

Other Records: Various papers, SR, DNA.

Indian Treaties Act [HR-20]

August 20, 1789

AN ACT PROVIDING FOR THE EXPENCES
WHICH MAY ATTEND NEGOTIATIONS OR
TREATIES WITH THE INDIAN TRIBES, AND
THE APPOINTMENT OF COMMISSIONERS FOR
MANAGING THE SAME

[1] BE IT ENACTED BY THE SENATE, AND HOUSE OF REPRESENTATIVES OF THE UNITED STATES OF AMERICA, IN CONGRESS ASSEMBLED, that a sum not exceeding Twenty thousand Dollars, arising from the duties on imports and tonnage, shall be, and the same is hereby appropriated, to defraying the expence of negotiating and treating with the Indian Tribes.

[2] AND BE IT FURTHER ENACTED that each of the Commissioners, who may be appointed for managing such negotiations and treaties, shall be entitled to an allowance, exclusive of his expences at the place of treaty, of eight dollars Per day during his actual service, to be paid out of the monies so appropriated.

FREDERICK AUGUSTUS MUHLENBERG
Speaker of the House of Representatives
JOHN ADAMS
Vice-President of the United States, and
President of the Senate

Approved August
the Twentieth
1789

GO. WASHINGTON
President of the United States

I certify that this Act did originate in
the House of Representatives.
JOHN BECKLEY—Clerk

Enrolled Acts, RG 11, DNA.

Calendar

Date	House	Senate
1789		
Aug. 7	*Message from the president,* transmitting *report of the secretary of war with en-closures,* received and read.	Message from the president, transmitting report of the secretary of war with en-closures, received.
Aug. 8	Message and enclosures debated in secret session of COWH;[1] *resolution* agreed to by House and referred to Clymer, Ames, and Moore.	
Aug. 10	Clymer presented "a bill providing for the expences which may attend negociations or treaties with the Indian tribes, and the appointment of commissioners for manag-ing the same," which was read.	
Aug. 11	Read; debated in COWH; motion by Sedgwick to strike "that commis-sioners, not exceeding three" agreed to; motion by Jackson, to add a clause empowering the president to raise troops and call up militia if the Creeks refused to treat, debated and withdrawn;[2] amendments reported by COWH and agreed to by House.	

---

[1] *CR,* Aug. 8.
[2] *GUS,* Aug. 12; *CR,* Aug. 11. Jackson's motion is printed as a resolution with the Troops Act [HR–27].

Date	House	Senate
1789		
Aug. 12	Read; motion to fill blank with $41,000 disagreed to by a vote of 24–23; motion by Madison to fill blank with $40,000 agreed to by a recorded vote of 28–23; bill debated in COWH; blank in clause allowing a compensation to the commissioners filled with $8 per day;[3] COWH amendment agreed to by House.	
Aug. 13	Read and agreed to.	Received and read.
Aug. 14		Read; committed to Few, Ellsworth, King, Lee, and Butler.
Aug. 17		*Committee report* presented and disagreed to; *resolutions* disagreed to.
Aug. 18		Debated; motion to strike "eight dollars" from clause providing compensation for the commissioners and insert "five dollars" disagreed to; motion to insert "at the discretion of the President" after "eight dollars per day" disagreed to; motion to strike the compensation figure of "eight dollars" and insert "six dollars" disagreed to; bill read; motion to change figure allotted for negotiating an Indian treaty from 40 thousand dollars to twenty thousand dollars

[3] *GUS*, Aug. 15; *CR*, Aug. 12.

Date	House	Senate
1789		
		agreed to by a recorded vote of 12–7; consideration of a proposed *resolution* superseded by a motion for the previous question; bill agreed to with an amendment.
Aug. 19	Senate amendment debated; motion by Baldwin to amend the amendment by inserting "for holding treaties with the Indians south of the Ohio" debated; motion by Fitzsimons, seconded by Madison, to postpone debate, disagreed to; Baldwin motion disagreed to;[4] amendment agreed to.	
Aug. 20	Signed by speaker and by president.	Signed by vice president.

[4] *GUS,* Aug. 26; *CR,* Aug. 19.

Message from the President
August 7, 1789

GENTLEMEN of the HOUSE of REPRESENTATIVES,

THE business which has been under the consideration of Congress, has been of so much importance, that I was unwilling to draw their attention from it to any other subject, but the disputes which exist between some of the United States, and several powerful tribes of Indians within the limits of the Union, and the hostilities which have in several instances been committed on the frontiers, seem to require the immediate interposition of the General Government.

I have therefore directed the several statements and papers which have been submitted to me on this subject by General Knox, to be laid before you for your information.

While the measures of government ought to be calculated to protect its citizens from all injury and violence, a due regard should be extended to those Indian tribes whose happiness, in the course of events, so materially depends on the national justice and humanity of the United States.

If it should be the judgment of Congress, that it would be most expedient to terminate all differences in the southern district, and to lay the foundation for future confidence, by an amicable treaty with the Indian tribes in that quarter, I think proper to suggest the consideration of the expediency of instituting a temporary commission for that purpose, to consist of three persons, whose authority should expire with the occasion.

How far such a measure, unassisted by posts, would be competent to the establishment and preservation of peace and tranquillity on the frontiers, is also a matter which merits your serious consideration.

Along with this object, I am induced to suggest another, with the national importance and necessity of which I am deeply impressed; I mean some uniform and effective system for the militia of the United States. It is unnecessary to offer arguments in recommendation of a measure, on which the honor, safety, and well-being of our country so evidently, and so essentially depend.

But it may not be amiss to observe, that I am particularly anxious it should receive as early attention as circumstances will admit; because it is now in our power to avail ourselves of the military knowledge disseminated throughout the several States, by means of the many well instructed officers and soldiers of the late army, a resource which is daily diminishing by deaths and other causes.

To suffer this peculiar advantage to pass away unimproved, would be to neglect an opportunity which will never again occur, unless unfortunately we should again be involved in a long and arduous war.

GEORGE WASHINGTON

NEW-YORK, August 7, 1789

HJ, pp. 137–38.

Report of the Secretary of War and Enclosures
August 7, 1789

War Office June 15th. 1789.

Sir.

The time it will require to complete a full statement of the department of War, induces me to submit to your view in a series of numbers such parts thereof as seem to claim an immediate attention.

As most of the nations of indians within the limits of the United States are at present discontented and some of them turbulent, I have conceived it proper to commence by a statement of the indian department—In the performance of this business, I have not barely confined myself to facts, but I have taken the liberty of suggesting such measures as appear to my mind to be necessary for the happiness and reputation of the public.

By the ordinance of Congress of the 7th August 1786 for the regulation of indian affairs which is herewith submitted the department is divided into the Northern and Southern districts.

The report on the treaties of Fort Harmar submitted the 23d. of May last will shew the situation of those tribes with whom the United States have formed treaties since the conclusion of the War with Great Britain.

I have now the honor to transmit a paper number 1 relative to the Wabash indians—Were the subsisting disorders with those indians quieted, and they attached to the interests of the United States, it is not probable that any further troubles with the more distant indians would soon arise.

Number 2 which will be submitted shortly will shew the situation of the Southern indians, and contain some observations on the difficulties subsisting between them and the frontier people of the States of Georgia and North Carolina.

I have the honor to be
With the highest respect
Sir
Your Most Obedient
Humble Servant
H. KNOX

The President of the United States

GENERAL STATEMENT
OF THE
DEPARTMENT OF WAR

Number 1.
Indian Department
Wabash Nations

War Office June 15th. 1789

By information from Brigadier General Harmar the commanding officer of the troops on the frontiers it appears that several murders have been lately committed on the inhabitants by small parties of indians probably from the Wabash country.

Some of the said murders having been perpetrated on the south side of the Ohio, the inhabitants on the waters of that river are exceedingly alarmed for the extent of six or seven hundred miles along the same.

It is to be observed that the United States have not formed any treaties with the Wabash indians—On the contrary, since the conclusion of the War with great Britain hostilities have almost constantly existed between the people of Kentuckey and the said indians—The injuries and murders have been so reciprocal, that it would be a point of critical investigation to know on which side they have been the greatest.

Some of the inhabitants of Kentuckey during the year past roused by recent injuries made an incursion into the Wabash country, and possessing an equal aversion to all bearing the name of indians—they destroyed a number of peaceable Piankeshaws who prided themselves in their attachment to the United States.

Things being thus circumstanced it is greatly to be apprehended that hostilities may be so far extended as to involve the indian tribes with whom the United States have recently made treaties—It is well known how strong the passion for War exists in the mind of a young savage, and how easily it may be inflamed so as to disregard every precept of the older and wiser part of the tribes who may have a more just opinion of the force of a treaty.

Hence it results that unless some decisive measures are immediately adopted to terminate those mutual hostilities, they will probably become general among all the indians north west of the Ohio.

In examining the question, how the disturbances on the frontiers are to be quieted, two modes present themselves, by which the object might perhaps be effected—The first of which is by raising an Army and extirpating the refractory tribes entirely, or 2dly. By forming treaties of peace with them, in which their rights and limits, should be explicitly defined, and the treaties observed on the part of the United States with the most rigid justice, by punishing the whites, who should violate the same.

In considering the first mode, an enquiry would arise, whether under the existing circumstances of affairs, the United States have a clear right, consistently with the principles of justice and the laws of nature to proceed to the destruction or expulsion of the savages on the Wabash, supposing the force for that object easily attainable.

It is presumable that a nation solicitous of establishing its character on the broad basis of justice, would not only hesitate at, but reject every proposition to benefit itself, by the injury of any neigbouring community, however contemptible and weak it might be, either with respect to its manners or power.

When it shall be considered that the indians derive their subsistence cheifly by hunting, and that according to fixed principles, their population is in proportion to the facility with which they procure their food, it would most probably be found that the expulsion or destruction of the indian tribes have nearly the same effect—for if they are removed from their usual hunting ground they must necessarily encroach on the hunting grounds of another tribe who will not suffer the encroachment with impunity—hence they destroy each other.

The Indians being the prior occupants possess the right of the soil—It cannot be taken from them unless by their free consent, or by the right of conquest in case of a just War—To dispossess them on any other principle would be a gross violation of the fundamental Laws of nature, and of that destributive justice which is the glory of a nation.

But if it should be decided on an abstract view of the question to be just, to remove by force the Wabash indians from the territory they occupy, the finances of the United States would not at present admit of the operation.

By the best and latest information it appears that on the Wabash and its communications, there are from 1,500 to 2,000 Warriors, an expedition against them with the view of extirpating them, or destroying their towns, could not be undertaken with a probability of success with less than an Army of 2,500 men—The regular troops of the United States on the frontiers, are less than six hundred—of that number not more than four hundred could be collected from the posts for the purpose of the expedition—To raise, pay, feed, arm, and equip 1,900 additional men with their necessary officers for six months, and to provide every thing in the Hospital, and Quarter Masters line would require the sum of 200,000 dollars—A sum far exceeding the ability of the United States to advance consistently with a due regard to other indispensible objects.

Were the representations of the people of the frontiers, (who have imbibed the strongest prejudices against the indians, perhaps in consequence of the murders of their dearest friends and connections) only to be regarded, the circumstances before stated would not appear conclusive—an expedition however inadequate, must be undertaken.

But when the impartial mind of the great public sits in judgement, it is necessary that the cause of the ignorant indians should be heard as well as those who are more fortunately circumstanced—It well becomes the public to enquire before it punishes—to be influenced by reason, and the nature of things, and not by its resentments.

It would be found on examination that both policy and justice unite in dictating the attempt of treating with the Wabash indians—For it would be unjust in the present confused state of injuries to make War on those tribes without having previously invited them to a treaty, in order amicably to adjust all differences—If they should afterwards persist in their depredations the United States may with propriety inflict such punishment as they shall think proper.

But at present were the measure just, the Union could not command an army for coercion but at the expence of some great national object.

In case no treaty should be held, the events which are rising in rapid succession on the frontiers must be suffered to take their own course—Their progress and issue will deeply injure, if not utterly destroy, the interests and Government of the United States in the Western territory.

The estimates of the Governor of the Western Territory herewith submitted will shew that in addition to the property already in his possession, a treaty with the Wabash indians may be effected for the sum of 16,150 Dollars—If additional territory should be the object it would require the further sum of   Dollars.

It is however to be remarked that it is very possible that this sum may not effect the object intended—It can be considered only as an experiment dictated by a regard to public justice which ought in all cases to govern the conduct of a nation.

The United States having come into the possession of sovereignty, and an extensive territory, must unavoidably be subject to the expences of such a condition.

The time has arrived when it is highly expedient, that a liberal system of justice should be adopted for the various indian tribes within the limits of the United States.

By having recourse to the several indian treaties made by the authority of Congress since the conclusion of the War with Great Britain, excepting those made January 1789 at Fort Harmar, it would appear, that Congress were of opinion that the treaty of peace of 1783 absolutely invested them with the fee of all the indian lands within the limits of the United States—That they had the right to assign, or retain such portions as they should judge proper.

But it is manifest, from the representations of the confederated indians at the Huron Village in December 1786 that they entertained a different opinion, and that they were the only rightful proprietors of the soil—and it appears by the resolve of the 2d. of July 1788, that Congress so far conformed to the idea as to appropriate a sum of money soley to the purpose of extinguishing the indian claims to lands they had ceded to the United States, and for obtaining regular conveyances of the same—This object was accordingly accomplished at the treaty of Fort Harmar in January 1789.

The principle of the indian right to the lands they possess being thus conceded, the dignity and interest of the nation will be advanced by making it the basis of the future administration of justice towards the indian tribes.

The whole number of indian Warriors south of the Ohio, and east of the

Mississippi may be estimated at 14,000—Those to the Northward of the Ohio, and to the southward of the lakes at about 5,000—In addition to these the old men, women, and children may be estimated at three for one Warrior the whole amounting to 76,000 souls.

It is highly probable that by a conciliatory system, the expence of managing the said indians and attaching them to the United States for the next ensuing period of fifty years may on average cost 15,000 dollars annually.

A system of coercion and oppression, pursued from time to time for the same period as the convenience of the United States might dictate, would probably amount to a much greater sum of money—But the blood and injustice which would stain the character of the nation, would be beyond all pecuniary calculation.

As the settlements of the whites shall approach near to the indian boundaries established by treaties—The game will be diminished, and the lands being valuable to the indians only as hunting grounds, they will be willing to sell further tracts for small considerations—By the expiration therefore of the above period, it is most probable that the indians will by the invariable operation of the causes which have hitherto existed in their intercourse with the whites, be reduced to a very small number.

These general reflections have arisen on considering the particular case of the Wabash indians respecting whom one observation more may be added.

The United States must soon possess the posts within their limits on the Lakes—This circumstance will either awe the Wabash indians, or in case of their continuing refractory, enable the Union to operate against them with a much greater prospect of success than at present.

All which is humbly submitted to the President of the United States.

H. Knox

By the United States in Congress assembled
August 7, 1786
An Ordinance for the Regulation of Indian Affairs

Whereas the safety and tranquillity of the frontiers of the United States, do in some measure, depend on the maintaining a good correspondence between their citizens and the several nations of Indians in amity with them: And whereas the United States in Congress assembled, under the ninth of the articles of confederation and perpetual union, have the sole and exclusive right and power of regulating the trade, and managing all affairs with the Indians not members of any of the states; provided that the legislative right of any state within its own limits be not infringed or violated.

Be it ordained by the United States in Congress assembled, That from and after the passing of this ordinance, the Indian department be divided into two districts, viz. The *southern*, which shall comprehend within its limits, all the nations in the territory of the United States, who reside southward of the river Ohio; and the *northern*, which shall comprehend all the other Indian nations within the said territory, and westward of Hudson river: Provided that all councils, treaties, communications and official transactions, between the superintendant hereafter mentioned for the northern district, and the Indian nations, be held, transacted and done, at the outpost occupied by the troops of the United States, in the said district. That a superintendant be appointed for each of the said districts, who shall continue in office for two years, unless sooner removed by Congress, and shall reside within or as near the district for which he shall be so appointed, as may be convenient for the management of its concerns. The said superintendants, shall attend to the execution of such regulations, as Congress shall from time to time establish respecting Indian affairs. The superintendant for the northern district, shall have authority to appoint two deputies, to reside in such places as shall best facilitate the regulations of the Indian trade, and to remove them for misbehaviour. There shall be a communications of all matters relative to the business of the Indian department, kept up between the said superintendants, who shall regularly correspond with the secretary' at war, through whom all communications respecting the Indian department, shall be made to Congress; and the superintendants are hereby directed to obey all instructions, which they shall from time to time receive from the said secretary at war. And whenever they shall have reason to suspect, any tribe or tribes of Indians, of hostile intentions, they shall communicate the same to the executive of the state or states, whose territories are subject to the effect of such hostilities. All stores, provisions or other property, which Congress may think necessary for presents to the Indians, shall be in the custody and under the care of the said superintendants, who shall render an annual account of the expenditures of the same, to the board of treasury.

And be it further ordained, That none but citizens of the United States, shall be suffered to reside among the Indian nations, or be allowed to trade with any nation of Indians, within the territory of the United States. That no person, citizen or other, under the penalty of five hundred dollars, shall reside among or trade with any Indian or Indian nation, within the territory of the United States, without a license for that purpose first obtained from the superintendant of the district, or one of the deputies, who are hereby directed to give such license to every person, who shall produce from the supreme executive of any state, a certificate under the seal of the state, that he is of good character and suitably qualified, and provided for that employment, for which license he shall pay the sum of fifty dollars to the said superintendant for the use of the United States. That no license to trade with the Indians shall be in force for a longer term than one year; nor shall permits or passports be granted to any other persons than citizens of the United States to travel through the Indian nations, without their having previously made their business known to the superintendant of the district, and received his special approbation. That previous to any person or persons obtaining a license to trade as aforesaid, he or they shall give bond in three thousand dollars to the superintendant of the district, for the use of the United States, for his or their strict adherence to, and observance of such rules and regulations as Congress may from time to time establish for the government of the Indian trade. All sums to be received by the said superintendants, either for licenses or fines, shall be annually accounted for by them with the board of treasury.

And be it further ordained, That the said superintendants, and the deputies, shall not be engaged, either directly or indirectly in trade with the Indians, on pain of forfeiting their offices, and each of the superintendants shall take the following oath, previous to his entering on the duties of his appointment—"I, A.B. do swear, that I will well and faithfully serve the United States in the office of superintendant of Indian affairs, for the   district: That I will carefully attend to all such orders and instructions as I shall from time to time receive from the United States in Congress assembled, or the secretary at war: That I will not be concerned, either directly or indirectly in trade with the Indians, and that in all things belonging to my said office, during my continuance therein, I will faithfully, justly and truly, according to the best of my skill and judgement, do equal and impartial justice, without fraud, favor or affection." And the superintendant for the northern district, shall administer to his deputies, the following oath, before they proceed on the duties of their office, "I, A.B. do swear, that I will well and faithfully serve the United States, in the office of deputy superintendant of Indian affairs in the northern district, that I will carefully attend to all such orders and instructions as I shall from time to time receive from the United States in Congress assembled, the secretary at war, or the superintendant of the district aforesaid, and that in all things belonging to my said office, during my continuance therein, I will faithfully, justly and truly, according to the best of my skill and judgement, do equal and impartial justice, without fraud, favor or affection." And the said superintendants, and deputy-superintendants, shall each of them give bond with surety to the board of treasury, in trust for the United States; the superintendants each in the sum of six thousand dollars, and the deputy-superintendants each in the sum of three thousand dollars, for the faithful discharge of the duties of their office.

And it is further ordained, That all fines and forfeitures which may be incurred by contravening this ordinance, shall be sued for and recovered before any court of record within the United States, the one moiety thereof to the use of him or them who may prosecute therefor, and the other moiety to the use of the United States. And the said superintendants, shall have power, and hereby are authorised, by force to restrain therefrom, all persons who shall attempt an intercourse with the said Indians without a license therefor obtained as aforesaid.

And be it further ordained, That in all cases where transactions with any nation or tribe of Indians shall become necessary to the purposes of this ordinance, which cannot be done without interfering with the legislative rights of a state, the superintendant in whose district the same shall happen, shall act in conjunction with the authority of such state.

Done, &c.

CHAS. THOMSON secy.

New York June 14. 1789

Sir.

I have been honored with your letter of the 12th. and in reply have to observe, that by the resolution of Congress of the 29th. of August 1788, I was directed to repair to the Missisippi, in order to hold a treaty with the Indians who inhabit the country upon that river, for the extinguishing their claims to lands, within certain limits, if any such claims existed, and to lay out certain donations of land to the ancient inhabitants. from thence I was to proceed to post St. Vincennes upon the Wabash and lay out like donations for the inhabitants there, but the Instructions contained no directions to make any purchase about the post, from a presumption, I suppose, that a Cession had been made there to the crown of France. With the remainder of the goods from former treaties, and the warrants I have received from the Board of Treasury, there is sufficient, I suppose in my hands to defray the expence of the treaty with the Missisippi Indians, exclusive of the provisions. what they may amount to I cannot ascertain as I am ignorant of the indian numbers. they are inconsiderable; but an immediate provision for the payment of the provisions, either for that, or any other Treaty is not necessary, the contractors being obliged to furnish all rations that may be required by the United States.

Should it be thought proper to treat with the indians of the Wabash and Miami, a further sum will be necessary, and I have enclosed an estimate of what the expence would probably amount to. It appears indeed of absolute necessity that these savages should be brought to peace either by treaty or by Force.

It is impossible for me to Judge what sum would induce them to extend the Northern Boundary of the last cession to the Missisippi, neither is it very well known what nations are the proprietors of the country that would be obtained by that extension. perhaps a provisional power to make such agreements, and limiting the sum might not be improper, as the expence of another meeting for that purpose might be avoided if the proprietors attended at the treaty in contemplation. The stipulations could be made then, and the payment at an after period.

I have the honor to be
Sir
Your Most obedient servant
Signed Ar. St. Clair

Major General Knox

Estimate of the expence, with which a treaty with the Indians of the Wabash and Miami Rivers would probably be attended, their numbers are supposed to be from twelve to fifteen hundred men.

	Dollars
Indian goods assorted to the value of	6,000.
Stores and necessaries	650.
Transportation	2,500.
Messengers & Interpreters	1,000.
Store Keeper	300.
Commissioners wages	500.
Contingencies	200.
	11,150.
The provisions cannot be estimated at less than 30,000 rations, which at contract price will amount to	5,000.
	16,100.

Many circumstances may occur to occasion the expenditure of a larger quantity of provisions a lesser quantity ought not to be reckoned upon.

Signd Ar. St. Clair

Indian Department

Southern District

The Creeks

This nation of indians is divided into two districts, the upper and the lower Creeks.

The former reside cheifly on the waters of the Albama river in about 60 towns or villages—The latter on the waters of the Apalachicola river in about 40 towns—The Creeks are principally within the limits of the United States, but some of the most southern towns of the lower Creeks or Semanolies, are within the territory of Spain stretching towards the point of Florida—The Gun-men or warriors of the whole nation are estimated at 6,000.

Besides the cheifs of the respective towns the Creeks appear at present to be much under the influence and direction of Alexander McGillivray.

The father of this person was an inhabitant of Georgia, and adhering to Great Britain in the late war his property was confiscated by that State—His mother was a principal woman of the upper Creeks.

He had an english education—his abilities and ambition appear to be great—his resentments are probably unbounded against the State of Georgia for confiscating his fathers estate, and the estates of his other friends, refugees from Georgia, several of whom reside with him among the Creeks—He is said to be a partner of a trading house which has the monopoly of the trade of the Creeks—The communications to the indian country are through the Floridas under the protection of the Spanish Colonies—The profits of this commerce center in Great Britain, and one of the Bahama Islands is the intermediate place of deposit.

The State of Georgia is engaged in a serious War with the Creeks—and as the same may be so extended and combined, as to require the interference of the United States, it will be highly proper that the causes thereof should be stated and examined.

The first treaty between the State of Georgia and the Creeks after the conclusion of the War with Great Britain was held at Augusta in November 1783—at this treaty certain lands on the Oconee were ceded by the Creeks to the State of Georgia—A copy of this treaty is not among the papers of Congress—but the purport as it respects the boundaries then established, is recited by the Legislature of the State of Georgia in their report on indian affairs hereunto annexed.

The second treaty was held at Galphinton on the 12th. of November 1785—By which the boundary lines defined by the treaty of Augusta in November 1783 were confirmed, and a new boundary line obtained, to extend from the forks of the Oconee and Oakmulgee to the source of the St. Marys—A copy of this treaty is hereunto annexed in the papers marked A. also a letter from the Commissioners of the United States—and a report of a Committee accepted by the Legislature of Georgia on the 11th. of February 1786.

A third treaty was held by the Commissioners of Georgia and the Creeks at Shoulder bone on the 3d. of November 1786—At this treaty it would appear that the Creeks acknowledged the violation of the two former treaties, recognized, and ratified the former boundaries, and gave six hostages for the faithful execution of the conditions.

On the one side—The Creeks object entirely to the validity of the said treaties stating that the cessions to the State of Georgia were made by the cheifs of two towns only, whereas the lands ceded were the property of the whole nation—as will more fully appear by the letters of Alexander McGillivray marked B, and numbered, 1, 2, 3 & 4.

The letter of Benjamin Hawkins, Andrew Pickens, Joseph Martin, and Lach. McIntosh Esqrs. Commissioners of the United States dated at the Keowee the 17th. of November 1785—marked A. states that as there were only two towns properly represented at Galphinton instead of about one hundred, the number in the whole nation, they could not treat with them on behalf of the United States—But that "the day after they left Galphinton, the Agents of Georgia held a treaty with the few indians then present, and obtained a cession of all the lands south of the Altamaha, and eastward of the line to be run south west from the junction of the Oakmulgee, and Oconee rivers 'till it shall strike St. Marys, with a confirmation of the lands ceded to the State by the same towns north-east of the Oconee river in 1783."

The letter of James White Esqr. Superintendant of the United States for the Southern District, and the proceedings held by him with the lower Creeks at Cusetahs will further show the sentiments of the said lower Creeks of the said treaties—marked C.

On the other side, the Legislature of Georgia by their Committee 23d. October 1787 marked D States that the Cherokees by a treaty made at Augusta on the 3d. of May 1783, and the Creeks by the treaty of Augusta in the succeeding November both nations made the same relinquishment of the lands on the Oconee, on account of mutual claims which had not before been settled between them.

That it was not untill a few months after the treaty of Galphinton that uneasinesses began to be fermented in the nation, and some murders were committed.

That this conduct of the Creeks was considered by the Government of Georgia as an infraction of the treaties, and they demanded reparation accordingly—That Commissioners were appointed with full powers to enquire into the causes, and restore peace, but with powers also if unavoidable to take eventual measures of defence.

That this proceeding of Georgia produced the treaty at Shoulder bone, whereby the violence was acknowledged, the boundaries confirmed, and hostages given.

"That the Committee cannot forbear to observe that during the course of all these transactions, the communications were made in solemn, open, and ancient form, and the articles of the treaties were mutually respected untill the aggression posterior to that of Galphinton.

And that whilst it is admitted on the one hand, that there was no principle of representation of the parts of the nations known in civilized governments, it cannot be denied on the other, that it was such as had been common, and the indians acknowledged without doubt, and regret their forming a part, and being members of the State."

The Committee after stating some circumstances relative to the proceedings of James White Esqr. the Superintendant—"Report it as their opinion that the ultimate causes of the War, were the too sudden interferences with the treaties of the State, by which the minds of the indians were perplexed— and the impression induced, that in a War they should not have the strength of the Union to fear, and that another disposition would be made of the territory, than that which considers it as part of the State—That representations to this effect should be immediately transmitted to Congress, and the support of the Union demanded."

That the papers whereon this statement is founded, and the general subject of the said dispute between the State of Georgia and the Creeks, have several times been discussed and considered in the late Congress.

That the report of the Committee of Congress as stated on the Journals of the 3d. of August 1787, will show the perplexities of this case.

That the subject was further debated in Congress on June 27th. and decided on July 15th. 1788 will appear by their Journals.

That in obedience to the order of Congress of the 15th. of July 1788, the Secretary at War made the report marked E.

That in consequence of the Resolve of Congress of the 26th. of October 1787 Commissioners were appointed by the States of South Carolina and Georgia—That the time for which the Superintendant was elected expired on the 29th. of November 1788.

That the proceedings of the said Commissioners and Superintendant as communicated by the latter are hereunto attached marked F.

That in addition to the information of the Superintendant it appears from the public news paper marked G, that the two Commissioners from Georgia and South Carolina have given a further invitation to a treaty to be held at Oconee during the present month.

But it also appears from the public news papers that instead of the proposed treaty, parties of indians have been making inroads into Georgia, and that the outrages committed by them have excited an alarm which has extended itself to Savannah the Capital of the State.

Hence it will appear from this general Statement of facts

1st.   That hostilities still rage between the State of Georgia, and the Creek indians.

2dly.   That the cause of the War is an utter denial on the part of the Creeks of the validity of the three treaties stated to have been made by them with the State of Georgia.

3dly.   That the United States in Congress assembled by their resolve of the 15th. of July 1788, have caused it to be notified to the Creeks "that should they persist in refusing to enter into a treaty upon reasonable terms, the arms of the United States shall be called forth for the protection of that frontier."

From this result the following questions arise

1st.   Whether the circumstance of the Commissioners not having received an answer from Alexander McGillivray to their letter of November 28th. 1788 and his letter to Andrew Moor Esqr. of the 4th. of January, and to his Excellency the Governor of South Carolina of the 26th. of February 1789, (letter B) together with the recent irruption of parties of Creeks into the State of Georgia, amount to a refusal to treat on reasonable terms, and of consequence form that crisis of affairs in which the Arms of the Union are to be called forth agreeably to the resolve of Congress of the 15th. of July 1788?

2dly.   Whether the final report of the Commissioners is necessary to be received before decision can be made on the case?

or 3dly.   Whether in the present state of public affairs any proper expedients could be devised for effectually quieting the existing hostilities between the State of Georgia, and the Creek Nation, other than by raising an Army?

All which is humbly submitted to the President of the United States

H. KNOX

War office July 6th 1789

A

Containing

1st.   A letter from the Commissioners of the United States dated Keowee 17th November 1785.

2.   A copy of the treaty made by the Commissioners of Georgia at Galphinton 12th. of November 1785.

3.   The report of a Committee to the legislature of Georgia and accepted 11th. of February 1786. in which the state Commissioners are Justified &

approved; and the attempt of the Continental Commissioners to treat at Galphinton and the treaty at Hopewell, are disapproved.

A No. 1.

Keowee the 17th. November 1785

Sir,

Agreeable to our appointment we arrived at Galphinton on the 24th and 28th of October, to meet and treat with the Creeks, having previously procured every thing necessary for this purpose—By the 29th the Chiefs of two towns with sixty men arrived, and from them as well as those we sent to invite the Indians to meet and treat with us we received assurances that the Chiefs of all the Towns would certainly come; that they were very much pleased with the intention of Congress and very desirous of establishing with them a permanent peace.

On the 7th of November we were informed that some false reports had been circulated through the Nation which had created Jealousies among them and discouraged them from coming to meet us and that we had only to expect the Tallissee King with twenty young men in addition to those already arrived. On the next day we agreed to meet the Indians and explained to them the object of our Commission at the same time remarking we could not treat with so few of their Nation, there being but two Towns properly Represented, instead of about one hundred the number in the whole Nation. As those Towns had been always friendly to the United states we gave them some presents and left them.

The Commissioners of Georgia visited us previous to our conference with the Indians and delivered us the protest marked A to which we returned the answer marked B. The day after we left Galphinton the agents of Georgia held a treaty with the few Indians then present and obtained a Cession of all the lands South of the Alatamaha and Eastward of a line to be run South west from the junction of the Oakmulgee and Oconee Rivers till it shall strike St. Mary's with a confirmation of the lands ceded to the state by the same towns North-East of the Oconee River in 1783.

By various informations we have had from the Creek nation, the accounts Colonel Martin brought us from the Cherokees and a letter wrote by McGilivrey a half breed, to general Pickens marked C (which we enclose to shew Congress the ability of this man who has great influence among his Country men) it appears that he is forming a dangerous confederacy between the several Indian Nations, the Spaniards and British agents with whom he is connected—His resentment is chiefly against the Citizens of Georgia who banished his Father and confiscated a capital property which he had in that state.

There is a Capital British Company of Merchants engaged by licence from the Court of Spain to supply all the Indian Nations to the southward with goods through East Florida in which Company it is said McGillivrey is a partner, and they have their agents in all the Towns from Tennessee Southwardly.

We are with due Respect

Sir

Your Most Obedient and
Humble Servants

        (Signed)   BENJAMIN HAWKINS
                                    ANDREW PICKENS
                                    JOS. MARTIN
                                    LACHN. McINTOSH

The Honorable
   Charles Thomson Esquire
Secretary to the United states in Congress assembled
   The above is a copy from the files in the Office of the Secretary of Congress.
CHAS. THOMSON secy.
N.B. The protest marked A and the answer Marked B have been taken off the files of Congress by some committee and never returned.

A. No. 2.

ARTICLES of a Treaty concluded at Galphinton on the 12th day of November 1785 between the Underwritten Commissioners in behalf of the state of Georgia of the one part and the Kings, head men and warriors in behalf of themselves and all the Indians in the Creek Nation of the other, on the following Conditions.

Art. 1st. The said Indians for themselves and all the ~~Indians~~ tribes or Towns within their Respective Nations within the limits of the state of Georgia, have been, and now are members of the same (since the day and date of the Constitution of the state of Georgia).

Art. 2d. If any Citizen of this State or other person or persons shall attempt to settle any of the lands reserved to the Indians for their hunting grounds, such person or persons may be detained untill the Governour Shall demand him or them, and then it shall be lawful for any of the Tribes near such offenders to come and see the punishment according to such laws, as now are or hereafter shall be enacted by the said state for trying such offenders.

Art. 3d. It Shall in no case be understood that the punishment of the innocent under the the idea of Retaliation shall be practiced on either side.

Art. 4th. If any Citizen of this State or other white person or persons shall commit a robbery or murder or other Capital crime on any Indian such offenders shall be delivered up to Justice and shall be tryed according to the Laws of the state, and due notice of such intended punishment shall be sent to some one of the Tribes.

Art. 5th. If any Indian shall commit a Robbery or murder or other Capital crime on any white person such offenders shall receive punishment adequate to such Offence, and due Notice of such intended punishment shall be given to his Honour the Governour.

Art. 6th. In case of any design being formed in any neighbouring tribe against the peace or safety of the state which they Shall know or suspect, they shall make known the same to his Honor the Governour.

Art. 7th. All white person or persons shall be at liberty, and conducted in safety into the settled parts of the state when they shall require it, except such persons as Shall come under the restrictions pointed out in the second Article.

Art. 8th. The Indians Shall restore all the Negroes, Horses and other property that are or may be among them belonging to any Citizen of this state or any other person or persons whatsoever, to such person as the Governour shall direct.

Art. 9th. That the trade with the said Indians Shall be carried on as heretofore.

Art. 10th. All horses belonging to any Indian that shall be found in the said state such horses shall be Restored to such person as the head of the Tribe where such Indian may reside shall direct.

Art. 11th. The present temporary line reserved to the Indians for their hunting grounds, shall be agreeable to a Treaty held at Augusta in the year 1783—and that a new temporary line shall begin at the forks of the Oconee and Oakmulgee Rivers—thence in a Southwest direction until it shall intersect the most Southern part of the stream called St. Mary's River, including all the Islands and waters of the said stream—thence down the said stream to the old line—And all the ground without the said new temporary line, when run and compleated shall be reserved to the said Indians for their hunting grounds as aforesaid.

In Witness whereof the parties have hereunto affixed their Hands and Seals the day and year before written.

While the Commissioners of the United states were at Galphinton, the Commissioners of Georgia copied their draught of the Articles intended to be proposed to the Creeks, and which were afterwards the Basis of the Treaty with the Cherokees.

B.H.[1]

---

[1] "B. H." is Benjamin Hawkins, one of the commissioners for southern Indians.

The above n. 2 is a copy from the files in the office of the secretary of Congress.

CHAS. THOMSON secy.

A. No. 3
Georgia

In General Assembly Saturday 11th February 1786
The Committee to whom was Referred the proceedings of the State Commissioners appointed to attend the Continental Commissioners to a meeting with the Cherokees and other Indians to the Southward—

REPORT,

That is appears to your Committee certain Commissioners of the United states in Congress Assembled, at Galphinton, did attempt a Treaty with the Creek Indians, and did also at Hopewell in the state of South Carolina enter into a pretended Treaty with some of the Cherokees and some parts of other tribes there in Named, which said pretended Treaty, and all other proceedings that have yet transpired, are a manifest and direct attempt to violate the retained sovereignty and Legislative right of this state, and repugnant to the principles and harmony of the federal Union; in as much as the aforesaid Commissioners did attempt to exercise powers that are not delegated by the Respective states to the United states in Congress assembled: Wherefore your Committee recommend the following Resolutions

1st. That the Delegates of this state be directed to make a Representation of the conduct of the said Commissioners to the United states in Congress Assembled, and to move and contend for an immediate abolition of their powers; as the continuation of such appointment would tend to weaken and destroy that entire confidence in the wisdom and Justice of Congress which this state wishes ever to preserve.

2d. That the Delegates be requested to apply for and immediately send to the Governour authenticated copies of the Commissioners instructions, and all proceedings thereon of the said Commissioners, in order that such measures may be taken as will most effectually preserve the sovereign Territorial and Legislative Rights of this State as well as the rights & Privileges to which each Citizen is entitled by the Confederation and by the laws of the land.

3d. That all and every act and thing done or intended to be done within the limits and Jurisdiction of this state by the said Commissioners inconsistent of the before mentioned rights and privileges shall be, and the same are hereby declared to be null and void.

4th. That the thanks of this house be given to the Honorable Edward Telfair, and to John King and Thomas Glasscock Esquires, Commissioners on the part of this state, for their patriotism and vigilance in discharging the duties required of them at the aforesaid meetings; That each of them be allowed three dollars ℔ day, during their actual attendance on the said business; and that the Governour and Council take order accordingly.

Which was agreed to

Extract from the Minutes

JAS. M. SIMMONS Clk. G. A.

The foregoing is a copy from the files in the office of the Secretary of Congress.

CHAS. THOMSON secy.

B

Containing

No. 1. A letter dated the 5th. of September 1785. from Alexander McGillivray, to Andrew Pickens Esquire Commissioner &c.

No. 2. A letter dated April 8th. 1787. from Alexander McGillivray to James White Esqr. Superintendant of Indian affairs, for the United States.

No. 3. A letter dated 4th January 1789 from Alexander McGillivray, to Andrew Moor Commissioner from Virginia, to the Cherokees.

No. 4. A letter dated 26th February 1789. from Alexander McGillivray, to Thomas Pinckney Esquire Governor of South Carolina.

B. No. 1

Little Tallassie 5th September 1785

Sir.

I am favored with your letter by Brandon who after detaining it near a month sent it by an Indian a few days ago, he perhaps has some reasons for keeping himself at a distance from this; he caused old Mr. McQueen to take charge of this letter in answer to yours he being shortly to set out for Augusta.

The notification you have sent us, is agreeable to our wishes, especially as the meeting is intended for the desirable purpose of adjusting and settling matters on an equitable footing between the United States and the Indian Nations. At same time cant avoid expressing my Surprise that a measure of this nature should have been so long delayed on your parts; when we found that the American Independency was confirmed by the peace, We expected that the New government would soon have taken some steps to make up the differences that subsisted between them and the Indians during the war; and to have taken them into protection and confirm to them their hunting grounds—such a Conduct would have reconciled the minds of the Indians and secured to the states their attachment and friendship, and considered them as their Natural guardians and Allies. Georgia whose particular interest it was to have endeavored to conciliate the friendship of this Nation; but instead of which I am sorry to observe that violence and prejudice had taken place of good policy and reason in all their proceedings with us. They attempted to avail themselves of our supposed distressed situation. Their talks to us breathed nothing but Vengeance; and being entirely possessed with the Idea that we were wholly at their mercy. They never once reflected that the Colonies of a powerful Monarch were nearly surrounding us, and to whom in any extremity we might apply for Succour and protection; and who to answer some end of their policy might grant it to us. However we yet deferred any such proceeding, still expecting we could bring them to a sense of their true interest; But still finding no alteration in their conduct towards us, we sought the protection of Spain and treaties of friendship and Alliance were mutually entered into. They to guarantee our hunting grounds and Territory, and to grant us a free trade in the ports of the Floridas.

How the Boundary or limits between the spaniards and the states will be determined a little time will shew, as I believe that matter is now on foot. However we know our own limits and the extent of our hunting grounds, and as a free Nation we have applied, as we have a right and have obtained protection for—So that we shall pay no regard to any limits that may prejudice our Claims that were drawn by an American and confirmed by a British Negotiator.

Yet notwithstanding we have been obliged to adopt these measures for our preservation, and from real Necessity—We sincerely wish to have it in our power to be on the same footing with the states as before the late unhappy war. To effect which is intirely in your power—we want nothing from you but justice—we want our hunting grounds preserved from encroachments— They have been ours from the beginning of time, and I trust that with the assistance of our friends we shall be able to maintain them against every attempt that may be made to take them from us.

Finding our representations to the state of Georgia of no effect in restraining their incroachments we thought it proper to call a meeting of the Nation—on the matter, we then came to a Resolution to send out parties to remove the people and effects from off the lands in question in the most peaceable manner possible.

Agreeable to your requisition and to convince you of my sincere desire to restore a good understanding between us—I have taken the Necessary steps to prevent any future predatory excursions of my people against any of your settlements. I could wish that the people of Cumberland shewed an equal good disposition to do what is right. They were certainly the first agressors since the peace, and acknowledged it in a written Certificate left at the Indian Camp they had plundered.

I have only to add that we shall prepare ourselves to meet the Commissioners of Congress whenever we shall receive notice, in expectation that every matter of difference will be made up and settled with that liberality and Justice worthy the Men who have so gloriously assisted the cause of liberty and Independency, and that we Shall in future consider them as Brethern and defenders of the land.

> I am with much Respect
> Sir
> Your Most obedt. servant
> (signed) ALEXR. McGILLIVRAY

Honorble. Andrew Pickens Esqr.

I should be sorry that your interest should suffer in the hands of Brandon, but he has committed so many thefts in horses, and to satisfy the people we given him up to be made an example of, and I imagine his goods are gone for Satisfaction. He is a very unfit person for a trader—as I have pretty well cleared the Nation of such kind of people he must not look for indulgence in these parts.

> A. McG.

The foregoing letter is a copy from the files in the Office of the secretary of Congress.

> CHAS. THOMSON secy.

B. No. 2

> Little Tallassie　8th of April 1787

Sir

I had the pleasure to receive the letter that you favored me with by Mr. Miller on your arrival at the Cusitaks.

It is with real satisfaction that I learn of your being appointed by Congress, for the laudable purpose of enquiring into and settling the differences that at present subsist between our nation and the Georgians. It may be necessary for you to know the cause of those differences, and of our discontents, which perhaps have never come to the Knowledge of the honorable body that has sent you to our country.

There are chiefs of two towns in this Nation, who during the late war, were friendly to the state of Georgia, and had gone at different times to that State, and once after the general peace, when the people of Augusta, demanded a cession or grant of lands, belonging to, and enjoyed as hunting ground by the Indians of this nation in common, on the east of the Oconie River, which demand was rejected by those chiefs, on the plea that those grounds were hunting lands of the nation, and could not be granted by two individuals; but after a few days, a promise was extorted from them, that on their return to their own country, they would use their influence to get a grant confirmed. Upon these mens reporting this affair on coming home, a general convention was held at the Teickibatik Town, when those two chiefs were severally censured for their conduct, and the chiefs of Ninety Eight towns, agreed upon a talk to be sent to Savannah disapproving in the strongest manner of the demand made upon their nation, and denied the right of any two of their country to making any cession of land, which could only be valid by the unanimous voice of the whole, as joint proprietors in common. Yet these two, regardless of the voice of the nation, continued to go to Augusta and other places within that State, continuing to make such promises, to obtain presents, our customs not permitting us to punish them for the crime; we warned the Georgians of the dangerous consequences that would certainly attend the settleing of the lands in question; Our Just remonstrances were treated with contempt, and those lands were soon filled with settlers. The nation Justly alarmed at the encroachments, resolved to use force to maintain their rights, yet being averse to shedding the blood of a people whom we would rather consider as friends, we made another effort to awaken in them a sense of Justice and equity, but we found from experience, that entreaty could not prevail, and party's of warriors were sent out to drive off all intruders, but to shed no blood, only where self preservation made it necessary.

This was in May 1786—in October following we were invited by Commissioners of the State of Georgia to meet them in conferrence at the Oconie, professing a sincere disire for an amicable adjustment of our disputes, and "pledging their sacred Honours, for the safety and good treatment of all those that should attend and meet them." It not being convenient for many of us to go to the proposed conferrence, a few towns, say their chiefs, attended, most of whom, merely from motives of curiosity, and were surprized to find an armed body of men, prepared for, and professing hostile intentions, than peacable commissioners, apprehensions for personal safety induced those chiefs to subscribe to every demand that was asked by the army and its Commissioners. lands were again demanded, and the lives of some of our chiefs were required, as well as some innocent traders, as a sacrafice to appease their anger. assassins have been employed to effect some part of their attrocious purposes. If I fall by the hand of such, I shall fall a victim in the noblest of causes, that of falling in maintaining the Just rights of my country. I aspire to the honest ambition of meriting the appellation of the preserver of my country, equally with those chiefs among you, whom from acting on such principles, you have exalted to the highest pitch of glory; And if after every peacable mode of obtaining a redress of grievances having proved fruitless, the having recourse to arms to obtain it, be marks of the Savage and not of the Soldiers, What Savages must the americans be, and how much undeserved applause have your Cincinnatus, your Fabius obtained. if war names had been necessary to distinguish those chiefs in such a case, the Man-Killer, the great destroyer &c. would have been the proper appellations.

I had appointed the Cussitikes, for all the chiefs of the lower creeks to meet in convention. I shall be down in a few days, when from your timely arrival, you will meet the chiefs, and will learn their sentiments, and I sincerely hope that the propositions that you shall offer us will be of such a nature that we can safe accede to—The talks of the former Commissioners of Congress at Gelphinton, were much approved of, and your coming from the white town (seat of Congress) has raised great expectations, that you will remove the principal and almost only Cause of our disputes, that is, securing to us all our possessions and hunting grounds entire, and clear them of encroachments, when we meet we shall talk these matters over, mean time, I have the honor to be with regard,

Sir

Your Most Obedt. Servt.

(Signd) ALEX. MCGILLVERAY

The Indians that were detained
as hostages in Augusta must
speedily be liberated, or hostilities
will soon commence, as their
relations are uneasy on their
accounts.

the foregoing
is copied from
the files of the
War Office.

H. KNOX

(Copy)

Honble. James White Esqr. Supdt. of Indn. affairs for the U. States

B. No. 3.

Little Tallassie upper Creeks—
January 4th 1789.

Sir.

I take this opportunity to write to you, in answer to a letter which you did me the favor to write me in September last from Seneca, in which was enclosed a proclamation issued by Congress, requiring all the whites that are settled on the lands of the Cherokees to remove from off them immediately; this measure, together with the talk from the Governor of Virginia, appears to have given much satisfaction to the Cherokees. The little Turkey, or Coweta King, with some warriors, relations to the dragging Canoe, have been to consult me on these subjects, bringing with them all the talks that they had received for some time past. I gave it as my opinion to them, that the talks in question might be safely relied on, that the talk of Congress was a strong one, to their people, who would obey it, and the Governor being a principal chief and ruler, he would not speak with a forked Tongue, and that in the ensuing spring there would be a great meeting for the purpose of concluding a general peace, the terms of which would be very favorable to them: In the meantime, the chiefs should advise all the young Warriors to attend Closely to hunting, during the winter, instead of risquing their lives for a scalp, which when obtained would not purchase clothing for their famely's. and that, considering them as an oppressed people, I had agreed to give them assistance to enable them to obtain a good peace: but they were not to Consider me as engaged to support them in an unjust and an unnecessary war.

The people of your state, who complain of our people molesting them, are not rightly informed, for besides that I always have endeavored to confine the excursions of our warriors, to the people with whom we have ground of quarrel. the state of Virginia and its dependencies are very far distant. and I never knew that a creek had ever been near Kentucke, at least from the nation. there are several who have wives and famelys among the Cherokees, and constantly reside there. those I cannot answer for, being to be reckoned as Cherokees; it is the custom of a Creek to disregard all Connexions and Country, and Cleave to his wife, those that have wives abroad never return to their native land.

The Gentlemen, my friends, do me justice when them inform you that I am disirous of peace. I have been now five years in laboring to bring about one with the state of Georgia, but in vain; more than a twelve month after the general peace, was spent by us, in representing to them in friendly terms, the cruelty and injustice of their proceedings of wresting forcibly from us, a large portion of our hunting lands, and which were in a great measure necessary for our support. that we were not situated as several other Indian nations were, with immense wildernesses behind us. on the contrary, we were surrounded from west to North, by the Choctaws, Chickasaws, Cumberland and Cherokees; and on every other side by the Whites; so that our hunting grounds were already very insufficient for our purposes; to all which we were always answered in haughty and contemptuous language, with threats to drive us over the Missisippi—So that having nothing to hope from their justice or humanity, it was resolved to raise up the red hatchet for self preservation. as our Cause was Just, so fortune has favored our exertions in driving them from the contested ground tho' the war has reduced them to an extremity of distress, yet their stubborness of pride is such, they take no measures to retract the conduct which has brought them to it. they have spurned every attempt that Congress has offered at, to accomodate, by its Interference the disputes between us, the new Congress will equally find them obstinate and intractable, the only method they can adopt, will be to leave the Georgians to their fate; and in another season 'tis probable that they will be brought to reason.

I shall be glad to be favored with an account, when convenient, soon after the meeting of the new Congress, and in what manner the new Constitution is finally Settled. Any thing that I can serve you in, pray freely command.

> I remain with regard
> your most obedient servant
> ALEX. McGILLIVRAY

Hon. Andrew Moor Esquire
Commissioner for treating with the Cherokees
for State of Virginia

> copied from the original
> H. KNOX

B. No. 4

Little Tallassie Upper Creek Nation 26th. February 1789

Sir.

Your Excellencys letter of 6th. November is just come to hand inclosed in one from the Superintendant and Commissioners by which I find that the respectable State of South Carolina viewing with concern the continuance of the destructive contests carrying on between our nation the Creeks and their sister State of Georgia have been induced from their good intentions to both, to offer their interference to bring about an amicable adjustment of the disputes subsisting between us, which offer we can have no good reason for objecting to, and as your Excellency as Chief of the State has stept forward as the Mediator it is very necessary that you in that capacity should be informed of the real grounds of such dispute, and from the account which I shall give you of it, you will readily admit that we had the best reasons for opposition. Directly after the conclusion of a general peace was announced to us all, the Georgians sent up an invitation to our Chiefs to meet them in Treaty at Augusta, professing it was with an intention of burying the Hatchet and with it the remembrance of every injury which they had sustained from us in the War of Britain. The call being at an inconvenient season, the proper Chiefs not being in the way a few people who during the War pretended to neutrality, attended the Call at Augusta and on conferrences then held the leading people of the upper parts of that State made a demand of a large cession of lands comprehending our best hunting grounds, as a compensation for the injuries sustained by them in the War and which was inforced by bands of armed men who at the same time surrounded them, threat'ning them with instant death if it was refused, the two chiefs then present being of the second rank, truly told them that the demand was unexpected and were unprepared to answer it, and being only two men, could not promise that any grant that they should be forced to consent to make, would be confirmed by the Chiefs of the Nation, as it was not unknown to the white people that it was necessary that the joint voice of the whole Nation should make and confirm such grants, this reply not satisfying the Georgians, they persisted and renewed their threats—then these men to escape the Threatned danger consented as far as what concerned them, but could not engage to bind the whole to their act; when these men arrived in the Nation a general Convention was immediately called to deliberate on this affair the Chiefs of more than forty Towns assembled when they reprobated the transactions of the two inferior Chiefs in strong terms, and refused to consent to any such Cession, and desired me to inform the Georgians of the same and to warn them that if the threat'ned encroachments were made, a War would immediately insue, which I did in a letter to Mr. Houstoun the Governor—this is a true account of the transactions of the first of three pretended treaty's which the Commissioners mention in their letter to me—the second invitation which we received to treat was made by Colonel Hawkins and General Pickins under the appointment of Congress as they informed me, and mentioned that they had not at that time fixed upon any place to meet us but when that point was settled they would give a second notification and which I never received—soon after I learned that the Georgians took up the matter, and smuggled a Treaty at Galphinton on OGeechee to which place they secretly invited a few of our people whom they had bribed and secured to their interests and who they were sure would agree to any thing that was asked of them, and there of course a Cession was again asked of them, with a large addition—Sometime after I received a letter from Colonel Hawkins desiring to know my reasons for not meeting at OGeechee at the same time remarking that he did not consider the few that attended a proper representation of the Creek Nation he said nothing to them; the authority of the Commissioner of Congress I expect will be sufficient evidence to overset any claim that is founded on as a grant of this Treaty.

Another Convention protested through me in warm terms to the Georgians respecting their conduct in offering to make pretentions to Cessions of land obtained from a few beggars who only want to obtain presents—The third invitation which was sent to us to treat was from the Georgians only through their Commissioners at the head of whom was Mr. M. Habersham President of the Executive Council and he proposes the Oconee River for the place of meeting, in the letter they "pledged their Sacred Honor" for the safety and welfare of every one that would attend their conferrences, but I being so often threatened and having the worst opinion of the back people as they are called did not go, but sent a few Coweta Warriors to report to me on their return, during the conferrences of Oconee an additional Cession was demanded which was strongly opposed by the Cowetas and others, for which they were violently insulted by a Colonel Clark in the presence of the Commissioners who could not prevent it, and though their sacred honors were pledged for maintaining good order yet several warriors of different Towns were forcibly seized upon by Armed Men and conveyed to Augusta more as Prisoners, than Hostages to be kept as a pledge that my life and six more of leading men should be taken—Such a conduct convinced the whole nation that it was full time to adopt measures for the general safety; a general Convention was appointed to be held in May for that purpose and a few days before it was opened, a Doctor White arrived in the Nation with an appointment of Superintendant of Indian Affairs from Congress, the Chiefs assembled shewed him every attention, and on account of his arrival the two men who had given the grants as before related were called upon to attend (for they had not mingled themselves with the others for shame) that Doctor White should know the truth he very minutely interrogated those Men concerning the foregoing matters, and they gave him the same account of the first Treaty as it is called and of the rest as I have done, the Doctor used his best ability to get the Chiefs in Convention to consent to the disputed Cession but in vain on the contrary the Chiefs by their Speaker, the King of the Cowetas told Doctor White that before they would give more lands, they would rather risque an attempt to resume what the nation had formerly been deprived of— The Doctor on his going away required of me a written representation of the causes of our discontents to be shewn to Congress, which I gave him, and am certain that it is in the possession of that Honorable body: the subject of which made part of the deliberations of a Committee ordered to sit upon Indian Affairs and to report the same a printed report of that Committee I have now in the House, and from sentiments contained in it I had great hopes that it would form the Basis for accommodating matters between us and the Georgians, and which would be very satisfactory to us—I beg leave next to remark to you that if the Georgians after the peace had conducted themselves to us with moderation and humanity we should not have fallen out with them for trifles, and they have brought the War on themselves by manifesting at the outset an unaccommodating and persecuting spirit towards us; our situation does by no means admit of our giving away our lands; We are already closely surrounded and our hunting grounds much circumscribed—There is the State of Georgia on the east—South East, and South West by the Spanish Floridas, west by the nations of the Choctaws and Chikisaws on the North by the Cherokees and Cumberland; we are not situated as the Western and Northern Nations with immense desarts at our back, all this tells us that we must either struggle hard to preserve our hunting grounds and perish to a man in its defence, for where can we go to possess ourselves of new ones? such forcible considerations with us may weigh nothing in the minds of those who think that Indians are only Animals fit to be exterminated, and this is a language which I know is held in many places in your Country; but let us be what we may, let it be attempted when it will, it will be found no very easy enterprize—I have given your Excellency a very circumstantial account of the origin of the contest between us and the Georgians, from which you will find that the Georgians have no well founded cause of quarrell with us, and that they can have no just claim to your assistance; for to support them in this contest is to side with injustice and oppression; a reproach which I firmly believe that the respectable State over which you preside will not subject its Magnanimity and Honor to—"very far am I Sir from spurning at your offered Mediation but the letter of the Commissioners (puts it out of my power) or rather makes it of no effect, as they declare that it is impossible for them to comply with our requisition to restore to us the territory usurped from us by the Georgians" wishing us to "reconsider the matter, as the Georgians claims is founded on three Treaties signed by our head men and Warriors."

The Treaties alluded to have been faithfully reported to you—one of the new Commissioners Genl. Pickens, formerly by letter acknowledged to me, that he was in Augusta at the time the first Treaty as it was called, was held, and the manner in which a consent to a Cession was extorted was very unfair, the General as a Gentleman will not deny his assertion—I cannot take upon myself to engage to meet the Commissioners to enter into an investigation of this subject; it will be attended with no good effect, the claims will be endevored to be maintained, and we shall be as firm in attempting to over-throw it, and disagreeable if not bloody consequences would be the result of such conferrences—I understand your Excellency very well when you say that you are not unprepared for a change of circumstances; that is, we shall or must purchase peace of the Georgians at the expence of sacrificing our rights properties, and life itself, or you are resolved to join that State in hostility against us—The Commissioners also say that Congress is resolved to do justice to Georgia—all this has the most formidable appearance. I by no means make light of the great power which thus menaces, if 'tis determined as I suspect it is the case, to attempt at a conquest of our Country, we will be found as determined to oppose it—Spain is bound by Treaty to protect and support us in our claims and properties, we shan't want for means of defence but still I hope, for I earnestly desire that your influence and power will be used to set every matter to rights in a peaceable manner, rather than to exercise the Calamities of War.

I am returned a month or two since from a tour thro' the principal of the lower Towns and Semanolies, which I made for the purpose of urging them to a strict observance of the truce and I believe I can venture to assure your Excellency that no complaints will be made for any breaches of it throughout Winter.

> I have the Honor to be with most respectful considera[tion]
> Your Excellencys Most Obedient Servant
> (Signed) ALEX. MCGILLIVRAY

His Exy. Tho. Pinckney Esqr.   ⎫
Govr. of the state of So. Carolina ⎭
    A true Copy taken from the Original sent by his Excellency the Govr.
to the House of Representatives.
                             (Signed) JOHN SANDFORD DART C.H.R.
                             April 3d. 1789.
                             Charlestown
copied from the [origina]l
certified Copy.
   [H. KN]OX

C

Contains

No. 1. A letter dated May 24th. 1787. from James White Esquire Superin-
tendant of Indian affairs to the Secretary at war.
No. 2. A letter dated April 4th 1787. from James White Esqr. &c. to
Alexander McGillivray.
No. 3. A Talk delivered on the 10th April 1787. to the lower Creeks—by
the Superintendant.
No. 4. Proceedings of the meeting of the lower Creeks on the 10 April 1787.
Mr. McGillivray and the principal chiefs, of the lower Towns
present.

C. No. 1.

                                 Fayetteville May 24th 1787
Sir.
    Being lately returned from the Creek Nation which occasioned the alarm in
Georgia last summer, I do myself the honor of sending you an account of the
state of those indians.
    The invasion which threatened that State had subsided ere my arrival; and
first appearances seemed to promise tranquility: for hostages had been given
by some of the indians to give satisfaction, and enlarge the boundary of the
state. I soon discovered these hostages were but of imaginary Consequence;
they were taken from the Cusitash, a town not only without imputation of
offence on this occasion, but at all times attached to the white people in a
singular manner; My tour to the nation convinced that these men answered
no other purpose by their detention, than to alienate the minds of such of the

indians as might be favorably disposed: they have since been dismissed, all but a Youth who in his impatience of confinement put himself to death; The further creeks who had insulted the state, continue in the same disposition; and if their hatchet has been hitherto restrained, it has been thro' their respect to the United States; Their dispositions had been favorably inclined by the liberal sentiments of the former Commissioners from Congress, and they had got information that there was an agent now coming to them from that hon'ble body. This witheld their resentment to the state of Georgia. They have all along been avowedly opposed to the new Settlements of the white people. the sentiments of the *lower towns* seemed not so well known 'till I went out; But at a full meeting of these latter, they also protested against what they termed the Georgian encroachments, which they declared they would repel by force. From a sketch of the proceedings at that meeting (paper No. 1.) you may see that the very indians, said to have made the grants, were the first to accuse the state of having extorted land from them under pretence of cessions All their expressions, indeed, were mingled with respect for the power that had delegated the Superintendant to whom they addressed their talk. "But there was a third party, (the Georgians) they said, which evidently meant injustice and oppression." The meeting upon the whole, Concluded so unfavorably, that there was room to apprehend an immediate invasion. To that however, a temporary stop was put by an idea of their influential chief, McGillivray. In this there was something so singular, that perhaps I may be excused for relating it circumstantially. The following, therefore, was nearly the address of that indian chief. "Notwithstanding that, as the guardian of the indian rights, I prompt them to defend their lands; yet I must declare that I look upon the United States as our most natural allies. Two years I waited before I would seek for the alliance I have formed. I was compelled to it. I could not but resent the greedy encroachments of the Georgians; to say nothing of their scandalous and illiberal personal abuse. Notwithstanding which, I will now put it to the test whither they or myself entertain the most generous sentiments of respect for Congress. If that honorable body can form a government to the southward of the Altamaha, I will be the first to take the oath of allegiance thereto. and in return to the Georgians for yielding to the United States that claim, I will obtain a regular and peacable grant of the lands, on the Oconie on which they have deluded people to Settle under pretence of grants from the indians, you yourself have seen how ill founded. however if this takes place I will put this matter out of dispute for them. I will give you to the first of August for an answer."

I hope I shall be excused for relating this unexpected proposal in his own words as nearly as I can recollect; his motives were probably inclination as well as interest, I could discover his natural biass is not towards his Spanish allies, and he is a trader of a company that imports largely, from which the

Government of Pensacola exacts an exorbitant impost. on the other hand, he would not only expect a more moderate duty thro' the altamaha, but the Indian country is more accessable thro' that way.

The strength of these indians is about 6,000 gun-men mostly well armed with rifles, they extend down the waters of the Alabama and Apalachicola rivers along to the point of Florida, thro' the spanish territories; thro' which they could have a Convenient retreat in case they were forced by an expedition against them. It is beyond a doubt that they receive every encouragement, from the Jealous policy of the spaniards, against us—From this source they are already provided with ammunition; magazines of which are dispersed thro' their towns, and reserved for a public occasion. I am well informed, that when the creeks were threatened from Georgia, the Spanish influence, in favor of those indians, was very active with the Choctaws.

With what conveniency the United States Could carry on a war with the creeks, I cannot determine, but I may be permitted to remark that the State of Georgia, only in holding a partial treaty with some of them, last autumn was obliged to have recourse to a paper medium. which is already depreciated 400 ℔ cent, and it was with great difficulty that the troops raised for this indian business, could be Kept together till it terminated in the unsubstantial manner it did.

The causes that excite an unfriendly disposition in the indians may in part be gathered from Mr. McGillivray's letter which comes enclosed to you. Besides there are the following, among other causes.

The natural reluctance of the indians to part with any of their lands, for to use their own expression, they look on their lands as their blood and their life, which they must fight for rather than part with 2d. Because in obtaining the new purchase, a sufficiently general consent of the nation was wanting; and even that partial consent extorted by threats as they pretend. 3rd. The white people on the frontier continuing their encroachments; they pursue their Surveys into the indian country and destroy the game there.

Much also of the indian animosity may be ascribed to the instigations of Mr. McGillveray, who is said to be in spanish pay, and entertains a personal resentment to the state of Georgia. To this may be added habits of enmity contracted during the war, and their connection with the british. In like manner the spanish influence now succeeds to that.

I have sent you the letter from Mr. McGillveray, not only as it may serve to give some idea of the character of the man; but also as it Contains a State of Indian complaints.

The two papers (No. 2 & 3.) from the Legislature and executive of the State of Georgia, will help to shew in what manner that government has received the institution of a Superintendant within the claim of their jurisdiction.

Permit me to enclose also a letter to McGillveray, and a talk to the lower Creeks you will please to Judge if any of the contents may be proper to offer to the attention of Congress: it appeared necessary for me to mention at least the proposal, as above, from McGillveray.

I am with the greatest respect
Sir
Your Obedient and
Humble Servant
JAMES WHITE

The Honorable
Major Genl. Knox

Copied from the files
of the War office.
H. KNOX

C. No. 2
(Copy.)

Cassetash April 4th. 1787

Sir.

I flattered myself I should have been able in person to deliver you the enclosed—Unfortunately the decline of my health has disappointed me in that expectation—It is with difficulty indeed that I have reached thus far; but I am encouraged by reflecting that if our efforts are successful in removing the misunderstanding which seems to have taken place between the people of Georgia, and some part of the Creek Nation; we shall have rendered good offices perhaps equally to both—That this can be effected I the more readily hope as each party seems to entertain an inclination to avoid the further effusion of human blood on the occasion—I assure you Sir the better and more moderate people among us appear to wish there may be no cause to proceed to extremes.

As for the United States the very nature of their Government is averse to violence, and if through the ties of the confederation there is a necessity to turn the force of the Continent into this quarter, it will not be without regret that there is occasion for the disagreeable measure.

In like manner it is with pleasure I perceive by your letters, that the Indians only wish their rights may not be violated—Let both parties therefore condescend a little—For my part the very small share of persuasion I possess among the white people, shall be exerted for so good a purpose, as indeed it has not been hitherto neglected: your more powerful influence among this people cannot certainly take place to a better end—Matters may be amicably settled—It will prove a mutual advantage.

I confess, among the herd of white people there are many who may be ripe for precipitating themselves into measures as injurious to others, as destructive to themselves—The same, no doubt, among the indians—To restrain this temper is the duty of more sober reflection.

As for the occasion of these animosities, which I am sorry has subsisted— The territory of the State is I own in my opinion, amply extensive: and this consideration is a security for the indians that there will be no similar ground for complaint in future; as it cannot be an object with government to disperse its subjects still more widely, while there is so much internal room for cultivation, I can take upon me to assure you that measures, are adopted with strict severity for curbing the licentiousness of any who might be disposed to give offence to this people.

On the other hand the white people are not without heavy complaints— They alledge that the assassination in cold blood of their unsuspecting fellow citizens can scarcely be atoned for—Barbarities which may indeed raise the indignation of a civilized people; but as you well know it requires a different spirit to bring them to any terms; so you will be the first to discountenance these marks not of the soldier—but the savage.

With respect to the subject that produced these enormities if I may be permitted to remark without the imputation of partiality; it is obvious that as the Creeks have no written Laws or customs, it was to be supposed the people of Georgia would in reason, view that purchase as good which they were to make ~~from the people~~ from the people who were in the indisputed possession and use—The case of your lower towns—However as the subject of grievances is at all times a tender one, I am sorry if I have not touched it with a finger sufficiently delecate. Let us rather turn our views to the means of future peace, and happiness—For this purpose I am anxious for an early meeting— and I hope I am not deceived in thinking you will heartily concur in endeavours of so humane a tendency.

As I propose going to the Northward as soon as I see this business in any regular train, it would do me pleasure to convey any word to your correspondent Mr. H. who thinks of you with sentiments of singular esteem, and who is a man of a benevolence and Philanthropy expanded beyond party and national contractedness.

I am with great esteem
Your Obedt. Servt.
(Signed) JAMES WHITE

Honble. Alexander McGillivray Esqr.
One of the Chiefs of the creek Nation

for the answer

copied from the files of the War office
    H. KNOX

to this letter
vide B.

C. No. 3.

At a Meeting of the Lower Creeks April 10th. 1787.

Friends and Brothers

The occasion that brings me here to see you is I believe partly of the same nature as that for which you have met together. But before I enter upon the business, I cannot help expressing the pleasure I feel at seeing so many of our particular friends assembled. The lower towns of the Creek nation have always shewn a moderation, and a prudence, which I feel, and admire. If this disposition is continued it will establish such a friendship and commerce, as will be infinitely better than quarreling and bloodshed.

There are many present who are already informed that I am sent here by the great Council which in peace and War, directs the affairs of all the 13 United Nations of white men of which the Virginians your neighbours make a very small part, I come now from the center of their government; at the distance from here of a whole moons journey on strong Horses.

BROTHERS,

The Virginians of Georgia, who form one of the thirteen fires of our great Council, complained at the meeting last autumn that their Country was attacked, and their people killed by some bad men of the Creek Nation— They demanded assistance, if due satisfaction was not given against the offenders—But the Old and Wise men of the great Council, the Congress, before they would send out a strong Army to assist in killing their Brothers the indians, with whom they would rather be at peace, wished first to enquire into the matter, and see if all things could not be amicably settled—For this purpose they have sent me out.

NOW, BROTHERS,

From peace may we not all reap advantage? There can be none from spilling each others blood—The master of Breath, lends us that breath but for a little while; why then should we snatch it from one another sooner than he designs? For this reason I hope both parties will be moderate. Perhaps it hath been a little the fault of both parties that any of the human blood hath been spilt on the occasion—I hope that now each will yield a little to the other—When our friends of the Creek nation who are now at Augusta, come up they will tell you how much I inculcated this to the white people: I was happy to find them disposed to it; except a few of their mad young men, who are too apt to be disposed to war. But their nation will not be rigorous in their demands; they have presents in waiting for the indians, who I hope will go down and receive the goods—I am convinced that this nation will not in the end lose any thing, by confirming the grant of such lands as many of the respectable men of the nation have thought might be spared, and have already granted: which gift it would look unmanly to retract, if it could be done—but it cannot.

BROTHERS,

I have carefully avoided to mention any old cause of quarrels, and I hope there will be none for the future. You will find that the Head-men among the Virginians have lately made provision for severely punishing any of their bad folks who shall disturb their friends the indians.

I will not trouble you further, but to mention one thing which concerns us all, and which I feel from my heart: the red people and the white are equally interested in it. We are countrymen, we live in the same land; we breath the same air, we should be Brothers. The Kings and people who live over the great Water will wish to subdue us all. They will use cunning and force. Perhaps at this very time there are men employed among you to set you against us. It is not so long since but you must remember how one of these powers made violent efforts of this kind, even upon us, the white people their children. But to tell you what is done by others of them to people of your colour towards the mid-day sun would fill you with horror.

Ought we not therefore, to grasp one another with a strong arm of friend-ship, the more easily to repel these foreigners? Go down then and receive the presents which are kept for you as marks of friendship when you run the line; as you have agreed. You will be assured that every care has been taken by the Virginians to prevent your receiving any offence; as you I flatter myself will also do by them. For my part, when I return from whence I came, I shall have the pleasure to tell the great Council of Congress this; then they far from sending an Army into the Creek Nation will exert themselves to give trade and the comforts of life to you, and your families. This will make the chain of our friendship brighter, and indeed will be better for us all.

Before I make an end, I must inform you that our friend CHE-WOCLEYMICHO and his companions the hostages are in good health and spirits. I have sent down to request they may be brought up, that it may not appear hard to keep our friends too long from their relations. But I hope the time passes away agreeably with them; for when I left them they had nothing to do but to drink rum and be merry—If there is any just cause of complaint I now beg it may be known, that I may use my best endeavours to find a remedy. All we have to request is, that you go and receive your presents; and attend at running the line according to your agreement at the Treaty.

Copied from the files of
the War Office. H. KNOX

C. No. 4
(Copy.)

Proceedings of a Meeting of the Lower Creeks April 10th 1787
Present

The Principal Chiefs of the lower towns; also the Talissee, or half way house king; and from the further Creeks, Alexr. McGillivray—Of the white people, besides the Superintendant of indian affairs, the two State Commissioners Messrs. Barnard & Golphin.

Mr. McGillivray opened the business by telling the indians "they knew for what purposes this meeting was called: he regretted it had not been earlier, that their sentiments respecting the white peoples settling their lands, might have been certainly known: that the Virginians (i.e., Georgians) had falsely persuaded the rest of the white people they had purchased those lands from them; there was now a gentleman come out to enquire into this business; that he came from a different quarter, and would be a good witness to the truth— He (McGillivray) had no doubt they would treat him with the highest respect, and with every attention to what he might have to say to them."

He then requested the Superintendant to put any questions, or make any proposals he thought proper—During the talk of the Superintendant the indians observed a singular decorum and attention 'till he came to request them to go down and run the line; at which they interrupted by asking if the white people wanted to make any more of them prisoners (i.e. hostages).

In answer to the talk, the talissee King spoke first—He said that "he was glad the Superintendant had come out that he might make known his complaints of which he had many—He had always been a friend to the white people; that after the War he was invited to Augusta, where he expected to be treated like a friend; instead of which the white people, their long knives in their hands, insisted on his making a cession of land, which he had no right to do; but that after three days importunity he was obliged to consent, on condition the nation would agree to it."

The hallowing King of the Cowetas, seemed principally to undertake to speak for the indians in general—He expressed their thankfulness to the Superintendant for coming so great a journey with the good intention of settling the quarrel between them and the Georgians. If the matter rested between them and Congress, no doubt it could be amicably concluded; but there was a third party who had no mind to do justice—He gave an historical account of the progress of the white people, from even before their establishment to the southward of the Savannah, as he had seen himself or been informed by older men—But says he "these last strides tell us they never mean to let their foot rest—Our lands are our life and our breath, if we part with them we part with our blood—We must fight for them."

The Superintendant then endeavoured to shew the difficulty, nay the impossibility of evacuating the lands on which people had settled, after buying them in the opinion that they were granted by the indians in atonement for the many unprovoked injuries the State had sustained—He adduced many reasons to make it probable the Talissee King had made the grants unconstrained—He promised them every security should be given them against all future encroachments; and he offered to take off several conditions of the late Treaty that might seem to bear too hard—But they insisted, the great grievance was taking their land; and that they could not dispense with—When they were desired to declare if nothing would do but relinquishing the lands on the Oconie; they answered, that, or war.

The Superintendant took his leave, assuring them of his good wishes to the nation; and that he would always use his endeavours in obtaining for them whatever might be fair and reasonable; but that he was sorry to think their demands in the present case were neither.

Mr. McGillivray's proposal was made next day.
Copied from the files of the War office
H. KNOX.

D

Containing

No. 1. a letter dated 15th November 1787. from George Mathews Esquire Governor of Georgia to the president of Congress.

No. 2. a Report of a Committee of the General Assembly of the State of Georgia.

D No. 1
(Copy)

Augusta, Georgia 15 Novr. 1787
Sir.

I do myself the honour to enclose to your Excellency a Report of a Committee of the General Assembly of this state respecting the Creek Indians—it so fully informs your Excellency of the unavoidable necessity there is for a war with that Nation that little is left for me to say on the subject—In my letter to our Delegates of the 9th of August I inform them of the murders Committed by the Indians, and by their answer it appears the letter was laid before Congress, since which time our frontiers have been the scene of blood and Ravages—they have killed thirty one of our Citizens wounded twenty and taken four prisoners—they have burnt the Court house and Town of Greensburgh in the County of Greene and a number of other houses in different parts of the Country—The Assembly fully convinced that the state never can have a secure and lasting peace with that perfidious Nation until they have severely felt the effects of war—have ordered three thousand men to be raised, and given the Executive power, to call forth fifteen hundred more should the first not be adequate. The arming and equiping these Troops will be attended with such expence that the aid of the Union will be required in addition to our exertions, and I flatter myself the United States will grant such assistance as will enable us to prosecute the war with vigour and establish us in the blessings of peace—I would also take the liberty of remarking that I have reason to think the Creek Indians are supplied with arms and ammunition from the Spanish government of West Florida, and whether it may not be proper for Congress Officially to remonstrate against such supplies being granted them whilst engaged in a war with us.

I have the honour to be with respect
Your Excellency's
Most Obedt. Huml. Servt.
(Signed) GEO. MATHEWS

~~The f~~ Copy from the files in the office of the Secy. of Congress.

CHAS. THOMSON secy.

D. No. 2
(Copy)

HOUSE OF ASSEMBLY
Tuesday the 23d. October 1787

The House proceeded to take into consideration the Report of the Committee to whom was referred the message of His Honor the Governour of the 18th Instant together with such parts of the dispatches accompanying the same as relates to the Creek Indians—and the same being read and amended was agreed to by the house and is as follows.

"THE COMMITTEE consisting of General Clarke, Mr. Telfair, Mr. Joseph Habersham Mr. Seagrove and Mr. Walton to whom were Referred the papers marked No. 1 accompanying the Governours Message of the 18th Instant respecting Indian Affairs REPORT,

THAT in examining the letters and documents, committed to them they have Necessarily been led to a Reference to the Treaties, and principal transactions with the Indians which have taken place since the Revolution, and the establishment of peace with Great Britain. And they find that on the thirty first day of May in the year One thousand seven hundred and eighty three the CHEROKEES by a Treaty held at Augusta among others agreed to and subscribed the following clause.

CLAUSE 3rd. 'That a new line shall be drawn without delay, between the present settlements in the said State, and the hunting ground of the said Indians to begin on SAVANNAH River, where the present line strikes it, thence up the said River to a place on the most Northern branch of the same (commonly called Keowee) where a north East line to be drawn from the top of the OCUNNA mountain shall intersect, thence along the said line on a Southwest direction to the top of the said mountain, thence in the same direction to TUEGOLA River, thence to the top of the Currahee mountain, thence to the head or source of the most southern branch of the Oconee River including all the waters of the same, and thence down the middle of the said branch to the Creek line.'

And that on the first day of November following by a treaty also held at Augusta, among others the Creeks agreed to and subscribed a similar clause, for establishing the same line for their hunting grounds. And both Nations made the same Relinquishment on account of mutual claims which had not before been settled between them; and this boundary was again acknowledged and confirmed at another treaty held with the Creeks at Galphinton the 12th day of November one thousand Seven hundred and Eighty five, and extended from the confluence of the Oconee and Okemulgey Rivers to the source of St. Mary's. That it is true that some few months after the holding of this latter Treaty some uneassinesses began to be fomented in the Nation, and some murders were committed. This was considered and declared to be an infraction of the treaty, and Reparation was demanded—It was made a serious object of Government, and the Legislature being convened, our domestic situation, and our relative one with the Union were considered with all possible attention and respect. Commissioners were appointed with full powers to enquire into the causes and to restore peace; but with power also, if unavoidable, to take eventual measures of defence. This proceeding produced another Treaty which was held at SHOULDER-BONE on the third of November one thousand seven hundred and Eighty six, whereby the violation was acknowledged, the boundaries contained in the former treaties again recognized and ratified; and Seven hostages were pledged for the faithful execution of the Condition—Your Committee cannot forbear here to observe that during the course of all these transactions, the communications were made in solemn, open and antient form and the Articles of the treaties were mutually respected, until the aggression posterior to that of Galphinton. And that whilst it is admitted on the one hand there was no principle of representation of the parts of the Nation known in Civilized Government; it cannot be denied on the other that it was such as had been common, and the Indians acknowledged without doubt, and Regret their forming a part, and being members of the state.

Peace being thus Restored by the Treaty of shoulder-bone but before the Articles were yet carried into full effect the state received the appointment of a superintendant of Indian Affairs by the Congress of the United states for the southern department, and on the 15th January in the present year the same was acknowledged by the following Resolutions of the Legislature

'That this house have a due sense of the attention of Congress to the affairs between this state and the Indians within its Territory.

RESOLVED that his honour the Governour be Requested to communicate to the said Superintendant that the Government of this state on the former part of the last year Received certain advice that it was the intention of the Creek Indians to make war against the white inhabitants of the same; and that a short time after they did actually commit hostilities.

That in consequence thereof, and agreeably to the Articles of Confederation and perpetual Union, which this state holds as the Rule of its good faith, and as the evidence of its portion of sovereignty of the Union measures were taken which had for their object the present security of the state, and the Restoring of peace and tranquility by the most expeditious and certain means—and that under providence the measures have been attended with the desired success.

That immediately after the measures before mentioned were determined on, the delegates of this state were directed to make full representation of the same to Congress with the motives which compelled the state to the same, without the delay which would unavoidably have arisen from the Remote distance of the state from the Residence of Congress which no doubt has been done accordingly.'

And afterwards a Committee was appointed to confer with the said superintendant on the subject of his mission, and on the 6th of February they reported, and of which the following are extracts.

'Your Committee report that they have confered with the Honorable the superintendant of the United states and have laid before him the papers and instructions committed to their care to which he has been pleased to return the following answer.

Gentlemen of the Committee for Indian affairs accept my thanks for your polite communication of the different materials in your possession to assist in acquiring an idea of the situation of Indian affairs in this district—The not having been engaged in this line till very lately will hardly permit me to remark on the subject as you Request. I will only express my satisfaction, in observing the moderation as well as spirit with which this state persued her plan of checking the savage insolence on the late occasion—The Report I have to make to the United states in Congress, taking its complexion from these circumstances will probably induce them to a more cheerful participation of the expence.

The Spirit and prudence of the state will no doubt farther dictate means of future tranquility, as well as those of invigorating the hands of the superintendant of Indian Affairs, so far, as is conducive to the execution of his Office, within the limits of this state.

I wish to do myself the honour of assuring the honorable the Legislature, that as they may think it adviseable for me, in my official capacity to be present at making the temporary line, I will cheerfully to attend to that or any other measure they will favour me with pointing out in the line of my duty, and that in every official transaction I Shall observe a most sacred Respect to the Rights of the state of Georgia.

I am With great Respect
Your Humble Servt.
(Signed) JAS. WHITE'

The same Committee having Reported the expediency of New Regulations for Indian affairs, a bill was brought in for that purpose, and being carried into effect, a board of Commissioners were appointed of which the said Superintendant was one—The Commissioners having convened, entered upon the duties of their office; and it was expected that the Indians would be down some time in the Spring on the fulfilment of the shoulderbone treaty. That in the mean time the appointment of Commissaries, with some other arrangements were made, and the superintendant determined to visit the Nation. When there, he wrote to the Governour from the Buzzard-roost on the 12th March, stating the appearances of mischief with some of the Indians, the probable good effects of his mediation, and of the giving up the hostages, which he recommended, It was also said—'There is no doubt but the upper Creeks may be reconciled to the boundary as wished' and by a letter from Mr. John Galphin one of the Commissaries, written at the same time, and on the same Sheet he says 'I saw Mr. McGilivray lately who says he only waits for Doctor White, and if he comes, he will have the line run between the Indians and the Georgians by the first of May' and he also advised that the hostages should be given up. Upon the foundation of these letters the surrender of the hostages was agreed to, and two of the principal ones went on with the answers, and the others were to accompany the Commissioners.

But that on the 13th. of April following another letter from the superintendant to the Governour dated from the Cussatas advises to prepare for War in any event; adding that his personal safety was assured to be in danger, should he threaten the Nation with the force of the Union; and upon his return to augusta on the 23d of April in a farther address to the Governour he ascribes the suspension of hostilities between the Indians and the state to propositions communicated to him by Mr. McGilivray for a new state to be laid off South of the Altamaha, and mentions that he had acceded to a truce until the first of August.

And here ends the knowledge of your Committee of transactions with, or by the superintendant. It was but a little while however before several Murders were committed on our frontier, and which have been Repeated from time to time, until mutual hostilities have at length taken place on the whole length of our border, and a war by the savages is now raging with all its horrors.

And here too, the task of your Committee becomes distressingly difficult. As lovers of their Country, and as servants of the state, it is equally their desire and their duty to be true and to be just, and while they wish to treat the servants of the Union with the strictest Respect, they ought to guard our Government at home against the improper imputation of wrong. They therefore Report it as their Opinion that the ultimate causes of the war were the too sudden interferences with treaties of the state, by which the minds of the Indians were perplexed, and the impression induced that, in a war with the state, they Should not have the strength of the Union to fear; and that another disposition would be made of the Territory, than that which considers it as part of the state. That representations to this effect should be immediately transmitted to Congress, and the support of the Union demanded.

That in the mean time the most Vigorous and decisive measures be taken by the Government of this state for suppressing the bloody violences of the Indians.

For which purpose your Committee advise, that a law be passed as speedily as possible for raising and forming Magazines of Arms, ammunition, Stores and provisions in kind, and for inlisting of men for the protection of the state."

Extracts from the Minutes
(signed) JAS. M. SIMMONS
Clk. G. A.

Copy from the files in the office of
the Secy. of Congress.
  CHAS. THOMSON secy.

E

Contains

No. 1. The report of the Secretary at war, of a plan for the protection of the frontier of Georgia July 26th. 1788.

E. No. 1.

The Secretary of the United States for the Department of War in obedience to the order of Congress of the 15th. instant to report a plan for the protection of the frontier of Georgia agreeably to the principle of the resolve of Congress of the 21st. of July 1787.

REPORTS

That he conceives it is intended the protection to be afforded the State of Georgia should be complete, in case the Creek Indians should persist in refusing to enter into a treaty on reasonable terms, and to comprehend all operations offensive as well as defensive that may be deemed necessary for the full accomplishment of the object.

That unless vigorous exertions be made in the first instance calculated to terminate effectually the contest in one campaign, the United States will hazard the event of being drawn into a tedious, expensive and inglorious War.

That the strength of the Wabash indians who were principally the object of the resolve of the 21st. of July 1787, and the strength of the Creek Indians is very different—That the said Creeks are not only greatly superior in numbers but are more United, better regulated, and headed by a man whose talents appear to have fixed him in their confidence.

That your Secretary humbly apprehends the regular troops of the Union on the Ohio were considered as the basis of the before recited resolve of the 21st. July 1787. That the militia intended to have been drawn forth were to have acted as auxiliaries to the said regular troops, and that all the arrangements were to have been made under the direction of the commanding officer of the said troops—That the case is widely different on the frontiers of Georgia, no troops of the United States being there, nor is it easily practicable to remove any considerable body from the Ohio, were the measure expedient in other respects.

That this difference of circumstances will require a different and more extensive arrangement for the protection of the frontier of Georgia, than any that were contemplated by the aforesaid resolve of the 21st. of July 1787.

That the frontier of Georgia may be protected either by a large body of militia detached from time to time, or by a corps of troops regularly organized and enlisted for a certain period—That a consideration of the expence and irregularity of detachments of mere militia, compared with the oeconomy and vigor of a corps of troops properly organized would evince the great superiority and advantage to be derived to the public by an adoption of the organized troops.

That from the view of the object your Secretary has been able to take he conceives that the only effectual mode of acting against the said Creeks in case they should persist in their hostilities, would be by making an invasion of their Country with a powerful body of well regulated troops, always ready to combat and able to defeat any combination of force the said creeks could oppose, and to destroy their towns and provisions.

Your Secretary humbly conceives, that any interference on the part of the United States with less force and energy would cherish the hostilities of the Creeks instead of extinguishing them.

That he conceives the operation herein stated would require an Army of two thousand eight hundred non commissioned officers and privates of the different species of troops to be raised for the term of nine months.

That the said troops should be commanded by one Major General, and one Brigadier General to be appointed by Congress, who should also appoint an Inspector and Quarter Master to said troops.

That the pay and emoluments of said Officers be fixed by Congress.

That the organization of the troops should be as follows.

Three regiments of Infantry of seven hundred each—One regiment of Cavalry of five hundred and sixty—One corps of Artillery of one hundred and forty.

That if Congress should approve of these numbers they might be apportioned as follows.

Georgia—one Regiment of Infantry	700	
" five companies of Cavalry of 70 each	350	
		1050
South Carolina—one Regt. of Infantry	700	
two companies of Artillery of 70 each	140	
		840
North Carolina—one Regiment of Infantry	700	
three companies of Cavalry	210	
		910
		2800

That all the regimental officers be appointed by the said States respectively according to the proportions to be specified by the Secretary at War.

That the said troops should be mustered and inspected in the manner to be directed by the Secretary at War which musters should be considered as essential vouchers in the settlement of the accounts of the troops.

That the said troops should be paid by the States in which they are respectively raised according to the rates of pay established for the troops of the United States.

That suitable clothing to the value of ten dollars be allowed each non-commissioned officer and private who should enlist for the said term of nine months which with tents, the necessary camp-equipage, and waggons or other means of transportation agreeably to the proportions to be specified by the Secretary at War should be furnished to the troops by the States in which they shall be raised.

That the States of North and South Carolina should also subsist their quotas respectively until their arrival at the place of rendezvous to be appointed by the commanding Officer.

That the rations and forage of said Army should be provided by Contract by the State of Georgia while acting within the said State, and also for the quotas of South and North Carolina until they should return to the places of dismission within the said States respectively.

That the issues of the rations of provision and forage should be checked in the manner to be directed by the Secretary at War, and for every ration of provision allowed accordingly the United States should be charged a sum not exceeding   parts of a dollar, and for every ration of forage not exceeding   parts of a dollar.

That the amount of pay, transportation and subsistence of said troops should be settled in the manner and forms to be previously established by the Board of Treasury, and the same when completed should be passed to the credit of said states on the existing requisitions according to the amount they may have respectively furnished.

That as it is highly probable that the said States may be deficient in Arms, accoutrements and ammunition, the same be furnished out of the Arsenals of the United States, and be transported, by the Secretary at War, by water to such ports within the said States as may be most convenient and addressed to the executives of the same.

That ten pieces of light field artillery with their necessary apparatus, and a suitable quantity of ammunition be also transported by the Secretary at War to Savannah in Georgia for the purposes of the said expedition, addressed to the Major General who may be appointed for the expidition.

That the expences of every species which would be incurred for the various objects of the said Army for nine months, may be estimated at four hundred and fifty thousand dollars.

All which is humbly submitted to Congress.

H. KNOX

War Office 26th. July 1788
Copied from the Register of the War office. H. KNOX

F

Contains letters and enclosures, of the Superintendant & Commissioners for treating with the Southern nations of Indians

No.   Instructions to the Commissioners.

No. 1. A letter of 15th June 1788. from Richard Winn Esqr. to the Secretary at war.

No. 2 A letter of 19th March 1788. from Samuel Johnson Esqr. Governor of North Carolina to the Governor of South Carolina.

No. 3 An Estimate of the expences that would attend a treaty.

No. 4 A letter of 5th. August 1785. from Richard Winn Esqr. to the Secretary at war.

~~No. 5~~ ~~A letter dated 6th August 1788. from Andrew Pickens Commissioner to Richard Winn Superintendant of Indian affairs.~~

No. 6 A letter of August 8th. 1788. from Richard Winn Esqr. to the Secretary at war.

No. 7. A letter of 14th of October 1788. from Richard Winn Esqr. to the Secretary at war.

No. 8 A letter of the 14th of August 1788. from the Governor of Georgia to the Superintendant and Commissioners of Indian affairs.

No. 9 A letter of 16th July 1788. from the Superintendant and Commissioners to Alexander McGillivray.

No. 10 A letter of the 12th of August 1788. from Alex. McGillivray to the superintendant and Commissioners of Indian affairs.

No. 11 A letter of the 8th December 1788. from Richard Winn Esquire to the Secretary at war.

No. 12 A letter of the 15. September 1788. from Alexander McGillivray to the Superintendant and Commissioners of Indian affairs.

No. 13 A letter of the 28th of November 1788. from the Superintendant and Commissioners of Indian affairs, to Alexander McGillivray.

No. 14 A letter of 19th December 1788. from Richard Winn Esqr. to the Secretary at war.

No. 15. A letter of 1st. March 1789 from Richard Winn Esqr. to the Secretary at war.

the above copied from the files of the War office.

H. Knox

(Copy.)

In Congress October 26th. 1787

Instructions to the Commissioners for negotiating a treaty with the tribes of Indians in the Southern department for the purpose of establishing peace between the United States and the said tribes.

Gentlemen,

Several circumstances rendering it probable that hostilities may have commenced, or are on the eve of commencing between the State of North-

Carolina and the Cherokee Nation of Indians, and between the State of Georgia and the Creek Nation of Indians—you are to use every endeavour to restore peace and harmony between the said States and the said Nations on terms of justice and humanity.

The great source of contention between the said States and the Indian tribes being boundaries—you will carefully enquire into and ascertain the boundaries claimed by the respective states, and altho' Congress are of opinion that they might constitutionally fix the bounds between any State, and an Independent tribe of Indians, yet unwilling to have a difference subsist between the general government, and that of the individual States, they wish you so to conduct the matter, that the States may not conceive their Legislative rights in any manner infringed, taking care at the same time that whatever bounds are agreed upon they may be described in such terms as shall not be liable to misconstruction and misrepresentation but may be made clear to the conceptions of the Indians as well as whites.

The present treaty having for its principal object the restoration of peace— no cession of land is to be demanded of the indian tribes.

You will use the utmost care to ascertain who are the leading men among the several tribes—the real head men and Warriors—these you will spare no pains to attach to the interest of the United States—by removing as far as may be all causes of future contention or quarrels—by kind treatment and assurances of protection by presents of a permanent nature—and by using every endeavour to conciliate the affections of the white people inhabiting the frontiers towards them.

You will encourage the Indians to give notice to the Superintendant of Indian Affairs of any designs that may be formed by any neighbouring Indian tribe, or by any person whatever against the peace of the United States.

You will insist that all prisoners of whatever age, sex, or complexion be delivered up, and that all fugitive slaves belonging to Citizens of the United States be restored.

A Copy from the Journal of Congress at the request of the Secretary at War
(Signed) Attest. R. ALDEN D. Secy.

F. No. 1.

                                            Winnsborough 25 June 1788
Sir.

I beg leave to lay before you the steps taken by the Commissioners to bring about a treaty with the Creek Indians agreably to the resolves of Congress.

A talk was sent to that nation, the 29th of March last addressed to Mr. McGillivray, and the head men and warriors, urging the necessity there was to treat, and in the most pointed terms insisting as a first principle, that every hostile proceedure should instantly cease. a Mr. Whitfield was the bearer, he is a respectable character and has formerly traded with them, he writes us that the Indians are highly pleased with what Congress has done, and willing to treat on the principles of justice and equity. on that ground they will meet the Superintendant and Commissioners, in the interim all hostilities to cease. this, I have the pleasure to inform you is the case at present, and the sooner it can be effected the better as it is the wish of the Indians that the treaty be held as speedy as possible.

The above accounts I laid before the Executive of the State of Georgia who agreed with me in opinion that the 15th. September next is as early as this matter can be begun on—the reason is obvious. The state of No. Carolina not complying with the resolves of Congress in forwarding the needful, nor is it to be expected that they intend it. (see a copy of the Governors letter enclosed) and even supposing they had, upon a general calculation—the sum allowed by Congress, would have been too small to carry into effect a treaty with the Creeks alone, considering the greatness of their Nation—presents, I make no doubt are expected by them. The goods on hand from the last treaty, amount to not more than to £ 400 "—" and many of them consists of perishable articles which of course have Suffered.

The two Commissioners General Pickens and Mathews with myself made an estimate a few days ago at Augusta, a copy of which you have herewith. as these Gentlemen as well as myself calculated on the lowest scale—I make no doubt you will think with me that a further supply is necessary. there is every reason to beleive there will be present from 1000 to 1500 Indians, and each Indian, Genl. Pickens (who has been on similar occasions of this kind before) assures me, at such a time, which cannot well be denied them, ~~expects double~~ expects *double rations.* upon the whole I trust on a matter of such consequence to the States, Georgia in particular, that Congress will give it a reconsideration, and make such provision as they conceive best on this business. The treaty as I before mentioned will take place on the 15 September next, therefore no time ought to be lost.

I beg leave further to observe, that my commission as superintendant expires the 29th of August, it will be necessary to prolong the time if tis the wish of Congress to continue to be represented in the Southern department. I shall conclude with assuring you that the States of So. Carolina, and Georgia, will contribute every thing in their power towards facilitating the treaty under the auspices of Congress; before whom I beg you will lay the purport of this without delay. they may depend on my utmost exertions in forwarding a plan so highly necessary. I have the honor to be

Sir

Your Most obedient Servant
Signd. RICHARD WINN

General Knox Secretary at war

F. No. 2
(Copy)

Edenton 19th March 1788

Sir

The resolution of Congress of 26th. October to which you refer in the letter you did me the honor of addressing to me on the 18th. day of February last, did not come to me till after the adjournment of the assembly, and as I considered that the settling the boundary between this state and the indians, a subject of too much importance for me to act in without the direction of the legislature I laid aside the consideration of it, till since I had the honor of receiving your Excellencys letter.

I yesterday laid all the papers relating to this business, before the council of State for their consideration, who concurred with me in opinion that the powers of the executive department of this state, did not extend so far as to comprehend all the objects contained in the instructions sent forward by Congress, for the Government of the Commissioner to be appointed by this state, and tho' the resolution of Congress passed as early as the 26th of October, no hostilities have hitherto been committed on the inhabitants of this state by the Cherokees, nor have we any intimation from the inhabitants of the frontier that any such hostilities are at present apprehended. I have not therefore appointed a commissioner to treat with the Cherokees. Should the States of South Carolina, and Georgia, be of opinion that the co-operation of this state can in any manner facilitate the negociation with the Creeks, we will be ready to adopt any measure that may have a tendency to promote the peace and Security of the State of Georgia, at any time when they may think proper to favor us with an intimation in what manner we can be useful to them.

I have the honor to be with the
highest consideration & respect
Sir &c

Signed   SAML. JOHNSTON

His Excellency
The Governor of
South Carolina

F. No. 3.

An Estimate of money necessary to be advanced by Southern States for carrying on a treaty with the Creek Indians

Dr.

		£	None	£
none expected	To the Commissioner of No. Carolina		None	
The Commissioners of So. Carolina and Georgia are supposed to be in actual service 60 days each, or perhaps longer.	the Commissioner of So. Carolina 70.. .. the Commissioner of Georgia 70.. ..		140	
It is supposed that the shortest treaty will hold 20 days. therefore it will take the men 10 days to go and return from the place where the treaty is to be held.	1 Major 30 days @ 13/ 19..10.. 2 Captains do. @ 10/ 30.. .. 4 Lieuts. do. @ 7/ 42.. .. 100 privates do @ 1/6 225.. .. Rations for the above @ 6d. ⅌ day each 85.. 5..0		401 15	
Genl. Pickens says at the last treaty with the Cherokees, there were 1500 indians—a Nation much inferior to the Creeks—this representation may be greater—so says Mr. Whitfield.	ditto for 1000 Indians 20 days @ 9d.		750	
No person can be got to go to the Indians under 4 dollars ⅌ day. Mr. Whitfield has been out now Near three months.	To money advanced to persons going to and from the nations with talks and to expresses to other places		150	

Cr.

	£		
By money advanced by No. Carolina	466	13	4
By ditto advanced by So. Carolina	466	13	4
By ditto advanced by Georgia	400	8	
By amount of Goods supposed to be on hand			
Deficiency now wanting to carry the Treaty into effect	958	8	4

(continued)

F. No. 3 (*continued*)

Description		Amount
The goods and provisions will be transported a considerable distance—houses must be built to receive the public stores— 10 or 12 waggons will be wanted.	To Waggon hire, transporting the goods and provisions to the place where the treaty is to be held, and the building 2 rough houses for the reception of goods & for the accomodation of the Commissrs.	200
Two Linguisters must be employed—One on the side of the Commissioners the other for the indians—Commissarys must also be employed.	To 2 Linguisters, Commissary's & money for supporting the Commissioners Table	50
The Commissioners think the presents ought to be as considirable as possible, as the indians expect them so.	To presents necessary to be given the indians	600
	Total	£2,291 15

£2,291 15

This calculation made at Augusta in the state of Georgia the 13th day of June 1788 by the Commissioners, and a true copy

Signed RICHARD WINN

F. No. 4

Winnsborough 5th. August 1788

Sir

By talks received from the head men and warriors of the Cherokee nation dated the 30th. June last, I am given to understand that a party from North-Carolina (called Franklin State) with Servier at their head came over and destroyed several of their towns, killed near thirty of the Indians, made one prisoner, and obliged the remainder to fly with their famelys to some of the lower towns for protection. notwithstanding these outrages, there are at this present time near thirty of their Towns in friendship with the white people, whose wish is to remain so, as their talks run continually, for a lasting peace to be established between them and the whites. The Overhills, the other part of the nation, where the above affair happen'd, seem determined for war, of which I shall make the Governor of North Carolina acquainted. The daily encroachments made on the Territories of this set of people, is such as to induce them through me, to lay their distressed situation before Congress which this opportunity gives me the honor of now doing, presuming they will see with me, the real necessity there is, for an accommodation taking place with this nation; and order the necessary supplies accordingly for carrying the treaty into effect. I must beg leave to add, that could I have been supplied with the needful, I should have called this nation to a permanent treaty long ere this.

I have the honor to be

Sir

Your Obedient Servant,

RICHARD WINN

Sir. This moment General Pickens's letter came to hand which I have taken the liberty to inclose to you.

R. WINN

General Knox
Secretary at war

F. No. 6

Winnsborough 8th. August 1788.

Sir.

The gentleman who was sent to the Creek Nations, with talks from the Commissioners, has returned with answers which appear to be friendly. The indians are willing to come to a treaty next month, therefore the 15th. day is set for that purpose—the meeting will be on the Tugelo River, at the house of a Mr. Larkland Cleaveland on the Georgia Side, in consequence of which hostilities have ceased on both sides.

I make no doubt the wish of Congress will be fully answered, provided the assembly of Georgia repeal a law which in some measure militates against the resolves of Congress in carrying into effect the treaty with that nation. The assembly are now setting on the business, which I hope will have the disired effect.

I have the honor to be
Sir
Your humble Servant
RICHARD WINN

General Knox }
Secretary at war }

F. No. 7.

Winnsborough October 14th. 1788

Sir.

I have had the honor of receiving your several letters, with the duplicates of each enclosing the different resolves of Congress of July 15th. August 4th. and 14th. respecting Indian affairs, and shall at all times be happy through you to lay before that honorable body such information as offers in that department.

From several conferrences with the commissioners relative to the Creek Indians and opening a correspondence with McGillivray who is their head man, we were led to believe that our negociations would terminate in a peace between that nation and the state of Georgia, and agreeably to what I before informed you, had actually appointed the time and place for holding a treaty, not doubting when we met to get over every obstacle in bringing it to an issue, however not having the supplies necessary in time, and receiving a letter (see No. 1 enclosed) from the Governor of Georgia, we wrote to McGillivray and the head men and warriors, to postpone the treaty until the spring of next year, to this we have had no answer as yet, but have received a letter from him (see No. 2 enclosed) wherein he insists as a leading principle, upon having the boundaries the same as they were when the state of Georgia was a british province; these terms of treaty he mentions in his first letter to the Commissioners, but neither they nor myself imagined this would operate in his breast or with the indians, as a barrier to the treaty, when we produced the different articles of peace entered into since, with the bounds prescribed, and mutually agreed to by both parties, (see a copy of our letter to which No. 2 is an answer). It evidently appears by his last, if we are to expect peace with these Indians, it must be on his own terms. from these considerations, we may think it our duty to reply in a different manner to what we have: as soon as we have an answer to our last respecting the postponing the treaty, I shall do myself the honor of transmitting you a copy of it.

Before I quit the subject of the Creek indians it will be necessary to inform you (in order to make the Governor of Georgias meaning appear more clear), that the Georgians have at this time a law existing, wherein they have given as bounty land to their Soldiers, a large tract of Country which belongs to the Indians.

This I remonstrated to the executive of that state, and this was another motive for the treaty's being postponed, as such a law should be repealed before an accomodation could take place.

With due respect
I have the honor to be
Sir.
Your Most Obedient
Servant
(Signed)   RICHARD WINN

The honorable General Knox
Secretary at war

F. No. 8.
(Copy)   Augusta Georgia 14th August 1788

Gentlemen.

The disagreeable and unhappy situation of our State affairs, are such, that I am sorry on this occasion to be under the necessity to declaim against their inability of carrying into effect the business fully of the proposed treaty with the Creek nation of Indians.

In order to obviate the many difficulties and insufficiency that appeared in the operation of the said treaty—I did with the advice of the executive call the Legislature to convene in Augusta the 22nd. ulto. but without effect—and the executive have it not in their power to make any appropriations. I have, and will continue to exert myself in endeavoring to obtain a credit from the mercantile line, either on public or private faith, and if successful will give you early notice thereof. but in this I doubt.

I would therefore, (if Congress does not appropriate a further sum for carrying on the said treaty, as the superintendant I presume represented the whole to that honorable body) most seriously recommend that you endeavor, all in your power to have the said treaty postponed if possible. I promise you the sight of the business shall not be put off, but every preparation in our power shall be exerted, you have to urge, on your parts, the reason for postponing the treaty to be, that of the change of Government, and of other matters; that I dare say would be sufficient particularly to Mr. McGillivray who is a sensible intelligent man. if possible that the same could be postponed until the Spring of the next year it would be well, but at any rate for two or three months. this matter would be best managed by the person you appoint to go to the nation, who ought to be a sensible man; I shall engage that peace be observed by the citizens of this state against the Creek Nation as far as is in my power to enforce, You will please also to urge the observance of the same on their parts, against the citizens of this State.

I flatter myself gentlemen; taking a review of our situation, that you will do all in your power to obtain peace with the Indians within your district, and the citizens of the United States.

I have the honor to be
with every sentiment of respect
Your most obedient humble Servt.
(Signed) GEO. HANDLEY

Honble. Richard Winn Esquire Superintendant
and the honble. Geo. Mathews, & Andrew Pickens Esqrs.
Commissrs. of Indian affairs

F. No. 9

Fort Charlotte July 16th 1788.

To Alexander MGillivray Esquire and others the chief men and warriors of the Creek nation.

This day your letter was opened which you were pleased to address to us, as also the talks of the hallooing king of the lower, and mad dog of the upper Creeks, in answer to the one sent you by Mr. Whitefield.

We are happy to find that you are willing to meet us in treaty, so as to convince the world that your conduct and the leading men of the Indians is such as to dispose you to do that which is right and just; on such grounds we are equally willing to meet.

You mention you expect a requisition will be made by us to the people of Georgia, to retire from the Oconie river, within the bounds claimed under the british government, this we are not authorised to do, but will write to the governor of Georgia, requesting him to issue his proclamation that no further tresspasses be committed and that all hostilities do cease. We make no doubt you will lose sight of all matter of little weight and bring fully into view the grand object of the treaty agreably to the resolves of Congress so as to restore peace and harmony once more between the citizens of Georgia and the Creek Indians on the principles of Justice and humanity; as we do firmly assure you 'tis what we ardently wish.

As to the time and place for holding the treaty, this power was fully vested in the superintendant and the executive of Georgia, and they had previous to any advice received from Mr. Whitfield (except his letter of May 15th.) appointed the 15 Septr. next, the day on which the treaty is to begin, on the river Tugoolo, the dividing line between South Carolina, and Georgia, at the house of Larkland Cleaveland on the Georgia side, at which time and place we hope to meet you and the Creek Chiefs, as brothers. we wish to see every thing conducted in the greatest friendship.

We conclude thanking you for your polite attention to Mr. Whitefield, and shall be disposed to make you a like return in future.

We have the honor to be
Your Obedient Servants

signed
{
RICHARD WINN Supt.
ANDREW PICKENS Commissr. for So. Caroa.
GEORGE MATHEWS Commissr. for Georgia
}

(Copy)

F. No. 10
(True Copy)

Little Tallassee 12th. August. 1788

Gentlemen

I have received your letter of the 16th. July. this day.

It is with equal surprize and concern, that I learn from you that the honorable the Congress has not authorised you its Commissioners to give us a full redress of our complaints, and to give us full satisfaction in what concerns our territory which the Georgians are attempting to wrest from us forcibly; all which we were taught to expect from the Justice and humanity of that honorable body, from the measure adopted by them in sending Doctor White among us to be fully and truly informed of the cause of the war between us and Georgia; we had great expectations that we Should soon experience the good effects of it, in having the causes of our discontents removed; and more particularly on Mr. Whitefields coming here we did so firmly beleive that we were on the point of obtaining a satisfactory peace, that we were eager to meet you and conclude one, but your letter discovers to me that nothing has been done, and all is yet to do.

It was expected that the requisition which I made to you for removing the Georgians from the disputed lands, was to be considered by you as it was meant by us, as an indispensible preliminary to form the basis on which the treaty of peace was to be concluded.

I feel much pleasure in your approving of the leading sentiments as expressed in my letter by Mr. Whitfield, and it is with regret that I remark that our enemy does not manifest an equal disposition with us to terminate the war, by agreeing to equitable terms of peace, and as we ask no concession from them as the price of peace, so they ought not to demand any on our side.

When I next meet the chiefs which will be early in September, I will explain to them the contents of your letter.

Mean time I answer you; as well knowing that they will not consent to treat unless they see their requisition enforced.

I have the honor to be, with
most respectful consideration
Your most obedient Servant
(Signed)   ALEXAR. McGILLIVRAY

To the Honorable Generals Richard Winn
Andrew Pickens &
George Mathews Commissioners appointed

by the Honorable the Congress. to treat with the southern nations of Indians. True Copy. (RICHARD WINN)

F. No. 11.

Winnsborough 8th. December 1788

Sir.

I do myself the honor to enclose you a copy of McGillivrays last letter to the Commissioners and myself together with our answer, by which you will discover if the Indians evade coming to a treaty they mean war, and will in my opinion come down in great force against the state of Georgia.

On the receipt of his letter which never came to hand 'till the 13th. of last month tho dated so early as the 15th of September, I immediately directed a meeting of the Commissioners at Hopewell, when it was agreed on that the treaty could not take place sooner than next May or June, as it was thought necessary the Indians should have time to consult and finally determine on the last talk sent them, which is the answer alluded to; wherein we expressly request their reply to be pointed and decisive, and that it be dispatched to us as soon as possible. Should they do this, it will give Congress and the Georgians timely notice to prepare for the worst or otherwise as it may happen.

Not long since a fort between french broad and Holstien rivers, was taken by the Cherokees and Creeks—Ten persons were killed and about 30 were made prisoners. the war is still carried on between North Carolina, and the Cherokees—by a talk I lately held with one of the Chiefs of that nation, he says "Notwithstanding what has happened between them, their principal men wish for peace, that they are now holding a great talk among their head men and warriors," the result of which was not determined but he thinks they would gladly bury the hatchet.

I have every reason to believe that McGillivray is trying to Unite the two nations—the Creeks and Cherokees, the so. Carolina and Georgia Commissioners think with me, that if the state of North Carolina would Send forward their Commissioner, with the Supplies, a treaty might be effected with the Cherokees before a junction with the Creeks could take place.

Sir, with regard
I have the honor to be
Your Most obedient
Servant
RICHARD WINN

The Honorable Major General Knox
Secretary at war.

F. No. 12.

Little Tallassia 15th Septr. 1788

Gentlemen

I have received your letter of 28 August wherein you disire that the proposed treaty between us may be deferred untill the spring of the next year; the reasons you give us for that measure is good, and to which we do agree, hoping that a new Congress acting on the principles of the new Constitution of america. will set every thing to rights between us on the most equitable footing, so that we may become real friends to each other, settling on the same land and having but one interest.

We expected that upon Mr. Whitfields return, a truce of arms would have been directly proclaimed in Georgia, and can't account for the delay of that measure, and in fact there has been no observance of it on their part, from June 'till now, they have been driving and plundering our hunting camps, of horses and skins, &c. and it is only lately, that a Coweta indian brought me a paper, which he found fastened to a tree near to Flint river, which upon a close examination I find to be a threatening letter directed to me, it is wrote on the back of an advertisement with gunpowder, a part of it rub'd out as it dry'd, and with the carriage, the writing says something of the war, and your savage subjects—and—an establishment of peace you must "not expect, until all our damages are made good at the treaty and Satisfaction we will have for our grievances." from all which I foresee great difficulty in the attempt to preserve strict suspension of hostility. I can only assure you that we shall regulate ourselves by the conduct of the Georgians, and act according to circumstances. The writing I mention is signed Jam. Alexander 5. August 1788. The Cherokees are daily coming in to me complaining of acts of hostility committed in the most barbarous manner by the americans, and numbers are taking refuge within our territory, who are permitted to settle and build villages under our protection. Such acts of violence, committed at the time that the Congress through you is holding out to the whole nations and tribes, professions of the most friendly nature, makes it appear to all, that such professions are only deceitful snares to lull them into a security, whereby the americans may the more easily destroy them.

Be not offended Gentlemen, at the remark, 'tis true that it is universal through the Indians.

> I am with great respect
> Gentlemen
> Your humble Servant
> Signed ALEX. MCGILLIVRAY

The Honorable Generals, Richard Winn,
Andrew Pickens, & George Mathews
Commissioners for treating with the
Southern Nations of Indians
(True Copy)

F. No. 13.
(True Copy.)   Hopewell on Kiowee. November 28th. 1788

Sir

Your letter of the 12th. August and 15th. September are now before us, with regard to the former wherein you mention. *Nothing has been done, and all is yet to do,* give us leave to tell you, that every thing in our power has been done in order to bring forward a Treaty, and, under the authority of Congress, to give you full and ample redress in what concerns your territory, at the same time we must observe that, that honorable body will not loose sight of doing equal Justice to the state of Georgia, whose claim to what you call the disputed lands, is confirmed by three different treaties, signed by your head men and warriors: Therefore we earnestly recommend you and the chiefs seriously to consider, under these circumstances, how impossible it is for us to comply with your requisition, relative to removing the people from the Oconie lands, this can only be the business of the treaty, after a full investigation of the right of Claim.

In answer to your last, where you so pointedly attack that body under whom we have the honor to act, we cannot be silent, least it should be tortured into a conviction of Guilt. narrow and illiberal indeed must be that mind, that could for a moment suppose, that Congress, after withstanding one of the greatest powers of Europe with her allies, together with almost the whole of the Indian tribes combined, Should at this day have recourse to base artifice, in order to accomplish the ruin of a few Indian tribes, while She's enjoying the blessings of peace at home, and an honorable name among the nations of the world.

We have already enclosed you the Governor of Georgia's proclamation dated July the 31st. last for a truce of arms, which has been as strictly adhered to as possible, and any thing that has happened in violation of it, had you been more explicit, and mentioned the time and place where the Indians horses and skins were plundered, Strict enquiry might have been made and the offenders punished.

If we take a view of the conduct of the Indians on your part, we have more right to complain. we daily hear of the most cruel depredations, committed by the Creeks on the Georgians, the man you allude to (Alexander) we are credibly informed was in pursuit of a party of Creeks that had stole twelve horses from Green County, and notwithstanding we have had every assurance given us that hostilities should cease; the Governor of Georgia has lately handed us a list of the different Counties that have recently Suffered. To wit

Liberty County—between 25 and 30 Negroes & several large stocks of Cattle.

Effingham—one man killed.

Wilkes—from 6 to 10 horses plundered

Greene—from 21 to 27 horses ditto

Washington—6 horses   ditto

Franklin—from 16 to 20 horses ditto—One man wounded. We must add to the above list a pair of fine dunn geldings taken from general Martin, about a mile from his plantation, by some of the Coweta Indians, while he was acting under Congress as agent for the Cherokees and Chicasaws.

The Simenolian Indians are likewise doing a deal of mischief, we know not whither they belong to any part of the Creeks, but wish to be informed. from these violations committed, what can the union expect, unless a stricter compliance on your part is observed in putting a Stop to hostilities. we are well assured Congress will not look on in silence and see any part of the union robbed of its citizens. enclosed you will find a late resolve of Congress, and a proclamation relative to the Cherokees.

It is our sincere wish that you will meet us the Eighth day of June next at the place appointed before, but should this appear to you at too distant a period, a month sooner will be no object with us in holding a treaty, in the interim, we fully assure you nothing shall be wanting on our parts in the observance of a strict suspension of arms, on a presumption that you will act in like manner, we request that you will consult the head men and warriors, on this occasion, and send us a pointed and decisive answer signed Jointly, as soon as possible.

We are Sir, with due respect
Your Obedient Servants.
RICHARD WINN
ANDREW PICKENS
GEORGE MATHEWS

To Alexander McGillivray Esqr.
and the head men and warriors
of the Creek nation.

F. No. 14

Winnsborough December 19th 1788

Sir.

Since I had the honor of writing you last I have received by express from the Governor of North Carolina, that the legislature of that state has appointed a John Steele Esquire Commissioner on indian affairs, and voted their quota, agreably to the resolves of Congress, they have also requested the Governor to issue his proclamation that hostilities do cease against the Cherokees, and to send a talk to Mr. McGillivray, that it is their wish to be at peace with the Creeks—These steps being taken on the part of North-Carolina, there is not the least doubt of a friendly treaty taking place with the cherokees which persuades me will lead to one with the Creeks. The Executive of that State think the last of May the best time for holding a treaty.

> I have the honor to be
> Sir
> Your most obedient
> Servant
> Signd. RICHARD WINN

Honble. Majr. Genl. Knox

F. No. 15.

Winnsborough March 1. 1789

Sir.

I think it necessary to inform you that a treaty will take place with the Cherokee Indians the third monday in may next, at the upper war-ford on French broad river, in the neighbourhood of Swananao—State of North Carolina.

The Creek Indians 'tis supposed will also treat, they are now holding a great talk in their nation, the result of which is not yet come to hand.

> I have the honor to subscribe
> Myself
> Your Most
> Obedient Servant.
> RICHARD WINN

The Honorable Major General Knox

G.

An extract from the Gazette of the United States of the 17th of June 1789.

A Talk, lately sent by the Commissioners of Indian affairs, in the southern Department to the Creeks correspondent.

To the head men, Chiefs, and Warriors of the Creek nation.

We last year appointed a time and place for holding a treaty with you to establish a lasting peace between you and us, that we might again become as one people; you all know the reasons why it was not held at that time.

We now send you a talk, inviting you to a treaty on your bank of the Oconee river, at the rock landing. We wished to meet you at that place on the 8th. of June, but, as that day is so near at hand, you might not all get notice. We therefore shall expect to meet you on the 20th. of June.

We have changed the place of meeting from that of the last year; so that none of you should have reason to complain; it is your own ground and on that land we wish to renew our former trade and friendships, and to remove every thing that has blinded the path between you and us.

We are now governed by a President, who is like the old King over the great water; he Commands all the warriors of the Thirteen great Fires. He will have regard to the welfare of all the Indians: and when peace shall be established, he will be your father and you will be his Children, so that none shall dare to do you harm.

We know that lands have been the cause of dispute between you and the white people; but we now tell you that we want no new grants; our object is to make a peace, and to unite us all under our great Chief Warrior and President, who is the father and Protector of all the white people; Attend to what we say. Our traders are very rich, and have houses full of such goods as you used to get in former days; it is our wish that you should trade with them and they with you, in Strict friendship.

Our brother George Galphin will carry you this talk; listen to him, he will tell you nothing but truth from us:

Send us your answer by him.

April 20th. 1789

ANDREW PICKENS H. OSBORNE	⎫ Commissioners of the ⎬ United States for ⎪ Indian affairs in the ⎭ Southern Department

(A True Copy from the original) C. SWAN

G

Containing

No. 1. A letter of the Governor of Georgia dated August the 9th 1787. Stateing the circumstances of the hostilities between them and the creeks.

No. 2. Talk of the lower Creeks 14 June 1787.

No. 3. Answer to the talk of the lower Creeks June 29th. 1787.
No. 4. Talk of the lower Creeks July 27. 1787.
No. 5. Answer to the talk of the lower Creeks Augt. 7. 1787.

G. No. 1.
(Copy)

Augusta 9th August 1787

Gentlemen,

From a wish that you may be informed, and through you the Honorable the Congress of the United States, of the situation of this State with the Creek Indians, I do myself the pleasure to enclose you two talks I have received from that Nation, with my answers thereto, from which it appears there is reason to expect this state will be compelled to engage in a war with them; it would ill become a free people and more particularly those of Georgia to give satisfaction for the warriors that have been killed for murders committed on our peaceable inhabitants in violation of the most solemn treaties entered into with us. As this State had experienced many and repeated injuries from that nation during the late war with Great Britain, such as killing our inhabitants, and plundering us of our property, all of which we were willing to sacrifice rather than continue the war a day longer than the United States wished to crown the Union with peace.

That you may be as well informed as the Nature and situation of matters will admit, it is needful that I should inform you that from letters I received from James White Esqr. agent for Indian affairs for the Southern department, dated last march, and April there was some reason to think the Indians were not perfectly for peace, and on his return to the state he informed me that they assured him that no hostilities should be committed or injury done to this state before August, or until they receive an Answer from Congress or him, but in direct violation of this promise they did on the 29th day of May in the County of Greene, kill and Scalp two of our Men and carried off a Negro and fourteen horses, a party of Militia crossed the Oconee River in pursuit of the murderers, fell in with some Indians of that nation, and killed twelve, which from the first talk I received appears to be of the lower Towns, and the murderers from the upper Towns, which is the distinction they make, from their talk; I thought we were to have peace, as they remark, it was impossible for us to tell, whether it was the upper or lower Creeks that had done the murder, or been killed by our men—Their talk of the 27th of July insolently demands the Officer that Commanded the party, and as many of his men to be delivered to them as will make satisfaction for the twelve warriors they have lost. Candor compels me to say, when I think of this insolent demand, the repeated alarms they have given our frontiers and the injury the state sustains from them, that I feel my blood run warm in my veins, and a just impulse to Chastise them for their insolence and perfidy, and think it my indispensable duty if they commit hostilities on this state to take the most effectual means in my power for the defence of the same by carrying the war into their Country, or such other measures as may be most for the safety and happiness of the inhabitants of this Country.

>I have the Honor to be with much
>Respect and Real esteem
>Gentlemen
>Your Most obedt. servt.
>(Signed) GEO. MATHEWS

Copied from the files in the office of the Secy. of Congress.

>CHAS. THOMSON Secy.

G. No. 2
(Copy)

>Cusetas 14th June 1787

The beloved man from Congress was here, and we had talk with him, what was agreed upon there did not answer—then Mr. McGilivray came over here and matters were settled—Mr. White and Mr. McGilivray came upon terms and it was told to them and they agreed to it, till such time as Col. White sent an answer back, we then thought that matters were settled, and we did nothing but mind our business—Mr. McGilivray promised to acquaint the upper towns of this, and for them to lie still, we then expected that Mr. White would inform the state of Georgia of this, and tell them that we were their friends, we minded nothing but our hunting, we always talk together and always agreed, and promised that if any thing happened we would not go on rashly but let one another know our grievances; you always promised that the innocent should not suffer for the guilty, you certainly knew us, we were always among the houses, we did not know of the upper towns doing any mischief, nor did we think that our friends would kill us, for what other bad people did, you could not think, that it was any of the lower Towns did you any mischief, when we were at your houses and living with you in a manner that you might be sure it was not us. We knew nothing of these bad people going out to do any mischief, or we would have sent you word, and we dont think but you must have known that we were your friends or we should not have been among you a hunting, and hope you will send us an answer, and tell us the reason that you have killed your friends for what other people did. It is not the Rule of the Indians to acquaint you of this, but to take satisfaction, but we were always your friends, and we will not take rash steps, unless you will throw us away and not have us as friends, we always were your friends and will be let what will happen, is the reason we lie still, although we have lost nine of our people innocently, but still we wont take rash steps, we must have an answer immediately that we may know what to do, hope you will consider us the lower Towns to be your friends, we look upon all white people as one, and suppose you look upon all Indians as one, is the reason you have killed your friends, who was your friends in the time of the last war and is yet. We have had a meeting lately with the Northward Indians, we told them and so did Mr. McGilivray that we had settled matters with the Virginians and could not go to war. The Oakjeys went unknown to any of the rest of the towns and killed some of your people, not as many as you killed of your friends, but we wont take rash steps as we are your friends, and we would be glad of an answer to know what to do, we have told you the number killed, we have a number of people out a hunting, we dont know but there is more killed innocently, but we will lie still and hope you will send us an answer, it shall be received as friends to us still, as we look upon you as friends still, we are sure that you must been sensible that it was not the people that was among you did the murder. It was your rule that the innocent should not suffer for the guilty, hope you will send an answer that we may know what to do—We speak the voice of the whole lower Towns and hope you will consider us as friends—we hope you will send us an answer and a white flag with it, that we may still be friends, and we will have all the Towns together and hear your answer, and then we will be friends again. No person need be afraid to come up, as the whole Nation will be acquainted with this, who brings an answer will bring a White flag upon a pole in his hand, we shall wait for an answer, and Nothing shall be done to you, no hurt whatever. The talk you sent to Mr. Barnard by John Galphin, he delivered to Mr. Barnard a good while ago, two days after he arrived, which we have not heard yet, nor seen Mr. Barnard, as he has not come to Town yet to tell us the talk, we hope you will consider us as friends, as you are sensible we are your friends, for when the English offered us great presents to go and kill you, we told them we would not, that you were our friends and brothers, we were born in one land, and we were your friends and brothers, and will be to the last day, tho' you have not treated us as friends, but it might be a mistake, and hope my friends that you will not delay an answer, but let it come up with speed, there is a fellow down there belonging to our Town the Cusetas we hope he wont be hurt, but let him and John Galphins Negro that he went down with, if you are afraid to send up, if you will send up the Talk by John Galphins Negro and the Indian that is there if you will be so good as to send them safe over the Oconee, then we shall be good friends and try to keep the path white between us. You will likewise appoint somebody to give out the Talks up here and let a man be here constantly, that when there is any bad people wants to do mischief that they can send word down to alarm the settlements, so that we may then live like brothers, and let us try to keep peace, for peace is better than war. We cant blame you for taking satisfaction, if you had not taking satisfaction from those people who were at the houses with you every day, and if it is done in a mistake we must try and take satisfaction from those bad people that went down and did the first mischief. However I hope you will send us a good Talk as soon as possible the sooner it comes the better for both parties, that we may take one another by the hand again, see one another once more in friendship as we always will. By request of the lower Creeks the two Chiefs, the Hollowing King of the Cewetas and the fat King of the Cusatas.

JOHN GALPHIN
JAS. DOUZEAZEAUX
Interpreter

(Copy) J. Merewether Secy. E.C.
Copied from the files in the office of the Secy. of Congress.

CHAS. THOMSON secy.

G. No. 3
(Copy)

To the head men and warriors of the
lower Creeks 29th June 1787

Friends & Brothers,

Your friendly talk we have just received by our Commissary Mr. Barnard, and are very sorry to be informed that some of your people our friends should have been killed through mistake by our Warriors to revenge the murders of some of our peaceable inhabitants—Yourselves must be fully convinced that our people have not been the agressors in this instance, as soon as the murders were committed by the Indians, our warriors crossed the River and unfortunately fell in with your people, it was impossible then to distinguish whether you were our friends or enemies, we never knew until we received your Talk by whom our people were murdered, whether by upper or whether by lower Creeks—We have repeatedly assured you it was our desire to be at peace with the whole of your Nation—we still have the same wish notwithstanding what has passed.

Brothers, Remember the caution we now give you, should any acts of hostilities be in future committed against our people, or should any property be taken from them be assured it will be impossible to prevent our warriors from doing themselves Justice—Our great Council are to meet in a day or two, previous to which had we not received your talk a large Army would have been sent into your Nation what consequences would have attended this your are capable of judging. We have sent orders to our warriors not on any pretence to cross the Oconee River, We wish you to give your people the same instructions, this will be the means of preventing any disputes in future.

Brothers—Should the Conduct of the upper Creeks render it necessary to march an army into the Nation be assured we will consider your Towns as friends and Brothers and treat you as such.

Brothers—If you have the friendship for us you express, it is your duty to keep a Watchful eye on the conduct of those who you may suppose have a wish or desire to disturb our friendship; Mr. Barnard or Mr. Galphin are always among you, if you hear of any mischief intended against our settlements it is your duty to inform one or both of them of it immediately, this you are particularly bound to observe by an Article of the last Treaty entered into with our Commissioners at Shoulderbone.

You acknowledged that the beloved man of the upper Creeks Mr. McGilivray made a promise to our beloved man who was sent from the White Town that no mischief whatever should be done; after having this assurance our people considered themselves safe and looked upon all the Indians of your Nation as friends and Brothers—have you not often entered into the most solemn engagements with us? and have not you as often violated them? what had our people to expect when they saw their peaceable Countrymen murdered, they determined to take satisfaction for the repeated injuries they had received, and it was with great difficulty that we the grand Council could prevent our young warriors from marching in a body into the heart of your Nation, from your late conduct and the assurance you have given us in your talk, rest satisfied that we consider you the lower Towns as our best friends and brothers and if you do not long continue to hold fast the Chain of our friendship it will not be the faults of the white people.

You express a wish in your Talk to have one of your people who has been some time at Mr. Galphins sent to you, we have enquired for him and find he has been gone several days and hope he is now safe among you. Mr. Barnard who is always with you will carefully attend to all Talks that we may send, and deliver them out to you as soon as they arrive among you.

Brothers, We really regret the loss of your innocent people who have lately been killed, it is your duty as men and warriors to do yourselves justice by taking satisfaction of the persons who were the cause of it, in doing this we shall be fully convinced of your Brotherly love and friendship towards us.

Brothers it is our wish to see you and the upper Creeks one people but should they continue to create differences between you and us, and you should think yourselves unable to take satisfaction we will as all friends and Brothers ought to do, be ever ready to give any assistance you may require.
(Copy)   (Signed) J. MEREWETHER Secy. E.C.
Copied from the files in the Office of the Secy. of Congress.

                                        CHAS. THOMSON secy.

G. No. 4

> In a meeting of the lower Creeks
> in the Cussetahs 27th. July 1787
> Talk of the Fat King to his honour Governour Mathews and the Council.

Friends and Brothers,

The talk you sent us in answer to ours by your Commissary Mr. Barnard we have seen this day, and as that talk is not satisfactory to our people we have agreed upon to send you this one more.

Friends, Tis not we that have forgot the talks at Shoulderbone, but you, among other things it was proposed by you and agreed to by us that no hasty revenges should be taken in future by either side, and in the late affairs tis you that have been rash, for when the injury was done to you, you did not wait, but for a little while and look around you, to find out from whence the blow came, but fell directly upon our people your real friends, who were daily among your houses and whose persons you well knew, and some that were taken declared themselves and towns to you, which you disregarded, it might have been from people of another Nation for what you knew at that time.

Friends, you ought not to think of making us accountable for any measures of the upper Towns our brothers, they had two men killed last summer and they can answer for themselves, they went against you unknown to McG. or us, and he did not mean to break the promise he made to Mr. White, as he had declared to the whole Nation and a talk from him is still expected by us.

Friends, you must give us immediate satisfaction, life for life an equal number for twelve of our people destroyed by you—The leader of these mad people that did the mischief, and so many of his people should fall for satisfaction (tis our Custom to give it) then the tears of the Relations of the dead will be dried up, and our hearts not continue hot against you, for it is in vain that you call us friends and brothers and dont consider and treat us as such, and as you wish the Chain of friendship to be kept bright between us, we expect you will not fail to give us the desired satisfaction, as we should have give you had we been in fault.

When you do this, you will then send a gentleman into our land to renew friendship, as we have often gone into yours for such purposes.

(Signed) by A.McGilivray

In twenty days from the date that Mr. Galphin setts out, we shall expect the return of Mr. Galphin.

(Copy)   (Signed) J.Mereweth. Sy. E.C.

Copied from the files in the office of the Secy. of Congress.

Chas. Thomson secy.

G. No. 5.

> To the Fat King and other head men
> of the lower Creeks. 7th August 1787.

When we received your talk by Mr. Barnard our Commissary, we considered you as friends and brothers, in the one you now send us, there appears to be much reason to suspect you of deceit, and that you were then as well as now secretly our enemies—whether this sudden change has been owing to the duplicity of your beloved man Mr. McGilivray, or whether you assume this conduct it matters not. On what principle can you demand satisfaction—your warriors were killed for the Murder of our innocent inhabitants committed by your Nation in direct violation of the most solemn treaties entered into with us—We wished and still do wish we could forget the many and repeated injuries you have done us during and since the late war with Great Britain—It is in vain to talk of Satisfaction, did you not last summer kill six of our peaceable frontier inhabitants, and did you not at Shoulderbone engage to have an equal number of your men put to death for them—have you done this—No—did you not just before we received your last Talk murder two of our people on the Oconee, and did you not also at the very time Mr. Barnard was down from you kill two white men; have you complyed with a single Article of the Treaties of Augusta, Galphinton and Shoulderbone? No—instead of complying with your several engagements you have repeatedly murdered our innocent people, burned their houses and carryed off their property—all these outrages we have submitted to rather than enter into a War with you—your conduct towards us long since have authorised our putting flames to your Towns and indiscriminately killing your people, but a wish to be at peace with you, and to spare the effusion of human blood have prevented this—Now open your ears *wide* and hear what we tell you, should any act of hostility or depredations be committed on our people by your Nation, be perfectly assured we ~~shall~~ will not hesitate to do ourselves ample Justice, by carrying war into your Country, burning your Towns and staining your land with blood, you will then be compelled to fly for refuge to some other Country.

It now rests with you whether we engage in War or not, if we do, remember yourselves are answerable for the consequences—the Hatchet once lifted is not easily buried.

(Copy)   J. MEREWETHER Secy. E.C.

Copied from the files in the office of the Secy. of Congress.

               CHAS. THOMSON secy.

War Office July 28th. 1789

Sir,

Having examined the report of the Commissioners for treating with the southern indians dated the 30th. of June last and the papers accompanying the same, I have the honor to observe.

That it is the opinion of the said Commissioners, that the Creek nation of Indians are generally disposed to enter into a treaty with the United States, for the purpose of establishing a permanent peace.

That it is of great importance that the favorable dispositions of the said Creek nation should be embraced immediately, in order to terminate by an equitable peace, the disturbances and hostilities which have for some years past existed on the southern frontiers.

That the said Commissioners having been appointed by the States of South Carolina and Georgia in consequence of the resolves of the late Congress of the 26th. of October 1787, it may be considered that their powers expired with the late confederation.

That therefore it may be proper to institute a Commission to consist of three persons to be appointed conformably to the Constitution, who should be invested with full powers to enquire into and decide on all causes of complaint between the Citizens of the United States and the Southern nations and tribes of indians and to negociate and conclude with them firm treaties of peace on principles consistent with the national justice and dignity of the United States.

> I have the honor to be
> With the highest respect,
> Sir
> Your most Obedient
> Humble Servant,
> H. KNOX

The President
Of the United States[2]

In Council Augusta June 19th. 1789

To the end that no interruption, or personal interference may take place between the Hon. the Commissioners and the Indians, in the progress of the Treaty at the Rock Landing; It is unanimously ordered, in the most express terms, that no person or persons whatsoever, do approach the Treaty ground, or cross over the Oconee to the south side, during the time of holding the same, or within ten days thereafter, without special permission from the

---

2 The report of the southern Indian commissioners, dated June 30, 1789, and mentioned in Henry Knox's letter, is printed in the *SEJ*, pp. 188–99. This report is pages 241–83 of the manuscript.

Commissioners, for that purpose; and, any breach of this order will be punished with the utmost severity.

Extract from the Minutes
J. MERIWETHER, S.E.C.

Council Chamber June 19th. 1789

In pursuance of the above order of Council, the Governor and Commander in Chief orders and directs, that the Officers of the Militia guard to the Commissioners, and of the State Troops, do see, at their respective stations, that the same be not violated; And any neglect herein will be deemed a breach of duty, and punished accordingly.

(Signed) GEORGE WALTON[3]

SOUTHERN DISTRICT

THE CHEROKEES

This nation of indians consisting of separate towns or villages are seated principally on the head waters of the Tennessee which runs into the Ohio—Their hunting grounds extend from Cumberland river along the frontiers of Virginia North and South Carolina and part of Georgia.

The frequent Wars they have had with the frontier people of the said States have greatly diminished their numbers—The Commissioners estimated them in November 1785 at 2,000 Warriors—but they were estimated in 1787 by Colonel Joseph Martin who was well acquainted with them at 2,650—But it is probable they may be lessened since by the depredations committed on them.

The United States concluded a treaty with the Cherokees at Hopewell on the Keowee the 28th. of November 1785, which is entered on the printed Journals of Congress April 17th. 1786—The negociations of the Commissioners on the part of the United States is hereunto annexed marked A.

It will appear by the papers marked B, that the State of North Carolina by their Agent protested against the said treaty as infringing and violating the Legislative rights of that State.

By a variety of evidence which has been submitted to the late Congress it has been proved that the said treaty has been entirely disregarded by the

---

[3] The orders of the Executive Council and the Governor of Georgia were enclosures in enclosure number 10 of the report of the southern Indian commissioners.

White people inhabiting the frontiers styling themselves the State of Franklin.

The proceedings of Congress on the first of September 1788, and the Proclamation they then issued on this subject, will show their sense of the many unprovoked outrages committed against the Cherokees.

The information contained in the papers marked C from Colonel Joseph Martin the late Agent to the Cherokees, and Richard Winn Esqr. will further evince the deplorable situation of the Cherokees, and the indispensible obligation of the United States to vindicate their faith, justice, and national dignity.

The letter of Mr. Winn the late Superintendant of the 1st. of March informs, that a treaty will be held with the Cherokees on the 3d monday of May of the upper War-ford on french broad river.

But it to be observed that the time for which both he and Colonel Joseph Martin, the Agent to the Cherokees and Chickasaws were elected has expired, and therefore they are not authorized to act on the part of the Union—If the Commissioners appointed by North Carolina, South Carolina and Georgia by virtue of the resolve of Congress of the 26th. of October 1787 should attend the said treaty, their proceedings thereon may soon be expected.

But as part of the Cherokees have taken refuge within the limits of the Creeks, it is highly probable, they will be under the same direction—and therefore as the fact of the violation of the treaty cannot be disputed, and as the Commissioners have not power to replace the Cherokees within the limits established in 1785, it is not probable even if a treaty should be held as stated by Mr. Winn, that the result would be satisfactory.

All which is humbly submitted to the President of the United States.

H. KNOX

War office July 7th 1789

A

Contains

No. 1. a letter of the 2nd. December 1785, from the commissioners of Indian affairs to the President of Congress.

No. 2. A Map of the territorial claim of the Indians.

No. 3. Negociations of the Commissioners with the Cherokee Indians.

Received from the office of the late secretary of Congress

H. KNOX

A. No. 1.

Hopewell on the Keowee 2 Decemr. 1785

Sir,

We enclose to your Excellency a Treaty which we entered into on the 28th. Ultimo with all the Cherokees at this place—We had invited the Chiefs only of the respective Towns, but they having some reason to expect ill treatment from some disorderly people in that part of the westward of North Carolina where the exercise of an Independent Government has lately been assumed, were under the Necessity of bringing their young warriors, their wives and Children who were most exposed to be protected, so that from this Nation we have had nine hundred and eighteen.

Previous to entering into the Treaty, we with interpreters who understood the Cherokee language well, explained the occurrences of the late War, with the extent of Territory ceded to us by the King of Great Britain. We also explained every article of the Treaty, so that they could comprehend it perfectly. after it was signed they expressed their obligations to the United states of America for taking them under protection and treating them with such unexpected justice.

The agents of Georgia and North Carolina attended the Treaty as will appear by their protest herewith enclosed—The Commissioners in establishing the boundary which is the Chief cause of all the complaints of the Indians, were desirous of accommodating the southern states and their western Citizens in anything consistent with the duty we owed to the United states.

We established the line from forty miles above Nashville on the Cumberland agreeable to the deed of sale to Richard Henderson and Co. as far as the Kentucky ford; thence to the mountain six miles south of Nolchuckey agreeable to the Treaty in 1777 with Colonel William Christie, William Preston and Evan Shelby on the part of Virginia, and Waitstill Avery Attorney General, Colonel Robert Lanier, William Sharp, and Joseph Winston on the part of North Carolina—thence by agreement South to the North Carolina line, and to the South Carolina Indian boundary—Thence to the Tugelo river the treaty at Duets corner in 1777 with states of South Carolina and Georgia—Thence over the Currahee mountain to the South fork of Oconee the Treaty at Augusta of 1783—The line from Duck river is now given by the Cherokees to accomodate the people of Nashville and others South of the Cumberland (which River is the Southern boundary of the lands sold to Richard Henderson and Company) as it would be difficult to remove them as well as very distressing to the Citizens.

There are some few people settled on the Indian lands who we are to remove and those in the fork of French Broad and Holston, being numerous the Indians agreed to refer their particular situation to Congress and abide their decision. We told them there were too many for us to engage positively to order off, altho' they had settled espressly against the Treaty entered into by Virginia and North Carolina with the Cherokees in 1777.

The Commissioners know not what is best to be done in this case. They see that Justice, humanity and good policy require that some compensation should be made to the Indians for these lands but the manner of doing it probably would be difficult. However a small sum we think could be raised on the unlocated lands as well as from those already Settled, and which if appropriated to the purpose of teaching them some useful branches of Mechanics would be of lasting advantage. Some of the women have lately learnt to spin, and many of them are very desirous that some method should be fallen on to teach them to raise flax, Cotton and Wool, as well as to Spin and weave it.

We have required the aid of the agent of North-Carolina and the Commissioners of Georgia in the execution of the Treaty, and we foresee that difficulties will frequently arise, and indeed rendered it ineffectual, if these two states should refuse their Co-operation.

We have given the Indians some presents, but our Stock was so small, compared with the number of Indians and their naked distressed condition that the dividend was triffling indeed. We told them that we invited and expected the Headmen and warriors only—that the object of our Commission was altogether for their benefit, and we had made provision accordingly.

The Spaniards and the French from New Orleans are making making great efforts to engross the trade of the Indians, several of them are on the Northside of the Tennessee and well supplied with proper goods for the trade. The Governour of New Orleans or West Florida has sent orders to the Chickasaws to remove all traders from that Country except those who had or should take the Oath of Allegiance to the Catholic King; and also had appointed ten traders who were down after goods, when our informant a man of Respectability left that Country.

We sent a very intelligent honest man with our invitation to the Choctaws and Chickasaws to treat with us, and he brought us assurances from them that they would attend the treaty, and some of the former set out before he left the Chickasaw Nation, but none of them have as yet arrived, and we cannot account for it. Unless we give credit to Reports which contradict expressly all assurances of their attachment to the United States, and joy on the first Notification of the resolution of Congress appointing Commissioners to treat with them and receive them into the favour and protection of the United states—The Cherokees say that the Northern Indians have their emissaries among the southern tribes endeavouring to prevail on them to form an alliance offensive against the United states and to commence hostilities against us, in the Spring or next fall at farthest, they also say that not only the British emissaries are for this measure, but that the spaniards have extensive

Claims to the southward, and have been endeavouring to poison the minds of the Indians against us, and to win their affections by large Supplies of arms military stores and Cloathing.

We are at a loss what to do, to compleat the object of our Commission, the sum to which we are limited is already by our disappointments and expences attendant thereon so diminished that we are unable to fix on any place, and therefore must await the further order of Congress.

We have for the information of Congress collected as near as may be the number of Indians in the four Southern states, and we find the gun-men of the Cherokees 2,000
The upper and lower Creek Nation from an agent who resided seven years in their Towns and employed by John Stewart for the purpose 5,400
The Chickasaws 800
The Chocktaws 6,000

14,000

There are also some remains of tribes settled among these as Shawnees, Eutchees &c. &c.

At a moderate calculation we may reckon the women the Children and the old men unfit for hunting to four times the number of gun-men.

We have the Honor to be with due Respect
Sir,
Your Excellency's
Most obedient and
Humble Servants
(signed) BENJAMIN HAWKINS
ANDREW PICKENS
JOS. MARTIN
LACHN. MCINTOSH

His Excellency
Richard Henry Lee Esqr.
President of
Congress

A. No. 3.

Hopewell on Keowee the 18th November 1785
The Commissioners of the United states in Congress assembled appointed to treat with the Cherokees and all other Indians southward of them within the limits of the United states, Assembled.

Present Benjamin Hawkins, Andrew Pickens Joseph Martin and Lauchlin McIntosh, from the state of North Carolina, The Honorable

William Blount Esqr. who produced his Commission as agent for that state.

The Commissioners ordered a Return to be made of the Indians, and there were five hundred—The head-men and warriors having informed, that the present Representation of their tribe was not compleat, but would be so, in a few days, it was agreed to post-pone treating with them until the whole representation Should arrive.

November 21st.

The Head-men and warriors of all the Cherokees assembled. Ordered that the Interpreters inform the Indians that Commissioners will meet them to morrow at 10 o'Clock under the Bower erected for that purpose.

November the 22nd.

The Commissioners assembled—Present Benjamin Hawkins, Andrew Pickens, Joseph Martin and Lauchlin McIntosh

From the State of North Carolina William Blount agent

From the state of Georgia John King & Thomas Glasscock Commissioners

From all the tribes or Towns of the Cherokees The Head-men and Warriors—

James Madison }
Arthur Coody }   Interpreters

The Commissioners delivered the following address to the Indians—

Head-men and warriors of all the Cherokees

We are the men whom you were informed came from Congress to meet you the Head men and warriors of all the Cherokees—to give you peace and to receive you into the favour and protection of the United states: and to remove as far as may be all causes of future Contention or quarrels—That you your people, your wives and your Children may be happy and feel and know the blessings of the new change of Sovereignty over this land which you and we inhabit.

We sincerely wish you to live as happily as we do ourselves, and to promote that happiness as far as is in our power, regardless of any distinction of ~~power~~ colour or of any difference in our customs our manners or particular situation.

This humane and generous act of the United states, will no doubt be received by you with ~~great~~ gladness; and held in grateful remembrance, and the more so as many of your young men, and the greatest number of your warriors during the late war were our enemies and assisted the King of Great Britain in his endeavours to conquor our Country.

You yourselves know, that you refuse to listen to the good talks Congress sent you—That the cause you espoused was a bad one—That all the adherents of the King of Great Britain are compelled to leave this Country never more to return.

Congress is now the Sovereign of all our Country which we now point out to you on the map. A.[4] They want none of your lands or any thing else which belongs to you; and as an earnest of their regard for you we propose to enter into Articles of a Treaty perfectly equal, and conformable to what we now tell you.

If you have any grievances to complain of, we will hear them, and take such measures in consequence thereof as may be proper. We expect you will speak your minds freely, and look upon us as the Representatives of your Father and friend the Congress who will see justice done you. you may now retire and reflect on what we have told you, and let us hear from you to morrow or as soon as possible.

November 23d.
Present as yesterday.

After seting some time in silence, the Tassel of Chota arose and addressed the Commissioners as follows.

I am going to let the Commissioners hear what I have to say to them. I told you yesterday I would do this to day—I was very much pleased at the talk you gave us yesterday, it is very different from what I expected when I left home: The head-men and warriors are also equally pleased with it.

Now I shall give you my own Talk—I am made of this Earth on which the great man above placed me to possess it—and what I am about to tell you I have had in my mind for many years.

This land we are now on, is the land we were fighting for, during the late contest, B,[5] and the great man made it for us to subsist upon; you must know the Red people are the aborigiens of this land and that it is but a few years since the White people found it out. I am of the first stock as the Commissioners know, and a native of this land; and the white people are now living on it as our friends—From the beginning of the first friendship between the

---

[4] The commissioners' explanation "A," which was inserted at the bottom of the manuscript page, reads:
A We used McMurrays map: and explained with great pains the limits of the United states as well as the occurrences of the late war; and we believe they comprehend us—some of the Indians had visited the six Nations. some had been up the Wabash and down the Miami to lake Erie and others had been at Fort-pitt, the Natches, Pensacola, St. Augustine, Savannah, Charleston, and Williamsburg.
B.H.

[5] The commissioners' explanation "B," which was inserted at the bottom of the manuscript page, reads:
B. Hopewell is fifteen miles above the junction of the Keowee and Tugalo, it is a seat of General Pickens in sight of Seneca an Indian town at the commencement of the late war inhabited by one hundred gun-men, but at present a waste. Dewets corner is forty miles east of this, and that was the Eastern Indian boundary till the treaty of 1777.
B.H.

white and red people beads were given as an emblem thereof: and these are the beads I give to the Commissioners of the United states as a confirmation of our friendship, and as a proof of my opinion of what you yesterday told us.

A string of white Beads

The Commissioners have heard how the white people have encroached on our lands, on every side of us that they could approach.

I remember the talks I delivered at the long Island of Holston—and I remember giving our lands to Colonel Christie and others who treated with us, and in a manner compelled me thereto, in 1777—I remember the talks to Colonel Christie when I gave the lands at the mouth of Clouds Creek eighteen Springs past. At that treaty we agreed upon the line near the mouth of lime stone—The Virginia line and part from the mouth of Clouds Creek to Cumberland mountain near the gap was paid for by Virginia.

From Clouds creek a direct line to the Chimneytop mountain, thence to the mouth of Big limestone on Nolichucky, thence to the first mountain about six miles from the River on a line a cross the sun, was never paid for by the Carolina which joins the Virginia line—I wish the Commissioners to know every thing that concerns us, as I tell nothing but the truth: They, the people of North Carolina have taken our lands for no consideration, and are now making their fortunes out of them. I have informed the Commissioners of the line I gave up, and the people of North Carolina and Virginia have gone over it, and encroached on our lands expressly against our inclination— They have gone over the line near little River, and they have gone over Nine mile Creek, which is but Nine miles from our Towns—I am glad of this opportunity of geting redress from the Commissioners—If Congress had not interposed I and my people must have moved—They have even marked the lands on the Bank of the River near the Town where I live; and from thence down in the fork of the Tennessee and Holston.

I have given into you a detail of the abuse and encroachments of these two states—We shall be satisfied if we are paid for the lands we have given up, but we will not nor cannot give up any more—I mean the line I gave to Colonel Christie.

I have no more to say, but one of our beloved women has, who has born and raised up warriers—a string of Beads.

The war woman of Chota then address'd the Commissioners.

I am fond of hearing that there is a peace and I hope you have now taken us by the hand in real friendship—I have a pipe and a little Tobacco to give the Commissioners to smoak in friendship; I look on you and the Red people, as my Children—your having determined on peace is most pleasing to me, for I have seen much trouble during the late war. I am old, but I hope yet to bear Children, who will grow up and people our Nation, as we are now to be under the protection of Congress, and shall have no more disturbance.

A string, little old pipe and some Tobacco—The talk I have given is from the young warriors I have raised in my Town, as well as myself—They Rejoice that we have peace, and we hope the Chain of friendship will never more be broke.

A string of Beads

The Commissioners to the Tassel—

We want the boundary of your Country you must recollect yourself and give it to us, particularly the line between you and the Citizens with any information you have on that subject—If Necessary you may consult your friends, and inform us tomorrow or as soon as possible with conveniency.

Tassell—I will let you know the line Tomorrow I have done speaking for this day.

UNSUCKANAIL,

of New-Cusse in the middle settlement I speak in behalf of Kowé New-Cusse and Watoge, I am much pleased with the Talks between the Commissioners and the Tassel who is the beloved man of Chota—I remember the talks given out by you yesterday, I shall always I hope remember, that if we were distressed in any manner we should make our Complaints to the Commissioners that Justice may be done. There are around us young men and warriors who hear our talks and who are interested in the success of this Treaty, particularly as their lands are taken from them, on which they lived entirely by hunting—and I hope, and they all anxiously hope it is in the power of the Commissioners to do them Justice. The line mentioned by the beloved man of Chota is in truth as he expressed it; I remember it and it was formerly our hunting grounds.

The encroachments on this side of the line have entirely deprived us of our hunting grounds; and I hope the Commissioners will remove the white people to their own side—This is the desire of the three Towns I speak for—The settlements I mean are those on pigeon River and Swanano. It was the desire of the Commissioners that the Indians should tell all their grievances and I hope they will do justly therein. when any of my young men are hunting on their own grounds, and meet the white people, they, the white people order them off and claim our deer.

A string of white beads.

CHESCOENWHEE,

I am well satisfied with the Talks of this day I intended to speak but as the day is far spent I will decline it till tomorrow, I will go home and consider on it.

November 24th. 1785

Present as yesterday.

TUCKASÉE

I remember the Talks when I made peace, I have appointed Chescoenwhee to speak for me to-day

CHESCOENWHÉE

I rejoice that the Commissioners have delivered their talks to the Head men of the different towns.

I am in hopes that these our talks will always remain unbroken—what you hear from the representatives of the Towns the young warriors will invariably adhere to.

I am in hopes it is now in the power of the Commissioners from their talks of yesterday and the day before to see Justice done to us; to see that we may yet have a little land to hunt upon; I was sent here to settle all matters Respecting my Country, and being under the protection of the United states, I shall return satisfied—we have been formally under the protection of Great Britain—and then when I saw a white man I esteemed him as a friend, and I hope that the Commissioners of Congress will see that times may be as formerly—I wish what I say may be deemed strictly true, for so it is, and that I may be always looked on as friend to the thirteen United states and that they will see justice done me.

The talks of the Commissioners are the most pleasing to us, as they do not want any lands. Formerly when I had peace talks, the first thing the white people expressed was a desire for our lands. I am in hopes you will adjust and settle our limits, so that we may be secured in the possession of our own. I will abide by what hitherto has been said on this subject, but cannot cede any more lands.

A string of Beads

I am in hopes the Commissioners will deliver to us our prisoners who are in their lands: Neither the Commissioners or any of the Citizens of the United states can suppose that we can be at peace on their account, they are our own flesh and blood and we desire them out of your Country—I am in hopes of Seeing them with the assistance of the Commissioners, they have been long detained, and we often were promised by Colonel Martin that we should see them—one of them was taken from Talksoa, three girls and one boy from Erejoy, and one boy from Tuckareechée—we do not know how old they are, we are a people who do not know how to count by years, they are in North Carolina and were taken by an army from thence.

OONANOOTÉE,

I am to deliver the talks in answer to what I heard at Oostanawie. I was sent down from different Towns to receive the Talks of the Commissioners, and to be governed by them, I do expect by the time I return home from the Commissioners the young men of the Towns of our Nation will be there to hear me repeat what you have or shall say to me, I was told by all of them when I set out, that they expected I would return with good talks—It was the desire of the Commissioners that we should tell all our grievances: The encroachment on our hunting grounds is the source of all ours; and I hope they can, and will take measures to see justice done in our land. I have attended to the talks of the Commissioners, and our beloved men, and I sincerely wish they may always abide by them, I am in hopes it is in your power to see our distresses redressed, and that you will order off the people who are settled on our lands, and protect for us our hunting grounds.

A string of Beads

I wish the Commissioners to take in hand the case of the traders in our Country, and settle what respects them during the late war; so that they may not be seized on and plundered by bodies of armed men as they pass to and from the Nation. I am come down as one to make peace with the Commissioners of the United states of America, and I hope the traders may pass through the Country—I wish the Commissioners would prevent such acts of injustice as robbing the traders, several of them have been plundered in Georgia and South Carolina and their lives endangered if they Should attempt to Recover their property—as for my part I mean to keep the path clear, for the traders as far as our line, and I hope the Commissioners will do the same on their part—Here are the Chiefs of all our Nation who hear me, the traders have been out for goods, and returned without any, having been robbed, and I hope it will not be the case again—I sincerely desire that our talks and complaints may go up to Congress, that they may know how we are distressed about our Country—I have delivered the Talks to the Commissioners, and laid the beads on the beloved table, and as to my part of the Country I will keep the path clear.

TASSEL. We have said all we intend to-day, if the Commissioners have anything to say, we will hear it and answer them.

COMMISSIONERS,

We want the boundary of your Country, particularly to the Northward and Eastward—this we told you yesterday, when we can agree upon the bounds of the lands we mean to allot to you; we will prepare the draught of a Treaty on the plan we mentioned to you in our address.

TASSEL, I expected to give the bounds of our Country but it is too late in the day, and I will do it tomorrow.

November 25th.

Present as yesterday.

The Head-men after some conversation together requested the Commissioners to give them some paper and a pencil, and leave them to themselves, and they would draw the map of their Country.

November 26th

Present as yesterday.

The Head-men produced their map and the Tassel addressed the Commissioners as follows—

I will give the bounds of the land as far as I claim, Colonel Martin is present and heard our talks at the Long Island of Holsten, and he knows every thing I shall say to be true. The line which I have marked beginning on the Ohio above Kentucky, and running thence to where the Kentucky Road crosses Cumberland River thence to the Chimney-top mountain and by the mouth of Big limestone to the mountain six miles south of Nolichucky is justly our boundary with the white people, the Indians from the middle settlements will extend the line and Shew their Claim.

I know that Richard Henderson says he purchased the lands at Kentuckey, and as far South as Cumberland, but he is a rogue and a liar, and if he was here I would tell him so. He requested us to let him have a little lands on Kentuckey River for his Cattle and horses to feed on, and we consented, but told him at the same time, he would be much exposed to the depredations of the Northern Indians, which he appeared not to regard; provided we gave our consent. If Attacullaculla signed his deed we were not informed of it; but we know that Oconestoto did not, and yet his name we hear is to it, Henderson put it there and he is a rogue.

COMMISSIONERS

You know Colonel Henderson, Attacuttaculla and Oconestoto are all dead, what you say may be true; but here is one of Hendersons deeds, which points out the line, as you have done, nearly till it strikes Cumberland, thence it runs down the waters of the same to the Ohio, thence up the said river as it meanders to the beginning. Your memory may fail you, this is on record and will remain forever. The parties being dead, and so much time elapsed since the date of the deed, and the Country being settled, on the faith of the deed, puts it out of our power to do any thing respecting it—you must therefore be content with it, as if you had actually sold it, and proceed on to point out your Claim exclusive of this land.

TASSEL—I know they are dead and I am sorry for it, and I suppose it is now too late to recover it—if Henderson was living I should have the pleasure of telling him he was a liar; but you told us to give you our bounds and therefore we marked the line, but we will begin at Cumberland, and say nothing more about Kentuckey altho' it is justly ours.

COMMISSIONERS—You must also make provision if practicable for the people settled at Nashville, and for such other bodies of people if numerous as may be within what you have pointed out as your claim. Our object in treating with you is to fix a permanent boundary, and to keep our faith in whatever we promise you, and you must not expect from us any promise which we know cannot be done but with great inconveniency to our Citizens. The Chickasaws we are informed by Col. Martin and the agent of North Carolina claim the lands at Nashville, and they are content that the people should live there, and you must mark a line for them.

TASSEL and TUSKEGATAHEE,

We understand you perfectly we wish to post-pone this matter if the

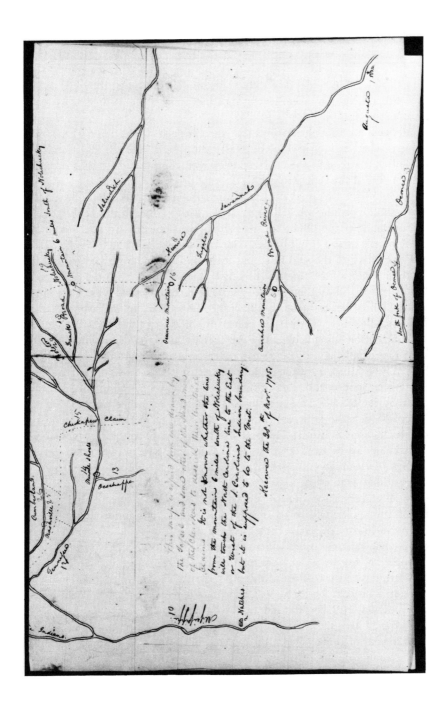

Chickasaws would come; it is a kind of common right in all the Indians, and they had no right of themselves to give it.

COMMISSIONERS

We have now no expectations that the Chickasaws will meet us, and you know the necessity of having the Treaty completed, that we may as early as possible put a stop to the encroachments you complain of, if they do exist.

TASSEL and TUSKEGATAHÉE

We know the Necessity of completing the Treaty; and we will mark a line for the white people, we will begin at the Ridge between the Tennessee and Cumberland on the Ohio; and run along the same till we get around the white people as you think proper—we will also mark a line from the mouth of Duck River to the said line, and leave the remainder of the lands to the South and west of the lines to the Chickasaws, we will from the ridge go to Cumberland, and up the same to where the Kentucky road crosses the same. Colonel Christie run the remainder of the line with us, as we have marked it; and he said we were at liberty to punish or not as we pleased, any person who should come on our side to violate the Treaty; But this we have not done, and the white people have come over it a great way as we have told you—In the fork of French broad river and Holsten there are three thousand souls—This is a favorite spot of land, and we cannot consent to their having of it, and they must be removed—there are some few settled on other parts whom the Commissioners we hope will remove—We cannot mark a line around the people on French Broad. Those lands are within twenty five miles of our Towns and we prize them highly—The people have settled there several springs past, and they ought to be removed.

COMMISSIONERS,

We expect some sort of provision will be made for these people and you had better think seriously of it. They are too numerous for us to engage to remove—you say they have been there for along time and ought to have been removed—while you were under the protection of the King of Great Britain he ought to have removed them for you, but he Neglected it, and we cannot stipulate positively to do any thing respecting them, unless you choose to mark around them for the present they must remain as they are, all the others you mention shall be removed.

TASSEL, I have shewn you the bounds of my Country on my map, which I drew in your presence, and on the map of the United states—If the Commissioners cannot do me Justice in removing the people from the fork of French broad and Holsten, I am unable to get it of myself—Are Congress who conquered the King of Great Britain unable to remove those people? I am satisfied with the Promises of the Commissioners to remove all the people from within our lines, except those within the fork of Holsten and French Broad—and I will agree to be content that the particular situation of the

People settled there, and our claims to the lands should be Referred to Congress as the Commissioners may think just, and I will abide by their decision.

UNSUCKANAIL,

I and my people are to extend their line, and altho' our Claims are well founded to a large portion of the Mountains, which are of little advantage to any but hunters, and of great value to them, yet I am willing to extend the line to the Southward until we come to the South Carolina Indian boundary, and we have a right formed on the Treaties at Duets corner and at Augusta to make that line as far as the south fork of Oconée our boundary against the white people.

November 28th. 1785

The Commissioners assembled—Prest. Benjamin Hawkins, Andrew Pickens, Joseph Martin and Lauhlin McIntosh

From the state of North Carolina William Blount agent.

From the state of Georgia, John King and Thomas Glascock Commissioners,

The Head men and warriors of all the Cherokees—

James Madison ⎫
Arthur Coody ⎭ sworn Interpreters

Major Samuel Taylor, Major William Hazzard Captain Commandant, John Cowen, John Owen and George Ogg, merchants, with several other Reputable Characters.

The Commissioners produced a draught of a treaty on the plan they originally proposed to the Indians which was read and interpreted to them with great attention, so that they agreed, that they perfectly understood every article, and would with pleasure unanimously sign the same, accordingly two Copies were signed by the Commissioners and all the Head-men, the one for the United States and the other for the Cherokees.

Previous to the signing, the agent from North-Carolina and the Commissioners of Georgia delivered their protests against the same.

After the Treaty was signed sealed and witnessed The Commissioners told the Head-men that Congress from motives of humanity had directed some presents to be made to them for their use and comfort, and that on the next day, they would direct the presents to be distributed accordingly.

November 29th.

Present as yesterday

The Commissioners ordered a return of the Indians, and there were nine hundred and eighteen, and goods to the amount of 1,311 10/90 Dollars were distributed among the head men of every Town.

The Indians having expressed a desire to say something farther to the Commissioners, they attended accordingly.

TASSEL—

I will now inform you of some farther complaints against your people—I remember the Treaty with Colonel Cristie, and in all our Treaties that we reserved the Long Island of Holsten for ourselves as beloved ground to hold our treaties on—I remember the Commissioners yesterday in an article of the Treaty demanded all their property and prisoners—I am now going to make my demand—I desire that Colonel Martin may be empowered to find and get our prisoners, he is our friend, and he will get them for us—I am now done my Talks, and I hope the Commissioners will be as good as their promise yesterday in the Treaty—The white people have taken so much of our lands we cannot kill as many deer as formerly—The traders impose on us greatly, and we wish our trade could be Regulated and fixed Rates on our goods—our traders are frequently robbed when coming to, and going from our Nation— John Benge was among others Robbed of about £ 150 sterlings worth of leather in the state of Georgia.

TUSKEGATAHÉE,

I am not a chief, but will speak for my Country I Shall always pay great regard to what I have heard respecting the treaty, as well as what may be sent us from Congress hereafter, and as I am within the limits of the United States, I shall always expect their protection and assistance—Our young men and warriors have heard what has passed—I expect as our boundaries are ascertained Congress may be informed of them—and that as peace is now firmly established and we are all friends we may be allowed to hunt on each others lands without molestation—On my part being in peace and friendship with you I shall feel myself safe wherever I go—many of your people on Cumberland and Kentucky loose their horses in our lands, and Should we find them I wish Colonel Martin to Receive them.

NOWOTA,

I am fond to hear the Talks of the beloved men of Congress and of ours— you Commissioners remember the talks, and I shall always endeavour to support the peace and friendship now established I remember your talks by Colonel Martin, and I promised to be attached to America, But until the present I was afraid to be in your Country—I am now perfectly happy as you are to protect us—your prisoner at Chickamanga I will deliver you—Formerly Captain Commeron saw justice done to us in our land; he is gone and I now depend on the Commissioners—If any thing depends on me to strengthen our friendship I will faithfully execute it—you are now our protectors— when I go and tell to those of our people who could not come to hear your talks what I have seen and heard, they will rejoice—I have heard your declarations of a desire to do us any service in your power, I believe you, and in Confidence shall rest happy.

COMMISSIONERS,

We will give you provisions for the Road, and wish you may be happy. We will send up to Congress all our Talks.

B
Contains

No. 1. A letter of 22nd. November 1785 from Colonel William Blount to the Commissioners, with an extract of the Constitution of North-Carolina.

No. 2. second letter of 28th November 1785. from Colonel Blount agent for North Carolina to the commissioners—Colonel Blounts protest against their proceedings, and their answer to his correspondence.

Received from the office of
the late secretary of Congress
H. KNOX

B. No. 1
Copy

Hopewell on Keowee Novr. 22d 1785
Gentlemen,

Having yesterday had the honor to to lay before you my Commission as agent on the part of North Carolina, I now consider it my duty to call your attention to the following extract from the Constitution of that state which was agreed to and published to the world on the eighteenth day of December in the year 1776.

"The property of the soil in a free government, being one of the essential rights of the collective body of the people it is Necessary in order to avoid future disputes, that the limits of the state should be ascertained with precision, and as the former Temporary line between North and south Carolina was confirmed and extended by Commissioners appointed by the Legislatures of the two States agreeable to the order of the late King George the second in Council: That line and that only should be esteemed the southern boundary of this state That is to say beginning on the sea side at a Cedar stake at or near the mouth of Little river (being Southern boundary of Brunswick County) and running from thence a Northwest course through the Boundary house which stands in thirty three degrees fifty six minutes to thirty five degrees North latitude, and from thence a west course so far as is mentioned in the Charter of King Charles the second to the late proprietors of Carolina—Therefore all the Territory, Seas, waters and harbours with their appurtenances lying between the line above described and the south line of the state of Virginia which begins on the Sea shore in thirty six degrees thirty minutes north latitude, and from thence runs West agreeable to the said Charter of King Charles, are the right and property of the people of this state to be held in Sovereignty."

And to remark to you that years after the state of North Carolina was received into and signed the Articles of Confederation.

> I have the honour to be
> Your Most obedient Humble sert.
> (Signed) WM. BLOUNT, agent
> for North Carolina

Benjamin Hawkins
Andrew Pickens Joseph
Martin and Laughlin McIntosh
Esquires, Commissioners for Negotiating
with the southern Indians

B. No. 2
Second letter
A Copy

> Hopewell on the Keowee Novr. 28th. 1785

Gentlemen,

The State of North Carolina have at this time a law in force and use, alloting the lands contained in the following bounds to the Cherokee Indians—"Beginning on the Tenessee River where the southern boundary of the state of North Carolina intersects the same nearest the Chickamawga Towns thence up the middle of the Tennessee and Holston Rivers to the middle of Frenchbroad River, thence up the Middle of the said French Broad river (which lines are not to include any Island) to the mouth of big Pigeon River thence up the same to the head thereof thence along the dividing Ridge between the waters of Pigeon River and Tuckasegée River to the said Southern boundary thence west with the said boundary to the beginning."

Should you by Treaty fix any other boundaries than the before mentioned within the limits of the said state of North Carolina between the said Cherokee Indians and her Citizens that State will consider such Treaty a violation and infringement upon her Legislative Rights—The lands contained within the limits of Davidson County, which begins on Cumberland river where the

Northern boundary of the said state of North-Carolina first intersects the same, thence South forty five miles, thence west to the Tennessee river, thence down the Tennessee ~~River~~ to the said Northern boundary, thence East with the said boundary to the beginning have been appropriated by the State of North Carolina to the payment of the bounties of land promised to the officers and Soldiers of the Continental line of that state, and it is said that the Militia in that County are in number about seven hundred. And the state of North Carolina have sold to her Citizens for a valuable consideration several Millions of Acres of the land situate, lying and being between the Missisippi and the line as fixed by Colonel Christie and others in the year 1777 and without the limits of Davidson County on which lands several thousands of people are settled.

I have the Honor to be
Your most Obedient
Humble servt.
(Signed)   WM. BLOUNT, agent
for North Carolina

Benjamin Hawkins, Andrew
Pickens, Joseph Martin and
Laughlin McIntosh Esquires
Commissioners for treating with
the southern Indians

Copy of Col. Blounts protest
    The under written agent on the part of the State of North Carolina protests against the Treaty at this instant about to be signed and entered into between Benjamin Hawkins, Andrew Pickens Joseph Martin and Laughlin McIntosh Commissioners on the part of the United states, and the Cherokee Indians on the other part, as containing several stipulations which infringe and violate the Legislative Rights of the state.

Hopewell on Keowee Novemr. 28th 1785
WM. BLOUNT

A Copy of the Commissioners answer to Colo. Blounts letters and protest.

Hopewell on Keowee 28th Novr. 1785
Sir,
    We received your letters of the 22d of November with an extract from the Constitution of your state declarative of the limits thereof—of the 28th inclosing an abstract of an Act allotting certain lands to the Indians of the Cherokee Nation, and your protest of the same date against the Treaty

entered into between the Commissioners of the United states of America, and all the Cherokees, which we shall transmit to Congress.

We enclose two articles of the Treaty to you, which we hope, as agent of the state of North Carolina you will take measures to see executed so far as the same may respect the Citizens of that state: or the faith of the Commissioners pledged for the restoration of the prisoners now held there. We are informed that the late Governour Martin made an unsuccessful effort to restore them, and that there are five, three girls and two boys in the possession of General McDowel and Col. Miller—We are certain that a steady adherence to the Treaty alone can insure confidence in the Justice of Congress and remove all causes of future contention or quarrels.

The local policy of Some states is certainly much opposed to Federal measures which can only in our opinion make us Respectable abroad and happy at home.

> We are with due respect
> Sir
> Your Most obedt. and
> Most Humble servts.
> B. HAWKINS
> A. PICKENS
> J. MARTIN
> L. McINTOSH

The Honorable
William Blount Esqr.
Agent for North Carolina
B. The two articles inclosed are the second and fourth.

C
Contains

No. 1. a letter of 13th. October 1788. from Richard Winn Esqr. to the Secretary at war.

No. 2. a letter of 29th. August 1788. from Richard Winn Esqr. to General Martin and others commanding Officers and inhabitants beyond the mountains.

No. 3. A letter of 31. August 1788. from the Governor of North Carolina to Richard Winn Esquire.

No. 4. A letter of 13th Decr. 88. from Richard Winn Esqr. to the Secretary at war.

No. 5.   Talk of the head men of the Cherokees, addressed to Richard Winn Esquire. November 20th. 1788.

No. 6.   Letter of 15 January 1789 from Jos. Martin Esqr. to the Secretary at war.

No. 7.   Talk of the head men and warriors of the Cherokees addressed to Brigadier General Martin Novr. 1. 1788.

No. 8.   Talk of William Elders.

No. 9.   a letter of 2nd. February 1789. from Jos. Martin Esqr. to the Secretary at war.

No. 10. letter of 1st. March 1789. from Richard Winn Esqr. to the secretary at war.

Copied from the files of the War office.
H. KNOX

C. No. 1.

Winnsborough October 13th. 1788

Sir,

I do myself the honor of writing you the different occurrences respecting the people on the frontiers of North Carolina, and the Cherokee Indians transpired since my last.

In consequence of hearing that several outrages had been committed by the people of Franklin (formerly called the new State) upon the Cherokees I dispatched a letter to the Governor of North Carolina to put a stop to any further hostilities, as it was the wish of Congress to carry into effect a treaty with that nation; not receiving an immediate answer from him, and having reason to believe these depredations continued, I sent a copy of the enclosed, addressed to the Officers commanding on the frontiers of that State, which I hope will be attended with every good Consequence. You will also find enclosed a Copy of a letter, I have lately received from the Governor, on comparing these, it will point out to you the similarity of our ideas relative to the establishment of peace in that quarter, previous to the late resolution of Congress coming to hand.

I shall avail myself of the earliest oppertunity of making known to the executive of North Carolina the further supplies granted by Congress for carrying the treaty into effect, which I hope may take place without the trouble and expence of marching troops from the Northward, urging the Governor to send on their Commissioner with the needful and to name the time and place. the answer with their determination you may rely on having transmitted you as soon as possible. I beg leave farther to observe, I have enclosed to the Cherokees the proclamation of Congress, and at the same time requested a suspension of hostilities should take place.

I have the honor to be
with esteem
Sir,
your most humble Servant
RICHARD WINN

P.S. your favor of the 4th September enclosing the Proclamation of Congress, with the duplicate I have to acknowledge since writing the above.

The Honorable General Knox
    Secretary at war

C. No. 2
(True Copy)

Winns Borough 29th August 1788

Friends & Brother soldiers

I write this to you in behalf of the United States to intreat you to desist from any further hostilities against the Cherokees, as it is the wish of Congress to be at peace with every tribe of Indians whatever, And as they have directed me to secure that peace by a permanent treaty, your own good sense, must convince you how impossible it will be for me to effect it while these outrages on both sides exist. Besides, what have we not to apprehend, if it is not put a Stop to? a Junction may take place with the southern Indians, and both United, may involve the innocent lives of thousands. perhaps when by a well timed peace nothing of the kind could ever happen.

I have daily expected an interference between you and the Indians would have taken place, from the Governor of North Carolina, but as I have received no accounts from him of that nature, I cannot consistent with my duty to the union, hear of these unhappy dissentions continuing, without emotion, therefore let me again, in the most friendly manner, exhort you to a suspension of arms 'till such times as I hear from Congress, to whom I have wrote for farther supplies to facilitate a treaty as soon as possible, at which time I am Convinced all grieviances will be adjusted, the Indians I shall write to—to the same purport, and as I have been at a deal of Pains to get proper persons to bear to both parties my Ideas on the matter, I hope it will be attended with every good consequence. by your religiously observing on both sides a strict neutrality, till the treaty is brought about. Any further Information You can receive from Capt. Baker who is the bearer of this, and who is a gentleman I particular recommend to your notice. wishing to hear from you as soon as possible.

I am

friends & brother soldiers
Your Obedient Servant
(Signed) RICHARD WINN

To General Martin and Others ⎫
the Commanding Officers and ⎬
inhabitants beyond the mountains ⎭

C. No. 3.

Edenton 31st. August 1788

Sir,

The information which you did me the honor to favor me with in your letter of the Ninth had reached me some time past. I had given orders for a process to issue to apprehend Sevier, and had directed the Commanding Officer on the frontier, to persue a line of Conduct similar to that pointed out in your letter, it gives me pleasure to find that your ideas in this particular so intimately corresponds with the measures I have adopted to restore and preserve the peace of the frontier.

I am with great respect
Sir,
Your most obedient Servt.
(Signed) SAML. JOHNSON

To Richard Winn Esquire
Superintendant of Indian
affairs for the southern
Department

True Copy
RICHARD WINN

C. No. 4

Winnsborough December 13th. 1788

Sir.

Notwithstanding I have received no late accounts from Congress, I Judge it necessary to continue giving every information that occurs relative to the Indians in this department.

Since I wrote you last, the enclosed Talk from the head men and warriors of the Cherokee Nation came to hand, which fully points out their disposition to come to a friendly treaty, I have urged the same to the state of north Carolina trusting they will send forward their Commissioner and supplies, should this step not be taken, and that state still continue to do them injury, I fear the disappointment of the Indians will be attended with bad consequences, as in all probability, the Union may be involved in a bloody and unnecessary war, whereas a well timed Peace would prevent it.

Sir,

I have the honor to be

with respect

Your Obedient Servant

RICHARD WINN

The honorable Major General ⎱
H. Knox—Secretary at war ⎰

C. No. 5.

A TALK from the head men and Warriors of the CHEROKEE nation, at a meeting held at Ustinare the beloved Town 20th November 1788—addressed to the honorable Richard Winn Esquire Superintendant for the southern department, in answer to a talk sent by him dated the 12th. Octer. 1788.

FRIEND & BROTHER.

We received your talk likewise the Resolves of Congress dated 1st. September 1788. likewise a copy of a letter from the Governor of North Carolina to you, and the proclamation from Congress, all which affords us much satisfaction, that we have in you a real friend, who tells us the truth and endeavours to do us Justice. it like wise gives us much Satisfaction to hear from Congress and Virginia.

BROTHER. You have opened our eyes and likewise our hearts. the talks we received from you pleases us much, that Congress is determined to have our hunting grounds open, so that our young men may hunt and kill deer to purchase goods of our traders, to Clothe ourselves, and famelies, our hunting grounds was very small, now it gives us the greatest Satisfaction that it will be soon enlarged, as appears by the proclamation from Congress—it likewise gives us much satisfaction that we have a view of returning from the woods where we have been droven, and once more settling again in our old Towns, which we propose to do, when we are certain that the white people have quitted our hunting grounds.

BROTHER. It affords us much satisfaction that a friendly talk will soon take place, you inform us, you have wrote to the Governor of North Carolina to fix a time and place for that purpose. At that time we will talk over all matters, and smoke the pipe of friendship.

The head men and warriors from the middle settlement was on their way to *Ustinaire,* but being informed that it was good talks, and that white beads and tobacco was sent from Ustinaire to all the Towns in the nation, they went back fearing that some of their young men might go out again and do mischief, the head men are determined to put a stop to all hostilities and for the time to come to live like brothers and friends as long as the sun shines, and water runs.

The following talk comes from the Little Turkey.

FRIEND and BROTHER. Your talk I have heard which gives me the greatest satisfaction, likewise all our beloved men in my part of the nation, it is a talk from you, our great beloved brother, who I am informed is appointed by Congress to see justice done us, we have now heard from our beloved brothers from New York, likewise from Virginia, which now opens our eyes and our hearts, for they are the men we must abide by—your talks are good and your friendships we look on sincere, for the good of our land. I have seen the resolves of Congress likewise the proclamation for all the white people Settled on our hunting grounds, to go off without loss of time.

FRIEND and BROTHER. I have the satisfaction to inform you that Alexander McGillivray, Chief of the Creek Nation has taken your talks, likewise the talks from Congress and Virginia, and means to hold them fast, and when they meet will take his white brothers by the hand as we do, and hopes to live in peace and friendship as long as the grass grows and the water runs.

A Copy of this talk you will please to send to Congress and Virginia, it will be two moons before every thing can be Settled to your entire satisfaction, because some of our beloved men are out a hunting. as for the prisoners, it is impossible to send them to Seneca at this time because they are Scattered through the nation, but they shall be restored to their friends as soon as possible, we shall have all them collected together—orders are given out that they may be used well, that my people Should not be reflected upon hereafter for using their prisoners Ill—this you will please to acquaint their friends, and hope they will make themselves easy for a Short-time.

FRIEND and BROTHER. We must inform you that we look upon the white people that live in the new State, very deceitful, we have experienced them, and are much afraid of them, we are now obliged to keep Spies out continually on the frontiers, fearing they will return and do us an injury as they did before.

FRIEND & BROTHER. we must inform you that there are some Creeks out and some of our people that are not yet come in, if any mischief should be done that is contrary to our desire, but on their return will all be stopt and all hostilities cease against the white people and the path made white, we must inform you that several talks that has been directed to the head men and warriors at ustinaire has been opened before we received them Your last talk came under Cover to Mr. Gegg, and by him delivered in the Square at Ustinare to our beloved men we do not approve of any person opening any talks that comes from our White Brothers, except Mr. Gegg who explains them to us or our linguister James Carrey. The boy we had prisoner at Coosowattee we are informed is delivered to Jesse Spears, in order that he may be conveyed down to Seneca, the girl is not yet come to her friends, but we presume She is in the land—We now have finished our talk in token of friendship and peace, We have enclosed a String of White Wampum.

The Little Turkey	Yellow Bird	Chickhesattee	Dak
Killy Geshee	Thigh	Cowetthee	Glass
Badger	Second man	Dragon Canoe	Humingbird
The Jobberson	Ale Chesnutt	Norrawahee	Prince
The Warrior Nephew	Bear Coming } out of a hole	Hanging Maw	Nottley
		Watts	
		Fool Warrior	

(True Copy)

C. No. 6

Long Islands Holston River 15th. day Jany. 1789

Sir.

I had the honor to receive two letters from your office, bearing date the 22nd. of August last past, one by way of Virginia, the other North Carolina, enclosing sundry resolves of Congress, also proclamations, they came to hand the 9th day of October last, That day being appointed by the field officers of Washington District, to Meet and concert some plan for carrying an expedition against the Cherokee Indians, which was agreed on in the following manner—resolved that 1500 men be immediately draughted out of Washington district, that each Captain of a company see their men well armed and ten days provision for each man—before the council rose, your dispatches came to hand, which I immediately laid before them, which put a final stop to any further proceeding on that head.

The next morning I set for my plantation in South Carolina, where some of the Indians had retreated to, in order to escape Mr. Savier, with a view to send some runners of them through their nation and Collect their Chiefs together, that I would meet them at any place they might disire, and lay before them several resolves of Congress, which would be very satisfactory to them, also a letter from the governor of North Carolina. But on my way thither at Major Taylors at Seneca was informed, a few hours before my arrival there, two gentlemen from Virginia, by order of Government, had Called two of the indian Chiefs there and had done some business with them, and the Indians set out for their nation; on which I dispatched a runner after them and brought them back, and read to them the resolves of Congress, and the proclamation, on which the hanging mow, rose up and took me by the arm and said by this holt I will settle all further quarrels, you and myself are allways the men that makes peace, when our young men differ we are the men that makes every thing strait—I will instantly go to my nation, and put a stop to war, you shall shortly hear from me, the talks we then had together. I sent them with a copy which I expect has come to your hand long before now; the next talk I had I enclosed you No. 1. I then dispatched a messenger to eastewley requesting some of the chiefs of my acquaintance to come to my plantation where we might talk face to face—they attended accordingly. I then and there read to them the several resolves of Congress to me directed, also the proclamation, and impressed on their minds, the Justness of Congress for their Safety, also the consequence that might attend to those regardless of that power, after which Will. Elders one of their Chief Warriors rose up and Spoke which you will see in No. 2. after he had finished his talk, he tells me his nation was for peace, and was disirous of returning to their old Towns, but that they had no way of Sustenance, that while they lived out in the hunting ground they could get meat, and those that went to the Creeks could get Corn that he feared they must all Join the Creek Indians or perish; I then asked him if they could get corn if they all would return to their old Towns, his answer was, they most certainly would, if the white people were moved off their lands. I then told him I would at my own expence furnish Citico a Town I formerly lived in, and would lay a state of their distressed situation before Congress—Perhaps they might take pity on them—which seemed to have a wonderfull effect on this Warrior in a short time after, several old women from that Town apply'd to me for Salt, to purchase corn with from other Towns all of whom I furnished and sent them back well pleased. In the intermediate time I went over to a plantation I had in Georgia, the evening of my arrival at that place I was attacked by a partie of Creek Indians, In the skirmish my overseer was badly wounded, I was obliged to take to the house, leaving them masters of the field they took of my horses with several Others, leaving one of their warriors dead on the ground.

I am well assured that with prudent means we may have the Cherokee Indians our friends, but it is to be feared there is a partie that has such a thirst for the Cherokee lands, they will take every measure in their power to prevent a treaty—You will observe in the talks sent on in October last, that the hanging-maw Said all hostilities should cease—Before he reached the nation 400 Creek Indians were come out was Joined by 1200 Cherokees, had marched against the frontiers, and had storm'd a fort and took 28 prisoners before the runners overtook them—the whole frontier Country seemed then to be in their Power; The then hostile Indians had several companies of horse, equipt from the Creek nation commanded by white men from that quarter—as soon as runners overtook them and informed that Congress had sent to them, they returned leaving a letter addressed to Mr. Savier & Myself—saying they were then on their own ground, and did not intend to go any farther—that the prisoners they should take Care of, That they did not wish to spill any more blood, that they would allow the people thirty days to move off their lands. After which the superintendant sent to them to meet him at hopewell on Keowee, which they did, two of the Commissioners met also, who gave the Indians the greatest reasons to beleive all hostilities between them and the white people would cease, the Indians went off well pleased; but a few days after when all the Indians was ordered out by their warriors to make their winters hunts; that war was no longer to be dreaded by them, being well assured by the Commissioners of the same. Mr. Savier went to one of their Towns, took off 29 Prisoners and plundered the Town—which actings of Mr. Savier, made great confusion again, but by the early interposition of General Pickens and some others that affront was allay'd, alledging those indian prisoners taken by Mr. Savier, was to exchange for those taken by them. another misfortune happened shortly after that, a party of men went to where some Indians was hunting, under a colour to trade with them for furrs which they had at their Camp, took an advantage and Shot two of the Indians dead and plundered their camp.

I fear no regulations to conserve a peace, so much the desire of the well disposed Citizen, will take place until the arrival of the troops ordered by Congress.

I have promised to see the Indians again some time in april next If Congress thinks proper to send on any talks to them, I think it will be of essential service towards forwarding the treaty.

Any Commands you will honor me with will meet me at my seat at Fort-Patrick Henry—Long Islands, holston River, Sullivan County North Carolina.

> I have the honor to be
> Your Most obedient
> and most Humble Servant,
> Jos. Martin

The Honorable
H. Knox secretary at war
or in his absence the next
in Command.

No. 1

C. No. 7

A Talk from the head men and Warriors of the CHEROKEES, now met at their beloved Town of Ustinaire 1st. November 1788 Addressed to Brigadier General Martin.

Friend and Brother.

We hear you are at Tascolo and that you are the great warrior of North Carolina and the new State—Your people provoked us first to war by Settling on our lands and killing our beloved men; however we have laid by the hatchett and are Strongly for peace—now we have heard from our brother, also from Congress, likewise the Governor of Virginia, who tells us that the people settled on our hunting grounds shall be removed without loss of time, which gives us great satisfaction—As we told you before we are strongly for peace we do not want any more war, we hope you will keep your people now at peace, and not to disturb us as they have done; when these People move we shall all be friends, and Brothers. There is a great many Creeks out—if they should do your people any Injury, we hope you will not lay the blame on us. for all our head men and warriors, will prevent our young people for the future to do the white people any Injury, but they expect they will move off their Land.

The talk from Congress, and the talk likewise from the Governor of Virginia, we have taken fast hold of and will remember because they are good, and strongly desirous to live in the greatest friendship with their red Brothers. we should be glad to receive a talk from you if it is a good one, and for hereafter to live in peace and friendship. We disire you will let our friends and Brothers in North Carolina hear this talk which we hope will be the means to procure that peace and friendship we strongly disire—We are your Friends and Brothers.

The Badger	Killygiskee	Thigh
The Crane	Yellow Bird	Pumpkin Vine
Bloody fellow	Bear coming out ⎱	Chesnutt
Jobbers Son	of the tree ⎰	
The Lyin Fawghn	Hanging Maw	
	the Englishman &c.	

Dear Sir.

I send you a talk from the head men and warriors met at ustinaire 1st. Instant which I hope will give you Satisfaction and prevent a war, I should always be glad to receive a line from you,

I am Dear Sir
your most obedient
Humble Servant
THO. GEGG

Pine Logg
3d November 1788

(No. 2)

C. No. 8

BROTHER

We have been long acquainted with you and know you to be our friend, but what is the reason Congress has not moved those people from off our lands before now, you was one of the beloved men that spoke for Congress at

Keowee three years ago—you then said the people Should move off in Six moons from that time but near forty moons are past and they are not gone yet, We will remember whenever we are invited into a treaty as observed by us at that time, and bounds are fixed, that the white people Settle much faster on our lands than they did before—It must certainly be the case, they think we will not break the peace directly, and they will strengthen themselves and keep the lands, you know this to be the case, you told us at the treaty, if any white people settled on our lands we might do as we pleased with them. They come and settle close by our Towns, and some of the Chicamoga people come contrary to our disire and killed a famely; and the white people came and drove us out of our Towns, and killed some of our beloved men, and several women and little Children—altho we could not help what the Chicamoga people does—you know that well—We are now like wolves ranging about the woods to get something to eat. Nothing to be seen in our towns, but bones, weeds, and grass. But for all this, we will lie still, we will not do any more mischief if the white people will Stop—I am but a boy, but my eyes are open, and wherever I turn them, many young men turn with them—I here give you this string of White beads, as a token of my friendship to you, also I present you with a string in the name of your brother John Watts he says he holds you fast by the hand, but he cannot see you yet, as he is in great trouble about his uncle.

The Corn-tassel but will come to your house towards the spring, and stay a great while with you as it will be very hungry times with him then.

WILL. ELDERS

A true Copy.

C. No. 9

Fort Patrick Henry 2d. Febry. 1789
Sullivan County North Carolina

Sir,

I have certain accounts that some designing men on the Indian lands have assembled themselves to the number of fifteen, and calls themselves a Convention of the people, and have entered into several resolves, which they say they will lay before Congress; one of which resolves, is to raise men by subscription to defend themselves—as the Legislature of North Carolina refuses to protect them on the Indian lands; but on the Contrary have directed and ordered those people off the Indian lands—A certain Alexander Outlaw by name, I am informed is to wait upon Congress on behalf of this new Plan. I think it my duty to say the truth of him: shortly after the murder of the Corn-tassel and two other chiefs, this said Outlaw collected a partie of men and went into an Indian Town called Citico, where he found a few helpless women and children which he inhumanly murdered, exposing their private parts in a most shameful manner. leaving a young child with both arms broke alive, at the breast of its dead mother; These are facts well known and cannot be denyed in this country. Mr. Outlaw has done every thing in his power to drive the Indians to desperation—Altho I find some complaint by the said Outlaw, against me for carrying on an expedition against the Cherokee Indians, without orders of Government I have once stated that matter to you, but least that may not have come to hand, I beg leave to state the facts to you—In the month of may last a boat richly laden, was going down Tennessee to Cumberland, the crew was decoyed by the Chiccamaga Indians and Creeks together all of which Crew were killed and taken prisoners after which doings, the Corntassel informed me of the cruel murder they had committed, also the repeated murders and robbery's they were Constantly committing on the frontiers of Cumberland and Kentuckey, also on the Kentuckey road in Company with the Creeks—there was not the least hopes of reclaiming them, as long as they lived so far detached from their nations. That the Corn Tasil had talked to them until he found it was of no use. That he with the other Chiefs advised and thought it best to go against them and burn their Towns, by which means they would return to their allegiance—That then they would have it in their power to govern them. This the Indian chiefs urged in the strongest terms, which account I laid before the executive of North Carolina who advised that peace should be offered them, and if refused by the Indians, that then, the principal officers of Washington district should persue such measures, as to them should appear most likely to put a stop to those merciless Indians on the frontiers and roads, it was unanimously agreed to march against Chiccamoga, but by no means to give offence to the Cherokees, which has been a means of uniting the Chiccamoga Indians to the Other Indians. It will now be our own faults if we do not make all that race of Indians our friends.

So great is the thirst for Indian lands prevails that every method will be taken by a party of peoples to prevent a treaty with the Indians. They are now labouring to draw some of the Indians to a treaty, as they may purchase their Country. this party say if they can purchase of the Indians, they will have it without the consent of any other power. That the Indians have an undoubted right to it and not Congress, that if they could only prevail on a few of the lower Class to Come into their scheme, they would get conveyances made and contend for the right, this I have heard from them.

I this moment have received a talk from the Chicasaw Indians which I enclose you.

I have the honor with much respect
to be your most humble &
Most Obedient Servant
Jos. MARTIN

The Honorable H. Knox
Secretary at war or in
his absence to the next in
Command

C. No. 10   ,

                               Winnsborough March 1st. 1789
Sir.

I think it necessary to inform you that a treaty will take place with the Cherokee Indians the third monday in May next at the upper war-ford, on french broad River in the neighborhood of Swananno, State of North Carolina.

The Creek Indians 'tis supposed will also treat, they are now holding a great talk in their nation, the result of which is not yet come to hand.

                                 I have the honour
                                     to subscribe myself
                                     Your most
                                     Obedient Servant
                                     RICHARD WINN

The Honorable
Major General Knox

SOUTHERN DISTRICT

THE CHICKASAWS

This nation of indians were estimated by the Commissioners in 1785 at 800 Warriors, other opinions make them amount to 1200.

The lines of their territory between the Cherokees and Choctaws do not appear precisely fixed—Their limits established by the Treaty hereafter mentioned are bounded on the north by the ridge which divides the waters running into the Cumberland, from those running into the Tennessee—The Mississippi on the west—The Choctaws and the Creeks on the South, and the Cherokees on the East.

The United States formed a treaty with the Chickasaw nation at Hopewell the 10th. of January 1786, which was entered on the Journals of Congress April 17th. 1786.

By this treaty they acknowledge themselves to be under the protection of the United States, and of no other Sovereign whosoever—a tract of land is reserved for a trading post to the use and under the government of the United States of a circle of five miles diameter, at the lower post of the Muscle Shoals at the mouth or junction of the Ocochappo with the Tennessee—The land transportation from the head of the Ocochappo, to the head of the most northerly part of the Mobile river is said not to exceed thirty five miles.

The distance of this nation from the frontier settlements being so great is the principal reason that no complaints have been made of the encroachments of the Whites.

In the year 1787 they sent one of the Warriors of their nation to Congress to represent the distressed situation of the Cherokees, and that unless the encroachments of the Whites were restrained they should be obliged to join the Cherokees—and also to enforce the establishment of trade agreeably to the Treaty.

THE CHOCTAWS

This nation of indians were estimated by the Commissioners of the United States at 6,000 warriors—other opinions state them at 4,500, or 5,000.

Their principal towns or villages are on the head waters of the Passagoula and Pearl rivers—They are mostly to the northward of the 31st. degree of latitude but some of them are to the Southward of it within the territory of Spain.

Both the Chickasaws and Choctaws are represented as candid, generous, brave and honest, and understanding each others language.

The Commissioners of the United States, concluded a treaty with the Choctaws at Hopewell on the 3d of January 1786, and the same is entered on the Journals of Congress the 16th. of April 1786.

By this treaty the Choctaws acknowledged themselves to be under the protection of the United States and of no other Sovereign whosoever—And three tracts or parcels of land, each of six miles square for the establishment of trading posts are reserved to the use of the government of the United States at such places as they shall think proper.

The distance of the Choctaws has also prevented hitherto those encroachments which have been complained of by the Cherokees.

In the year 1787 they sent TOBOCAH, one of their great medal Cheifs to Congress principally in order to solicit the establishment of trade.

All which is humbly submitted to the President of the United States

H. KNOX

War office 7th day of July 1789

No. 4

No. 1. A letter of 30th. December 1785. from the commissioners of Indian affairs to Charles Thomson Esq. Secretary of Congress.

No. 2. A letter of the 4th January 1786. from the Commissioners of Indian affairs to the President of Congress.

No. 3. a letter of the 14th of January 1786 from the Commissioners of Indian affairs to the President of Congress.

No. 4. The ~~Treaty~~[6], proceedings with the Chickasaws, ~~and the Choctaw Indians~~.

> Received from the Office of
> the late secretary of Congress.
>
> H. KNOX

4—No. 1

Seneca on Keowee the 30th December 1785

Sir,

The Commissioners have been much longer executing the duties of the Commission than they at first had any idea of. as I informed you from Charleston of the last of September, we were under the Necessity of postponing the time of meeting both at Galphinton and this place one month later than the original appointment, that the Indians might have full time, and that all delays be avoided. Accordingly the Commissioners Mr. Perry excepted met at Galphinton the 24th and 28th of October, and although we had had assurances that the Chiefs of the Creek Nation would meet us there, yet from some cause not clearly known we were met only by the Representatives of two Towns who had been friendly to us—This disappointment was the more unexpected as we knew a majority of the Nation to be pleased with our invitation and very anxious of establishing with us a permanent peace— perhaps I might attribute it to the intreagues of the Neighbouring spanish Officers and to Alexander McGillivray a half breed of great abilities and consequential Rank in his Nation, and who has lately had permission to form connections with, and establish British Commercial houses for the supply of the Indians. He is also an agent of Spain with a salary of Six hundred dollars ℗ annum paid monthly.

We did not think proper to enter into a Treaty with the heads of these Towns only, and after explaining to them the object of the United states we dismissed them with a few presents as they had been friendly to us most of the late war.

The Commissioners of Georgia attended and protested against everything we had done or should do founded on our Commission "except in such cases only, as may or Shall lead to continue principles of Friendship, and to explain the great occurrences of the late war"—And after we left Galphinton the

---

[6] Henry Knox crossed out "treaty" and wrote "proceedings" above it.

agents of that state entered into a treaty with the Indians then present, and obtained from them a Cession of all the lands South of the Alatamaha and Eastward of a line to be run Southwest from the junction of the Oconee and Oakmulgee untill it shall strike St. Mary's with a confirmation of the Cession North East of the Oconee in 1783.

The 17th of November we arrived here, and were met in a few days by nine hundred and eighteen Cherokees with whom on the 28th we entered into a Treaty, they were anxiously desirous of being under the protection of the United states thereby to be secured in the possession of their hunting grounds from the avidity of land speculation. They had for some time past lost all confidence in promises made them by the Neighbouring states as well as the Citizens thereof. They saw their situation with despondency until they were informed of the humane and liberal views of Congress; and then with Joy and gladness they embraced the protection we offered them, and I believe would have submitted their fate to the decision of the United states without a Negative—Colonel William Blount as agent for North Carolina is with us, and he has entered a protest against the Treaty, and the Commissioners of Georgia were present and gave us a second protest, which with the Treaty and all our proceedings thereon I shall send forward as early as practicable.

The 4th. Instant the Commissioners agreed to adjourn and Report their proceedings—and Joseph Martin and Laughlin McIntosh set out for their Respective homes leaving Mr. Pickens and myself to discharge the Indians, to wind up every thing and close the Report—The Ninth, we received advice from Captain Woods that the Chiefs of the Choctaws were on the way, and would be here in this Month—Mr. Martin hearing of it returned on the 27th. but Mr. McIntosh was so far on his way home as to prevent his having advice in time, although I wrote for him immediately on the receipt of the information—The Choctaws arrived on the 26th, after a fatiguing Journey of seventy seven days, the whole of them almost Naked. The Creeks endeavoured all they could to prevent their coming by false information, stealing of horses & ca. but they have apparently a rooted aversion to the Spaniards and Creeks, and are determined to put themselves under the protection of the United states. This day we Shall commence our Negotiations with them, we should have done it sooner, but the Chiefs told us, they were so naked they must first receive some Cloathing, and we yesterday, gave to eighteen, Coats in the Uniform of the late Army, with other Necessaries to dress them, and we foresee that there are no difficulties to oppose, but that in a few days we shall finish our Treaty with them—some of the Chickasaws are here, and the representation from the Nation expected to arrive every day, and the same spirit actuates them as the Choctaws; so that in a few days our Negotiations will be complete, except with the Creeks, and all difficulties Respecting them Removed.

On the Article of expence, we have had our fears and knowing the sum to which we were limited would be exhausted too soon, unless we contracted our Original plan, we were under the Necessity of dismissing our guard three weeks past, and do our business without one—This opportunity does not admit our writing farther.

We are with due Respect
Sir,
Your most Obedient servts.
(Signed)   BENJAMIN HAWKINS
ANDREW PICKENS

The Honorable
Charles Thomson Esqr.

4 No. 2

Hopewell the 4th. of January 1786

Sir,

The 28th of November we had the honour to enclose your Excellency the Treaty we entered into with the Cherokees, and all the papers Respecting the same. at that period we did not suppose we should be able to meet any other of the tribes this winter—a few days afterwards we received an express from Colonel John Woods informing us of the approach of the Choctaws, and they arrived here on the 26th.—They had been on the path from the 16th of October, and had experienced great difficulties from the badness of the way, the scarcity of Cloathing and provisions, and the frequent interruptions of the Creeks by stealing their horses; and we were from motives of humanity at their arrival under the Necessity of Cloathing the whole of them, as the weather was very cold and they were nearly naked, before we commenced our Negotiations with the Chiefs—The third Instant we concluded a Treaty with them which we enclose to your Excellency with our Journal and other papers respecting the same.

The Indians seem to comprehend very well every article, and we have taken great pains to explain it to them, as well as the humane views of Congress towards all the tribes of Indians within the United States of America.

We had some difficulty in finding out how we should ascertain the bounds of the lands alloted to the Choctaws, and could not fix them other than as in the third Article; And knowing the avidity of land speculation, would take any possible advantage, we fixed on the 29th of November 1782 the day before the signing of our preliminary Articles with Great Britain that being as we conceived the earliest period in our power.

The Indians were well satisfied with the Treaty and with the treatment they met with, and expressed their gratitude for it. But we could perceive their strong hankering after presents could not be abated, by the prudent method we adopted of Cloathing them comfortably, or by our liberality in the Treaty. They are the greatest beggars and the most indolent creatures we ever saw, and yet honest simple, and regardless of any situation of distress. Their passion for gambling and drinking is very great; we have had instances of their selling blankets at a pint of Rum each, and gambling them away when they had no prospect of replacing them, and knew they must return this winter five hundred miles to their Nation with a shirt only—They were very little accustomed to traveling, and we should not have had them here, had we not supplyed them with Provisions on the road—and that they may return without starving through indolence, we were necessitated to pack up some proper goods, and put them under the care of the interpreter and the four Chiefs, for the purpose of procuring provisions.

The Spaniards were desirous of preventing them from meeting us—and Mr. McGillivray by their order took pains to stop them as they passed through the Creeks. But they were determined to go to Congress rather than not form some connexion with us. They have strong regard for the British and an exalted idea of the Military prowess of the United States, and they urge that as the latter conquered the former, they are the fittest persons on earth for them to apply to for protection.

The Chiefs produced their medals and Commissions and were very desirous of exchanging for those under the United states—They were also desirous of having three stand of Colours for their upper and lower towns and six Villages, and an agent to superintend their business—Captain John Woods is recommended by two of the Chiefs, and he is a man of some enterprize and ability but much addicted to strong drink—he came in with the Indians, and has been at much trouble with them.

We have appointed John Pitchlynn our interpreter of the Choctaw tongue, we have told him that we did not know, whether Congress would annex any salary to such an appointment; he is a very honest sober young man, and has lived twelve years in the Nation and is much respected by the Chiefs as an interpreter.

The presents we have given the Indians, and the goods for the purchase of provisions amount to 1,181 Dollars.

We have the Honor to be with sincere esteem Sir
Your Excellencys most obedient Humble Servts.
(Signed) BENJAMIN HAWKINS
ANDREW PICKENS
JOS. MARTIN

His Excellency
John Hancock Esqr.
President of Congress

4—No. 3

Hopewell the 14th January 1786

Sir,

We have the honour to enclose to your Excellency a treaty we entered into with the Chickasaws on the 10th Instant; They had been as long on the path as the Choctaws, but coming through the Cherokees were better supplyed with provisions and experienced less difficulties, except from the villanous practice of horse stealing which has taken deep root among them as well as the Creeks.

We found no difficulty in our Treaty with these Indians, who are the most honest and well informed as well as the most orderly and best governed of any we have seen—The trading posts reserved to the use of the United states is situated in the most convenient place within the whole of their lands; It is within sixty miles of their towns and one hundred of the Choctaws upper Towns. The lands on the North side of the River very fit for cultivation and for grazing.

Through the whole of our Negotiations we have paid particular attention to the rights and interests of the United states as far as our abilities could comprehend them, regardless of the protests of the adjoining states against us—Finding from the delays of the Indians and the particular circumstances attending the Negotiations that our expences would exceed the sums we had provided for, and even the sum to which we were restricted by Congress, and without compleating the object of our Commission—We were Necessitated to discharge our guard early in december, and meet the Indians without them, and curtail every expence that could possibly be avoided—and yet after all they have exceeded our wishes.

By this treaty the boundary of the lands allotted to the respective tribes is closed on every side from the south fork of Oconée around Northerly and Westwardly, and we verily believe that if the Adjoining states were disposed to carry the Treaties into effect, the Indians would be happy in the new change of Sovereignty, and in constant amity with us.

The Chickasaws will leave us tomorrow, we have given them presents amounting to 639 3/5 Dollars including some goods for the purchase of provisions—The Choctaws left us on the 12th.

The Commissioners of Georgia returned home after the Treaty with the Cherokees—The agent of North Carolina continued with us, and we enclose his letter and protest.

We have the honor to be with
sincere esteem
    Sir,
       your Excellency's
       Most obedient Humble Servts.

(Signed)   BENJAMIN HAWKINS
ANDREW PICKENS
JOS. MARTIN

1st—4. No. 4

Hopewell the 7th. January 1786

The Commissioners plenipotenitary of the United states in Congress Assembled appointed to treat with the Cherokees, and all other Indians Southward of them within the limits of the United states assembled—Present Benjamin Hawkins, Andrew Pickens and Joseph Martin.

From the state of North Carolina
William Blount Esqr. Agent
James Cole Interpreter.

The Commissioners were informed that the leading Chiefs of the Chickasaws with their followers had arrived, and were desirous of seeing the Commissioners and entering upon their business as early as practicable—That they had been long on the path and detained by the Villany of the Cherokees, some of whom had stolen several of their horses—They were introduced and expressed a most friendly disposition towards the United states, and an earnest desire of entering into a treaty of peace and protection with them. The Commissioners after explaining the object of their Commission informed the Chiefs, that they would on Monday, or as early as would be convenient for them enter upon the Business.

9th. of January

Present as on the 7th.

The leading Chiefs attended at 10 o'Clock, and after some friendly conversation—The Commissioners addressed the leading Chiefs as follows Vizt.

Leading Chiefs, who represent the Chickasaws

We are the Commissioners plenipotentiary from the United states in Congress assembled, who sent an invitation to you the leading Chiefs who represent the Chickasaws to meet us at this place—to give you peace and to receive you into the favor and protection of the United States—and to remove as far as may be all causes of future contention or quarrels—That you your wives and your Children may be happy, and feel and know the blessings of the New change of Sovereignty over this land which you and we inhabit.

This humane and generous Act of the United states will no doubt be received by all the Chickasaws with Joy and gladness, and held in grateful remembrance, particularly as it flows unsolicited from their Justice, their humanity and their attention to the rights of human Nature.

On our own parts we sincerely wish you to live as happily as we do ourselves, and to promote that happiness as far as in our power, regardless of any distinction of colour or of any differences in our customs or manners or particular situation; and as a proof of the sincerity of our declarations, we propose to enter into Articles of a treaty as equal as may be comfortable to what we now tell you.

After this address the Chiefs were told that at some future period the occurrences of the late war and the extent of Territory within the United states would be fully explained to them—To which Piomingo—replyed he wished to hear every thing intended to be communicated to him prior to his talks—The whole was accordingly explained, and apparently to their satisfaction and comprehension; The draught of the Treaty was also explained with which they seemed to acquiesce most heartily.

The leading Chiefs then in turn addressed the Commissioners.

PIOMINGO,

The period has arived, that I have visited you to see you, and to regulate everything that respects us. These Beads are our Credentials of peace and friendship, and two of us have come to bring the talks of the Nation—These white Beads are of little value but in our Nation where they are kept even by our Children with veneration as tokens of peace and friendship. When I take you by the hands, the day will never come, that discord will break my hold— although I may not be eloquent, yet I wish my talks to be as much esteemed as if I was, it being my sincere desire that what I say should be construed most friendly—my talks are not long and I hope when you see these Beads you will remember my friendship—Eight strands of Beads.

MINGATUSHKA,

The day is come when I have met you to talk with you, and I am well pleased, and now you shall hear what I have to say.

I have come to see you and you are not strangers to us, you are a white people I claim as our eldest and first Brothers—These beads in my hand are a token of friendship, and I hope friendly ideas will arise in your minds whenever you see them—my predecessor loved you white people in his time, and I mean to do the same—Our two old leading men are dead, and we two come as their successors in business with the same friendly talks as they had which were always friendly—although our old King and leading man is dead, we wish their friendly talks may live and be remembered with you as with us and for that purpose we come to renew them. I hope when your Children and our Children grow up they will remember the old peace and friendship of this day, and strictly adhere to it. This is the day I have come to see you, and I have been informed of the peace of the United states of America with all Nations, and I am glad of it; and wish sincerely it may long continue. The substance of my talks is done, and when we red people talk we give Beads as a proof of friendship, and I give these—my talks are short and true—when people are prolix they some times are false.

A string of Beads.

PIOMINGO,

I now represent Latopoia—He is a particular man, when he gives his word or acquiescence he never lets go, and this is his belt—he and I are related, our sentiments are the same—Our talks are short but his token of friendship is great.

A Broad belt of Wampum

our talks are done, our predecessors are dead, and we come and give in our talks, and now we will hear further from you.

MINGATUSHKA,

The great man of our Nation who wore this medal I shew you, is dead, and I am his Nephew and a leader; on the death of this great man, he left a daughter who took care of this Medal, and she Judged it was proper when I came that I Should bring it—That you might see it, and know such a thing belonged to our family, and accordingly She and her mother sent it.

PIOMINGO,

You see this now (pointing to the Medal) it was worn by our great man, he is dead, his daughter sent it for you to see it: I take place as head leading warrior of the Nation to treat with all Nations.

COMMISSIONERS,

We are glad you rember with pleasure the virtues of your old and worthy predecessors and we are pleased that the daughter of one of them has sent us this Medal, with the reasons for so doing in return we will give you some present for her.

As you are well pleased with the draught of our Treaty we shall prepare two Copies thereof to be Signed tomorrow, the one for you and the other for the Congress.

When the first Article was read, the Chief Piomingo said he had no prisoners of ours in his Nation or property of any kind—To the reservation in the third Article he at first seemed much opposed; but on being assured by the Commissioners that they were not desirous of getting his land, and that all, that would be Necessary for the United states, as a trading post, would be five or Six miles square, he readily acquiesced, and marked the Article in the map describing its diameter to be five miles, and remarked at the same time that the lands on the North of the River was fine for cultivation and grazing, and he would have no objection to our using what we might think proper for the conveniency of traders.

10th of January
Present as yesterday.

The Commissioners produced two Copies of the draught agreed on, and a Map of the lands in question partly drawn by themselves, and partly by the Indians, and instead of agreeing to the line between the respective tribes, they doted only with black ink, which the Chief observed and said he wished

Congress would point out his lands to him, he wanted to know his own—
The line was then extended as in the third Article, and the Commissioners
told the Chiefs that they must agree with the Neighbouring tribes respecting
their boundary, and that then Congress would send a white man to be present
with the Indians and see them mark it.

The treaty was then read over again, and every Article explained with great
attention, and the Indians acquiesced with them, and at the close the Commissioners asked if they comprehended the whole, and were willing to sign,
they answered, yes, and that it was all straight, meaning it was proper and
satisfactory to them; it was then signed, but previous thereto the agent of
North Carolina delivered a letter to the Commissioners referring them to his
former letters to them respecting the Constitutional claims of North Carolina
to all the lands within the bounds described in their Bill of Rights—He also
gave in his protest against the Treaty.

The Commissioners informed the Chiefs, that on tomorrow, in pursuance
of the humane and liberal views of Congress they would make them some
present for their use and comfort.

11th. of January.
Present as yesterday.

It being very wet and rainy the Chiefs postponed receiving the presents till
tomorrow—In the evening the principal Warrior Piomingo visited the Commissioners and addressed them as follows—Vizt. I am now going to inform
you of the situation of the white people in our land—There are a great many
of them who have numerous stocks of Cattle and Horses, and they are not
traders or of any advantage to us, and when a white man comes they without
our permission or even asking of it, build a house for him, and settle him
among us—I do not wish to be cross to them, or do them any injury, and I
desire they may go in peace with their stocks to their own lands. such people
as they, are of no use to us, on the contrary very injurious. If they were traders
I should be pleased at their being with us—They are not those in our Towns
only, who have stocks, but some are settled out Thirty or forty miles who
keep Cattle and Horses; and if an Indians horse or Colt should get among
their stocks, they brand him and Claim him to the injury of the owner—
Some pedlars come also to us, who are a pest, as they Steal more than they
purchase of our horses—If we had merchant traders who would set down with
us and trade properly I should be pleased with it, such men would be a
valuable acquisition to us as they would supply us our Necessary wants in
exchange for our property. you the Commissioners have told me that we shall
be properly supplied with goods, and I depend on their promise, such men as
come properly to trade with us will be very welcome, and any thing we have
is at their service—But the Class of Settlers we now have are a pest, and I
wish they would go with their property to their own lands, and enjoy it.

COMMISSIONERS,

Your remarks are very proper, and we have in an Article of the Treaty provided against a repetition of the abuse—and you will have the Right to punish these, if you think proper—we shall send the Treaty and all our talks with you to Congress, and they will issue a proclamation warning the white people of their danger, and this will be by some person communicated to the Chiefs of all the Southern tribes—when you return you may by our Interpreter communicate the Article of the Treaty respecting these people, that they may see their situation.

12th of January
Present as yesterday.

Piomingo addressed the Commissioners as follows—

The people I complained of last ~~evening~~ Night I imagine will not pay attention to what I say respecting their removal—and I wish that Colonel Martin would come and see them removed—my talk is a short one—I am only desirous that Colonel Martin may come and adjust every thing between the Red people and white people.

The Chickasaw Chiefs had also informed the Commissioners, That on the way hither they saw two Companies of Creeks going to Cumberland to plunder the Citizens and very probably to get some scalps—That Piomingo represented to them the injustice of the act, as well as their folly—and expressly told them that the white people on Cumberland and their property was equally dear to him with his own. and that although the Creeks were numerous compared with the Chickasaws yet if they continued to Robb and plunder on his lands, his own, or the hunters and traders of the white people; he would take such steps as would be proper.

The Commissioners then distributed presents among the Chiefs and Indians amounting including the goods to purchase provisions to   Dollars—they were perfectly satisfied, with the presents, and the treatment they met, and expressed their gratitude for it; and prepared to set out to their own Nation—In the evening the Cherokees gave the Chief a proof of their ingenuity in Robbing of packs as well as stealing horses—two of them Robbed the Chief of all his presents, and the goods given to purchase provisions, and within sight of the Chickasaws—The Commissioners issued a proclamation offering a reward for the goods and the Robbers, and sent runners to the Neighbouring Towns to proclaim the same as well as to call on the Chiefs to interpose immediately and apprehend the Robbers, and send them to Hopewell to be punished.

15th January

The Chief of Chetugoh with three young men brought the goods and informed the Commissioners that they had pursued the Robbers, and endeavored to apprehend them, but could not—They came up with them and fired at them and wounded one.

The Commissioners paid the reward and told the Chief that they had done very properly, and that in future he should be noticed for his attention to this order, and prompt execution of it.

[OBSERVATIONS BY THE SECRETARY AT WAR ON THE DIFFICULTIES
SUBSISTING BETWEEN THE SOUTHERN INDIANS
AND THE FRONTIER PEOPLE][7]

The report of the 23d. of May 1789, on the treaties at Fort Harmar, by the Governor of the Western Territory, and the paper Number 1. of the Indian department, contain such a general statement of the circumstances relative to the indian tribes, within the limits of the United States, North West of the Ohio, as will probably render their situation sufficiently understood.

The numbers, two, three, and four, comprehend a general view of the nations south of the Ohio.

But the critical situation of affairs between the State of Georgia and the Creek nation, require a more particular consideration—In discussing this subject it will appear that the interest of all the indian nations south of the Ohio as far as the same may relate to the whites is so blended together, as to render the circumstance highly probable, that in case of a war, they may make it one common cause.

Although each nation or tribe may have latent causes of hatred to each other on account of disputes of boundaries and game, yet when they shall be impressed with the idea that their lives and lands are at hazard all inferior disputes will be accomodated, and an Union as firm as the six northern nations may be formed by the southern tribes.

Their situation entirely surrounded on all sides, leads naturally to such an Union; and the present difficulties of the Creeks and Cherokees may accelerate and complete it—Already the Cherokees have taken refuge from the violence of the frontier people of North Carolina within the limits of the Creeks, and it may not be difficult for a Man of Mr. McGillivrays ability to convince the Choctaws and Chickasaws, that their remote situation is their only present protectio[n] that the time must shortly arrive when their troubles will commence.

In addition to these causes impelling to a general confederacy, there is another of considerable importance—The policy of the Spaniard, The jealousy that power entertains of the extension of the United States would lead them into considerable expence to build up if possible an impassable bar-

---

[7] This document has been titled by the editors, using Knox's own description of it in his letter to the President of the U.S., dated June 15, 1789.

rier—They will therefore endevor to form and cement such an union of the Southern indians.

Mr. McGillivray has stated that Spain is bound by treaty to protect the Creeks in their hunting grounds—Although it may be prudent to doubt this assertion for the present, yet it is certain that Spain actually claims a considerable part of the territory ceded by Great Britain to the United States.

These circumstances require due weight in deliberating on the measures to be adopted respecting the Creeks.

Although the case of the Creeks will be a subject of Legislative discussion and decision, it may be supposed that after due consideration they will in substance adopt one or the other of the following alternatives to wit,

1st. That the national dignity and justice require that the arms of the Union should be called forth in order to chastise the Creek nation of indians for refusing to treat with the United States on reasonable terms and for their hostile invasion of the State of Georgia or 2dly.

That it appears to the Congress of the United States that it would be highly expedient to attempt to quiet the hostilities between the State of Georgia and the Creek Nation of indians, by an amicable negociation, and for that purpose there be a bill brought in to authorize the President of the United States to appoint three Commissioners to repair to the State of Georgia in order to conclude a peace with the said Creek nation and other nations of indians to the southward of the Ohio, within the limits of the United States.

Supposing that any measure similar to either of the said alternatives should be adopted it may be proper to examine into the manner which they are to be executed.

The most effectual mode of reducing the Creeks to submit to the will of the United States and to acknowledge the validity of the treaties stated to have been made by that nation with Georgia, would be by an adequate Army to be raised and continued untill the objects of the War should be accomplished.

When the force of the Creeks be estimated and the probable combinations they might make with the other indian nations, the army ought not to be calculated at less than 5,000 men, The number on paper would not probably afford, at the best, more than 3,500 effectives—The delays and contingencies inseparable from the preparations and operations of an army, would probably render its duration necessary for the term of two years—An operating Army of the above description, including all expences could not be calculated at less than one million, five hundred thousand dollars annually.

A less Army than the one herein proposed would probably be utterly inadequate to the object, an useless expence, and disgraceful to the nation.

In case the second alternative should be agreed upon, the negociation should be conducted by three Commissioners with an adequate compensation for the trouble of the business, as an inducement for proper persons to accept the trust.

The Commissioners should be invested with full powers to decide all differences respecting boundaries between the State of Georgia and the Creek indians, unconstrained by treaties said to exist between the said parties, otherwise than the same may be reciprocally acknowledged.

The Commissioners also should be invested with powers to examine into the case of the Cherokees, and to renew with them the treaty made at Hopewell in November 1785, and report to the President such measures as shall be necessary to protect the said Cherokees in their former boundaries.

But all treaties with the indian nations however equal, and just they may be in their principles will not only be nugatory but humiliating to the Sovereign unless they shall be guaranteed by a body of troops.

The angry passions of the frontier indians and whites are too easily enflamed by reciprocal injuries, and are too violent to be controuled by the feeble authority of the civil power.

There can be neither justice or observance of treaties, where every man claims to be the sole judge in his own cause, and the avenger of his own supposed wrongs.

In such a case the sword of the Republic only, is adequate to guard a due administration of justice, and the preservation of the peace.

In case therefore of the Commissioners concluding a treaty, the boundaries between the Whites and indians must be protected by a body of at least five hundred troops.

The posts which they should occupy should be without the limits or jurisdiction of any individual State, and within the territory assigned to the indians for which particular provision should be made in the treaties.

All offences committed by individuals contrary to the treaties should be tried by a Court Martial agreeably to a law to be made for that purpose.

By this arrangement, the operation of which will soon be understood, the indians would be convinced of the justice and good intentions of the United States, and they would soon learn to venerate and obey that power from whom they derived security against the avarice and injustice of lawless frontier people.

Hence it will appear that troops will be necessary in either alternative—An Army in case of an adoption of the first, and after all the success that could reasonably be expected by means thereof, a corps to be continued and stationed on the frontiers of five hundred men—In case of the adoption of the second, the corps of five hundred only will be wanted, provided proper treaties can be effected.

But in any event of troops the subject must necessarily be considered and determined by Congress.

The disgraceful violation of the treaty of Hopewell with the Cherokees, requires the serious consideration of Congress—If so direct and manifest contempt of the authority of the United States be suffered with impunity it will be in vain to attempt to extend the arm of Government to the frontiers—The indian tribes can have no faith in such imbecile promises, and the lawless whites will ridicule a Government which shall on paper only, make indian treaties, and regulate indian boundaries.

The policy of extending trade under certain regulations to the Choctaws and Chickasaws under the protection of military posts will also be a subject of Legislative deliberation.

The following observations, resulting from a general view of the indian department, are suggested with the hope that some of them might be considered as proper principles to be interwoven in a general system for the Government of indian affairs.

It would reflect honor on the new Government, and be attended with happy effects were a declarative Law to be passed that the indian tribes possess the right of the soil of all lands within their limits respectively and that they are not to be divested thereof but in consequence of fair and bona fida purchases, made under the authority, or with the express approbation of the United States.

As the great source of all indian wars are disputes about their boundaries, and as the United States are from the nature of the Government liable to be involved in every war that shall happen on this or any other account it is highly proper that their authority and consent should be considered as essentially necessary to all measures for the consequences of which they are responsible.

No individual State could with propriety complain of invasion of its territorial rights—The independent nations and tribes of indians ought to be considered as foreign nations, not as the subjects of any particular State—each individual state indeed will retain the right of pre-emption of all lands within its limits, which will not be abridged—But the general Sovereignty must possess the right of making all treaties, on the execution or violation of which depend peace or war.

Whatever may have been the conduct of some of the late British Colonies in their separate capacities toward the indians, yet the same cannot be charged against the national character of the United States.

It is only since they possess the powers of Sovereignty, that they are responsible for their conduct.

But in future the obligations of policy, humanity and justice, together with that respect which every nation sacredly owes to its own reputation unite in requiring a noble, liberal, and disinterested administration of indian affairs.

Although the disposition of the people of the States to emigrate into the indian country cannot be effectually prevented, it may be restrained and regulated.

It may be restrained by postponing new purchases of indian territory, and by prohibiting the citizens from intruding on the indian Lands.

It may be regulated by forming Colonies under the direction of Government, and by posting a body of troops to execute their orders.

As population shall encrease, and approach the indian boundaries, Game will be diminished, and new purchases may be made for small considerations—This has been and probably will be the inevitable consequence of cultivation.

It is however painful to consider that all the Indian tribes once existing in those States, now the best cultivated and most populous, have become extinct—If the same causes continued, the same effects will happen, and in a short period the idea of an indian on this side the Mississippi will only be found in the Page of the historian.

How different would be the sensation of a philosophic mind to reflect that instead of exterminating a part of the human race by our modes of population that we had persevered through all difficulties and at last had imparted our knowledge of cultivation, and the arts, to the Aboriginals of the Country by which the source of future life and happiness had been preserved and extended. But it has been conceived to be impracticable to civilize the indians of north America—This opinion is probably more convenient than just.

That the civilization of the indians would be an operation of complicated difficulty—That it would require the highest knowledge of the human character, and a steady perseverence in a wise system for a series of years cannot be doubted—But to deny that under a course of favorable circumstances it could not be accomplished is to suppose the human character under the influence of such stubborn habits as to be incapable of melioration or change—a supposition entirely contradicted by the progress of society from the barbarous ages to its present degree of perfection.

While it is contended that the object is practicable under a proper system, it is admitted in the fullest force to be impracticable according to the ordinary course of things, and that it could not be effected in a short period.

Were it possible to introduce among the indian tribes a love for exclusive property it would be a happy commencement of the business.

This might be brought about by making presents from time to time to the Cheifs or their wives of Sheep and other domestic animals—and if in the first instance persons were appointed to take charge and teach the use of them a considerable part of the difficulty would be surmounted.

In the administration of the indians every proper expedient that can be devised to gain their affections, and attach them to the interest of the Union should be adopted—The British Government had the practice of making the indians presents of silver medals and Gorgets, uniform Clothing, and a sort of military Commission—The possessors retained an exclusive property to these articles—and the Southern indians are exceedingly desirous of receiving similar gifts from the United States for which they would willingly resign those received from the British Officers—The policy of gratifying them cannot be doubted.

Missionaries of excellent moral character should be appointed to reside in their nation, who should be well supplied with all the implements of husbandry and the necessary stock for a farm.

These men should be made the instruments to work on the indians—presents should commonly pass through their hands or by their recommendations—They should in no degree be concerned in trade, or the purchase of lands to rouse the jealousy of the indians—They should be their friends and fathers.

Such a plan although it might not fully effect the civilization of the Indians would most probably be attended with the salutary effect of attaching them to the interest of the United States.

It is particularly important that something of this nature should be attempted with the southern nations of indians, whose confined situation might render them proper subjects for the experiment.

The expence of such a conciliatory system may be considered as a sufficient reason for rejecting it.

But when this shall be compared with a system of coercion it would be found the highest oeconomy to adopt it.

The commanding Officers of the troops on the frontiers of the Southern and Northern districts as they possess the sword should be the indian Agents and for which they should have a consideration.

Every article given to the Indians should be accounted for and witnessed by two commissioned officers.

The commanding officer should not receive any presents from the indians but in every respect conduct towards them in the most friendly and just manner.

All which is humbly submitted to the President of the United States.

H. Knox

War Office 7th. July 1789

Transcribed Reports and Communications from Executive Departments, 1789–1814, (War Department, Southern Indians), Records of the Secretary, SR, DNA.

House Resolution
August 8, 1789

RESOLVED, That it is the opinion of this committee, that an act ought to pass, providing for the necessary expences attending any negociations or treaties which may be held with the Indian tribes, or attending the appointment of commissioners for those purposes.

HJ, p. 140.

Senate Committee Report
August 17, 1789

Resolved that there be allowed and paid to a Superintendant of Indian affairs for the So. Department that may be nominated by the President and appointed by and with the advice and consent of the Senate, the sum of
       per day including his expences for the time he may be employed in attending a treaty proposed to be held by the Commissioners of the United States and the Creek Indians at the Rock landing in the State of Georgia on the 15th day of Septr. next.

Resolved that in case the proposed treaty should fail in the desired object of establishing peace between the Citizens of the United States and Creek Indians, Congress will make such Grants of money and pursue such other measures as will be necessary for the protection and safety of the Inhabitants
                                         best
of the Southern frontiers and ∧ secure the peace of the United States.

The report, in the hand of Few, is in Various Select Committee Reports, SR, DNA. Otis wrote "Passed in the Negative." at the bottom.

Senate Resolutions
August 17, 1789

RESOLVED, That the President of the United States be requested to nominate a fit person for Superintendant of Indian Affairs in the Southern Department, in order that he may be sent forward as soon as may be, to act with the Commissioners of Indian Affairs in the Southern Department, appointed pursuant to a resolution of Congress, passed on the   day of
and aid them in carrying into effect a Treaty that is proposed to be held with the Creek Nation, on the 15th day of September next, in the State of Georgia, at the Rock-Landing—

That the sum of   dollars be delivered to the said Superintendant, to be appropriated for the immediate purpose of the said Treaty, for which sum he shall be accountable—

That the President of the United States be requested to instruct the said Superintendant and Commissioners, to hear and fully investigate all the complaints and grievances, of the said Creek Indians, and to use all the means in their power to quiet their minds and do them ample justice, agreeably to the aforesaid resolution of Congress, and instructions heretofore given for that purpose: That if the said Indians should prove refractory, or refuse to treat and establish peace on just and reasonable terms, then and in that case, the said Superintendant and Commissioners be directed to make immediate report thereof to the President of the United States, and Congress will make such grants of money, and pursue such other measures, as will be necessary for the safety and protection of the inhabitants of the Southern frontiers, and best secure the peace of the United States.

RESOLVED, That the President of the United States be authorised and empowered, and he is hereby authorised and empowered, should the Creek Indians decline to make peace with the State of Georgia, to take effectual measures for covering the State of Georgia from the incursions of the Indians, either by ordering some of the troops now at Fort Harmar to march to the frontiers of Georgia, or by embodying such a number of the militia as he shall think sufficient to insure to the citizens of Georgia protection, and the cultivation of their lands in peace and security, and that he be empowered to draw on the Treasury for defraying the expenses of the same.

SLJ, pp. 122–23. A draft of the second resolution, in the hand of Otis, is in Various Select Committee Reports, SR, DNA. Otis noted on it, "Motion by Mr. Butler."

<h2 style="text-align:center">Senate Resolution
August 18, 1789</h2>

RESOLVED, That Congress will make provision for the discharging of any expenses that may be incurred by such military arrangements, as the President of the United States may think proper to make, for the purpose of protecting the citizens of Georgia from the depredations of the Creek Indians, should peace not take place with them, or should they, having agreed to a peace, violate the same.

SLJ, p. 124.

Indian Treaty Act [HR-50b]
July 22, 1790

AN ACT PROVIDING FOR HOLDING A
TREATY OR TREATIES TO ESTABLISH PEACE
WITH CERTAIN INDIAN TRIBES

BE IT ENACTED BY THE SENATE AND HOUSE OF REPRESENTATIVES OF THE UNITED STATES OF AMERICA IN CONGRESS ASSEMBLED, That in addition to the balance unexpended of the sum of twenty thousand dollars appropriated by the Act intituled "An Act providing for the expences which may attend negociations or treaties with the Indian tribes, and the appointment of Commissioners for managing the same," a farther sum not exceeding twenty thousand dollars arising from the duties on imports and tonnage, shall be, and the same is hereby appropriated for defraying the expences of negociating, and holding a treaty or treaties, and for promoting a friendly intercourse, and preserving peace with the Indian tribes.

FREDERICK AUGUSTUS MUHLENBERG
    Speaker of the House of Representatives
JOHN ADAMS
    Vice-President of the United States, and
    President of the Senate

Approved July
  the Twenty second
    1790

GO. WASHINGTON
    President of the United States

I certify that this Act did originate
in the House of Representatives.
JOHN BECKLEY—Clerk

Enrolled Acts, RG 11, DNA.

Calendar

Date	House	Senate
1790		
Jan. 12	President's message enclosing a report of the secretary of war received and partly read.[1]	
Jan. 13	Report read and referred to Wadsworth, Brown, Boudinot, Burke, and Baldwin.	
Jan. 14	Livermore, Ames, Laurance, Scott, and Smith (Md.) added to committee.	
Jan. 20	Wadsworth presented committee report, which was read.	
Jan. 21	Read; debated and agreed to in COWH; House debated report.	
Jan. 22	Secret session of House apparently agreed to COWH report.[2]	
Mar. 3	Secret session.[3]	
Mar. 5	Secret session.[4]	
Mar. 25	Secret session.[5]	
Mar. 29		*An Act providing for holding a treaty or treaties, to establish peace with certain Indian tribes* received and read.

[1] The president's message is printed in the *SLJ*, p. 221. The secretary's report is printed with the Military Establishment Act [HR-50a]. The actions of January 12, 13, 20, and 21, although reported in the *HJ*, took place in secret sessions, according to the newspaper accounts (*GUS*, Jan. 13; *NYJ*, Jan. 14; *NYDG*, Jan. 21; *NYDA*, Jan. 22).

[2] *GUS, NYWM*, Jan. 23.

[3] *NYP*, Mar. 4. It is probable that this bill was discussed in this secret session, as well as those of March 5 and 25.

[4] *GUS*, Mar. 6.

[5] *GUS*, Mar. 27.

Date	House	Senate
1790		
Apr. 5		Read and postponed.
May 4		Debated and postponed.
July 9		Committed to Schuyler, Gunn, and Langdon.
July 16		Schuyler presented *committee report;* committee *amendment* adopted as an amendment to the bill.[6]
July 17	Senate amendment agreed to.	Read and agreed to with an amendment.
July 20	Signed by speaker.	Signed by vice president.
July 22	Signed by president.	

[6] A *report of the secretary of war,* dated July 15, and sent to Schuyler as the chairman of the committee, was used to prepare the report of July 16.

Indian Treaty Bill [HR-50b]
March 29, 1790

An Act providing for holding a treaty or
treaties to establish peace with certain
Indian tribes

BE IT ENACTED BY THE SENATE AND HOUSE OF REPRESENTATIVES OF THE UNITED STATES OF AMERICA IN CONGRESS ASSEMBLED, That in addition to the balance unexpended of the sum of twenty thousand dollars appropriated by the Act intituled "An Act providing for the expences which may attend negociations or treaties with the Indian tribes, and the appointment of Commissioners for managing the same," a farther sum not exceeding twenty thousand dollars arising from the duties on imports and tonnage, shall be, and the same is hereby appropriated for defraying the expences of negociating, and holding a treaty or treaties[1] with the Indian tribes.

The bill as it passed the House has not been located. The above is a reconstruction of the text of the bill at this point.

[1] The Senate inserted "and for promoting a friendly intercourse and preserving peace" at this point. *SLJ,* p. 421n.

Report of the Secretary of War
July 16, 1790

STATEMENT of 20,000 dollars appropriated by Congress on the 20th August 1789 for the expences of negociations with Indian Tribes.

Expended by the Commissioners for treating with the southern indians, including an advance of 500 dollars to Governor St. Clair, & 425.51 dollars to equip George M. White Eyes as pr. Statement made 31. Decr. 1789.   6,768.46

Balance unexpended, rendered in statement made 31. December 1789   4,951.40

Received from the sales of goods in Georgia since 31. December 1789   1,988.51   6,939.91

This sum or the greater part thereof may be required to defray the expences which have arisen or may arise in consequence of the visit of the Creek chiefs.

The amount of goods remaining in Georgia and the charges thereon   6,291.63

Many of the indian goods remaining on hand are liable to waste and damage, being of a perishable nature.

Dollars   20,000.

War-office
July 15, 1790
    H. KNOX
The Honble. Mr. Schuyler—Chairman of the Committee of the Senate

Reports from the Secretary of War, SR, DNA.

Senate Committee Report
July 16, 1790

The Committee to whom was referred the bill, providing for holding a treaty or Treaties to Establish peace with Certain Indian tribes Beg leave to report.

That It appears from a statement delivered to Your Committee by the Secretary for the department of war that of the 20,000 Dollars appropriated by Act of the 20th Augst. 1789 there remains

unexpended in Cash   6,939.91 Dollars

And in goods lodged in the State of Georgia, to the amount of   6,291.63

That the unexpended Cash may be required to defray the Expences which have arisen & may arise in consequence of the Intended visit of the Creek chiefs.

That the said Secretary ᐱverbally informed Your Committee—that in Addition to the goods in Georgia—such further Goods and Money would probably be wanted for carrying into full Effect the treaty ~~as~~ contemplated with the Creeks, and with ~~other treaties with~~ ᐱ ~~different~~ tribes,ᐱtogether with douceurs to the most influential Characters amongst the Indians ~~as~~ would require a further appropriation of 20,000 dollars.

Your Committee are therefore of Opinion that the bill should pass to a third reading with the following amendment If the same should be adopted by the Senate.

Between the words *treaties* and *with* in the last line except one, insert, *and for preserving a friendly intercourse.*

Various Select Committee Reports, SR, DNA, hand of Schuyler.

Inspection Act [HR-48]

April 2, 1790

AN ACT TO PREVENT THE EXPORTATION OF GOODS NOT DULY INSPECTED ACCORDING TO THE LAWS OF THE SEVERAL STATES

BE IT ENACTED BY THE SENATE AND HOUSE OF REPRESENTATIVES OF THE UNITED STATES OF AMERICA, IN CONGRESS ASSEMBLED, That the Collectors and other Officers of the Customs in the several ports of the United States, be, and they are hereby directed to pay due regard to the Inspection-laws of the States in which they may respectively act, in such manner, that no Vessel having on board Goods liable to inspection, shall be cleared out until the Master or other proper person shall have produced such Certificate that all such Goods have been duly inspected as the laws of the respective States do, or may require to be produced to Collectors or other Officers of the Customs.

> FREDERICK AUGUSTUS MUHLENBERG
> Speaker of the House of Representatives
> JOHN ADAMS
> Vice President of the United States and
> President of the Senate

Approved April
the second
1790

> GO. WASHINGTON
> President of the United States

I certify that this Act did originate in the House of Representatives.
JOHN BECKLEY—Clerk

Enrolled Acts, RG 11, DNA.

Calendar

Date	House	Senate
1790		
Mar. 3		*Izard* introduced a *resolution* relative to inspection of vessels.
Mar. 4		Upon motion of Ellsworth,[1] resolution committed to Izard, Strong, and Bassett.
Mar. 5	Senate resolution received.	Izard reported for committee and *resolution* as reported agreed to.
Mar. 8	Resolution committed to White, Tucker, and Contee to prepare a bill; White presented "a bill to prevent the exportation of goods not duly inspected according to the laws of the several states," which was read.	
Mar. 9	Read.	
Mar. 10– 25	Postponed as order of the day; motion to consider made by Smith (S.C.?) on March 13.[2]	
Mar. 26	Debated and amended in COWH;[3] House agreed to amendment.	
Mar. 29	Read; agreed to.	Read.
Mar. 30		Read.
Mar. 31		Read; agreed to.
Apr. 1	Signed by speaker.	Signed by vice president.
Apr. 2	Signed by president.	

[1] This motion, in the hand of Ellsworth and labeled "Mr. Ellsworths motion to commit Mr. Izards motion" is in Senate Simple Resolutions, SR, DNA.
[2] *NYDG,* Mar. 15.
[3] *GUS,* Mar. 27; *NYDG,* Mar. 29.

Izard Resolution
March 3, 1790

Resolved by the Senate, & House of Representatives, that the Secretary of the Treasury direct the respective Collectors in the several Ports of the United States, not to clear out any Vessel having Articles on board, subject to inspection by the Laws of the State, from which such Vessel shall be about to depart, without having previously obtained such Manifests, & other Documents as are enjoined by the said Laws.

Senate Simple Resolutions, SR, DNA, hand of Izard.

Senate Resolution
March 5, 1790

Resolved by the Senate, & House of Representatives of the United States in Congress assembled—That the respective Collectors in the several Ports of the United States be directed not to grant a clearance for any Ship, or Vessel having articles on board, subject to inspection by the Laws of the State from which such Ship, or Vessel shall be about to depart, without having previously obtained such Manifests, & other Documents as are enjoined by the said Laws.

Senate Simple Resolutions, SR, DNA, hand of Izard.

Invalid Officers Bill [HR-59]

Calendar

Date	House	Senate
1790		
Apr. 28	Burke gave notice of intention to move for appointment of a committee to bring in a bill for relief of a certain description of officers.[1]	
Apr. 29	Burke motion "that a committee be appointed to bring in a bill for directing the Commissioners of Army Accounts to issue certificates in favor of a certain description of officers," debated and agreed to; motion by Vining "that proper officers be authorized to issue certificates to a certain description of invalid officers" debated;[2] committee to prepare bill appointed (Burke, Contee, and Coles).	
Apr. 30	Burke presented a bill, which was read.	
May 3	Read.	

[1] *NYDG*, Apr. 20. The Senate disagreed to the Officers Bill [HR-53] on April 23.
[2] *NYDG*, Apr. 30.

Date	House	Senate
1790		
May 4	Read; blanks filled; agreed to as *An act to authorize the issuing of certificates to a certain description of invalid officers.*	Received and read.
May 5		Read; committed to Schuyler, Hawkins, and Ellsworth.
July 7		Schuyler presented committee report; bill read and disagreed to.

Invalid Officers Bill [HR-59]
May 4, 1790

AN ACT to authorise the issuing of Certificates to a certain description of invalid Officers

[1] BE IT ENACTED by the Senate and House of Representatives of the United States of America in Congress assembled, that such of the Commissioned Officers of the late Army as have received the Commutation of their Half-pay for life, and who having been examined in their State respectively were adjudged entitled to receive Pensions as Invalids at a less rate than half their monthly pay, shall be entered on the invalid list of the United States, when they shall return to the public such proportion of their Commutation, as their respective pensions shall bear to half their Monthly pay while in Service. PROVIDED ALWAYS, that such of the aforesaid description of Officers, as shall not avail themselves of the benefit of this Act before the first day of one thousand seven hundred and   shall ever thereafter be precluded therefrom.

[2] AND BE IT FURTHER ENACTED, that such of the Officers of the late Army as have been admitted on the invalid list, at a less pension than half their monthly pay, and who were entitled to the Commutation of half pay for life, and have returned or have not received the same, shall be entitled to receive, or in case of their death, their Representatives shall be entitled to receive of the Commissioner of Army Accounts, such proportion of the

Commutation aforesaid, as their pensions shall be less than half their monthly pay while in service.

1790. the 4th. of May.

Read the third time and passed the House of Representatives

JOHN BECKLEY, Clerk

Engrossed House Bills, HR, DNA.

Invalid Pensioners Act [HR-29]

September 29, 1789

AN ACT PROVIDING FOR THE PAYMENT OF THE INVALID PENSIONERS OF THE UNITED STATES

BE IT ENACTED BY THE SENATE AND HOUSE OF REPRESENTATIVES OF THE UNITED STATES OF AMERICA IN CONGRESS ASSEMBLED, that the Military pensions which have been granted and paid by the States respectively, in pursuance of the Acts of the United States in Congress assembled, to the Invalids who were wounded and disabled during the late War, shall be continued and paid by the United States, from the fourth day of March last, for the space of one year, under such regulations as the President of the United States may direct.

FREDERICK AUGUSTUS MUHLENBERG
Speaker of the House of Representatives
JOHN ADAMS
Vice President of the United States, and
President of the Senate

Approved September
the Twenty ninth
1789

GO. WASHINGTON
President of the United States

I certify that this Act did originate
in the House of Representatives.
JOHN BECKLEY—Clerk

Enrolled Acts, RG 11, DNA.

Calendar

Date	House	Senate
1789		
June 29	Petition of William Finnie, for "a reimbursement of monies expended by him in the public service" as deputy quartermaster general in the southern department during the late war, presented by Parker[1] and read.	
Sept. 4	Petition of James Gibbon, "praying that his claim for military services, rendered during the late war, may be liquidated and satisfied," presented and read; petition of invalid pensioners of Pennsylvania, "praying relief in consideration of the payments of their pensions being stopped by an act of the legislature of that state," presented by Hiester and read; on a motion by Partridge,[2] the latter petition, together with other petitions of invalid pensioners previously received, was referred to Hiester, Wadsworth, and Gilman to bring in a bill.	
Sept. 5	Petition of Archibald McAlister, "praying that his claim for military services during the late war,	

---

[1] *GUS,* July 1.
[2] *GUS,* Sept. 5.

Calendar

Date	House	Senate
1789		
	may be liquidated and satisfied," presented, read, and referred, with the petitions of James Gibbon and William Finnie, to the above committee.	
Sept. 18	Hiester presented a bill,[3] which was read.	
Sept. 19	Read and committed to COWH.	
Sept. 21– 23	Postponed as order of the day.	
Sept. 24	Debated in COWH and reported without amendment; recommitted to select committee.	
Sept. 25	Hiester reported an amendment, which was agreed to; bill read and agreed to as "An act making provision for the invalid pensioners of the United States."	Received.
Sept. 26		Read; committed to Read, Butler, King, Ellsworth, and Morris.
Sept. 28		Read reported concurrence; bill read twice and agreed
	Signed by speaker.	to; signed by vice president.
Sept. 29	Signed by president.	

[3] The *NYDA*, Sept. 19, printed a summary of the bill as follows:
 This bill provides that inspectors shall be appointed, one in each state, to whom the invalids shall resort for examination, except those who may be incapable of moving, in which case the inspectors shall examine them at their place of abode, or procure by other measures the necessary information of their situation and merit—and that a certain part of the avails of the Impost be appropriated to pay the pension list. Provided, that no commissioned officer who has received commutation, shall be entitled to the benefits of the act.

Invalid Pensioners Act [HR-80]
July 16, 1790

AN ACT FURTHER TO PROVIDE FOR THE PAYMENT OF THE INVALID PENSIONERS OF THE UNITED STATES

BE IT ENACTED BY THE SENATE AND HOUSE OF REPRESENTATIVES OF THE UNITED STATES OF AMERICA IN CONGRESS ASSEMBLED, That the Military pensions which have been granted and paid by the States respectively, in pursuance of former Acts of the United States in Congress assembled, and such as by Acts passed in the present Session of Congress, are, or shall be declared to be due to Invalids who were wounded and disabled during the late War, shall be continued and paid by the United States, from the fourth day of March last, for the space of one year, under such regulations as the President of the United States may direct.

> FREDERICK AUGUSTUS MUHLENBERG
>> Speaker of the House of Representatives
>
> JOHN ADAMS
>> Vice-President of the United States, and
>> President of the Senate

Approved July the 16th. 1790

> GO. WASHINGTON
>> President of the United States

I certify that this Act did originate in the House of Representatives.
JOHN BECKLEY—Clerk

Enrolled Acts, RG 11, DNA.

Calendar

Date	House	Senate
1790		
Feb. 1	On a motion by Hiester,[1] committee to prepare appointed (Hiester, Partridge, and Hathorn).	
June 29	Hiester presented a bill, which was read.	
June 30	Read.	
July 1	Read; agreed to as *An act further to provide for the payment of the invalid pensioners of the United States.*	Received.
July 2, 6		Read.
July 7		Read; agreed to with an *amendment.*
July 9	Senate amendment agreed to.	
July 12	Signed by speaker.	Signed by vice president.
July 16	Signed by president.[2]	

[1] *NYDA,* Feb. 2.
[2] The provisions of this act were extended to March 4, 1792, by the Mitigation of Forfeitures Act [S-24].

Invalid Pensioners Bill [HR-80]
July 1, 1790

An Act further to provide for the payment of the invalid pensioners of the United States

Be it enacted by the Senate and House of Representatives of the United States of America in Congress assembled, That the Military pensions which have been granted and paid by the States respectively, in pursuance of former Acts of the United States in Congress assembled, and such as by Acts passed in the present Session of Congress, are[1]

[1] The Senate inserted "or shall be" at this point.

declared to be due to Invalids who were wounded and disabled during the late War, shall be continued and paid by the United States, from the fourth day of March last, for the space of one year, under such regulations as the President of the United States may direct.

The bill as it passed the House has not been located. The above is a reconstruction of the text of the bill at this point. The amendment is from the *SLJ*, p. 402n.

Judicial Officers Bill [HR-126]

Calendar

Date	House	Senate
1790		
Mar. 24	Motion by Sedgwick, to appoint committee "to consider and report what provisions shall be made for the support of the officers of the supreme judicial court," tabled.[1]	
July 30	Motion by Sedgwick, to appoint committee "for making provision for the officers of the judiciary courts of the United States, and for jurors, &c.," agreed to and Smith (S.C.), Benson, and Vining appointed.[2]	
Aug. 5	Motion by Benson, to discharge committee and to have the attorney general report on the subject in the next session, agreed to.[3]	
1791		
Jan. 13	Sedgwick gave notice of intention to move to di-	

---

[1] *GUS*, Mar. 27.
[2] *NYDG*, July 31. The *HJ* for this date records no action on this subject.
[3] *NYDA*, *NYDG*, Aug. 6. The *HJ* for this date records no action on this subject.

Date	House	Senate
1791		
	rect the attorney general to report a bill.[4]	
Feb. 3	On a motion by Sedgwick,[5] committee appointed (Sedgwick, Sturges, and Contee) to bring in a bill "to establish a temporary provision for the clerks of the several judicial courts of the United States, for the marshals of districts, and for the attendance and services of jurors in the circuit and district courts."	
Feb. 11	Sedgwick presented a bill "providing compensations for clerks, marshals and jurors," which was read twice and committed to COWH.	
Feb. 12	Petition of John Tucker, "praying compensation for his past services and expences, as clerk to the supreme court of the United States," referred with the bill to the COWH.	
Feb. 15–18	Bill postponed as order of the day.	
Feb. 19	Debated in COWH.	
Feb. 21	Debated in COWH; COWH agreed to an amendment that would	

[4] *PaM*, Jan. 15.
[5] *FG*, Feb. 3.

Date	House	Senate
1791		
	"leave the compensations to arise altogether from fees"; amendment amended and agreed to by House; bill and amendment recommitted to Sherman, Benson, Seney, White, and Livermore to report a table of fees.[6]	

[6] *GUS,* Feb. 23. The committee reported the Judicial Officers Bill [HR-133] on February 24.

Judicial Officers Act [HR-133]

March 3, 1791

An Act providing compensations for
the officers of the Judicial Courts of
the United States and for Jurors and
Witnesses, and for other purposes

[1] Be it enacted by the Senate and House of Representatives
of the United States of America in Congress assembled, that there
be allowed to the several officers following in addition to the fees (except
milage to the marshals) to which they are otherwise by law intitled, and also
to jurors and witnesses, in the Courts of the United States, the following
respective compensations, that is to say: To the Attorney of the United States
for the district, for his expenses and time in traveling from the place of his
abode to any Court of the United States, on which his attendance shall be
requisite, at the rate of ten Cents per mile going, and the same allowance for
returning; to the Clerk of the District Court, for attending in the district or
circuit Court, five dollars per day, and the like compensation for traveling, as
is above allowed to the Attorney for the district; to the Clerk of the Supreme
Court for attending in Court eight dollars per day; to the Marshal of the
district, for attending the Supreme, Circuit or District Courts, five dollars
per day; for summoning a Grand Jury three dollars, and for summoning a
Petit Jury two dollars, and for serving and returning a Writ, five cents per
mile for his necessary travel; to the grand and petit Jurors, each fifty cents per
day for attending in Court, and for traveling, at the rate of fifty cents for
every ten miles from their respective places of abode, to the place where the
Court is held, and the like allowance for returning; to witnesses summoned
on the part of the United States, or in behalf of any prisoner to be tried for any
capital offence in any of the Courts thereof, the same compensation as is above
allowed to grand and petit Jurors. That the several officers above specified
shall be deemed to have been intitled to the above respective compensations,
from the time of their respective appointments; and that the grand and petit
Jurors and witnesses, who have heretofore attended, shall also be deemed
intitled to the above compensation, in like manner as those who shall hereafter attend. That there shall also be paid to the Marshal, the amount of the

expense for fuel, candles, and other reasonable contingencies for holding a Court, as hath accrued or shall accrue; and the compensations to the grand and petit Jurors and Witnesses shall be included in the account of, and paid to the Marshal, to the use of, and be by him accordingly paid over to the several persons intitled to the same: And the accounts of the several officers for the compensations aforesaid, (except milage to the Marshal, for the service of Writs in civil causes) having been previously examined and certified by the Judge of the district, shall be passed in the usual manner at, and the amount thereof paid, out of the Treasury of the United States. And a sum arising from the fines and forfeitures to the United States, and equal to the amount thereof, is hereby appropriated for the payment of the above accounts.

[2] AND BE IT FURTHER ENACTED, that instead of the provisions in that respect heretofore made, the first sessions of the Circuit Courts in the Eastern Circuit, after the passing of this Act, shall commence at the times following; that is to say: In NEW YORK district, on the fifth, and in CONNECTICUT district, on the twenty fifth days of April next; in MASSACHUSETTS district, on the twelfth, and in NEW-HAMPSHIRE district on the twenty fourth days of May next; and in RHODE-ISLAND district, on the seventh day of June next; and the subsequent Sessions in the respective districts, on the like days of every sixth Calendar month thereafter; except when any of those days shall happen on a Sunday, and then the sessions shall commence on the next day following. And the Sessions of the said Circuit Court shall be held in NEW HAMPSHIRE district at Portsmouth and Exeter alternately, beginning at the first: In MASSACHUSETTS district, at Boston, In RHODE ISLAND district at Newport and Providence, alternately, beginning at the first; In CONNECTICUT district at Hartford and New Haven, alternately, beginning at the last: And in NEW YORK district at the City of New York only.

[3] AND BE IT FURTHER ENACTED, that from and after the passing of this Act, instead of the provisions in the Act for that purpose, the Sessions of the Circuit Court for the district of VIRGINIA shall be holden in the City of Richmond only.

[4] AND BE IT FURTHER ENACTED that this Act shall continue in force until the end of the next Session of Congress and no longer.

> FREDERICK AUGUSTUS MUHLENBERG
> Speaker of the House of Representatives
> JOHN ADAMS
> Vice President of the United States and
> President of the Senate

Approved March
the third
1791

> GO. WASHINGTON
> President of the United States

I certify that this Act did originate
in the House of Representatives.
                JOHN BECKLEY—Clerk

Enrolled Acts, RG 11, DNA.

Calendar

Date	House	Senate
1791		
Feb. 24	Sherman, on behalf of the committee to which the Judicial Officers Bill [HR-126] was recommitted, presented "an amendatory bill providing compensation for the officers of the several courts of law, and for jurors and witnesses," which was read twice and committed to COWH; 100 copies ordered printed.[1]	
Feb. 25–26	Postponed as order of the day.	
Feb. 28	Debated in COWH; House agreed to add a section altering the times of holding the district courts in the eastern circuit; another amendment, making Richmond the only place where the circuit court for the district of Virginia could be held, was agreed to; a third amendment was also agreed to.[2]	

[1] *FG*, Feb. 24.
[2] *GA*, Mar. 1.

Date	House	Senate
1791		
Mar. 1	Read; agreed to by a recorded vote of 30–23 as *An act providing compensations to the officers of the judicial courts of the United States, and to jurors and witnesses, and for other purposes.*	Read; ordered printed.
Mar. 2		Read; committed to Ellsworth, Henry, and King.
Mar. 3		Ellsworth reported amendments, which were agreed to; bill read and agreed to with *amendments;*
	Senate amendments considered; some agreed to, others disagreed to;	3rd and 4th amendments which were disagreed to by House, receded from; signed by vice president.
	signed by speaker and by president.	

Judicial Officers Bill [HR-133]
March 1, 1791

An ACT providing compensations for the officers of the judicial courts of the United States, and for jurors and witnesses, and for other purposes

Sect. I. BE it enacted by the Senate and House of Representatives of the United States of America, in Congress assembled, That there be allowed to the several officers following, in addition to the fees (except mileage to the Marshals) to which they are otherwise by law entitled, and also to jurors and witnesses, in the courts of the United States, the following respective compensations; that is to say, To the Attorney of the United States for the district, for his expences and time in travelling from the place in the State where the office of the Clerk of the district court is kept, to the other place in the district where a circuit court is directed to be held,[1] at the rate of ten cents per mile going, and the same allowance for returning.

To the Clerk of the district court, for attending in the district or circuit court, five dollars per day, and the like compensation for travelling as is above allowed to the Attorney for the district.

To the Clerk of the supreme court, for attending in court, eight dollars per day.

To the marshal of the district, for attending the supreme circuit or district courts, five dollars per day; for summoning a grand jury three dollars, and for summoning a petit jury two dollars, and for serving a writ five cents per mile from the place where the office of the clerk of the district court is kept, to the place where the writ shall be served, but there shall not in any case be an allowance of mileage to the marshals exceeding one hundred miles;[2] to the grand and petit jurors, each fifty cents per day, for attending in court, and for travelling, at the rate of fifty cents for every ten miles, from their respective places of abode, to the place where the court is held, and the like allowance for returning;[3] to witnesses summoned on the part of the United States, or in behalf of any prisoner to be tried for any capital offence in any of the courts thereof, the same compensation as is above allowed to grand and petit jurors.[4] That the several officers above specified, shall be deemed to have been entitled to the above respective compensations, from the time of their respective appointments, and that the grand and petit jurors and witnesses who have heretofore attended, shall also be deemed entitled to the above compensation, in like manner as those who shall hereafter attend.

That there shall also be paid to the marshal the amount of the expence for fuel, candles and other reasonable contingencies for holding a court, as hath accrued or shall accrue, and the compensations to the grand and petit jurors, and witnesses, shall be included in the account of, and paid to the marshal, to the use of and be by him accordingly paid over to the several persons entitled to the same: And the accounts of the several officers for the compensations aforesaid (except mileage to the marshal, for the service of writs in civil

---

[1] The Senate struck out from "in the State where" through "directed to be held" and inserted "of his abode, to any court of the United States, on which his attendance shall be requisite."

[2] The Senate struck out from "a writ five cents" through "one hundred miles"; and inserted "and returning a writ, five cents per mile, for his necessary travel."

[3] The Senate struck out from "each fifty cents per day" through "allowance for returning" and inserted "such compensations respectively as they would by law be entitled to for attending the courts of the State of which they are citizens." The House disagreed to this amendment.

[4] The Senate struck out "the same compensation as is above allowed to grand and petit jurors," and inserted "each fifty cents per day for attending in court, and for travelling five cents per mile, from their respective places of abode to the place where the court is held, and the like allowance for returning." The House disagreed to this amendment.

causes) having been previously examined and certified by the Judge of the district, shall be passed in the usual manner at, and the amount thereof paid out of the Treasury of the United States. And a sum arising from the fines and forfeitures to the United States, and equal to the amount thereof, is hereby appropriated for the payment of the above accounts.

Sect. II. And be it further enacted, That instead of the provisions in that respect heretofore made, the first session of the circuit courts in the Eastern Circuit, after the passing of this act, shall commence at the times following; that is to say—In New-York district, on the fifth, and in Connecticut district, on the twenty-fifth days of April next; in Massachusetts district, on the twelfth, and in New-Hampshire district, on the twenty-fourth days of May next; and in Rhode-Island district, on the seventh day of June next; and the subsequent sessions in the respective districts, on the like days of every sixth callender month thereafter, except when any of those days shall happen on a Sunday, and then the sessions shall commence on the next day following. And the sessions of the said circuit court shall be held in New-Hampshire district, at Portsmouth and Exeter alternately, beginning at the first; in Massachusetts district, at Boston; in Rhode-Island district, at New-Port and Providence alternately, beginning at the first; in Connecticut district, at Hartford and New-Haven alternately, beginning at the last; and in New-York district, at the city of New-York only.

Sect. III. And be it further enacted, That from and after the passing of this act, instead of the provisions in the act for that purpose, the sessions of the circuit court for the district of Virginia, shall be holden in the city of Richmond only.

Sect. IV. And be it further enacted, That this act shall continue in force until the end of the next session of Congress, and no longer.

March 1st, 1791, Passed the House of Representatives.

Before the Senate, for concurrence.

Printed by JOHN FENNO

House Bills, SR, DNA. The amendments are from the *SLJ*, p. 694.

Judiciary Act [S-1]

September 24, 1789

An Act to establish the Judicial Courts of the United States

[1] Be it enacted by the Senate and House of Representatives of the United States of America in Congress assembled, That the Supreme Court of the United States shall consist of a Chief Justice and five associate Justices, any four of whom shall be a quorum and shall hold annually at the seat of government two sessions, the one commencing the first Monday of February, and the other the first Monday of August. That the associate Justices shall have precedence according to the date of their Commissions, or when the Commissions of two or more of them bear date on the same day, according to their respective ages.

[2] And be it further enacted, That the United States shall be, and they hereby are divided into thirteen districts to be limited and called as follows, to wit: One to consist of that part of the State of Massachusetts which lies easterly of the State of New-Hampshire, and to be called Main district; One to consist of the State of New Hampshire, and to be called New-Hampshire district; One to consist of the remaining part of the State of Massachusetts, and to be called Massachusetts district; One to consist of the State of Connecticut, and to be called Connecticut district; One to consist of the State of New York, and to be called New York district; One to consist of the State of New Jersey, and to be called New Jersey district; One to consist of the State of Pennsylvania, and to be called Pennsylvania district; One to consist of the State of Delaware, and to be called Delaware district; One to consist of the State of Maryland, and to be called Maryland district; One to consist of the State of Virginia, except that part called the district of Kentucky, and to be called Virginia district; One to consist of the remaining part of the State of Virginia, and to be called Kentucky district; One to consist of the State of South Carolina, and to be called South Carolina district; and one to consist of the State of Georgia, and to be called Georgia district.

[3] And be it further enacted, That there be a Court called a district Court in each of the afore mentioned districts to consist of one Judge, who shall reside in the district for which he is appointed, and shall be called a

district Judge, and shall hold annually four Sessions, the first of which to commence as follows, to wit, in the districts of New York, and of New Jersey on the first, in the district of Pennsylvania on the second, in the district of Connecticut on the third, and in the district of Delaware on the fourth Tuesdays of November next, in the districts of Massachusetts, of Main and of Maryland on the first, in the district of Georgia on the second, and in the districts of New Hampshire, of Virginia and of Kentucky on the third Tuesdays of December next; and the other three Sessions progressively in the respective districts on the like Tuesdays of every third Calendar Month afterwards; and in the district of South Carolina, on the third Monday in March and September; the first Monday in July, and the second Monday in December of each and every year, commencing in December next; and that the district Judge shall have power to hold special Courts at his discretion. That the stated district Court shall be held at the places following, to wit, in the district of Main at Portland and Pownalsborough alternately, beginning at the first; in the district of New Hampshire at Exeter and Portsmouth, alternately, beginning at the first; in the district of Massachusetts at Boston and Salem, alternately, beginning at the first; in the district of Connecticut alternately at Hartford and New Haven beginning at the first; in the district of New York at New York; in the district of New Jersey alternately at New Brunswick and Burlington beginning at the first; in the district of Pennsylvania at Philadelphia and York Town alternately beginning at the first; in the district of Delaware alternately at New Castle and Dover beginning at the first; in the district of Maryland alternately at Baltimore and Easton beginning at the first; in the district of Virginia alternately at Richmond and Williamsburgh beginning at the first; in the district of Kentucky at Harrodsburgh; in the district of South Carolina at Charleston; and in the district of Georgia alternately at Savannah and Augusta beginning at the first; and that the special Courts shall be held at the same place in each district as the stated Courts, or in districts that have two at either of them in the discretion of the Judge, or at such other place in the district, as the nature of the business and his discretion shall direct. And that in the districts that have but one place for holding the district Court, the Records thereof shall be kept at that place, and in districts that have two, at that place in each district which the Judge shall appoint.

[4] AND BE IT FURTHER ENACTED, That the before mentioned districts except those of Main and Kentucky shall be divided into three Circuits, and be called the eastern, the middle and the southern Circuit. That the eastern circuit shall consist of the districts of New Hampshire, Massachusetts, Connecticut, and New York; that the middle Circuit shall consist of the districts of New Jersey, Pennsylvania, Delaware, Maryland and Virginia; and that the southern Circuit shall consist of the districts of South Carolina and Georgia;

and that there shall be held annually in each district of said Circuits two Courts, which shall be called circuit Courts, and shall consist of any two Justices of the Supreme Court, and the district Judge of such districts, any two of whom shall constitute a quorum: PROVIDED that no district Judge shall give a vote in any case of appeal or error from his own decision, but may assign the reasons of such his decision.

[5] AND BE IT FURTHER ENACTED, That the first session of the said circuit Court in the several districts shall commence at the times following, to wit, in New Jersey on the second, in New York on the fourth, in Pennsylvania on the eleventh, in Connecticut on the twenty second, and in Delaware on the twenty seventh days of April next, in Massachusetts on the third, in Maryland on the seventh, in South Carolina on the twelfth, in New Hampshire on the twentieth, in Virginia on the twenty second, and in Georgia on the twenty eighth days of May next; and the subsequent sessions in the respective districts on the like days of every sixth calendar month afterwards, except in South Carolina where the session of the said Court shall commence on the first, and in Georgia where it shall commence on the seventeenth day of October, and except when any of those days shall happen on a Sunday, and then the session shall commence on the next day following. And the sessions of the said circuit Court shall be held in the district of New Hampshire at Portsmouth and at Exeter alternately, beginning at the first; in the district of Massachusetts at Boston; in the district of Connecticut alternately at Hartford and New Haven beginning at the last; in the district of New York alternately at New York and Albany beginning at the first; in the district of New Jersey at Trenton; in the district of Pennsylvania alternately at Philadelphia and York Town beginning at the first; in the district of Delaware alternately at New Castle and Dover beginning at the first; in the district of Maryland alternately at Annapolis and Easton beginning at the first; in the district of Virginia alternately at Charlottesville and Williamsburgh beginning at the first; in the district of South-Carolina alternately at Columbia and Charleston beginning at the first; and in the district of Georgia alternately at Savannah and Augusta beginning at the first. And the circuit Courts shall have power to hold special sessions for the trial of criminal Causes at any other time at their discretion, or at the discretion of the Supreme Court.

[6] AND BE IT FURTHER ENACTED, That the Supreme Court may, by any one or more of its Justices being present, be adjourned from day to day until a quorum be convened; and that a Circuit Court may also be adjourned from day to day by any one of its Judges, or if none are present by the Marshal of the district, until a quorum be convened; and that a district Court, in case of the inability of the Judge to attend at the commencement of a session, may by virtue of a written Order from the said Judge directed to the Marshal of the

district, be adjourned by the said Marshal to such day, antecedent to the next stated Session of the said Court, as in the said order shall be appointed; and in case of the death of the said Judge, and his vacancy not being supplied, all process, pleadings, and proceedings of what nature soever, pending before the said Court, shall be continued of course until the next stated Session after the appointment and acceptance of the Office by his Successor.

[7] AND BE IT ENACTED, That the Supreme Court, and the district Courts, shall have power to appoint Clerks for their respective Courts; and that the Clerk for each district Court shall be Clerk also of the circuit Court in such district; and each of the said Clerks shall, before he enters upon the execution of his Office, take the following oath or affirmation, to wit, "I, A.B. being appointed Clerk of   do solemnly swear, or affirm, that I will truly and faithfully enter and record all the orders, decrees, judgments, and proceedings of the said Court; and that I will faithfully and impartially discharge and perform all the duties of my said Office, according to the best of my abilities and understanding. So help me God." Which words so help me God, shall be omitted in all cases where an affirmation is admitted instead of an Oath. And the said Clerks shall also severally give Bond with sufficient sureties (to be approved of by the Supreme and district Courts respectively) to the United States in the sum of Two thousand dollars, faithfully to discharge the duties of his Office, and seasonably to record the decrees, judgments, and determinations of the Court, of which he is Clerk.

[8] AND BE IT FURTHER ENACTED, That the Justices of the Supreme Court, and the district Judges, before they proceed to execute the duties of their respective Offices, shall take the following Oath or affirmation, to wit, "I, A.B. do solemnly swear or affirm, that I will administer Justice without respect to Persons, and do equal right to the Poor and to the rich; and that I will faithfully and impartially discharge and perform all the duties incumbent on me as   according to the best of my abilities and understanding, agreeably to the Constitution and laws of the United States. So help me God."

[9] AND BE IT FURTHER ENACTED, That the district Courts shall have, exclusively of the Courts of the several States, cognizance of all crimes and offences that shall be cognizable under the authority of the United States, committed within their respective districts, or upon the high Seas; where no other punishment than whipping, not exceeding Thirty stripes, a fine not exceeding one hundred Dollars, or a term of imprisonment not exceeding six Months, is to be inflicted; And shall also have exclusive original cognizance of all civil causes of admiralty and maritime jurisdiction, including all seizures under laws of impost, navigation or trade of the United States, where the seizures are made, on waters which are navigable from the Sea by Vessels of ten or more tons burthen, within their respective districts as well as upon the

high seas. Saving to Suitors, in all cases, the right of a common law remedy where the common law is competent to give it: And shall also have exclusive original cognizance of all seizures on land, or other waters, than as aforesaid, made, and of all suits for penalties and forfeitures incurred, under the laws of the United States. And shall also have cognizance, concurrent with the Courts of the several States, or the circuit Courts, as the case may be, of all Causes where an Alien sues for a tort only in violation of the law of Nations or a Treaty of the United States. And shall also have cognizance, concurrent as last mentioned, of all suits at common law where the United States sue, and the matter in dispute amounts, exclusive of costs, to the sum or value of One hundred Dollars. And shall also have jurisdiction exclusively of the Courts of the several States, of all suits against Consuls or Vice Consuls, except for offences above the description aforesaid. And the trial of issues in fact, in the district Courts, in all causes except civil Causes of admiralty and maritime jurisdiction, shall be by Jury.

[10] AND BE IT FURTHER ENACTED, That the district Court in Kentucky district shall, besides the jurisdiction aforesaid, have jurisdiction of all other causes, except of appeals and Writs of Error, herein after made cognizable in a circuit Court, and shall proceed therein in the same manner as a circuit Court. And Writs of error and appeals shall lie from decisions therein to the Supreme Court in the same causes, as from a circuit Court to the Supreme Court, and under the same regulations. And the district Court in Main district, shall besides the jurisdiction herein before granted, have jurisdiction of all causes, except of Appeals and Writs of error herein after made cognizable in a circuit Court, and shall proceed therein in the same manner as a circuit Court: And Writs of error shall lie from decisions therein to the circuit Court in the district of Massachusetts in the same manner as from other district Courts to their respective circuit Courts.

[11] AND BE IT FURTHER ENACTED, That the circuit Courts shall have original cognizance, concurrent with the Courts of the several States, of all suits of a civil nature at common law or in equity, where the matter in dispute exceeds, exclusive of costs, the sum or value of Five hundred Dollars, and the United States are Plaintiffs or Petitioners; or an Alien is a Party, or the suit is between a Citizen of the State where the suit is brought, and a Citizen of another State. And shall have exclusive cognizance of all crimes and offences cognizable under the authority of the United States, except where this Act otherwise provides, or the laws of the United States shall otherwise direct, and concurrent jurisdiction with the district Courts of the crimes and offences cognizable therein. But no Person shall be arrested in one district for trial in another, in any civil action before a circuit or district Court. And no civil suit shall be brought before either of said Courts against an inhabitant of the United States by any original process in any other district than that

whereof he is an inhabitant, or in which he shall be found at the time of serving the Writ; nor shall any district or circuit Court have cognizance of any Suit to recover the contents of any Promissory Note or other chose in action in favor of an Assignee, unless a suit might have been prosecuted in such Court to recover the said contents if no assignment had been made, except in cases of foreign Bills of exchange. And the circuit Courts shall also have appellate jurisdiction from the district Courts under the regulations and restrictions herein after provided.

[12] AND BE IT FURTHER ENACTED, That if a Suit be commenced in any State Court against an Alien, or by a Citizen of the State in which the Suit is brought against a Citizen of another State, and the matter in dispute exceeds the aforesaid sum or value of Five hundred Dollars, exclusive of costs, to be made to appear to the satisfaction of the Court, and the Defendant shall, at the time of entering his appearance in such State Court, file a Petition for the removal of the cause for trial into the next circuit Court to be held in the district where the suit is pending, or if in the district of Main to the district Court next to be holden therein; or if in Kentucky district to the district Court next to be holden therein, and offer good and sufficient surety for his entering in such Court, on the first day of its session, copies of said process against him, and also for his there appearing and entering special bail in the cause if special bail was originally requisite therein; it shall then be the duty of the State Court to accept the surety, and proceed no further in the cause; and any bail that may have been originally taken shall be discharged, and the said Copies being entered as aforesaid, in such Court of the United States, the Cause shall there proceed in the same manner as if it had been brought there by original process. And any attachment of the goods or estate of the defendant by the original process, shall hold the goods or estate so attached to answer the final judgment in the same manner as by the laws of such State they would have been holden to answer final judgment, had it been rendered by the Court in which the suit commenced. And if in any action commenced in a State Court the title of land be concerned, and the parties are Citizens of the same State, and the matter in dispute exceeds the sum or value of Five hundred Dollars, exclusive of costs, the sum or value being made to appear to the satisfaction of the Court, either party, before the trial, shall state to the Court and make affidavit if they require it, that he claims and shall rely upon a right or title to the land under a grant from a State other than that in which the suit is pending, and produce the original grant or an exemplification of it, except where the loss of public records shall put it out of his power, and shall move that the adverse party inform the Court, whether he claims a right or title to the land under a grant from the State, in which the suit is pending, the said adverse shall give such information, or, otherwise not be allowed to plead such grant or give it in evidence upon the trial; and if he informs that

he does claim under such grant, the party claiming under the grant first mentioned, may then, on motion, remove the cause for trial to the next circuit Court to be holden in such district; or if in the district of Main, to the Court next to be holden therein; or if in Kentucky district, to the district Court next to be holden therein; but if he is the defendant, shall do it under the same regulations as in the before mentioned case of the removal of a cause into such Court by an Alien: And neither party removing the cause, shall be allowed to plead or give evidence of any other title than that by him stated as aforesaid, as the ground of his claim. And the trial of issues in fact in the circuit Courts shall, in all suits except those of equity and of admiralty and maritime jurisdiction, be by Jury.

[13] AND BE IT FURTHER ENACTED, That the Supreme Court shall have exclusive jurisdiction of all controversies of a civil nature, where a State is a Party except between a State and its Citizens; and except also between a State and Citizens of other States or Aliens, in which latter case it shall have original but not exclusive jurisdiction. And shall have exclusively all such jurisdiction of suits or proceedings against Ambassadors, or other public Ministers, or their domestics or domestic servants, as a Court of law can have or exercise consistently with the law of Nations; and original, but not exclusive jurisdiction of all suits brought by Ambassadors, or other public Ministers, or in which a Consul or Vice-Consul shall be a Party. And the trial of issues in fact in the Supreme Court, in all actions at law against Citizens of the United States, shall be by Jury. The Supreme Court shall also have appellate jurisdiction from the circuit Courts and Courts of the several States, in the cases herein after specially provided for: And shall have power to issue Writs of Prohibition to the district Courts when proceeding as Courts of admiralty and maritime jurisdiction; and Writs of mandamus, in cases warranted by the principles and usages of law, to any Courts appointed, or persons holding office, under the authority of the United States.

[14] AND BE IT FURTHER ENACTED, That all the before mentioned Courts of the United States shall have power to issue Writs of Scire facias, habeas corpus, and all other Writs not specially provided for by Statute, which may be necessary for the exercise of their respective jurisdictions, and agreeable to the principles and usages of law. And that either of the Justices of the Supreme Court, as well as Judges of the district Courts, shall have power to grant Writs of Habeas Corpus for the purpose of an enquiry into the cause of commitment. PROVIDED that Writs of Habeas Corpus shall in no case extend to prisoners in Gaol, unless where they are in custody under or by color of the authority of the United States, or are committed for trial before some Court of the same, or are necessary to be brought into Court to testify.

[15] AND BE IT FURTHER ENACTED, That all the said Courts of the United States, shall have power in the trial of actions at law, on motion and

due notice thereof being given, to require the parties to produce books or writings in their possession or power which contain evidence pertinent to the issue, in cases and under circumstances where they might be compelled to produce the same by the ordinary rules of proceeding in chancery: And if a Plaintiff shall fail to comply with such order, to produce books or writings, it shall be lawful for the Courts respectively, on motion, to give the like judgment for the Defendant as in cases of nonsuit; and if a Defendant shall fail to comply with such order, to produce books or writings, it shall be lawful for the Courts respectively, on motion as aforesaid, to give judgment against him or her by default.

[16] AND BE IT FURTHER ENACTED, That suits in equity shall not be sustained in either of the Courts of the United States, in any case where plain, adequate and complete remedy may be had at law.

[17] AND BE IT FURTHER ENACTED, That all the said Courts of the United States shall have power to grant new trials, in cases where there has been a trial by Jury, for reasons for which new trials have usually been granted in the Courts of law: and shall have power to impose and administer all necessary Oaths or affirmations, and to punish by fine or imprisonment, at the discretion of said Courts, all contempts of authority in any cause or hearing before the same; and to make and establish all necessary rules for the orderly conducting business in the said Courts, provided such rules are not repugnant to the laws of the United States.

[18] AND BE IT FURTHER ENACTED, That when in a circuit Court, Judgment upon a Verdict in a civil Action shall be entered, execution may, on motion of either Party, at the discretion of the Court, and on such conditions for the security of the adverse Party as they may judge proper, be stayed Forty two days from the time of entering judgment, to give time to file in the Clerk's Office of said Court, a Petition for a new trial. And if such Petition be there filed within said term of Forty two days, with a Certificate thereon from either of the Judges of such Court, that he allows the same to be filed, which Certificate he may make or refuse at his discretion, execution shall of course be further stayed to the next session of said Court. And if a new trial be granted the former judgment shall be thereby rendered void.

[19] AND BE IT FURTHER ENACTED, That it shall be the duty of circuit Courts, in causes in equity and of admiralty and maritime jurisdiction, to cause the facts on which they found their Sentence or decree, fully to appear upon the Record either from the pleadings and decree itself, or a state of the case agreed by the Parties, or their Council, or if they disagree, by a stating of the case by the Court.

[20] AND BE IT FURTHER ENACTED, That where in a circuit Court, a Plaintiff in an action, originally brought there, or a Petitioner in equity, other than the United States, recovers less than the sum or value of Five

hundred Dollars, or a Libellant, upon his own appeal less than the sum or value of Three hundred Dollars, he shall not be allowed but at the discretion of the Court may be adjudged to pay Costs.

[21] AND BE IT FURTHER ENACTED, That from final decrees in a district Court in causes of admiralty and maritime jurisdiction, where the matter in dispute exceeds the sum or value of Three hundred Dollars, exclusive of costs, an appeal shall be allowed to the next circuit Court to be held in such district: PROVIDED NEVERTHELESS, that all such Appeals from final decrees as aforesaid from the district Court of Main, shall be made to the circuit Court, next to be holden after each appeal in the district of Massachusetts.

[22] AND BE IT FURTHER ENACTED, That final decrees and judgments in civil Actions in a district Court, where the matter in dispute exceeds the sum or value of Fifty Dollars, exclusive of costs, may be re-examined, and reversed or affirmed in a Circuit Court holden in the same district upon a writ of error whereto shall be annexed and returned therewith at the day and place therein mentioned, an authenticated transcript of the record, an assignment of errors, and prayer for reversal, with a citation to the adverse Party, signed by the Judge of such district Court or a Justice of the Supreme Court, the adverse Party having at least Twenty days notice. And upon a like Process, may final judgments and decrees in civil Actions and suits in equity in a circuit Court brought there by original process or removed there from Courts of the several States, or removed there by appeal from a district Court where the matter in dispute exceeds the sum or value of Two thousand Dollars exclusive of Costs, be re-examined and reversed or affirmed in the supreme Court, the citation being in such case signed by a Judge of such circuit Court or Justice of the supreme Court, and the adverse Party having at least Thirty days notice. But there shall be no reversal in either Court on such Writ of error for error in ruling any Plea in abatement, other than a plea to the jurisdiction of the Court, or such Plea to a Petition or bill in equity as is in the nature of a demurrer, or for any error in fact. And Writs of error shall not be brought but within Five years after rendering or passing the judgment or decree complained of, or in case the Person entitled to such Writ of error be an Infant feme Covert, non compos mentis or imprisoned, then within Five years as aforesaid, exclusive of the time of such disability. And every Justice or Judge signing a citation on any Writ of error as aforesaid, shall take good and sufficient security, that the Plaintiff in error shall prosecute his Writ to effect, and answer all damages and costs if he fail to make his Plea good.

[23] AND BE IT FURTHER ENACTED, That a Writ of error as aforesaid shall be a Supersedeas and stay execution in cases only where the Writ of error is served, by a Copy thereof being lodged for the adverse Party, in the Clerk's Office where the Record remains, within Ten days, Sundays exclusive, after rendering the judgment or passing the degree complained of. Until the

expiration of which term of Ten days, executions shall not issue in any case where a Writ of error may be a Supersedeas; and where, upon such Writ of error the supreme or a circuit Court shall affirm a judgment or decree, they shall adjudge or decree to the Respondent in error just damages for his delay, and single or double costs at their discretion.

[24] AND BE IT FURTHER ENACTED, That when a judgment or decree shall be reversed in a circuit Court, such Court shall proceed to render such judgment or pass such decree as the district Court should have rendered or passed; and the Supreme Court shall do the same on reversals therein, except where the reversal is in favor of the Plaintiff or Petitioner in the original suit, and the damages to be assessed, or matter to be decreed, are uncertain, in which case they shall remand the cause for a final decision. And the supreme Court shall not issue execution in causes that are removed before them by Writs of error, but shall send a special mandate to the circuit Court to award execution thereupon.

[25] AND BE IT FURTHER ENACTED, That a final judgment or decree in any suit, in the highest Court of law or equity of a State in which a decision in the suit could be had, where is drawn in question the validity of a treaty or statute of, or an authority exercised under the United States, and the decision is against their validity; or where is drawn in question the validity of a statute of, or an authority exercised under any State, on the ground of their being repugnant to the Constitution, treaties or laws of the United States, and the decision is in favor of such their validity; or where is drawn in question the construction of any clause of the constitution, or of a treaty or statute of, or commission held under the United States, and the decision is against the title, right, privilege or exemption specially set up or claimed by either Party, under such clause of the said Constitution, treaty, statute or commission, may be re-examined and reversed or affirmed in the supreme Court of the United States, upon a Writ of error, the citation being signed by the chief Justice or Judge or Chancellor of the Court rendering or passing the judgment or decree complained of, or by a Justice of the supreme Court of the United States, in the same manner and under the same regulations, and the Writ shall have the same effect, as if the judgment or decree complained of had been rendered or passed in a circuit Court; and the proceeding upon the reversal shall also be the same, except that the Supreme Court instead of remanding the cause for a final decision as before provided, may at their discretion, if the cause shall have been once remanded before, proceed to a final decision of the same, and award execution. But no other error shall be assigned or regarded as a ground of reversal in any such case as aforesaid, than such as appears on the face of the Record and immediately respects the before mentioned questions of validity or construction of the said constitution, treaties, statutes, commissions or authorities in dispute.

[26] AND BE IT FURTHER ENACTED, That in all causes brought before either of the Courts of the United States to recover the forfeiture annexed to any articles of agreement, covenant, bond or other speciality, where the forfeiture, breach or non-performance shall appear, by the default or confession of the Defendant, or upon demurrer, the Court before whom the action is, shall render judgment therein for the Plaintiff to recover so much as is due according to equity. And when the sum for which judgment should be rendered is uncertain the same shall, if either of the Parties request it, be assessed by a Jury.

[27] AND BE IT FURTHER ENACTED, That a Marshal shall be appointed in and for each district, for the term of Four years; but shall be removeable from office at pleasure; whose duty it shall be, to attend the district and circuit Courts when sitting therein, and also the supreme Court in the district in which that Court shall sit: And to execute throughout the district, all lawful precepts directed to him, and issued under the authority of the United States; and he shall have power to command all necessary assistance in the execution of his duty, and to appoint, as there shall be occasion, one or more Deputies, who shall be removeable from office by the Judge of the district Court, or the circuit Court sitting within the district, at the pleasure of either; and before he enters on the duties of his Office, he shall become bound for the faithful performance of the same, by himself and by his Deputies, before the Judge of the district Court, to the United States, jointly and severally, with two good and sufficient sureties, inhabitants and freeholders of such district, to be approved by the district Judge, in the sum of Twenty thousand Dollars, and shall take before said Judge, as shall also his Deputies, before they enter on the duties of their appointment, the following Oath of Office "I, A.B. do solemnly swear or affirm, that I will faithfully execute all lawful precepts directed to the Marshal of the district of   under the authority of the United States, and true Returns make, and in all things well and truly, and without malice or partiality, perform the duties of the office of Marshal (or Marshal's Deputy as the case may be) of the district of   during my continuance in said Office, and take only my lawful fees. So help me God."

[28] AND BE IT FURTHER ENACTED, That in all causes wherein the Marshal or his Deputy shall be a Party, the Writs and Precepts therein shall be directed to such disinterested Person as the Court or any Justice or Judge thereof may appoint: And the Person so appointed is hereby authorised to execute and return the same: And in case of the death of any Marshal, his deputy or deputies shall continue in Office, unless otherwise specially removed; and shall execute the same, in the name of the deceased, until another Marshal shall be appointed and sworn: And the defaults or misfeasances in Office of such deputy or deputies in the mean time as well as before, shall be adjudged a breach of the condition of the bond given as before directed by the

Marshal who appointed them; and the executor or administrator of the deceased Marshal shall have like remedy for the defaults and misfeasances in Office of such deputy or deputies during such interval, as they would be entitled to if the Marshal had continued in life and in the exercise of his said Office, until his Successor was appointed and sworn or affirmed: And every Marshal or his Deputy when removed from office, or when the term for which the Marshal is appointed shall expire, shall have power notwithstanding to execute all such precepts as may be in their hands respectively at the time of such removal or expiration of Office, and the Marshal shall be held answerable for the delivery to his Successor of all Prisoners which may be in his custody at the time of his removal, or when the term for which he is appointed shall expire, and for that purpose may retain such Prisoners in his custody until his Successor shall be appointed and qualified as the law directs.

[29] AND BE IT FURTHER ENACTED, That in cases punishable with death the trial shall be had in the County where the offence was committed, or where that cannot be done without great inconvenience, Twelve petit Jurors at least, shall be summoned from thence: And Jurors in all cases to serve in the Courts of the United States, shall be designated by lot or otherwise in each State respectively, according to the mode of forming Juries therein now practiced, so far as the laws of the same shall render such designation practicable by the Courts or Marshals of the United States; and the Jurors shall have the same qualifications as are requisite for Jurors by the laws of the State of which they are Citizens, to serve in the highest Courts of law of such State, and shall be returned as there shall be occasion for them, from such parts of the district from time to time as the Court shall direct, so as shall be most favorable to an impartial trial, and so as not to incur an unnecessary expense or unduly to burthen the Citizens of any part of the district with such services. And Writs of venire facias when directed by the Court shall issue from the Clerk's office and shall be served and returned by the Marshal in his proper Person or by his deputy, or in case the Marshal or his Deputy is not an indifferent Person or is interested in the event of the cause, by such fit Person as the Court shall specially appoint for that purpose, to whom they shall administer an Oath or affirmation that he will truly and impartially serve and return such Writ. And when from challenges or otherwise there shall not be a Jury to determine any civil or criminal cause, the Marshal or his deputy shall, by order of the Court where such defect of Jurors shall happen return Jurymen de talibus circumstantibus sufficient to complete the pannel; and when the Marshal or his Deputy are disqualified as aforesaid, Jurors may be returned by such disinterested Person as the Court shall appoint.

[30] AND BE IT FURTHER ENACTED, That the mode of proof by oral testimony and examination of Witnesses in open Court shall be the same in all the Courts of the United States, as well in the trial of causes in equity and

of admiralty and maritime jurisdiction as of actions at common law. And when the testimony of any Person shall be necessary in any civil cause depending in any district in any Court of the United States, who shall live at a greater distance from the place of trial than One hundred miles, or is bound on a voyage to sea, or is about to go out of the United States or out of such district, and to a greater distance from the place of trial than as aforesaid, before the time of trial, or is ancient or very infirm, the deposition of such Person may be taken de bene esse before any Justice or Judge of any of the Courts of the United States, or before any Chancellor Justice or Judge of a supreme or superior Court, Mayor or chief Magistrate of a City, or Judge of a County Court or Court of common Pleas of any of the United States not being of Counsel or Attorney to either of the Parties, or interested in the event of the cause; provided that a notification from the Magistrate before whom the deposition is to be taken to the adverse Party, to be present at the taking of the same, and to put interrogatories if he think fit, be first made out and served on the adverse Party or his Attorney as either may be nearest, if either is within one hundred miles of the place of such caption, allowing time for their attendance after notified, not less than at the rate of one day, Sundays exclusive, for every Twenty miles travel. And in causes of admiralty and maritime jurisdiction, or other cases of seizure when a libel shall be filed, in which an adverse Party is not named, and depositions of Persons circumstanced as aforesaid shall be taken before a claim be put in, the like notification as aforesaid shall be given to the Person having the Agency or possession of the property libelled at the time of the capture or seizure of the same, if known to the Libellant. And every Person deposing as aforesaid shall be carefully examined and cautioned, and sworn or affirmed to testify the whole truth, and shall subscribe the testimony by him or her given after the same shall be reduced to writing, which shall be done only by the Magistrate taking the deposition, or by the Deponent in his presence. And the depositions so taken shall be retained by such Magistrate, until he deliver the same with his own hand into the Court for which they are taken; or shall together with a certificate of the reasons as aforesaid of their being taken, and of the notice if any given to the adverse Party, be by him the said Magistrate sealed up and directed to such Court, and remain under his Seal until opened in Court. And any Person may be compelled to appear and depose as aforesaid in the same manner as to appear and testify in Court. And in the trial of any cause of admiralty or maritime jurisdiction in a district Court, the decree in which may be appealed from, if either party shall suggest to and satisfy the Court that probably it will not be in his power to produce the Witnesses there testifying, before the circuit Court should an appeal be had, and shall move that their testimony be taken down in writing, it shall be so done by the Clerk of the Court: And if an appeal be had, such testimony may be used on the trial of the same, if it shall appear to the satisfaction of the Court which shall try the appeal, that the Witnesses are then dead, or gone out of the United States, or to a greater distance than as aforesaid from the place where the Court is sitting, or that by reason of age, sickness, bodily infirmity or imprisonment they are unable to travel and appear at Court, but not otherwise: And unless the same shall be made to appear on the trial of any cause; with respect to Witnesses whose depositions may have been taken therein, such depositions shall not be admitted or used in the cause: PROVIDED that nothing herein shall be construed to prevent any Court of the United States from granting a dedimus potestatem, to take depositions according to common usage, when it may be necessary to prevent a failure or delay of justice; which power they shall severall possess; nor to extend to depositions taken in perpetuam rei memoriam, which if they relate to matters that may be cognizable in any Court of the United States, a circuit Court, on application thereto made as a Court of equity, may, according to the usages in Chancery, direct to be taken.

[31] AND BE IT ENACTED, That where any suit shall be depending in any Court of the United States, and either of the Parties shall die before final judgment, the executor or administrator of such deceased Party who was Plaintiff, Petitioner or Defendant, in case the cause of action doth by law survive, shall have full power to prosecute or defend any such suit or action until final judgment; and the Defendant or Defendants are hereby obliged to answer thereto accordingly; and the Court before whom such cause may be depending is hereby impowered and directed to hear and determine the same, and to render judgment for or against the executor or administrator, as the case may require. And if such executor or administrator having been duly served with a Scire facias from the office of the Clerk of the Court where such suit is depending Twenty days beforehand, shall neglect or refuse to become a Party to the suit, the Court may render judgment against the estate of the deceased party, in the same manner as if the executor or administrator had voluntarily made himself a party to the suit: And the executor or administrator who shall become a party as aforesaid, shall, upon motion to the Court where the suit is depending, be entitled to a continuance of the same until the next term of the said Court. And if there be two or more Plaintiffs or Defendants, and one or more of them shall die, if the cause of action shall survive to the surviving Plaintiff or Plaintiffs, or against the surviving defendant or defendants, the Writ or Action shall not be thereby abated, but such death being suggested upon the record, the Action shall proceed at the suit of the surviving Plaintiff or Plaintiffs against the surviving defendant or defendants.

[32] AND BE IT FURTHER ENACTED, That no summons, Writ, declaration, Return, process, judgment, or other proceedings in civil causes in any

of the Courts of the United States, shall be abated, arrested, quashed or reversed, for any defect or want of form, but the said Courts respectively shall proceed and give judgment according as the right of the cause and matter in law shall appear unto them, without regarding any imperfections, defects, or want of form in such Writ, declaration or other pleading, Return, process, judgment, or course of proceeding whatsoever, except those only in cases of demurrer, which the party demurring shall specially set down and express together with his demurrer as the cause thereof: And the said Courts respectively shall and may, by virtue of this act from time to time, amend all and every such imperfections, defects and wants of form, other than those only which the party demurring shall express as aforesaid, and may at any time permit either of the parties to amend any defect in the process or pleadings, upon such conditions as the said Courts respectively shall in their discretion, and by their rules prescribe.

[33] AND BE IT FURTHER ENACTED, That for any crime or offence against the United States, the offender may, by any Justice or Judge of the United States, or by any Justice of the Peace, or other Magistrate of any of the United States where he may be found, agreeably to the usual mode of process against offenders in such State, and at the expence of the United States, be arrested and imprisoned or bailed as the case may be, for trial before such Court of the United States as by this act has cognizance of the Offence: And Copies of the process shall be returned as speedily as may be into the Clerk's Office of such Court, together with the recognizances of the Witnesses for their appearance to testify in the case; which recognizances the Magistrate before whom the examination shall be, may require on pain of imprisonment: And if such commitment of the offender, or the Witnesses shall be in a district other than that in which the offence is to be tried, it shall be the duty of the Judge of that district where the delinquent is imprisoned, seasonably to issue, and of the Marshal of the same district to execute a warrant for the removal of the offender and the Witnesses, or either of them, as the case may be, to the district in which the trial is to be had. And upon all arrests in criminal cases, bail shall be admitted except where the punishment may be death, in which cases it shall not be admitted but by the supreme or a circuit Court, or by a Justice of the supreme Court, or a Judge of a district Court, who shall exercise their discretion therein, regarding the nature and circumstances of the offence, and of the evidence, and the usages of law. And if a Person committed by a Justice of the Supreme or a Judge of a district Court, for an Offence not punishable with death, shall afterwards procure bail, and there be no Judge of the United States in the district to take the same, it may be taken by any Judge of the Supreme, or superior Court of law of such State.

[34] AND BE IT FURTHER ENACTED, That the laws of the several States except where the Constitution, treaties or statutes of the United States shall

otherwise require or provide, shall be regarded as rules of decision in trials at common law in the Courts of the United States in cases where they apply.

[35] AND BE IT FURTHER ENACTED, That in all the Courts of the United States the Parties may plead and manage their own causes personally or by the assistance of such Counsel or Attornies at law as by the rules of the said Courts respectively shall be permitted to manage and conduct causes therein. And there shall be appointed in each district a meet Person, learned in the law, to act as Attorney for the United States in such district, who shall be sworn or affirmed to the faithful execution of his office, whose duty it shall be to prosecute in such district all delinquents for crimes and offences, cognizable under the authority of the United States, and all civil actions in which the United States shall be concerned, except before the Supreme Court in the district in which that Court shall be holden: And he shall receive as a compensation for his services such fees as shall be taxed therefor in the respective Courts before which the suits or prosecutions shall be. And there shall also be appointed a meet Person, learned in the law, to act as Attorney General for the United States, who shall be sworn or affirmed, to a faithful execution of his Office; whose duty it shall be to prosecute and conduct all suits in the supreme Court in which the United States shall be concerned, and to give his advice and opinion upon questions of law when required by the President of the United States, or when requested by the heads of any of the departments, touching any matters that may concern their departments; and shall receive such compensation for his services as shall by law be provided.

> FREDERICK AUGUSTUS MUHLENBERG
> Speaker of the House of Representatives
> JOHN ADAMS
> Vice-President of the United States, and
> President of the Senate

Approved September
the Twenty fourth
1789

> GO. WASHINGTON
> President of the United States

I do certify that this Act did
originate in the Senate.
Attest, Sam. A. Otis Secretary

Enrolled Acts, RG 11, DNA.

Calendar

Date	House	Senate
1789		
Apr. 7		Committee appointed to prepare a bill for organizing the judiciary of the United States (Ellsworth, Paterson, Maclay, Strong, Lee, Bassett, Few, and Wingate).
Apr. 13		On a motion by Ellsworth, seconded by Johnson, Carroll and Izard added to the committee in order to include a member from each state.
May 11		Drafting subcommittee established by committee.[1]
June 12		Lee presented *a bill to establish the Judicial Courts of the United States,* which was read.[2]
June 22		Read; sections 1 and 2 postponed; section 3 debated and motion to approve of district courts in principle agreed to; motion by Lee, to confine federal courts to admiralty and maritime jurisdiction.[3]
June 23		Lee motion disagreed to; section 1 agreed to.[4]
June 24		Bill, including section 4 which was agreed to, through section 9, debated; *amendment* proposed.[5]

[1] Maclay, May 11.
[2] Maclay, June 12, states that the bill was printed. According to Thomas Greenleaf's account in the Records of the Secretary of the Senate: Concerning printing, SR, DNA, 250 copies were printed on June 16, and an additional 120 copies on June 23.
[3] Maclay, June 22.
[4] Maclay, June 23.
[5] Maclay, June 24.

Date	House	Senate
1789		
June 25		Bill debated; amendment to section 9 disagreed to; section 9 struck.[6]
June 26–27		Debated.
June 29		Bill, including section 15, to which *amendments* were proposed, debated.[7]
June 30		Bill debated; amendments to section 15 voted on; on motion of Lee, section 13, which had been postponed, was debated.[8]
July 1		Bill debated, including section 16, which was agreed to.[9]
July 2		Bill debated, including section 25, which was postponed.[10]
July 3		Bill debated; *amendment* to section 31 disagreed to.[11]
July 6		Debated.
July 7		Read;[12] bill debated, including section 4, which was *amended*.[13]
July 8		Bill debated, including section 12, which was *amended*.
July 9		Bill debated; *amendment* to section 18 agreed to;[14]

[6] Maclay, June 25.
[7] Maclay, June 29.
[8] Maclay, June 30.
[9] Maclay, July 1.
[10] Maclay, July 2.
[11] Maclay, July 3.
[12] The Judiciary Bill had two third readings. According to Maclay, July 6, the second reading had been in the committee of the whole Senate, and therefore amendments were allowed during the third reading.
[13] Maclay, July 7.
[14] Maclay, July 10.

Date	House	Senate
1789		
		amendments to section 27 disagreed to.
July 10		Bill debated; *amendments* to sections 18 and 28–31 agreed to.[15]
July 11		Bill debated, including section 16, which was struck, and section 20 [21], to which an amendment was made; new section added between sections 17 and 18 [19]; several *amendments* disagreed to.
July 13		Bill debated, including sections 9, 18 [19], and 21 [22] which were amended, section 16 [15] which was restored and *amended,* and section 27 to which an *amendment* was made and disagreed to; recommitted.
July 17		Read; agreed to by a recorded vote of 14–6, as *An Act to establish the Judicial Courts of the United States.*[16]
July 20	Received, read twice, and committed to the COWH; 100 copies ordered printed.[17]	
July 27– Aug. 22	Postponed as order of the day.	

---

[15] Ibid.

[16] According to Maclay, July 17, the motion printed in the *SLJ*, p. 84, regarding members' rights to enter a protest against bills in the *Journal*, was submitted by Butler during debate on the Judiciary Bill.

[17] *GUS*, July 22.

Date	House	Senate
1789		
Aug. 4	Petition of Freeholders of Cumberland County, Pennsylvania, "praying that the District and Circuit Judicial Courts of the United States, to be established in the said state, may be fixed at some central place therein, convenient to the citizens thereof at large," presented by Hiester[18] and tabled.	
Aug. 24	Sections 1 through 3 debated and *amended* in COWH; *amendment* to section 3 debated.[19]	
Aug. 25–28	Postponed as order of the day.	
Aug. 29	Section 3 debated in COWH; petition of the inhabitants of East New Jersey, "praying that the district court of the United States to be held within the said state, may be fixed at Perth–Amboy, as a place most central and convenient to the inhabitants of the said state at large," presented by Boudinot and tabled.[20]	
Aug. 31	Section 3 debated; amendment proposed Aug. 24 disagreed to.[21]	

[18] *GUS*, Aug. 5.
[19] *GUS*, Aug. 26.
[20] *NYDA*, Aug. 31, Sept. 1; *GUS*, Sept. 2, 5.
[21] *NYDA*, Sept. 1; *GUS*, Sept. 5, 9.

Date	House	Senate
1789		
Sept. 1–7	Postponed as order of the day.	
Sept. 8	Petition of the inhabitants of the state of New Jersey, "praying that the seat of the federal district and circuit courts for that state may be fixed at Perth Amboy," presented by Boudinot; section 4 of bill debated in COWH.[22]	
Sept. 9	Sections 5–9 debated and amended in COWH.[23]	
Sept. 10	Petitions of the inhabitants of the counties of Monmouth and Essex, in the state of New Jersey, "praying that the seat of the federal district and circuit courts for that state may be fixed at Perth Amboy," presented by Boudinot[24] and tabled; postponed as order of the day.	
Sept. 11	Sections 10–15 debated in COWH.[25]	
Sept. 12	Sections 16–27 debated in COWH.[26]	
Sept. 14	Sections 28–35 debated in COWH; section 29 *amended;* COWH amendments reported to the House.[27]	

[22] *GUS*, Sept. 9.
[23] *GUS*, Sept. 12.
[24] *NYDA*, Sept. 11.
[25] *GUS*, Sept. 12.
[26] *GUS*, Sept. 16.
[27] Ibid.

Date	House	Senate
1789		
Sept. 15	Petition of the inhabitants of Bergen County, New Jersey, "praying that the district court of the United States, to be held within the said state, may be at Burlington and Newark alternately," presented and tabled; COWH amendments debated; two additional *amendments* disagreed to.[28]	
Sept. 16	COWH amendments amended and agreed to.	
Sept. 17	Read, debated, and agreed to with *amendments* by an unjournalized recorded vote of 37–16 called for by Burke.[29]	House amendments committed to Ellsworth, Butler, and Paterson.
Sept. 19		Ellsworth reported for committee and report agreed to; four House amendments disagreed to; one agreed to with an *amendment;* others agreed to.
	Senate action considered.	
Sept. 21	Amendments disagreed to by Senate receded from; Senate amendment agreed to.	

[28] *NYDA*, Sept. 16; *GUS*, Sept. 19.

[29] The *GUS*, Sept. 19, gives this vote as follows:
AYES. *Messrs*. Ames, Baldwin, Benson, Boudinot, Brown, Cadwallader, Carroll, Clymer, Contee, Fitzsimons, Foster, Gale, Gilman, Goodhue, Griffin, Hartley, Heister, Huntington, Lawrance, Lee, Madison, Moore, P. Muhlenberg, Page, Schureman, Scott, Sherman, Silvester, Sinnickson, Smith, (Md.) Smith, (S.C.) Thatcher, Trumbull, Vining, Wadsworth, White, Wynkoop. 37.
NOES. *Messrs*. Bland, Burke, Coles, Floyd, Gerry, Grout, Hathorn, Jackson, Livermore, Matthews, Parker, Van Ransellaer, Seney, Stone, Sumpter, Tucker. 16.

Date	House	Senate
1789		
Sept. 22	Signed by speaker.	Signed by vice president.
Sept. 24		Signed by president.

Judiciary Bill [S-1]
June 12, 1789

A Bill[1]   the[2]
~~A Bill entitled, An Act to reorgani~~ ∧ to establish [*lined out*] ∧ Judicial
Courts of the United States

Be it enacted by the Senate and Representatives of the United States of America in Congress assembled, That the Supreme Court of the United States
other   associate
shall consist of a Chief Justice and five ~~puisne~~ ∧ Justices, any four of whom shall be a Quorum, and shall hold annually at the Seat of the federal Government two Sessions, the one commencing the first Monday of February, and
associate
the other the first Monday of August. That the ~~puisne~~ ∧ Justices shall have Precedence according to the Date of their Commissions, or when the Commissions of two or more of them bear Date on the same Day, according to
respective ages.
their ~~*Seniority.*~~ ∧
                    by the Authority aforesaid,
    2. And be it further enacted ∧ that the United States shall be and they hereby are divided into eleven[3] Districts to be [de]limited and called as follows, to wit,[4] one to consist of the State of New Hampshire and that Part of the State of Massachusetts, which lies easterly of the State of New Hampshire,[5] and to be called New Hampshire District; one to consist of the remaining Part of the State of Massachusetts, and to be called Massachusetts District; one to consist of the State of Connecticut, and to be called Connecticut District; one to consist of the State of New York, and to be called New York District; one to consist of the State of New Jersey and to be called New Jersey District; one to consist of the State of Pennsylvania and to be called Pennsylvania District; one to consist of the State of Delaware, and to be called Delaware District;

---

[1] The words "A Bill" were inserted by Otis.
[2] The word "the" was inserted by Otis.
[3] The Senate struck out "eleven" and inserted "thirteen."
[4] The Senate inserted "One to consist of that part of the State of Massachusetts, which lies easterly of the State of New-Hampshire, and to be called Main district" at this point.
[5] The Senate struck out "and that Part" through "New Hampshire."

of
one to consist of the State Maryland and to be called Maryland District; one to
consist of the State of Virginia,[6] and to be called Virginia District;[7] one to
consist of the State of South Carolina, and to be called ~~the~~ South Carolina
District; and one to consist of the State of Georgia, and to be called Georgia
District.

3. And be it further enacted by the Authority aforesaid, That there be a
Court called a District Court in each of the aforementioned Districts to
consist of one Judge, who shall reside in the District for which he is appointed, and shall be called a District Judge, and shall hold annually four Sessions,
the first of which to commence as follows, to wit, in the District of New
York, and of New Jersey on the first, in the District of Pennsylvania on the
second, in the District of Connecticut on the third, in the District of Dela-
ware and of South Carolina on the fourth Tuesdays of November next; in the
District of Massachusetts[8] and of Maryland on the first, in the District of
Georgia on the second, and in the District of New Hampshire and[9] of
Virginia[10] on the third Tuesdays of December next; and the other three
Sessions progressively in the respective Districts on the like Tuesdays of every
third Calendar Month afterwards; and that the ~~said~~ District Judge shall have
Power to hold special Courts at his Discretion. That the stated District Court
shall be held at the Places following, to wit,[11] in the District of New
Hampshire alternately[12] at Portsmouth and Portland beginning at the first;[13]
in the District of Massachusetts at Boston; in the District of Connecticut at
Middle Town;[14] in the District of New York at New York; in the District of
New Jersey alternately at New Brunswick & Burlington beginning at the
first; in the District of Pennsylvania at Philadelphia; in the District of
Delaware[15] at[16] Dover[17] in the District of Maryland[18] at Baltimore[19] in the
District of Virginia alternately at Richmond and Williamsburgh beginning
at the first;[20] in the District of South Carolina at Charles Towne and in the

---

[6] The Senate inserted "except that part heretofore called the district of Kentucky"
at this point.
[7] The Senate inserted "one to consist of the remaining part of the State of Virginia,
and to be called Kentucky district" at this point.
[8] The Senate inserted "of Main" at this point.
[9] The Senate struck out "and."
[10] The Senate inserted "and of Kentucky" at this point.
[11] The Senate inserted "in the district of Main at Portland" at this point.
[12] The Senate struck out "alternately."
[13] The Senate struck out "and Portland beginning at the first."
[14] The Senate struck out "at Middle Town" and inserted "alternately at Hartford
and New Haven beginning at the first."
[15] The Senate inserted "alternately" at this point.
[16] The Senate inserted "New-Castle and" at this point.
[17] The Senate inserted "beginning at the first" at this point.
[18] The Senate inserted "alternately" at this point.
[19] The Senate inserted "and Easton, beginning at the first" at this point.
[20] The Senate inserted "in the district of Kentucky at Harrodsburgh" at this point.

District of Georgia alternately at Savannah and Augusta beginning at the
in each district
first; and that the special Courts shall be held at the same Place as the stated
Courts, or in Districts that have two at either of them in the Discretion of the
Judge, or at such other Place in the District as the Nature of the Business and
his Discretion shall direct. And that, in the Districts that have but one Place
for holding the District Court, the Records thereof shall be kept at that Place,
and in Districts that have two, at that Place in each District which the Judge
shall appoint.

4. And be it further enacted by the Authority aforesaid, that the before-
mentioned Districts[21] shall be divided into three Circuits, and be called the
Eastern, the Middle, and the Southern Circuit. That the Eastern Circuit shall
consist of the Districts of New Hampshire, Massachusetts, Connecticut, and
New York; that the middle Circuit shall consist of the Districts of New
Jersey, Pennsylvania, Delaware, Maryland, and Virginia; and that the Southern Circuit shall consist of the Districts of South Carolina and Georgia; and
that there shall be held annually in each District[22] two Courts, which shall be
called Circuit Courts, and shall consist of any two Justices of the Supreme
Court, and the District Judge of such District, in which any two of whom
shall constitute a Quorum.[23]

5. And be it further enacted by the Authority aforesaid, That the first
Session of the said Circuit Court in the several Districts shall commence at the
Times following, to wit, in the District of New Jersey on the second, in New
York on the fourth, in Pennsylvania on the eleventh, in Connecticut on the
twenty second, in South Carolina on the twenty fifth, and in Delaware on the
twenty seventh Days of April next; in Massachusetts on the third, in Maryland on the seventh, in Georgia on the tenth, in New Hampshire on the
twentieth, and in Virginia on the tw twenty second Days of May next, and
the subsequent Sessions in the respective Districts on the like Days of every
sixth Calendar Month afterwards, exp except when any of those Days shall
happen on a Sunday, and then the Session shall commence on the next Day
following. And the Sessions of the said Circuit Court shall be held in the
and Portland beginning at the first[25]
District of New Hampshire alternately[24] at Portsmouth ; in the District of

---

[21] The Senate inserted "except those of Main and Kentucky" at this point.

[22] The Senate inserted "of said Circuits" at this point.

[23] The Senate inserted the following proviso, proposed by Maclay on July 7
(Maclay, July 7), at this point:
> Provided always, that no District Judge shall sit in Judgment or give a Vote in
> any Case of Jud Appeal or Error from his own Decision, but may assign the
> reasons of such his decission.
The draft amendment is filed with the bill. The first part, through "his own Deci-
sion," is in the hand of Paterson; the remainder is in the hand of Ellsworth.

[24] The word "alternately" was struck out by the Senate.

[25] The words "and Portland beginning at the first" were struck out by the Senate.

Massachusetts at Boston; in the District of Connecticut at Middle Town;[26] in the District of New York ~~at~~ alternately at New York and Albany beginning at the first; in the District of New Jersey at Trenton; in the District of Pennsylvania at Philadelphia; in the District of Delaware alternately at New Castle and Dover beginning at the first in the District of Maryland alternately at Annapolis and Easton beginning at the first in the District of Virginia alternately at Richmond and Williamsburgh beginning at the first; in the District of South Carolina alternately at Charles Town & Cambden, beginning at the first and in the District of Georgia[27] at[28] Augusta.[29]

6. And be it further enacted by the Authority aforesaid, That the Supreme Court may, by any one or more of its Justices being present, be adjourned from Day to Day till a Quorum be convened; and that a Circuit Court may also be adjourned from Day to Day by any one of its Judges[30] till a Quorum be convened; and that a District Court, in Case of the Inability of the Judge to attend at the Commencement of a Session, may, by Virtue of ~~one~~ a written Order from the said Judge directed to the Marshal of the District, be adjourned by the said Marshal to such Day, antecedent to the next stated Session of the said Court, as in the said Order shall be appointed; and in Case of the Death of the said Judge, and his Vacancy not being supplied, all Process, Pleadings and Proceedings of what Nature soever pending before the said Court shall be continued of Course till the next stated Session.[31]

7. And be it enacted by the Authority aforesaid, that the Supreme Court and the District Courts shall have Power to appoint Clerks for their respective Courts; ~~that each of the said Clerks shall, before he enters upon the Execution of his Office, take and subscribe an Oath or Affirmation before the Court appointing him well and faithfully to execute the Duties of the said Office;~~ and that the Clerk of each District Court shall be Clerk also of the Circuit Court ~~when sitting~~ in such District; ~~and shall as such take an Oath or Affirmation before the Circuit Court for the faithful Execution of the Duties~~

---

[26] The Senate struck out "at Middle Town" and inserted "alternately at Hartford and New-Haven, beginning at the first." Both the engrossed and the printed bill say "last" instead of "first," but this error was corrected in the enrolled act.

[27] The Senate inserted "alternately" at this point.

[28] The Senate inserted "Savannah and" at this point.

[29] The Senate inserted the following at this point:
  beginning at the first.
                    for the trial of criminal causes
    And the circuit-courts shall have power to hold special Sessions‸at their discretion—or at the discretion of the Supreme Court.
The draft of the new paragraph is filed with the bill. The first part, through "discretion," is in the hand of Ellsworth; the remainder is in the hand of Otis.

[30] The Senate inserted "or if none are present by the Marshall of the district" at this point. A draft of this amendment, in the hand of Ellsworth, is filed with the bill.

[31] The Senate inserted "after the appointment and acceptance of the Office by his Successor." A draft of this amendment, in the hand of Strong, is filed with the bill.

~~of his Office.~~ and ~~that~~ each of the said Clerks shall, before he enters upon the Execution of his Office, take the following Oath or Affirmation, to wit.

"I A. B. being appointed Clerk of   do solemnly swear or affirm, that I will truly and faithfully enter and record all the Orders, Decrees, Judgments, and Proceedings of the said Court, and that I will faithfully and impartially discharge and perform all the Duties of my said Office, according to the best of my Abilities, and Understanding. So help me God."[32]

                                                                    the
8. And be it further enacted by the Authority aforesaid, That ∧ ~~every~~ Justices of the Supreme Court and the District Judges, before they proceed to execute the Duties of their respective Offices, shall take the following Oath or Affirmation, to wit.

"I A.B. do solemnly swear or affirm, that I will administer Justice without Respect to Persons; and do equal Right to the poor & to the rich, and that I will faithfully and impartially ~~exec~~ discharge and perform all the Duties incumbent on me as   according to the best of my Abilities and Understanding, agreeably to the Constitution and Laws of the United States. So help me God."

9. And be it further enacted, that in all Cases wherein by Law an Oath shall be allowed, authorized, directed, or required, the solemn Affirmation of any of the People called Quakers shall be allowed and taken instead of such Oath.[33]

                              by the authority aforesaid
10. And be it further enacted, ∧ that the district courts shall have, ex-
                              Several
clusively of the courts of the ~~respective~~ ∧ States, cognizance of all crimes & offences that shall be cognizable under the Authority of the United States & defined by the laws of the same,[34] committed within their respective districts or upon the high seas; where other corporal punishment than whipping, not exceeding (30)   stripes, a higher fine than (100)   dollars, or a

---

[32] The Senate inserted the following at this point:
   which words So help me God, shall be omitted in all cases where an affirma-
                              the said Clerks
   tion is admitted instead of an oath. And ∧ shall also severally give Bond with sufficient Sureties (to be approved of by the District Judg[e)] to the United States in the Sum of 2,000 Dollars faithfully to discharge the Duties of his office, and seasonably to record the Decrees Judgments and Determinations of the Court of whi[ch] he is Clerk.
Drafts of the first part, through "oath," in the hand of Ellsworth, and of the second part, in the hand of Strong, are filed with the bill.

[33] The Senate struck out this section. According to Maclay (June 24 and 25), this action occurred on June 25, following a motion by Maclay on June 24 to allow all persons opposed to oaths to substitute an affirmation. The motion to strike this section was also made by Maclay.

[34] The Senate struck out "& defined by the laws of the same."

JUDICIARY ACT [S–1]   1177

longer term of imprisonment than (6)   months, is not to be inflicted;
except where the laws of the United States shall otherwise direct; & the trial
of facts shall be by Jury.[35] And shall also have exclusive original cognizance of
all civil causes of admiralty & maritime jurisdiction, ~~except of crimes above
the description aforesaid~~, including[36] all seizures under laws of impost,
navigation or trade of the United States, where the seizures ~~shall be~~ are
              which are   by   or more
made on waters ˄ navigable from the sea ~~with~~ ˄ vessels of (10)   tons ˄ burthen, within their respective districts as well as upon the high seas. Saving to
Suitors in all cases the right of a common law remedy where the common law
is competent to give it.[37] And shall also have cognizance, concurrent with the
courts of the several States or the circuit courts, as the case may be, of all
causes where a forreigner sues for a tort only in violation of the law of nations
or a treaty of the United States. And shall also have cognizance, concurrent as
last mentioned, of all ~~civil~~ suits at common law where the United States, or a
common informer as well for himself as the United States,[38] Sue, & the
matter in dispute amounts, exclusive of costs, to the sum or value of
(100)   dollars.[39] And the trial of facts[40] in both cases last mentioned[41]
shall be by jury.[42]

---

[35] The Senate struck out "& the trial of facts shall be by Jury." A draft of this
amendment, in the hand of Ellsworth, is filed with the bill.

[36] The word "including" was written over "& of" by Ellsworth.

[37] The Senate inserted the following at this point:
 And shall also have exclusively of the courts of the several States jurisdiction of
 all seizures ~~by C~~ on land or other waters than as aforesaid made, & of all Suits for
 penalties & forfietures incurred under the laws of the United States; ~~& the trial of~~
 ~~& the trial of facts shall be by Jury.~~
This draft amendment, in the hand of Ellsworth, is filed with the bill.

[38] The Senate struck out "or a common informer as well for himself as the United
States."

[39] The Senate inserted the following at this point:
 And shall also have jurisdiction, exclusively of the Courts of the several States, of
 all suits against Consuls or Vice-Consuls, except for offences, above the discrip-
 tion aforesaid.
This draft amendment, in the hand of Ellsworth, is filed with the bill.

[40] On July 13 the Senate struck out "facts" and inserted "issues in fact." The *SLJ*,
p. 83, refers to this amendment as one to section 9 because the original section 9 had
been struck out.

[41] The Senate struck out "both cases last mentioned" and inserted "the district
Courts, in all Causes, except civil Causes of Admiralty and Maritime jurisdiction." A
draft of this amendment, in the hand of Ellsworth, is filed with the bill.

[42] The Senate inserted the following section at this point:
 And be it further enacted, That the district Court in Kentucky district shall,
 besides the jurisdiction aforesaid, have jurisdiction of all other Causes, except of
 Appeals and Writs of error, herein after made cognizable in a circuit Court, and
 shall proceed therein in the same manner as in a circuit Court. And Writs of
 error shall lie from decisions therein to the Supreme Court in the same Causes, as
 from other district Courts to a circuit Court, or from a circuit Court to the
 Supreme Court, and under the same regulations.

~~by the Authority aforesaid~~

11. And be it further enacted,ₐthat the circuit courts shall have original cognizance concurrent with the courts of the several States, or the supreme

of a civil nature

court, as the case may be,[43] of all Suitsₐat common law or in equity, where the matter in dispute exceeds, exclusive of costs, the sum or value of 500[44]

~~or a State is plaintiff or petitioner & the Suit is against~~

dollars & the United States are plaintiffs or petitioners;ₐ~~& where it~~ ~~exceeds~~   ~~dollars &~~ or a forreigner or citizen of another State than that in which the suit is brought is a party.[45] And shall have exclusively ~~cog-~~ ~~nizance~~ cognizance of all crimes & offences cognizable under the authority of

this act otherwise provides or

the United States, & defined by the laws of the same,[46] except whereₐthe laws of the United States shall otherwise direct; & concurrent jurisdiction with the district courts of the crimes[47] & offences cognizable therein. But no person

brought to trial

shall beₐ ~~arrested for trial~~ in any civil ~~cause~~ action before any other circuit

that

~~Court~~ or district Court thanₐ~~those of~~ within the district where the ~~arrest~~ ~~shall be made.~~ [with?]~~in any other district than that whereof the defendant is~~ ~~an inhabitant or in which he shall be found at the time of Serving the Writ.~~ ~~And neither of the courts above mentioned shall have cognizance of any action~~ ~~to recover the contents of any promissary note or other chose in action in~~ ~~favour of any assignee unless an action might have been prosecuted in such~~ ~~court to recover the said contents if no assignment had been made.~~[48] & offences cognizable therein. But no person shall be arrested in one district for trial in another, in any civil action before a circuit or district court. And no civil Suit shall be brought before either of said[49] courts against an inhabitant of the United States by any original process in any other district than that whereof he is an inhabitant or in which [he] shall be found at the time of

Nor shall any

Serving the Writ ~~and neither~~ [lined out] ~~And no~~ ₐdistrict or circuit court

---

[43] The Senate struck out "or the supreme court, as the case may be."

[44] "500" was written over another number in parentheses.

[45] The Senate struck out "or a forriegner" through "a party" and inserted "or an Alien is a Party, or the suit is between a Citizen of the State where the suit is brought, and a Citizen of another State." A draft of this amendment, in the hand of Ellsworth, is filed with the bill.

[46] The Senate struck out "& defined by the laws of the same."

[47] This section is garbled in the manuscript from this point to the words "& offences cognizable therein" following the lined out passage below. Ellsworth started to revise this section, but then stopped and placed an asterisk in the margin, referring to a separate sheet of paper, now filed with the amendments, on which he rewrote part of the section. The text from this separate sheet follows the long lined out passage and continues the section up to "And the circuit Courts. . . ."

[48] The words "[with?] in any other district" through "had been made" were inserted along the side of the page by Ellsworth.

[49] The word "said" was written over "such" by Ellsworth.

~~shall~~ have cognizance of any action[50] to recover the contents of any promissary note or other chose in Action in favour of an assignee, unless an action[51] might have been prosecuted in such court to recover the Said contents if no assignment had been made.[52] And the circuit Courts shall also have appellate jurisdiction from the district courts under the regulations & restrictions herein after provided.[53]

12. And be it further enacted ~~by the authority aforesaid~~, that if a Suit be commenced in any State court against a forriegner, or citizen of another State than that in which the Suit is brought,[54] & the matter in dispute exceeds the aforesaid sum or value of (500)   dollars, exclusive of costs; & such Forriegner or Citizen[55] shall, at the time of entering his appearance in such State Court, file a motion for the removal of the cause for trial into the next circuit court to be held in the district where the suit is pending,[56] and offer good & sufficient surety for his entering in such circuit court, on the first day of its session, copies of said process against him, & also for his there appearing in the cause if Special bail was originally requisite therein; it shall then be the duty of the State Court to accept the Surety & dismiss further proceedings[57] in the cause; & any bail that may have been originally taken shall be discharged; & the said copies being entered as aforesaid in the circuit court,[58] the cause shall there proceed in the same manner as if it had been brought there by original process. And any ~~lien put upon~~ ^attachment of^ the goods or estate of the defendant by the original process shall still[59] hold to respond the final judgement.[60] And if in any action commenced in a State Court the title of

50 The Senate struck out "action" and inserted "suit."

51 The Senate struck out "an action" and inserted "a suit."

52 The Senate inserted "except in cases of foreign Bills of exchange" at this point.

53 The Senate inserted "And Main district shall, for every purpose affecting the jurisdiction of a circuit Court, be considered as a part of Massachusetts district" at this point.

54 The Senate struck out "a forriegner, or citizen of another State than that in which the Suit is brought" and inserted "an Alien, or by a Citizen of the State in which a suit is brought against a Citizen of another State."

55 The Senate struck out "& such Forriegner or Citizen" and inserted "to be made to appear to the satisfaction of the Court, and the Defendant."

56 The Senate inserted "or if in the District of Main to the circuit Court next to be holden in Massachusetts district, or if in Kentucky district to the district Court next to be holden therein" at this point.

57 The Senate struck out "dismiss further proceedings" and inserted "proceed no further."

58 The Senate struck out "the circuit court" and inserted "such Court of the United States."

59 The Senate struck out "still."

60 The Senate inserted the following at this point:
in the same manner as by the laws of such State they would have been holden to respond final judgment had ^it^ ~~the same~~ been rendered in a court of ~~such State~~ the same.

The draft amendment, in the hand of Ellsworth and endorsed, "July 8" by Otis, is filed with the bill.

land be concerned, & the parties are citizens of the same State, & the matter in dispute exceeds, the Sum or value of (500)   dollars, exclusive of
                or value
costs, the sum being made to appear to the Satisfaction of the court, & the defendant in his plea in barr shall set up a title under a grant from another State than that in which the Suit is pending, & move that the plaintiff also set forth his title, the plaintiff shall set it forth in his replication, & if he founds it upon a grant from another State than that ~~in which the suit is~~ under whose grant the defendant claims;[61] the defendant may then, on motion, have the cause removed to the circuit court for trial; in the same manner & under the same regulations as in the case before mentioned of the removal of a cause into that court by a forreigner ~~&c~~. And the defendant shall in such case abide by his plea in barr.[62] And the trial of facts[63] in the circuit courts shall, in all suits, except those of equity & of admiralty & maritime jurisdiction be by jury.

13. And be it further enacted by the authority aforesaid that the supreme court shall have exclusive jurisdiction of all controversies of a civil nature, where any of the United States ~~is a party~~ or a forriegn State[64] is a party, except between a State & its citizens; & except also between a State & citizens

---

61 Instead of "another State than that under whose grant the defendant claims," the printed copy of the bill as introduced reads "the state in which the suit is pending."

62 The Senate struck out "& the defendant in his plea in barr" through "abide by his plea in bar" and inserted the following:

either party, before the trial, shall state to the court, & make affidavit if they require it, that he claims & shall rely upon a right or title to the land under a grant from a State other than that in which the Suit is pending, & produce an exemplification of such grant, except where the loss of publick records shall put it out of his power, & shall move that the adverse party inform the court, whether he claims a right or title to the land under a grant from the State in which the suit is pending, the said adverse party shall give such information, or, otherwise not be allowed to plead ~~or give~~ such grant or give it in evidence upon the trial; and if he informs that he does claim under such grant, the party claiming under the grant first mentioned, may then, on motion, remove the cause for trial to the next circuit court to be holden in such district; but if he is the defendant, shall do it under the same regulations as in the before mentioned case of the removal of a cause into such court by a foreigner; and neither party removing the cause shall be allowed to plead or give evidence of any title aliene to the grant by him stated as aforesaid as the ground of his claim.

This draft amendment, in the hand of Ellsworth, is filed with the bill. The version of the amendment passed by the Senate substituted "the original grant or an exemplification of it," for "an exemplification of such grant." The final amendment also included "or if in the district of Main, to the circuit Court next to be holden in Massachusetts district; or if in Kentucky district, to the district Court next to be holden therein" after "such district." Also in the final amendment, "an alien" was substituted for Ellsworth's "a forreigner."

63 The Senate struck out "facts" and inserted "issues in fact."

64 The Senate struck out "any of the United States or a forriegn State" and inserted "a State."

of other States or forriegners,[65] in which latter case it shall have original, but not exclusive jurisdiction. And shall have exclusively all such jurisdiction of Suits or proceedings against ambassadors, other publick ministers or consuls, or their domesticks or domestick servants, as a court of law can have or exercise consistantly with the law of nations; And original, but not exclusive jurisdiction of all Suits for trespasses brought by ambassadors, other publick ministers or consuls, or their domesticks or domestick servants.[66] And the
trial of facts[67] ~~in~~ the supreme court, in all actions at law against citizens of the United States, shall be by jury. The Supreme court shall also have appellate jurisdiction from the circuit courts & courts of the several States in the cases herein after specially provided for. And shall have power to issue writs of prohibition to the district courts when proceeding as courts of Admiralty & maritime jurisdiction; and writs of *mandamus,* in cases warranted by the principles & usages of law, to any courts appointed, or persons holding office, under the authority of the United States.

14. And be it further enacted ~~by the authority aforesaid,~~ that all the before mentioned Courts of the United States shall have power to issue writs of *Scire-facias, ~~subpoena & protection for witnesses,~~ Habeas Corpus,* & all other writs not specially provided for by Statute, which may be necessary for the exercise of their respective jurisdictions, & agreeable to the principles & usages of law. And that either of the Justices of the supreme court, ~~as~~ as well as Judges of the district courts, shall have power to grant writs of *habeas corpus* for the purpose of an enquiry into the cause of commitment. Provided that writs of *habeas corpus* shall in no case extend to prisoners in gaol unless where they are in custody under or by colour of the Authority of the United States, or are committed for trial before some court of the same, or are necessary to be brought into court to testify.

15. And be it further enacted by the Authority aforesaid, that all the said Courts of the United States, shall have power in the trial of ~~civil~~ actions at law, on motion & due notice thereof being given, to require the parties to produce books or papers in their possession or power which contain evidence perti-

---

[65] The Senate struck out "forriegners" and inserted "aliens."
[66] The Senate struck out from "And shall have exclusively" to this point and inserted the following:
And shall have exclusively all such jurisdiction of Suits or proceedings against Ambassadors, or other publick Ministers, or their domesticks or domestick servants, as a court of law can have or exercise consistantly with the law of nations; & original but not exclusive jurisdiction of all Suits brot. by Ambassadors or other publick ministers, or in which a consul or vice-consul shall be a party.
This draft amendment, in the hand of Ellsworth, is filed with the bill.
[67] The Senate struck out "facts" and inserted "issues in fact."

nent to the issue, in cases & under circumstances where they might be compelled to produce the same by the ordinary rules of proceeding in chan-

& due notice thereof ~~being given,~~ as aforesaid

cery; or, on motion of a plaintiff,ˆand his rendering it probable to the satisfaction of the court that he has by casualty & without fault or negligence of his own been deprived of evidence necessary to support his action,[68] to

or her

require the defendant to disclose on ~~his~~ oath hisˆKnowledge in the cause,[69] in cases & under circumstances where a respondent might be compelled to make such disclosure on oath by the aforesaid rules of proceeding in chancery:[70] And if a plaintiff shall fail to comply with such order, to produce books or papers,[71] it shall be lawful for the courts respectively, on motion, to give the like judgment for the defendant as in cases of nonsuit; & if a defendant shall fail to comply with such order, either to produce books or papers or to disclose on oath,[72] ~~the~~ it shall be lawful for the courts respectively, on

or her

motion as aforesaid to give judgment against himˆby default.

16. And be it further enacted by the authority aforesaid that Suits in equity shall not be sustained in either of the courts of the United States, in any case where[73] remedy may be had at law ~~Nor shall depositions be admitted in either of said courts in suits in equity, or in causes of admiralty or maritime jurisdiction or when other circumstances or regulations~~ [than in trial?] ~~at common law.~~

And the mode of receiving testimony in suits in equity & in ca[us]es of admiralty & maritime jurisdiction shall be the same ~~in sd. Courts~~ as in trials at common law, or as is herein after specially provided.[74]

---

68 The words "and his rendering" through "action" were inserted along the side of the page by Ellsworth.

69 The word "cause" was written over "case."

70 On June 29 Paterson, seconded by Maclay, moved to strike out "or, on motion of a plaintiff" through "in chancery." Ellsworth moved instead to insert a clause requiring the plaintiff, at the request of the defendant, to swear to his knowledge of the case. On June 30 Paterson's motion was agreed to and Ellsworth's disagreed to. (Maclay, June 29, 30)

71 The Senate struck out "papers" and inserted "writings."

72 The Senate struck out "either to produce" through "oath" and inserted "to produce books or writings."

73 On July 13 the Senate inserted "plain, adequate and complete" at this point. (SLJ, p. 83)

74 On a motion by Paterson, this section was struck out on July 11. Both the SLJ, p. 82, and a note by Otis filed with the bill, "Paterson moves to dele. Sect. 15 Courts of Equity," number this section as 15 rather than 16, because section 9 had been struck out. On July 13, on a motion by Ellsworth, seconded by Maclay, the section was restored. (Maclay, June 13)

The words "or in causes of admiralty" through "specially provided" were inserted along the side of the page by Ellsworth. The sentence "And the mode" through "specially provided" does not appear in the printed bill or in the engrossed bill.

the courts respectively, on motion as aforesaid to
give judgment against him ~~or her~~ by default.

16   And be it further enacted by the authority
aforesaid that suits in equity shall not be sustained in either of the courts of the United States,
in any case where remedy may be had at
law.* ~~Nor shall depositions be admitted in either of said courts in suits in equity~~

17   And be it further enacted ~~by the~~
~~authority aforesaid~~, that all the said courts
of the United States shall have power to grant
new trials, in cases where there has been a
trial by jury, for reasons for which new trials
have usually been granted in the courts of
law. — And shall have power to impose &
administer all necessary oaths, & to punish
by fine or imprisonment, at the discretion
of said courts, all contempts of authority
in any cause or hearing before the ~~same~~ same,
& to make & establish all necessary rules
for the orderly conducting business in the
said courts, provided such rules are not
repugnant to the laws of the United States.

And be it further enacted by the authority
aforesaid,

Judiciary Bill [S-1], June 12, 1789. (Courtesy of the National Archives)

17. And be it further enacted ~~by the Authority aforesaid,~~ that all the said courts of the United States shall have power to grant new trials, in cases where there has been a trial by jury, for reasons for which new trials have usually been granted in the courts of law. And shall have power to impose & administer all necessary oaths,[75] & to punish by fine or imprisonment, at the discretion of said Courts, all contempts of authority in any cause or hearing before ~~them~~ same; & to make & establish all necessary rules for the orderly conducting business in the said courts, provided such rules are not repugnant to the laws of the United States.

[18.] And be it further enacted by the authority aforesaid That when ~~Judgment shall be entered~~ in a circuit court, ~~in a upon a verdict~~ judgment upon a verdict in a civil action shall be entered, execution may, on motion of either party, at the discretion of the court, & on Such conditions for the security of the adverse party as they may Judge proper, [be stayed (42)] days from the time of entering judgment, to give time to file in the Clerks office of said Court, a motion for a new trial. And if such motion be there filed within said term of (42)   days, with a certificate thereon from either of the judges of such court, that he allows the same to be filed, which certificate he may make or refuse at his discretion, execution shall of course be further stayed to the next session of said court. And if a new trial be granted the former judgment shall be thereby rendered void.[76]

18 [19.] And be it further enacted ~~by the authority aforesaid,~~ that where in a circuit court, a plaintiff in an action originally brought there,

---

[75] The Senate inserted "or affirmations" at this point.

[76] On July 9 the Senate agreed to an amendment, to be inserted at or near this point, to the effect "that in the Circuit Courts, under the name of equity, they should have all the depositions copied and sent up on an appeal to the Supreme Court, as evidence on the rehearing of facts." On July 10, on a motion by Ellsworth, seconded by Strong, this amendment was reconsidered and apparently disagreed to. (Maclay July 10)

On July 11, on a motion by Ellsworth, the Senate inserted the following section at this point:

> And be it further enacted that it shall be the duty of circuit courts in causes in equity & of ~~circuit & district courts in causes of~~ admiralty & maritime jurisdiction, to cause the facts on which they found their sentence or decree fully to appear upon the record, either from the pleadings & decree ~~itself~~ itself, or a state of the case agreed by ~~their~~ parties or their counsel, or, if they disagree, by a stating of the case by the court. (Senate Bills, SR, DNA, hand of Ellsworth)

A motion by Johnson to strike out "facts" in this new section and insert "evidence" was disagreed to, as was a motion by Paterson to postpone Ellsworth's amendment in favor of the following:

> And be it further enacted, That it shall be the duty of circuit courts in the trial of causes in equity and of admiralty and maritime jurisdiction, where facts are contested, to cause the evidence exhibited at the hearing to be reduced to writing, if either of the parties require it, or a state of the facts to be made, if the parties agree thereto. (Senate Bills, SR, DNA, hand of Paterson)

The *SLJ*, p. 81, omits the words "and maritime" in Paterson's motion.

other than the United States
or a petitioner in equity,ᴧrecovers less than the Sum or value of (500)
    dollars, or a libellant, upon his own appeal less than the Sum or value
of (300)   dollars, he shall not be allowed, but shall[77] pay costs.

    19 [20.] And be it further enacted by the Authority aforesaid, that from
~~all~~ final decrees in a district court in causes of admiralty & maritime
jurisdiction where the matter in dispute exceeds the sum or value of (300)
    dollars, exclusive of costs, an appeal shall be allowed to the next
circuit court to be held in such district.

    20 [21.] And be it further enacted ~~by the Authority aforesaid,~~ that final
                               in a district court
decrees & judgments ~~& Judgments~~ in civil actions,ᴧwhere the matter in
dispute exceeds the sum or value of (50)   dollars, exclusive of costs,
may be reexamined, & reversed or affirmed in a circuit court holden in the
Same district, upon a petition in[78] error, containing[79] an authenticated
transcript of the record, an assignment of errors, & prayer for reversal with a
citation to the adverse party annexed[80] signed by the Judge of such district
court or a Justice of the Supreme court, the [adverse] party having at least
[(20)]   days notice. And upon a like process, may final ~~decrees &~~
                 ~~brought or removed there, otherwise~~
    & decrees & suits in equity   ~~than by Petitions in Error~~
judgementsᴧin civil actionsᴧin a circuit courtᴧbrought there by original process
[or removed there] from Courts of the Several States, or, [if the matter] in
dispute exceeds the Sum or value of [(2,000)]   dollars exclusive of
                                     re
costs, removed there by [appeal] from a district court;[81] beᴧ examined &
reversed or affirmed in the Supreme Court, the citation being in such case
                             a
signed by a Judge of such circuit court orᴧ Justice of the supreme court, & the
adverse party having at least [(30)]   days notice. But there shall be no
reversal in either court[82] for error in ruling any plea in abatement, other
than[83] to the jurisdiction of the court, or such plea to a petition or bill in

---

    77 On July 13 the Senate struck out "shall" and inserted "at the discretion of the
Court may be adjudged to." The engrossed act substitutes "at" for "in." A draft of
this amendment, in the hand of Read, is filed with the bill.
    78 The Senate struck out "petition in" and inserted "Writ of."
    79 On July 11 the Senate struck out "containing" and inserted "whereto shall be
annexed and returned therewith at the day and place therein mentioned." (*SLJ*, p. 82)
A draft of this amendment, in the hand of Read, is filed with the bill.
    80 The Senate struck out "annexed."
    81 The phrase from "brought there by original process" through "district court"
was inserted along the side of the page by Ellsworth.
    82 The Senate inserted "on such Writ of error" at this point.
    83 The Senate inserted "a plea" at this point.

equity as ~~admits the facts~~ is in nature of a demurrer.[84] And Petitions in[85] error shall not be brought but within (3)[86]   years after ~~the renderin~~ rendering or passing the judgment or decree complained of except or in case the person entitled to Such petition in[87] error be[88] *non compos mentis* or imprisoned, then within three[89] years as aforesaid exclusive of the time of ~~his or her~~ such insanity or imprisonment.[90] And every Justice or Judge signing a citation on any petition in[91] error as aforesaid shall take good & sufficient security, that the Petitioner[92] shall prosecute his petition[93] to effect, & answer all damages & costs if he fail to make his plea good.

21 [22.] And be it further enacted ~~by the authority aforesaid,~~ that petitions in[94] error as aforesaid shall be a *Supersedeas* & stay execution in cases only where the matter in dispute, exclusive of costs, exceeds, if in a district court, the sum or value of (300)   dollars, or if in a circuit court, the sum or value of (2,000)   dollars, & the petition[95] is served, by a copy thereof being ~~left~~ lodged for the adverse party, in the clerks office where the record remains, within (10)   days, sundays exclusive, after ~~the~~ rendering the judgment or passing the decree complained of. Until the expiration of which term of (10)   days, executions shall not issue in any case where a petition in[96] error may be a *Supersedeas*. And where the matters in dispute, do not, in the respective courts exceed the several sums aforesaid, petitioners in error, failing of a reversal, shall pay double costs.[97] And where upon a petition in error [that has] stayed execution[98] the supreme or a circuit court shall affirm a Judgment or decree, [they shall] adjudge or decree to the respondent [in] error just damages for his delay, as well as his costs.[99]

---

[84] The Senate inserted "or for any error in fact" at this point.
[85] The Senate struck out "Petitions in" and inserted "Writs of."
[86] The Senate struck out "3" and inserted "Five."
[87] The Senate struck out "petition in" and inserted "Writ of."
[88] The Senate inserted "an Infant feme Covert" at this point.
[89] The Senate struck "three" and inserted "Five."
[90] The Senate struck out "insanity or imprisonment" and inserted "disability."
[91] The Senate struck out "petition in" and inserted "Writ of."
[92] The Senate struck out "Petitioner" and inserted "Plaintiff in error."
[93] The Senate struck out "petition" and inserted "Writ."
[94] The Senate struck out "petitions in" and inserted "Writs of."
[95] On July 13 on a motion by Bassett (Maclay, July 13), the Senate struck out "matter in dispute" through "petition" and inserted "Writ of error." (*SLJ*, p. 82)
[96] The Senate changed "petition in" to "writ of."
[97] The Senate struck out from "And where the" through "double costs."
[98] On July 13 the Senate struck out "petition in error that has stayed execution" and inserted "such Writ of error."
[99] On July 11 Ellsworth moved:
  That ~~Justice~~ in the trial of causes in the Supreme Court upon a writ of Error from a circuit Court the Justices who sat in the trial of the cause shall not vote in the decission of the cause except where the court shall be equally divided but may assign the reasons of their former decission.
The draft amendment, in the hand of Ellsworth, is filed with the bill. This amend-

22 [23.] And be it further enacted by the Authority aforesaid, that when a judgment or decree shall be reversed in a circuit Court, such court shall proceed to renderʌjudgment or pass such decree as the district court should have rendered or passed; &̶ g̶r̶a̶n̶t̶ e̶x̶e̶c̶u̶ And the supreme Court shall do the same on reversals b̶e̶f̶o̶r̶e̶ [̶t̶h̶e̶r̶i̶n̶?̶]̶ therin, except where the reversal is in favour of the plaintiff or petitioner in the original Suit, & the damages to be assessed, or matter to be decreed, are uncertain, in which case they shall send the cause back for a final decision. And the Supreme Court shall not issue execution in causes that are removed before them by petitions in[100] error but shall send a special mandate to the circuit court to award execution thereupon.

23 [24.] And be it further enacted by the authority aforesaid, that a final judgment or decree in any Suit, in the highest court of law or equity of a State in which a decision in the Suit could be had; where is drawn in question the validity of a treaty or statute of, or an authority exercised under the United States, & the decission is against their validity; or where is drawn in question the validity of a Statute of or an authority exercised under t̶h̶ a̶n̶y̶ any state, on the ground of their being repugnant to the constitution, treaties or laws of the United States, & the decission is in favour of such their validity; or where is drawn in question the construction of a̶ t̶r̶e̶a̶t̶y̶ t̶h̶e̶ any clause of the constitution or of a treaty or statute of, or commission held under the United States, & the decission is against the title, right, priviledge or exemption specially set up or claimed by either party, under such clause of the said constitution, treaty, statute or commission; may be reexamined & reversedʌ or &̶ affirmed in the Supreme court of the United States, upon a petition in[101] error, the citation being signed by the chief Justice or Judge or Chancellor of the court rendering or passing the judgment or decree complained of, or by a Justice of the Supreme court of the United States, in the same manner & under the same regulations, & the petition[102] shall have the same effect, as if the judgment or decree complained of had been rendered or passed in in a circuit court; & the proceedings[103] upon the reversal shall also be the same, except that the Supreme Court instead of Sending back the cause for a final

---

ment, which probably would have been inserted at or near this point, did not pass. The following replacement motion was then offered, but it was not agreed to:

> But no Judge of the Supreme Court shall sit i̶n̶ j̶u̶d̶g̶m̶e̶n̶t̶ on any cause where in he has giv'n judgement in a circuit Court.

The draft amendment, in the hand of Otis, is filed with the bill.

On July 13, the Senate struck out "as well as his costs" and inserted "and single or double costs at their discretion." (*SLJ*, p. 83)

[100] The Senate struck out "petitions in" and inserted "writs of."
[101] The Senate struck out "petition in" and inserted "writ of."
[102] The Senate struck out "petition" and inserted "Writ."
[103] The word "proceedings" was changed to "proceeding."

decission as before provided, may at their discretion, if the cause shall have
been once so sent back before, proceed to a final decission of the same & award
execution. But no other error shall be assigned or regarded as a ground of
reversal in any such case as aforesaid, than Such as[104] immediately respect[105]
the before mentioned questions of validity or construction of the said Con-
                commissions [*lined out*] or authorities
stitution, treaties, Statutes, &c. in dispute.

24 [25.] And be it further enacted that in all Causes brought before either
of the Courts of the United States to recover the Forfeiture annexed to any
Articles of Agreement Covenant Bond or other Specialty, where the Forfeiture Breach or nonperformance shall be found by Jury[106] by the Default or
Confession of the Defendant or upon Demurrer the Court before whom the
Action is, shall render Judgment therein for the Plaintiff to recover so much
as is due according to Equity.[107]

And be it further enacted, that all Suits between a State and the Citizens of
another State or between Citizens of different States or between the Citizens
of a State and foreign States Citizens or Subjects [*three lines obliterated by water
stains*] when a suit shall be commenced in any other District than as above
directed the Writ shall be abated and the Defendant allowed double Costs.
And neither of the Courts abovementioned shall have Cognizance of any
Action to recover the Contents of a promissory Note or other Chose in Action
in favor of any Assignee unless an Action might have been prosecuted in such
Court to recover the said Contents if no assignment had been made.

[26.] And be it further enacted, That a Marshall shall be appointed in and
for each District, for the Term of four years; [but] shall be removable from
Office at Pleasure; whose duty it shall be, to attend the District & Circuit
Courts when sitting therein, and also the Supreme Court in the District in
which that Court shall sit: and to execute throughout the District, all lawful
precepts directed to him, and issued under the authority of the United States;
and he shall have Power to command all necessary assistance in the Execution
of his Duty, and to appoint, as there shall be occasion, one or more Deputies,
who shall be removeable from Office by the Judge of the District Court, or
the Circuit Court, sitting within the District at the pleasure of either; and
before he enters on the duties of his Office, he shall become bound for the
faithful Performance of the same, by himself and by his Deputies, before the
Judge of the District Court, to the Treasurer of[108] the United States, jointly

---

104 The Senate inserted "appears on the face of the record and" at this point.
105 The Senate changed "respect" to "respects."
106 The Senate struck out "be found by Jury" and inserted "appear."
107 The Senate inserted "And when the sum for which judgment should be rendered is uncertain the same shall, if either of the Parties request it, be assessed by a
Jury" at this point.
108 The Senate struck out "the Treasurer of."

& severally, with two good and sufficient Sureties Inhabitants and Free-holders of such District, to be approved by the District Judge, in the sum of (30,000)[109]   dollars, and shall take before said Judge, as shall also his Deputies, before they enter on the duties of their Appointment, the following Oath of Office.

I, A.B. do solemnly swear or affirm, that I will faithfully execute all lawful Precepts directed to the Marshall of the District of   under the authori-ty of the United States, and true Returns make, and in all Things well and truly, and without Malice or Partiality, perform the duties of the Office of Marshall (or Marshalls Deputy as the Case may be) of the District of during my Continuance in said Office, and take only my lawful Fees.

So help me God.[110]

And in all Causes wherein the Marshall or his Deputy shall be a party, the Writs and Precepts therein, shall be directed to such disinterested Person, as the Court or any Justice thereof may appoint: and the Person so appointed is hereby authorised to execute and return the same—And in Case of the Death of any Marshall, his Deputy or Deputies shall continue in Office, unless otherwise specially removed; and shall execute the same, in the name of the deceased, until another Marshall be appointed & sworn—And the Defaults or Misfeasances in Office of such Deputy or Deputies in the mean Time as well as before shall be adjudged a Breach of the Condition of the Bond given as before directed by the Marshall who appointed them; and the Executor or Administrator of the deceased Marshall shall have like Remedy for the De-faults & Misfeasances in Office of such Deputy or Deputies during such interval, as they would be entitled to if the marshall had continued in Life and in the [exercise] of his said Office, [until his successor] was appointed and sworn:[111] And every Marshall or his Deputy, when removed from Office, or when the Term for which the Marshall is appointed shall expire, shall have Power notwithstanding to execute all such Precepts as may be in their hands respectively at the Time of such removal or Expiration of Office. And the Marshall shall be held answerable for the Delivery to his Successor of all which may be
Prisoners in his Custody at the Time of his [Removal] or when the Term for which [he is appointed shall expire, and for that purpose may retain such prisoners in his custody until his sucessor] shall be appointed and qualified as the [law directs].

[27.] And be it further enacted, that Grand and petit Jurors who shall be summoned to serve in the Courts of the United States shall have the same Qualifications as are requisite for Jurors by the Laws of the State of which they

---

[109] The Senate struck out "30,000" and inserted "Twenty thousand."

[110] In the engrossed bill, this section ends at this point and the next paragraph is a new section.

[111] The Senate inserted "or affirmed" at this point.

are Citizens, to serve in the highest Courts of Law of such State, and[112] shall be returned as there shall be occasion for them, from such parts of the District from Time to Time as shall be most favorable to an impartial Trial and as the Court shall direct, so as not͜ incur an unnecessary Expense or unduly to burthen the Citizens of any part of the District with such services[113]—And Writs of Venire facias when directed by the Court shall issue from the Clerks Office and shall be served and returned by the Marshall in his proper Person or by his Deputy out of such List as shall be given him by the Marshall, or in case the Marshall or his Deputy is not an indifferent Person or is interested in the Event of the Cause, by such fit Person as the Court shall specially appoint for that purpose to whom they shall administer an Oath[114] that he will truly & impartially serve and return such Writ—And when from Challenges or otherwise there shall not be a Jury to determine any civil or criminal Cause the Marshall or his Deputy shall by order of the Court where such Defect of Jurors shall happen return Jurymen de talibus circumstantibus sufficient to complete the Panel and when the Marshall or his Deputy are disqualified as aforesaid Jurors may be returned by such disinterested Person as the Court shall appoint.

[28.] And be it enacted by the Authority aforesaid, that the mode of Proof by oral Testimony and Examination of Witnesses in open Court shall be the same in all the Courts of the United States as well in the Trial of Causes in Equity and of Admiralty and Maritime Jurisdiction as of Actions at Common Law—And when the Testimony of any Person shall be necessary in any Civil Cause depending in any District in any Court of the United States who shall live out of such District and at a greater Distance from the place of Trial than one hundred Miles or is bound on a Voyage to Sea or is about to go out of the United States or out of such District, and to a greater Distance from the Place of Trial than as aforesaid, before the Time of Trial—the Deposition of such Person may be taken de bene esse before any Justice or Judge of any of the Courts of the United States, or before any Chancellor Justice or Judge of a Supreme or Superior Court, Mayor of a City or Judge of a County Court or Court of Common Pleas of any of the United States not being of Counsel or Attorney to either of the Parties or interested in the Event of the Cause,

---

[112] On July 9 the Senate disagreed to a motion to insert "That Grand Jurors in all cases whatever, and petit Jurors in all cases not punishable with death" at this point.

[113] On July 9 the Senate disagreed to a motion to insert "That petit Jurors, in all cases punishable with death, shall be returned from the body of the county in which the offence was committed" at this point. (*SLJ*, p. 80) On July 13 the Senate disagreed to a motion by Lee, seconded by Grayson, to reconsider this action and insert the following proviso:

> Provided always, that in criminal cases where the punishment is capital, the petit jury shall come from the body of the county where the fact was committed. (*SLJ*, p. 83)

[114] The Senate inserted "or affirmation" at this point.

provided that a Notification from the Magistrate before whom the Deposition is to be taken to the adverse Party to be present at the taking of the same and to put Interrogatories if he think fit, be first made out and served on the adverse Party or his Attorney as either may be nearest, if either is within such District or within one hundred Miles of the Place of such Caption allowing Time for their attendance after [notified, not less than at the] rate of one Day, [Sundays] exclusive, [for every twenty miles travel. And in causes of admiralty and maritime jurisdiction,[115] when a libel shall be filed, in which an adverse] party is not named, and depositions of persons circumstanced as aforesaid shall be taken before a Claim be put in, the like Notification as aforesaid shall be given to the Person having the Agency or Possession of the Property libelled at the Time of the Capture or Seizure of the same if known to the Libellant—And every Person deposing as aforesaid shall be carefully examined and cautioned and sworn[116] to testify the whole Truth, and shall subscribe the Testimony by him or her given after the same shall be reduced to writing which shall be done only by the Magistrate taking the Deposition or by the Deponent in his presence—And the Depositions so taken shall be retained by such Magistrate until he deliver the same with his own hand into the Court for which they are taken, or shall together with a Certificate of the Reasons as aforesaid of their being taken and of the Notice if any given to the adverse Party, be by him the said Magistrate sealed up and directed to such Court and remain under his Seal until opened in Court—and any Person may be compelled to depose as aforesaid in the same manner as to appear and testify in Court—And in the Trial of any Cause of Admiralty or Maritime Jurisdiction, in a District Court,[117] the Decree in which may be appealed from, if either Party shall suggest to and satisfy the Court, that probably it will not be in his power to produce the Witnesses there testifying before the Circuit Court[118] should an Appeal be had, and shall move that their Testimony be taken down in writing, it shall be so done by the Clerk of the Court—And if an appeal be had, such Testimony may be used on the Trial of the same, if it shall appear to the satisfaction of the Court which shall try the Appeal, that the Witnesses are then[119] gone out of the United States or out of the District where the Trial is, and to a greater Distance than as aforesaid, from the place where the Court is sitting, or that by Reason of Age sickness bodily Infirmity or Imprisonment they are unable to travel and appear at Court, but not otherwise—And unless the same shall be made to appear on

---

[115] The Senate inserted "or other cases of seizure" at this point.

[116] The Senate inserted "or affirmed" at this point.

[117] On July 10 the Senate reconsidered a motion to insert "or on any hearing of a cause in equity in a circuit court" at this point, and the amendment was struck out.

[118] On July 10 the Senate reconsidered an amendment inserting "or supreme court, as the case may be" at this point, and the amendment was struck out.

[119] The Senate inserted "dead or" at this point.

the Trial of any Cause with Respect to Witnesses whose Depositions may have been taken therein, such Depositions shall not be admitted or used in the Cause—Provided that nothing herein shall be construed to prevent any Court of the United States from granting a dedimus potestatem to take Depositions according to common usage when it may be necessary to prevent a failure or delay of Justice which power they shall severally possess—Nor to extend to Depositions taken in perpetuam Rei Memoriam which if they relate to Matters that may be Cognizable in any Court of the United States, a Circuit Court on application thereto made as a Court of Equity may according to the usages in Chancery direct to be taken.

Suit[120]

[29.] And be it enacted, That where any ~~Action~~ shall be depending in any Court of the United States and either of the Parties shall die before final Judgment, the Executor or Administrator of such deceased Party who was Plaintiff, Petitioner or Defendant in Case the Cause of Action doth by Law survive, shall have full Power to prosecute or defend any such Suit or Action until final Judgment, and the Defendant or Defendants are hereby obliged to answer thereto accordingly, And the Court before whom such Cause may be depending is hereby impowered & directed to hear and determine the same and to render Judgment for or against the Estate of the deceased in the hands of such[121] Executor or Administrator as the Case may require—And if such Executor or Administrator having been duly served with a Scire facias from the Office of the Clerk of the Court when such Suit is depending (20)
days before hand, shall neglect or refuse to become a Party to the Suit the Court may render Judgment against the Estate of the deceased Party in the same manner as if the Executor or Administrator had voluntarily made himself a Party to the Suit—And the Executor or Administrator who shall become a Party as aforesaid shall upon Motion to the Court where the Suit is depending be entitled to a [continuance of] the same until the next Term of the said Court—And if there be [two or more plaintiffs or defendants, and one or more of them shall die,] if the cause of [~~said~~?] action shall [survive to the surviving] Plaintiff or Plaintiffs, or against the surviving Defendant or Defendants, the Writ or Action shall not be thereby abated, but such Death being suggested upon the Record, and Action shall proceed at the Suit of the surving Plaintiff or Plaintiffs against the surviving Defendant or Defendants.

[30.] And be it further enacted, That no Summons Writ Declaration Return Process Judgment or other Proceedings in ~~either~~ any of the Courts of the United States shall be abated arrested quashed or reversed, for any Defect or

---

[120] The word "Suit" was inserted by Otis.

[121] On July 10 the Senate struck out "Estate of the deceased in the hands of such." (*SLJ*, p. 81) The *SLJ* also says that the words "or by" were inserted, but they would have made the phrase unintelligible and were not included in the engrossed bill.

want of Form, but the said Courts respectively shall proceed and give Judgment according as the right of the Cause and Matter in Law shall appear unto them without regarding any Imperfections Defects or want of Form in such Writ Declaration or other Pleading Return Process Judgment or Course of Proceeding whatsoever, except those only in Cases of Demurrer, which the Party demurring shall specially set down and express together with his Demurrer as the Cause thereof—And the said Courts respectively shall and may by virtue of this Act from Time to Time amend all and every such Imperfections Defects & Wants of Form other than those only which the Party demurring shall express as aforesaid. [122]

[31.] And be it further enacted by the authority aforesaid, [123] that every Justice of the Supreme Court and Judge of a District Court may either upon his own knowledge or the Complaint of others [124] cause any Person to be apprehended for any Offence against the Laws of the United States and brought before himself for Examination and if he shall think proper may bail or commit such Offender or send him by Warrant to the District where the Offence was committed—And [125] for any Crime or Offence against the Laws of [126] the United States, the Offender may [127] by any Justice of the Peace or other Magistrate of any of the United States where he may be found agreeably to the mode of Process against Offenders in such State accustomed, and at the Expence of the United States be arrested and imprisoned or bailed as the Case may be, for Trial before such Court of the United States as by this Act has Cognizance of the Offence—And Copies of the Process shall be returned as speedily as may be into the Clerks Office of such Court together with the Recognizances of the Witnesses for their appearance to testify in the Case, which Recognizances the Magistrate before whom the Examination shall be may require on pain of Imprisonment—And if such Committment of the Offender or the Witnesses shall be in a District other than that in which the Offence is to be tried, it shall be the Duty of the Judge of that District where the Delinquent is imprisoned, seasonably to issue and of the Marshall of the same District to execute a Warrant for the Removal of the Offender and the

---

[122] On July 10 the Senate inserted the following at this point:
and may, at any time permit either of the parties to amend any defect in the process or pleadings, upon such conditions as the said courts respectively shall in their discretion, and by their rules prescribe. (Ibid.)
[123] On July 10 the Senate struck out "by the authority aforesaid" in this section and in all other cases where the words were redundant. (Ibid.)
[124] On July 3 a motion by Maclay, seconded by Lee, to strike out "either upon his own" through "of others" and insert "upon oath or affirmation made and reduced to writing and signed by the party, stating sufficient reason in law," was disagreed to. (Maclay, July 3)
[125] On July 10 the Senate struck out "every Justice" through "committed—And." (SLJ, p. 81)
[126] The Senate struck out "the Laws of."
[127] The Senate inserted "by any Justice or Judge of the United States, or" at this point.

Witnesses or either of them, as the Case may be, to the District ~~to the District~~ in which [the] Trial is [to be had.] And upon all arrests in criminal [cases,] bail shall be admitted, except where the punishment may be death, in which cases it shall not be admitted but by the Supreme or a circuit court, or two Justices of the supreme [court, or one] justice of the supreme & a Judge of a district court, who shall [exercise] their discretion therein, regarding the nature & circumst[ances of the] offence, & of the evidence & the usages of law.[128]

[32.] And be it further enacted, that in all the courts of the United States, the Parties may plead & [manage] their own Causes personally or by the assistance of such Counsel or Attorneys at Law as by the Rules of the said Courts respectively shall be permitted to manage and conduct Causes therein—And each District Court shall appoint[129] a meet Person learned in the Law to act as Attorney for the United States in such District, and shall swear him[130] to the faithful Execution of his Office, whose duty it shall be to [prosecute] in such District all Delinquents for Crimes & Offences, cognizable under the authority of the United States and all [ci]vil Actions [in which the United States shall be concerned, except] before the Supreme Court in the District in which that Court shall be holden—And he shall receive as a compensation for his services such Fees as shall be taxed therefor in the respective Courts before which the Suits or Prosecutions shall be—And the Supreme Court shall also appoint[131] a meet Person learned in the Law to act as

---

[128] The words "And upon all arrests" through "usages of law" were inserted along the side of the page by Ellsworth.

The Senate inserted the following clause at this point:

                           not punishable with death

And if a person committed as aforesd. for ~~want of ba~~ an ~~bailable~~ offence shall afterwards procure bail & there be no Judge of the United States in the district to take the same, it may be taken by any Judge of the Supreme or superior Court of law of such State.

The amendment, in the hand of Ellsworth, and another draft in the hand of Otis, are filed with the bill.

The Senate also inserted the following additional section at this point:

                           Laws

And be it further enacted, That the ~~Statute law~~ of the several States ~~in force for the time being, & their unwritten or common law now in use, whether by adoption from the common law of England, the ancient Statutes of the same or otherwise,~~ except where the constitution Treaties or Statutes of the United States shall otherwise require or provide, shall be regarded as rules of decission in [*lined out*] trials at common law in the courts of the United States in cases where they apply.

This draft amendment, in the hand of Ellsworth, is filed with the bill.

[129] The Senate struck out "each District Court shall appoint" and inserted "there shall be appointed in each district."

[130] The Senate struck out "and shall swear him" and inserted "who shall be sworn or affirmed."

[131] The Senate struck out "And the Supreme Court shall also appoint" and inserted "And there shall also be appointed."

Attorney General for the United States and shall swear him[132] to a faithful Execution of his Office whose duty it shall be to prosecute and conduct all Suits in such[133] Court in which the United States shall be concerned, and to give [his] advice and opinion upon Questions of Law when required by the President of the United States, or when requested by the Heads of any of the Departments touching any matters that may concern their Departments and shall receive such Compensation for his services as shall by Law be provided.

Senate Bills, SR, DNA. Sections 1–9 were written by Paterson, 10–24 by Ellsworth, 25 by Strong, and 25–32, including the unnumbered cancelled section, by a Senate clerk. From this we have concluded that the subcommittee to draft this bill consisted of at least Paterson, Ellsworth, and Strong. A printed copy, which differs from the manuscript in two places, indicated in the notes, is in the Broadside Collection, RBkRm, DLC.

The manuscript bill is heavily lined out and annotated, and in some places was made illegible by water stains. We supplied the illegible words from the printed copy; these appear in brackets.

The Senate amendments not printed in the *SLJ*, pp. 80–83, or filed with the bill were determined by comparing the bill as introduced with the engrossed bill. Other proposed amendments, which do not appear in the engrossed bill, are printed separately below.

---

[132] The Senate struck out "and shall swear him" and inserted "who shall be sworn or affirmed."

[133] The Senate struck out "such" and inserted "the Supreme."

Proposed Amendments
June 22–July 9, 1789

That no subordinate federal jurisdiction be established in any State, other than for Admiralty or Maritime causes but that federal interference shall be limited to Appeal only from the State Courts to the supreme federal Court of the U. States.

Senate Bills, SR, DNA, hand of Lee.

         the Jugds. &c. may
~~upon~~ that,ᴧ for any offence against the L. of the U.S. upon ~~the~~ complaint exhibited on oath or affirmation; or if the offence be committed in their
              [*lined out*] ~~what is~~ is   able with corporal
presence & with actual force,ᴧ or ~~when~~ corporal punishᴧ ~~ment may be in-~~
         punishment
~~flicted,~~ may upon their own Knowledge.

for any offence against the laws of the United States, upon complaint ~~on oa~~ exhibited on oath or affirmation, or where the offence is committed in his presence, & with actual force or is an offence for which corporal punishment may be inflicted, may, upon his own Knowledge cause any person to be apprehended & brot. before himself for examination.

The above two drafts are in Senate Bills, SR, DNA and in the hand of Ellsworth and are apparently of the same amendment.

Judiciary Bill [S-1]
July 17, 1789

AN ACT to establish the Judicial Courts of the UNITED STATES

1. BE IT ENACTED BY THE SENATE AND HOUSE OF REPRESENTATIVES OF THE UNITED STATES OF AMERICA IN CONGRESS ASSEMBLED, That the Supreme Court of the United States shall consist of a Chief Justice[1] and five associate Justices, any four[2] of whom shall be a quorum, and shall hold annually at the seat of the federal[3] government two sessions, the one commencing the first Monday of February, & the other the first Monday of August. That the associate Justices shall have precedence according to the date of their Commissions, or when the Commissions of two or more of them bear date on the same day, according to their respective ages.

2. AND BE IT FURTHER ENACTED, That the United States shall be, and they hereby are divided into thirteen districts, to be limited and called as follows, to wit, One to consist of that part of the State of Massachusetts which lies easterly of the State of New-Hampshire, and to be called Main district; One to consist of the State of New-Hampshire, and to be called New-Hampshire district; one to consist of the remaining part of the State of Massachusetts, and to be called Massachusetts district; one to consist of the State of Connecticut, and to be called Connecticut district; one to consist of the State of New-York, and to be called New-York district; one to consist of the State of New-Jersey, and to be called New-Jersey district; one to consist of the State of Pennsylvania, and to be called Pennsylvania district; one to consist of the State of Delaware,[4] and to be called Delaware district; one to consist of the State of Maryland, and to be called Maryland district; one to consist of the State of Virginia, except that part heretofore called the

---

[1] On August 24, a motion by Burke to strike out "a Chief Justice" was withdrawn. (*GUS,* Aug. 26)

[2] On August 24, the COWH disagreed to a motion by Livermore to strike out "four" and insert "three." (Ibid.)

[3] On August 24, on a motion by Benson, the COWH struck out "the federal." (Ibid.)

[4] On September 15, the House disagreed to a motion by White to add the Eastern Shore of Maryland and Virginia to the Delaware district and certain counties in northern Virginia to the Maryland district. (*NYDA,* Sept. 16; *GUS,* Sept. 19)

district of Kentucky, and to be [ca]lled Virginia district; one to consist of the remaining part of the State of Virginia, and to be [calle]d Kentucky district;[5] one to consist of the State of South-Carolina, and to be called South Carolina district; and one to consist of the State of Georgia, and to be called Georgia district.[6]

[3.] AND BE IT FURTHER ENACTED, That there be a Court called a district Court in each of the afore-mentioned districts to consist of one Judge, who shall reside in the district for which he is appointed, and shall be called a district Judge, and shall hold annually four Sessions, the first of which to commence as follows, to wit, in the districts of New York, and of New-Jersey on the first, in the district of Pennsylvania on the second, in the district of Connecticut on the third,[7] in the districts[8] of Delaware and of South-Carolina[9] on the fourth Tuesdays of November next; in the [distri]cts of Massachusetts, of Main and of Maryland on the first, in the district of Georgia on the [second], and in the districts of New-Hampshire, of Virginia and of Kentucky on the third Tuesdays [of] December next; and the other three Sessions progressively in the respective districts on the like Tuesdays of every third calendar Month afterwards;[10] and that the district Judge shall have power to hold special Courts at his discretion. That the stated district Court shall be held at the places following, to wit, in the district of Main at Portland;[11] in the district of New-Hampshire at[12] Portsmouth;[13] in the district of Massachusetts at Boston;[14] in the district of Connecticut alternately at Hartford and New Haven beginning at the first; in the district of New-York at New York; in the district of New Jersey alternately at New Brunswick and Burlington beginning at the first; in the district of Pennsylvania at Philadelphia;[15] in the district of Delaware alternately at New-Castle[16]

---

[5] On August 24, the COWH disagreed to a motion by Livermore to strike out the clause establishing the Kentucky district. (*GUS,* Aug. 26)

[6] On August 24, the COWH disagreed to a motion by Tucker, seconded by Sumter, to strike out section 2. (Ibid.)

[7] The House inserted "and" at this point.

[8] The House changed "districts" to "district."

[9] The House struck out "and of South-Carolina."

[10] The House inserted the following at this point:
and in the district of South Carolina, on the third Monday in March and September; the first Monday in July, and the second Monday in December of each and every year, commencing in December next.

[11] The House inserted "and Pownalsborough alternately, beginning at the first" at this point.

[12] The House inserted "Exeter and" at this point.

[13] The House inserted "alternately, beginning at the first" at this point.

[14] The House inserted "and Salem alternately, beginning at the first" at this point.

[15] The House inserted "and York Town alternately, beginning at the first" at this point.

[16] In the engrossed bill, "New-Castle" was underlined, indicating that the ninth House amendment, which was rejected by the Senate, appeared at this point.

and Dover beginning at the first; in the district of Maryland alternately at Baltimore and Easton[17] beginning at the first; in the district of Virginia alternately at Richmond and Williamsburgh beginning at the first; in the district of Kentucky at Harrodsburgh; in the district of South Carolina at Charleston; and in the district of Georgia alternately at Savannah and Augusta beginning at the first; and that the special Courts shall be held at the same place in each district as the stated Courts, or in districts that have two at either of them in the discretion of the Judge, or at such other place in the district as the nature of the business and his discretion shall direct. And that, in the districts that have but one place for holding the district Court, the records thereof shall be kept at that place, and in districts that have two, at that place in each district which the Judge shall appoint.[18]

4. AND BE IT FURTHER ENACTED, That the before-mentioned districts except those of Main and Kentucky shall be divided into three circuits, and be called the eastern, the middle, and the southern circuit. That the eastern circuit shall consist of the districts of New Hampshire, Massachusetts, Con-
consist
necticut, and New York; that the middle circuit shall of the districts of New-Jersey, Pennsylvania, Delaware, Maryland and Virginia; and that the southern circuit shall consist of the districts of South Carolina and Georgia; and that there shall be held annually in each district of said Circuits two Courts, which shall be called circuit Courts, and shall consist of any two Justices of the Supreme Court, and the district Judge of such districts, any two of whom shall constitute a quorum: Provided that no district Judge shall give a vote in any Case of appeal or error from his own decision, but may assign the reasons of such his decision.

5. AND BE IT FURTHER ENACTED, That the first Session of the said circuit Court in the several districts shall commence at the times following, to wit, in New-Jersey on the second, in New-York on the fourth, in Pennsylvania on the eleventh, in Connecticut on the twenty second, in South Carolina on the twenty fifth,[19] and in Delaware on the twenty seventh days of April next; in Massachusetts on the third, in Maryland on the seventh, in Georgia on the tenth,[20] in New Hampshire on the twentieth, and[21] in Virginia on the twenty second[22] days of May next; and the subsequent Sessions in the respec-

---

[17] On September 15, the House disagreed to a motion by Seney to strike "Easton" and insert "Chestertown" by a recorded vote of 23–20. (*GUS,* Sept. 15)

[18] On August 31, the COWH disagreed, 33–11, to a motion made by Livermore on August 24 to strike section 3. (*GUS,* Aug. 26, Sept. 2; *NYDA,* Sept. 1. The *CR,* Aug. 31, reports the vote as 31–11.)

[19] The House struck out "in South Carolina on the twenty fifth."

[20] The House struck out "in Georgia on the tenth" and inserted "in South Carolina on the twelfth."

[21] The House struck out "and."

[22] The House inserted "and in Georgia on the twenty eighth" at this point.

tive districts on the like days of every sixth calendar month afterwards, except[23] when any of those days shall happen on a Sunday, and then the session shall commence on the next day following. And the sessions of the said circuit Court shall be held in the district of New Hampshire at Portsmouth;[24] in the district of Massachusetts at Boston; in the district of Connecticut alternately at Hartford and New Haven beginning at the last; in the district of New York alternately at New-York and Albany beginning at the first; in the district of New-Jersey at Trenton; in the district of Pennsylvania[25] at Philadelphia;[26] in the district of Delaware alternately at New Castle[27] and Dover beginning at the first; in the district of Maryland alternately at Annapolis and Easton beginning at the first; in the district of Virginia alternately at Richmond[28] and Williamsburgh beginning at the first; in the district of South Carolina alternately at[29] Charleston and Cambden[30] beginning at the first; and in the district of Georgia alternately at Savannah and Augusta beginning at the first. And the circuit Courts shall have power to hold special sessions for the trial of Criminal Causes[31] at their discretion, or at the discretion of the Supreme Court.

6. AND BE IT FURTHER ENACTED, That the Supreme Court may, by any one or more of its Justices being present, be adjourned from day to day until a quorum be convened; and that a circuit Court may also be adjourned from day to day by any one of its Judges, or if none are present by the Marshall of the district, until a quorum be convened; and that a district Court, in case of the inability of the Judge to attend at the commencement of a Session, may, by virtue of a written Order from the said Judge directed to the Marshall of the district, be adjourned by the said Marshall to such day, antecedent to the next stated session of the said Court, as in the said order shall be appointed; and in case of the death of the said Judge, and his vacancy not being supplied, all process, pleadings, and proceedings of what nature soever, pending before the said Court, shall be continued of course until the next stated session after the appointment and acceptance of the Office by his Successor.

7. AND BE IT ENACTED, That the Supreme Court, and the district Courts, shall have power to appoint Clerks for their respective Courts; and that the

---

[23] The House inserted "in South Carolina where the session of the said Court shall commence on the first, and in Georgia where it shall commence on the seventeenth day of October, and except" at this point.

[24] The House inserted "and at Exeter alternately, beginning at the first" at this point.

[25] The House inserted "alternately" at this point.

[26] The House inserted "and York Town beginning at the first" at this point.

[27] In the engrossed bill, "New Castle" was underlined, indicating that the sixteenth House amendment, which was rejected by the Senate, appeared at this point.

[28] The House struck out "Richmond" and inserted "Charlottsville."

[29] The House inserted "Columbia and" at this point.

[30] The House struck out "and Cambden."

[31] The House inserted "at any other time" at this point.

Clerk of[32] each district Court shall be Clerk also of the circuit Court in such district; and each of the said Clerks shall, before he enters upon the execution of his Office, take the following oath or affirmation, to wit; "I, A.B. being appointed Clerk of   do solemnly swear, or affirm, that I will truly and faithfully enter and record all the orders, decrees, judgments, and proceedings of the said Court; and that I will faithfully and impartially discharge and perform all the duties of my said Office, according to the best of my abilities, and understanding. So help me God." Which words So help me God, shall be omitted in all cases where an Affirmation is admitted instead of an oath. And the said Clerks shall also severally give bond with sufficient sureties (to be approved of by the district Judge[33]) to the United States in the sum of Two thousand dollars, faithfully to discharge the duties of his Office, and seasonably to record the decrees, Judgments, and determinations of the Court of which he is Clerk.

8. AND BE IT FURTHER ENACTED, That the Justices of the Supreme Court, and the district Judges, before they proceed to execute the duties of their respective Offices, shall take the following oath or affirmation, to wit, "I, A.B. do solemnly swear, or affirm, that I will administer Justice without respect to Persons, and do equal right to the poor and to the rich; and that I will faithfully and impartially discharge and perform all the duties incumbent on me as   according to the best of my abilities and understanding, agreeably to the constitution and laws of the United States. So help me God."

9. AND BE IT FURTHER ENACTED, That the district Courts shall have, exclusively of the Courts of the several States, cognizance of all crimes and offences that shall be cognizable under the authority of the United States, committed within their respective districts, or upon the high Seas; where[34] other corporal[35] punishment than whipping, not exceeding Thirty stripes, a higher fine than[36] One hundred Dollars, or a longer[37] term of imprisonment than[38] Six Months, is not[39] to be inflicted; except where the laws of the United States shall otherwise direct.[40] And shall also have exclusive original cognizance of all civil Causes of Admiralty and Maritime Jurisdiction, including all seizures under laws of impost, navigation, or trade of the United States, where the seizures are made, on waters which are navigable from the

---

[32] The enrolled act reads "for" in place of "of."

[33] The House struck out "district Judge" and inserted "Supreme and district Courts respectively."

[34] The House inserted "no" at this point.

[35] The House struck out "corporal."

[36] The House struck out "a higher fine than" and inserted "a fine not exceeding."

[37] The House struck out "longer."

[38] The House struck out "than" and inserted "not exceeding."

[39] The House struck out "not."

[40] The House struck out "except where the laws of the United States shall otherwise direct."

sea by Vessels of ten or more tons burthen, within their respective districts as well as upon the high Seas. Saving to Suitors, in all cases, the right of a common law remedy where the common law is competent to give it: And shall also have exclusively, of the Courts of the several States, jurisdiction[41] of all seizures on land, or other waters, than as aforesaid made, and of all suits for penalties and forfeitures incurred, under the laws of the United States. And shall also have cognizance, concurrent with the Courts of the several States, or the circuit Courts, as the case may be, of all Causes where a foreigner[42] sues for a tort only in violation of the law of Nations or a treaty of the United States. And shall also have cognizance, concurrent as last mentioned, of all suits at common law where the United States sue, and the matter in dispute amounts, exclusive of costs, to the sum or value of One hundred dollars. And shall also have jurisdiction exclusively, of the Courts of the several States, of all suits against Consuls, or Vice Consuls, except for offences above the description aforesaid. And the trial of issues in fact, in the district Courts, in all Causes except civil Causes of Admiralty and Maritime jurisdiction, shall be by Jury.

10. AND BE IT FURTHER ENACTED, That the district Court in Kentucky district shall, besides the jurisdiction aforesaid, have jurisdiction of all other Causes, except of Appeals and Writs of error, herein after made cognizable in a circuit Court, and shall proceed therein in the same manner as a circuit Court. And Writs of error[43] shall lie from decisions therein to the Supreme Court in the same Causes, as from other district Courts to a circuit Court, or from[44] a circuit Court to the Supreme Court, and under the same regulations.[45]

11. AND BE IT FURTHER ENACTED, That the circuit Courts shall have original cognizance, concurrent with the Courts of the several States, of all suits of a civil nature at common law or in equity, where the matter in dispute exceeds, exclusive of costs, the sum or value of Five hundred dollars and the United States are Plaintiffs or Petitioners; or an Alien is a party, or the suit is between a Citizen of the State where the suit is brought, and a Citizen of another State. And shall have exclusive cognizance of all crimes and

---

[41] The House struck out "exclusively, of the Courts of the several States, jurisdiction" and inserted "exclusive original cognizance."

[42] The House struck out "a foreigner" and inserted "an alien."

[43] The House inserted "and appeals" at this point.

[44] The House struck out "other district Courts to a circuit Court, or from."

[45] The House inserted the following at this point:

And the district Court in Main district, shall besides the jurisdiction herein before granted, have jurisdiction of all causes, except of Appeals and writs of error herein after made cognizable in a circuit Court, and shall proceed therein in the same manner as a circuit Court: And writs of error shall lie from decisions therein to the circuit Court in the district of Massachusetts in the same manner as from other district Courts to their respective circuit Courts.

offences cognizable under the authority of the United States, except where this act otherwise provides, or the laws of the United States shall otherwise direct, and concurrent jurisdiction with the district Courts of the crimes and offences cognizable therein. But no Person shall be arrested in one district for trial in another, in any civil action before a circuit or district Court. And no civil suit shall be brought before either of said Courts against an inhabitant of the United States by any original process in any other district than that whereof he is an inhabitant, or in which he shall be found at the time of serving the Writ; nor shall any district or circuit Court have cognizance of any suit to recover the contents of any promissory note or other chose in action in favor of an Assignee, unless a suit might have been prosecuted in such Court to recover the said contents if no assignment had been made, except in cases of foreign Bills of exchange. And the circuit Courts shall also have appellate jurisdiction from the district Courts under the regulations and restrictions herein after provided—And Main district shall, for every purpose affecting the jurisdiction of a circuit Court, be considered as a part of Massachusetts district.[46]

12. AND BE IT FURTHER ENACTED, That if a suit be commenced in any State Court against an Alien, or by a Citizen of the State in which the suit is brought against a Citizen of another State, and the matter in dispute exceeds the aforesaid sum, or value of Five hundred dollars, exclusive of costs, to be made to appear to the satisfaction of the Court, and the Defendant shall, at the time of entering his appearance in such State Court, file a motion[47] for the removal of the Cause for trial into the next circuit Court to be held in the district where the suit is pending, or if in the district of Main to the circuit[48] Court next to be holden in Massachusetts district,[49] or if in Kentucky district to the district Court next to be holden therein, and offer good and sufficient surety for his entering in such Court, on the first day of its session, copies of said process against him, and also for his there appearing[50] in the Cause if special bail was originally requisite therein; it shall then be the duty of the State Court to accept the surety, and proceed no further in the Cause; and any bail that may have been originally taken shall be discharged; and the said copies being entered as aforesaid, in such Court of the United States, the Cause shall there proceed in the same manner as if it had been brought there by original process. And any attachment of the goods or estate of the defendant by the original process, shall hold to respond the final judgment, in the same manner as by the laws of such State, they would have been holden to

---

46 The House struck out "And Main district" through "Massachusetts district."
47 The House struck out "motion" and inserted "Petition."
48 The House struck out "circuit" and inserted "district."
49 The House struck out "in Massachusetts district" and inserted "therein."
50 The House inserted "and entering special bail" at this point.

respond final Judgment, had it been rendered in a Court of the same.[51] And if in any Action commenced in a State Court the title of land be concerned, and the parties are Citizens of the same State, and the matter in dispute exceeds the sum or value of Five hundred dollars, exclusive of costs, the sum or value being made to appear to the satisfaction of the Court, either party, before the trial, shall state to the Court and make affidavit if they require it, that he claims and shall rely upon a right or title to the land under a grant from a State other than that in which the suit is pending, and produce the original grant or an exemplification of it, except where the loss of public Records shall put it out of his power, and shall move that the adverse party inform the Court, whether he claims a right or title to the land under a grant from the State, in which the suit is pending, the said adverse party[52] shall give such information, or, otherwise not be allowed to plead such grant or give it in evidence upon the trial; and if he informs that he does claim under such grant, the party claiming under the grant first mentioned, may then, on motion, remove the cause for trial to the next circuit Court to be holden in such district; or if in the district of Main, to the circuit[53] Court next to be holden in Massachusetts district;[54] or if in Kentucky district, to the district Court next to be holden therein; but if he is the defendant, shall do it under the same regulations as in the before mentioned case of the removal of a Cause into such Court by an Alien: And neither party removing the Cause, shall be allowed to plead or give evidence of any title aliene to the grant[55] by him stated as aforesaid, as the ground of his Claim. And the trial of issues in fact in the circuit Courts shall ∧in all suits except those of equity and of admiralty and maritime jurisdiction, be by Jury.

13. AND BE IT FURTHER ENACTED, That the Supreme Court shall have exclusive jurisdiction of all controversies of a civil nature, where a State is a party, except between a State and its Citizens; and except also between a State and Citizens of other States or Aliens, in which latter case it shall have original but not exclusive jurisdiction. And shall have exclusively all such jurisdiction of suits or proceedings against Ambassadors, or other public Ministers, or their domestics or domestic servants, as a Court of law can have or exercise consistently with the law of Nations; and original, but not ex-

---

[51] The House struck out "to respond the final judgment" through "the same" and inserted the following:

the goods or estate so attached to answer the final judgment in the same manner as by the laws of such State they would have been holden to answer final judgment, had it been rendered by the Court in which the suit commenced.

[52] The enrolled act omits "party."

[53] The House struck out "circuit."

[54] The House struck out "in Massachusetts district" and inserted "therein."

[55] The House struck out "title aliene to the grant" and inserted "other title than that."

clusive jurisdiction of all suits brought by Ambassadors, or other public Ministers, or in which a Consul or Vice-Consul shall be a party. And the trial of issues in fact in the Supreme Court, in all actions at law against Citizens of the United States, shall be by Jury. The Supreme Court shall also have appellate jurisdiction from the circuit Courts and Courts of the several States, in the cases herein after specially provided for: And shall have power to issue Writs of prohibition to the district Courts when proceeding as Courts of admiralty and Maritime jurisdiction; and Writs of Mandamus, in cases warranted by the principles and usages of law, to any Courts appointed, or persons holding office, under the authority of the United States.

14. AND BE IT FURTHER ENACTED, That all the before mentioned Courts of the United States shall have power to issue Writs of Scire facias, habeas Corpus, and all other Writs not specially provided for by Statute, which may be necessary for the exercise of their respective jurisdictions, and agreeable to the principles and usages of law. And that either of the Justices of the Supreme Court, as well as Judges of the district Courts, shall have power to grant Writs of Habeas Corpus for the purpose of an enquiry into the cause of commitment. Provided that Writs of Habeas Corpus shall in no case extend to Prisoners in Gaol, unless where they are in custody under or by color of the authority of the United States, or are committed for trial before some Court of the same, or are necessary to be brought into Court to testify.

15. AND BE IT FURTHER ENACTED, That all the said Courts of the United States, shall have power in the trial of actions at law, on motion and due notice thereof being given, to require the parties to produce books or writings in their possession or power which contain evidence pertinent to the issue, in cases and under circumstances where they might be compelled to produce the same by the ordinary rules of proceeding in chancery; And if a Plaintiff shall fail to comply with such order, to produce books or writings, it shall be lawful for the Courts respectively, on motion, to give the like judgment for the defendant as in cases of nonsuit; and if a defendant shall fail to comply with such order, to produce books or writings, it shall be lawful for the Courts respectively, on motion as aforesaid, to give judgment against him or her by default.

16. AND BE IT FURTHER ENACTED, That suits in equity shall not be sustained in either of the Courts of the United States, in any case where plain, adequate and complete remedy may be had at law.

17. AND BE IT FURTHER ENACTED, That all the said Courts of the United States shall have power to grant new trials, in cases where there has been a trial by Jury, for reasons for which new trials have usually been granted in the Courts of law: And shall have power to impose and administer all necessary oaths or affirmations, and to punish by fine or imprisonment, at the discretion of said Courts, all contempts of authority in any Cause or hearing before

the same; and to make and establish all necessary rules for the orderly conducting business in the said Courts, provided such rules are not repugnant to
the laws of the United States.

18. AND BE IT FURTHER ENACTED, That when in a circuit Court, judgment upon a Verdict in a civil Action shall be entered, execution may, on
Motion of either Party, at the discretion of the Court, and on such conditions
for the security of the adverse Party as they may judge proper, be stayed Forty
two days from the time of entering judgment, to give time to file in the
Clerk's office of said Court, a Motion[56] for a new trial. And if such Motion[57]
be there filed within said term of Forty two days, with a Certificate thereon
from either of the Judges of such Court, that he allows the same to be filed,
which Certificate he may make or refuse at his discretion, execution shall of
course be further stayed to the next session of said Court. And if a new trial be
granted the former judgment shall be thereby rendered void.

19. AND BE IT FURTHER ENACTED, That it shall be the duty of circuit
Courts, in Causes in equity and of admiralty and maritime jurisdiction, to
cause the facts on which they found their sentence or decree, fully to appear
upon the Record either from the pleadings & decree itself, or a state of the
Case agreed by the Parties, or their Council, or if they disagree, by a stating
of the Case by the Court.

20. AND BE IT FURTHER ENACTED, That where in a circuit Court, a
Plaintiff in an action, originally brought there, or a Petitioner in equity,
other than the United States, recovers less than the sum or value of Five
hundred dollars, or a libellant, upon his own appeal less than the sum or
value of Three hundred dollars, he shall not be allowed but at the discretion
of the Court may be adjudged to pay Costs.

21. AND BE IT FURTHER ENACTED, That from final decrees in a district
Court in causes of admiralty and maritime jurisdiction, where the matter in
dispute exceeds the sum or value of Three hundred dollars, exclusive of costs,
an appeal shall be allowed to the next circuit Court to be held in such
district.[58]

22. AND BE IT FURTHER ENACTED, That final decrees and judgments in
civil Actions in a district Court, where the matter in dispute exceeds the sum
or value of Fifty dollars, exclusive of costs, may be re-examined, and reversed
or affirmed in a circuit Court holden in the same district, upon[59] a Writ of
error whereto shall be annexed and returned therewith at the day and place

---

[56] The House struck out "Motion" and inserted "petition."
[57] The House struck out "Motion" and inserted "Petition."
[58] The House inserted the following proviso at this point:
  Provided nevertheless, that all such Appeals from final decrees as aforesaid from the
  district Court of Main, shall be made to the circuit Court, next to be holden
  after each appeal in the district of Massachusetts.
[59] In the engrossed bill, "upon" was underlined, indicating that the forty-first
House amendment, which was rejected by the Senate, appeared at this point.

therein mentioned, an authenticated transcript of the record, an assignment of errors, and prayer for reversal, with a citation to the adverse Party, signed by the Judge of such district Court or a Justice of the supreme Court, the adverse Party having at least Twenty days notice. And upon a like process, may final judgments and decrees in civil Actions and suits in equity in a circuit Court brought there by original process or removed there from Courts of the several States, or if the matter in dispute exceeds the sum or value of Two thousand dollars exclusive of Costs,[60] removed there by appeal from a district Court;[61] be re-examined and reversed or affirmed in the Supreme Court, the citation being in such case signed by a Judge of such circuit Court or Justice of the Supreme Court, and the adverse Party having at least Thirty days notice. But there shall be no reversal in either Court on such Writ of error for error in ruling any plea in abatement, other than a plea to the jurisdiction of the Court, or such plea to a Petition or bill in equity as is in the nature of a demurrer, or for any error in fact. And Writs of error shall not be brought but within Five years after rendering or passing the judgment or decree complained of, or in case the Person entitled to such Writ of error be an Infant feme Covert, Non compos Mentis or imprisoned, then within Five years as aforesaid, exclusive of the time of such disability. And every Justice or Judge signing a citation on any Writ of error as aforesaid shall take good and sufficient security, that the Plaintiff in error shall prosecute his Writ to effect, and answer all damages and costs if he fail to make his plea good.

23. AND BE IT FURTHER ENACTED, That Writs[62] of error as aforesaid shall be a Supersedeas and stay execution in cases only where the Writ of error is served, by a Copy thereof being lodged for the adverse Party, in the Clerk's Office where the record remains, within Ten days, Sundays exclusive, after rendering the Judgment or passing the decree complained of. Until the expiration of which term of Ten days, executions shall not issue in any case where a Writ of error may be a Supersedeas; and where, upon such Writ of error the supreme or a circuit Court shall affirm a judgment or decree, they shall adjudge or decree to the respondent in error just damages for his delay, and single or double costs at their discretion.

24. AND BE IT FURTHER ENACTED, That when a judgment or decree shall be reversed in a circuit Court, such Court shall proceed to render such judgment or pass such decree as the district Court should have rendered or passed; and the Supreme Court shall do the same on reversals therein, except where the reversal is in favor of the Plaintiff or Petitioner in the original suit, and the damages to be assessed, or matter to be decreed, are uncertain, in

---

60 The House struck out "if the matter" through "Costs."
61 The House inserted "where the matter in dispute exceeds the sum or value of Two thousand Dollars exclusive of Costs" at this point.
62 The House struck out "Writs" and inserted "a Writ."

which case they shall send the Cause back[63] for a final decision. And the Supreme Court shall not issue execution in Causes that are removed before them by writs of error, but shall send a special Mandate to the circuit Court to award execution thereupon.

25. AND BE IT FURTHER ENACTED, That a final judgment or decree in any suit, in the highest Court of law or equity of a State in which a decision in the suit could be had; where is drawn in question the validity of a treaty or statute of, or an authority exercised under the United States, and the decision is against their validity; or where is drawn in question the validity of a statute of, or an authority exercised under any State, on the ground of their being repugnant to the constitution, treaties or laws of the United States, and the decision is in favor of such their validity; or where is drawn in question the construction of any clause of the constitution, or of a treaty or statute of, or commission held under the United States, and the decision is against the title, right, privilege or exemption specially set up or claimed by either party, under such clause of the said Constitution, treaty, statute or Commission; may be re-examined and reversed or affirmed in the Supreme Court of the United States, upon a Writ of error, the citation being signed by the chief Justice or Judge or Chancellor of the Court rendering or passing the judgment or decree complained of, or by a Justice of the Supreme Court of the United States, in the same manner and under the same regulations, and the Writ shall have the same effect, as if the judgment or decree complained of had been rendered or passed in a circuit Court; and the proceeding upon the reversal shall also be the same, except that the Supreme Court instead of sending back[64] the cause for a final decision as before provided, may at their discretion, if the cause shall have been once so sent back[65] before, proceed to a final decision of the same, and award execution. But no other error shall be assigned or regarded as a ground of reversal in any such case as aforesaid, than such as appears on the face of the record and immediately respects the before-mentioned questions of validity or construction of the said constitution, treaties, statutes, commissions, or authorities in dispute.

26. AND BE IT FURTHER ENACTED, That in all causes brought before either of the Courts of the United States to recover the forfeiture annexed to any articles of Agreement, covenant, bond or other speciality, where the forfeiture, breach or non-performance shall appear, by the default or confession of the defendant, or upon demurrer, the Court before whom the action is, shall render judgment therein for the Plaintiff to recover so much as is due according to equity. And when the sum for which judgment should be rendered is uncertain the same shall, if either of the Parties request it, be assessed by a Jury.

---

[63] The House struck out "send the Cause back" and inserted "remand the Cause."
[64] The House struck out "sending back" and inserted "remanding."
[65] The House struck out "so sent back" and inserted "remanded."

27. AND BE IT FURTHER ENACTED, That a Marshall shall be appointed in and for each district, for the term of Four years; but shall be removeable from office at pleasure; whose duty it shall be, to attend the district and circuit Courts when sitting therein, and also the Supreme Court in the district in which that Court shall sit: And to execute throughout the district, all lawful precepts directed to him, and issued under the authority of the United States; and he shall have power to command all necessary assistance in the execution of his duty, and to appoint, as there shall be occasion, one or more deputies, who shall be removeable from Office by the Judge of the district Court, or the circuit Court sitting within the district, at the pleasure of either; and before he enters on the duties of his office, he shall become bound for the faithful performance of the same, by himself and by his deputies, before the Judge of the district Court, to the United States, jointly and severally, with two good and sufficient sureties, inhabitants and freeholders of such district, to be approved by the district Judge, in the sum of Twenty thousand dollars, and shall take before said Judge, as shall also his Deputies, before they enter on the duties of their appointment, the following Oath of Office: "I, A.B. do solemnly swear or affirm, that I will faithfully execute all lawful precepts directed to the Marshall of the district of   under the authority of the United States, and true returns make, and in all things well and truly, and without malice or partiality, perform the duties of the Office of Marshall (or Marshall's deputy, as the case may be) of the district of   during my continuance in said Office, and take only my lawful fees. So help me God."

28. AND BE IT FURTHER ENACTED, That in all causes wherein the Marshall or his deputy shall be a party, the Writs and precepts therein shall be directed to such disinterested Person as the Court or any Justice or Judge thereof may appoint: And the Person so appointed is hereby authorised to execute and return the same: And in case of the death of any Marshall, his deputy or deputies shall continue in Office, unless otherwise specially removed; and shall execute the same, in the name of the deceased, until another Marshall be appointed and sworn: And the defaults or misfeasances in Office of such deputy or deputies in the mean time as well as before, shall be adjudged a breach of the condition of the bond given as before directed by the Marshall who appointed them; and the executor or administrator of the deceased Marshall shall have like remedy for the defaults and misfeasances in office of such deputy or deputies during such interval, as they would be entitled to if the Marshall had continued in life and in the exercise of his said Office, until his Successor was appointed and sworn or affirmed: And every Marshall or his deputy when removed from Office, or when the term for which the Marshall is appointed shall expire, shall have power notwithstanding to execute all such precepts as may be in their hands respectively at the time of such removal or expiration of Office, and the Marshall shall be held answerable for the delivery to his Successor of all Prisoners which may be in

his custody at the time of his removal, or when the term for which he is appointed shall expire, and for that purpose may retain such Prisoners in his custody until his Successor shall be appointed and qualified as the law directs.

29. AND BE IT FURTHER ENACTED, That grand and petit Jurors who shall be summoned to serve in the Courts of the United States,[66] shall have the same qualifications as are requisite for Jurors by the laws of the State of which they are Citizens, to serve in the highest Courts of law of such State, and shall be returned as there shall be occasion for them, from such parts of the district from time to time[67] as shall be most favorable to an impartial trial, and as the Court shall direct,[68] so as not to incur an unnecessary expense or unduly to burthen the Citizens of any part of the district with such services. And writs of Venire facias when directed by the Court shall issue from the Clerk's office and shall be served and returned by the Marshall in his proper Person or by his deputy out of such list as shall be given him by the Marshall,[69] or in case the Marshall or his deputy is not an indifferent Person, or is interested in the event of the cause, by such fit Person as the Court shall specially appoint for that purpose, to whom they shall administer an oath or affirmation that he will truly and impartially serve and return such Writ. And when from challenges or otherwise there shall not be a Jury to determine any civil or criminal cause, the Marshall or his deputy shall, by order of the Court where such defect of Jurors shall happen return Jurymen de talibus circumstantibus sufficient to complete the pannel; and when the Marshall or his deputy are disqualified as aforesaid, Jurors may be returned by such disinterested Person as the Court shall appoint.

30. AND BE IT FURTHER ENACTED, That the mode of proof by oral testimony and examination of Witnesses in open Court shall be the same in all the Courts of the United States, as well in the trial of causes in equity and of admiralty and maritime jurisdiction as of actions at common law.[70] And

---

[66] On September 14, the House amended the phrase, "That grand and petit Jurors" through "United States." Motions by Burke, to add a clause requiring indictments and trials for felonies or treason to be held in the locality where the crime was committed, and by Smith (S.C.), specifying that juries should be formed according to state laws, were agreed to. (GUS, Sept. 16) Burke's amendment was House amendment number forty-eight, which was amended to read as follows by the Senate before being accepted:

> That in cases punishable with death, the trial shall be had in the county where the offence was committed, or where that cannot be done without great inconvenience, twelve petit Jurors, at least, shall be summoned from thence. And Jurors, in all cases, to serve in the Court of the United States, shall be designated by lot or otherwise, in each State respectively, according to the mode of forming Juries therein, now practised, so far as the laws of the same shall render such designation practicable by the Courts or Marshalls of the United States, and the Jurors. (SLJ, p. 179)

[67] The House inserted "as the Court shall direct, so" at this point.
[68] The House struck out "as the Court shall direct."
[69] The House struck out "out of such list as shall be given him by the Marshall."
[70] In the engrossed bill, "law" was underlined, indicating that the fifty-second House amendment, which was disagreed to by the Senate, appeared at this point.

when the testimony of any person shall be necessary in any civil Cause depending in any district in any Court of the United States, who shall live out of such district, and[71] at a greater distance from the Place of trial than one hundred Miles, or is bound on a Voyage to Sea, or is about to go out of the United States or out of such district, and to a greater distance from the place of trial than as aforesaid, before the time of trial, or is ancient or very infirm, the deposition of such Person may be taken de bene esse before any Justice or Judge of any of the Courts of the United States, or before any Chancellor, Justice or Judge of a Supreme or Superior Court, Mayor[72] of a City, or Judge of a County Court or Court of common Pleas of any of the United States not being of Counsel or Attorney to either of the Parties, or interested in the event of the cause; provided that a notification from the Magistrate before whom the deposition is to be taken to the adverse Party, to be present at the taking of the same, and to put interrogatories if he think fit, be first made out and served on the adverse Party or his Attorney as either may be nearest, if either is within such district, or[73] within one hundred Miles of the Place of such Caption, allowing time for their attendance after notified, not less than at the rate of one day, Sundays exclusive, for every Twenty miles travel. And in causes of admiralty and maritime jurisdiction, or other cases of seizure when a libel shall be filed, in which an adverse Party is not named, and depositions of Persons circumstanced as aforesaid shall be taken before a claim be put in, the like notification as aforesaid shall be given to the Person having the agency or possession of the property libelled at the time of the capture or seizure of the same, if known to the Libellant. And every Person deposing as aforesaid shall be carefully examined and cautioned, and sworn or affirmed to testify the whole truth, and shall subscribe the testimony by him or her given after the same shall be reduced to writing, which shall be done only by the Magistrate taking the deposition, or by the deponent in his presence. And the depositions so taken shall be retained by such Magistrate, until he deliver the same with his own hand into the Court for which they are taken; or shall, together with a Certificate of the reasons as aforesaid of their being taken, and of the notice if any given to the adverse Party, be by him the said Magistrate sealed up and directed to such Court, and remain under his Seal until opened in Court. And any Person may be compelled to appear and depose as aforesaid in the same manner as to appear and testify in Court. And in the trial of any cause of admiralty or maritime jurisdiction in a district Court, the decree in which may be appealed from, if either Party shall suggest to and satisfy the Court that probably it will not be in his power to produce the Witnesses there testifying, before the circuit Court should an appeal be had, and shall move that their testimony be taken down in writing, it shall be so done by the

---

[71] The House struck out "out of such district, and."
[72] The House inserted "or chief Magistrate" at this point.
[73] The House struck out "within such district, or."

Clerk of the Court: And if an appeal be had, such testimony may be used on the trial of the same, if it shall appear to the satisfaction of the Court which shall try the appeal, that the Witnesses are then dead, or gone out of the United States, or out of the district where the trial is, and[74] to a greater distance than as aforesaid from the place where the Court is sitting, or that by reason of age, sickness, bodily infirmity or imprisonment they are unable to travel and appear at Court, but not otherwise: And unless the same shall be made to appear on the trial of any cause, with respect to Witnesses whose depositions may have been taken therein, such depositions shall not be admitted or used in the cause. Provided that nothing herein shall be construed to prevent any Court of the United States from granting a dedimus Potestatem, to take depositions according to common usage, when it may be necessary to prevent a failure or delay of justice; which Power they shall severally possess; nor to extend to depositions taken in Perpetuam Rei Memoriam, which, if they relate to matters that may be cognizable in any Court of the United States, a circuit Court, on application thereto made as a Court of equity, may, according to the usages in Chancery, direct to be taken.

31. AND BE IT ENACTED, That where any suit shall be depending in any Court of the United States, and either of the Parties shall die before final judgment, the executor or administrator of such deceased Party who was Plaintiff, Petitioner, or defendant, in case the cause of action both by law survive, shall have full power to prosecute or defend any such suit or action until final judgment; and the defendant or defendants are hereby obliged to answer thereto accordingly; and the Court before whom such cause may be depending is hereby impowered and directed to hear and determine the same, and to render judgment for or against the executor or administrator, as the case may require. And if such executor or administrator having been duly served with a scire facias from the office of the Clerk of the Court where such suit is depending Twenty days beforehand, shall neglect or refuse to become a Party to the suit, the Court may render judgment against the estate of the deceased Party, in the same manner as if the executor or administrator had voluntarily made himself a Party to the suit: And the executor or administrator who shall become a Party as aforesaid, shall, upon motion to the Court where the suit is dependening, be entitled to a continuance of the same until the next term of the said Court. And if there be two or more Plaintiffs or defendants, and one or more of them shall die, if the cause of action shall survive to the surviving Plaintiff or Plaintiffs, or against the surviving defendant or defendants, the Writ or action shall not be thereby abated; but such death being suggested upon the record, the action shall proceed at the suit of the surviving Plaintiff or Plaintiffs against the surviving defendant or defendants.

32. AND BE IT FURTHER ENACTED, That no summons, Writ, declaration,

---

[74] The House struck out "out of the district where the trial is, and."

return, Process, judgment, or other Proceedings[75] in any of the Courts of the United States, shall be abated, arrested, quashed or reversed, for any defect or want of form, but the said Courts respectively shall proceed and give judgment according as the right of the cause and matter in law shall appear unto them, without regarding any imperfections, defects, or want of form in such Writ, declaration or other Pleading, return, process, judgment, or course of proceeding whatsoever, except those only in cases of demurrer, which the Party demurring shall specially set down and express together with his demurrer as the cause thereof: And the said Courts respectively shall and may, by virtue of this Act from time to time, amend all and every such imperfections, defects and wants of form, other than those only which the Party demurring shall express as aforesaid, and may at any time permit either of the Parties to amend any defect in the process of pleadings, upon such conditions as the said Courts respectively shall in their discretion, and by their rules prescribe.

33. AND BE IT FURTHER ENACTED, That for any crime or offence against the United-States, the offender may, by any Justice or Judge of the United States, or by any Justice of the Peace, or other Magistrate of any of the United States where he may be found, agreeably to the[76] mode of process against offenders in such State accustomed,[77] and at the expence of the United States, be arrested and imprisoned or bailed as the case may be, for trial before such Court of the United States as by this act has cognizance of the offence: And copies of the process shall be returned as speedily as may be into the Clerk's Office of such Court, together with the recognizances of the Witnesses for their appearance to testify in the case; which recognizances the Magistrate before whom the examination shall be, may require on pain of imprisonment: And if such commitment of the offender, or the Witnesses shall be in a district other than that in which the offence is to be tried, it shall be the duty of the Judge of that district where the delinquent is imprisoned, seasonably to issue, and of the Marshall of the same district to execute a warrant for the removal of the offender and the Witnesses, or either of them, as the case may be, to the district in which the trial is to be had. And upon all arrests in criminal cases, bail shall be admitted, except where the punishment may be death, in which cases it shall not be admitted but by the Supreme or a circuit Court, or two Justices of the Supreme Court, or one Justice of the Supreme and[78] a Judge of a district Court, who shall exercise their discretion therein, regarding the nature and circumstances of the offence, and of the evidence, and the usages of law. And if a Person committed by a Justice of the Supreme or a Judge of a district Court, for an offence not punishable with death, shall

---

[75] The House inserted "in civil causes" at this point.
[76] The House inserted "usual" at this point.
[77] The House struck out "accustomed."
[78] The House struck out "or two Justices of the Supreme Court, or one Justice of the Supreme and" and inserted "or by a Justice of the supreme Court, or."

afterwards procure bail, and there be no Judge of the United States in the district to take the same, it may be taken by any Judge of the Supreme, or Superior Court of Law of such State.

34. AND BE IT FURTHER ENACTED, That the laws of the several States except where the constitution, treaties or statutes of the United States shall otherwise require or provide, shall be regarded as rules of decision in trials at common law in the Courts of the United States in cases where they apply.

35. AND BE IT FURTHER ENACTED, That in all the Courts of the United States, the Parties may plead and manage their own causes personally or by the assistance of such Counsel or Attornies at law as by the rules of the said Courts respectively shall be permitted to manage and conduct causes therein. And there shall be appointed in each district a meet Person, learned in the law, to act as Attorney for the United States in such district, who shall be sworn or affirmed to the faithful execution of his office, whose duty it shall be to prosecute in such district all delinquents for crimes and Offences, cognizable under the authority of the United States, and all civil actions in which the United States shall be concerned, except before the Supreme Court in the district in which that Court shall be holden: And he shall receive as a compensation for his services such fees as shall be taxed therefor in the respective Courts before which the suits or prosecutions shall be. And there shall also be appointed a meet Person, learned in the law, to act as Attorney General for the United-States, who shall be sworn or affirmed, to a faithful execution of his Office; whose duty it shall be to prosecute and conduct all suits in the Supreme Court in which the United States shall be concerned, and to give his advice and opinion upon questions of law when required by the President of the United States, or when requested by the heads of any of the departments, touching any matters that may concern their departments; and shall receive such compensation for his services as shall by law be provided.

UNITED STATES OF AMERICA
IN SENATE July the 17th. 1789
Read the third time and Passed
SAM. A. OTIS Secy.

Engrossed Senate Bills and Resolutions, SR, DNA. The first page of the bill is torn; we supplied the missing words and letters, in brackets, from a printed copy in the Broadside Collection, RBkRm, DLC. Unless otherwise mentioned, we determined the House amendments by comparing the engrossed bill with the enrolled act. Four House amendments, numbers 9, 16, 41, and 52, which correspond to footnotes 16, 27, 59, and 70, were rejected by the Senate. We were able to identify the places at which these appeared because they, like the location of the other House amendments, were underlined in the engrossed bill. The Senate committee report recommending the disagreement to the four amendments and an amendment to House amendment 48 (note 66) is in Senate Select Committee Reports, SR, DNA, in the hand of Ellsworth.

Kentucky and Vermont
Representatives Act [S-20]

February 25, 1791

AN ACT REGULATING THE NUMBER OF
REPRESENTATIVES TO BE CHOSEN BY THE
STATES OF KENTUCKY AND VERMONT

BE IT ENACTED BY THE SENATE AND HOUSE OF REPRESENTATIVES OF
THE UNITED STATES OF AMERICA IN CONGRESS ASSEMBLED, That until the
representatives in Congress shall be apportioned according to an actual enu-
meration of the inhabitants of the United States, the States of Kentucky and
Vermont shall each be entitled to choose two representatives.

FREDERICK AUGUSTUS MUHLENBERG
    Speaker of the House of Representatives
JOHN ADAMS
    Vice President of the United States, and
    President of the Senate

Approved February
the Twenty fifth
1791

GO. WASHINGTON
    President of the United States

I do certify that this Bill
did originate in the Senate.
Attest,
SAM A. OTIS Secretary

Enrolled Acts, RG 11, DNA.

Calendar

Date	House	Senate
1791		
Feb. 11		By unanimous consent, King permitted to bring in "a Bill

Date	House	Senate
1791		
		regulating the number of Representatives to be chosen by the States of Kentucky and Vermont," which was read twice.[1]
Feb. 12		Read; agreed to.
	Received; read twice; committed to COWH.	
Feb. 14–18	Postponed as order of the day.	
Feb. 19	Debated in COWH; read and agreed to.	
Feb. 22	Signed by speaker.	
Feb. 23		Signed by vice president.
Feb. 25		Signed by president.

[1] This bill was originally a section of the Vermont Statehood Bill [S-19].

Kentucky Statehood Act [S-16]

February 4, 1791

An Act declaring the consent of
Congress that a new State be formed
within the jurisdiction of the
Commonwealth of Virginia, and
admitted into this Union by the name
of the State of Kentucky

Whereas the legislature of the commonwealth of Virginia, by an Act entitled "An Act concerning the erection of the district of Kentucky into an independant State," passed the eighteenth day of December one thousand seven hundred and eighty nine, have consented that the District of Kentucky within the jurisdiction of the said Commonwealth and according to its actual boundaries at the time of passing the Act aforesaid, should be formed into a new State, And Whereas a Convention of Delegates chosen by the People of the said District of Kentucky, have petitioned Congress to consent that on the first day of June one thousand seven hundred and ninety two the said District should be formed into a new State and received into the Union by the name of "the State of Kentucky."

[1] Be it enacted by the Senate, and House of Representatives of the United States of America in Congress assembled, and it is hereby enacted and declared that the Congress doth consent that the said District of Kentucky, within the jurisdiction of the Commonwealth of Virginia, and according to its actual boundaries on the eighteenth day of December one thousand seven hundred and eighty nine, shall, upon the first day of June one thousand seven hundred and ninety two, be formed into a new State separate from and independant of the said Commonwealth of Virginia.

[2] And be it further enacted and declared, that upon the aforesaid first day of June one thousand seven hundred and ninety two, the said new State, by the name and stile of the State of Kentucky, shall be received and admitted into this Union, as a new and entire member of the United States of America.

FREDERICK AUGUSTUS MUHLENBERG
Speaker of the House of Representatives
JOHN ADAMS
Vice President of the United States, and
President of the Senate

Approved February ⎫
the fourth   ⎬   GO. WASHINGTON
1791   ⎭   President of the United States

I do certify that this Act did originate
in the Senate of the United States.
Attest,
SAM. A. OTIS, Secy.

Enrolled Acts, RG 11, DNA.

Calendar

Date	House	Senate
1790		
Dec. 9	Presidential message received, transmitting papers relating to Kentucky statehood.	Presidential message received, transmitting papers relating to Kentucky statehood.[1]
Dec. 14		On motion by Schuyler,[2] committee appointed to report on Kentucky papers (Schuyler, Monroe, and Johnson).
1791		
Jan. 3		Schuyler presented *committee report;* report agreed to and committee ordered to bring in a bill.
Jan. 4		Committee presented *a bill declaring the consent of Congress to the independence of the Dis-*

[1] The message and documents are printed in the *SLJ*, pp. 502–4.
[2] The motion, in the hand of Schuyler and endorsed by Otis, "General Schuylers motion to Commit the Kentucky papers," is in Senate Simple Resolutions and Motions, SR, DNA.

Date	House	Senate
1791		
		trict of Kentucky, which was read.
Jan. 5		Read; ordered printed.
Jan. 7		Debated and postponed.
Jan. 12		Read; agreed to as *An Act declaring the consent of Congress that a new state be formed within the jurisdiction of the Commonwealth of Virginia, and admitted into this union by the name of the State of Kentucky.*[3]
	Received and read.	
Jan. 13	Read; committed to COWH.	
Jan. 17–27	Postponed as order of the day.	
Jan. 28	On motion by Brown,[4] debated in COWH; read; agreed to.	
Jan. 31	Signed by speaker.	Signed by vice president.
Feb. 4		Signed by president.

[3] The title recorded in the *SLJ* on January 12 was "An Act providing that the district of Kentucky should become an independent State, and be admitted as a member of the United States of America." This copyist's error was corrected on January 28.
[4] *GUS*, Jan. 29.

Senate Committee Report
January 3, 1791

The committee which was directed to take into consideration the papers referred to in the president's speech in relation to Kentucky
Beg leave to report
That it appears to your committee, the General Assembly of the common-
the district of Kentucky,
wealth of virginia, did (upon the application of the inhabitants residing in͵
part of the commonwealth of Virginia, to be seperated therefrom, to the

intent, that the said district might become an Independent state, and a member of the union of the united states of America,) by act of the legislature, passed on the 18th day of December 1789, (Authenticated (copy whereof is filed in the office of the Secretary of State of the united states) intitled "An Act concerning the erection of the district of Kentucky into an independant state" Assent to the Independance of the said district on certain conditions stipulated and contained in the said Act, a printed copy whereof is herewith submitted.

That It appears from the papers referred to the consideration of your Committee, That a convention of deputies from the several counties in the said district, was convened in conformity to the said Act, which in the name, and in behalf, of the people whom they represented, declared It, as the will of the said good people to be erected into an independant state, on the terms and conditions specifyed In the said Act of the commonwealth of Virginia.

That by the memorial of the said convention bearing to Congress bearing date the 28th of July 1790 praying to be recieved into the foedral union by the name of the state of Kentucky, It is declared that the people of the said district "are as warmly devoted to the American union, and as firmly attatched to the present happy establishment of the fedral government as any of the citizens of the united states."

That from General such information as Your committee have been able to procure, the Inhabitants resident in the said district are sufficiently numerous for all the purposes of an Independant state.

That from these facts your committee opinion have concluded that It would be proper for Congress to consent that the said district should become an Independant state, and be admitted as a member of the united states of America, and that a bill should be prepared for that purpose.

Various Select Committee Reports, SR, DNA, hand of Schuyler.

Kentucky Statehood Bill [S-16]
January 4, 1791

An Act declaring the consent of Congress to the
independance of the district of Kentucky

Whereas The Legislature of the common wealth of[1] Virginia having in hath by and by an Act Intitled "An Act concerning the erection of the District of Ken-

---

[1] The word "of" was written over another word, which is illegible.

tucky into an Independant state" passed on the 18th day of December 1789, assented that the said district should become a state seperate from and Indebeing pendant of the said Common Wealth, And ~~whereas~~ congress is willing to Consent thereto, Therefore

Be It enacted by the Senate and house of Representatives of the united States of America and It is hereby enacted and declared that in conformity with the powers vested in Congress by the third section of the fourth Article of the Constitution of the united States of America, The Congress doth consent that on the first day of June 1792 the district of Kentucky as composed of the counties specified in the first section of the said Act of the legislature of ~~Virginia~~ the Commonwealth of Virginia passed on the 18th day (Authenticated of December 1789 ~~copy whereof is filed in the office of the Secretary for the department of state of the united states)~~ shall be received and Admitted as a distinct member of the united states of America and as a state seperate from and Independant of the said commonwealth of Virginia by the name and Style of the state of Kentucky[2] ~~provided~~

~~Provided nevertheless that nothing in this Act contained shall be of any force or validity unless a convention to be held in the said district shall before the said first day of June 1792 have adopted and ratified the constitution of the united states of America.~~

Senate Bills, SR, DNA, hand of Schuyler.

---

[2] The phrase "and as a state" through "Kentucky" was written in the margin to be inserted at this point.

Kentucky Statehood Bill [S-16]
January 12, 1791

An act declaring the consent of Congress that a new
State be formed within the Jurisdiction of the Commonwealth
of virginia, & admitted into this Union by the name of
the State of Kentucky

Whereas the legislature of the commonwealth of Virginia by an act, intitled "an act concerning the erection of the District of Kentucky into an independant State," passed the 18th. day of December, 1789, have consented that being the District of Kentucky within the Jurisdiction of the said Commonwealth ~~& composed of the Counties of Jefferson, Nelson, Mercer, Lincoln, Madison,~~

                                                    and   its
~~Fayette, Woodford, Bourbon & Mason~~ ∧according to∧ ~~their~~ actual boundaries
at the time of passing the act aforesaid, should be formed into a new State,
and whereas a Convention of Delegates chosen by the People of the said
District of Kentucky, have petitioned Congress to consent that on the first
day of June 1792 the said District should be formed into a new State and
~~admit~~ received into the Union by the name of "the State of Kentucky—"

[1] Be it enacted by the Senate, and house of Representatives of the U.S. of
America in Congress assembled, and it is hereby enacted and declared that
the Congress doth consent that the said District of Kentucky, ~~being~~ within
the Jurisdiction of the commonwealth of Virginia, ~~& composed of the counties aforesaid of the of Jefferson, Nelson, Mercer, Lincoln, Madison, fayette,~~
                                        and   its
~~Woodford, Bourbon & Mason,~~ ∧according to∧ ~~their~~ actual Boundaries ~~at the time of the pa~~ on the 18th. day of December 1789, shall upon the first day of
June 1792 be formed into a new State separate from & independant of the said
Commonwealth of Virginia.

[2] And be it further enacted & declared, that upon the aforesaid 1st. day
of June 1792 the said ~~District of Kentucky~~ new State, by the name & Stile of
the State of Kentucky shall be received & admitted into this Union, as a new
& entire member of the U.S. of America.

Senate Bills, SR, DNA, hand of King.

Land Office Bill [HR-17]

Calendar

Date	House	Senate
1789		
May 26	Scott gave notice of intention to bring in a bill for a land office. [1]	
May 28	Motion by Scott, to consider land office in COWH, agreed to; motions by Scott, seconded by Vining, to establish land office in western territory and determine the mode of disposing of lands, debated; motion by Boudinot, to strike establishment of land office from the resolutions, debated; COWH rose; motion by Gerry, for a committee to inquire into the state of unappropriated lands in the western territory and report what steps should be taken for their sale, divided and first part agreed to, second part disagreed to;[2] Scott, Huntington, and Sherman appointed to	

---

[1] *GUS*, May 27.
[2] *NYDA, NYDG*, May 29; *GUS*, May 30.

Date	House	Senate
1789		
	"consider the state of the unappropriated lands in the western territory, and to report thereupon."	
June 15	Scott presented committee report "that a law ought to be passed establishing a land office, and regulating the terms and the manner of disposing of the western lands";[3] report referred to COWH.	
June 29	Motion by Scott to consider report in COWH disagreed to.[4]	
July 13	On a motion by Scott, committee report debated and agreed to in COWH; resolution that land office be under the direction of the governor of the western territory debated; motion by Sedgwick to strike "governor of the western territory" and insert "secretary of the treasury."[5]	
July 22	On a motion by Scott,[6] land office debated in COWH; *resolution* reported and agreed to; committee to prepare a bill appointed (Scott, Silvester, and Moore).	
July 31	Scott presented "a bill establishing a Land Office,	

---

[3] *NYDA,* July 14.
[4] *NYDA,* June 30. The *HJ* for this date records no action on this subject.
[5] *NYDA, NYDG,* July 14; *GUS,* July 15.
[6] *GUS,* July 25.

Date	House	Senate
1789		
	in, and for the Western Territory," which was read.	
Aug. 3	Read; 100 copies ordered printed.[7]	

[7] *GUS,* Aug. 5.

House Resolution
July 22, 1789

RESOLVED, That an act of Congress ought to pass for establishing a Land-Office, and for regulating the terms and manner of granting vacant and unappropriated lands, the property of the United States—That the said office be under the superintendance of the Governor of the Western Territory—That the land to be disposed of, be confined to the following limits, viz.

That the tracts or parcels to be disposed of to any one person, shall not exceed   acres; that the price to be required for the same shall be   per acre; and that every person actually settled within the said limits shall be entitled to the pre-emption of a quantity not exceeding   acres, including his settlement.

HJ, p. 119.

Land Office Bill [HR-114]

Calendar

Date	House	Senate
1790		
Jan. 18	Petition of Hannibal W. Dobbyn, "setting forth that he is desirous of becoming a citizen of the United States, and of making a considerable purchase of the public lands; and praying that the Secretary of the Treasury may be authorised to contract with him for that purpose," presented, read, and referred to Page, Scott, and Partridge.	
Jan. 19	Page presented *committee report,* which was read.	
Jan. 20	Report debated; *amendment* debated and not admitted; motion by Boudinot, seconded by Sedgwick, to refer report to the secretary of the treasury with a request that he report a uniform system for the sale of public lands, disagreed to; motion by Baldwin, to table report and ask the secretary to report a system; motion	

Date	House	Senate
1790		
	divided and report tabled; on a motion by Sherman,[1] committee report of June 15, 1789, on unappropriated western lands referred to secretary.	
Jan. 27	Motion by Lee, to submit Dobbyn petition to "the secretary of the treasury who had been directed to report a plan for the disposition of the western lands of the United States, to make provision for such cases," debated; on a motion by Sherman, latter part of motion struck out and Dobbyn petition referred to secretary for his information.[2]	
Mar. 2	Petition of George Scriba, "praying to be permitted to purchase of the United States, a tract of Western Territory, not less than two million, and not exceeding four millions of acres, on the terms therein mentioned," presented, read, and referred to the secretary of the treasury for his information.	
Mar. 11	Petition of Scriba, "praying that the Secretary of the Treasury may be authorised to report on a	

[1] *NYDG,* Jan. 21; *GUS, NYP,* Jan. 23.
[2] *GUS,* Jan. 30.

Date	House	Senate
1790		
	petition of the memorialist, which was presented on the second instant," presented and read; secretary ordered to report on the petitions of Scriba and Dobbyn.	
Apr. 3	Petition of Dobbyn, praying final disposition of his former memorial, received and read.[3]	
July 22	*Report of the secretary of the treasury* on the disposition of the public lands received.	
July 28	Upon motion of Smith (S.C.), report committed to COWH; vote on motion was 23–23 with speaker breaking the tie.[4]	
July 30	Report debated in COWH.[5]	
Aug. 2	Smith (S.C.?) laid on the table two resolutions on the disposition of the public lands during the recess of Congress.[6]	
Dec. 15	On a motion by Boudinot, report of the secretary of the treasury committed to COWH; 100 copies ordered printed.[7]	

[3] *GUS*, Apr. 7.
[4] *NYDG*, July 29.
[5] *NYDA*, July 31.
[6] *GUS*, Aug. 4.
[7] *GA*, Dec. 16.

Date	House	Senate

1790

Dec. 27   Report debated in
COWH; motion by
Boudinot, that "it is the
sense of the committee,
that a land-office be es-
tablished at the seat of
the general government,
under the direction of
          commissioners";
motion by Sherman, that
there be a general land
office established, agreed
to; motion by Boudinot,
for two subordinate land
offices, one north of the
Ohio river and one south
of it, agreed to; motion
by Boudinot, "that all
sales made at the general
land office shall be above
          acres"; Scott
moved to fill blank in
Boudinot motion with
"one thousand"; White
moved for "five thou-
sand"; Scott and White
motions withdrawn;
Boudinot motion agreed
to; Boudinot motion, that
all smaller quantities be
sold at subordinate land
offices, agreed to; Smith
(S.C.?) motion, that it be
determined who should
manage the subordinate
land offices, delayed;
Boudinot motion, that no
lands be sold previous to
settling Indian claims,

Date	House	Senate
1790		

agreed to; Scott motion,
"that such districts as
shall be set apart for sale
shall include the actual
settlements, and be left to
be indiscriminately lo-
cated," disagreed to;
Fitzsimons motion, to
strike out limitation of
100 acres to each settler
from report, agreed to
with an amendment by
Scott leaving it to Con-
gress to fix the limitation;
Scott moved that the
tracts set apart for sale be
within the seven ranges
already surveyed, rather
than in ten mile town-
ships and as otherwise
suggested in the report.[8]

Dec. 28   Report debated in
COWH; Scott's final mo-
tion of Dec. 27 agreed to;
Scott motion, to strike
out "thirty cents" as
amount to be paid per
acre, disagreed to; motion
by Sedgwick, "that the
price shall not be less
than thirty cents," dis-
agreed to; Scott proposal
"that no difference be
made in the value of the
different public securities,
whether 6 per cents, three
per cents, or deferred, as
received for the land that
Congress was about to

---

[8] *GA,* Dec. 29, 30.

Date	House	Senate
1790		
	dispose of" disagreed to; Laurance motion, to strike out public securities as a form of payment, disagreed to; Tucker's proposal "that by virtue of warrants granted to soldiers, the holders be entitled to take up land in any part and not be confined to particular tracts" disagreed to.[9]	
Dec. 29	Report debated in COWH.[10]	
Dec. 31	Report debated and resolutions agreed to in COWH and reported to House.	
1791		
Jan. 3	Resolutions 1–8 debated; first through fourth resolutions agreed to; fifth resolution, providing that "convenient locations shall be set off for actual settlers," struck out on a motion by Scott; Scott substitute disagreed to; seventh resolution agreed to with an amendment by Burke that "for every chain surveyed and sold on the bank of a navigable river, the purchaser shall be obliged to take chains back"; on a motion by Boudinot,	

[9] *GA,* Dec. 31; Jan. 1, 4; *GUS,* Jan. 1, 5.
[10] *GA,* Dec. 30.

Date	House	Senate
1791		
	seconded by Steele, eighth resolution on the price of land was altered to read "that gold and silver or public securities, (without discrimination) should be received in payment for the land"; motion to strike out 30 cents disagreed to.[11]	
Jan. 4	Resolutions 8–25 debated; motion by Sedgwick, to strike out "gold and silver and public securities" from the eighth resolution on the price of land, agreed to;[12] *resolutions* agreed to; Scott, White, and Bloodworth appointed to committee to prepare a bill.	
Jan. 14	White presented "a bill to establish offices for the purpose of granting lands within the territories of the United States," which was read twice and committed to the COWH; 100 copies ordered printed.[13]	
Jan. 20– Feb. 9	Postponed as order of the day.	
Feb. 10	Debated in COWH.	
Feb. 11	COWH reported amendments.	
Feb. 12–14	Amendments debated.	

---

[11] *GUS*, Jan. 5.
[12] Ibid.
[13] *GUS*, Jan. 15.

Date	House	Senate
1791		
Feb. 15	House debated and agreed to amendments; motion by Sherman, to strike out "the Attorney General" for the purpose of inserting "the secretary of the Treasury" as superintendent of the general land office, disagreed to; *motion* by *Gerry* agreed to by a recorded vote of 34–21.[14]	
Feb. 16	Read; blanks filled; principal blank filled with "twenty-five cents. per acre";[15] agreed to as *An act to establish offices for the purpose of granting lands within the territories of the United States.*	Received, read, and ordered printed.
Feb. 17–18		Read and postponed.
Feb. 21		Read; committed to Strong, Ellsworth, Foster, King, and Monroe.[16]

[14] *GUS*, Feb. 16.
[15] *FG*, Feb. 16.
[16] The vote for this committee is in Other Records: Yeas and nays, SR, DNA, and was as follows:

Mr. Bassett	II	
" Butler	ℍℍ II	
" Carroll	III	
" Dalton	I	
" Dickinson	IIII	
" Ellsworth	ℍℍ ℍℍ I	
" Elmer		
" Few	ℍℍ II	
" Foster	ℍℍ ℍℍ	
" Gunn	ℍℍ	
" Hawkins	I	
" Henry	II	
" Johnson	ℍℍ	
" Johnston	ℍℍ	
" Izard	III	

Date	House	Senate
1791		
Feb. 26		Strong reported that the committee recommended postponing further consideration of the bill until next session; report postponed; bill debated and recommitted.
Mar. 1		Strong reported a resolution,[17] which was agreed to; bill postponed to next session.

"	King	⟦⟧ ⟦⟧
"	Langdon	⟦⟧
"	Lee	⟦⟧ I
"	Maclay	III
"	Monroe	⟦⟧ IIII
"	Morris	I
"	Read	⟦⟧
"	Schuyler	II
"	Stanton	
"	Strong	⟦⟧ ⟦⟧ IIII
"	Wingate	II

[17] For this resolution see Resolution on Unclaimed Western Lands.

House Committee Report
January 19, 1790

THAT the Secretary of the Treasury of the United States, ought to be empowered to contract with the said Hannibal William Dobbyn, for the sale of any quantity of unappropriated lands in the Western territory, at a price not less than   per Acre, in specie, or public Securities of the United States:[1] Provided, that the said quantity of land shall not be less than fifty thousand Acres, and shall be contained in one Survey.

Various Select Committee Reports, HR, DNA.

---

[1] On January 20, the House did not admit a motion by Scott to amend the report by adding the following at this point:
    That one third be paid down, one third at the end of seven years, and the other third at the end of twelve years, with interest at six per cent. on the two thirds unpaid, from the time of closing the contract. (*GUS*, Jan. 23)

Report of the Secretary of the Treasury
July 22, 1790

TREASURY-DEPARTMENT, July 20th. 1790.
In obedience to the order of the House
of Representatives of the 20th. of
January last,
The Secretary of the Treasury,

RESPECTFULLY REPORTS;

That in the formation of a plan for the disposition of the vacant lands of the United States, there appear to be two leading objects of consideration; one, the facility of advantageous sales according to the probable course of purchases; the other, the accommodation of individuals now inhabiting the Western Country, or who may hereafter emigrate thither.

The former, as an operation of finance, claims primary attention: the latter is important, as it relates to the satisfaction of the inhabitants of the Western Country. It is desirable, and does not appear impracticable to conciliate both.

Purchasers may be contemplated in three classes. Monied individuals and companies, who will buy to sell again. Associations of persons, who intend to make settlements themselves. Single persons, or families now resident in the Western Country, or who may emigrate thither hereafter. The two first will be frequently blended, and will always want considerable tracts. The last will generally purchase small quantities. Hence a plan for the sale of the Western lands, while it may have due regard to the last, should be calculated to obtain all the advantages which may be derived from the two first classes. For this reason, it seems requisite, that the general Land-office should be established at the seat of Government. 'Tis there, that the principal purchasers, whether citizens or foreigners, can most easily find proper agents, and that contracts for large purchases can be best adjusted.

But the accommodation of the present inhabitants of the Western Territory, and of unassociated persons and families who may emigrate thither, seems to require that one office, subordinate to that at the Seat of Congress, should be opened in the North western, and another in the South western Government.

Each of these offices, as well the general one as the subordinate ones, it is conceived, may be placed with convenience under the superintendance of three Commissioners, who may either be pre-established officers of the Government, to whom the duty may be assigned by law, or persons specially appointed for the purpose. The former is recommended by considerations of Oeconomy, and, it is probable, would embrace every advantage which could be derived from a special appointment.

To obviate those inconveniences, and to facilitate and ensure the attainment of those advantages which may arise from new and casual circumstances springing up from foreign and domestic causes, appears to be an object for which adequate provision should be made, in any plan that may be adopted. For this reason, and from the intrinsic difficulty of regulating the details of a specific provision for the various objects which require to be consulted, so as neither to do too much nor too little for either, it is respectfully submitted, whether it would not be advisable to vest a considerable latitude of discretion in the Commissioners of the General Land Office, subject to some such regulations and limitations as follow. Vizt.

That no land shall be sold, except such, in respect to which the titles of the Indian tribes shall have been previously extinguished.

That a sufficient tract or tracts shall be reserved and set apart for satisfying the subscribers to the proposed loan in the public debt, but that no location shall be for less than five hundred Acres.

That convenient tracts shall from time to time be set apart for the purpose of locations by actual settlers, in quantities not exceeding to one person one hundred acres.

That other tracts shall, from time to time, be set apart for sales in townships of ten miles square, except where they shall adjoin upon a boundary of some prior grant, or of a tract so set apart, in which cases there shall be no greater departure from such form of location, than may be absolutely necessary.

That any quantities may, nevertheless, be sold by special contract, comprehended either within natural boundaries or lines, or both.

That the price shall be thirty Cents per acre to be paid, either in gold or silver, or in public securities, computing those which shall bear an immediate interest of six per cent, as at par with gold and silver, and those which shall bear a future or less interest, if any there shall be, at a proportional value.

That Certificates issued for land upon the proposed loan, shall operate as warrants within the tract or tracts which shall be specially set apart for satisfying the subscribers thereto, and shall also be receivable in all payments whatsoever for land by way of discount, Acre for Acre.

That no credit shall be given for any quantity, less than a township of ten miles square, nor more than two years credit for any greater quantity.

That in every instance of credit, at least one quarter part of the consideration shall be paid down, and security other than the land itself, shall be required for the residue. And that no title shall be given for any tract or part of a purchase, beyond the quantity for which the consideration shall be actually paid.

That the residue of the tract or tracts set apart for the subscribers to the proposed loan, which shall not have been located within two years after the same shall have been set apart, may then be sold on the same terms as any other land.

That the Commissioners of each subordinate office shall have the management of all sales, and the issuing of Warrants for all locations in the tracts to be set apart for the accommodation of individual settlers, subject to the superintendency of the Commissioners of the general Land-office, who may also commit to them the management of any other sales or locations, which it may be found expedient to place under their direction.

That there shall be a Surveyor General, who shall have power to appoint a Deputy Surveyor General, in each of the Western Governments, and a competent number of Deputy Surveyors to execute, in person, all Warrants to them directed by the Surveyor General or Deputy Surveyors General within certain districts to be assigned to them respectively. That the Surveyor General shall also have in charge, all the duties committed to the Geographer General by the several resolutions and ordinances of Congress.

That all warrants issued at the General Land Office, shall be signed by the Commissioners or such one of them as they may nominate for that purpose, and shall be directed to the Surveyor General. That all warrants issued at a subordinate office shall be signed by the Commissioners of such office, or by such one of them, as they may nominate for that purpose, and shall be directed to the Deputy Surveyor General within the government. That the priority of locations upon Warrants shall be determined by the times of the applications to the Deputy Surveyors; and in case of two applications for the same land at one time, the priority may be determined by Lot.

That the Treasurer of the United States shall be the receiver of all payments for sales made at the General Land-office, and may also receive deposits of money or securities for purchases intended to be made at the subordinate offices, his receipts or certificates for which shall be received in payment at those offices.

That the Secretary of each of the Western Governments, shall be the receiver of all payments arising from sales at the office of such Government.

That controversies concerning rights to patents or grants of land shall be determined by the Commissioners of that office, under whose immediate direction or jurisdiction, the locations, in respect to which they may arise, shall have been made.

That the completion of all contracts and sales heretofore made, shall be under the direction of the Commissioners of the General Land Office.

That the Commissioners of the General Land Office, Surveyor General, Deputy Surveyors General, and the Commissioners of the Land Office, in each of the Western Governments, shall not purchase, nor shall others purchase for them in trust, any public lands.

That the Secretaries of the Western Governments shall give security for the faithful discharge of their duty, as receivers of the Land Office.

That all patents shall be signed by the President of the United States, or by the Vice-President or other officer of government acting as President, and shall be recorded in the office, either of the Surveyor General, or of the Clerk of the Supreme Court of the United States.

That all officers acting under the laws establishing the Land Office, shall make oath faithfully to discharge their respective duties, previously to their entering upon the execution thereof.

That all Surveys of land shall be at the expense of the purchasers or grantees.

That the fees shall not exceed certain rates to be specified in the law, affording equitable compensations for the services of the Surveyors, and establishing reasonable and customary charges for patents and other Office papers for the benefit of the United States.

That the Commissioners of the General Land Office shall, as soon as may be, from time to time, cause all the rules and regulations which they may establish, to be published in one gazette, at least, in each State, and in each of the Western Governments, where there is a Gazette, for the information of the citizens of the United States.

Regulations, like these, will define and fix the most essential particulars which can regard the disposal of the Western lands, and where they leave any thing to discretion, will indicate the general principles or policy intended by the Legislature to be observed; for a conformity to which the Commissioners will, of course, be responsible.

They will, at the same time, leave room for accommodating to circumstances which cannot, beforehand, be accurately appreciated, and for varying the course of proceeding, as experience shall suggest to be proper, and will avoid the danger of those obstructions and embarrassments in the execution which would be to be apprehended from an endeavor at greater precision and more exact detail.

All which is humbly submitted
ALEXANDER HAMILTON
Secretary of the Treasury

A Record of the Reports of the Secretary of the Treasury, vol. I, HR, DNA.

House Resolutions
January 4, 1791

RESOLVED, That it is the opinion of this committee, that it is expedient that a general land-office be established and opened at the seat of the government of the United States.

That two subordinate land-offices be established and opened; one in the government north-west of the Ohio, and the other in the government south of the Ohio.

That all contracts for the sale of land above the quantity of   acres, shall be exclusively made at the general land office.

That no land shall be sold, except such in respect to which the titles of the Indian tribes shall have been previously extinguished.

That the seven ranges already surveyed, be sold in lots as laid out.

That any quantities may be sold by special contract comprehended either within natural boundaries or lines, or both, but no survey shall in any case be made on a river, but in the proportion of   chains back from such river for every chain along the bank thereof.

That the price shall be thirty cents per acre.

That warrants for military services be put on the same footing with warrants issuing from the land office, and that the exclusive right of locating the same in districts set apart for the army, cease after the   day of

That no credit shall be given for any quantity less than a township of six miles square, nor more than two years credit for any quantity.

That in every instance of credit, at least one quarter part of the consideration shall be paid down, and security, other than the land itself, shall be required for the residue. And that no title shall be given for any tract or part of a purchase, beyond the quantity for which the consideration shall be actually paid.

That the   of each subordinate office, shall have the management of all sales, and the issuing of warrants for all locations in the tracts to be set apart for the accommodation of individual settlers, subject to the superintendency of the   of the general land office, who may also commit to them the management of any other sales or locations, which it may be found expedient to place under their direction.

That preference be given for a limited time to those actual settlers, whose titles are not secured by the former governments of that country, and the existing ordinances and acts of Congress.

That there shall be a surveyor-general, who shall have power to appoint a deputy surveyor-general in each of the western governments, and a competent number of deputy surveyors, to execute in person all warrants to them directed by the surveyor-general, or the deputy surveyor-generals, within certain districts to be assigned to them respectively. That the surveyor-general shall also have in charge all the duties committed to the geographer-general by the several resolutions of Congress.

That all warrants issued at the general land-office, shall be signed by   and shall be directed to the surveyor-general. That all warrants issued at a subordinate office, shall be signed by   and shall be directed to the deputy surveyor-general within the government. That the priority of locations upon warrants shall be determined by the times of the applications to the deputy surveyors: and in case of two applications for the same land at one time, the priority may be determined by lot.

That the treasurer of the United States shall be the receiver of all payments for sales made at the general land-office, and may also receive deposits of money for purchases intended to be made at the subordinate offices; his receipt or certificate for which shall be received in payments at those offices.

That the secretary of each of the western governments shall be the receiver of all payments arising from sales at the office of such government.

That controversies concerning rights to patents or grants of land, shall be determined by the   of that office, under whose immediate direction or jurisdiction the locations, in respect to which they may arise, shall have been made.

That the   of the general land-office, surveyor-general, deputy surveyor-general, and the   of the land-office in each of the western governments, shall not purchase, nor shall others purchase for them in trust, any public lands.

That the secretaries of the western governments, shall give security for the faithful execution of their duty as receivers of the land-office.

That all patents shall be signed by the President of the United States, and shall be recorded in the office of the Secretary of State.

That all officers, acting under the laws establishing the land-office, shall make oath or affirmation, faithfully to discharge their respective duties, previously to their entering upon the execution thereof.

That all surveys of land shall be at the expense of the purchasers or grantees.

That the fees shall not exceed certain rates to be specified in the law, affording equitable compensations for the services of surveyors, and establishing reasonable and customary charges for patents and other office papers, for the benefit of the United States.

That the   of the general land-office, shall, as soon as may be, from time to time, cause all the rules and regulations which they may establish to be published in one gazette at least, in each state, and in each of the western governments where there is a gazette, for the information of the citizens of the United States.

HJ, pp. 653–55.

Gerry Motion
February 15, 1791

Provided always, That any purchaser of lands, when the payment thereof shall be due, may proffer in payment any of the certificates of the funded debt of the United States, at the same rates as the Treasurer shall have allowed for such certificates respectively, in the last purchase which he shall have made thereof, prior to such payment.

HJ, p. 717.

Land Office Bill [HR-114]
February 16, 1791

AN ACT to establish Offices for the purpose of granting lands within the territories of the United States

SECTION 1st BE IT ENACTED by the Senate and House of Representatives of the United States of America in Congress assembled, That an office shall be established at the seat of the Government of the United States, for the purpose of granting lands within the territories of the United States: And that two subordinate offices shall be established for the same purpose, one in the territory North West of the Ohio, and the other in the territory South of the Ohio. That no lands shall be sold or granted, except those to which the titles of the Indian tribes shall have been previously extinguished. That the seven ranges of Townships already surveyed, shall be sold in lots as they are laid out. That any quantities of other land may be sold by special contract. That convenient tracts from time to time be set apart for the purpose of locations by actual settlers. That the superintendants of each subordinate office shall have the management of all sales, and the issuing of Warrants for all locations in the tracts to be set apart for the accommodation of individual settlers, subject to the direction of the superintendant of the general land Office, who may also commit to them the management of any other sales or locations which it may be found expedient to place under their direction.

SECTION 2nd.   AND BE IT FURTHER ENACTED. That the price of all land sold or granted by the United States shall be (*twenty five Cents*) per Acre, except such as may be sold by special contract, and such as may be granted as bounties for military services; the Warrants for which last mentioned lands shall be located, surveyed and patented in the same manner as Warrants issuing from the land office in consideration of the payment of money; and the exclusive right of locating such Warrants in districts set apart for the army, shall cease from and after the (*first*) day of (*May*) One thousand seven hundred and ninety (four:) PROVIDED ALWAYS, that any purchaser of lands, when the payment thereof shall be due, may proffer in payment any of the Certificates of the funded debt of the United States, at the same rates as the Treasurer shall have allowed for such Certificates, respectively, in the last purchase which he shall have made thereof prior to such payment.

SECTION 3rd.   AND BE IT FURTHER ENACTED, That no credit shall be given for any quantity of land less than twenty three thousand Acres and no credit shall be given for any quantity, unless one quarter part of the price shall be paid down, and sufficient security (other than the land sold) given for the payment of the residue within two years. And that no patent shall issue, or title be made for any part of a tract of land purchased, beyond the proportion for which the money shall be actually paid.

SECTION 4th.   AND BE IT FURTHER ENACTED, That all persons who have really and bona fide settled on unappropriated land in either of the said territories, and have made improvements thereon, the titles to which lands are not, or might not have been secured by the Governments of those territories, or by the Acts or Ordinances of Congress, shall be entitled to six hundred and forty Acres each, including their respective improvements, PROVIDED that such settlers shall within twelve Months after the passing of this Act, pay to the Secretary of the territory in which the settlement hath been made, the stated price for the land to which such settler is entitled by virtue of his improvement, or for so much thereof as he shall incline to take, and prove by the oath or affirmation of two or more credible persons, their residence and improvements, a certified copy of which oath or affirmation shall be produced to the said Secretary, to be by him filed in his office.

SECTION 5th.   AND BE IT FURTHER ENACTED, That a Surveyor of lands shall be appointed in each of the said territories, who may appoint as many deputy surveyors as may be necessary to assist them in executing all Warrants to them respectively directed, which warrants shall be signed by the superintendant of the respective offices, and directed to the surveyor of the territory in which the land to be located lies. The priority of location of Warrants shall be determined by the time of application to the surveyor, and in case of two applications at the same time for the same land, the priority shall be determined by lot.

SECTION 6th.   AND BE IT FURTHER ENACTED, That the Treasurer of the United States shall be the receiver of all monies to be paid for lands granted at the general land office, and that the Secretaries of the government established in the said territories shall be the receivers of all monies arising from the sales or grants of land at the Offices of their respective territories. And that any person paying into his or their hands, a sum of money for the purchase of land, shall be entitled to a receipt expressing the sum paid, and the quantity of land to be granted in consideration thereof; On producing of which receipt to the Superintendant of the proper Office, and lodging the same with him to be recorded, the Superintendant shall issue a warrant directed to the Surveyor of the territory, specifying the quantity of land purchased, and authorizing him to cause the same to be surveyed agreeably to the established rules of the land Office. And where the money shall be paid

for a settlement right, the receipt shall so express; on producing which receipt
to the Superintendant of the land Office of the territory in which the land
may be, a Warrant shall issue, and the same proceedings be had thereon, as in
cases of money paid to the Treasurer of the United States for the like
quantity.

SECTION 7th.   AND BE IT FURTHER ENACTED, That the Superintendant of the general land Office, the Surveyor, and the superintendants of the
land Offices in each of the said territories, shall not purchase any public
lands, and shall be incapable of holding any such lands as may be purchased
by them, or by any person for their use, during their continuance in Office.

SECTION 8th.   AND BE IT FURTHER ENACTED, That all patents shall
be signed by the President of the United States, and shall be recorded in the
Office of the Secretary of State.

SECTION 9th.   AND BE IT FURTHER ENACTED, That all Officers to be
appointed by virtue of this Act, shall take an Oath or Affirmation before some
judge or Magistrate of the United States, that they will faithfully discharge
the duties of their respective Offices; a certificate of which Oath or Affirmation shall be returned to the general land Office, or to the land Office of the
territory in which the duties are to be performed, previous to their entering
upon the execution of their Offices.

SECTION 10th.   AND BE IT FURTHER ENACTED, That the Secretaries
of the said governments shall give bond, with sufficient sureties in the sum of
ten thousand dollars each for the faithful discharge of their duty, as receivers
of the money arising from the sale of land at their respective Offices.

SECTION 11th.   AND BE IT FURTHER ENACTED, That the Superintendant of the general land Office may agree with any person or persons for the
sale of any quantity of land, not less than twenty-three thousand Acres, to be
located in one body, and particularly described by natural boundaries, or by
lines to be run and plainly marked by the Surveyor of the district or territory
in which the land may lie, at the expence of the purchaser or purchasers,
provided the price be not less than (twenty Cents) per Acre.

SECTION 12th.   AND BE IT FURTHER ENACTED, That the Superintendant of the general land Office, shall have power to establish all such rules
and regulations as he shall judge necessary respecting the form, time, and
manner of locating Warrants for lands, of making and returning Surveys,
issuing patents thereupon, entering caveats, and proceedings preparatory to
the trial thereof, and all such other rules and regulations as shall be necessary
to carry this Act into effect, according to the true intent and meaning thereof;
which rules he shall cause to be published, in one gazette at least, in each of
the United States, and in each of the said territories in which there may be a
gazette.

SECTION 13th.   AND BE IT FURTHER ENACTED, That controversies concerning rights to patents or grants, shall be determined by the Superintendant of that Office under whose immediate direction or jurisdiction the locations in respect to which they may arise, shall have been made: Provided, that no determination of such Superintendants shall be construed to prevent either of the parties from bringing their Action or Actions, Suit or Suits in law or equity, for the final decision of their rights to the lands in dispute, or for recovering damages for waste or trespass committed thereon.

SECTION 14th.   AND BE IT FURTHER ENACTED, That the Attorney General of the United States, shall, by virtue of his Office, be superintendant of the general land Office: And that the governors of the said territories, shall, by virtue of their Offices, be superintendants of the subordinate land Offices, within their respective governments.

SECTION 15th.   AND BE IT FURTHER ENACTED, That a separate Account shall be kept at the Treasury of the monies arising from the sale of the aforesaid lands, and the said monies shall be, and they are hereby appropriated to the purchase of the debt of the United States, according to the terms of the Act "making provision for the reduction of the public debt."
1791, February the 16th.

      Read the third time and passed the House of Representatives

JOHN BECKLEY—Clerk

Engrossed House Bills, HR, DNA.

Liability of Shipowners Bill [HR-107]

Calendar

Date	House	Senate
1790		
Dec. 23	Fitzsimons gave notice of intention to present bill.[1]	
Dec. 24	Committee to prepare a bill appointed (Fitzsimons, Foster, and Silvester).	
Dec. 27	Fitzsimons presented *a bill to ascertain how far the owners of ships and vessels shall be answerable to the freighters*, which was read.	
Dec. 28	Read; 100 copies ordered printed.[2]	

[1] *FG*, Dec. 23.
[2] *FG*, Dec. 28.

Liability of Shipowners Bill [HR-107]
December 27, 1790

A BILL *to ascertain how far the* OWNERS *of* SHIPS *and* VESSELS *shall be answerable to the* FREIGHTERS

SEC. 1. BE *it enacted by the* SENATE *and* HOUSE *of* REPRESENTATIVES *of the United States of America in Congress assembled,* That from and after the passing of this act, no person or persons, who is or shall be owner or owners of any ship or vessel, shall be liable to answer for or make good any loss or damage which may happen to any goods or merchandize, which after the time aforesaid shall be shipped in any such ship or vessel, by reason of any fire happening on board such ship or vessel.

Sec. 2. *And be it further enacted,* That from and after the   day of next, no master, owner or owners of any ship or vessel, shall be subject to, or be liable to answer for, any loss or damage which may happen to any gold or silver, diamonds, jewels, precious stones, or watches, which shall be shipped on board any such ship or vessel, by reason of any robbery, embezzlement, making away with or secreting thereof, unless the owner or shipper shall at the time of shipping the same, insert in his bill or bills of lading, or otherwise declare in writing, to the master, owner or owners of such ship or vessel, the true nature, quality and value of such gold, silver, diamonds, jewels, precious stones, or watches.

Sec. 3. *And be it further enacted,* That from and after the said   day of no owner or owners of any ship or vessel, shall be liable for the payment of any loss or damage which may accrue by reason of any robbery, embezzlement, secreting or making away with any goods or merchandize, or any gold, silver, diamonds, jewels, or precious stones, shipped on board any ship or vessel, or for any act done or forfeiture incurred, *without the privity or knowledge of such owner or owners,* further than the value of such ship or vessel, and the full amount of the freight due, or to grow due during the voyage wherein such robbery, embezzlement, secreting or making away with as aforesaid, shall be made, committed or done.

Sec. 4. *And be it further enacted,* That if several freighters or proprietors of any such goods or merchandize, or any such gold, silver, diamonds, jewels, precious stones, or watches, shall suffer any loss or damage by any of the means aforesaid, in the same voyage (fire only excepted;) and that the value of the ship or vessel, with all her appurtenances, and the freight due or to grow due during such voyage, shall not be sufficient to make full compensation to all and every of them, then such freighters or proprietors shall receive their satisfaction thereout in proportion to their respective losses and damages. And in every such case, it shall be lawful for such freighters or proprietors, or any of them, on behalf of himself, and all other such freighters or proprietors, or for the owners of such ship or vessel, or any of them, on behalf of himself and the other part owners of such ship or vessel, to exhibit a bill, in any court of equity in the United States, for the discovery of the total amount of such losses or damages, and also of the value of such ship or vessel, her appurtenances and freight, and for an equal distribution thereof, amongst such freighters or proprietors, in proportion to their respective losses and damages.

Broadside Collection, RBkRm, DLC. This undated printed bill was annotated on the back by Johnson, a senator in the First Congress. Since Johnson resigned from the Senate at the end of the First Congress, we have concluded that the bill is the one introduced on December 27.

Lighthouses Act [HR-12]

August 7, 1789

AN ACT FOR THE ESTABLISHMENT AND SUPPORT OF LIGHT-HOUSES, BEACONS, BUOYS, AND PUBLIC PIERS

[1] BE IT ENACTED BY THE SENATE AND HOUSE OF REPRESENTATIVES OF THE UNITED STATES OF AMERICA, IN CONGRESS ASSEMBLED, That all expences which shall accrue from and after the fifteenth day of August, One thousand seven hundred and eighty nine, in the necessary support, maintenance, and repairs of all Light houses, beacons, buoys, and public Piers, erected, placed, or sunk before the passing of this Act, at the entrance of, or within any bay, inlet, harbour, or port of the United States, for rendering the Navigation thereof easy and safe, shall be defrayed out of the Treasury of the United States: PROVIDED NEVERTHELESS, that none of the said expences shall continue to be so defrayed by the United States, after the expiration of one year from the day aforesaid, unless such Light-houses, beacons, buoys, and public Piers shall in the mean time be ceded to, and vested in the United States, by the State or States respectively in which the same may be, together with the lands and tenements thereunto belonging, and together with the jurisdiction of the same.

[2] AND BE IT FURTHER ENACTED, That a Light house shall be erected near the entrance of the Chesapeake Bay, at such place when ceded to the United States in manner aforesaid, as the President of the United States shall direct.

[3] AND BE IT FURTHER ENACTED, That it shall be the duty of the Secretary of the Treasury, to provide by contracts which shall be approved by the President of the United States, for building a Light house near the entrance of Chesapeake bay, and for rebuilding when necessary, and keeping in good repair the Light houses, Beacons, Buoys, and Public Piers in the several States, and for furnishing the same with all necessary supplies, and also to agree for the salaries, wages, or hire of the person or persons appointed by the President for the superintendance and care of the same.

[4] AND BE IT FURTHER ENACTED, That all pilots in the bays, inlets, rivers, harbours, and ports of the United States, shall continue to be regulated in conformity with the existing laws of the States respectively, wherein

such pilots may be, or with such laws as the States may respectively hereafter enact for the purpose, until further legislative provision shall be made by Congress.

FREDERICK AUGUSTUS MUHLENBERG
Speaker of the House of Representatives
JOHN ADAMS
Vice-President of the United States, and
President of the Senate

Approved August
the 7th.
1789

GO. WASHINGTON
President of the United States

I certify that this Act did originate
in the House of Representatives.
JOHN BECKLEY—Clerk

Enrolled Acts, RG 11, DNA.

Calendar

Date	House	Senate
1789		
Apr. 11	Committee appointed, consisting of one member from each state present, to prepare a bill for collecting the imposts and tonnage (Gilman, Gerry, Sherman, Laurance, Cadwalader, Fitzsimons, Gale, Madison, and Tucker).	
June 2	On a motion by Laurance,[1] committee instructed to bring in a bill for regulating lighthouses.	
June 12	Vining, Stone, and Jackson added to committee.	
July 1	Gerry presented *a bill for*	

---

[1] *NYDA, NYDG,* June 3.

Date	House	Senate
1789		
	the establishment and support of light-houses, beacons, and buoys; and for authorising the several states to provide and regulate pilots, which was read.	
July 2	Read and committed to COWH.	
July 8–15	Postponed as order of the day.	
July 16	On a motion by Laurance,[2] debated in COWH.	
July 17	Debated and *amended* in COWH; House agreed to *amendments.*	
July 20	Read; blanks filled; agreed to as *an Act for the establishment and support of light-houses, beacons and buoys.*	Received.
July 21		Read.[3]
July 23		Read and committed to Morris, Langdon, and Dalton.[4]
July 24		Committee reported amendments; *amended bill* ordered printed.[5]
July 28–30		Debated and *amended.*

---

[2] *NYDG,* July 17.

[3] According to Thomas Greenleaf's account in the Records of the Secretary of the Senate: Concerning printing, SR, DNA, 50 copies of this bill were printed on July 21.

[4] During its deliberations on the bill, the committee relied on a *suggested substitute lighthouses bill,* which was enclosed in a letter dated July 16, 1789, from a committee of Philadelphia merchants to the Pennsylvania delegation in Congress.

[5] According to Thomas Greenleaf's account in the Records of the Secretary of the Senate: Concerning printing, SR, DNA, 50 copies of this bill were printed on July 24.

Date	House	Senate
1789		
July 31		Read and agreed to with *amendments*.
Aug. 3	Senate amendments agreed to.	
Aug. 6	Signed by speaker.	Signed by vice president.
Aug. 7	Signed by president.	

Lighthouses Bill [HR-12]
July 1, 1789

A BILL for the Establishment and Support of LIGHT HOUSES, BEACONS, and BUOYS, and for authorising the several States to provide and regulate Pilots[1]

[1] BE IT ENACTED by the Senate and House of Representatives of the United States of America in Congress assembled,[2] That from and after the [3] day of [4] the light-house or light-houses of any State in the union, upon application[5] of such State to the Secretary of the Treasury of the United States, shall be provided with an overseer or overseers, and with the necessary materials for keeping the lights, and such State shall be reimbursed the expense of supporting the lights after the said [6] day of [7] next;[8] and when a cession is made to the United States of such lighthouse or light-houses, and of the land appropriated to[9] the same, they shall be kept in good repair at the expense of the United States.

---

[1] The House struck "and for authorising" through "Pilots" from the title.

[2] On July 16, Tucker moved to strike the entire bill except for the enacting clause and substitute language which would:

> place the establishment both of lighthouse and pilots in the hands and under the controul of the state government, the former to be supported by the appropriation of a certain proportion of the duty on tonnage of vessels, not exceeding six cents per ton—and in case that were insufficient, that each state should have power to lay an additional tonnage duty on all vessels entering the ports where such houses were erected, and that pilots should be under the direction of the states.

This motion was disagreed to on July 17. (*NYDA*, July 17)

[3] The House filled this blank with "first."

[4] The House filled this blank with "August next."

[5] The House inserted "of the Governor or Executive authority thereof, in behalf" at this point.

[6] The House filled this blank with "first."

[7] The House filled this blank with "August."

[8] The House inserted "PROVIDED application for such re-imbursement be made within twelve months after the passing of this Act" at this point.

[9] The House changed "to" to "for."

[2] AND BE IT FURTHER ENACTED, That the beacons or buoys[10] provided by any State, shall at the request thereof[11] be kept in good repair at the expense of the United States.

[3] AND BE IT FURTHER ENACTED, That a light-house shall be erected near the entrance of the Chesapeake-Bay, at such place when ceded to the United States as the President of the United States shall direct.

[4] AND BE IT FURTHER ENACTED, That it shall be the duty of the Secretary of the Treasury to provide by contracts for the maintenance of the light-houses, and also for keeping in good repair the beacons and buoys which shall be the property or under the care and direction of the United States.[12]

[5] AND BE IT FURTHER ENACTED, That the legislatures of the several States, may provide by law, which shall be subject to the revision and controul of Congress, for the establishment and regulation of pilots for the ports, rivers, and harbours, in such States respectively.[13]

Fisher Family Papers, PHi. E–45647. Unless otherwise noted, we determined the amendments by comparing this bill with the House engrossed bill.

---

[10] The House inserted "already" at this point.

[11] The House struck out "at the request thereof" and inserted "on application thereof as aforesaid."

[12] The House struck out "the maintenance" through "United States" and inserted the following:

> placing and keeping in good repair, all necessary Buoys and Beacons, and rebuilding when necessary, the Light-Houses in the several States, and for furnishing the same with all necessary materials, PROVIDED, that no Light-House shall be rebuilt at the expense of the United States, unless the land on which the same is to be rebuilt, shall be ceded to the United States.

[13] On July 17, the House agreed to a motion by Smith (S.C.) to strike out this section. (NYDA, July 18)

Lighthouses Bill [HR-12]
July 20, 1789

AN ACT for the Establishment and Support of LIGHT-HOUSES, BEACONS, and BUOYS[1]

[1] BE IT ENACTED BY THE SENATE AND HOUSE OF REPRESENTATIVES OF THE UNITED STATES OF AMERICA, IN CONGRESS ASSEMBLED, That[2] from

---

[1] The Senate struck out "and" before "Buoys" and inserted "And public piers" at this point.

[2] The Senate struck out the remainder of this section and inserted the following:

> All expenses which shall accrue from and after the 15th day of August, 1789, in the necessary support, maintenance and repairs of all Light-Houses, Beacons, Buoys, and Public Piers, erected, placed, or sunk before the passing of this act, at the entrance of, or within any bay, inlet, harbour, or port of the

and after the first day of August next, the Light-house, or Light-houses of any State in the union, upon application of the Governor or Executive authority thereof, in behalf of such State to the Secretary of the Treasury of the United States, shall be provided with an Overseer or Overseers, and with the necessary materials for keeping the Lights; and such State shall be re-imbursed the expense of supporting the Lights after the said first day of August next, PROVIDED application for such re-imbursement be made within twelve months after the passing of this Act; and when a cession is made to the United States of such Light-house, or Light-houses, and of the land appropriated for the same, they shall be kept in good repair at the expense of the United States.

[2] AND BE IT FURTHER ENACTED, That the Beacons or Buoys, already provided by any State, shall on application thereof as aforesaid, be kept in good repair at the expense of the United States.[3]

[3] AND BE IT FURTHER ENACTED, That a Light-House shall be erected near the entrance of the Chesapeake-Bay, at such place when ceded to the United States,[4] as the President of the United States shall direct.

[4] AND BE IT FURTHER ENACTED, That it shall be the duty of the Secretary of the Treasury to provide by contracts[5] for placing and keeping in good repair, all necessary Buoys and Beacons, and rebuilding when necessary, the Light-Houses in the several States, and for furnishing the same with all necessary materials, PROVIDED, that no Light-House shall be rebuilt at the expense of the United States, unless the land on which the same is to be rebuilt, shall be ceded to the United States.

1789, July 20th.
Read the third time, and passed the House of Representatives.

[NEW-YORK, PRINTED BY THOMAS GREENLEAF.]

Broadside Collection, RBkRm, DLC. The Senate amendments are printed in the *SLJ*, pp. 102–3.

United States, for rendering the navigation thereof easy and safe, shall be defrayed out of the Treasury of the United States: PROVIDED NEVERTHELESS, That none of the said expenses shall continue to be so defrayed by the United States, after the expiration of one year from the day aforesaid, unless such Light-Houses, Beacons, Buoys, and Public Piers, shall in the mean time be ceded to and vested in the United States, by the State or States respectively in which the same may be, together with the Lands and Tenements thereunto belonging, and together with the jurisdiction of the same.

3 The Senate struck out this section.
4 The Senate inserted "in manner aforesaid" at this point.
5 The Senate struck out the remainder of this section and inserted the following: which shall be approved by the President of the United States for building a Light-House near the entrance of Chesapeake-Bay; and for rebuilding when necessary, and keeping in good repair the Light-Houses, Beacons, Buoys, and Public Piers in the several States, and for furnishing the same with all necessary

supplies, and also to agree for the salaries, wages, or hire of the person or persons appointed by the President for the superintendance and care of the same.

AND BE IT FURTHER ENACTED, That all pilots in the bays, inlets, rivers, harbours, and ports of the United States, shall continue to be regulated in conformity with the existing laws of the States respectively, wherein such pilots may be, or with such laws as the States may respectively hereafter enact for the purpose, until further Legislative provision shall be made by Congress.

Suggested Substitute Lighthouses Bill
July 23, 1789

A Bill for the Support & Establishment of Light Houses Beacons, Buoys & public Piers and for authorising the several States to regulate Pilots

For preserving the Accommodations now subsisting & further rendring the Navigation of the Bays, Inlets Rivers Harbours & Ports of the United States more safe Be it enacted by the Senate & House of Representatives of the United States of America in Congress assembled That all the Expences which shall have accrued from & after the first Day of August *next* in the necessary Support Maintenance & Repair of all Light Houses, Beacons, Buoys, & Public Piers, which before the passing of this Act have been erected, placed or sunk at the Entrance of or within any Bay, Inlet, Harbour or Port of the
for rendring the Navigation thereof easy & safe
United States which have not been or shall not be provided for by the State to whom the same respectively belong shall be defrayed out of the Treasury of the United States, upon such States Applying & ceding to the President for the Use of the United States such Light Houses, Beacons, Buoys & public Piers & the Lands & Tenements thereto belonging; and after such Cession, the same shall be supported maintaind & kept in Repair at the Charge of the United States by such Persons as the President shall from time to appoint for those Purposes.

And be it further enacted that such other Light Houses, Beacons, Buoys & public Piers as the President of the United States shall approve of shall be erected, placed, sunk supported maintaind & repaird at the Charge of the United States at the Entrance of or within any Bay, Inlet, Harbour or Port of the United States, the State requesting the same having first ceded to the President for the Use of the United States such or so much Land as shall be judgd necessary to be appropriated for the Use & Support thereof.

And be it further enacted that the Legislatures of the several States may provide by Laws which whether now subsisting or hereafter to be made shall be in Force until otherwise declared by Congress, for the Establishment &

Regulation of Pilots in the Bays Inlets, Rivers, Harbours & Ports in such States respectively.

Fisher Family Papers, PHi. This draft was enclosed in a letter dated July 16, 1789, from a committee of Philadelphia merchants to the Pennsylvania delegation in Congress. Morris was chairman of the Senate committee on this bill.

Lighthouses Bill [HR-12]
July 24, 1789

AN ACT for the Establishment and Support of LIGHT-HOUSES, BEACONS, BUOYS, and[1] PIERS

SEC. 1st. BE IT ENACTED BY THE SENATE AND HOUSE OF REPRESENTATIVES OF THE UNITED STATES OF AMERICA IN CONGRESS ASSEMBLED, That all the expenses which shall have accrued[2] from and after the   3 day of   next,[4] in the necessary support, maintenance and repair of all Light-Houses, Beacons, Buoys, and Public Piers, before the passing of this act,[5] erected, placed, or sunk, at the entrance of, or within any bay, inlet, harbour, or port, of the United States, for rendering the navigation thereof easy and safe, which have not been, or shall not be provided for by the State to whom the same respectively belong,[6] shall be defrayed out of the Treasury of the United States,[7] upon application of the Governor or executive authority of such States, to be made within twelve months after the passing of this act, to the Secretary of the said Treasury,[8] and ceding to the United States all such Light-Houses, Beacons, Buoys, and Public Piers; Together with the Lands and Tenements thereto belonging; And after such cession, the same shall be supported, maintained and kept in repair at the charge of the United States, by such person, or persons, as the President shall from time to time appoint for that purpose.[9]

---

[1] Johnson inserted "public" at this point.
[2] Johnson changed "have accrued" to "accrue."
[3] Johnson filled this blank with "15th."
[4] Johnson struck out "next" and filled the blank with "Augt. 1789."
[5] Johnson struck out "before the passing of this act" and inserted the same phrase after "or sunk."
[6] Johnson struck out "which have not been" through "belong."
[7] Johnson inserted a parenthesis at this point and wrote "but so continued only 1. year unless Ceded." in the margin, summarizing the Senate's revision of the last part of this section.
[8] Johnson changed "Secretary of the said Treasury" to "President of the United States."
[9] This section is a paraphrase of the first section of the bill suggested by the Philadelphia merchants.

Sec. 2d. AND BE IT FURTHER ENACTED, That a Light-house shall be erected near the entrance of the Chesapeake-Bay, at such place when ceded to the United States,[10] as the President of the United States shall direct:[11] PROVIDED the States of Virginia and Maryland, shall first pay into the Treasury of the United States, the amount of all the monies collected by tonnage on shipping, or otherwise, for the express purpose of building such Light-house.[12]

Sec. 3d. AND BE IT FURTHER ENACTED, That such other Light-Houses, Beacons, Buoys and Public Piers, as to the President of the United States shall appear necessary and proper, upon representation made by the executive authority of any one or more States in the union, shall be erected, placed, sunk, supported, maintained and repaired, at the charge of the United States, at the entrance of, or within any bay, inlet, harbour or port of the United States,[13] the State or States requesting the same, having first ceded to the United States, such, or so much land, as shall be judged necessary for the use and support thereof.[14]

Sec. 4th. AND BE IT FURTHER ENACTED, That it shall be the duty of the Secretary of the Treasury[15] to provide by contracts, which shall be approved by the President, for building or[16] re-building such[17] Light-Houses, and for erecting,[18] placing or sinking such Buoys, Beacons and Public Piers, as may be necessary; And for supplying[19] the same with all necessary materials;[20] And also to agree on reasonable terms[21] for the salaries, wages or hire, of the person or persons appointed by the President, for the superintendance and care of the same.

Sec. 5th. AND BE IT FURTHER ENACTED, That the Legislatures of the several States may provide by Laws, which, whether now subsisting or here-after to be made, shall be in force, until otherwise declared by Congress, for

---

[10] Wingate inserted "in manner aforesaid" at this point.

[11] Johnson inserted a brace and wrote "restored" in the margin beside the first part of this section.

[12] Johnson inserted a brace and wrote "struck out" beside this proviso.

[13] Wingate inserted a brace at this point, probably to indicate that the following phrase was moved to the first section.

[14] This section is virtually the same as the second section of the bill suggested by the Philadelphia merchants.

[15] Johnson inserted "to be approved by the Prest." at this point.

[16] Johnson struck out "building or" and inserted "building the Light House at Chesapeak Ba[y] &" at this point.

[17] Johnson struck out "such" and inserted "when necessary & keeping in repair such."

[18] Johnson struck out "and for erecting" and inserted "when" above "Houses."

[19] Johnson wrote "furnishing" over "supplying."

[20] Johnson struck out "materials" and substituted "supplies."

[21] Johnson struck out "on reasonable terms."

the establishment and regulation of Pilots in the Bays, Inlets, Rivers, Harbours and Ports in such States respectively. [22]

[NEW-YORK, PRINTED BY THOMAS GREENLEAF]

A copy of the bill, with annotations by Johnson, is in the Broadside Collection, RBkRm, DLC. Another copy, annotated by Wingate, is in the Dartmouth College Library. This printing is a transitional stage of the bill and incorporates only the amendments made in committee prior to debate on the Senate floor. The committee's amendments were influenced by the suggestions of the Philadelphia merchants, printed above; we have pointed out the affected sections in the footnotes. The annotations by Johnson and Wingate indicate the direction taken by the Senate floor debate on and amendments to the committee's version of the bill, but do not show all the final changes made by the Senate. We have noted the changes made by Johnson and included Wingate's only where they differ.

---

[22] This section is the same as the third section of the bill suggested by the Philadelphia merchants.

Lighthouses Act [HR-84]
July 22, 1790

AN ACT TO AMEND THE ACT FOR THE
ESTABLISHMENT AND SUPPORT OF LIGHT-
HOUSES, BEACONS, BUOYS, AND PUBLIC
PIERS

BE IT ENACTED BY THE SENATE AND HOUSE OF REPRESENTATIVES OF THE UNITED STATES OF AMERICA IN CONGRESS ASSEMBLED, That all expences which shall accrue from and after the fifteenth day of August next for the necessary support, maintenance and repairs of all lighthouses, beacons, buoys and public piers within the United States, shall continue to be defrayed by the United States, until the first day of July one thousand seven hundred and ninety one, notwithstanding such lighthouses, beacons, buoys and public piers, with the lands and tenements thereunto belonging, and the Jurisdictions of the same, shall not in the mean time be ceded to or vested in the United States by the State or States respectively in which the same may be, and that the said time be further allowed to the States respectively to make such Cessions.

> FREDERICK AUGUSTUS MUHLENBERG
> Speaker of the House of Representatives
> JOHN ADAMS
> Vice-President of the United States, and
> President of the Senate

Approved July
the twenty Second
1790

> GO. WASHINGTON
> President of the United States

I certify that this Act did originate
in the House of Representatives.
JOHN BECKLEY—Clerk

Enrolled Acts, RG 11, DNA.

Calendar

Date	House	Senate
1790		
July 13	Motion for amendatory lighthouses bill made by Smith (S.C.).[1]	
July 14	Committee to prepare appointed (Smith, Sinnickson, and Foster); Smith presented "a bill to amend the act 'for the establishment and support of light-houses, beacons, buoys, and public piers,'" which was read twice.	
July 15	Read; agreed to.	
July 16		Received and read.
July 17		Read.
July 19		Read; agreed to.
July 20	Signed by speaker.	Signed by vice president.
July 22	Signed by president.[2]	

[1] *GUS,* July 14.
[2] The provisions of this act were extended to July 1, 1792, by the Mitigation of Forfeitures Act [S-24].

Maryland Act {HR-115}

February 9, 1791

AN ACT DECLARING THE CONSENT OF
CONGRESS TO A CERTAIN ACT OF THE
STATE OF MARYLAND

BE IT ENACTED BY THE SENATE AND HOUSE OF REPRESENTATIVES OF
THE UNITED STATES OF AMERICA IN CONGRESS ASSEMBLED, That the
consent of Congress be and is hereby granted and declared to the operation of
an Act of the General Assembly of Maryland, made and passed at a Session
begun and held at the City of Annapolis on the first Monday in November
last intituled "An Act to empower the wardens of the port of Baltimore to
levy and collect the duty therein mentioned," until the tenth day of January
next, and from thence until the end of the then next Session of Congress and
no longer.

> FREDERICK AUGUSTUS MUHLENBERG
> Speaker of the House of Representatives
> JOHN ADAMS
> Vice President of the United States, and
> President of the Senate

Approved February
the ninth
1791.

> GO. WASHINGTON
> President of the United States

I certify that this Act did originate
in the House of Representatives.
JOHN BECKLEY—Clerk

Enrolled Acts, RG 11, DNA.

Calendar

Date	House	Senate
1791		
Jan. 7	Notice of intention to bring in a bill given by Stone.[1]	
Jan. 17	Presidential message[2] received, communicating an *act of the state of Maryland.*	
Jan. 18	On a motion by Smith (Md.),[3] committee appointed to prepare a bill (Smith [Md.], Seney, and Mathews); Seney presented a bill, which was read.	
Jan. 19	Read; committed to COWH.	
Jan. 24–27	Postponed as order of the day.	
Jan. 28	Debated and amended in COWH; House agreed to amendments.	
Jan. 31	Read; blanks filled; agreed to as "An act declaring the consent of Congress to a certain act of the state of Maryland."	Received and read.
Feb. 1		Read.
Feb. 2		Read; agreed to.
Feb. 8	Signed by speaker.	Signed by vice president.
Feb. 9	Signed by president.	

[1] *FG*, Jan. 7.
[2] The message is printed in the *HJ*, p. 669.
[3] *FG*, Jan. 18.

Act of the State of Maryland
January 17, 1791

(Copy)

(Seal appendant)

AN ACT to empower the Wardens of the Port of Baltimore to levy and collect the duty therein mentioned

WHEREAS, many useful Regulations have taken place in consequence of the Powers heretofore granted to the Wardens of the Port of Baltimore and to enable them to carry the said Regulations into full effect

[1] BE IT ENACTED by the General Assembly of Maryland that the Wardens of the said Port of Baltimore shall have full power and Authority, to assess, levy, and collect, on every Vessel, arriving at the said Port of Baltimore from Sea, a sum of money not exceeding two Cents per Ton, to be appropriated and applied by the said Board of Wardens, to carry into effect the Rules and Regulations, which they may, from time to time make respecting the Harbour and Port of Baltimore.

[2] AND BE IT FURTHER ENACTED, that so much of the Act of Assembly entitled "an Act appointing Wardens for the Port of Baltimore Town in Baltimore County" which empowers the said Board of Wardens to assess and levy a duty of one penny per Ton on every Vessel entering or clearing at the said Port, and also so much of another Act of Assembly, entitled a suppliment to the Act entitled an Act appointing Wardens for the Port of Baltimore Town in Baltimore County, which empowers the Board of Wardens to assess, levy, and collect on every Vessel arriving at the said Port of Baltimore except Pilot Boats and Vessels not coming from Sea, belonging to Citizens of this State, a sum of money not exceeding two pence Current money per Ton be and are hereby repealed.

PROVIDED ALWAYS, that this Act of Assembly shall not operate and take effect until the same be ratified and confirmed by an Act of the Congress of the United States.

By the Senate Decr. 8th 1790   By the House of Delegates
Read & assented to   December 10th 1790
    By Order   Read & assented to
(signed) H. RIDGLEY JR. Clk.   By Order
                     (signed)   WM. HARWOOD Clk.

            (signed) J. E. HOWARD

I certify that the aforegoing is a true copy of the Original engrossed Act—
(signed) T. JOHNSON JR. Clk. of Council
MARYLAND SS.   In testimony that Thomas Johnson Junior is Clerk of the
Executive Council for the State of Maryland I have hereunto affixed the Great
Seal of said State   Witness my hand this eleventh Day of January
Anno Domini 1790—
(signed) SAMUEL HY. HOWARD Reg. Cor. Can.
A true Copy of the Act transmitted to the President of the United States.
TOBIAS LEAR
Secretary to the President
of the United States.

President's Messages: Suggesting legislation, SR, DNA, hand of Tobias Lear.

Merchant Seamen Act [HR-61]

July 20, 1790

An Act for the government and regulation of Seamen in the Merchants service

[1] BE IT ENACTED BY THE SENATE AND HOUSE OF REPRESENTATIVES OF THE UNITED STATES OF AMERICA IN CONGRESS ASSEMBLED, That from and after the first day of December next, any master or commander of any ship or vessel bound from a port in the United States to any foreign port, or any Ship or Vessel of the burthen of fifty tons or upwards, bound from a port in one State to a port in any other than an adjoining State, shall, before he proceed on such voyage, make an agreement in writing, or in print, with every seaman or mariner on board such ship or vessel, (except such as shall be apprentice or servant to himself or owners) declaring the voyage or voyages, term or terms of time, for which such seaman or mariner shall be shipped. And if any master or commander of such ship or vessel shall carry out any seamen or mariner (except Apprentices or Servants as aforesaid) without such contract or agreement being first made and signed by the seamen and mariners, such master or commander shall pay to every such seaman or mariner, the highest price or wages, which shall have been given at the port or place where such seaman or mariner shall have been shipped for a similar voyage, within three months next before the time of such shipping; PROVIDED such seaman or mariner shall perform such Voyage: or if not, then for such time as he shall continue to do duty on board such Ship or Vessel; and shall moreover forfeit twenty Dollars for every such seaman or mariner, one half to the use of the person prosecuting for the same, the other half to the use of the United States: And such seaman or mariner, not having signed such Contract, shall not be bound by the regulations, nor subject to the penalties and forfeitures contained in this Act.

[2] AND BE IT ENACTED, that, at the foot of every such Contract, there shall be a memorandum in writing of the day and the hour, on which such seaman or mariner, who shall so ship and subscribe, shall render themselves on board, to begin the voyage agreed upon. And if any such seaman or mariner shall neglect to render himself on board the Ship or Vessel, for which

he has shipped, at the time mentioned in such memorandum, and if the master, commander, or other Officer of the ship or vessel, shall, on the day on which such neglect happened, make an entry in the log-book of such ship or vessel, of the name of such seaman or mariner, and shall, in like manner, note the time that he so neglected to render himself (after the time appointed); every such seaman or mariner shall forfeit for every hour, which he shall so neglect to render himself, one day's pay—according to the rate of Wages agreed upon, to be deducted out of his Wages. And if any such seaman or mariner shall wholly neglect to render himself on board of such ship or vessel, or having rendered himself on board shall afterwards desert and escape, so that the ship or vessel proceed to sea without him, every such seaman or mariner shall forfeit and pay to the master, owner, or consignee of the said ship or vessel, a sum equal to that which shall have been paid to him by advance at the time of signing the Contract, over and besides the sum so advanced, both which sums shall be recoverable in any Court, or before any Justice or Justices of any State, City, Town or County within the United States, which, by the laws thereof, have cognizance of debts of equal value, against such seaman or mariner, or his Surety or Sureties, in case he shall have given surety to proceed the Voyage.

[3] AND BE IT ENACTED, that if the Mate or first Officer under the master, and a majority of the Crew of any ship or vessel, bound on a Voyage to any foreign port, shall, after the Voyage is begun (and before the ship or vessel shall have left the land) discover that the said ship or vessel is too leaky, or is otherwise unfit in her Crew, Body, Tackle, Apparel, Furniture, Provisions or Stores, to proceed on the intended Voyage, and shall require such unfitness to be enquired into, the master or commander shall, upon the request of the said mate, (or other Officer) and such majority, forthwith proceed to, or stop at, the nearest or most convenient port or place where such enquiry can be made, and shall there apply to the Judge of the District-Court, if he shall there reside, or if not, to some Justice of the peace of the City, Town or place, taking with him two or more of the said Crew who shall have made such request; and thereupon such Judge or Justice is hereby authorized and required to issue his precept directed to three persons in the neighborhood the most skilful in maritime affairs that can be procured, requiring them to repair on board such ship or vessel, and to examine the same in respect to the defects and insufficiencies complained of, and to make report to him, the said Judge, or Justice, in writing under their hands, or the hands of two of them, whether in any, or in what, respect the said ship or vessel is unfit to proceed on the intended voyage, and what addition of men, provisions or stores, or what repairs, or alterations in the body, tackle or apparel will be necessary; and upon such report the said Judge or Justice shall adjudge and determine, and shall endorse on the said Report his Judgment, whether the said ship or vessel

is fit to proceed on the intended voyage, and if not, whether such repairs can be made, or deficiencies supplied, where the ship or vessel then lays, or whether it be necessary for the said ship or vessel to return to the port from whence she first sailed, to be there refitted, and the master and crew shall, in all things, conform to the said Judgment; and the master or commander shall, in the first instance, pay all the Costs of such view, report and judgment, to be taxed and allowed on a fair Copy thereof certified by the said Judge or Justice. But if the Complaint of the said Crew shall appear, upon the said report and judgment, to have been without foundation, then the said master, or the owner, or consignee of such ship or vessel, shall deduct the amount thereof, and of reasonable damages for the detention, (to be ascertained by the said Judge or Justice) out of the Wages growing due to the complaining Seamen or Mariners. And if, after such Judgment, such ship or vessel is fit to proceed on her intended voyage, or, after procuring such men, provisions, stores, repairs or alterations as may be directed, the said seamen or mariners, or either of them, shall refuse to proceed on the Voyage, it shall and may be lawful for any Justice of the peace to commit by Warrant under his hand and seal every such seaman or mariner (who shall so refuse) to the common Gaol of the County, there to remain without bail or mainprize, until he shall have paid double the sum advanced to him at the time of subscribing the Contract for the voyage, together with such reasonable costs as shall be allowed by the said Justice, and inserted in the said Warrant, and the Surety or Sureties of such seaman or mariner (in case he or they shall have given any) shall remain liable for such payment; nor shall any such seaman or mariner be discharged upon any Writ of Habeas corpus, or otherwise, until such sum be paid by him or them or his or their surety or sureties, for want of any form of commitment, or other previous proceedings; PROVIDED that sufficient matter shall be made to appear upon the return of such Habeas Corpus, and an examination then to be had to detain him for the causes herein before assigned.

[4] AND BE IT ENACTED, that if any person shall harbor or secrete any seaman or mariner belonging to any ship or vessel, knowing them to belong thereto, every such person, on conviction thereof, before any Court in the City, Town or County, where he, she or they may reside, shall forfeit and pay ten dollars for every day which he, she or they shall continue so to harbor or secrete such seaman or mariner, one half to the use of the person prosecuting for the same, the other half to the use of the United States; and no sum exceeding one dollar shall be recoverable from any seaman or mariner by any one person, for any debt contracted during the time such seaman or mariner shall actually belong to any ship or vessel, until the voyage, for which such seaman or mariner engaged, shall be ended.

[5] AND BE IT ENACTED, that if any seaman or mariner, who shall have

subscribed such Contract as is herein before described, shall absent himself from on board the ship or vessel in which he shall so have shipped, without leave of the master, or officer commanding on board; And the mate, or other Officer having charge of the Logbook, shall make an entry therein of the name of such seaman or mariner, on the day on which he shall so absent himself, and if such seaman or mariner shall return to his duty within forty eight hours, such seaman or mariner shall forfeit three days pay, for every day which he shall so absent himself, to be deducted out of his Wages; but if any seaman or mariner shall absent himself for more than forty eight hours at one time, he shall forfeit all the Wages due to him, and all his Goods and Chattels which were on board the said ship or vessel, or in any store where they may have been lodged at the time of his desertion, to the use of the Owners of the ship or vessel, and moreover shall be liable to pay to him or them, all damages, which he or they may sustain, by being obliged to hire other seamen or mariners in his or their place, and such damages shall be recovered with Costs in any Court, or before any Justice or Justices having Jurisdiction of the recovery of debts to the value of ten dollars or upwards.

[6] AND BE IT ENACTED, that every seaman or mariner shall be entitled to demand and receive from the master, or commander, of the ship or vessel to which they belong, one third part of the wages which shall be due to him, at every port where such ship or vessel shall unlade and deliver her Cargo, before the voyage be ended, unless the contrary be expressly stipulated in the contract, and as soon as the voyage is ended, and the Cargo or Ballast be fully discharged at the last port of delivery, every seaman or mariner shall be entitled to the Wages which shall be then due according to his Contract; and if such Wages shall not be paid within ten days after such discharge, or if any dispute shall arise between the master and seamen or mariners, touching the said Wages, it shall be lawful for the Judge of the District where the said ship or vessel shall be, or, in case his residence be more than three miles from the place, or of his absence from the place of his residence, then for any Judge, or Justice of the peace, to summon the master of such ship or vessel to appear before him, to shew cause why process should not issue against such ship or vessel, her tackle, furniture and apparel, according to the course of Admiralty-Courts, to answer for the said Wages; and if the master shall neglect to appear, or appearing shall not shew that the Wages are paid, or otherwise satisfied or forfeited, and if the matter in dispute shall not be forthwith settled, in such case, the Judge or Justice shall certify to the Clerk of the Court of the District, that there is sufficient cause of complaint, whereon to found Admiralty-process, and thereupon the Clerk of such Court shall issue process against the said ship or vessel, and the suit shall be proceeded on in the said Court, and final Judgment be given according to the course of Admiralty-Courts in such cases used, and in such suit all the seamen or mariners (having cause of complaint of the like kind against the same ship or

vessel) shall be joined as Complainants, and it shall be incumbent on the master or commander to produce the Contract, and Logbook if required, to ascertain any matters in dispute, otherwise the Complainants shall be permitted to state the contents thereof, and the proof of the contrary shall lie on the master or commander; but nothing herein contained shall prevent any Seaman or Mariner from having or maintaining any Action at Common Law, for the recovery of his Wages, or from immediate process out of any Court having Admiralty-jurisdiction, wherever any ship or vessel may be found, in case she shall have left the port of delivery where her Voyage ended before payment of the Wages, or in case she shall be about to proceed to sea before the end of the ten days next after the delivery of her Cargo or Ballast.

[7] AND BE IT ENACTED, that if any seaman or mariner, who shall have signed a Contract to perform a Voyage, shall, at any port or place, desert, or shall absent himself from such ship or vessel without leave of the master, or officer commanding in the absence of the master, it shall be lawful for any Justice of peace within the United States (upon the complaint of the master) to issue his Warrant to apprehend such deserter, and bring him before such Justice; and if it shall then appear by due proof, that he has signed a Contract within the intent and meaning of this Act, and that the Voyage agreed for is not finished, altered, or the Contract otherwise dissolved, and that such seaman or mariner has deserted the ship or vessel, or absented himself without leave, the said Justice shall commit him to the house of correction, or common Gaol of the City, Town or place, there to remain until the said Ship or Vessel shall be ready to proceed on her voyage, or till the Master shall require his discharge, and then to be delivered to the said master, he paying all the cost of such Commitment, and deducting the same out of the Wages due to such seaman or mariner.

[8] AND BE IT ENACTED, that every ship or vessel belonging to a Citizen or Citizens of the United States, of the burthen of one hundred and fifty tons or upwards, navigated by ten or more persons in the whole, and bound on a voyage without the limits of the United States, shall be provided with a Chest of Medicines put up by some Apothecary of known reputation, and accompanied by directions for administering the same; and the said medicines shall be examined by the same or some other Apothecary, once at least in every year, and supplied with fresh medicines, in the place of such as shall have been used or spoiled; and in default of having such medicine-chest so provided, and kept fit for use, the master, or commander of such ship or vessel, shall provide and pay for all such advice, medicine or attendance of Physicians, as any of the Crew shall stand in need of, in case of sickness, at every port or place, where the ship or vessel may touch or trade at, during the voyage, without any deduction from the wages of such sick seaman or mariner.

[9] AND BE IT ENACTED, that every ship or vessel, belonging as aforesaid, bound on a voyage across the Atlantic Ocean, shall, at the time of leaving the last port from whence she sails, have on board, well secured under deck, at least sixty gallons of water, one hundred pounds of salted flesh meat, and one hundred pounds of wholesome ship-bread, for every person on board such ship or vessel, over and besides such other provisions, stores and live-stock, as shall by the master or passengers be put on board, and in like proportion for shorter or longer voyages; and in case the Crew of any ship or vessel, which shall not have been so provided, shall be put upon short allowance in water, flesh or bread, during the voyage, the master or owner of such ship or vessel shall pay to each of the Crew, one day's wages beyond the wages agreed on, for every day they shall be so put to short allowance, to be recovered in the same manner as their stipulated Wages.

FREDERICK AUGUSTUS MUHLENBERG
Speaker of the House of Representatives
JOHN ADAMS
Vice-President of the United States and
President of the Senate

Approved July ⎱ 1790
the Twentieth ⎰

GO. WASHINGTON
President of the United States

I certify that this Act did originate
in the House of Representatives.
JOHN BECKLEY—Clerk

Enrolled Acts, RG 11, DNA.

Calendar

Date	House	Senate
1790		
Apr. 29	On a motion by Fitzsimons,[1] committee to prepare appointed (Fitzsimons, Smith [Md.], and Sturges).	

---

[1] *NYDG,* Apr. 30.

Date	House	Senate
1790		
May 3	Fitzsimons presented *a bill for the government and regulation of seamen in the merchants service,* which was read twice and committed to the COWH; 400 copies ordered printed.[2]	
May 10–26	Postponed as order of the day.	
May 27	Recommitted to Gilman, Goodhue, Parker, Fitzsimons, and Smith.	
June 17	Gilman reported *amendments;* motion by Fitzsimons for debate on bill disagreed to.[3]	
June 25	Committee amendments agreed to.	
June 28	Read and agreed to.	Received and read.
July 1		Read and committed to Dalton, Morris, and Langdon.
July 7		Dalton reported *amendments,* which were agreed to.
July 8		Agreed to with amendments.
July 10	Senate amendments agreed to, except the third.	
July 12		Amendment disagreed to by House receded from.
July 17	Signed by speaker.	Signed by vice president.
July 20	Signed by president.	

[2] *NYDG,* May 4.
[3] *NYDG,* June 18.

Merchant Seamen Bill {HR-61}
May 3, 1790

A BILL FOR THE GOVERNMENT AND REGULATION OF SEAMEN
IN THE MERCHANTS SERVICE

SEC. 1. BE *it enacted by the* SENATE *and* HOUSE *of* REPRESENTATIVES *of the*
United States of America in Congress assembled, That from and after the
day of   [1] next, every master or commander of any ship or
vessel, bound from a port in the United States to any foreign port, or of any
ship or vessel of the burthen of   [2] tons or upwards, bound from a port
in one State to a port in another[3] State, by sea,[4] shall before he proceed on
such voyage, make an agreement in writing or in print, with every seaman or
mariner on board such ship or vessel (except such as shall be apprentice or
servant to himself or owners) declaring the voyage or voyages, term or terms
of time for which such seaman or mariner shall be shipped. And if any master
or commander of such ship or vessel shall carry out any seaman or mariner
(except apprentices or servants as aforesaid) without such contract or agreement being first made and signed by the seamen and mariners, such master or
commander shall pay to every such seaman or mariner the highest price or
wages which shall have been given at the port or place where such seaman or
mariner shall have been shipped, for a similar voyage, within three months
next before the time of such shipping, provided such seamen or mariner shall
perform such voyage; or if not, then for such time as he shall continue to do
duty on board such ship or vessel; and shall moreover forfeit   [5] dollars
for every such seaman or mariner, one half to the use of the person prosecuting for the same, the other half to the use of the United States.[6] And such
seaman or mariner, not having signed such contract, shall not be bound by
the regulations, nor subject to the penalties and forfeitures contained in this
act.

SEC. 2. *And be it enacted,* That at the foot of every such contract, there shall
be a memorandum in writing, of the day and the hour on which such seaman
or mariner who shall so ship and subscribe, shall render themselves on board,
to begin the voyage agreed upon. And if any such seaman or mariner shall
neglect to render himself on board the ship or vessel for which he has shipped,
at the time mentioned in such memorandum, and if the master, commander

---

[1] The House filled these blanks with "first" and "December."
[2] The House filled this blank with "fifty."
[3] The Senate struck out "another" and inserted "any other than an adjoining."
[4] The Senate struck out "by sea."
[5] The House filled this blank with "twenty."
[6] The Senate struck out from "and shall moreover forfeit" through "United States." The House disagreed to this amendment and the Senate receded from it.

or other officer of the ship or vessel, shall on the day on which such neglect happened, make an entry in the log-book of such ship or vessel, of the name of such seaman or mariner, and shall in like manner note the time that he so neglected to render himself (after the time appointed); every such seaman or mariner shall forfeit, for every hour which he shall so neglect to render himself, one day's pay, according to the rate of wages agreed upon, to be deducted out of his wages when the voyage shall be ended.[7] And if any such seaman or mariner shall wholly neglect to render himself on board of such ship or vessel, or having rendered himself on board, shall afterwards desert and escape, so that the ship or vessel proceed to sea without him; every such seaman or mariner shall forfeit and pay to the master, owner or consignee of the said ship or vessel, a sum equal to that which shall have been paid to him by advance, at the time of signing the contract, over and besides the sum so advanced, both which sums shall be recoverable in any court, or before any justice or justices of any state, city, town or county within the United States, which by the laws thereof have cognizance of debts of equal value, against such seaman or mariner, or his surety or sureties, in case he shall have given surety to proceed the voyage.

SEC. 3. *And be it enacted,* That if the mate or first officer under the master, and a majority of the crew of any ship or vessel, bound on a voyage to any foreign port, shall, after the voyage is begun, (and before the ship or vessel shall have left the land) discover that the said ship or vessel is too leaky, or is otherwise unfit, in her crew, body, tackle, apparel, furniture, provisions or stores, to proceed on the intended voyage, and shall require such unfitness to be enquired into; the master or commander, shall, upon the request of the said mate, (or other officer) and such majority, forthwith proceed to, or stop at, the nearest or most convenient port or place, where such enquiry can be made, and shall there apply to the judge of the district court, if he shall there reside, or if not, to some justice of the peace, of the city, town, or place, taking with him two or more of the said crew, who shall have made such request; and thereupon, such judge or justice is hereby authorized and required to issue his precept, directed to three persons in the neighborhood, the most skilful in maritime affairs that can be procured, requiring them to repair on board such ship or vessel, and to examine the same in respect to the defects and insufficiencies complained of, and to make report to him the said judge or justice, in writing, under their hands, or the hands of two of them, whether, in any, or in what respect the said ship or vessel is unfit to proceed on the intended voyage, and what addition of men, provisions or stores, or what repairs or alterations in the body, tackle or apparel, will be necessary; and upon such report the said judge or justice shall adjudge and determine, and shall endorse on the said report his judgment, whether the said ship or

---

[7] The Senate struck out "when the voyage shall be ended."

vessel is fit to proceed on the intended voyage; and if not, whether such repairs can be made, or deficiencies supplied where the ship or vessel then lays; or whether it be necessary for the said ship or vessel to return to the port from whence she first sailed, to be there refitted; and the master and crew shall in all things conform to the said judgment; and the master or commander shall, in the first instance, pay all the costs of such view, report and judgment, to be taxed and allowed, on a fair copy thereof, certified by the said judge or justice. But if the complaint of the said crew, shall appear, upon the said report and judgment, to have been without foundation, then the said master, or the owner or consignee of such ship or vessel, shall deduct the amount thereof, and of reasonable damages for the detention, (to be ascertained by the said judge or justice), out of the wages growing due, to the complaining seamen or mariners. And if, after such judgment, such ship or vessel is fit to proceed on her intended voyage, or, after procuring such men, provisions, stores, repairs, or alterations, as may be directed, the said seamen or mariners, or either of them, shall refuse to proceed on the voyage, it shall and may be lawful for any justice of the peace, to commit by warrant under his hand and seal, every such seaman or mariner (who shall so refuse) to the common gaol of the county, there to remain without bail or mainprize, until he shall have paid double the sum advanced to him at the time of subscribing the contract for the voyage, together with such reasonable costs as shall be allowed by the said justice, and inserted in the said warrant; and the surety or sureties of such seaman or mariner (in case he or they shall have given any) shall remain liable for such payment; nor shall any such seaman or mariner be discharged upon any writ of *habeas corpus,* or otherwise, until such sum be paid by him or them, or his or their surety or sureties, for want of any form of commitment, or other previous proceedings; provided, that sufficient matter shall be made to appear upon the return of such *habeas corpus,* and an examination then to be had to detain him for the causes herein before assigned.

SEC. 4. *And be it enacted,* That if any person shall harbor or secrete any seaman or mariner, belonging to any ship or vessel, knowing them to belong thereto, every such person, or conviction thereof, before any court of record in the city, town or county, where he, she or they may reside, shall forfeit and pay   8 dollars for every day, which he, she or they shall continue so to harbor or secrete such seaman or mariner, one half to the use of the person prosecuting for the same, the other half to the use of the United States; and no sum exceeding   9 dollars, shall be recoverable from any seaman or mariner, by any one person, for any debt contracted during the time such seaman or mariner shall actually belong to any ship or vessel. 10

---

8 The House filled this blank with "ten."

9 The House filled this blank with "three." The Senate struck out "three" and inserted "one."

10 The House inserted "until the voyage for which such seaman or mariner engage, shall be ended" at this point.

SEC. 5. *And be it enacted,* That if any seaman or mariner, who shall have subscribed such contract as is herein before described, shall absent himself from on board the ship or vessel in which he shall so have shipped, without leave of the master,[11] and that[12] the mate, or other officer having charge of the log-book, shall make an entry therein, of the name of such seaman and[13] mariner, on the day on which he shall so absent himself; and that[14] such seaman or mariner shall return to his duty within forty-eight hours, such seaman or mariner shall forfeit three days pay for every day which he shall so absent himself, to be deducted out of his wages; but if any seaman or mariner shall absent himself for more than forty-eight hours at one time, he shall forfeit all the wages due to him, and all his goods and chattels which were on board the said ship or vessel, or in any store where they may have been lodged at the time of his desertion, to the use of the owners of the ship or vessel, and moreover shall be liable to pay to him or them, all damages which he or they may sustain by being obliged to hire other seamen or mariners in his or their place, and such damages shall be recovered with costs in any court, or before any justice or justices having jurisdiction of the recovery of debts to the value of   [15] or upwards.

SEC. 6. *And be it enacted,* That every seaman or mariner shall be entitled to demand and receive from the master or commander of the ship or vessel to which they belong, one third part of the wages that shall be due to him at every port where such ship shall unlade and deliver her cargo, before the voyage be ended, unless the contrary be expressly stipulated in the contract, and as soon as the voyage is ended, and the cargo or ballast be fully discharged at the last port of delivery, every seaman or mariner shall be entitled to the wages, which shall be then due, according to his contract; and if such wages shall not be paid within ten days after such discharge, or if any dispute shall arise between the master and seamen or mariners, touching the said wages, it shall be lawful for the judge of the district where the said ship or vessel shall be, or in case his residence be more than three miles from the place, or of his absence from the place of his residence, then for any judge or justice of the peace to summon the master of such ship or vessel to appear before him to shew cause why process should not issue against such ship or vessel, her tackle, furniture and apparel, according to the course of admiralty courts, to answer for the said wages, and if the master shall neglect to appear, or appearing shall not show that the wages are paid, or otherwise satisfied or forfeited, and if the matter in dispute shall not be forthwith settled, in such case the judge or justice shall certify to the clerk of the court of the district, that there is sufficient cause of complaint whereon to found admiralty pro-

---

[11] The House inserted "or officer commanding on board" at this point.
[12] The engrossed bill omits "that."
[13] The engrossed bill reads "or" in place of "and."
[14] The engrossed bill reads "if" in place of "that."
[15] The House filled this blank with "ten."

cess, and thereupon the clerk of such court shall issue process against the said ship or vessel, and the suit shall be proceeded on in the said court, and final judgment be given according to the course of admiralty courts in such cases used, and in such suit, all the seamen or mariners (having cause of complaint of the like kind against the same ship or vessel) shall be joined as complainants, and it shall be incumbent on the master or commander, to produce the contract and log-book, if required, to ascertain any matters in dispute, otherwise the complainants shall be permitted to state the contents thereof, and the proof of the contrary shall lie on the master or commander; but nothing herein contained shall prevent any seaman or mariner from having or maintaining any action at common law, for the recovery of his wages, or from immediate process out of any court, having admiralty jurisdiction wherever any ship or vessel may be found, in case she shall have left the port of delivery, where her voyage ended before payment of the wages, or in case she shall be about to proceed to sea before the end of the ten days next after the delivery of her cargo or ballast.

SEC. 7. *And be it enacted,* That if any seaman or mariner, who shall have signed a contract to perform a voyage, shall at any port or place desert, or shall absent himself from such ship or vessel without leave of the master, or officer commanding in the absence of the master, it shall be lawful for any justice of peace within the United States, (upon the complaint of the master) to issue his warrant to apprehend such deserter, and bring him before such justice, and if it shall then appear by due proof, that he has signed a contract within the intent and meaning of this act, and that the voyage agreed for is not finished, altered, or the contract otherwise dissolved, and that such seaman or mariner has deserted the ship or vessel, or absented himself without leave, the said justice shall commit him to the house of correction, or common jail of the city, town or place, there to remain until the said ship or vessel shall be ready to proceed on her voyage, or till the master shall require his discharge, and then to be delivered to the said master, he paying all the cost of such commitment, and deducting the same out of the wages due to such seaman or mariner; and the consuls of foreign nations, resident in the United States, and recognized as such, shall have the powers of a justice of the peace over mariners not being citizens of the United States, and belonging to ships or vessels of their respective nations, who shall so desert as aforesaid, while in any port of the United States.[16]

SEC. 8. *And be it enacted,* That every ship or vessel belonging to a citizen or citizens of the United States, of the burthen of one hundred and fifty tons or upwards, navigated by ten or more persons in the whole, and bound on a voyage without the limits of the United States, shall be provided with a chest

---

[16] The House struck out from "and the consuls of foreign nations" through the end of this section.

of medicines, put up by some apothecary of known reputation, and accompanied by directions from the same apothecary[17] for administering the same, signed by him, and certified to contain what shall be necessary and sufficient for the number of persons on board, according to the intended voyage for one year;[18] and the said medicines shall be examined by the same, or some other apothecary, once at least in every year, and supplied with fresh medicines in the place of such as shall have been used or spoiled; and in default of having such medicine chest so provided and kept fit for use, the master or commander of such ship or vessel, shall provide and pay for all such advice, medicine, or attendance of physicians, as any of the crew shall stand in need of, in case of sickness, at every port or place where the ship or vessel may touch or trade at during the voyage, without any deduction from the wages of any such sick seaman or mariner.

SEC. 9. *And be it enacted,* That every ship or vessel, belonging as aforesaid, bound on a voyage across the Atlantic ocean, shall at the time of leaving the last port from whence she sails, have on board, well secured under deck, at least sixty gallons of water, one hundred and fifty pounds of salted flesh meat, and one hundred and fifty pounds of wholesome ship bread for every person on board such ship or vessel, over and besides such other provisions, stores, and live stock, as shall by the master be thought necessary,[19] and in like proportion for shorter or longer voyages, and in case the crew of any ship or vessel, which shall not have been so provided, shall be put upon short allowance in water, flesh or bread during the voyage, the master or owner of such ship or vessel, shall pay to each of the crew, one days wages beyond the wages agreed on for every day they shall be so put to short allowance, to be recovered in the same manner as their stipulated wages.

PRINTED BY FRANCIS CHILDS AND JOHN SWAINE.

Broadside Collection, RBkRm, DLC. We determined the House amendments, all of which were reported by the committee, by comparing the bill as introduced with the engrossed House bill. We are not printing the latter because of its close similarity to the earlier version. The Senate amendments are printed in the *SLJ,* p. 403n. A draft of the Senate amendments, in the hand of Dalton, is in Various Select Committee Reports, SR, DNA.

---

[17] The Senate struck out "from the same apothecary."
[18] The Senate struck out from "signed by him, and" through "for one year."
[19] The Senate struck out "be thought necessary" and inserted "or Passengers be put on board."

Military Establishment Act [HR-50a]
April 30, 1790

AN ACT FOR REGULATING THE MILITARY ESTABLISHMENT OF THE UNITED STATES

[1] BE IT ENACTED BY THE SENATE, AND HOUSE OF REPRESENTATIVES OF THE UNITED STATES OF AMERICA IN CONGRESS ASSEMBLED, That the commissioned Officers herein after mentioned and the number of one thousand two hundred and sixteen non-commissioned Officers, privates and Musicians, shall be raised for the service of the United States for the period of three Years, unless they should previously by law be discharged.

[2] AND BE IT FURTHER ENACTED that the non-commissioned Officers and Privates aforesaid shall, at the time of their inlistments respectively, be able-bodied men, not under five feet six inches in height without shoes, nor under the age of eighteen, nor above the age of forty six Years.

[3] AND BE IT FURTHER ENACTED, that the commissioned Officers herein after mentioned, and the said non-commissioned Officers Privates and Musicians shall be formed into one Regiment of Infantry to consist of three Battalions, and one Battalion of Artillery. The Regiment of Infantry to be composed of one Lieutenant-Colonel Commandant, three Majors, three Adjutants, three Quarter Masters, one Paymaster, one Surgeon, two Surgeon's Mates and twelve Companies, each of which shall consist of one Captain, one Lieutenant, one Ensign, four Serjeants, four Corporals sixty six privates and two Musicians. The Battalion of Artillery shall be composed of one Major-Commandant, one Adjutant, one Quarter Master, one Paymaster, one Surgeon's Mate and four Companies; each of which shall consist of one Captain, two Lieutenants, four Serjeants, four Corporals, sixty six privates and two Musicians: PROVIDED ALWAYS, that the Adjutants, Quarter Masters, and Paymasters shall be appointed from the line of Subalterns of the aforesaid Corps respectively.

[4] AND BE IT FURTHER ENACTED, that the President of the United States may from time to time appoint one or two Inspectors as to him shall seem meet to inspect the said Troops who shall also muster the same, and each of whom shall receive the like pay and subsistence as a Captain and be allowed ten dollars per month for forage.

[5] AND BE IT FURTHER ENACTED, that the Troops aforesaid shall receive

for their Services the following enumerated monthly rates of pay Lieutenant Colonel Commandant sixty dollars: Major Commandant of Artillery forty five dollars: Majors forty Dollars: Captains thirty dollars: Lieutenants twenty two dollars: Ensigns eighteen dollars: Surgeons thirty dollars: Surgeon's Mates twenty four dollars: Serjeants five dollars; Corporals four dollars; privates three dollars; Senior musician in each Battalion of Infantry, and in the Battalion of Artillery, five dollars; Musicians three dollars, Provided always, that the sums herein after specified shall be deducted from the pay of the non-commissioned Officers, Privates and Musicians stipulated as aforesaid, for the purposes of forming a fund for Clothing and Hospital Stores. From the monthly pay of each Serjeant and senior Musician there shall be deducted for uniform Clothing the sum of one dollar and forty Cents, and the farther sum of ten Cents for Hospital Stores; and from the monthly pay of each Corporal for Uniform Clothing, one dollar and fifteen Cents, and the farther sum of ten Cents for Hospital Stores, and from the Monthly pay of each private and Musician for uniform clothing the sum of ninety Cents, and the further sum of ten Cents for Hospital Stores.

[6] AND BE IT FURTHER ENACTED, that the Subalterns who may be appointed to act as Adjutants shall each receive for the same in addition to their regimental pay ten dollars per month: and Quarter and Pay-masters so appointed each five dollars per month.

[7] AND BE IT FURTHER ENACTED, that the Commissioned Officers aforesaid shall receive for their daily subsistence the following number of Rations of Provisions *to wit,* Lieutenant Colonel Commandant six, a Major four, a Captain three, a Lieutenant two, an Ensign two, a Surgeon three, a Surgeon's Mate two, or money in lieu thereof at the option of the said Officers, at the contract price at the posts respectively where the rations shall become due.

[8] AND BE IT FURTHER ENACTED, that the Commissioned Officers, herein after described shall receive monthly the following enumerated sums, instead of forage: Lieutenant Colonels Commandant twelve dollars: Major Commandant of Artillery, Majors, and Surgeon each ten dollars, Surgeon's Mates each six dollars.

[9] AND BE IT FURTHER ENACTED, that every non-commissioned Officer, Private and Musician aforesaid shall receive annually the following Articles of Uniform clothing; One Hat or Helmet, one Coat; one Vest; two pair of woollen and two pair of linen Overalls; four pair of Shoes; four Shirts; two pair of Socks; one Blanket; one Stock and Clasp, and one pair of Buckles.

[10] AND BE IT FURTHER ENACTED, that every non-commissioned Officer, Private and Musician aforesaid shall receive daily the following rations of Provisions or the value thereof; one pound of Beef, or three Quarters of a pound of Pork; one pound of bread or flour; half a gill of rum, brandy, or

whiskey, or the value thereof at the contract price where the same shall become due; and at the rate of one quart of Salt, two Quarts of Vinegar, two pounds of Soap and one pound of Candles to every hundred Rations.

[11] AND BE IT FURTHER ENACTED, that if any commissioned Officer, non-commissioned Officer, Private or Musician aforesaid, shall be wounded or disabled while in the line of his duty in public Service, he shall be placed on the list of the invalids of the United States at such rate of pay, and under such regulations as shall be directed by the President of the United States for the time being: PROVIDED ALWAYS, that the rate of Compensation for such wounds or disabilities, shall never exceed for the highest disability, half the monthly pay received by any commissioned Officer, at the time of being so wounded or disabled; and that the rate of Compensation to non commissioned Officers, Privates, and Musicians shall never exceed five dollars per month; AND PROVIDED ALSO, that all inferior disabilities shall entitle the persons so disabled to receive only a sum in proportion to the highest disability.

[12] AND BE IT FURTHER ENACTED, that every commissioned Officer, non-commissioned Officer, Private and Musician aforesaid shall take and subscribe the following Oath or Affirmation, to wit "I, A.B. do solemnly swear or affirm (as the case may be) to bear true Allegiance to the United States of America, and to serve them honestly and faithfully against all their enemies or opposers whomsoever, and to observe and obey the Orders of the President of the United States of America, and the Orders of the Officers appointed over me according to the Articles of War."

[13] AND BE IT FURTHER ENACTED, that the commissioned Officers, non-commissioned Officers, Privates, and Musicians aforesaid, shall be governed by the rules and articles of War, which have been established by the United States in Congress assembled, as far as the same may be applicable to the Constitution of the United States, or by such rules and articles as may hereafter by law be established.

[14] AND BE IT FURTHER ENACTED, that the "Act for recognizing and adapting to the Constitution of the United States, the establishment of the Troops raised under the resolves of the United States in Congress assembled and for other purposes therein mentioned," passed the twenty ninth day of September, one thousand seven hundred and eighty nine, be, and the same is hereby repealed. PROVIDED ALWAYS, that the non-commissioned Officers and Privates continued and engaged under the aforesaid Act of the twenty ninth day of September, one thousand seven hundred and eighty nine, and who shall decline to reinlist under the establishment made by this Act shall be discharged whenever the President of the United States shall direct the same. PROVIDED FURTHER, that the whole number of non commissioned Officers, Privates, and Musicians, in the service of the United States, at any one time, either by virtue of this Act, or by virtue of the aforesaid Act passed

the twenty ninth day of September one thousand seven hundred and eighty nine, shall not exceed the number of one thousand two hundred and sixteen.

[15] AND BE IT FURTHER ENACTED, that for the purpose of aiding the Troops now in service, or to be raised by this Act in protecting the inhabitants of the frontiers of the United States, the President is hereby authorized to call into service from time to time such part of the Militia of the States respectively as he may judge necessary for the purpose aforesaid; and that their pay and subsistence while in service be the same as the pay and subsistence of the Troops above mentioned, and they shall be subject to the rules and Articles of War.

FREDERICK AUGUSTUS MUHLENBERG
    Speaker of the House of Representatives
JOHN ADAMS
    Vice President of the United States and
    President of the Senate

Approved
April 30th
1790

GO. WASHINGTON
    President of the United States

I certify that this Act did originate
in the House of Representatives.
JOHN BECKLEY—Clerk

Enrolled Acts, RG 11, DNA.

Calendar

Date	House	Senate
1790		
Jan. 12	Presidential message enclosing a *report of the secretary of war* received and partly read.[1]	
Jan. 13	Report read and referred to Wadsworth, Brown, Boudinot, Burke, and Baldwin.	

---

[1] The president's message is printed in the *SLJ*, p. 221. The actions of January 12, 13, 20, and 21, although reported in the *HJ*, took place in secret sessions, according to the newspaper accounts. (*GUS*, Jan. 13; *NYJ*, Jan. 14; *NYDG*, Jan. 21; *NYDA*, Jan. 22)

Date	House	Senate
1790		
Jan. 14	Livermore, Ames, Laurance, Scott, and Smith (Md.) added to committee.	
Jan. 20	Wadsworth presented committee report, which was read.	
Jan. 21	Committee report read; debated and agreed to in COWH; debated in House.	
Jan. 22	Secret session of House apparently agreed to COWH report.[2]	
Mar. 3	Secret session.[3]	
Mar. 5	Secret session.[4]	
Mar. 15	On motion by Jackson, secret session held.[5]	
Mar. 25	Secret session.[6]	
Mar. 26		*An Act for regulating the military establishment of the United States* received, read, and ordered printed.
Mar. 29		Read.
Mar. 30		Read; committed to Few, Ellsworth, Butler, Schuyler, Carroll, Langdon, and Strong.
Apr. 6		Few presented committee report, which was postponed.
Apr. 13–15		Debated.

---

[2] *GUS, NYWM,* Jan. 23.
[3] *NYP,* Mar. 4. It is probable that this bill was discussed in this secret session, as well as those of March 5, 15, and 25.
[4] *GUS,* Mar. 6.
[5] *GUS,* Mar. 17.
[6] *GUS,* Mar. 27.

Date	House	Senate
1790		
Apr. 16		Debated, *amended,* and recommitted.[7]
Apr. 20		Debated; Few presented *committee report,* which was adopted as amendments to bill.
Apr. 21	Motion to go into secret session apparently failed; motion by Gilman to adjourn agreed to.[8]	Bill read and agreed to with *amendments.*
Apr. 22	In secret session,[9] Senate amendments agreed to with an *amendment.*	
Apr. 23		House amendment agreed to.
Apr. 28	Signed by speaker.	Signed by vice president.
Apr. 30	Signed by president.	

[7] On April 19, Ellsworth used the opportunity of correcting the minutes of April 16 to delete a roll call vote and other action on this bill. (Maclay, Apr. 19; *SLJ,* pp. 288n–289n)

[8] *NYDG,* Apr. 22.

[9] *NYDG,* Apr. 23.

Report of the Secretary of War
January 12, 1790

A Statement of the Indian Department, and of the South Western Frontiers

War Office, January 4th, 1790

Sir

I humbly beg leave to submit to your consideration a general statement of the Indian Department, and of the South Western frontiers, the same being intimately blended together.

The invitation of the United States to the Creek Nation of Indians, to treat of peace on terms of mutual advantage has not been accepted—The report of the Commissioners A will fully show the precarious state of this business.

The assurances given by some of the Cheifs of the peaceable intentions of the Creek Nation, are too uncertain in their nature, even if sincere, for the United States to rely upon.

The case seems to require an adequate provisional arrangement which on the commission of any further depredations by the Creeks should be called into activity—After the solemn offer of peace which has been made and refused, it is incumbent on the United States to be in a situation to punish all unprovoked aggressions.

In case the conduct of the Creeks should render coercion indispensibly necessary; policy requires that it should be undertaken with a force adequate to the speedy accomplishment of the object—An Army of sufficient strength should be raised to march into their country and destroy their Towns, unless they should submit to an equitable peace.

The warriors of the Creeks have been stated at various numbers from four to six thousand, and are said to be generally well armed, and furnished with ammunition.

To march into the Country of the Upper and Lower Creeks so as to be superior to all opposition would require an Army to be raised of five thousand men—This number after making the necessary deductions for sickness—establishment of posts of communication—and convoys of provision, would probably be reduced to three thousand five hundred effectives.

The troops to be employed on this service ought to be enlisted for the occasion, subject however to be sooner discharged if necessary.

I have formed an Estimate of the expence of such an Army which is hereunto annexed marked No. 1. on the supposition that the pay of the noncommissioned officers and privates may be reduced to the sums therein specified.

But in either event of peace or War with the Creeks the establishment of a line of military posts on the south western frontier appears to be highly requisite. No peace with the Indians can be preserved unless by a military force—The lawless whites as well as Indians will be deterred from the commission of murders when they shall be convinced that punishment will immediately follow detection.

The situation of the Cherokee Nation looking up to the United States for protection in consequence of the treaty of Hopewell demands attention.

Although existing circumstances may require that the boundaries stated in the said treaty should be more accomodated to the inhabitants who cannot be removed—Yet the other general principles thereof ought to be preserved, and particularly the stipulated protection of the United States—This cannot be afforded but by troops—The friendship of the Chickasaws and Choctaws cannot be cultivated, and the trade stipulated by treaty cannot be extended to them but by means of the protection of troops.

The present military arrangement of the United States consists of one Battalion of Artillery of two hundred and forty non commissioned and privates, and one regiment of Infantry of five hundred and sixty non commissioned and privates—This force for the following objects is utterly inadequate—To prevent the usurpation of the lands of the United States—To facilitate the surveying and selling of the same, for the purpose of reducing the public debt—and for the protection of the frontiers from Georgia to Lake Erie—If it should be decided to erect a line of posts of that extent, and to leave small guards for the public Arsenals the following establishment would be required.

A Battalion of Artillery of two hundred and forty non commissioned officers and privates—And two Regiments of Infantry of seven hundred non commissioned officers and privates each—the total of the Artillery and Infantry amounting to sixteen hundred and forty non commissioned and privates.

The Estimate hereunto annexed marked No. 2. will exhibit the annual expence of such an establishment—It is to be observed that the Estimate is formed on the principle, that the present pay of the non-commissioned officers and privates may be considerably reduced—But the pay of a Lieutenant Colonel Commandant is enlarged from fifty to seventy five dollars per month—and the pay of the Major Commandant of Artillery to fifty dollars per month—This occasions an encrease for the Lieutenant Colonels and Major Commandant of sixty dollars per month—when the duty and expence of a Commanding Officer of a regiment or battalion be considered, it is presumed, that the proposed additional pay in these instances will promote the oeconomy and good of the service.

Although the proposed reduction of the pay cannot effect the existing stipulations to the troops now in service yet as they are liable to be discharged at any period it is highly probable that in preference thereto, they would accept the reduced pay.

The several representations herewith submitted marked B of the depredations committed by the Indians on the people along the south of the Ohio, and upon Cumberland river, show the exposed situation of those settlements—It seems the posts North West of the Ohio do not afford the necessary protection, and the people claim the employment of their own militia at the expence of the United States—A similar arrangement having been in operation until the organization of the General Government, at the expence of Virginia.

If it shall be decided to afford the protection requested, the propriety of employing the militia of the country for that purpose may be doubted—The oeconomy of disciplined troops is always superior to militia while their efficacy is at least equal—Hence if troops are employed within the district of Kentuckey as patroles or otherwise, they ought to be detachments from the regular troops of the United States under the orders of the Commanding Officer on the Ohio—About four companies acting as patroles or scouts would afford all the satisfaction to the settlements which could be derived from defensive measures—but it is only from offensive measures that full security could be obtained.

The various tribes seated on the Wabash river, extending up to the Miami Village, and the several branches of that river, are the indians from whom the settlements of Kentuckey principally receive injury.

But these depredations although perhaps effected with impunity as to the actual perpetrators, are not so to the Indians generally, for the whites frequently make incursions into the Wabash country north west of the Ohio, and it is probable that indiscriminate revenge is wreaked on all bearing the name of Indians—Hence a difficulty arises on the part of the United States, which requires a serious consideration.

That the people of Kentuckey are entitled to be defended, there can be no doubt—But as there seems to have been such a prevalence of hostilities as to render it uncertain who are right, or who wrong—The principles of justice which ought to dictate the conduct of every nation seems to forbid the idea of attempting to extirpate the Wabash indians until it shall appear that they cannot be brought to treat on reasonable terms—If after a treaty should be effected with them, it should be violated, or after an invitation to a treaty, which should be refused, and followed by hostilities, the United States will clearly have the right to inflict that degree of punishment which may be necessary to deter the Indians from any future unprovoked aggressions.

If this statement be just it would follow that the Governor of the Western territory should be instructed to attempt to effect a general treaty with the said Wabash tribes on terms of mutual advantage—If they should refuse, and continue, or suffer a continuance from any of their neighbouring tribes of the depredations upon the district of Kentuckey; the Arms of the Union ought to be exerted to chastise them.

The statement hereunto annexed No. 3. will show the application of the sum appropriated during the last session of Congress to indian treaties, and indian expences—The sum remaining unexpended might be applied to a treaty with the Wabash Indians.

Provisions must be furnished the indians during the treaty—Whether any presents shall be added thereto will depend on the decision of Congress—It seems to have been the custom of barbarous nations in all ages to expect and receive presents from those more civilized—and the custom seems confirmed by modern Europe with respect to Morocco, Algiers, Tunis and Tripoli.

The practise of the British Government and its colonies of giving presents to the indians of North America is well known—They seem to have been convinced that it was the cheapest and most effectual mode of managing the

Indians—The idea of fear, or purchasing a peace is not to be admitted in the cases above stated—But the conduct appears to have been dictated by wise policy—a comparative view of the expences of an hostile or conciliatory system towards the indians will evince the infinite oeconomy of the latter over the former.

The question then on the point of presents must be simply this—Is the situation of the United States such, with respect to the neighbouring European Colonies, as to render it good policy at this time to annihilate the indian customs and expectations of receiving presents, and thereby disgusting them in such a manner, as to induce them to connect themselves more closely with the said Colonies?

If it should be decided to the contrary, the Estimate of the Governor of the Western Territory for the object of the Wabash indians No. 4 would show the sum required, from which however must be deducted the balance remaining from the appropriation of the last year.

Although the information is not sufficiently accurate whereon to form a decided opinion of the number of indian Warriors within the limits of the United States, yet the evidence seems sufficient to warrant the supposition that they amount nearly to twenty thousand—If to this number we should add for every Warrior three old men women and children, the total number would be eighty thousand.

Since the United States became a nation, their conduct, and some of the States towards the indians seems to have resulted from the impulses of the moment—Until the treaty effected at Fort Harmar in January 1789, it seemed a prevailing opinion, that the treaty of peace with Great Britain instead of the pre-emption only, actually invested the United States with the absolute right of the indian Territory—and in pursuance of this idea treaties were made, and boundaries allotted to the indians—But by the directions of Congress of the 2d. of July 1788 to the Governor of the Western territory to extinguish the indian claims to lands they had ceded to the United States, and to obtain regular conveyances of the same it would appear, that they conceded the indian right to the soil.

The various opinions which exist on the proper mode of treating the indians, require that some system should be established on the subject.

That the Indians possess the natural rights of man, and that they ought not wantonly to be divested thereof cannot be well denied.

Were these rights ascertained, and declared by law—were it enacted that the indians possess the right to all their territory which they have not fairly conveyed, and that they should not be divested thereof, but in consequence of open treaties, made under the authority of the United States, the foundation of peace and justice would be laid.

The individual States claiming or possessing the right of pre-emption to territory inhabited by indians, would not be materially injured by such a declarative law, the exercise of their right would be restrained only, when it should interfere with the general interests—Should any State having the right of pre-emption desire to purchase territory, which the indians should be willing to relinquish, it would have to request the General Government to direct a treaty for that purpose, at the expence however of the individual State requesting the same.

But as indian Wars almost invariably arise in consequence of disputes relative to boundaries, or trade, and as the right of declaring War, making treaties, and regulating commerce, are vested in the United States it is highly proper they should have the sole direction of all measures for the consequences of which they are responsible.

I have the honor to be
Sir,
With the highest respect
Your Most Obedient
Humble Servant,
H. KNOX
secretary for the department
of War

The President
   of
The United States

An Estimate of the expences of an army for One Year, including the General Staff, Field and Company Officers, and Five thousand and forty noncommissd. offs. & privates

General Staff

		pay per mo.	dollars	p. mo.	12 mo.
1 Major General	pay per mo.	200			
	Subsistence	96		332	3,984
	Forage	36	80		
2 Aids de Camp	Pay	40	40		
	Subsistence	20	24	144	1,728
	Forage	12	200		
2 Brigadier Generals	Pay	100	96		
	Subsistence	48	36	332	3,984
	Forage	18	80		
2 Aids de Camp	Pay	40	40		
	Subsistence	20	24	144	1,728
	Forage	12			
1 Adjutant General	Pay	75			
	Subsistence	32		125	1,500
	Forage	18			
1 Deputy Adjut. General	Pay	40			
	Subsistence	20		72	864
	Forage	12			
1 Inspector General	Pay	75			
	Subsistence	32		125	1,500
	Forage	18			
1 Deputy Inspector	Pay	40			
	Subsistence	20		72	864
	Forage	12			
1 Quarter Masr. General	Pay	75			
	Subsistence	32		125	1,500
	Forage	18			

		dolls. p. mo.				
2 deputy Qr. Masters	Pay	40	80			
	Subsistence	20	40			
	Forage	12	24	144		1,728
1 Chief Physician & director	Pay	75				
	Subsistence	32				
	Forage	18		125		1,500
1 Chief Surgeon	Pay	75				
	Subsistence	32				
	Forage	18		125		1,500
1 Apothecary & surveyor	Pay	40				
	Subsistence	20				
	Forage	12		72		864
1 Chaplain	Pay	40				
	Subsistence	20				
	Forage	12		72		864
						24,108

REGIMENTAL OFFICERS

For 6 Regiments of Infantry—1 Regiment of Cavalry, and two Companies of Artillery.

Field & Regimental Staff

		dolls. p. mo.			
7 Lieutenant Colonels Commandant	Pay	75	525		
	Subsistence	32	224		
	Forage	18	126	12 mo. 875	10,500
			560		
14 Majors	Pay	40	280		
	Subsis.	20	168	1,008 12 mo.	12,096
	Forage	12			
7 Pay Masters	Pay	10	70		
7 Adjutants	Pay	10	70		
7 Quartermasters	Pay	10	70	210 12 mo.	2,520
for the above 21 Rations of forage p. mo. @			6	126 12 mo.	1,512

		dolls. p. mo.			
7 Surgeons	Pay	45	315		5,628
	Subsistence	16	112		
	Forage	6	42	469 12 mo.	
14 Surgeons Mates	Pay	30	420		6,384
	Subsistence	8	112	532 12 mo.	38,640

COMPANY OFFICERS

72 Captains	Pay p. mo.	35	2,520		40,608
	Subsistence	12	864	3,384 12 mo.	
74 Lieutenants	Pay	26	1,924		30,192
	Subsistence	8	592	2,516 12 mo.	
70 Ensigns & Cornets	Pay	20	1,400		23,520
	Subsistence	8	560	1,960 12 mo.	94,320

TWO COMPANIES OF ARTILLERY

8 Serjeants	5 dollars p. mo.		40		
8 Corporals	4 ,,		32		
4 Musicians	3 ,,		12		
120 Privates	3 ,,		360	444 12 mo.	5,328

ONE REGIMENT OF CAVALRY

40 Serjeants	5		200		
40 Corporals	4		160		
20 Musicians	3		60		
600 privates	3		1,800	2,220 12 mo.	26,640

SIX REGIMENTS INFANTRY

		dolls. p. mo.			
240 Serjeants	5		1,200		
240 Corporals	4		960		
120 Musicians	3		360		
3600 privates	3		10,800	13,320 12 mo.	159,840
				amount	191,808

From which deduct 1 $^{25}/_{100}$ dollars from each each Serjeant and Corporal pr. Month for Clothing, and $^{10}/_{100}$ from each for hospital Stores—also $^{90}/_{100}$ from each musician and private for Clothing and $^{10}/_{100}$ Dolls. from each for hospital Stores, which will

for Clothing amount to   46,044

& for Hospital Stores to   6,048   52,082   139,716

RATIONS

For 5,040 Non Commissioned Officers and privates for 365 days at one Ration per day is 1,839,600 Rations at 12 Cents per ration   220,752

CLOTHING

5040 Suits at 20 dollars each   100,800

HOSPITAL DEPARTMENT

     6,000

HORSES

For the Cavalry   700 at 75 dollars each   52,500

Forage for   700 horses at 5 dollars each per month for one year   42,000

Horse-furniture & equipment at 20 dolls. ea.   14,000   108,500

QUARTER MASTERS DEPARTMENT

Tents—Axes—Camp Kettles—Waggons—Horses Pack horses—Boats—and every means for the transportation of the army may be rated at   300,000

The artillery, arms, ammunition, and accoutrements, are not particularly estimated, they being generally in the public possession but they may be rated at   120,000

     Total Dollars   1,152,836

War Office December 31st. 1789
H. KNOX Secretary
for the department of War

AN ESTIMATE of the annual expence of a Corps to consist of Two Regiments of Infantry of Ten Companies each, and one Battalion of Artillery of four Companies, each Company to be composed of 4 Serjeants, 4 Corporals 2 musicians and 60 privates, amounting in the whole to 1680 Non-Commissioned Officers and privates.

Rank		Each	Total	Per mo.		Annual
1 Brigadier General	Pay	100				
	Subsistence	48				
	Forage	18		166	dolls. p. mo.	1,992
2 Lieutenant Colonels Comdt.	Pay	75	150			
	Subsistence	32	64			
	Forage	18	36	250 for 12 mo.		3,000
4 Majors	Pay	40	160			
	Subsistence	20	80			
	Forage	12	48	288	12 mo.	3,456
1 Major Comandt. of Artillery	Pay	50				
	Subsistence	20				
	Forage	12		82	12 mo.	984
2 pay masters						
2 quartermasters } Pay 10 dolls. forage 6 ea. p. mo. is 96					12 mo. is	1,152
2 Adjutants						
2 Surgeons	Pay	45	90			
	Subsistence	16	32			
	Forage	6	12	134	12 mo.	1,608
5 Mates	Pay	30	150			
	Subsistence	8	40	190	12 mo.	2,280
20 Captains of Infantry	Pay	35	700			
	Subsistence	12	240	940	12 mo.	11,280
20 Lieutenants	Pay	26	520			
	Subsistence	8	160	680	12 mo.	8,160
20 Ensigns	Pay	20	400			
	Subsistence	8	160	560	12 mo.	6,720
4 Captains of Artillery	Pay	35	140			
	Subsistence	12	48	188	12 mo.	2,256
8 Lieutenants do.	Pay	26	208			
	Subsistence	8	64	272	12 mo.	3,264
						46,152

TWO REGIMENTS OF INFANTRY

80 Serjeants	pay p. mo.	5 is	400	12 mo.	4,800
80 Corporals	"	4 is	320		3,840
40 Musicians	"	3 is	120		1,440
1,200 privates	"	3 is	3,600		43,200

ONE BATTALION OF ARTILLERY

16 Serjeants	pay p. mo.	5 is	80	12 mo.	960
16 Corporals	"	4 is	64	"	768
8 Musicians	"	3 is	24	"	288
240 Privates	"	3 is	720	"	8,640
					63,936

From which deduct $1 \, 25/100$ dollars per month from each Serjeants and Corporals pay per month for Clothing and $10/100$ dollars per month from each for hospital Stores—and also $90/100$ dollars per month from the pay of each musician and private for Clothing, and $10/100$ dollars from each per Month for hospital Stores, which will for Clothing amount to   18,749

& for Hospital Stores   2,016   20,765

43,171

CLOTHING

1,680 Suits   @ 20 dollars   33,600

RATIONS

1,680 Rations per day for 365 days is 613,200 Rations at 12 Cents per Ration   73,584

Total dollars   186,507[1]

THE ANNUAL EXPENCE OF THE PRESENT ESTABLISHMENT

Pay, Subsistence and forage to the Officers, and pay to 840 Non Commissioned Officers and privates Vizt. to Serjeants 6 to Corporals and musicians 5 and to privates 4 dollars per month & Clothing annually   90,164

Rations annually   36,792

126,956

THE ANNUAL EXPENCE OF THE PROPOSED ESTABLISHMENT

The Pay, Subsistence, and forage to Officers, and pay to 1680 Non Commissioned Officers and privates, as reduced Vizt. Serjeants 5 Corporals 4 musicians and privates 3 dollars, per month (from which is to be deducted the sum already noted for Clothing and hospital Stores) and their Clothing annually   112,923[2]

Rations annually   73,584

186,507[3]

The difference is dolls.   59,551[4]

---

[1] The word "Error" was written in before "186,507" and this figure was corrected to "196,507."
[2] This figure should be "122,923."
[3] This figure should be "196,507."
[4] This figure should be "69,551."

—NOTE—

The relative value of a Colonel in a tariff for the exchange of Prisoners during the late war, being much higher than a Lieutenant Colonel, and there being but few of the rank of Colonel in the British Army, employed in America, Occasioned the present Arrangement of field Officers to a Regiment, Consisting of a Lieutenant Colonel Commandant and two Majors.

But as the troops on the frontiers may act with Militia Commanded by Colonels, the Lieutenant Colonels may be Superseded in their command by militia Officers, to the extreme prejudice of the service.

The idea therefore is submitted to recur to the former arrangement of field Officers to a Regiment—to wit, a Colonel, a Lieutenant Colonel, and a Major.

The only difference of expence will be fourteen dollars per Month to the Lieutenant Colonel in addition to the pay and emoluments of a Major, as the Lieut. Colonels Commandant, were entitled to the pay and emoluments of a full Colonel.

War Office December 31st. 1789
H. KNOX
Secretary of the department of War

No. 3

STATEMENT of 20,000 Dollars appropriated by Congress on the 20th. of August 1789. for the expence of negociations with the Indian tribes

Expended by the Commissioners as per their statement Rendered the Auditor	5,842.95
* Provisions and Indian goods deposited by the Commissioners in Georgia, and the expences thereon	8,280.14
Advanced the superintendant of the Northern Department for the Uses thereof	500.
Expences incurred in equiping George M. White Eyes an indian Youth of the Delaware tribe, in order to return to his own Country, he having been educated by order, and at the expence of the United States	425.51
	15,048.60
Balance unexpended	4,951.40
Dollars	20,000.

*The Commissioners Stored the indian goods in Georgia in order that they might be ready, if a treaty should be held in the spring—The provisions and other articles liable to waste and damage were directed to be sold, and the whole accounted for and subject to the order of the Secretary at war.

War Office 31. December 1789
H. KNOX
Secretary for the department of War

No. 4

June 14. 1789

ESTIMATE of the expence with which a treaty with the Indians of the Wabash, and Miami Rivers would probably be attended—Their Numbers are supposed to be from twelve to fifteen hundred men.

Indian goods assorted to the value of	6,000
Stores and necessaries	650
Transportation	2,500
Messengers and interpreters	1,000
Store keepers	300

Commissioners wages	500
Contingencies	200
	11,150
The provisions cannot be estimated at less than 30,000 Rations which at ⎫ Contract Price will amount to ⎭	5,000
Dollars	16,150

Many circumstances may occur to occasion the expenditure of a larger quantity ⎫
of provisions—a lesser quantity ought not to be Reckoned upon. ⎭

Copy of the original ⎫
War Office 31. Decr. 1789 ⎭ /Signed/ Ar. St. Clair

Balance unexpended of the appropriation of the 20th of August 1789.	4,951.40
The sum which in case of a treaty would be required	11,199.60/100

H. Knox secretary of War

Reports and Communications from the Secretary of War, HR, DNA. Two of the enclosures, Instructions to the Commissioners for Southern Indians, August 29, 1789, and Report of the Commissioners for Southern Indians, November 17, 1789, are printed in the *SEJ*, pp. 202–41.

Military Establishment Bill [HR-50a]
March 26, 1790

An Act for regulating the Military Establishment of the United States[1]

Sec. 1. Be *it enacted by the Senate and House of Representatives of the United States of America, in Congress assembled,* That the commissioned Officers herein after mentioned, and the number of one thousand six hundred and eighty[2]

---

[1] On April 16, Maclay gave notice of his intention to move an amendment striking out "regulating the Military Establishment of the United States" and inserting the following:

> protection of the frontiers of the United States; facilitating the surveying and selling the public lands and preventing unwarrantable encroachments on the same.

This was moved, seconded by Lee, and disagreed to on April 20. Also on April 20, Ellsworth moved to strike out the same words and insert "for the defense of the frontiers and for other purposes." When this was not seconded, Ellsworth moved to change the title to "An act to raise the troops for the service of the United States." This motion was seconded by Butler and disagreed to by a vote of 10–10, decided by the vice president. (Maclay, April 16, 20)

[2] On April 16, a motion to strike out "one thousand six hundred and eighty" was agreed to by a recorded vote of 11–9. On April 19, the Senate agreed to a motion by Ellsworth to strike the recorded vote from the journal on the grounds that the Senate was in committee when the vote was required. (Journal of the Secretary of the Senate, Records of the Secretary, SR, DNA) On April 16, a motion by Ellsworth to insert "one thousand two hundred" was agreed to. (*SLJ*, p. 288n; Maclay, Apr. 16) The final figure agreed to by the Senate was "one thousand two hundred and sixteen."

non-commissioned Officers, Privates and Musicians, shall be raised for the service of the United States, for the period of three[3] years, unless they should previously by law be discharged.

SEC. 2. *And be it further enacted,* That the non-commissioned Officers and Privates aforesaid, shall, at the time of their inlistments, respectively, be able bodied men, not under five feet six inches in height, without shoes, nor under the age of eighteen, nor above the age of forty-six years.

SEC. 3. *And be it further enacted,* That the commissioned Officers herein after mentioned, and the said non-commissioned Officers, Privates, and Musicians, shall be formed into two regiments of Infantry, and one battalion of Artillery; each regiment of Infantry shall be composed of one Lieutenant-Colonel Commandant, two Majors, one Adjutant, one Quarter-Master, one Pay-Master, one Surgeon, two Surgeon's-Mates, and ten companies; each of which shall consist of one Captain, one Lieutenant, one Ensign, four Serjeants, four Corporals, sixty Privates, and two Musicians.[4] The battalion of Artillery shall be composed of one Major Commandant, one Adjutant, one Quarter-Master, one Pay-Master, one Surgeon's-Mate, and four companies; each of which shall consist of one Captain, two Lieutenants, four Serjeants, four Corporals, sixty[5] Privates, and two Musicians *Provided always,* That the Adjutants, Quarter-Masters, and Pay-Masters, shall be appointed from the line of Subalterns of the aforesaid corps respectively.

SEC. 4. *And be it further enacted,* That the President of the United States, may from time to time, appoint one or two of the commissioned Officers of the said regiments, as to him shall seem meet, to perform the office and duty of Inspectors and Muster-Masters to the said troops, who shall respectively receive fifteen dollars per month, extra pay.[6]

SEC. 5. *And be it further enacted,* That the troops aforesaid, shall receive for their services, the following enumerated monthly rates of pay,

Lieutenant Colonel Commandant, seventy-five[7] dollars;

---

[3] On April 20, a motion by Maclay to strike out "three" and insert "two" failed for want of a second. (Maclay, Apr. 20)

[4] The Senate struck out "two regiments of Infantry" through "two Musicians" and inserted the following:

> one Regiment of infantry to consist of three Battalions, and one Battalion of Artillery. The Regiment of infantry to be composed of one Lieutenant Colonel Commandant, three Majors, three Adjutants, three Quarter Masters, One Paymaster, one Surgeon, two Surgeons Mates and twelve Companies each of which shall consist of one Captain, one Lieutenant, one Ensign, four serjeants, four Corporals, sixty six privates and two Musicians.

[5] The Senate inserted "six" at this point.

[6] The Senate struck out "two of the commissioned" through the end of the section and inserted:

> inspectors as to him shall seem meet to inspect the said Troops who shall also muster the same, and each of whom shall receive the like pay and subsistence as a Captain and be allowed ten dollars per Month for forage.

[7] The Senate struck out "seventy-five" and inserted "sixty."

Major Commandant of Artillery, fifty[8]-five dollars;

Majors, forty-five[9] dollars;

Captains, thirty-five[10] dollars;

Lieutenants, twenty-six[11] dollars;

Ensigns, twenty[12] dollars;

Surgeons, forty-five[13] dollars;

Surgeon's Mates, thirty[14] dollars;

Serjeants, five dollars;

Corporals, four dollars;

Privates, three dollars;

Senior Musician in each regiment[15] of Infantry, and in the battalion of Artillery, five dollars;

Musicians, three dollars.

Provided always, That the sums herein after specified, shall be deducted from the pay of the non-commissioned Officers, Privates, and Musicians, stipulated as aforesaid, for the purposes of forming a fund for cloathing and hospital stores: From the monthly pay of each Serjeant and senior Musician, there shall be deducted for uniform cloathing, the sum of one dollar and forty cents, and the further sum of ten cents, for hospital stores; and from the monthly pay of each Corporal, for uniform cloathing, one dollar and fifteen cents, and the further sum of ten cents, for hospital stores; and from the monthly pay of each Private and Musician, for uniform cloathing, the sum of ninety cents, and the further sum of ten cents, for hospital stores.

SEC. 6. *And be it further enacted,* That the Subalterns who may be appointed to act as Adjutants, Quarter-Masters, and Pay-Masters aforesaid, shall each receive for the same, in addition to their regimental pay, ten dollars per month.[16]

SEC. 7. *And be it further enacted,* That the commissioned Officers aforesaid, shall receive monthly, the following enumerated sums for their subsistence: Lieutenant Colonels Commandant, thirty-two dollars; Major Commandant of Artillery, twenty-eight dollars; Majors, twenty dollars; Surgeons, sixteen

---

[8] The Senate struck out "fifty" and inserted "forty."

[9] The Senate struck out "five."

[10] The Senate struck out "five."

[11] The Senate struck out "six" and inserted "two."

[12] The Senate struck out "twenty" and inserted "eighteen."

[13] The Senate struck out "forty-five" and inserted "thirty."

[14] The Senate struck out "thirty" and inserted "eighteen." A House amendment changed this to "twenty-four."

[15] The Senate struck out "regiment" and inserted "battalion."

[16] The Senate struck out "Quarter-Masters, and Pay-Masters aforesaid" earlier in this section and inserted "and Quarter-Masters and Pay-Masters so appointed each five dollars per Month" at this point.

dollars; Surgeon's-Mates, eight dollars; Captains, twelve dollars; Lieutenants, eight dollars; Ensigns, eight dollars.[17]

SEC. 8. *And be it further enacted,* That the commissioned Officers herein after described, shall receive monthly, the following enumerated sums, instead of forage: Lieutenant Colonels Commandant, eighteen[18] dollars; Major Commandant of Artillery, fifteen dollars;[19] Majors, twelve dollars; Inspectors and Muster-Masters, Adjutants, Quarter-Masters, Pay-Masters, and Surgeons, each six dollars.[20]

SEC. 9. *And be it further enacted,* That every non-commissioned Officer, Private, and Musician aforesaid, shall receive annually, the following articles of uniform cloathing; one hat or helmet; one coat; one vest; two pair of woollen, and two pair of linen overalls; four pair of shoes; four shirts; two pair of socks; one blanket; one stock and clasp, and one pair of buckles.

SEC. 10. *And be it further enacted,* That every non-commissioned Officer, Private and Musician aforesaid, shall receive daily the following rations of provisions, or the value thereof; one pound of beef, or three quarters of a pound of pork; one pound of baked bread, or flour equivalent thereto;[21] half a gill of rum or whisky;[22] and at the rate of one quart of salt, two quarts of vinegar, two pounds of soap, and one pound of candles, to every hundred rations.[23]

SEC. 11. *And be it further enacted,* That any non-commissioned Officer,

---

[17] The Senate struck out "monthly, the following enumerated" through the end of the section and inserted the following:

> for their daily subsistence the following number of Rations of provisions to wit Lieutenant Colonel Commandant six, A Major four, a Captain three, a Lieutenant two, an Ensign two, a Surgeon three, a Surgeons Mate two, or Money in lieu thereof at the option of the Said Officers at the contract price at the ports respectively where the Rations shall become due.

[18] The Senate struck out "eighteen" and inserted "twelve."

[19] The Senate struck out "fifteen dollars,"

[20] The Senate struck out "twelve dollars" through the end of the section and inserted "and Surgeon each ten dollars, Surgeons Mates each six dollars."

[21] The Senate struck the words "baked" and "equivalent thereto" from this phrase.

[22] A committee amendment striking out "half a gill of rum or whisky" was apparently disagreed to by the Senate, but a floor amendment inserting "brandy" between "rum" and "or" in this phrase was agreed to. Another floor amendment adding "or the value thereof at the contract price where the same shall become due" after the word "whisky" was agreed to.

[23] The committee report contains the following proviso which was to appear at this point:

> *Provided* that It shall and may be lawful for the Commanding Officer of the regiment or of any battallion or commissioned Officer commanding any detachment, when on march during inclement weather, or for any Officer commanding a Garrisson when troops are employed on fatigue duty at the discretion of such Officers respectively to order to each non Commissioned Officer and private so marching or employed as aforesaid rum or Whiskey nor exceeding the rate of Half a Gill per day to each.

This proposed amendment was apparently disagreed to by the Senate.

Private, or Musician aforesaid, who, after having been duly inlisted, shall desert from the service, shall forfeit all arrearages of every sort, which may be due to him at the time of his desertion; besides being subjected, if apprehended, to such punishments as are, or shall be directed by the articles of war.[24]

SEC. 12. *And be it further enacted,* That if any commissioned Officer, non-commissioned Officer, Private or Musician aforesaid, shall be wounded or disabled, while in the line of his duty in public service, he shall be placed on the list of the invalids of the United States; at such rates[25] of pay, and under such regulations as shall be directed by the President of the United States, for the time being: *Provided always,* That the rate of compensation for such wounds or disabilities, shall never exceed for the highest disability, half the monthly pay received by any commissioned Officer, at the time of being so wounded or disabled; and that the rate of compensation to non-commissioned Officers, Privates and Musicians, shall never exceed five dollars per month: *And provided also,* That all inferior disabilities, shall entitle the persons so disabled, to receive only a sum in proportion to the highest disability.

SEC. 13. *And be it further enacted,* That every commissioned Officer, non-commissioned Officer, Private, and Musician aforesaid, shall take and subscribe the following oath or affirmation, to wit: *I A. B. do solemnly swear, or affirm (as the case may be) to bear true allegiance to the United States of America, and to serve them honestly and faithfully against all their enemies or opposers, whomsoever; and to observe and obey the orders of the President of the United States of America, and the orders of the Officers appointed over me, according to the articles of war.*

SEC. 14. *And be it further enacted,* That the commissioned Officers, non-commissioned Officers, Privates and Musicians aforesaid, shall be governed by the rules and articles of war which have been established by the United States in Congress assembled, as far as the same may be applicable to the Constitution of the United States, or by such rules and articles as may hereafter by law be established.

SEC. 15. *And be it further enacted,* That the "Act for recognizing and adapting to the Constitution of the United States, the establishment of the troops raised under the resolves of the United States in Congress assembled, and for other purposes therein mentioned," passed the twenty-ninth day of September, one thousand seven hundred and eighty-nine, be, and the same is hereby repealed. *Provided always,* That the non-commissioned Officers, and Privates continued and engaged under the aforesaid Act of the twenty-ninth day of September, one thousand seven hundred and eighty-nine, shall not be discharged, until the President of the United States shall direct the same.

---

[24] The Senate struck out this section.
[25] The letter "s" was struck out of the word "rates."

Provided nevertheless,[26] That the discharge of such of the said non-commissioned Officers and Privates, as shall decline to re-inlist under the establishment made by this Act, shall not be protracted to a longer period than the thirty-first day of December next ensuing: *And provided also,* That the whole number of non-commissioned Officers, Privates and Musicians, in the service of the United States, at any one time, either by virtue of this act, or by virtue of the aforesaid act, passed the twenty-ninth day of September, one thousand seven hundred and eighty-nine, shall not exceed the number of one thousand six hundred and eighty.[27]

SEC. 16. *And be it further enacted,* That for the purpose of[28] protecting the inhabitants of the frontiers of the United States from the hostile incursions of the Indians,[29] the President is hereby authorized to call into service, from time to time, such part of the Militia of the States respectively, as he may judge necessary for the purpose aforesaid; and that their pay and subsistence, while in service, be the same as the pay and subsistence of the troops above mentioned; the said Militia, when called into service, shall moreover be subject to the same rules and articles of war, with the troops established by this act.[30]

SEC. 17. *And be it further enacted,* That this Act shall continue and be in force until the twenty-sixth day of March, one thousand seven hundred and ninety-two.[31]

PRINTED by JOHN FENNO

Broadside Collection, RBkRm, DLC. The Senate amendments are from the *SLJ,* pp. 290n–291n and Maclay. Unless otherwise noted, the amendments were proposed by the Senate committee and agreed to by the Senate. The House amendment is from the *SLJ,* p. 293.

[26] The Senate struck out "shall not be discharged" through *"Provided nevertheless"* and inserted the following:
> *and who shall decline to reinlist under* the establishment made by this Act shall be discharged whenever the President of the United States shall direct the same, provided further

[27] The Senate struck out "six hundred and eighty" and inserted "two hundred and sixteen."

[28] The Senate inserted "aiding the Troops now in service or to be raised by this act in" at this point. A draft of this amendment, in the hand of Few and marked for insertion in the committee report, is filed with the report.

[29] The Senate struck out "from the hostile incursions of the Indians." A draft of this amendment, in the hand of Otis, is filed with the committee report.

[30] The Senate struck out "the said Militia" through the end of the section and inserted "and shall be subject to the Rules and articles of war."

[31] On April 20, the Senate struck out section 17. The committee report contains the following amendments to this section, which were crossed out and not agreed to:
> Sect. 17 Line 2d. expunge "twenty sixth" Substitute *twentyeth* Same line expunge "March" Substitute *April* at the end of the Section add *and no longer.*

On April 21, a motion by Maclay to restore this section was disagreed to, with only three votes in its favor. (Maclay, Apr. 21)

Senate Committee Report
April 20, 1790

Amendments to the Bill entitled, "An Act for regulating the Military Establishment of the united States"

Section 2d line 2d. expunge *"Six"* Substitute *"two"* [1]
    line 3d expunge ~~expunge~~ *"eighty"* Substitute *"Sixteen"*
Section 3d expunge from the word *"into"* in the second line to the word *"Musicians"* Inclueded
    "~~Provided~~" in the 5th line and substitute—*One regiment* of infantry to consist of three Battalions, and one battalion of Artillery[2] The regiment of infantry to be composed of one Lieutenant Colonel commandant, three Majors, three Adjutants, three Quarter Masters one paymaster. one Surgeon two surgeons mates and twelve Companies each of which shall consist of one Captain one lieutenant one Ensign four serjeants four Corporals, Sixty six privates and two Musicians
Section 3d Line 9th between *"sixty"* and *"privates"* Insert *Six*
Section 6th from the word *"two"* in 2d line expunge the remainder of the
                                        as to him shall seem meet
    section and Substitute Inspectors to inspect the said troops who
                                    each of
    shall Also muster the same, and whom shall receive the like pay and Subsistance as a Captain and be Allowed ten dollars per. month for forrage
Section 5th line 2d   Expunge *"Twenty five"* Substitute *Sixty*

line 3d	do.	*"fifty"*	do.	*Forty*
Same line	do.	*"five"*		
Same line	do.	*"five"*		
Line 4th	do.	*"Six"*	do.	*two*
Same line	do.	*"twenty"*	do.	*Eighteen*
Same line	do.	*"forty five"*	do.	*thirty*
line 5th	do.	*"thirty"*	do.	*Eighteen*
line 6	do.	*"regiment"*	do.	*Battallon*

Section 6. line 2d expunge *"Quarter masters and paymasters aforesaid"* and At the end of the Section Add *and Quarter masters and paymasters so appointed Each five dollars per month*
Sect. 7th Exc.[3] all except the first line, and Substitute *For their* daily subsistance the following number [4] of rations of provisions to wit

---

[1] The word "two" was written over another word, which is illegible.
[2] The word "Artillery" was written over the first letters of "infantry."
[3] "Exc." was written over another word, which is illegible.
[4] The word "number" was written over another word, which is illegible.

Lieut. Colonel Commandant	Six
A Major	four
A Captain	three
a lieutenant	two
An Ensign	two
A Surgeon	three
A Surgeons mate	two

or money in lieu thereof at the option of the said officers at the contract price at the posts respectively where the rations shall become due

insert 12 dollars[5]

Section 8 line 3d expunge "*eighteen dollars*" Also[6] "*fifteen dollars*" Same line expunge "~~twelve dollars~~" from "*Majors*" to the End of the section, and Substitute "~~*and ten dollars*~~ *and Surgeon Each ten dollars, Surgeons mates each Six dollars*

"*baked*" &[7]

Section 10 line 3 expunge "~~*flour*~~ "*equivalent thereto*" ~~Substitute~~ *one pound of flour*

~~same Line expunge "half a gill of rum or whisky" at the end of the Section Add, Provided that It shall and may be lawful for the Commanding officer of the regiment or of any battallion or com-missioned officer commanding any detachment, when on march during inclement weather, or for any officer commanding a Gar-risson when troops are employed on fatigue duty at the discretion of such officers respectively to order to each non Commissioned~~

Brandy[8] or

~~officer and private so marching or employed as aforesaid rum, Whiskey not exceeding the rate of Half a Gill per day to each.~~

Section 11th Expunge the whole.

Section 13th. line 6th. expunge from the word "*nine*" to the word "*That*" in the 9th line and Substitute *And who shall decline to re-inlist under* the establishment made by this Act shall be discharged when-ever the president of the united States shall direct the same, provided further

Section 15 last[9] line of the Section expunge "*six hundred and Eighty*" Sub-stitute *two hundred and Sixteen*

⊕   after the word "*mentioned*" expunge
Sect. 16 Line 5th. "~~*expunge when called into*~~" ~~Substitu~~ the remainder of the

---

[5] The words "insert 12 dollars" were inserted by Otis.
[6] The word "Also" was written over another word, which is illegible.
[7] The words "baked &" were inserted by Otis.
[8] The word "Brandy" was inserted by Otis.
[9] The word "last" was written over the word "line."

Section and Substitute *and shall be Subject to the rules & articles of war*

~~Sect. 17 Line 2d expunge *"twenty sixth"* Substitute *twentyeth*~~
~~Same line expunge *"March"* Substitute *April*~~
~~at the end of the Section add *and no longer*~~

⊕   Expunge the whole of the 17th Section

Sect. 16. Line 1. after "purpose of" insert[10]

Aiding the Troops now in service or to be raised by this act in[11]
16 Sect.

Line 2. And dele. "from the hostile incursions of the Indians" after the word "States"   16 Section[12]

The report, in the hand of Schuyler, is in House Bills, SR, DNA. It is undated, but Maclay's assertion (Maclay, Apr. 6) that the report of April 6 contained only "trifling amendments . . . in the compensation to the officers," shows that this long report must be that presented on April 20. Each amendment, except the one to section 17 line 2 and the last two, is followed by an "a" written by Otis, indicating Senate agreement.

---

[10] This line and the last two amendments are on a separate piece of paper.
[11] This amendment is in the hand of Few.
[12] This amendment was written by Otis, with the exception of "Line 2," which is in the hand of Schuyler.

Military Establishment Act [HR-126A]
March 3, 1791

AN ACT FOR RAISING AND ADDING ANOTHER REGIMENT TO THE MILITARY ESTABLISHMENT OF THE UNITED STATES, AND FOR MAKING FARTHER PROVISION FOR THE PROTECTION OF THE FRONTIERS

[1] BE IT ENACTED BY THE SENATE AND HOUSE OF REPRESENTATIVES OF THE UNITED STATES OF AMERICA IN CONGRESS ASSEMBLED, that there shall be raised an additional regiment of Infantry, which, exclusive of the commissioned officers, shall consist of nine hundred and twelve non commissioned officers, privates and musicians.

[2] AND BE IT FURTHER ENACTED, that the said regiment shall be organized in the same manner as the regiment of infantry described in the Act entituled "An Act for regulating the military establishment of the United States."

[3] AND BE IT FURTHER ENACTED, that the troops aforesaid by this Act to be raised, including the officers; shall receive the same pay and allowances, be subject to the same rules and regulations, and be engaged for the like term and upon the same conditions, in all respects, excepting the bounty hereinafter mentioned, as are stipulated for the troops of the United States, in the before-mentioned Act.

[4] AND BE IT FURTHER ENACTED, that each non-commissioned officer, private and musician, who has inlisted or shall inlist pursuant to the Act aforesaid, or who shall inlist pursuant to this Act shall be intituled to receive six dollars as a bounty.

[5] AND BE IT FURTHER ENACTED, that in case the President of the United States should deem the employment of a Major General, Brigadier-General, a Quarter Master and Chaplain, or either of them, essential to the public interest, that he be, and he hereby is empowered, by and with the advice and consent of the Senate, to appoint the same accordingly. And a Major-General so appointed may chuse his Aid-de-Camp, and a Brigadier-General, his Brigade Major, from the Captains or Subalterns of the line. PROVIDED ALWAYS, that the Major General and Brigadier General so to be

appointed shall, respectively, continue in pay during such term only, as the President of the United States in his discretion shall deem it requisite for the public service.

[6] AND BE IT FURTHER ENACTED, that in case a Major-General, Brigadier-General, Quarter-Master, Aid de Camp, Brigade-Major and Chaplain should be appointed their pay and allowances shall be, respectively, as herein mentioned. The Major-General shall be intituled to one hundred and twenty five dollars, monthly pay, twenty dollars allowance for forage monthly, and for daily subsistence fifteen rations, or money in lieu thereof at the contract-price. The Brigadier-General shall be intituled to ninety four dollars monthly pay, with sixteen dollars allowance for forage monthly, and for daily subsistence, twelve rations, or money in lieu thereof at the contract-price. That the Quarter-Master shall be intituled to the same pay, rations and forage, as the Lieutenant Colonel Commandant of a regiment. That the Aid de Camp be intituled, including all allowances, to the same pay, rations and forage as a Major of a regiment. That the Brigade-Major be intituled, including all allowances, to the same pay, rations and forage, as a Major of a regiment. That the Chaplain be intituled to fifty dollars per month, including pay, rations and forage.

[7] AND BE IT FURTHER ENACTED, that if, in the opinion of the President, it will be conducive to the good of the service, to engage a body of Militia to serve as Cavalry, they furnishing their own horses, arms, and provisions, it shall be lawful for him to offer such allowances to encourage their engaging in the service, for such time and on such terms, as he shall deem it expedient to prescribe.

[8] AND BE IT FURTHER ENACTED, that if the President should be of opinion, that it will be conducive to the public service, to employ troops inlisted under the denomination of Levies in addition to, or in place of the Militia, which in virtue of the powers vested in him by law, he is authorized to call into the service of the United States, it shall be lawful for him to raise, for a term not exceeding six months (to be discharged sooner, if the public service will permit) a Corps, not exceeding two thousand non-commissioned officers, privates and musicians, with a suitable number of commissioned officers. And in case it shall appear probable to the President, that the regiment, directed to be raised by the aforesaid Act and by this Act, will not be completed in time to prosecute such military operations as exigencies may require, it shall be lawful for the President to make a substitute for the deficiency, by raising such farther number of levies, or by calling into the service of the United States such a body of Militia as shall be equal thereto.

[9] AND BE IT FURTHER ENACTED, that the President be and he hereby is empowered to organize the said levies, and alone to appoint the commissioned officers thereof, in the manner he may judge proper.

[10] AND BE IT FURTHER ENACTED, that the commissioned and non-commissioned officers, privates and musicians of the Militia or said Corps of Levies shall, during the time of their service, be subject to the rules and articles of war; And they shall be intitled to the same pay, rations and forage, and, in case of wounds or disability in the line of their duty, to the same compensation as the troops of the United States.

[11] AND BE IT FURTHER ENACTED, that the non-commissioned officers, privates and musicians of the said corps of levies shall be intitled to receive such proportional quantity of clothing, as their time of service shall bear to the annual allowances of clothing to the troops of the United States, subject, however, to a proportional deduction from their pay.

[12] AND BE IT FURTHER ENACTED, that each of the non-commissioned officers, privates and musicians of the said Levies shall be intitled to receive three dollars as a bounty.

[13] AND BE IT FURTHER ENACTED, that in case the nature of the service, upon which the troops of the United States may be employed, should require a greater number of Surgeon's mates, than are provided for in the before-mentioned Act, the President of the United States may engage, from time to time, such additional number of Surgeon's mates, as he shall judge necessary.

[14] AND BE IT FURTHER ENACTED, that the commissioned officers, who shall be employed to recruit men for the said regiments, shall be [entitled] to receive for every recruit who shall be duly inlisted and mustered, the sum of two dollars.

[15] AND BE IT FURTHER ENACTED, that for defraying the expense, for one year, of the additional regiment to be raised by virtue of this Act; for defraying the expense, for a like term, of the officers mentioned in the seventh Section of this Act; for defraying the expense of the said Militia-horse, Militia-foot, and Levies, which may be called into, or engaged for the service of the United States, pursuant to this Act; for defraying the expense of such Surgeon's mates, as may be appointed pursuant to the fifteenth Section of this Act; for defraying the expense of recruiting the said two regiments; and for defraying the expense of any military posts which the President shall judge expedient and proper to establish, there be and hereby is appropriated a sum, not exceeding three hundred and twelve thousand six hundred and eighty six dollars and twenty cents, to be paid out of the monies, which, prior to the first day of January next, shall arise from the duties imposed upon spirits distilled within the United States, and from Stills, by the Act, intituled "An Act, repealing after the last day of June next, the duties heretofore laid upon distilled spirits imported from abroad, and laying others in their stead and also upon spirits distilled within the United States, and for appropriating the same;" together with the excess of duties which may arise from the duties imposed by the said Act on imported spirits, beyond those which

would have arisen by the Act intituled "An Act making farther provision for the payment of the debts of the United States."

[16] AND to the end that the public service may not be impeded for want of necessary means;

BE IT FURTHER ENACTED, that it shall be lawful for the President to take on loan the whole sum by this Act appropriated, or so much thereof as he may judge requisite, at an interest not exceeding six per centum per annum, and the fund established for the above-mentioned appropriation is hereby pledged for the repayment of the principal and interest of any loan to be obtained in manner aforesaid; and in case of any deficiency in the said fund, the faith of the United States is hereby also pledged to make good such deficiency.

> FREDERICK AUGUSTUS MUHLENBERG
> Speaker of the House of Representatives
> JOHN ADAMS
> Vice President of the United States and
> President of the Senate

Approved March
the third
1791
}

> GO. WASHINGTON
> President of the United States

I certify that this Act did originate
in the House of Representatives.
JOHN BECKLEY—Clerk

Enrolled Acts, RG 11, DNA.

Calendar

Date	House	Senate
1790		
Dec. 9	*Letter from the secretary of war* received, enclosing *statement of information on expedition against the Indians northwest of the Ohio, instructions to the governor of the northwest territory and the commanding officer,* and	

Date	House	Senate
1790		
	an estimate of expenses of the expedition. [1]	
Dec. 14	Presidential message received,[2] enclosing *communications relative to the expedition against the Indians northwest of the Ohio.*	
Dec. 15	*Resolution* of COWH agreed to and, on a motion by Sherman,[3] referred to the secretary of the treasury with instruction to report an appropriation for expedition against the northwest Indians.	
Dec. 30	Secret session,[4] probably concerning the expedition against the Indians.	
1791		
Jan. 24	Presidential message received, enclosing *report of the secretary of war on the frontiers with enclosures.* [5]	
Jan. 26	Secret session to discuss report received Jan. 24; report referred to select committee.[6]	
Jan. 27	Message from president, transmitting *information on*	

---

[1] The letter of the secretary also encloses several *additional letters of the secretary of war.*

[2] The message is printed in the *HJ*, pp. 630–31.

[3] *GA*, Dec. 16.

[4] *GA*, Dec. 31. The *HJ* for this date records no action on this subject.

[5] *FG*, Jan. 26; *PaG*, *PaJ*, Feb. 2. This message and statement are not mentioned in the *HJ*, but the message is printed in the *SLJ*, p. 538.

[6] *FG*, Jan. 26. The *HJ* for this date records no action on this subject.

Date	House	Senate
1791		
	depredations by Indians, received and referred to Ames, Wadsworth, Fitzsimons, Vining, Brown, Williamson, and Jackson.[7]	
Feb. 1	Secret session; *committee report* on message of Jan. 24 received.[8]	
Feb. 9	Secret session; committee report considered in COWH; first six resolutions in report agreed to and preparation of bill ordered; seventh and eighth resolutions tabled.[9]	
Feb. 10–12	Secret sessions;[10] bill probably presented, read, and agreed to.	
Feb. 12		*An Act for raising and adding another regiment to the military establishment of the United States, and for making further provision for the protection of the frontiers* received, read, and ordered printed, under injunctions of secrecy.
Feb. 14		Read and committed to

[7] The *HJ* records no report by this committee. It may be the same committee to which the president's message of January 24 was referred on the 26th, and which reported on February 1. The message is printed in the *HJ,* p. 686.

[8] *FG,* Feb. 1. The *HJ* for this date records no action on this subject. The *report of the secretary of war,* giving an estimate of expenses of an expedition against the Wabash Indians, was sent to this committee.

[9] *FG,* Feb. 9. The *HJ* for this date records no action on this subject. The information on the day's proceedings is from the headings of the report in A Record of the Reports of Select Committees, HR, DNA.

[10] *GA,* Feb. 11, 12, 14. The *HJ* for these dates records no action on this bill.

Date	House	Senate
1791		
		Gunn, Schuyler, Dickinson, Hawkins, and Strong.[11]
Feb. 15	Secret session, in which speaker made private communications, may have been related to this bill.[12]	
Feb. 17		Schuyler presented *committee report;* amendments reported by committee ordered printed.
Feb. 19		Bill and amendments considered; first section agreed to; *motion* to add a section disagreed to; committee report

[11] The vote for this committee is in Other Records: Yeas and nays, SR, DNA, and was as follows:

Mr. Bassett	I
" Butler	ℍℍ III
" Carroll	III
" Dalton	
" Dickinson	ℍℍ IIII
" Ellsworth	ℍℍ III
" Elmer	I
" Few	III
" Foster	ℍℍ I
" Gunn	ℍℍ ℍℍ ℍℍ
" Hawkins	ℍℍ IIII
" Henry	ℍℍ
" Johnson	II
" Johnston	I
" Izard	II
" King	IIII
" Langdon	IIII
" Lee	
" Maclay	II
" Monroe	ℍℍ I
" Morris	II
" Read	II
" Schuyler	ℍℍ ℍℍ II
" Stanton	
" Strong	ℍℍ IIII
" Wingate	ℍℍ

[12] *GUS,* Feb. 16.

Date	House	Senate
1791		
		agreed to; other *amendments* agreed to.
Feb. 21		Read; *amendment* disagreed to; bill agreed to with amendments.
Feb. 21, 23, 26	Senate amendments probably debated in secret sessions. [13]	
Feb. 28		House *amendments* to Senate amendments received and debated.
Mar. 1	Senate action on House amendments probably debated in secret session. [14]	House amendments, except the last two, agreed to.
Mar. 2	Senate action on House amendments probably debated in secret session; [15] bill signed by speaker.	Senate notified that House receded from its last two amendments; bill signed by vice president.
Mar. 3	Signed by president.	

[13] *FG*, Feb. 21, 24, 26. The *HJ* for these dates records no action on this bill.
[14] *FG*, Mar. 1. The *HJ* for this date records no action on this bill.
[15] *FG*, Mar. 2. The *HJ* for this date records no action on this bill.

Letter from the Secretary of War with Enclosures
December 9, 1790

War Department
December 8th. 1790

Sir/

In obedience to the Orders of the President of the United States, I have the honor respectfully to submit to the Senate, a statement of the Information, on which the expedition against the Indians North-west of the Ohio, has been founded—And also the instructions to the Governor of the Western territory, and the Commanding Officer of the troops relative to the same object;

together with an estimate of the expence with which the expedition will probably be attended.

> I have the Honor to be
> With great Respect
> Sir
> Your most Obedient &
> very hume. servt.
> H. KNOX
> secretary of War

The Honble.
The President of the Senate
of the United States

Statement of Information on the Expedition against the Indians Northwest of the Ohio

Information relative to the depredations of the Indians
North West of the Ohio

No. 1
John Evans, Lieut. of the county of Monongalia, to the Executive of Virginia

25th. April 1789

"On the 23d. instant the Indians committed hostilities on the frontiers of this county, killed a captain William Thomas, Joseph Cornbridge and wife, and two children on Dunker's creek—which has alarmed the people in such a degree as to occasion them to apply to me for assistance."

No. 2
Wm. McCleery to the Govr. of Virginia

Morgantown, 25th. April 1789

"An express came here this morning with the disagreable news of the indians having committed hostilities on one of our frontier settlements on the 23d. instant. two parties attacked nearly about the same time two families on Dunkard creek, about 20 to 25 miles from this place, and killed one man, out of one, and the man and his wife and two children, which was the whole of the other family—the alarm given to the frontier of this county generally by this murder hath become very serious, and unless some speedy assistance is given I am something of opinion that the Monongahela river (which runs by this place) will be our frontier line in a short time."

No. 3
Geo. Clendinen to the Govr. of Virginia

Greenbriar, 15th. June 1789

"I am also unhappy to find that the executive have received no official information respecting the disposition of the Indians westward of the Ohio, but let their disposition be what it may they or some Indians to us unknown, since my last by Mr. Renick, have killed and taken ten persons from the settlement on Clinch, and also several persons at the mouth of great Sandy, and I have reason to expect their blows hourly on Kanawa."

No. 4.
Robt. Johnson, Lt. of the county of Woodford to the President of the United States

District of Kentuckey Augt. 22d. 1789

"About the 10th. instant two men were fired on by a party of Indians but no damage sustained only one of the horses the men rode was killed: the Indians took the saddle & bridle and the night following they stole eleven horses, our men pursued them next day came up with them and retook all the horses, together with said saddle & bridle, and killed two (one of which was a white man). On Sunday the 16th. six negroes were taken by a party of Indians in ambuscade about three quarters of a mile from my house. they carried them about one quarter of a mile where they were surprised by the noise of some people riding near them, they tomahawked four, two of which died, two was left for dead which is now in a hopeful way of recovery the other two made their escape while they were murdering the rest. The day following the party was seen twice and the evening or night of the sixteenth they stole some horses from captain Buford we pursued them as quick as possible with about forty men to the Ohio, about twenty five miles below the mouth of Big Miami, where twenty six volunteers crossed the Ohio after them, we came to a large camp of them early in the morning of the 20th. about twelve miles from the Ohio, we divided our party and attacked them opposite, on each side, they fought us a short time in that position until they got their women & children out of the way, and then give back to a thick place of high weeds & bushes, where they hid very close we immediately drove up about forty of their horses and made our retreat across the Ohio, we lost three men & two wounded. The indians wounded one of our men as we returned. Thus they are going on from time to time in this country."

No. 5.
Convention to the President of the United States

Danville, 26th. July 1789

"We can assure your Excellency, that the militia of Kentuckey from their hardiness, alertness & bravery are able to render essential service to the inhabitants of the district, if they are employed in its defence.

And we beg leave further to observe that, from the present stations of the federal troops, it is absolutely impossible to give the commanders notice, so as to enable them, even if their force was sufficient, to render any service whatever."

No. 6
Robt. Johnson County Lieut. to the Govr. of Virginia

District of Kentuckey, Woodford county
Augt. 22d. 1789

"The hostile acts of the savages is so frequent in our country that it becomes troublesome to write you on every occasion. On the 10th. of this inst. a party fired on a young man in this county near the settlement, killed the horse and took the saddle & bridle and stole some horses, the night following we were in motion early next morning and soon found their trail and came up with them, and retook the horses & killed two of them, one of which was a white man; the 16th. following a party took six negroes within a mile of my house, killed two, wounded two with their tomahawks and left them for dead, and the other two made escape while they were murdering the rest: The second night after they stole some horses. About forty men followed them to the Ohio and twenty six crossed the river and followed them over the Ohio, about twelve miles, where we came up with a party at a large camp making salt at a salt spring, we divided the party and attacked them on each side, they soon gave back; we took some of their horses and returned to the Ohio, where we crossed. We lost three men killed and two wounded."

No. 7.
An Account of the depredations committed in the District of Kentuckey by the Indians since the first of May 1789
enclosed in No. 5

"In Jefferson county

On Floyd's fork two men killed; near the same time & place two persons were killed and three taken prisoner.

On Brashears's creek, two killed and two taken prisoners.

On the 17th. of July, Chinoweth's station was attacked by a number of Indians, who entered Chinoweth's house while the family was at supper. Three of Chinoweth's family were killed, and seven wounded. Three of the wounded are since dead & several others yet dangerous. The indians plundered the house of every thing they could carry away. There was at the same station before this date one man killed and one wounded. The number of horses stolen from this county exceed twenty.

Nelson.

Two men killed and two wounded and a number of horses stolen to the amount of about twenty.

Lincoln

One man and one child killed, and two women wounded. About twenty five horses stolen.

Madison.

On the first day of June the Indians broke into the house of Edmund Stephenson and wounded one person. They have stolen a number of horses from this county.

Bourbon.

Two men have been badly wounded, and about fifteen horses stolen.

Mason.

Two men killed and forty one horses stolen.

Woodford,

One boy killed and several horses stolen."

No. 8.
Col. Benja. Wilson to Govr. St. Clair

Harrison County 4th. Octor. 1789

"On the 19th. of september last a party of Indians killed and scalped four persons and captivated four, the family of a certain William Johnston within about nine miles of Clerksburg—on the 22d. the indians killed John Mauk's wife and two of his children, and burnt his house, the same evening burnt Jacob Stotzer's house—the family hardly escaped—on the 23d. burnt Jethro Thompson's house—and on the 26th. burnt John Simm's house, and on the 28th. stole from Randolph county, ten or eleven horses—the number of horses taken from this county is not yet truly ascertained, but certain, five horses taken, cattle, sheep & hogs killed. some part of this mischief done eleven or twelve miles in towards the interior parts of this county—Sir be assured the people of this part of the county are much alarmed and much confused—and in my humble opinion if something more than treaties made with part of the Indian tribes is not done shortly, it will be with difficulty the frontiers of this county can be kept from evacuating their settlements—this opinion I have gathered from my having taken a tour amongst the people whilst the mischief was doing."

No. 9.
Geo. Clendinen Lieut. of the county of Kanawa to the President of the United States

Richmond 27th. Decemr. 1789

"The indians have in the county of Kanawa committed many hostilities; some of which I beg leave to ennumerate, They killed a man, near Point pleasant; took a young man and a negro fellow prisoners; have shot at others who made their escape, and have took between twenty and thirty head of horse creatures, together with many other outrages to the manifest injury & distress of the inhabitants.

If protection is not immediately given I am sure the greater part of our frontier will be compelled to leave their homes, and either live in forts, or move into the strong settled parts of the neighbouring counties, which I conceive would do great public injury, as well as distress in a great degree the inhabitants, that are thus exposed, who are situated in a part of the country not only to become respectable but very useful."

No. 10.
Address of the general Assembly of Virginia to the President of the United States

"It has been a great relief to our apprehensions, for the safety of our brethen on the frontiers, to learn from the communications of the secretary of War, that their protection against the incursions of the Indians, has occupied your attention.

Knowing the power of the federal Executive to concentrate the american force, and confiding in the wisdom of its measures we should leave the subject unnoticed, but from a belief, that time has been wanting, to give the proper intelligence, and make the necessary arrangements of defence, for a country, so far remote from the seat of government.

Many members of the general Assembly now present, have been either witnesses of the recent murders and depredations committed by the savages, or have brought with them information, the truth of which cannot be questioned. It is unnecessary to enter into a detail of those hostilities. Permit us only to say, that those parts of Kentuckey and the southwestern and northern counties lying on the Ohio, and its waters which have generally been, the scene of indian barbarity, are now pressed by danger the most imminent.

We have been induced to suppose it possible, that for the purpose of affording effectual relief, it may be found expedient to carry war into the country of the indian enemy; should this be the case we take the liberty of assuring you, that this commonwealth will chearfully sustain her proportion of the expences which may be incurred in such an expedition."

No. 11.
From the Representatives of the frontier counties of Virginia,
to the President of the United States

Richmond 12th. Decr. 1789
"In addition to the address of the General Assembly on indian affairs, We the representatives of the counties of Ohio, Monongalia, Harrison and Randolph, are contrained, to take the liberty of stating to you the defenceless situation of those counties, in order that you may be able to direct such measures as may be necessary for their defence, as we have every reason to expect that the Indians will break in upon our settlements as soon as the weather will permit them in the spring. First from the northern boundary line where it crosses the Ohio river at the mouth of the little Beaver Creek, down the said river to the mouth of big Sandy Creek distant about three hundred miles we lay open to the ravages of the Indians who may attack our settlements in any quarter they may chuse, it may here be supposed that the troops stationed at Muskingum would check their progress in this business, but experience hath taught us, that they are of very little use for we find that the indians cross the river Ohio, both above and below that garrison undiscovered either on their way, to our country or returning to their own, and indeed such will always be our fate until more effectual measures are adopted for our defence, it may be further supposed that general Sinclair can grant all the relief that is necessary for our safety; in answer to which we beg leave to observe, that altho' we have the highest opinion of that gentleman's integrity and goodness, but from his necessary calls to visit the different posts on the Ohio river, even as low down as the rapids; we fear it will be out of his power to render us the necessary aid, besides 'tis impracticable for us to find him in the hour of distress. We further beg leave to suggest that whilst our operations were confined to a defensive plan, only, we have ever found the greatest degree of safety to our country arising from keeping out scouts and rangers on

our frontiers; indeed it was owing to that plan, and that only, that large tracts of our country hath not long 'ere now been depopulated. These scouts and rangers were composed of our own militia on whom our people could with confidence depend, as they are well acquainted with our woods, and with the paths the indians use to come in upon our settlements—Whilst we were thus covered we lived in perfect security, but as soon as they were withdrawn last spring we immediately felt the effects of indian cruelty, for from the month of April last to the month of October at which time we left home, there was killed and captivated, twenty persons, a considerable number of horse and other property carried off, and several houses burned in our country. All military regulations being submitted to you, we therefore beg leave to suggest our wishes, that you would continue to us the aforesaid mode of defence, should you approve of it; or direct to such other measures as you in your wisdom may think more adviseable, to be continued in our country until it may be thought necessary to carry on offensive war into the enemey's country as to bring about a lasting peace. Suffer us further to assure you, that we on the behalf of our bleeding country look up to you, and to you only, for that assistance that our necessities require, and shall conclude with praying that the great parent of the universe may conduct you under the eye of his special providence enabling you to fill that exalted station to which he hath called you, as well for the good of your fellow citizens as also for the happiness of mankind so far as they come within the bounds of your administration.

We have the honor to be with very
great regard and esteem your
Excellency's most obedt. servants.

signed	JOHN P. DUVALL, senator,	
	WM. MACMAHON, ACHD. WOODS }	Ohio,
	WM. McCLEERY THOS. PINDALL }	Monongalia,
	JOHN PRUNTY GEO. JACKSON }	Harrison
	JON. PARSONS CORN. BOGARD }	Randolph

No. 12.
Govr. St. Clair, to the secretary of War

Fort Stuben 26th Jany. 1790
"By a note this moment received from Louisville, I am informed that the indians have killed three men within twelve miles of Danville, at Carpenter's

station; and three more and broke the settlement up, upon Russell's creek, about forty miles from the same place. Some people who had been hunting on this side of the river about six miles below Limestone, were fired upon by indians and one man killed, just almost at the time major Doughty was passing, he landed & pursued them, but in vain."

No. 13.
Hon. Harry Innes judge for the districk of Kentuckey
to the Hon. John Brown

Danville Mar. 13th. 1790
"In the month of January a boat with ten persons were cut off about sixteen miles above Limestone. Nine found dead in the boat and one woman missing, during the massacre a boy who was a prisoner made his escape, he was up hicking, being out with two men on a hunting party who were killed. Three men were killed about the same time in the wilderness between Bickland creek and Stinking creek on the road two escaped. Old John Sloan and his son were killed on the head of the Roling fork. One man killed on Holin. A station on Russel creek was attacked about the 25th. of the month, Isaac & Nathan Farris, a son of Isaac Farris's, John Painter and one other man killed, a negro woman, a white woman wounded & a number of horses have been taken, but I can't enumerate them. One Harper was killed on State creek.

In February one man killed at the Mudlick; One killed at the mouth of Kentuckey and the people have evacuated the station from fear. In this month I have only heard of one man killed & one wounded on the Rolling fork. But from various reports there is too much reason to fear they will be hostile this spring."

No. 14
Wm. W. Dowell, to the hon. John Brown

4th. April 1790
"Although I wrote you a few days ago I feel a propensity to hand you every intelligence in my power. The indians have again made a capital stroke on the Ohio; they, to the number of about fifty are encamped near the mouth of the Sciota, and have by means of a white prisoner who they have with them; taken three boats and a periange, the periange contained six men, who were going up the river from Limestone, one of the boats belonged to Mr. John May, the six men together with Mr. May and the whole crew, were put to instant death by the savages. The other two boats, one of them belonged to families, the other was the property of colonel Edwards of Bourbon and Mr. Thomas Marshall and others who the day after May was taken, were at the

same place attacked by the savages; they in the first instance attempted to induce the boats, to come to shore, by means of the prisoner who was the only person exposed to view, and who affected the utmost distress & anxiety in order that he might be received on board and brought to Limestone; but finding their stratagem would answer no purpose, they immediately exposed themselves and began to fire on the boats but without effect; the devils then to the number of about thirty, jumped into May's boat and gave chase; by which means being better supplied with oars, they would soon have overtaken Marshall and the family boat, if it had not been for colonel George Thompson, who was owner to a third part in the same company; he threw out all the horses he had in his boat, and received colonel Edwards's crew, and the families all into his boat together with their oars, by which means the whole of the people escaped after sustaining a chase of about fifteen miles; The loss of property in the two boats, was seventeen horses, about fifteen hundred pounds worth of dry goods and a considerable quantity of household furniture. It is not known what May had on board, as no person was left alive.

I have also heard to day that the Indians have taken a boat on salt river which was laded with salt, and killed a John Prior, and two others who belonged to the boats crew.

These are the most material outrages that I now recollect. The consequences are truly alarming no preparation is yet made, neither can there be by us, who are not authorized to cross the river."

No. 15.
Govr. St. Clair to the secretary of War

Cahokia, 1st. May 1790

"The major (Hamtramck) understanding that there was some private difference between that indian and the person who served as interpreter to the messenger did, on the first of April send forward another messenger; and he has enclosed to me a letter from him, from Quitepiconnais, fifteen miles above Ouiatanon of the 15th. of that month; a translation of which is sent with this—By that letter you will observe that every thing is referred to the Miamies, which does not indicate a peaceable issue—The confidence these have in their situation—the vicinity of many other nations, either much under their influence or hostiley disposed towards the United States, and pernicious counsels of the british traders, joined to the immense booties obtained by their depredations on the Ohio, will most probably prevent them from listning to any reasonable terms of accommodation, so that it is much to be feared, that the United States, must prepare effectually to chastise them; and the consequence of not doing it may, very probably be the defection of those who are now at peace, and would remain so, with the entire alienation of the affections at least *of the people of the frontiers."*

N. B. Gamelin's information being unimportant, is not copied.

Representation from the field Officers of Harrison County

Virginia—Harrison County, February 2. 1790
The President of the United States

Sir,

The alarming predicament in which this County now stands as touching the state of Indian Affairs, and the small prospect of protection from His Excellency Arthur St. Clair, hath moved us the subscribers to meet this day in Council in order to concert measures as far in our power to calm the minds of our exposed frontiers Who expects early in the Spring to be again harrassed by the Savages.

It appears to us by the Address of the General Assembly of Virginia dated the 30th of October 1789—that official information has been given to your Excellency of the Indians wanton barbarity on the frontiers of this State; we also have the strongest assurance that the Members of the General Assembly from the Western District, did apply by a subsequent Address separate and apart from the said Address sent by the General Assembly which we trusted would have fell into your hands before Governor St. Clair left New-York, which now appears to us not to be the case—therefore the frontiers is left defenceless, the People who lays exposed is complaining they are neglected—that the interior parts of the United States has enjoyed peace since the year 1782, that Government has got thoughtless about the lives of their Citizens &c.

We would undertake to give a full Detail of the various incursions made on the frontiers of this Country, but expects our County Lieutenant will hand this Petition to your Excellency who we believe will better satisfy your enquiries than our Detail.

We presume the aforesaid Address of our Legislative body, and the separate Address sent by the Members of this Western district fully takes in our wishes as touching the mode of present and future Relief.

Therefore in the name and behalf of our suffering fellow Citizens over whom we preside as field Officers of the Militia, pray that your Excellency would take our distressed situation under your parental Care and grant us such relief as you in your wisdom shall think proper, and we in Duty bound shall pray—&c. &c.

BENJAMIN WILSON, Col.
(sign'd)   GEO. JACKSON Lieut. Col.
WILLIAM ROBINSON Major

Extract of a Letter from the Lieuts. of the Counties of Fayette
Woodford C   & Mercer to the Secy. of War

dated 14th April 1790

"We almost every day receive accounts of their horrid murders on our defenceless frontiers (which entirely surround us) and the taking of Horses and other Property to the ruin of a number of families—It is painful to repeat particulars, but some recent Acts of the Savages demand our Representation.

Several Boats have within a few Weeks past been attacked and taken on the Ohio River, and one in Salt River by strong parties of Indians, and their unhappy Crews, murdered or carried into Captivity.

We have reason to believe that there is a combination of several Tribes, and their numbers pretty numerous."

Majr. Hamtramck to Govr. St. Clair

Post Vincennes 22d May 1790

"I now enclose the proceedings of Mr. Gamelin, by which your Excellency can have no great hopes of bringing the Indians to a peace with the United States. The 8th of May Gamelin arrived, and on the 11th. some Merchants arrived and informed me that as soon as Gamelin had passed their Villages on his return, that all the Indians had gone to War—that a large party of Indians from Mishlimackinack and some Patowatomies had gone to Kentuckey, and that three days after Gamelin had left the Miami, an American was brought there and burnt."

Deposition of Charles Johnston
taken before the Secretary of War

July 29th 1790

"On the 20th. of March 1790, going down the River Ohio, in company with John May Esquire of Virginia, with four other Persons in our Boat (two of whom were Women) we were attacked by a party of 54 Indians, consisting chiefly of Shawnese and Cherokees. In this attack Mr. May, and one of the Women were killed—the rest of us made prisoners.

The day following, a Canoe coming up the River, with six men in it, were fired upon and all killed.

In a few hours afterwards two Boats (the Owners of which had abandoned them, and got on board a third Boat that was in Company) were taken by the Savages, with Goods and other property in them, which, in my opinion, must have amounted to several Thousand pounds value.

Two days afterwards the Indians divided themselves into several parties;

when they set off to this Town; and arrived in about 5 or 6 Weeks at Sandusky, where the Nation of Wyandot or Huron Indians live.

Whilst in the Indian Country, I was informed that one of our Party, whose name was Wilm. Flin, and whom on a division, had fallen to the Cherokees, was carried to the Nation of Miamies—there tied to a stake, and in the most inhuman manner was roasted alive.

I further understood that there are a number of Americans, who have been made prisoners by the Indians, and are now in the Shawanese and Miami Nations languishing under slavery and all its bitter appendages."

Col. Robt. Rankins to Col. Thos. Lewis

April 3d. 1790

"As I presume you have not heard of the late mischief I shall just beg leave to inform you that about six weeks ago, two men were taken off Cabin Creek who have been made use of to decoy Boats ashore, by which means six men in a Canoe going up the River attempted to escape after they found themselves ensnared were murdered, Mr. May's Boat taken, himself and one other killed the rest of the Crew made Prisoners, two Boats in which was a considerable amount of property belonging to Col. John Edwards of Bourbon, Capt. Thomas Marshal and a number of other Gentlemen taken, the Gentlemen themselves forced to crowd into Colonel George Thomson's Boat and row for life, the Indians having pursued them in Mr. May's boat armed for that purpose with unparalelled avidity.

Two men were also killed, and seven more one Woman & five Children taken Prisoners about six weeks ago in Kennaday's bottom on the Ohio, 20 miles above Limestone, where they were engaged in erecting a new Settlement. All this mischief has been done by the same Party of Indians who are still on the River and from information about the same place where the Boats and Canoe were taken 6 or 7 miles above the mouth of Scioto—and we are informed by the two men above mentioned who have escaped and come in, that they have sent the Plunder to their Town by a Party and expect a reinforcement—A party of men were raised in this settlement on the first intelligence of the disturbance, but a dispute arising among them respecting the object in view, they split and returned without doing of any service, except bringing away a boat which the Indians fitted up for their offensive operations; However such generally are the consequence of expeditions where the Officers who conduct them have only Power to advise and persuade; and it is much to be lamented, that the Government under which we live wants Power; or they who are at the Helm a disposition to protect its Citizens.

I have this moment received further intelligence of the depredations of those cursed Devils. A Boat from Greenbriar, in which was Colonel Ward,

Mr. R. Madison and three or four other Boats from Monogahala, were yesterday afternoon attacked at or near the place mentioned above, a Mr. Richards was killed and the Monogahalia people were obliged to abandon one of their Boats with about 100 Gallons of Whiskey, some other property besides several Horses and Cattle: A number of Horses were killed and wounded in the other Boats."

Judge Innes to the Secry. of War

Danville May 13th. 1790

"That you may have an idea of our unhappy situation, I beg leave to refer you to a Letter I wrote on the 20th ultimo, to the Honble. John Brown; since which the Indians have killed two white men and two Negroes in Jefferson County—in Nelson two Girls—scalped one Woman, and made one other woman prisoner."

Judge Innes to the Secretary of War

Danville July 7th. 1790

"I have been intimately acquainted with this District from November 1783, I can with truth say that in this period of time the Indians have always been the agressors; that any incursions made into their Country have been from reiterated injuries committed by them—that the depredatory mode of War and plundering carried on by them renders it difficult and almost impossible to discriminate what tribes are the Offenders—that since my first visit to this District which was the time above named, I can venture to say that above 1,500 souls have been killed & taken in the District and migrating to it—that upwards of 20,000 Horses have been taken and carried off—and other property such as money—merchandize—Household Goods—and wearing apparel hath been carried off and destroyed by these Barbarians to at least £15,000.

Repeated informations have been given of these injuries which continue to be daily perpetrated, and yet we have no satisfactory account of the intention of Government for our relief—the consequences to the District are of a serious & important nature—by them do we see the population of our Country decreased, by the murders committed on the emigrants and actual settlers, and by them do we find people intimidated from migrating to our Country, which lessens our rising strength—by them are the wealth of our Citizens diminished and the value of our Lands decreased. What will be the result?

Volunteer expeditions will be carried on into the Indian Countries upon the principle of *revenge, protection and self preservation* and Government will not be able to counteract them—the consequences will be, that the Volunteers who may thus embody will not discriminate between the Indians who are hostile and these who have treated—they will consider all as enemies that come in their way—and the supposed amicable Indians will no longer have any faith in Government—it will not only prevent the intended views of Government, but undo what hath been done.

I will Sir, be candid on this subject not only as Inhabitant of Kentucky, but as a friend to Society who wishes to see order and regularity preserved in the Government under which I live; The people say they have long groaned under their misfortunes—they see no prospect of relief—they are the strength and wealth of the Western Country—all measures which have been attempted are placed (for execution) in the hands of Strangers who have no interest among them—they are the general sufferers and yet have no voice in the business—they are accused as the Aggressors and have no Representative to justify. These are the general sentiments of the People and they begin to want faith in the Government and appear determined to revenge themselves; for this purpose a meeting was lately held in this place by a number of respectable characters to determine on the propriety of carrying on three Expeditions this fall; from a more general Representation of the District, the business was postponed until the meeting of our Convention which is about the 26th. instant, at which time there will be a very general meeting of influential Characters of the District, and unless some information is received before that time that will be satisfactory, I fully expect one or more expeditions will be determined on.

Impressed with the Idea that the foregoing Observations will not be unacceptable to you as an Officer of Government through whose department it may be properly communicated to the President, if worthy your attention I shall make no Apology for the length of my Letter."

From the same

July 8th

"I have this day received a Letter from Governor St. Clair dated the 5th Inst.—'At the rapids of Ohio' (he says) 'that the expectations of Peace which I much wished cannot be realized with the people on the Wabash, and in consequence I have come here sooner than I should otherwise have done to prepare for operating against them'—he has requested me to apprize the Field Officers of the District that he shall call for the proportions of the Militia they are to furnish in consequence of the Orders he has received from the President."

Alexr. S. Ballit Lt. Jefferson County to Judge Innes

May 24, 1790

"I now embrace the first opportunity which offers of informing you that a Man was wounded near Mr. Joseph Hites Plantation about a fortnight ago, I mention this instance as the last of several which have appeared this spring of mischief done by the Indians in this County."

Certificate of Robert Lemen Jacob Steulan & Wm. Price

"We the underwriters Inhabitants of Jefferson County on the waters of Brashear's Creek do Certify, that in the latter end of March last the Indians took a negro woman Prisoner the property of Anderson Long's two young men at work at the said Long's in his field, on Clear Creek and branch of Brashear's Creek.

That on Tick Creek a branch of Brashear's Creek in April the Indians killed two men at work in their field.

That in May two Boys were made prisoners from Loudon's station on the head of Drennon's Lick Creek.

That on the 23d Instant a party of Indians fired on a company of a people on Clear Creek as they were returning from meeting, killed one man on the spot and took a young woman Prisoner who they carried about ten miles and then Tomahawk'd & scalped her.

That on the 25th. Instant as a Company were bringing home the Corpse of the man and Woman, they were alarmed by their Dogs and sent a Party out to reconnoitre who discovered the Trail of some Indians.

Given under our hands this 28th Day of May 1790

(sign'd)   ROBERT LEMEN
JACOB SEULAN
WILM. PRICE

There was no Magistrate to be conveniently found when this Certificate was given or I would have had an Affadavit made of the facts.

(sign'd)   HARRY INNES

John Caldwell to Judge Innes

Nelson County May 12th. 1790

"On Tuesday morning about eleven Indians attacked the House of Miles Heart on Valley Creek a fork of Nole-Lin and killed Heart and one of his

Children, and his Wife and two more, which includes the whole family were made Prisoners."

Deposition of Saml. Winter taken before Chrisr. Greenup

"Mercer ss.   21. May. 1790

Samuel Winter came before me a Justice for the said County and being sworn saith—That he is an Inhabitant of Nelson County & resides on Nolin Creek, that a certain Miles Heart who lived on Valley Creek about six miles from the Deponent was murdered in his House on Tuesday the 11th Instant, and that the wife and two Children of the said Heart were taken Prisoners, that two of Hearts horses are missing which are supposed to be carried off by the Indians who did the mischief."

Chrisr. Greenup to Judge Innes

Mercer County 24th May 1790

"About four days ago the Indians stole four Horses from Mr. Meaux, a considerable distance within the inhabitants, this might have been prevented had there been Scouts."

John Caldwell to Judge Innes

June 4. 1790

"About the seventh of March last the Indians came to the Rolling fork and stole a number of Horses to the amount of 16—they were pursued by Captain Wilson and small party, who came up with them in about forty miles; but being over power'd they were obliged to retreat; Capt. Wilson was killed upon the spot."

Robt. Johnson to Judge Innes

May 13th, 1790

"I send you two Depositions containing an account of some mischief done lately by the Savages in this County, to wit, the killing McBride and McConnel in April last, and also taking a son of Mr. Tanners (on the Ohio) a Prisoner &c. I also inform you that last fall two men were killed by the Savages one of the name of Brown whose wife & children live now in Lexington, as I was with the Men who brought the Corpse into the neighbourhood I live in, besides this there hath been another party last winter who stole a number of Horses from the neighbourhood I live in and carried them off."

Deposition of John Garnett taken before Robt. Johnson M. for W. C.

"Woodford County ss.   May 12. 1790
John Garnett of full Age being duly sworn saith, That he was at Mr. John Tanner's station on the Ohio in said County about five miles below the mouth of the big Miami, and that said Tanner informed him that about the last of April or first of May five Indians came and lay in ambush a little over one hundred yards from his house between the house and his field and took a son of said Tanner's about nine years old and carried him off across the Ohio—and further saith that Indians hath been seen since within about two miles of said station—and this Deponent further saith not."

Deposition of Saml. Stephenson taken before Robt. Johnson M. for W. Cy.

"Woodford County ss.   May 12th. 1790
Samuel Stephenson of full Age being duly sworn saith, That about the 12th of April 1790, being called on to go out to bury James McBride &   McConnell who was killed by the Indians on the Road or Path from the mouth of Lickin to the settlement on Elkhorn—and this Deponent further saith that he assisted to bury two men which was both scalped—one was much cut with a Tomahawk & the other was shot through the hips and he believes them to be said McBride & McConnell. and this Deponent further saith not."

John Edwards to Judge Innes

Bourbon County May 12 1790
"This morning was killed within six or seven miles of this place by the Indians, a certain Lewis Parker who was at his work, it will be unnecessary for me to say any thing more with respect to the murder as I have enclosed you an Affidavit—and as to the murder of two more men I am satisfied of its certainty, but have had no opportunity of finding the man who was with them when they were killed, nor those who have since buried them, the names of the men were McBride & McConnell."

Deposition of David Rankin & James Hays
taken before Benjn. Harrison

"Bourbon ss.   1790
"This day came before me one of the Commonwealth's justices for said County the Subscribers and made Oath, that on the 12th of May inst. they saw Lewis Parker lying dead, he had received several wounds with Balls,

Tomahawks & Knives (he was scalped) that they ~~saw~~ found him the said Parker about one hour after he was killed, and that they verily believe he was thus murthered by Indians, and further saith not."

Certificate of Benj. Harrison

"Altho' I did not see the Indians kill Parker, I do verily believe they did do it, I saw his Body about two hours after he was killed, it happened at Michl. Hoggs not quite 3 miles from my house, and I followed the trails of those who committed the Murther near 10 miles, their direction was towards the Big bone Lick, the Indians has stole Two Horses from Mr. Coleman Lately, there is no Person on this quarter that knows any thing of McBride & McConnel's being killed, only from hearsay but is a matter of fact."

John Edwards Lieut. B. Couny. to Judge Innes

Bourbon May 12. 1790

"I am sorry to inform you since my last Letter that a man was killed by a party of Indians in his Corn field about seven miles from my house on Thursday last, also a Boat was taken about Eight or Ten miles above Limestone where five persons was found killed on the shore—I think we need no greater proof of the intentions of those Savage Barbarians to distress us."

Henry Lee Lieut. M. Couny. to Judge Innes

Mason County May 16. 1790

"On the night of the 11th Inst. four Boats (one of which contained an Officer & eight men of the United States troops) landed about nine miles above Limestone, and about 12 o'Clock was fired on by a party of Indians (supposed to be fifteen or twenty in number); three Boats made their escape without damage; the other containing sixteen souls fell into possession of the Enemy, five of those persons were killed and most horridly massacreed— three made their escape, one of which was wounded; the balance taken Prisoners, and from every discovery I have been able to make they have not yet re-crossed the River—On the 15th Instant, a trail of a party Indians (supposed to be about fifteen) was discovered crossing the Ohio within the bounds of our lower Settlements and directed their course towards the Blue Licks; this notice has put the neighbourhood in that quarter on their guard; I have had no further intelligence; but am under apprehensions every hour of the fatal consequences; our Surveyors and Hunters have all retired from the woods, the frequent signs of Indians render it unsafe for them to pursue their business."

John Logan to Judge Innes

Lincoln May 17. 1790

"Friday morning the 14th Instant, a Company was defeated on the other side Ingles's station, six of said Company are missing supposed to be killed. About ten or fifteen Indians took possession of all their Horses and Goods ready pack'd up to start."

James Barnett to Judge Innes

Madison—Mount Holley. 23 May 1790

"I can assure you Sir, that the frontier of this County (which is about forty miles) have considered themselves in imminent danger all the last Spring, but their fears are much encreased since the last hostilities committed on the Wilderness Road, and Indian signs discovered very lately upon Stacion Comp.

"The mischief above referred to was in Madison County about 40 miles from the Inhabitants—4 killed—2 wounded. 10 or 12 Horses with valuable property."

signed   H. INNES

Deposition of Joseph Barnett taken before Michl. Campbell

Nelson County ss.   June 8th. 1790

"This day came Joseph Barnett Esq. before me a Justice of the peace for said County and made Oath on the Holy Evangelists of Almighty God, That on the Eighteenth of April last past (being Lords day) about the hour of five in the Evening a party of Indians fell upon a few defenceless people who was returning from Hartford Town on Rough Creek to a station at the house of this Deponent being two miles distant, killed a Girl of twelve years old and Boy of eight years old cutting them in a cruel manner with Tomahawks (suppos'd)—cut an ancient Lady of both respectable family & character in her right arm, head & back in a cruel manner with a Symetar, and after having scalped her alive left her and his Symetar with her and carried off the Daughter of this Deponent a Girl near eleven years old into captivity—They were pursued by a party till night, which gave them an opportunity of escaping—The above mentioned Boy lived till Tuesday morning following, having his scull split with a Tomahawk and a great part of his brains on the outside of his wounded scalped scull—and the old Lady is yet alive notwithstanding all the misery she has endured—further this Deponent saith not."

Observe that the above persons was returning from Sermon.

No.
Brigr. General Harmar to the secretary of War

March 24th. 1790

"The indians still continue to murder and plunder the inhabitants, especially the boats going up and down the Ohio river—About the beginning of this month, they broke up Kenton's station a small settlement fifteen miles above Limestone, killing & capturing the whole of the people supposed to be ten or twelve in number.

Buckner Thruston Esqr. has just arrived here who informs me of a capital stroke of plunder which they made from the boats one of which he was on board, a small distance above the Sciota river—This gentleman is a member of the Virginia legislature and has given me the enclosed written report of the attack, by which you will please to observe that the property captured by the savages was estimated at 4,000 pounds.

He supposes them to have been Shawanese. No calculation will answer, but raising a sufficient force to effectually chastize the whole of those nations who are known to be hostile."

Report of Buckner Thruston esqr.

March 24th. 1790

"On the 21st. of March about 12 o'Clock we discovered on the indian shore a flat bottomed boat which appeared to be crowded with Indians; we were fortunately near the Virginia shore at the time we discovered the savages—on our coming opposite them a white man ran down on the beach and hallowed to us for god's sake to surrender, that there were fifty indians, and if we made resistance we should be massacred—we refused to surrender and immediately they fired on us for a considerable time perhaps to the number of one hundred guns, which gave us time to pass by them, they then embarked all hands aboard their boat (commonly called a Kentuckey boat, which they had taken a day or two before from Mr. Jno. May, who with four other men, it is supposed are either killed or taken) and gave chase to us, upon finding that we could not escape, there being three boats in company, we chose out the strongest boat, turned the horses adrift and embarked therein all the people belonging to the three boats, cut holes in her sides and put in the oars of the three boats, and made the best way we could for fifteen or twenty miles—the indians pursuing us with great earnestness. They left us after a chase of between two & three hours and we arrived without farther impediment at Limestone—We lost 28 horses, fifteen hundred pounds value of merchandise (as I am informed) besides private property of passengers and others to a considerable amount. We supposed the indians to be fifty or sixty in number; we had about twenty eight men, and sixteen or seventeen guns—a family of women and a few negroes—women & children—The principal sufferers among the passengers were Colonel Thompson, Colonel Edwards, Mr. Abner Field, Mr. Thomas Marshall."

No.
Brigr. General Harmar, to the secretary of War

June 9th. 1790

"At the solicitation of the inhabitants of Kentuckey (copies of which are enclosed) I was induced to endeavor to break up a nest of vagabond Indians, who had infested the river, and seemed to make it an object to establish themselves near the mouth of the Scioto, in order to interrupt the navigation of the Ohio, and to plunder and muder the emigrants—I am sorry that my endeavors were unsuccessful, as the villains had retreated—wolves might as well have been pursued—every exertion in my power was made without effect.

Having settled our plan of operations, which was to make a circuitous route and strike the Scioto pretty high, and from thence march down to its mouth in hopes to intercept some of their parties we took up our line of march on the same day (18th. April), and gained about twelve miles. On this first days march four mockinson tracks were discovered; General Scott detached a small party of horsemen, who fell in with the savages, killed them and brought the four scalps into Limestone.

Ensign Hartshorn's convoy of boats were attacked at midnight on the 12th (May) about nine miles above Limestone, from the Virginia side, and several of the emigrants killed, I have enclosed a copy of his report."

"Fort Washington May 30th. 1790

Sir

I beg leave to report as follows. On the 12th. instant, as I was coming down the Ohio in company with five other boats, in the evening before we came to Limestone by the request of the company we put to shore in order to stay until 2 o'Clock so that we might land at Limestone in daylight. I landed nine miles above Limestone, and the other boats landed about one hundred yards below me. About 12 o'Clock the Indians attacked the lowermost boat, after a number of shot they left it and fell on the other above them which they took, in this time my men fired five or six shot at the flash of their guns. I had much to do to keep the men in the boat from cutting her loose and leaving my men on shore, so I thought proper to order my men on board, for by every circumstance I thought them too strong for me with so few men; and it being very dark, I ordered the boat of from the shore and fell down into their fire, where we received a number of shot, and when I found that all the boats were not taken, I ordered them to go a head in case the indians did pursue us that I might check them. We arrived at Limestone at 3 o'Clock in the morning; I immediately wrote to the county lieutenant upon the matter—he with twenty men came down at 3 o'Clock in the afternoon, myself with five men went up to the place where we was attacked—we found one man, one woman and three children killed & scalped, which we put into the boat, with their property to Limestone. There is eight missing; the whole killed and missing is thirteen souls—they took none of the property but one horse.

I am sir
your most hum. servt.

(signed)   ASA HARTSHORNE

Ens. 1st. U.S. Regt."

Jas. Wilkinson to Genl. Harmar

Lexington 7th April 1790
"I write to you at the public request, on a subject deeply interesting to Kentuckey, our national honor, and to humanity.

For more than one month past a party of Savages have occupied the N. Western Bank of the Ohio a few miles above the mouth of Scioto, from whence they make attacks upon every Boat which passes, to the destruction of much property, the loss of many lives, and the great annoyance of all intercourse from the northward.

By very recent accounts we are apprized that they still continue in force at that Point, and that their last attack was made against five Boats, one of which they captured—It is the general, and I conceive a well founded opinion, that if this party is not dislodged and dispersed, the navigation of the Ohio must cease—In a case so very critical the people of this district conceive themselves justified in appealing to arms, because their dearest interests and the lives of their Bretheren are at hazard—but being extremely unwilling to proceed, except in a legal, regular and authorized way, they call upon you for your advice, succour and assistance, in the hope and the expectation, that you will be able to co-operate with a detachment of the troops under your command, and carry an immediate expedition against the before mentioned party of Savages, from Limestone, where it is proposed to rendezvous a Body of Militia Volunteers.

Colonel Paterson waits upon you on this occasion to know your determination, and to make such adjustments as may be deemed expedient."

Levy Todd to Genl. Harmar

Fayette 7th April 1790

Within a few days past a party of Indians who have taken post on the Ohio near the mouth of the Scioto have captured four Boats, killed and taken several people and much property, for the particulars I refer you to Col. Paterson who I expect will hand you this—From circumstances we may conclude this practice will be continued unless they are dislodged—The unhappy consequence which will result are too obvious to every discerning man, and too distressing to be borne—A party of Men from the Counties north of Kentuckey river are preparing to remove these troublesome fellows from their station—they will rendezvous at Lexington on thursday the 15th instant—at Limestone the Saturday following. The inhabitants of this District flatter themselves they will meet with every encouragement & protection from the Officers in the Western Government in every plan that will tend to secure their persons & property, and to protect in the enjoyment of those rights for which we have so often risqued our persons and expended property—I flatter myself that in the present instance we shall not only meet the approbation of His Excellency Genl. St. Clair, but with such instructions and assistance from you as you may judge best calculated for the execution of the intended design, that a peaceable emigration may be preserved to the Western Country.

I flatter myself that an account of the hostilities that are committed in the Western Country will by the earliest opportunity be transmitted to the President of the United States."

Col. Paterson to Genl. Harmar

Licking 9. April 1790

I was very desirous of handing you General Wilkinson's and Col. Todds Letters, but from an interruption on the way and my business at home puts it out of my power—Mr. Lemond who I expect will hand this with others can inform you particularly—I do not know that my personal attendance would have answered any purpose only to have informed you of our intention—We do not wish to infringe on the rights of the federal Government—it is well known that the Indians occupy both sides of the River—We know that it is not infringing to drive the Enemy from our own Door, but that will not answer any purpose in this case—We rest assured that we will not only meet with your approbation, but your assistance—You need not doubt but that on

Saturday the 17th. instant, there will be at Limestone five hundred men at least to co-operate with your troops and your directions—Our Men will be furnished with twelve days provisions expecting to continue out that time.

Govr. St. Clair to the Secretary at War

New York August 23d. 1790

"The Letter from Major Hamtramck, and Journal of Mr. Gamelin, copies of which accompany this, were received by me at Kaskaskies, after my return from Cahokia; and when I was on the point of setting out for the Ouabache—from the information that Journal contained, and the intelligence which the Major had received afterwards, as stated in the Letter, it appeared to me that there was not the smallest probability of an accommodation with the Indians of that River and of the Miami, and that, from the manner in which the proposal of an accommodation had been received by them, and their subsequent conduct, it would not be proper for me to go to Post St. Vincennes; I therefore took the Resolution to return by the Mississippi and Ohio Rivers to the Head quarters of the troops, in order to concert with General Harmar upon the means of carrying into effect the alternative contained in my Instructions from the President—that of punishing them; and accordingly embarked on the eleventh day of June, and arrived at Fort Washington on the 13th day of July.

Before my departure from Kaskaskies I put a Letter into the hands of Major Sargent informing him of my intended Journey, and that, as soon as I had embarked, he was to consider me as absent, and in consequence the Government devolved upon himself and desired him to proceed to the Post, lay out a County there, establish the Militia, and appoint the Civil & Military Officers—I was led to proceed in this manner from the little time there would be to digest the Business, and bring the necessary force together from so many and distant parts, before it would be necessary that they should move and the certainty there appeared to be that, if I went to the Post, the consuming a good deal of it would be unavoidable, and the season for operation be lost.

From the falls of Ohio, I took Mr. Elliot, one of the Contractors, with me to Head quarters, that he might, in person, give General Harmar information with respect to the certainty of supplies, without being assured of which it would be vain to think of the matter.

The number of Militia I was empowered to call for was, One thousand from Virginia and Five hundred from Pennsylvania, to act in conjunction with the Continental troops—these the General estimated at four hundred effective—the manner of employing this force, which was concluded upon, is this—Three hundred of the Militia of Virginia are to rendezvous at Fort Steuben, and with the Garrison of that Fort to march to Post St. Vincennes and join Major Hamtramck—the remaining Twelve hundred of the Militia to assemble at Fort Washington under the orders of General Harmar, which, with the Troops to be collected there, will form a body of Fifteen hundred—these are intended to march directly across the Country to the Miami village, while Major Hamtramck moves up the Ouabash to attack any of the Villages on that river to which his force may be equal; but as it is not so respectable as I could wish it, I took it upon myself to give him authority to call for aid from the Militia of Post St. Vincennes.

It would perhaps have been better that the whole should have been drawn together, and one solid effort been made; but it was next to impossible to form a junction of all the parts at any one proper place in time, and we were not without hopes that, as the movements will be made in concert, the success of both may be forwarded by each other—for that up the Ouabash will certainly I think, make those nations uneasy for themselves, and prevent them from aiding the Miamies; while the direct movement to their Village will have the same effect upon them.

I could indeed have wished that the force in both quarters had been more respectable—as far as it is possible their success should be put out of the chance of accidents; for a failure will be attended with the very worst consequences: I believe Sir, that if the President approves the Business and should think proper to add to the Numbers, it is not yet too late, being of opinion that many more men might be obtained from that part of Virginia from whence the others are called, on very short notice—You will observe Sir, by my Letter to the County Lieutenants that the rendezvous at Fort Washington is fixed for the 15th. of next month—their assembling there however was not counted upon before the 20th; and that they would be in readiness to march by the first of October—before that time I hope I shall be able to join them.

Mr. Elliot made very little hesitation about the provisions, tho' it will be impossible to furnish flour—Corn however it seems is still abundant in Kentuckey, and with that General Harmar is satisfied.

I am very apprehensive that some disappointment will be met with in the Quota of Pennsylvania—for I found that, in two of the four Counties from which that Militia is to be drawn, they have not had an Officer for upwards of two years, and there was a general complaint for want of Arms. I represented that matter to the Executive of the State and they think the first difficulty will be obviated by a voluntary enlistment, and have ordered a quantity of Arms to be sent forward. As a disappointment there would be fatal, perhaps the President may think proper to make some conditional provision against it—I hope it will not happen, but I fear it; and am extremely anxious about it, on account of the expence that will have been incurred to no purpose, and more so from the injury the Reputation of the Government would sustain.

I request the favor of you Sir, to lay this Letter before the President as soon as possible, for it is of importance that I should return without loss of time, as the assembling the Militia of Pennsylvania is appointed on the 3d, and their being in motion not to exceed the 10th of September.

I have added a Copy of my Letter to the County Lieutenants and to the Senior Officer of the Pennsya. Militia."

No.

Mr. Gamelin's journal

Memorandum of sundry speeches
held by Anthony Gamelin to the chiefs
of the Ouabache & Miami nations

"I Anthony Gamelin by order of major Hamtramck set off from Fort Knox, the 5th. of April to proceed to Miami Town, with the speeches of his excellency Arthur St. Clair and to receive answer of the Ouabache and Miami nations—the first village I arrived to is called Kikapouquoi, the name of the chief of this village is called les Jambes croches—him and his tribe have a good heart, and accepted the speech.

The second village is at the river du Vermilion called Piankishaws—the first chief and all the chief warriors were well pleased with the speeches concerning the peace; but they said they could not give presently a proper answer, before they consult the Miami nation their eldest brethren—they desired me to proceed to the Miami Town and by coming back to let them know what reception I got from them—the said head chief told me that he thought the nations of the Lakes has a bad heart, and were ill disposed for the americans—that the speeches would not be received, particularly by the Chaouanons*[1] at Miami Town.

The 10th. of April I met thirteen Kikapoos warriors I asked them the purpose of their journey; We are for war said they, not against the white people, but against the Chichashas—I told them to be friends with white people—I gave them a letter for the commanding officer of Post Vincennes desiring them to go and shake hands with him—they promised to do it.

The 11th. of April I reached a tribe of Kikapoos, the head chief and all the warriors being assembled I gave them two branches of white wampum, with the speeches of his excellency Arthur St. Clair, and those of Major Hamtramck (it must be observed that the speeches have been in another hand before me)—the messenger could not proceed further than the Vermilion, on account of some private wrangling between the interpreter and some chief men of the tribe—moreover something in the speech displeased them very much, which is included in the third article, which says, 'I do now make you

---

[1] The following notation appears in the margin of the document: "*by these are meant the Shawanese."

the offer of peace, accept it or reject it as you please'—these words appeared to displease all the tribes to whom the first messenger, they told me they were menacing, and found that it might have a bad effect, I took upon myself to exclude them—and after making some apology they answered that him and his tribe were pleased with my speech, and that I could go up without danger, but that they could not presently give me an answer, having some warriors absent, and without consulting the Ouiatanons being the owners of their lands—they desired me to stop at Quitepiconnae, that they would have the chiefs and warriors of Ouiatanons and those of their nation assembled there, and would receive a proper answer. they said that they expected by ~~one~~ me a draught of milk from the great chief and the commanding officer of the post, for to put the old people in good humour, also some powder and ball for the young men for hunting, and for to get some good broth for their women and children, that I should know a bearer of speeches, should never be with empty hands—they promised me to keep their young men from stealing, and to send speeches to their nations in the prairies for to do the same. One of the chiefs desired me to listen to his speech—'Is it true that a man called Lewis Coder has in last summer carried a letter, wrote with red ink upon black paper, directed to the chief of the Falls, by the french and american people of the post inviting him for to furnish his young men, for to destroy the Kikapoos? Yourself Gamelin, you wrote the said letter without giving notice to the chiefs of that place as reported to us—But the Chief of the Falls answered, I don't understand the meaning of writing a letter with vermilion—don't you know that the Kikapoos are my children as well as other nations—instead of destroying them, I want to contract a solid peace with them—that is a proof of a good heart of the great chief & we sincerely believe that what you say concerning the peace is very true. another proof of his good heart we heard, that Ducoign applied to the commanding officer of the Post for to go against us, with the french people his brethern, but he got a refusal.'

The 14th. of April the Ouiatanons and the Kikapoos were assembled—after my speech one of the head chiefs got up and told me—'You Gamelin my friend and son in law, we are pleased to see in our village, and to hear by your mouth the good words of the great Chief—we thought to receive a few words from the french people, but I see the contrary, none but the big knife is sending speeches to us—You know that we can terminate nothing without the consent of our elder brethern the Miamies—I invite you to proceed to their village, and to speak to them—there is one thing in your speech I don't like—I will not tell of it; even was I drunk I would perceive it, but our elder brethern will certainly take notice of it in your speech—you invite us to stop our young men, it is impossible to do it, being constantly encouraged by the british.' Another chief got up and said, 'The americans are very flattering in their speeches—many times our nation went to their rendezvous—I was once my self—some of our chiefs died on the route, and we always came back all naked, and you Gamelin, you come with speech with empty hands'—Another chief got up and said to his young men—'If we are so poor and dressed in deerskins, it is our own fault—our french traders are leaving us and our villages because you plunder them every day, and it is time for us to have another conduct.' Another chief got up and said—'Know ye that the village of Ouiatanon is the sepulchre of all our ancestors—the chief of America invites us to go to him if we are for peace—he has not his leg broke, having been able to go as far as the Illinois—he might come here himself and we should be glad to see him in our village—We confess, that we accepted the ax, but it is by the reproach we continually received from the english and other nations which received the ax first, calling us women—at the present time they invite our young men to war—as to the old people they are wishing for peace'—they could not give me an answer before they receive advice from the Miamies their eldest brethern.

The 18th. of April I arrived to the river à l'anguille. The chief of the village, and those of war were not present. I explained the speeches to some of the tribe, they said they were well pleased, but they could not give me an answer, their chief men being absent, they desired me to stop at their village coming back and they sent with me one of their men for to hear the answer of their eldest brethern.

The 23d. April I arrived at the Miami Town, the next day I got the Miami nation, the Chaouanons*[2] and Delawares all assembled—I gave to each nation two branches of wampum, and began the speeches before the french and english traders, being invited by the Chiefs to be present, having told them myself, I would be glad to have them present, having nothing to say against any body—after the speech I shewed them the treaty concluded at Muskingum between his excellency Governor St. Clair and sundry nations; which displeased them—I told them that the purpose of this present time was not to submit them to any condition, but to offer them the peace, which made disappear their displeasure. The great chief told me that he was pleased with the speech—that he would soon give me an answer—In a private discourse with the great chief he told me not to mind what the Chaouanons would tell me having a bad heart & being the perturbators of all the nations—he said the Miamies had a bad name on account of mischief done on the river Ohio, but he told me it was not occasioned by his young men, but by the Chaouanons, his young men going out only for to hunt.

The 25th. of April, Bluejacket, chief warrior of the Chaouanons invited me to go to his house, and told me. 'My friend by the name and consent of the Chaouanons and Delawares I will speak to you. We are all sensible of your speech and pleased with it, but after consultation we cannot give an answer without hearing from our father at Detroit, and we are determined to give

---

[2] The notation "*Shawanese" appears in the left margin of the manuscript.

you back the two branches of wampum, and to sent you to Detroit to see and hear the chief, or to stay here twenty nights for to receive his answer—from all quarters we receive speeches from the americans, and not one is alike— We suppose that they intend to deceive us—then take back your branches of wampum.'

The 26th. five Peotewatamies arrived here with two negro men which they sold to english traders—The next day I went to the great chief of the Miamies called le Gris—his chief warrior was present—I told him how I had been served by the Chaouanons—he answered me that he had heard of it—that the said nation behaved contrary to his intentions—he desired me not to mind those strangers, and that he would soon give me a positive answer.

The 28th. April the great chief desired me to call to the french traders, and receive his answer—Don't take bad said he, of what I am to tell you—'You may go back when you please—we cannot give you a positive answer—we must send your speeches to all our neighbours and to the lake nations—we cannot give a definitive answer without consulting the Commandant of Detroit,' And he desired me to render him the two branches of wampum refused by the Chaouanons, also a copy of speeches in writing—he promised me that in thirty nights he would send an answer to post St. Vincennes, by a young man of each nation—he was well pleased with the speeches, and said to be worthy of attention, and should be communicated to all their confederates having resolved among them not do any thing without an unanimous consent. I agreed to his requisition and rendered him the two branches of wampum and a copy of the speech—afterwards he told me that the five nations, so called or Iroquois were training something—that five of them and three Wyandots were in this village with branches of wampum—he could not tell me presently their purpose, but he said I would know of it very soon.

The same day blue Jacket chief of the Chaouanons—invited me to his house for supper, and before the other chiefs told me, that after another deliberation they thought necessary that I should go myself to Detroit, for to see the commandant, who would get all his children assembled for to hear my speech—I told them that I would not answer them in the night—that I was not ashamed to speak before the sun.

The 29th. April, I got them all assembled—I told them that I was not to go to Detroit—that the speeches were directed to the nations of the river Ouabache and the Miami, and that for to prove the sincerity of the speech and the heart of governor St. Clair, I have willingly given a copy of the speeches to be shown to the commandant of Detroit—that his excellency will be glad to hear that his speeches have been sent to Detroit—and according to a letter wrote by the commandant of Detroit to the Miamies, Chaouanons and Delawares mentioning to you to be peaceable with the americans, I would go to him very willingly, if it was my directions, being sensible of his sentiments—I told them that I had nothing to say to the commandant, neither him to me—you must immediately resolve if you intend to take me to Detroit, or else I am to go back as soon as possible. Bluejacket got up and told me. 'My friend we are well pleased with what you say, our intention is not to force you to go to Detroit, it is only a proposal, thinking it for the best—Our answer is the same as the Miamies. We will send in thirty nights a full and positive answer by a young man of each nation by writing to Post St. Vincennes.' In the evening Bluejacket chief of the Chaouanons having taken me to supper with him, told me in a private manner, 'that the nation Chaouanon was in doubt of the sincerity of the Bigknife, so called, having been already deceived by them—that they had first destroyed their lands, put out their fire and sent away their young men, being a hunting without a mouthful of meat; also had taken away their women, wherefore many of them would with great deal of pain forget these affronts—moreover that some other nations was apprehending that offers of peace would, may be, tend to take away by degrees their lands, and would serve them as they did before—a certain proof that they intend to encroach on our lands, is their new settlement on the Ohio—if they don't keep this side clear, it will never be a proper reconcilement with the nations, Chaouanons, Iroquois Wiandots and perhaps many others.' Le Gris chief of the Miamies asked me in a private discourse, what chief had made a treaty with the Americans at Muskingum. I answered him that their names were mentioned in the treaty—he told me that he had heard of it some time ago, but they are not chiefs, neither delegates who made that treaty—they are only young men, who without authority and instruction from their chiefs have concluded that treaty which will not be approved—they went to that treaty clandestinely, and they intend to make mention of it, in the next council to be held.

The 2d. of May I came back to the river à l'anguille. One of the chief men of the tribe being witness of the council at Miami Town, repeated the whole to them; and whereas the first chief was absent they said they could not for present time give answer, but they are willing to join their speech to those of their eldest brethren—'To give you proof of an open heart, we let you know, that one of our chiefs is gone to war on the Americans; but it was before we heard of you—for certain they would not have been gone thither.' They also told me that a few days after I passed by their village, seventy warriors, Sauteux and Outawais from Michilimachmac arrived there some of them were Poux who meeting on their route the Sauteux and Outawais joined them— 'We told them what we heard by you, that your speech is fair and true—We could not stop them from going to war. The Poux told us that as the Sauteux and Outawais were more numerous than them, they were forced to follow them.'

The 3d. of May I got to the Ouias—they told me, they were waiting for an answer from their eldest brethern—'We approve very much our brethern for not to give a definitive answer without informing of it, all the Lake nations— that Detroit was the place where the fire was lighted—then it ought first to be put out there—that the english commandant is their father, since he threw down our french father, they could do nothing without his approbation.'

The 4th. of May, I arrived at the village of the Kikapoos, the Chief presented me two branches of wampum, black & white, said 'My son we cannot stop our young men from going to war—every day some set off clandestinely for that purpose—after such behaviour from our young men we are ashamed to say to the great chief at the Illinois, and of the post St. Vincennes, that we are busy about some good affairs, for the reconcilement— but be persuaded that we will speak to them continually concerning the peace; and that when our eldest brethern will have sent their answer, we will join ours to it.'

The 5th. of May I arrived at Vermilion—I found nobody but two chiefs— all the rest were gone a hunting, they told me, they had nothing else to say but what I was told going up—They told me that, the grosse Tête, a warrior absent appears to have a bad heart."

(signed)   ANTOINE GAMELIN
Messenger

This 17th. day of May appeared before me Mr. Antoine Gamelin and sworn that the within is the truth the whole truth and nothing but the truth.

(signed)   FS. HAMTRAMCK
Major Commdt.

(signed)   AR. ST. CLAIR

Copy of a circular letter from Governor St. Clair
to the County Lieutenants

Head Quarter Fort Washington
July 15th. 1790

Sir,

The interest of the United States dictating a peace with the Indian nations on the Ouabache if it could be obtained upon reasonable terms, I was directed by the President to give them information of the disposition of the general government on that subject, and to try to effect it—at the same time I was instructed by him to take measures for the security of the frontier country in case of their continuing hostile—the following is extracted from his instructions to me on that head (here was inserted that part of my instructions relative to the militia). I have now to inform you that there is no prospect of peace with the said Indians at present, on the contrary they continue very ill disposed towards the United States in general and to Virginia in particular, and many parties, are, from information lately received, now actually gone to war. The commanding officer of the troops and myself have therefore concerted a plan of offensive operations against them, and in conformity with the above recited instructions I now call upon you, in the name of the President of the United States for   men rank & file, and properly officered according to the legal establishment of the militia of your State, to act in conjunction with the federal troops against the said Indians, and that they be at   on the   day of September next, armed, accoutred and equipped for a service of sixty days or more after they shall have joined the troops, unless the object in view shall be sooner accomplished.

The laudable desire, and ardent spirit to repress the incursions of the savages, by which the militia have been actuated upon all occasions leave not room for a doubt but the present opportunity to punish them for the many injuries & cruelties they have committed, will be embraced with zeal. But allow me to observe, that it is of the utmost importance that they be punctually at the rendezvous.

I have the honor &c.
(signed)   AR. ST. CLAIR

The counties of Virginia were called upon in the following proportion—which were assigned them from the best information, I could get of their respective strengths.

The county of Nelson	125	to rendezvous at Fort Steuben, on the 12th. of Sepr.
Lincoln	125	
Jefferson	50	
	300	
Maddison	125	
Mercer	125	
Fayette	200	to rendezvous at Fort Washington Septemr. 15th.
Bourbon	125	
Woodford	85	
Mason	40	
	700	

The counties of Pennsylvania the proportions of which were assigned them by the number of their representatives in assembly which being governed by the number of people from time to time appeared an equal rule, and was the only I had to go by, having been able to meet with but one of the lieutenants.

Washington county	220	to assemble at
Fayette	110	McMahen's creek,
Westmoreland	110	four miles below
Alleghany	60	Wheeling on 3d.
	500	Sepr.

Copy of a letter from governor St. Clair, to the senior officer
of the Pennsylvania militia assembled at McMahens creek

Pittsburgh, Augt. 7th. 1790

Sir

As soon as the detachments from the different counties are arrived you will proceed without loss of time to Fort Harmar at the mouth of the Muskingum, and there join the federal troops under the command of major Doughty, who will either conduct you to head quarters, or direct the manner in which you are to proceed to that place. I do hope and expect that nothing will prevent the whole quota of Pennsylvania from being assembled at the appointed place & time; after which you will remain on that ground not a moment longer than is necessary—At all events you must be in motion from thence on, or before the 10th. of September for the delaying beyond that period, even for one day, might create difficulties & embarrassments that would not be easily got over, if it did not render the expedition altogether abortive—I have mentioned the 10th. as the utmost period, but you are by no means to delay it to that time, if the different detachments are sooner arrived. Should it happen that any of them are not got up when you move leave directions for them to follow you with all possible expedition to Fort Washington without halting at Muskingum.

You will be sure to take the necessary measures for the security of your camp while you remain at the rendezvous, and on your way down the river possibly you may see no indians, or none that are hostile, but a surprise is ever to be guarded against, so that you will never encamp without establishing proper guards & patroles—nor even go ashore, for ever so short a time without the same precaution.

You will please to observe that many of the friendly indians, with whom the United States are engaged by treaty, may be in the neighbourhood of McMahen's creek, and that they have a right to hunt in that country—It is of great consequence that no injury be done to any of them, both for the sake of public faith, which has been pledged to them, and to keep them detached from those who are inimical—You will therefore impress the necessity of treating those indians with kindness should any of them be met, with upon the minds of the people under your command in the most forceable manner—indeed the success of the expedition in some measure depends upon it. They are the Wyandots and Delawares, if you see any of them assure them no harm is intended them, if they continue in peace.

(signed)   AR. ST. CLAIR

No.

The Govr. of the western territory, to the secretary of War

Marietta, 19th. Sepr. 1790

"The depredations on the Ohio and the Ouabache still continue—every day almost brings an account of some murder or robbery and yesterday a number of horses were taken from this settlement—not long ago a boat belonging to Mr. Vigo, a gentleman of post St. Vincennes was fired upon near the mouth of Blue river; this person the United States have been very much obliged to on many occasions and is in truth the most disinterested person I have almost ever seen—he had three men killed and was obliged in consequence to fall down the river—This party it seems had been designed to intercept me, for they reported that they had had three fair discharges at the governor's boat, and expected that they had killed him—in defending the river Mr. Vigo's boat fell in with Mr. Melchor's returning from Tennessee and attempted in company with him to ascend the Ouabache—here they were attacked again—Melchor escaped and fell down, it seems, to the Ance de la Graise, but the savages possessed themselves of Vigo's boat, which they plundered of all his and the crews personal baggage and arms, but as she was navigated by frenchmen they suffered them to depart with the peltries, telling them that if she had not been in company with Americans they would not have injured them, and that if they found them in such again they would put them to death—Captain McCurdy likewise was fired upon between Fort Washington and this place and had five or six men killed & wounded.

I am directed to write to the commanding officer at Detroit—I have enclosed a copy of that letter."

Govr. St. Clair to the commanding officer of Detroit

Marietta, 19th. Septemr. 1790

Sir

As it is not improbable that an account of the military preparations going forward in this quarter of the country may reach you, and give you some uneasiness while the object to which they are to be directed is not perfectly known to you: I am commanded by the President of the United States to give you the fullest assurances of the pacific disposition entertained towards Great Britain and all her possessions, and to inform you explicitly that the expedition about to be undertaken is not intended against the post you have the honor to command nor any other place at present in the possession of the troops of his britannic majesty, but is on foot with the sole design of humbling and chastising some of the savage tribes whose depredations are become intolerable, and whose cruelties have of late become an outrage not on the people of America only but on humanity, which I now do in the most unequivocal manner. After this candid explanation Sir, there is every reason to expect both from your own personal character and from the regard you have for that of your nation, that those tribes will meet with neither countenance nor assistance from any under your command, and that you will do what in your power lies to restrain the trading people, from whose instigations, there is too good reason to belive, much of the injuries committed by the savages has proceeded. I have forwarded this letter by a private gentleman in preference to that of an officer, by whom you might have expected a communication of this kind, that every suspicion of the purity of the views of the United States might be obviated."

No.
Govr. St. Clair to the secrey. of War

Fort Washington, 9th Octor. 1790
"On the 23d. ultimo I arrived at this place, and found every thing in a better state of preparation than I had flattered myself with, owing to the prudent care and attention of general Harmar and the indefatigable application of captain Ferguson—The militia that had been ordered from Kentuckey appeared on the day appointed, all except one hundred and forty, who have since come forward, and marched to join the army—Major Wyllis with the troops from the Falls got up on the 22d. and Major Doughty with part of the garrison of Fort Harmar arrived on the 25th.—From the failure on the part of Pennsylvania, the corps would have been rather too weak, and general Harmar was of opinion with me that it would be proper to ask for a reinforcement from Kentuckey and in Virtue of the powers granted to me by the President, I immediately called for five hundred from the counties Fayette & Woodford, which were the nearest and also the most populous, and requested that, if it could be done they might all be mounted; but as the other militia had been for some time here, and were beginning to grow impatient, it was thought best not to wait for the arrival of the reinforcement, and accordingly the corps, under the immediate command of Colonel Harding was put in motion on the 27th. with orders to advance about twenty miles, and to open a road from their camp to this place, for the passage of the artillery. By the accounts we have of the country, after the first twenty miles are passed, it becomes

level, and so thinly covered with wood that there will be little occasion to open roads. On the 30th. General Harmar moved with the troops, three pieces of artillery and the provisions for the campaign; the cattle and horses for the transportation of the flour having arrived in due season. On the 2d. instant Mr. Frothingham arrived with the remainder of the garrison of Fort Harmar, and proceeded to join the army on the third.

I have not heard from General Harmar since his second days march—the country was then hilly and difficult for the artillery, but some persons who had been viewing the country came in two days ago, who confirm the account of its very soon becoming level & open—they fell in upon the trace of the army, about seven miles from Mudriver and returned upon it—In that distance there had been occasion to make only one very small causeway with logs. They must be up with Chilicothay before now; and if they have not been opposed there, which I do not expect, as it is situated in a plain prairie; the Indians will be found assembled at the Miami village. Major Hamtramck had orders from general Harmar to move on the 25th. of the last month; and the militia would join him in time for him to comply with the orders within a day or two at farthest. The intelligence I receive shall be communicated from time to time by every opportunity, and by express, if any thing occurs of sufficient importance.

The little army moved in high spirits, and have had excellent weather ever since, one days rain excepted."

No.

Messrs. Elliot & Williams, contractors—
to the secretary of War

14th. Octor. 1790

"In consequence of orders received from general Harmar, dated the 15th. July, which we engaged to comply with by the first of October; We have before the 18th of September, furnished and equipped for the use of the army in the intended expedition against the savages, One hundred and eighty thousand rations of flour, two hundred thousand rations of meat, Eight hundred and sixty eight pack, and artillery horses, equipped with pack saddles, bags, ropes &c. and one horse master general, eighteen horse masters, one hundred & thirty pack horse drivers, all of which could not have been done upon so short a notice as we have had, if we had not have employed all our funds and pledged our credit to the extent, to the people of the western country where the supplies were principally furnished. The expedition we trust; cannot fail from any default of ours, for we have forwarded supplies in greater quantities than were required of us; and even more than our most sanguine expectations at the commencement of the business encouraged us to promise."

Extracted from letters and papers on file in the War office of the United States.

H. KNOX

War Office, 7th. Decemr. 1790   secy. of War

Instructions to the Governor of the Western territory and to the Commanding officer of the troops on the Ohio. and an Estimate of the expence of an expedition against the Wabash indians

Instructions from the President of the United States to Governor St. Clair

6th. Octor. 1789

To Arthur St. Clair Esqe. Governor of the territory of the United States, Northwest of the Ohio, and Superintendant of Indian Affairs for the Northern District

Sir,

Congress having by their Act of the 29th. of September last empowered me to call forth the Militia of the States respectively, for the protection of the frontiers from the incursions of the hostile Indians, I have thought proper to make this communication to you, together with the instructions herein contained.

It is highly necessary that I should as soon as possible possess full information whether the Wabash, and Illoinais indians are most inclined for War or Peace—If for the former it is proper that I should be informed of the means which will most probably induce them to peace—If a peace can be established with the said Indians on reasonable terms, the interests of the United States dictate that it should be effected as soon as possible.

You will therefore inform the said indians of the dispositions of the general Government on this subject, and of their reasonable desire that there should be a cessation of hostilities as a prelude to a treaty—If however notwithstanding your intimations to them they should continue their hostilities, or meditate any incursions against the frontiers of Virginia and Pennsylvania, or against any of the troops or Posts of the United States, and it should appear to you that the time of execution would be so near as to forbid your transmitting the information to me, and receiving my further orders thereon, then you are hereby authorised and empowered in my name to call on the Lieutenants of the nearest Counties of Virginia and Pennsylvania for such detachments of Militia as you may judge proper, not exceeding however one thousand from Virginia and five hundred from Pennsylvania.

I have directed Letters to be written to the Executives of Virginia and Pennsylvania, informing them of the before recited Act of Congress and that I have given you these conditional directions, so that there may not be any obstructions to such measures as shall be necessary to be taken by you for calling forth the Militia agreeably to the instructions herein contained.

The said Militia to act in conjunction with the federal troops in such Operations, offensive or defensive, as you and the commanding Officer of the troops conjointly shall judge necessary for the public service, and the protection of the inhabitants and the Posts.

The said Militia while in actual service to be on the Continental establishment of pay and rations—they are to arm and equip themselves, but to be furnished with public ammunition if necessary—and no charge for the pay of said Militia will be valid unless supported by regular musters made by a field or other Officer of the federal troops to be appointed by the Commanding Officer of the troops.

I would have it observed forcibly that a War with the Wabash indians ought to be avoided by all means consistently with the security of the frontier inhabitants, the security of the troops and the national dignity—In the exercise of the present indiscriminate hostilities, it is extremely difficult if not impossible to say that a War without further measures would be just on the part of the United States.

But if after manifesting clearly to the Indians the dispositions of the general Government for the preservation of Peace, and the extension of a just protection to the said Indians, they should continue their incursions, the United States will be constrained to punish them with severity.

You will also proceed as soon as you can with safety to execute the orders of the late Congress, respecting the Inhabitants at St. Vincennes, and at the Kaskaskies, and the other Villages on the Mississippi—It is a circumstance of some importance that the said inhabitants should as soon as possible possess the lands to which they are entitled by some known and fixed principles.

I have directed a number of Copies of the Treaty made by you at Fort Harmar with the Wyandots &c. on the 9th. of January last to be printed and forwarded to you, together with the ratification, and my Proclamation enjoining the observance thereof.

As it may be of high importance to obtain a precise and accurate knowledge of the several Waters which empty into the Ohio on the North West—and of those which discharge themselves into the lakes Erie and Michigan; the length of the Portages between, and nature of the ground, an early and pointed attention thereto is earnestly recommended.

Given under my hand in the City of New York, this 6th day of October, in the Year of our Lord One thousand seven hundred and Eighty nine, and in the thirteenth year of the Sovereignty & Independence of the United States.

Secry. of War to Genl. Harmar

7th June 1790

"The information contained in your Letter of the 24th of March last, relative to the depredations of the Indians is corroborated by several other Letters, with considerable additions. The reports of these several events have excited much disquietude in the Public mind generally, and more particularly in all men whose views or interests are westward.

A Letter from Judge Symmes dated at Lexington the 30th of April last mentions that you, with some Continental troops, and General Scott with some Volunteers from Kentucky, had made an expedition up the Ohio against the Indians, at or near the Sciota, who had annoyed the Boats in descending the Ohio, but without any considerable effect, having killed only four Indians.

The recent hostilities, according to the information, seems to have been committed by the remnants of the Shawanese, and the banditti from several tribes associated with them. Although the said Shawanese and banditti aggregately may not amount at the excess to two hundred fighting men, yet they seem sufficient to alarm the whole frontier lying along the Ohio; and in a considerable degree injure the reputation of the Government.

To extend a defensive and efficient protection to so extensive a frontier, against solitary, or small parties of enterprizing savages, seems altogether impossible. No other remedy remains but to extirpate utterly, if possible; the said banditti.

The President of the United States, therefore directs that you and the Governor of the Western territory consult together, upon the most practicable mode of effecting this object, in such manner as not to interfere with any treaties he may be about forming with any of the regular tribes of Indians on the Wabash.

At this distance, and under the information received, it would seem that an expedition of the nature herein described, might if conducted with great address and rapidity be attended with the desired effect.

The troops to be employed on this occasion, to be composed of one hundred Continental, and three hundred Militia, non-commissioned Officers and Privates, all picked men and properly Officered.

The Militia to be drawn from the nearest Counties of Kentucky—to rendezvous at Fort Washington or the mouth of the great Miami, or such other place as you may judge more proper—to be engaged for thirty days from their arrival at the rendezvous.

The Continental troops and Militia to be mounted on Horseback, and if in the judgment of the Governor and yourself that mode of transportation, would most probably ensure success, and horses could be obtained in a reasonable distance.

The Militia to be on Continental pay, according to the establishment, passed the 30th. of April last; and rations from the time of their arrival at the place of rendezvous.

A continental Officer to muster and inspect the Militia on their arrival, and none to be inserted in the pay abstracts, which must be certified by you unless so mustered—The Militia to find their own Arms and Accoutrements, but to be furnished by the Public, with ammunition if necessary.

The Militia Officers, non-commissioned Officers and Privates to be allowed for the hire and risque of their horses and horse accoutrements, such a sum per day as the Governor and you shall certify that the nature of the service required; provided however such sum shall not exceed half a dollar per day.

The horses to be hired for continental troops to be on the same terms or less, in proportion to the risque of the horses, which perhaps ought to be on account of the United States, according to the value of the Horses, which in that case ought to be appraized.

It is presumed that each horse besides the Rider ought to carry thirty days bread and pork or bacon, and about a bushel of Corn, or one quart per day, as fodder for the horses.

The Shawanese and banditti associated with them, are said to reside on the eastern branches of the Wabash river towards its head—I have learned from Major Doughty and Captain Ferguson that the Wabash has a more easterly course, than is laid down in Hutchin's Map. If this be so, the distance from the mouth of the great Miami Over, cannot greatly exceed the distance from the rapids over to Post St. Vincennes—But suppose the distance should be one Hundred and thirty or forty miles, it could be marched on horseback, in four days at furthest.

It would be unnecessary to enter into any further details—To the judgement of the Governor and you, the expedition may justly be confided—efficacy and the peace of the frontiers are the great objects, with these are to be blended due economy—But all future depredations of the Indians from the south west of the Ohio, in considerable numbers, must if possible be prevented—and for this purpose the orders now given, or even an extension of them, one or two hundred men must be considered as a standing order, until the object of extirpating the murderous banditti before mentioned be effected.

It is however strongly to be observed, that the highest precautions must be taken in all incursions into the indian country, that the friendly or even neutral tribes be uninjured—but that the strongest assurances be given to such tribes of the pacific and just dispositions of the United States, and at the same time of their firm intentions of inflicting severe punishment upon all those of a contrary nature.

Although these orders are to be considered as addressed conjointly to the Governor and yourself, yet in case of his absence, and a conviction in your own mind, that an expedition of the before mentioned description would not interfere or impede his negociations; you are to undertake it as if he were present."

Estimate of Expenses of the Expedition

The Secretary of War to the
Secretary of the Treasury

23d August 1790

"An estimate of the expence of employing, for three months, one thousand seven hundred Militia, and four hundred Continental troops, in an expedition against the Wabash indians—two hundred of the Militia to be mounted.

The Militia

The Pay	24,012	
The Subsistence & Rations @ $16/_{90}$ of a Dollar	31,302	
Forage for the field & staff Officers	234	55,548

The Continental Troops

Additional expence of subsistence & Rations to the continental troops during the same period. This expence arises from the contract—the Price of the Ration at Fort Washington is stated at six $1/_2$ ninetieths of a Dollar; But from that Post to the places of operation the price will be sixteen ninetieths   4,146

The Quarter Master's department, including the

hire of four hundred horses, purchase of Boats and

transportation	30,000
Contingencies	10,306
Dollars	100,000

The Contractors are to execute the duties of the Quarter Masters department, the extra services therefore, which will be required of them, independent of the sums set down for contingencies will amount to sixty five thousand, six hundred and eighty two dollars. One half of this sum may be
necessary to be advanced immediately, to enable them to perform effectually
the services required."

Additional Letters from the Secretary of War

The Secretary of War to
Govr. St. Clair

Augt. 23. 1790

"I have submitted to the President of the United States, your Letter of this
date, and the Papers therein referred to, containing the reasons on which you
have founded the proposed operation against the Wabash Indians.

While the President regrets exceedingly the occasion, he approves the
measures you have taken for preventing those predatory incursions of the
Wabash indians, which for a considerable period past have been so calamitous
to the frontiers lying along the Ohio.

The offers of peace which have been made upon principles of justice and
humanity to the Wabash indians, and refused, will fully justify the conduct
of the United States in the operations which have been directed, for the
prevention of future murders and robberies.

It is the earnest desire of the President that the operation should be
effectual, and produce in the Indians proper dispositions for Peace. He therefore confides in your Judgment and abilities, as being perfectly acquainted
with the force of the Indians, the nature of the operation, and all the circumstances of the case, whether any further force shall be added to that already
ordered. If upon due deliberation you should be of opinion that the force you
have directed should be inadequate to the end proposed, and that an additional number of Militia should be requisite he consents to the measure, and
hereby authorises you for that purpose.

In this case the additional number of Militia should be taken from the frontier counties of Virginia, on account of their vicinity to Fort Washington, the place of rendezvous.

And if you should be of the judgement that two hundred of the Militia should be mounted on Horseback, he also consents to such arrangement, under the regulations prescribed in my Letter to Brigadier General Harmar of the 7th. day of last June.

It may not however be improper to observe, in all the arrangements for the expedition, that while energy is the first principle to be observed, that it must be blended with a just economy.

There are existing Jealousies in the minds of the British Officers, in Canada, of the designs of the United States respecting the posts to have been relinquished by the last peace—It will be a point therefore of delicacy that you should take measures by sending some Officer or Messenger at a proper time, to assure the commanding Officer of the real object of the expedition— That the Shawanese and some others joined with them have committed such enormous offences against the Citizens of the United States as are any longer insupportable, but to assure him of the entire pacific dispositions of the United States towards Great Britain and its possessions.

You will also find it at some certain moment highly proper to inform the Indians with whom you have formed treaties, of your pacific dispositions towards them.

And it may also be proper under certain circumstances of humiliation of the Indians, to conclude with them treaties of peace, provided it can be done on proper security of their good behaviour, and consistently with the dignity and interest of the United States.

The President has directed me to observe that many important circumstances concur to press, that the operation should commence immediately after the assembling of the Militia—And as the main force will march from Fort Washington, it is his opinion, as far as an opinion can be formed from the Maps, that the march of the Troops from that Post should commence two or three days previous to those from Post Vincennes.

The Militia employed must be mustered previously to their march, and on their return before they are discharged, by a field Officer of the Continental troops agreeably to your instructions from the President dated the 5th of October 1789, and to Brigr. General Harmar dated the 7th of June last.

I have made an estimate for the object of the expedition and transmitted it to the Secretary of the Treasury, and I have requested him to advance a sum of Money to the Contractors in order to enable them to furnish the requisite supplies of Provision and Articles in the Quarter Masters Department.

I have also written to Mr. Hodgden, Commissary of Military Stores in Philadelphia to forward immediately by the way of Red stone and wheeling two tons of best Rifle and Musket Powder, four tons leaden bullets—Cartridge Paper—Case shot for 5 1/2 inch Howitzers and for three and six pounders.

I have written to Lieut. Ernest at Fort Pitt, directing him to repair to Red stone in order to receive said Stores, and to have them transported down the Monongahalia, by water, to Fort Harmar, or to Wheeling by land, and thence to Fort Harmar, as he shall find most convenient."

The Secrey. of War to Bridgr. Genl. Harmar

24th Augt. 1790

"I now acknowledge the receipt of your Letter of the 15 of last month by Governor St. Clair, who has stated to me the plan of the proposed expedition against the indians, and the same has been submitted to the President of the United States, who has approved thereof.

My Letter to the Governor of yesterday, which he will communicate to you, contains some circumstances which may not be necessary to repeat.

The expedition you are about to undertake is not only of great importance in itself, but it may be attended with extensive and remote consequences— Every consideration therefore of a public nature, as well as personal to yourself, require that it should be conducted in the most perfect manner, that there should not be any omissions, but all just arrangements made to produce a due execution of every Plan & order.

A knowledge of your enemy's strength, situation & designs must be essential to your success, you will therefore make the best arrangements for obtaining intelligence.

While on the one hand your movements and execution should be so rapid & decisive as to astonish your enemy, so on the other, every possible precaution in the power of human foresight should be used to prevent surprize. To enter into the details of the measures you ought to take to effect the former, or prevent the latter, would be to attempt to preclude the exercise of your abilities. The President of the United States is impressed with the conviction that you are aware of the importance of your command, and that you will endeavour to make the best arrangements to ensure success, and particularly that you will avail yourself on all occasions of the mature experience & judgment of Governor St. Clair.

I have agreeably to Major Doughty's report directed Mr. Hodgden to forward two tons of the best rifle & musket Powder, lead in proportion, cartridge-Paper, flints and the medicines you wrote for, the capital articles of which are doubled.

I have transmitted you by Governor St. Clair one thousand Dollars for contingent money, for which you will forward me triplicate receipts.

As it is probable that most of the Militia may be armed with rifles, which are certainly not good arms in a close fight, it may perhaps be proper for you to attempt to persuade some of them to arm themselves with the spare muskets, you have in store.

P. S. It will be necessary that you communicate the time of your setting out, the number of your command, the progress and termination of the expedition, and the various events proper for the President to know."

Secry. of War to the Governor of Virginia

2d Septr. 1790

"Governor St. Clair has in Person laid before the President the plan of the proposed operation, against the Wabash indians, which has been approved.

It being the anxious desire of the President that the expedition should be effectual and not require a repetition, all the arrangements are made to accomplish so desirable an end. For this purpose Govr. St. Clair has been further empowered to require if necessary an additional number of Men—If therefore there are any measures necessary to be taken by your Excellency and the Council in order to facilitate an additional number of men, the President of the United States hopes that they will be expedited with all possible dispatch.

It has been suggested that the expedition may be liable to miscarriage from a jealousy of the militia and regular troops. It is devoutly to be wished that such suggestion may be entirely unfounded. But if jealousies should exist it would be highly important that they should be entirely removed or suspended during the season of activity. I shall write particularly on this point to Governor St. Clair and to Brigadier Genl. Harmar to adopt the most conciliatory conduct.

It has also been mentioned as a circumstance of considerable importance to the success of the expedition that Colonels Logan and Selby should be induced to accompany the Militia on the expedition even as Volunteers, great confidence being placed in the character of these Gentlemen. Could your Excellency therefore influence those Gentlemen to go forth on this occasion, it would be highly acceptable and might tend greatly to the accomplishment of the public good—The expence of the expedition will be great, and if it should fail by any circumstances whatever, the public injury and disappointment will be in proportion.

It is thought proper for particular and political reasons to give the expedition the appearance of being levelled only at the Shawanese."

Secrey. of War to Messrs. Elliot & Williams at Baltimore

3d Septemr. 1790

"Your friend Colonel Samuel Smith has been here, and has made such arrangements with the Secretary of the Treasury respecting advances as are entirely satisfactory to him. You will therefore not find yourselves any ways restrained in your preparations for want of pecuniary assistance.

I am persuaded that you will endeavour by every possible exertion, to make adequate preparations both in the Commissary & Quarter Master's line for the proposed expedition.

On your making adequate and seasonable supplies the whole success of the expedition may depend. You will see therefore the urgent necessity of every thing being in perfect readiness."

The Secretary of War to Govr. St. Clair

Septemr. 12th. 1790

"I have not been unmindful of the suggestion you made at the moment of your departure from this City relative to the establishment of a Post at the Miami Village, in the event of the proposed expeditions succeeding in a certain degree—I have had a full communication on the subject with the President of the United States, to whom you had previously made the same suggestion, and the following ideas are the result thereof, and will serve for the direction of yourself and Brigadier General Harmar on the occasion.

In contemplating the establishment of Military Posts North-west of the Ohio, to answer the purposes of awing the Indians residing on the Wabash, the west end of lake Erie, St. Josephs and the Illinois, as much as Indians can be awed by Posts, and at the same time exhibiting a respectable appearance to the British troops at Detroit and Niagara, the Miami Village presents itself as superior to any other position, excepting the actual possession of the Posts on the lakes which ought to have been given up conformably to the treaty of peace—this opinion was given to me by the President in the year 1789, and has several times been held forth by me to Brigadier General Harmar.

But at the same time it must be acknowledged, that the measure would involve a much larger military establishment than perhaps the value of the object or the dispositions of the United States would justify and that it would be so opposed to the inclinations of the Indians generally, even with the tribes with whom we have made treaties, as to bring on inevitably an Indian War of some duration—In addition to which, it may be supposed that the British Garrisons would find themselves so uneasy with such a force impending over them as not only to occasion a considerable reinforcement of their upper

Posts, but to occasion their fomenting, secretly at least, the opposition of the Indians.

The proposed expedition is intended, to exhibit to the Wabash Indians our power to punish them for their hostile depredations, for their conniving at the depredations of others, and for their refusing to treat with the United States when invited thereto. This power will be demonstrated by a sudden stroke, by which their Towns and Crops may be destroyed. The principal means used will be the Militia.

Let us suppose the expedition to be successful, as I pray God it may, and let us estimate the force which would be fully required for establishing a Post at the Miami Village.

From the mode of Indian fighting, it will not be reasonable to conclude that their force will be greatly reduced, in the skirmishes they may have with Brigadier General Harmar, or Major Hamtramck. If therefore eleven hundred Warriors, according to your judgment delivered to me, could be brought into activity from the Wabash and its vicinity, to which may be added a much greater number, if we should suppose that the Wyandot—Delaware—St. Joseph's and Illinois Indians should be combined with them. The Post to be established ought not to have a less garrison than 750 men—Were it inferior to this number it would always be liable to be invested and to have its supplies cut off, even when arrived in its vicinity. Whether the Posts of communication, essentially necessary to the existence of the Miami Post should be up the Wabash, up the Miami of the Ohio, or the Miami of Lake Erie, they would require at different places at least 500 men.

To establish the Post in the first instance so as to render it superior to the Indian force in the neighbourhood, would require all the troops employed on the expedition, to wit: 2,000. For if a sudden stroke by which the attention and force of the Indians should be divided would require that number, the notoriety of establishing a Post and erecting fortifications at the Miami Village in the heart of the Indian Country, would require the same or a superior number—as the Indians would then have one object of their attention and exertion.

To complete the works at the Post, and the essential communications to it would require probably two Months—Would the Militia stay for that period? If so, would a part of them remain in Garrison afterwards for six months, for the four hundred Continental troops to be employed on the expedition would be *utterly* inadequate for all the services required.

Besides the Post could not be established unless it had a number of pieces of Cannon, and a proper quantity of stores, and also three months provision in the first instance—The transportation of these Articles would require considerable time and a great Apparatus.

It might be added further—That altho' the establishment of a strong Post at the Miami Village would awe the Indians, yet experience has demonstrated that Posts will not prevent the depredations of small parties against the frontiers.

To render the measure entirely effectual, and at the same time to guard the public lands from intrusion, the regular force to be employed North-West of the Ohio, ought to be increased to 1,800 men—This establishment would not be compatible either with the public views or the Public finances, unless it should result from mere necessity—A due consideration therefore of these several circumstances, renders the measure at this period inexpedient and therefore not to be undertaken.

The expedition will either incline the Indians to treat of Peace, or it will induce them to wage open war in the ensuing Spring. A further time is also required to know the intentions of the British Court respecting the delivery of Niagara & Detroit. The decision of this point, has an intimate connection with the peace of the frontiers.

The ultimate determination of Government must therefore depend on the result of the arrangements which have been directed, and which are in operation. It would not be wise to direct a measure, which would give a wrong bias to Affairs.

The President will be exceedingly desirous to learn the measures taken by yourself and Bridgadier General Harmar; from time to time, and above all he is exceedingly anxious that every arrangement should be made to render the proposed expedition entirely effectual."

Secrey. of War to Genl. Harmar

14 Septemr. 1790

"The expence of the proposed expedition will be great. But I have that confidence in your economical arrangements that you will not order more Pack-horses than shall be absolutely necessary consistent with efficacy. The Pack-horses for provisions, will be at the Contractors expence—It is true they will have an additional price for the Rations—But as you will not take Tents and in all other respects will be unincumbered and as light as possible, I do not conceive that you will want Pack horses for other objects than your Provisions. I have written to the Governor by this conveyance, respecting the Miami Village, which will be considered as a joint Letter. The President of the United States will be anxious to hear of the arrangements and success."

The Secretary of War to Genl. Harmar

3d Sepr. 1790

"Since the departure of Governor St. Clair I have been informed that there may be an aversion in the minds of the Militia to act with the regular troops. If this should really be the case, and any jealousies should arise to impede the success of the expedition, it would indeed be an unfortunate circumstance. Every precaution therefore should be taken by the Governor and yourself either to remove such dispositions if existing, or to prevent them arising among the Militia.

It has been suggested that could Cols. Logan & Selby of Kentucky, be induced to accompany the expedition as Volunteers, that they would have a powerful influence over the conduct of the Militia—I therefore submit the idea, that the Governor and you invite those characters to accompany you in the expedition, and that you treat them with the greatest cordiality."

Copies   H. KNOX secy. of War

War department 9 Decr. 1790

Reports and Communications from the Secretary of War, HR, DNA. The manuscript, in the hand of a war department clerk, was signed by Henry Knox.

Official Communications relative to the Expedition against the Indians North-west of the Ohio December 14, 1790

War-department, Decr. 14th. 1790

Sir.

Lieutenant Denny arrived last evening from Fort Washington, on the Ohio, charged with letters from Governor St. Clair and Brigadier General Harmar, copies of which I have the honor herewith to submit, and also extracts from the orders issued during the late expedition, also a return of the killed and wounded.

Lieutenant Denny reports verbally that after he left Fort Washington, he saw in Kentucky several men of the militia of that district, who had been out with Major Whitly under Major Hamtramck of the federal troops, who commanded a seperate expedition.

The said militia men informed Lieut. Denny, that Major Hamtramck had destroyed several of the hostile Indian towns on the Wabash, and had returned to his garrison at post Vincennes without having met any opposition.

I have the honor to be,
with the highest respect,
Sir,
Your most obedt. Servt.

The President   H. KNOX
of the United States   secy. of War

Govr. St. Clair to The Secy. of War

Fort Washington, Novr. 6th. 1790

"Sir—

On the 29th of last month,[1] I had the honor to inform you generally of the success that had attended General Harmar. I could not then give you the particulars as the General's letters had not reached me (the officer however who had them in charge got in a few days afterwards) it is not now necessary because he writes himself—One thing however is certain that the Savages have got a most terrible stroke, of which nothing can be a greater proof than that they have not attempted to harrass the army on its return—They arrived at this place on the 3rd. instant in good health & spirits—There is not yet any account from Major Hamtramck—I trust he also has been successful, but this I think is certain, that no great misfortune can have happened to him, for in that case we should certainly have heard of it.

Mr. Denny, the gentleman, who takes General Harmar's dispatches, I beg leave to mention to you in a particular manner, and if you will be pleased to do so to the President in his favor you may be assured he will not disappoint any expectations that may be formed—He has every quality that I could wish a young man to possess that meant to make the army his profession—There are however some traits in his character as a man that are not generally known, that would endear him—Out of the little pittance he receives he has maintained two aged parents for a long time."

Brigr. Genl. Harmar to The Secretary of War

Head Quarters, Fort Washington,
Nov. 4th 1790

"Sir

I have the honor to inform you, that on the 30th September, I marched with 320 federal troops, and 1,133 militia, total 1,453—After encountering a few difficulties, we gained the Miami village. It was abandoned before we entered it, which I was very sorry for—The villainous traders would have been a principal object of attention. I beg leave to refer you to my orders which are enclosed—The substance of the work is this—our loss was heavy, but the Head Quarters of iniquity were broken up—At a moderate computation not less than 100, or 120 Warriors were slain and 300 log-houses and Wigwam burned—Our loss about 180—The remainder of the indians will be ill off for sustenance 20,000 bushels of Corn in the ears was consumed, burned and destroyed by the army with vegetables in abundance—The loss of Major Wyllys and Lieutenant Frothingham of the federal troops, and a number of valuable militia officers I sincerely lament.

---

[1] The notation, "Note, the letter of the 29th of October has not been received," in the hand of Henry Knox, appears in the left hand margin of the document.

The bearer Lieut. Denny is my Adjutant. It will afford me great satisfaction to know that some mark of honor will be shewn to him. His long & faithful services merit it. There is a vast deal of business in this Western world—If there is no impropriety in giving me an Aid-de-Camp, I wish him to be the person.

In my next dispatches I shall enter into the minutiae of business, and give you a particular description of each day's march, with all the occurrences & observations.

N.B. My Adjutant is really & truly an officer."

Extracts from the orders

Note

The orders issued previously to the march of the troops and militia from Fort Washington and until they arrived at the Miami village relate to the arrangement of the troops, the order of march, of encampment, and of battle, and the discipline necessary to be observed, all of which are particularly detailed.

General Orders

"Camp at the Miami village, about 170 miles from Fort Washington— October 17th. 1790.

The general is highly pleased with the zeal and alacrity shewn by the army (particularly the corps which was detached under the command of Colonel Hardin) to come up with the savages, altho' it was impracticable, as they had evacuated their favorite towns before the Light corps could possibly reach them.

Leaving behind them such a vast quantity of corn & vegetables, is a certain sign that they decamped in the utmost consternation, and dare not face the army.

The army is to remain in its present position until further orders, in the mean time Quarter Master Pratt is to have the corn brought in and deposited in one place or in as many houses as he can find, and a guard is to be placed over it for its security. He will receive directions how it is to be distributed.

The superintendant of the Horse department (Mr. Caldwell) is to be responsible that his pack saddles are repaired, and put in as good order as possible, ready for the next movement of the army.

The General calls upon the commanding officers of battalions not to suffer their men to straggle from the encampment, otherwise they will certainly stand in danger of being scalped.

The guards are to be extremely vigilant, to which the field officer of the day is to pay the most pointed attentions.

A detachment under the command of Lieut. Col. Commdt. Trotter consisting of.

Federal troops	30
Major Fontaine's light corps	40
Active rifle men	230
Total	300

are to march to morrow early.

Lieut. Col. Commdt. Trotter will receive his orders from the general."

Jos. Harmar
Brigr. Genl.

General Orders

"Camp at the Miami Village, October 18th. 1790.

The General is much mortified at the unsoldierlike behaviour of many of the men in the army, who make it a practice to straggle from the camp in search of plunder. He in the most positive terms forbids this practice in future and the guards will be answerable to prevent it—no party is to go beyond the line of centinels without a commissioned officer, who if of the militia, will apply to Colonel Hardin for his orders—The regular troops will apply to the general—All the plunder that may be hereafter collected will be equally distributed amongst the army, the kettles and every other article already taken is to be collected by the commanding officers of Battalions and to be delivered to morrow morning to Mr. Belli, the Quarter Master that a fair distribution may take place.

The rolls are to be called a troop & retreat beating and every man absent is to be reported. The general expects that these orders will be pointedly attended to, they are to be read to the troops this evening.

The army is to march to morrow morning early for their new encampment at Chilicothy about two miles from hence."

Jos. Harmar
Brigr. Genl.

General Orders

"Camp at Chilicothy one of the Shawanoe towns on the Omee river
October 20th. 1790

The party under command of Capn. Strong is ordered to burn & destroy every house & wigwam in this village, together with all the corn &c., which he can collect.

A party of 100 men (militia) properly officered under the command of

Colonel Hardin is to burn & destroy effectually, this afternoon the Pickaway town with all the corn &c. which he can find in it and its vicinity.

The cause of the detachment being worsted yesterday was entirely owing to the shameful cowardly conduct of the militia who ran away & threw down their arms without firing scarcely a single gun. In returning to Fort Washington if any officer or men shall presume to quit their ranks or not march in the form that they are ordered, the general will most assuredly order the artillery to fire on them. He hopes the check they received yesterday will make them in future obedient to orders."

(signed)   Jos. Harmar
Brigr. Genl.

General Orders

"Camp at Chilicothy, October 21st. 1790.

The army having completely effected the object for which they were ordered, vizt. a total destruction of the Maumee Towns as they are generally called, with the vast abundance of corn & vegetables &c. in them and their vicinity, are now to commence their march and to return to Fort Washington.

The general was in fond hopes that he should be able to break up the Weea towns on his return, but the reduced state of the pack horses, and several other circumstance conspire to render it impracticable at present.

The General is to beat at nine, the assembly at half past nine and the whole army to take up the line of march precisely at ten this morning.

It is not improbable but the savages will attempt to harrass the army on its return, particularly the rear & flanks, it is therefore incumbent upon every officer to attend to the duties of his station and by no means to quit their ranks or create the least confusion, but on the contrary to keep silence and good order otherwise the artillery (agreably to the orders of yesterday) shall certainly be ordered to fire upon such men as are so lost to every principal of honor as to run away in the time of danger.

The cattle & pack horses are to be kept up in the most compact order and the officer commanding the rear battalion is to be responsible with the Field officer of the day that these orders are strictley carried into execution. Such horses as Mr. Caldwell may absolutely stand in need of are to be taken from the mounted militia not attached to Major Fontaine's corps for public service, if these should be found insufficient, the remainder must come from Major Fontaine's Corps."

(signed)   Jos. Harmar
Brigr. Genl.

General Orders

"Camp, 8 miles from the ruins of the Maumee Towns on the return to Fort Washington, October 22d. 1790.

The army is to remain at the present encampment until further orders."

After Orders

"The general is exceedingly pleased with the behaviour of the militia in the action of this morning—They have laid very many of the enemy dead upon the spot—Altho' our loss is great, still it is inconsiderable in comparison of the slaughter made amongst the savages. Every account agrees that upwards of One hundred warriors fell in the battle; it is not more than man for man, and we can afford them two for one—The resolution & firm determined conduct of the militia this morning has effectually retrieved their character in the opinion of the general. He now knows that they can & will fight.

The loss of Major Wyllis (with so many of the federal troops) and Major Fontaine two gallant officers, he sincerely & deeply laments, but it is the fortune of War.

The general begs Colonel Hardin & Major Mc. Millan & Major Hall of Lieut. Colonel Commdt. Trotter's regiment, together with the officers and privates of the militia under their command to accept his thanks for the bravery displayed by them upon this occasion.

The army is to march to morrow morning at 8 o'Clock precisely."

signed   JOS. HARMAR

Brigr. Genl.

General Orders

"Camp about 24 miles from the ruins of the Maumee Towns on the return to Fort Washington,

October 23d. 1790

The general did not know in time last evening of the good conduct of Brigade Major Ormsby in rallying a party of the militia and firing upon the savages, whereby he destroyed several of them, otherwise he should then have returned him his thanks. He now begs him to accept them for his cool & gallant behaviour at that time.

Altho' the enemy were so sorely galled in the action of yesterday they may still take it into their heads to hover about our encampment. The general therefore orders that the same vigilance & caution which has hitherto taken place with the guards must constantly be observed to which the Field Officer of the day is to pay the strictest attention.

The wounded militia are all to be collected into one place. Doctor Allison

& Doctor Carmichael are to attend them, dress them and give every necessary direction concerning them.

The army is to march to morrow morning at eight o'Clock precisely."

(signed) Jos. HARMAR
Brigr. Genl.[2]

General Orders

"Head Quarters, Fort Washington, 4th. Novr. 1790

The Kentuckey & Pennsylvania militia are to be mustered this afternoon at 2 o'Clock by Captain Zeigler. The order and regularity which the militia observed on their return to the Ohio river, was highly commendable; upon the whole the general is exceedingly pleased with their conduct during the expedition—Notwithstanding our loss was great yet when they reflect that the army in five weeks not only effected the capital object of destroying the Miami Village and the Maumee Towns, as they are generally called, with the vast quantity of corn & vegetables therein, but also killed upwards of one hundred of their warriors, it must afford every man the greatest satisfaction. The militia from Kentuckey are to receive pay until the tenth instant, provisions are to be drawn for them until that time—and to morrow morning they are to march to their respective homes.

The general returns his thanks to every officer and private for their good conduct, and hereby discharges them with honor & reputation. The wounded men are to be left under the care of Doctor Allison and his mates, who will take all possible care of them."

(signed) Jos. HARMAR
Brigr. Genl.

---

[2] The notation, "Note. From the date of the last order of the 23d. of October, until the return of the troops to Fort Washington, the orders exhibit only the common details and business of troops, no enemy having been seen after the action of the 22d of October," appears in the left hand margin of the manuscript. Beginning at "no enemy" the note is in the hand of Henry Knox.

Return of the killed & wounded upon the Expedition
against the Miami Towns under the command
of Brigadier General Harmar
Head Quarters Fort Washington Novembr. 4th. 1790

	killed						wounded				
	Majors	Captains	Lieutenants	Ensigns	Rank & file	Total	Captain	Lieutenants	Ensigns	Rank & file	Total
Federal Troops	1	''	1	''	73	75	''	''	''	3	3
Militia	1	3	2	4	98	108	''	2	1	25	28
Total	2	3	3	4	171	183	''	2	1	28	31

killed
- Major — Wyllys } Federal Troops
- Lieutt. — Frothingham }
- Major — Fontaine
- Captains — Tharp / Scott / McMurtrey
- Lieutents. — Clark / Rogers
- Ensigns — Sweet / Bridges / Higgens / Thielkeld } Militia

wounded
- Lieutt. — Sanders
- Lieutt. — Worley
- Ensign — Arnold

(Signed) E. DENNY
Lieutt. & Adjt. 1st U. S. R.
(Signed) JOS. HARMAR
Brigr. General

Brigadier General Harmar

Reports and Communications from Executive Departments, 1789–1814, Records of the Secretary, SR, DNA. The manuscript, in the hand of a war department clerk, is signed by Henry Knox.

House Resolution
December 15, 1790

RESOLVED, That it is the opinion of this committee, that immediate provision ought to be made for defraying the expenses incurred in the expedition against the Indians north-west of the Ohio.

HJ, p. 633.

Report of the Secretary of War on the Frontiers
with Enclosures
January 24, 1791

The Secretary of War to whom the President of the United States referred the consideration of various papers and information, relative to the frontiers of the United States.

Respectfully reports:

That the frontiers from several causes are at present so critically circumstanced, as to claim an immediate consideration, and such arrangements, as may upon investigation be found indispensibly necessary, for the preservation of good order, and the protection of the inhabitants exposed to the hostilities of certain indian tribes.

That in order to obtain a clear view of the existing circumstances of the frontiers the following summary statement is submitted, and also that a judgement may be formed of the measures necessary to be adopted on the occasion.

That in the first place it may be proper to explain the relative situation of the Government of the United States, with the Choctaw, Chickasaw, and Cherokee nations of indians. It will appear by the journals of the late Congress and the paper herewith submitted marked A No. 1.—that the United States did in November 1785, and in January 1786, form treaties with the Cherokee, Choctaw and Chickasaw nations of indians by which their boundaries were defined.

That the State of Georgia claims the right of pre-emption to nearly all the lands belonging to the said indian nations.

That it will appear by the Act of Legislature of the said state passed the 21st. day of December 1789, a copy of which is herewith submitted marked A. No. 2. that the said Legislature has granted and sold to three private companies its said right of pre-emption to almost the whole of the lands of the Choctaws and Chickasaws, and part of the Cherokees, amounting in all to 15,500,000 Acres.

That although the right of Georgia to the pre-emption of said Lands should be admitted in its full extent, yet it is conceived, that should the said State, or any companies or persons claiming under it, attempt to extinguish the indian claims, unless authorised thereto by the United States, that the measure would be repugnant to the aforesaid treaties, to the Constitution of the United States, and to the law regulating trade and intercourse with the indian tribes.

That the President of the United States, apprehensive that individuals belonging to said companies might from ignorance, or otherwise, pursue a line of conduct derogatory to the United States, caused the said treaties and the law to regulate trade and intercourse with the indian tribes to be published on the 25th. day of August 1790, together with his proclamation requiring all persons to govern themselves accordingly.

But notwithstanding this warning, it appears from the information contained in A. No. 3, that certain persons claiming under the said companies are raising troops for the purpose of establishing, by force, one or more settlements on the Lands belonging to the aforesaid indian nations.

The authority of the United States is thus set at defiance—their faith pledged to the said indians and their constitution and laws violated, and a general indian War excited on principles disgraceful to the government.

But, there is another point of view in which this subject may be placed—It is said, the Spanish Officers stationed on the Mississippi, alarmed at the proposed settlements have decided to prevent them by force—Although the settlements should be made in opposition to the government of the United States, yet the interference of the Spaniards would start a new subject of discussion which merits some consideration.

Hence arises the following question—Is not the general government bound, by the indispensible obligations of its own rights and dignity—by the principles of justice and good faith to the aforesaid indian nations—by the principles of humanity—as it respects the innocent inhabitants of the frontiers who may fall victims to an unjust indian war, to interpose its arm in an effectual manner to prevent the intended settlements?

That in the second place, the protection to be afforded the frontiers during the ensuing year, requires an immediate arrangement.

That it is to be apprehended the late expedition against the Miami indians will not be attended with such consequences as to constrain the said indians to sue for peace—But, on the contrary that their own opinion of their success, and the number of trophies they possess, will probably not only encourage them to a continuance of hostilities, but may be the means of their obtaining considerable assistance from the neighbouring tribes. In addition to which they will probably receive all possible assistance in the power of certain malignant whites, who reside among them.

That it therefore appears from the examination of this subject, to be incumbent on the United States to prepare immediately for another expedition against the Wabash indians with such a decided force as to impress them strongly with the power of the United States.

That the objects of the expedition will in a considerable degree regulate the nature and number of troops to be employed.

That if the measure of establishing a strong fortification and garrison at the Miami village should be decided upon as proper and necessary, a considerable Encrease of the regular force for that and the other objects, mentioned in this report, would be requisite.

That a strong post and garrison at the said Miami village with proper subordinate posts of communications, have always been regarded as but little inferior to the possession of the post at Detroit: But, while there were existing hopes of obtaining the latter, it did not appear proper to incur the expence of an establishment at the former place—These hopes however having vanished for the present, it seems to be a point of real importance to effect an establishment at the Miami Village.

That a post established at the said place as the consequence of a successful expedition, would curb and overawe not only the Wabash indians, but the Ottawas and Chipewas and all others who might be wavering and disposed to join in the War—The said post would more effectually cover the line of frontier along the Ohio, than by a post at any other place whatever.

That it would therefore of consequence afford more full security to the territory of the United States North West of the Ohio—In this point of view it would assist, in the reduction of the National debt, by holding out a security to people, to purchase and settle the public lands—The purchasers of land from the Government will have a right of protection, and there will be no doubt of their claiming it forcibly.

The regular force upon the frontiers seems utterly inadequate for the essential purposes of the United States.

The frontiers, from the North East to the South-West are nearly enclosed by the possessions, garrisons, and claims of two formidable foreign nations, whose interests cannot entirely coincide with those of the United States.

Numerous indian tribes reside in the vicinity, whose hostilities are easily excited by their jealousy of the encroaching settlements and rapid population of the frontiers.

Bold and unprincipled adventurers will arise, from time to time, who in advancing their own scheemes of avarice, or ambition, will be incessantly machinating against the public peace and prosperity.

These several circumstances, and the distance from the seat of Government, require that a wise and vigorous system should be adopted and executed, as well to protect effectually the inhabitants of the frontiers, as to curb the licentious, and prevent the evils of anarchy, and prevent the userpation of the public lands.

But, besides these considerations, it would appear from information, that the State of Georgia is desirous that more troops should be placed on its frontiers—There are at present three Companies in Georgia, and another is raising there. Those four companies amount to one quarter part of the establishment.

The paper marked B. No. 1. will shew the number and stations of the troops at present in service, and the numbers wanting to complete the establishment of one thousand two hundred and sixteen non-commissioned officers and privates.

If the intended settlements upon the Choctaw, Chickasaw and Cherokee lands are to be effectually prevented and the government enabled to place troops upon the Tenassee which would at once awe the Creeks, if turbulent, and thereby comply with the desires of Georgia, and prevent the projected settlement on the Muscle Shoals—And if an establishment should be made at the Miami Village, it would require that the establishment should be augmented so as to form a legionary corps of two thousand, one hundred and twenty eight, non-commissioned and privates.

If this augmentation should take place two modes present themselves by which the object could be effected, both of which, and estimates thereon, are contained in the paper marked B. No. 2. the one amounting to 101,466.40/100 dollars and the other to 98,542.40/100 dollars.

The question which arises on this subject is!

Whether the objects proposed to be accomplished by the troops will fully compensate for the additional expence?

The United States have come into existence as a nation embarrassed with a frontier of immense extent, which is attended with all the peculiar circumstances before enumerated, and even with others which are obvious, but which are unnecessary to recite.

The population of the lands lying on the western waters are encreasing rapidly—The inhabitants request and demand protection—if it be not granted seeds of disgust will be sown—sentiments of separate interests will arise out of their local situation, which will be cherished, either by insiduous domestic or foreign emissaries.

It therefore appears to be an important branch of the administration of the general government, to afford the frontiers all reasonable protection as well in their just rights as against their enemies—And at the same time it is essential to show all lawless adventurers that notwithstanding the distance, government possess the power of preserving peace and good order on the frontiers. It is true oeconomy to regulate events instead of being regulated by them.

But whether the regular establishment be encreased or not, it seems indispensible, that another expedition be made against the Wabash Indians—Affairs cannot remain where they are—Winter imposes peace for the present, but unless the attention of the indians are called to their own Country, they will upon the opening of the spring, spread general desolation on the frontiers by their small parties.

That the said Wabash indians amount to about eleven hundred warriors—to this number may perhaps be added of other more distant indians one thousand.

If this should be the case the army for the Campaign ought to consist of three thousand well arranged troops, in order to be superior to all opposition, and to prevent the trouble and expence of being repeated.

That the reports herewith submitted, marked C. No. 1. will exhibit the species of defensive protection permitted during the last year by the general government—the system directed by the Executive of Virginia during the Month of December 1790, and the plan of a regiment of rangers proposed to be raised on the frontiers to answer the same purpose, and an estimate of the expence thereof.

That in case the said plan of a regiment of rangers should be adopted the same would furnish five hundred non-commissioned and privates for the proposed expedition.

That the other force necessary to complete the number of three thousand might be raised under the term, *levies*—to serve for the expedition, which it is presumed would not exceed four months.

That to induce the men to engage voluntarily for the said object it is respectfully suggested that it might be proper to appoint the best and most popular officers in Kentucky and the frontier Counties to superior commands with delegated authority to appoint their subordinate officers—and the idea is also submitted how far a Bounty of five dollars in money or clothing would be proper.

That the result therefore of the ideas suggested herein and in the report marked C. No. 1. are—

First—That the situation of the frontiers requires an additional defensive protection, at least until offensive measures shall be put into operation—The plan of a regiment of rangers is therefore submitted.

Secondly—That the peculiar situation of the frontiers require the augmentation of one regiment of regular troops to consist of nine hundred and twelve non commissioned Officers and privates.

Thirdly—That another expedition which shall effectually dispose the Wabash and other hostile indians to peace, seems indispensible.

That the army for the said expedition might be thus composed.

Regular troops, if the same should be augmented	1,200
Rangers; if the same should be adopted	500
Levies; so called for the sake of distinction	1,300
	3,000

But, if the regulars should not be augmented, nor the rangers adopted, then the number of Levies ought to be proportionally encreased.

That a corps of Levies raised for the expedition whose Officers should be selected by the general government, and who should possess a pride of arrangement and discipline would be more efficacious, and more oeconomical, than drafting the Militia cannot be well questioned.

It is to be observed that the engagements of four hundred and twenty of the troops on the frontiers expire during the present year, and that by the last accounts only sixty of that number had reinlisted on the new establishment.

As the reduced pay of the late establishment has therefore discouraged the recruiting service, the idea is suggested that a bounty of eight dollars should be given to all the recruits who have or shall re-inlist for three years on the said establishment. Were Congress to authorise this bounty, the subscriber is of opinion that all the recruits required would be immediately obtained.

That the paper marked B. No. 3. contains an estimate of the expence of the proposed number of Levies.

That the paper marked B. No. 4. contains in one view the extraordinary expence which would be incurred by the rangers, levies and other objects of the proposed expedition.

All which is humbly submitted.

War department, }
January 22nd. 1791. }

H. KNOX
Secretary of War

A No. 2
An Act of the State of Georgia

AN ACT for disposing of certain vacant lands or territory within this State

A

Whereas divers persons from the States of Virginia North-Carolina, and South Carolina have made application for the purchase of certain tracts and parcels of land lying and bordering on the Tenessee, Tom or Don Bigby Yazoo and Mississippi rivers within this State, and have offered to engage to settle the same a part of which territory has been already settled on behalf of some of the applicants under and by virtue of an Act of the General Assembly of this State, bearing date the seventh of February one thousand seven hundred and eighty five at Savannah entitled "An Act for laying out a district of land situated on the river Mississippi within the limits of this State into a county to be called Bourbon"—Now THEREFORE—Be it enacted by the Senate and House of Representatives of the State of Georgia in General Assembly met—

That all that tract or part of territory of this State within the following limits—to wit—beginning at the mouth of Coles Creek on the Mississippi continuing to the head spring or source thereof from thence a due East course to the Tom or Don Bigby river—thence continuing along the middle of the said river up to the latitude thirty three—thence down along the latitude thirty three bounding on the territory of the Virginia Yazoo company a due west course to the middle of the Mississippi—thence down the middle of the Mississippi to the mouth of Coles Creek aforesaid, and containing about five millions of acres shall be reserved as a preemption for the south Carolina Yazoo company for two years from and after the passing of this Act, and if the said South Carolina Yazoo Company shall within the said term of two years pay into the public treasury of this State the amount of Sixty six thousand, nine hundred and sixty four dollars, then it shall be lawful for the Governor at the time being and he is hereby empowered and directed to sign and deliver a grant in the usual form to Alexander Moultrie, Isaac Huger, William Clay Snipes, and Thomas Washington Esquires, and the rest of their Associates and to their heirs and assigns forever in fee simple as Tenants in common all the tract of land included in the aforesaid boundaries—AND be it further Enacted—That all that tract or part of territory of this State included within the following limits that is to say, beginning at the mouth of Bear Creek on the south side of the Tenesee river running thence up the said Creek to the head or source—thence a due west course to the Tom or Don Bigby or twenty mile Creek—thence down the same to latitude thirty-three—thence along the said latitude bounding on the south Carolina Yazoo Company's line a due west course to the middle of the Mississippi thence up the said river in the middle thereof to the northern boundary of this State—thence along the said boundary line a due east course to the Tenessee river—thence up the middle of the said river to the beginning thereof, and containing seven millions of acres shall be reserved as a pre-emption for the Virginia Yazoo Company for the term of two years from and after the passing of this Act, and if the said company shall cause to be paid into the public treasury of this State within the said term of two years, the amount of ninety three thousand seven hundred and forty one dollars, then it shall be lawful for the Governor at the time being, and he is hereby empowered and required to sign and deliver in the usual form a grant of the aforesaid tract of land to Patrick Henry, David

Ross, William Cowan, Araham B. Venable, John B. Scott, William Cock Ellis, Francis Watkins, and John Watts Esquires, and the rest of their associates, and to their heirs and assigns forever in fee simple as Tenants in common of all the tract of land included in the aforesaid boundaries—And be it further enacted—That all that tract or part of the territory of this State included within the limits following, to wit—beginning at the mouth of Bear Creek on the south side of the Tenessee river in the latitude of thirty-four degrees forty three minutes, running thence up Bear Creek to the head or source thence a due west course to the Tom Bigby or twenty mile creek— thence down the said Bigby or twenty mile creek to the latitude thirty four degrees, thence a due east course one hundred and twenty miles—thence a due North course to the Northern boundary line of this State—thence a due west course along the Northern boundary line to the Great Tenessee river— thence up the middle of the said river Tenessee to the place of beginning and containing three millions and a half Acres shall be reserved as a pre-emption for the Tenessee company for the term of two years from and after the passing this Act, and if the said company shall cause to be paid into the public treasury of this State within the said term of two years, the amount of forty-six thousand, eight hundred and seventy five dollars, then it shall be lawful for the Governor for the time being, and he is hereby empowered and required to sign and deliver in the usual form a grant of the aforesaid tract of land to Zachariah Cox, Thomas Gilbert and John Strother Esquires, and to the rest of their associates, and to their heirs and assigns forever as Tenants in common of all the tract of land included in the aforesaid boundaries— PROVIDED—That the said Grantees of each seperate grant, shall forbear all hostile attacks on any of the Indian Hords which may be found on or near the said territory if any such there be and keep this State free from all charge and expences which may attend the preserving of peace between the said Indians and Grantees, and extinguishing the claims of the said indians under the authority of this State—AND provided further and it is hereby expressly conditioned that this State and the government thereof shall at no time hereafter be subject to any suit at law or in equity, or claim or pretention whatever for or on account of any deduction in the quantity of the said territory by any recovery which may or shall be had on any former claim or claims—And for the better direction of the Governor—Be it enacted that the treasurer of this State shall on application of any agent of either of the said companies within the said term of two years receive the sum or sums of money which they are hereby respectively directed to advance a certificate or certificates of which payments under the hand of the treasurer shall be a sufficient voucher for the governor to issue the grants to the respective companies as aforesaid.

And be it further enacted that all the remaining vacant territory belonging to this State shall be disposed of as this or a future General Assembly shall direct and in no other manner whatever.

SEABORN JONES—Speaker
of the House of Representatives
N. BROWNSON—President
of the Senate
Concurred—December 21. 1789
EDWD. TELFAIR Governor

Georgia

Secretary's Office 12th. Jany. 1790
The foregoing is a true copy taken from the
original deposited in this office
D. LONGSTREET
for
JOHN MILTON—Secy:

True Copy

War department, Jany. 21st. 1791
JNO. STAGG Junr.
Chf. Clk.

A No. 3

Extract of a letter from Lieutenant John Armstrong to the secretary of War. dated Philadephia the

20th. January 1791

"Sir

Being a public officer I shall take the liberty of communicating to you some conversation that passed between a Doctor O'Fallon & myself a few days before I left Kentuckey, and some other circumstances relative to a settlement about to take place at the Yazou on the Missisippi under the direction of that gentleman—Having seen a proclamation published by the President of the United States. I observed to Doctor O'Fallon that I thought the sanction of government was necessary, in order to give the colour of success to his undertaking, he replied, it was immaterial, that Congress were concerned with him, offered to read a letter from one of that honorable body, but who he was I don't recollect; in the course of conversation he assured me that many of the Gentlemen of Congress were concerned in the business. I was also informed that a Mr. Mitchel had raised a company of adventurers in the District of Kentuckey—I saw a Mr. Christy who informed me he had an appointment & expected in a little time to fill a company also.

I understood from him that the business of those men were to protect the settlement, they were to be fed and have a bounty of Land. O'Fallon had also contracted with a Mr. Kirby at the Rapids of Ohio to frame several houses, and have them ready to raft down the river early in the spring.

On my way to this place, travelling through a part of North Carolina, I was there informed that an extensive settlement would be formed at the Bigbend of the Tennessee. This was the general subject of conversation in the back parts of Virginia also; and from an advertisement, a copy of which I gave you, a number of families were to, and I doubt not, but they did meet on the 10th. instant, on French broad river, in order to proceed to the place above mentioned."

> True Extract from the original letter
> War-department. Jany. 21. 1791
> JNO. STAGG, Junr.
> Chf. Clk.

Advertisement of Proprietors of Tennessee Company

Georgia, 2d. sept. 1790

This is to inform those who wish to become adventurers to the Tennessee company purchase, that the said company will embark from the confluence of Holston and French Broad rivers, on the tenth day of January next, for the purpose of forming a settlement on the sd. purchase at or near the Muscle Shoals. And for the encouragement of migration to the aforesaid intended settlement the said Tennesee Company have thought proper to set apart, four hundred & eighty thousand acres of land in the said purchase; to lye in a true square, on the south side of the Tennessee river; which said Tract of country so set apart for the encouragement of migration will be first laid off into bounties of Five hundred acres of land each. And to every family who may become adventurers to the aforesaid settlement will be allowed a bounty as aforesaid of five hundred acres each; and to every single man half a bounty of (that is to say) two hundred and fifty acres each: until the whole of the land so let apart is appropriated.

Preference to the adventures will be given by ballot: It is desired that those who wish to become adventurers, will rendezvous at the place appointed for setting out, time enough, previous to the tenth of January, to have their boats and necessary provisions prepared to embark.

ZACHARIAH COX ⎫
THOMAS CARR ⎭ Agents to the Tennessee Company

Augusta, 2d sept. 1790

> True Copy
> War department, Jany. 21. 1791
> JNO. STAGG Junr.
> Chf. Clk.

Advertisement of Proprietors of Tennessee Company

Those who wish to be further interested in Land on the Tennessee river, may be supplied on reasonable terms, by applying at the above mentioned place of rendezvous, on the first of January next; at which time and place the proprietors of the Tennessee company purchase (as holding the land on the north side of the Tennessee river, commonly called the Bent) will open an office for the sale of the same. The said office will continue at the confluence of Holston and French Broad rivers, until the tenth of January, and after, at the intended settlement of the Tennessee, until the whole of the Land on that part of the Bent (included by the Tennessee company purchase) is sold, amounting in the whole to about six hundred thousand acres of the most valuable part of the said Bent.

Undoubted titles, in fee simple, to adventurers and purchasers, for land in the Tennessee company will be given.

Given under our hands, as proprietors to the Tennessee company, this second day of September 1790.

ZACHARIAH COX,	Proprietors
THOMAS GILBERT,	Tennessee
JOHN STROTHER.	Company.

True Copy—War-department. Jany. 21. 1791. JNO. STAGG Junr.

C.C.

James O'Fallon to the President of the United States

(Copy.)

Lexington, September 25th. 1790.

Sir.

Having, since the sealing up of the dispatches herein enclosed to your Excellency, noticed a clause in the late Creek treaty, and another in an Act of the legislature of the United States, of Monday, January the 4th of this year, and a third in the same act, respecting persons passing into Indian nations, holding treaties on the subject of *lands,* and trade with them; and as, in my present agency, I may occasionally have, from the Spanish and Indian borders, intelligence of vital import to transmit to your Excellency, to the Governor of Georgia, to the company, to the new Ally of the States, Mr. McGillivray, through the Choctaws and Chickasaws, and may likewise have to determine on the tradeing intercourse between these nations and the people of my colony, so remote from your Excellency or your Excellency's Indian superintendant and may further have to purchase *more lands* within the company's State Charter, from the Choctaws: I, in consequence, submit it to your Excellency, whether, or not, it would comport with your Excellency's arrangement and official plans to extend to me, as the Agent General of the company, sufficient authority in the premises, and to transmit it as speedily as may be—your Excellency may depend on my discretion, in the uses of such authority; and that your confidence will, in no one instance be abused without such trust—evils may happen.

In regard to *trade* and *purchases of the Choctaw tribes,* it would perhaps, be better to place this authority in the hands of the company; but the power of passing expresses from *one,* in the directions just mentioned, ought, I should presume, to be speedily invested in the acting general Agent of the colony— These are submitted to your Excellency's better judgement, with becoming diffidence; And am,

> Your Excellency's
> Most devoted and respectful humble servt.
> JAMES O'FALLON
> Agt. Genl. for, and Proprietr.
> with the So. Carola. Yazou Compy.

P.S.—By persons, just now arrived from General Harmar's army, it is handed about, very confidently, that the expedition against the Northern indians *must* prove abortive—The militia (then about half-ways to the indian towns) began to mutiny, for the want of *meat*—They had not at the time more beeves, than would last the army 5 days, *nor were any ordered on.* They lost near one hundred in the woods. This disgusts the people here, because (they think) it will inspirit the Savages to greater hostility—The expedition, it is said, has been by Genl. St. Clair too *precipitately* taken up, and hastily provided for— The country abounds with every supply, and the people if called on, are willing to support the expedition—But *they are not called on*—If it fails, a new uproar I fore-see will be set up against the Governor.

> True Copy from the original
> War-department, Jany. 21st. 1791
> JNO. STAGG Junr.
> Chf. Clk.

Return of the Officers of the Yazou Battalion

Officers of the Yazou battalion, commissioned as well as warranted: Their names & grades respectively

---

Battalion filled, mustered & enrolled on the 16th. day of September 1790.

Colonel Commandant		JOHN HOLDER Esquire
Lieutenant Colonel		THOMAS KENNEDY Esquire
Major,		HENRY OWEN Esquire
Horse.	Captain	EBENEZER PLATT, gentln.
	Lieutenant	CHARLES SCOTT, junr. gent.
	Cornet	SHERWOOD HARRIS, gent.

Artillery,	Captain		THOMAS REYNOLDS, gent.
	Lieutenant		JAMES NOLAN, gent.
	2d. Lieutenant		ANDREW MCCROSHIE, gent.
Infantry- *Riflemen*	Captains	1st.	JOHN MCINTIRE, gent.
		2d.	MARTIN NALL, gent.
		3d.	JOHN SAPPINGTON, gent.
		4th.	CHARLES HAZLEWRIGG, gent.
		5th.	FRANCIS JONES, gent.
		6th.	PHILIP ALSTON, gent.
		7th.	JAMES DROMGOLD, gent.
		8th.	JOSEPH BLACKBURN, gent.
	Lieutenants	1st.	GABRIEL HARDIN, gent.
		2d.	JOHN PRICE, gent.
		3d.	WILLIAM BRISCOE, gent.
		4th.	MARTIN JOHNSON, gent.
		5th.	ROBERT KNOX, gent.
		6th.	JOHN ALSTON, gent.
		7th.	DANIEL SCOTT, gent.
		8th.	GEORGE LOGAN, gent.
	Ensigns	1st.	FRANCIS MCDOWELL, gent.
		2d.	WILLIAM BOYD, gent.
		3d.	ASA SEAFROY, gent.
		4th.	JOHN HOLDIN, gent.
		5th.	PHILIP BUSH, gent.
		6th.	ANTHONY MCGUIRE, gent.
		7th.	TOBIAS TALMASH, gent.
		8th.	NATHL. HOWARD, gent.
Warranted *Officers*			
	Quarter Master		WILLIAM KENNAN,
	Q. M. serjeant		JOHN DRAKE,
	Adjutant of the batt.		JAMES MITCHEL,
	Surgeon of ditto		WILLIAM SAPPINGTON
	Serjeant Major		PATRICK IRWIN
	Adjutant of horse		CHARLES DAVIS

True Copy from the original
War department, Jany. 21. 1791
JNO. STAGG Junr.
Chf. Clk.

Military Articles of Contract

MILITARY ARTICLES, Proposals and Terms of Contract, hereby offered, made, and solemnly entered into; for and on behalf of the SOUTH-CAROLINA YAZOU COMPANY, (as proprietors of that extensive Territory, on the Mississippi, and adjoining to the Natchey District, now proposed for Populous Colonization, by them, under a Grant from the State of Georgia, and a Deed of Gift from the Chactaw Nation) by the underwritten, who, himself is a Co-proprietor—and likewise the said Company's General Agent in and over their Affairs, throughout the whole of the Western Territory of the United States; and in New-Orleans & Pensacola, on the One part, and the Officers & Privates, as undersigned, on the other—And this for the sole purpose of raising, recruiting and enlisting, and for that of placing on the spot of Settlement, a well-appointed, well-armed, and well-accoutred Military Corps, in full form & organization of a Regular Batallion, aptly detailed and apportioned into. . . . One Troop of Cavalry . . . one Company of Artillery, and eight Companies of Infantry-Riflemen, as in order arranged, at foot; enlisted, or to be enlisted for the space of Eighteen Months certain, to be computed from the time of the Batallion's arrival at the place destined & appointed, by the Company, or their Agent General, for the first establishment of the Colony, Capital, and Fort; or for a shorter time, if the said Company shall have thought proper: these Troops being intended, although no danger is, at present, apprehended, to ensure the greater security of the Companys Rights, and their own, as well as to the rest of their fellow settlers Lives, Liberties, and Properties.

DETAIL of Officers and Privates in this Batallion; with their apportionments of Stipendiary Lands, respectively.

	Acres		Acres
1 Colonel commandt.		1 Major	5,000
1 Lieutenant Colonel	6,000	1 Captain of Horse	3,600
1 Lieut. of Horse	2,400	1 Qr. Masr. Serjt.	400
1 Cornet of ditto	2,400	1 Adjutant of Horse	400
1 Capt. of Artillery	3,600	2 Serjeants of Do. }	
First Lieutt. of Ditto	2,400	350 each }	700
Second Lieut. of Ditto	2,400	16 Serjts. of Infantry }	
Eight Captains of }		300 Acres ea. }	4,800
Infantry 3,000 Acres }	24,000	2 Serjts. of Artillery }	
each }		350 each }	700

	Acres		Acres
Eight Lieuts. of Infantry 2,000 Acres each	16,000	47 privates of Horse each 250 Acres	11,750
Eight Ensigns of do. 2,000 Acres each	16,000	46 ditto of Artillery 250 each	11,550
1 Adjut. of the Battaln.	2,000	400 ditto of Infantry 200 each	80,000
1 Surgeon of Do.	2,000	2 Gunners for the Artillery 400 each	800
1 Quarter Master	2,000	Total of Acres	201,300
1 Serjeant Major	400		

In addition to the Stipendiary allotments of Plantation rights, as above mentioned; Each Private, as well as Officer is to have one Town-Lot of half an Acre, and one Out Lot of five Acres, adjoining to the Capital.

The Plantation Lands are to be laid out, and drawn for, consonant to Rank, in enumerated Sections of 400—350—300—250— & 200 Acres; all in the vicinage of the said Capital, where, it is presumed, the Land must, in quality, be excellent. The Town Lots are, likewise, to be enumerated and drawn for, in half Acre Sections; and the Out Lots in Sections of five Acres: the company drawing Lot for Lot with, alternately, with each Officer & Private, so that the Troops, (with respect to the quantity of their Lands) will be on an equal footing with the Company. These Military Lots within the Town, may exist in any of the Streets thereof, saving one; which the Agent, in behalf of the Company, shall reserve for such uses as the said Company may, hereafter, have them applied to.

The Battalion is, still additionally, to be maintained by the Company, in the Subsistence of daily Rations; so long as the Troops shall have been retained in the service of the said Company.

OFFICERS & PRIVATES DAILY RATIONS

Colonel Commandant	5 ℔ Day
Lieutenant Colonel	℔ Day
Major	4 ℔ Day
Captains	3 do. do.
Lieutenants & Ensigns	2 do. do.
Adjutant of the Batallions	2 do. do.
Surgeon	2 do. do.

| Quarter Master | 2 do. do. |
| All others | 1 do. do. |

RATIONS to consist of
Bacon, Salted Pork, Flour, or Indian Corn Meal 3/4 of a lb. or if

Bread, instead of Flour	1 lb.	or if
Corn, instead of these	1 quart	or if
Salted Beef, instead of Bacon, or Salted Pork,	1 lb.	or if
Fresh Meat, or Fish, instead of either of these	1 $^1/_2$ lb.	—

One Gill of Whiskey, or half a Gill of Taffia, pr. Day, shall accompany each Ration.

The Company engages, to receive of the Hunters & Fishermen, all the Fresh Meat, Fish & Peltry, which they shall bring into the Garrison, at the customary price. The Troops are to have their Plantation Lots & Lands laid out for them, as soon after their arrival, as may be; but not to receive their Grants, or final titles for the same, before they shall have been honorably discharged, at or before the expiration of Eighteen months, as the Company shall optionally determine on. The Time of enlistment, then, is to be for eighteen months certain, or for so long, (within that Period) as the company shall judge this Military Establishment of defensive Force absolutely necessary. The Company is to exact no other services of the Troops, but such as shall be purely Military. Should a Soldier labour for the Company in any other respect, it shall be voluntarily, and for a stipulated compensation. No Soldier whatsoever is, in any wise, to be punished, as such, for any crime, under a Military Tribunal, but by a forfeiture of his Stipendiary Lands & Lots, for the Greater Crimes, and this, by the solemn Tryal of a Court-Martial; or, for the Lesser Ones, by an abridgement of his Rations of Whiskey, or Taffia, as his proper Captain shall adjudge, in conjunction with the Subalterns of the same Company, or a Majority of them.

The Greater Crimes are, *Murder,* or *any Act tending to the same; Disobedience; Desertion; Cowardice; Mutiny; Neglect of appointed Duty; Drunkenness, while on Duty; Striking an Officer; Insult to his Authority,* and *Theft.*

The Lesser Crimes are all else, beside the above, which tend to *Unmilitary* or *immoral* Examples.

The Col. Comandt. (or, in his absence, the next to him in command) shall, with his Corps of Commissioned Officers, possess the exclusive authority, of arranging the system of Discipline, and of directing that of Duty, as well of the Officers, as of the private men; and of adjusting the mode and the manner of holding Courts-Martial. They shall, likewise, be invested with a similar authority, respecting the regulation, inspection, and issuing Military Stores & Provisions.

The   is to have the Command of the Batallion. The Lieutenant
Colonel shall command under him; and in the absence of these, the Command of the Batallion shall devolve upon the Senior Officer in Rank, then
present. The Captain of the Cavalry is to hold precedence of him of the
Artillery, and he of those of the Infantry-Riflemen. The same preference, in
Rank, is to hold good, in regard to the Lieutenants of *Horse* & *Artillery,* as
well with respect to each other, as to those two, and those also of the Infantry.
The Cornet of Dragoons is to rank above the oldest Lieutenant of Infantry. All
the Infantry Officers are to rank, in their respective grades, by priority;
consonant to the priority of the Dates of their Commissions. Forfeiture of
Lands & Lots (for the *Greater* Crimes, shall equally affect the Officers, as the
Soldiers, with the superadded Ignomiy of Cashierment, by sentence of
Court-Martial. No Officer, however, shall be put under arrest; but by a
Senior one, who shall not be the *Complainant*: and all such Complaints shall
be in writing).

The Troops, whether of Horse, Artillery, or Infantry, shall procure their
respective Manual Arms & Accoutrements. The Cavalry are to have themselves furnished with good Horses, and with compleat equipment for the
same; and all are to find their own Uniform and Habiliments. The Arms of
the Horse are, Swords, or Cutlases, Pistols, or Carbines. Their Uniforms is to
consist of, a Light-Horseman's Cap, covered with Bearskins; a short skirted
Coat of blue, faced with Buff, and yellow metal Buttons. The Arms of the
Artillery are to be Swords or Cutlases; and their Uniforms are to consist of,
Yellow Hunting-shirts, bound about the Waist, with broad, black, Leathern
Belts; of a Hat, with its leaf flapped up, behind, and the Crown thereof
covered with a piece of Bearskin; with Overalls of blue. The Infantry
Riflemen are to wear the same Uniform with the Artillery and their Arms are
to be, each, a good Rifle, or Musket, shot or Bullet-pouch, and powder-horn.
All Military Stores, and Ammunition *for Duty,* are to be furnished by the
Company.

Should any Person demise, while in service, his Stipendiary Lands are to
revert to his heirs, or to pass over to his Assigns, as fully, absolutely, &
legally, as if he had duly served out the whole period of his enlistment.

The Company will grant (as a bounty of encouragement to Female Adventurers, who shall have enterprized into this Territory, at the time the
Batallion moves to it) Five Hundred acres of Land to the first Woman who
shall land there; and Five hundred more to her, who shall bring forth in it,
the first live Child, Bastard or Legitimate.

All those (of whatever Class or Rank) who shall take Provisions of *solid*
Food, or Whiskey, down with them to this Settlement; shall be paid for the
same, in Cash, or in Goods, on the delivery of these Provisions to the Agents

orders—Every Woman married, or marriageable, who shall accompany the Troops to the place of Settlement, shall have One hundred acres of Land.

The Articles being obligatory on the Company, and on their Troops, the one to the other; are to be signed (for the Company) by the Agent General, and (for the Batallion) by the Officers & Privates thereof; as herein after specified by their signatures, respectively.

True Copy from the original
War department, Jany. 21st. 1791
JNO. STAGG Junr.
Chf. Clk.

B No. 1

STATEMENT of the Troops in the service of the UNITED STATES

			Officers, non-commissd. & privates
In Georgia	At St. Marys,	Burbeck's company consisting of	69
	Rock Landing,	Savage's	55
	Beard's Bluff	J. Smith's	57
	Augusta,	Rudolph's	20
Western frontiers	Fort Washington,	Six companies	295
	Fort Knox, St. Vincennes,	Two—ditto	142
	Fort Franklin,	Detachment,	18
	Fort Harmar,	Two companies	87
	Halifax No. Carolina,	recruiting; Montfort's compy.	50
	Kentuckey, recruiting,	B. Smith's	12
	West Point, detachment,		21
		In Service	820
		Wanting to complete	396
		Establishment	1,216

War Office
22d. January 1791
H. KNOX secy. of War

B Nos. 2 & 3
Estimates of the two modes of Augmentation of the troops and
the Expence of 1,500 levies

The present Military establishment of the United States consists of one regiment of Infantry and one battalion of Artillery the whole number of non commissioned & Privates amount to 1,216.

The Regiment of Infantry is composed as follows
Regimental Staff

---

1 Lieutenant Colonel Commandant
1 Paymaster
1 Surgeon
2 Surgeon mates
    And three battalions each of which consists
1 Major
1 Adjutant
1 Quartermaster
    And four companies each of
1 Captain
1 Lieutenant
1 Ensign
4 Serjeants
4 Corporals
2 Musicians
66 Privates

The battalion of Artillery is of the same formation as the battalions of Infantry excepting having a paymaster.

If it should be thought proper to augment the establishment with another regiment of Infantry of the same proportions the establishment would consist of 2,128 non commissioned & privates formed as follows.

Infantry 1,824 non commissioned & privates

---

2 Regiments each of 3 Battalions, each battalion of four companies, each company of 76 non commissioned and privates

Artillery 304 non commissioned & privates

---

1 battalion of 4 Companies each 76 non commissioned & privates

A

In this case the following would be an estimate of the expences for one Year.

Pay

1 Lt. col. Commandant	at	D.	60	pr.	month	D. 720.
3 Majors	"	"	40	"	"	1,440.
12 Captains	"	"	30	"	"	4,320.
12 Lieutenants	"	"	22	"	"	3,160.
12 Ensigns	"	"	18	"	"	2,592.
3 Surgeon mates	"	"	24	"	"	864.
1 Adjutant	"	"	10	"	"	120.
1 Paymaster	"	"	5	"	"	60.
1 Quarter master	"	"	5	"	"	60.
3 Serjeants Majors	"	"	6	"	"	216.
3 Qr. Master Serjeants	"	"	6	"	"	216.
48 Serjeants	"	"	5	"	"	2,880.
48 Corporals	"	"	4	"	"	2,304.
24 Musicians } 784 privates }	"	"	3	"	"	29,088.

                                        D.   48,048.

deductions

54 Serjeants	D.	1 41/100 pr. month D.	907.20			
48 Corporals	"	1 15/100 "	"	"	662.40	
808 Musicians & Privates	"	90/100 "	"	"	8,726.40	10,296.

                                 amount of Pay   D   37,742.

Subsistence

1 Lt. Col. Commt.	6 Rations	"	2,190. Rs.	
3 Majors	4	"	"	4,330. "
12 Captains	3	"	"	13,140. "
12 Lieutenants	2	"	"	8,760. "
12 Ensigns	2	"	"	8,760. "
3 Surgeon mates	2	"	"	2,190. "
910 non com. & priv.	1	"	"	332,150. "

                                       "   371,570. Rs.

at 12 Cts. per Ration   "44,588.40

Forage

1 Lt. Col. Commt.	D.	12 pr. month D.	144.		
3 Majors	"	10 "	"	" 360.	
1 Adjutt. 1 paymaster 1 Quarter Master	"	6 each	"	" 216.	
3 Surgeon Mates	"	6	"	" 216.	936.

Clothing

910 Non Commissd. & Privates at D. 20   18,200.

                                      Doll.   101,466.40

But if the principle of the augmentation should be agreed to, but not the foregoing mode, then the following plan is submitted.

The whole establishment of Infantry and Artillery to consists of 20 companies each company of 108 non commissioned and privates amounting in total to 2,160.

Each company in consideration of the augmentation from 76 to 108 to have an additional Lieutenant, 2 Serjeants and 2 Corporals, and to be formed as follows.

1 Captain
2 Lieutenants
1 Ensign
6 Serjeants
6 Corporals
2 Musicians
94 privates

The Infantry to be formed into two Regiments, each of two battalions of four companies.

The artillery to remain formed into one battalion of four companies:

In this case the following Statement would be the precise number of the augmentation and an estimate of the expences thereof.

Pay

1 Lt. Col. Commt.	at D.	60	pr. month D.				720.
One battalion complete							
1 Major	at D.	40	"	"	"		480.
4 Captains	" "	30	"	"	"		1,440.
8 Lieutenants	" "	22	"	"	"		2,112.
4 Ensigns	" "	18	"	"	"		864.
1 Adjutant	" "	10	"	"	"		120.
1 Quartermaster	" "	5	"	"	"		60.
1 Paymaster	" "	5	pr. month D.				60.
1 Serjeant Major	" "	6	"	"	"		72.
1 Qr. Master Serjt.	" "	6	"	"	"		72.
24 Serjeants	" "	5	"	"	"		1,440.
24 Corporals	" "	4	"	"	"		1,152.
8 Musicians } 376 Privates }	" "	3	"	"	"		12,624.

deductions

26 Serjeants	D.	1 40/100	pr. month	D.		436.80
24 Corporals	"	1 15/100	"	"	"	331.20
334 Musicians & privates	"	90/100	"	"	"	4,147.20

	4,915.20
Amount of pay	D. 16,300.80

Subsistence

1 Lt. Colonel Commt.	6 Rations "		2,190 Rs.
1 Major	4 " "		1,460 "
4 Captains	3 " "		4,380 "
8 Lieutenants	2 " "		5,840 "
4 Ensigns	2 " "		2,920 "
434 non comm. &			
priv.	1 " "		158,410 "
	"		175,200 Rs.

at 12 Cts. pr. Ration   21,024.

Forage

1 Lt. Col. Commt.	D. 12 pr. month D.	144.	
1 Major	" 10 " " "	120.	
1 Adjutt. 1 Qr. Master			
1 paymaster each	" 6 " " "	216.	480.

Clothing

434 non commissd. & privates at D. 20			" 8,680.
16 additional Lieutenants			
to the 16 existing			
companies of Infantry			
& artillery at	D. 22 pr. mo. D.	4,224.	
32 Addl. Serjeants	5 " " "	1,920.	
32 Corporals	4 " " "	1,536.	
448 privates being 28 additionals to each of the			
aforesaid companies of artillery & Infantry at			
3 D.		16,128.	
	D.	23,808.	

Deductions

32 Serjeants D.	1 40/100	D.	537.60	
32 Corporals "	1 15/100	"	441.60	
448 privates "	90/100	"	4,838.40	
		"	5,817.60	" 17,990.40

Subsistence

16 Lieutenants	2 Rations "	11,680 R.	
512 non comms.			
& Privates	1 "	186,880 "	
		198,560 Rs.	

at 12 Cts. pr. Ration   23,827.20

Clothing

512 non commissioned & Privates @ 20 D.   "10,240

                                                    D. 98,542.40

By this plan the additional non commissioned officers & privates would
amount to   944
By the first mode to   912

                                                    difference   32

It appears that the difference of expence would be greater for the former
than the latter mode by the sum of D. 2,924. But the Secretary of war
Submits it as his opinion that the additional Regiment of three battalions
would be the best formation considering the nature of the service to be
performed on the frontiers.

But if the augmentation should take place in either mode, or indeed if it
should not take place it seems essential for the public interests that an officer
of high Rank & responsibility should command on the frontiers—the public
interest in that quarter require the best Security to be obtained the idea is
therefore hereby Suggested that a Major general should be appointed to the
command of the troops on the frontiers. In this case the following expence
would be incurred.

The pay of a Major general, 166 D. pr. mth.   D. 1,992.
    Subsistence 15 Rs. ℔ day, 5,475 Rs. @ 12/c   657.
    Forage 24 D. ℔ month   288.

                                                    D. 2,937.

Quartermaster[1]

Pay D. 60 pr. month   D. 720.
Subsistence 6 Rations is 2,190 at 12/cts.   " 262.80
Forage D. 12 pr. Month   " 144.

                                                    D. 1,126.80

---

[1] The following explanation appears in the left margin of the document:
    The articles in the Quarter Masters department is at present supplied by the
    contractors. But it is apprehended that a Quartermaster to the troops would be
    more oeconomical. The idea is therefore submitted that a Quarter Master
    should be appointed, who should govern himself by such regulations respect-
    ing his said duty as the President of the United States should from time to time
    direct. It is proposed that the Quarter Master should have the pay, Rations &
    forage of a Lieutenant Colonel Commandant.

AN ESTIMATE of the Expence of the corps of Levies consisting of 1,500 non commissioned & privates for four Months

Pay

1 Brigadier General	@	D.	100	pr. month D.		400.
2 Lt. Colonels	"	"	60	" " "		480.
5 Majors	"	"	40	" " "		800.
20 Captains	"	"	30	" " "		2,400.
20 Lieutenants	"	"	22	" " "		1,760.
20 Ensigns	"	"	18	" " "		1,440.
1 Adjutant	"	"	10	" " "		40.
1 Quarter Master	"	"	5	" " "		20.
1 Paymaster	"	"	5	" " "		20.
5 Surgeon mates	"	"	24	" " "		480.
80 Serjeants	"	"	5	" " "		1,600.
80 Corporals	"	"	4	" " "		1,280.
40 Musicians & } 1,300 Privates }	"	"	3	" " "		16,080.

Amount of Pay   D. 26,800.

Subsistence

1 Brigadr. General	8 Rs.	960 Rs.	
2 Lt. Colonels	6 "	1,440 "	
5 Majors	4 "	2,400 "	
20 Captains	3 "	7,200 "	
20 Lieutenants	2 "	4,800 "	
20 Ensigns	2 "	4,800 "	
5 Surgeon mates	2 "	1,200 "	
1500 non coms. & Privs.	1 "	180,000 "	

202,800 Rs.
@ 12 Cts.   24,336.

Forage

1 Brigadr. Genel.	D.	18	D.	72.
2 Lt. Colonels	"	12	"	96.
5 Majors	"	10	"	200.
1 Adjutant	"	6	"	24.
1 Quarter Master	"	6	"	24.
1 Paymaster	"	6	"	24.
5 Surgeon mates	"	6	"	120.

560.

In order that the Levies should be upon a footing with the regular troops, they ought to have for the 4

Months service one third part of the clothing of the said
regulars, but subject to a proportional deduction, the
clothing so given should be of the most usefull kind so
as to enable the Levies to render the most Service. It is
to be observed that many of the militia are soon
rendered unfit for Service by want of clothing.

The clothing therefore for the aforesaid 1,500 non
commissioned and privates amount at D. 6 2/3 to D.
10,000 from which the following deductions are to be
made agreeably to Law.

80 Serjeants $\frac{46^2/_3}{100}$ pr. mth. D.   149.34

80 Corporals $\frac{38^1/_3}{100}$ "   "   "   122.66

1,340 mus. & priv. 30/100   "   "   "   1,608.

1,880	8,120.
D.	59,816.

If only 1,300 levies should be raised than 2/15 part
of the above sum would be deducted—on the contrary
if the levies should be augmented to 2,000 then the
aforesaid estimate to be increased one fourth part viz.

If 1,300, there is to be deducted   D.   7,962.
If 2,000, there is to be added   D.   14,954.

War office Jany. 22 1791
H. KNOX
Secy. of War

B. No. 4

A GENERAL ESTIMATE of the Extraordinary Expences which would be incurred by an expedition against the Wabash Indians calculated for four
Months and the expence of a proposed regiment of Rangers for Nine months

The Rangers as pr. estimate marked C. no. 6	D.	49,454.
The Levies as pr. estimate marked the greatest sum being taken	"	74,770.
The difference between the price of 2,500 Rations pr. day on the ohio, and the proposed place of operation		

the one being stated 6.3/4/Cts. and the other 15$^1/_4$ Cts. calculated at 120 days 300,000 Rs. at 8$^1/_2$ Cts. diffe.	"	25,500.
The same difference for 600 continental Troops	"	6,120.

Quarter Masters department

Camp Equipage of all Sorts, Boats, horses, Tents &c. and the transportation including hospital Stores and baggage for the Army, and cannon & stores to establish a post at the miami, estimated in the gross	"	50,000.
Medical & Hospital Stores.	"	4,000.
Arms & ammunition are not estimated, the principal articles being in the public stores.		
Contingencies	"	25,000.
Dollars		234,844.

War office 22 January 1791
H. KNOX Secy. of War

C No. 1

Report of the Secretary of War with enclosures

The Secretary of War to whom the President of the United States was pleased to refer a letter of His Excellency the Governor of Virginia, dated the 10th. of December last, enclosing the joint Memorial addressed to him, of the Delegates of Ohio, Monongahalia, Harrison, Randolph, Kinhawa, Greenbrier, Montgomery, and Russell Counties, on the Ohio—

REPORTS,

That the said Memorial states, that the said Counties form a line of nearly four hundred miles along the Ohio—exposed to the hostile invasions of their indian enemies—and destitute of every kind of support.

That notwithstanding all the regulations of the General Government in that Country, the Memorialists have reason to lament that they have hitherto been ineffectual.

That the arrangements and regulations for their defence as declared by the Secretary of War are impossible to be complied with.

That the old experienced mode of keeping out Scouts and Rangers for the information and protection of the inhabitants, is exploded as the Memorialists are informed because the new plan is less expensive.

That there is reason to fear the defeat of the army on the frontiers will be severely felt, as there is no doubt but the Indians will in their turn flushed with victory, invade the settlements.

That the Memorialists therefore for the reasons assigned, think the only measure which will establish the confidence of the frontier people in the Government, and also bring about the proposed end—to wit, their safety and protection, is to empower the County Lieutenants in each of those Counties, to send out a few Scouts to watch the passes of the enemy when the Winter breaks up, and to place some rangers on the outside of the settlements.

That this arrangement be temporary, until more effectual measures are adopted for the protection of the Country.

That the expence of the Scouts and Rangers to be settled by the Auditor of Virginia, and the Government debited with the amount thereof.

That if the Executive Council of Virginia should not possess sufficient power to extend to the Memorialists that relief that necessities require, that the Governor would lay the Complaints before the proper tribunal where they may be redressed.

On the subject of this Memorial the Secretary of War observes, that on the 26th. of February 1790, a report upon the subject of Scouts, and an estimate thereof, was submitted to the President of the United States, who was pleased to lay the same before the Congress; a copy of which with the estimate is herewith submitted No. 1.

That as the danger of some of the frontier Counties was imminent, the President of the United States was pleased to permit a certain number of Scouts to be called forth under the regulations described in Paper marked No. 2.

That as it did not appear to be the judgment of Congress, to authorise the Scouts upon any higher rate of pay than the Militia—and as offensive measures were directed on the 7th. of June, the President of the United States directed that the employment of the Scouts should be discontinued, and in lieu thereof, that the Militia should be employed as Rangers under the regulations described in the paper herewith annexed No. 3.

It however appears from the Memorialists, that the permission has been rendered nugatory by the regulations prescribed, and that the Memorialists propose in lieu of the former arrangement, that the County Lieutenants should be invested with discretionary power on the occasion to call forth Scouts and Rangers.

It is to be observed that no partial measures can be adopted by the government—That any arrangement for the eight Counties to which the Memorialists belong, must also comprehend the County of Washington in Pennsylvania—eight Counties in Kentuckey—the exposed parts of Cumberland settlements, and the settlements lying upon and between the Holstein and french broad River, making in all, districts or divisions equal to twenty two Counties.

That it is to be observed, that the Scouts so called are the most active hunters or Woodsmen, well acquainted with the paths by which Indians enter the Country—That experience of their utility seems to have stamped an extraordinary value upon their services in the opinion of the frontier people. They seem however from information, to have received an exceeding high pay, and greatly disproportioned to any known compensation for military services.

But considering the confidence of the frontier people in the said Scouts, the Secretary of War is inclined to the opinion, that it might be proper to indulge them therein—Provided their services could be obtained for a reasonable pay, and regulated in such manner as to prevent abuse. The pay allowed by Virginia was five sixths of a dollar Pr. day for each person or Scout, but no rations.

The Secretary of war is of opinion, that pay at the rate of ten or twelve dollars per month, and one ration per day, to be given for each person acting as a Scout, would be as high a sum as ought to be given for any military service—that no greater number than six or eight should be allowed to any County. And in no instance a greater number, than have heretofore been allowed by Virginia.

That conformably to these ideas the estimate is herewith submitted No. 4—in order to shew the greatest aggregate expence of this business.

That this measure be adopted only as a temporary expedient, and be continued no longer, than the President of the United States shall judge necessary.

It ought however to be observed, that while the pay of the troops is greatly reduced, and the pay of this species of Militia greatly advanced, that it may have the effect to prevent the recruiting of the regular troops on the established pay—and to create discontents in the minds of those already in service on the frontiers. But it is conceived that although this objection may occur, yet perhaps it is not of sufficient importance to prevent the adoption of such reasonable measures, as may conciliate and attach the people of the frontiers to the General Government.

If therefore it should be judgment of the President of the United States, that it would be proper to adopt the Scouts, it will be necessary to lay the subject before the Congress for their consideration and approbation. For if a species of troops are to be adopted at a higher rate of pay than the rate established by Law, it will be necessary to make the provision for that purpose by a special Act.

The Rangers are a species of Militia, for which an higher rate of pay does not seem to be necessary.

All which is humbly submitted to the President of the United States.

War Department   }
5th. January 1791 }

H. KNOX
Secretary of War

No. 1
[Secretary of War to George Washington]

War Office, February 26th. 1790

Sir,

In obedience to your orders I have received the communications, of Colonel John Pierce Duval, Lieutenant of Harrison County in Virginia, the result of which I have the honor to submit to you.

The paper No. 1. is a representation from the field Officers of the said County on the subject of their exposed situation.

Colonel Duval states that there are five Counties of Virginia, lying on the Western Waters, exposed to the incursions of the Indians—all of which are to the east of the Kentuckey line—to wit, Monongahalia—Ohio—Randolph—Harrison—Kenhawa.

That these Counties have been permitted to keep out for their immediate protection, at the expence of Virginia, certain parties of Scouts and Rangers.

That during the last year the Governor of Virginia directed the said Scouts and Rangers to be discharged, in consequence of a letter from the President of the United States; a copy of which, with the letter from the said Governor, is herewith submitted—marked—No. 2.

That since the discharge the said Scouts and Rangers, the said Counties have suffered great injury from the Indians; and that Harrison County in particular, has had fifteen persons killed, besides Houses burnt and horses stolen.

That the object of the said Colonel Duval is, that he should be permitted to call into service again, the said Scouts and Rangers at the expence of the United States.

That the expence of the said Scouts and Rangers would, according to his information, for the ensuing season, and for Harrison County only, amount to Three thousand four hundred and forty dollars—agreeably to the estimate herewith submitted, marked No. 3.

That this arrangement would give perfect satisfaction to the inhabitants of said County.

On this information it may be observed, That an arrangement of this nature for one County, involves a similar arrangement, not only for the other four Counties of Virginia, but for the nine Counties of the district of Kentuckey, all of which are exposed in a greater or less degree as Harrison County.

That it would be proper that this Representation, from Harrison County, together with the Memorial of the Representatives of the Counties of the district of Kentuckey, dated the 28th of November 1789, requesting a Post to be established at Great-bone lick; and the Petition from the inhabitants of

Miro settlement, dated the 30th. of November 1789—should be laid before the Congress for their information, in addition to other Papers of the same nature, which you were pleased to lay before them on the 4th of January last. An Estimate of the expence of a guard of one Captain and 30 Rangers, and eight men termed Scouts, for the period of seven months, required by the Lieutenant of Harrison County for the protection of the same against the depredations of parties of Indians—the estimate being formed from information given the subscriber by Col. Duval, the Lieutenant of said County.

40 Rations @ 6 d. per day	£214.	
The pay of 1 Captain for 7 months at 35 dollars per month	73.10	
The pay of 2 Serjeants for 7 months at 6 dollars per month	25.04	
The pay of 28 privates for the same period at 4 $^1/_2$ dollars per month	264.12	
The pay of 8 Scouts for 7 months say 214 days @ 5∫ pr. day	428.	
Powder & Lead furnished by Government. . .suppose	30.	£1,035.6
	or Dollars	3,451.

If protection be given to the other four Counties of Virginia, and the nine Counties of the district of Kentuckey, and the same be estimated on the above scale—the expence would amount to 48,314 Dollars.

War-Office
Februy. 26th. 1790 }

No. 2
To Governor St. Clair—or, Brig. Genl. Harmar. pr. Col. Duval

War-Office, 3rd March 1790

Sir.

In pursuance of powers vested in the President of the United States, by the Act of Congress passed the 29th day of September 1789, he authorized you by his instructions dated the 6th of October following in certain cases and in the proportions therein specified to call forth the militia of Virginia and Pennsylvania for the protection of the frontiers, against the depredations of the indians.

Since transmitting you the aforesaid instructions, he has received several applications for protection, from the inhabitants of the frontier counties of Virginia lying along the south side of the Ohio—These applications are founded on the depredations of small parties of indians during the last year, who it seems have murdered many of the unguarded inhabitants, stolen their horses, and burned their houses.

Until the last year, an arrangement of the following nature existed at the expence of Virginia—The lieutenants of the exposed counties under certain restrictions, were permitted to call forth a number of active men as patroles or scouts as they are generally termed, and parties of rangers—But the government of that State thought proper to discontinue that arrangement on the organization of the general government, to which the inhabitants of the said counties now apply for protection.

All applications of this nature have been placed before the Congress for their information and in order that they may adopt such measures as the case may require. But as the season is fast approaching in which the inhabitants are apprehensive of a repetition of the injuries suffered the last year, they seem to be of an opinion that their situation requires some conditional security previously to the measures which may result from the deliberations of Congress.

The President of the United States has therefore so far conformed to their apprehensions on this point, as to refer the case to you or in your absence to Brigadier General Harmar, and to give you the authority herein described.

1st. That if from good and sufficient information it should be your judgement, or in your absence the judgment of the commanding officer aforesaid, that any of the frontier Counties of Virginia lying along the south of the Ohio, are under existing circumstances threatened immediately with incursive parties of indians, that you or the said commanding officer under your hands and seals empower the lieutenants of such exposed counties to call forth a particular *number of scouts* in proportion to the danger of the said counties not however exceeding for one county the number of eight men—The said scouts to be continued in service no longer than the danger shall exist according to the judgment of the county-lieutenants.

2'nd—That when the said service shall be performed, the following evidence thereof shall be required.

Firstly—A return of the names, ages and residence of the said scouts.

Secondly—An abstract of the pay of the said scouts, specifying the exact days in which they were so employed. The pay to be regulated by the lowest price in the respective counties in which the service may be performed, and on this point you and the commanding officer will be particularly accurate. I have been informed that 5/ Virginia currency per day has been given to each of the scouts—If this high price has been given, it must form the excess to be given on the part of the United States.

Thirdly—An account of rations, each ration being stated at not a higher rate than 6 d. Per ration.

Fourthly—All these papers must be signed and certified on Oath by the County lieutenants or commanding officer of each county, and transmitted to Brigadier General Harmar, in order to be delivered to the pay-master of his regiment who will have the accounts passed and draw the money for the same—The money so drawn to be paid by him to the County lieutenants who must produce to him the receipts of the individuals for whom the money was so drawn. The commanding officer will also issue a reasonable quantity of powder and ball for the said scouts to the county lieutenants.

It is however to be strongly remarked, that all measures of this nature are uncertain opposed to the principles of regularity, and to be adopted only in cases of exigence, and to cease the moment the said exigencies shall cease— That therefore you, or the commanding officer aforesaid will not confer the authority herein contained, but in cases of the most conspicuous necessity, and that when such cases do arise, that you or he transmit to this office a particular detail of the evidences whereon you have formed your judgment.

To the Lieutenants of the Counties of Harrison—Randolph—Ohio— Monongahala—and Kenhawa—The same to the Lieutenant of Russell County April 29th. 1790 with the alterations as in the margin

War-Office, April 13th. 1790

Sir.

The President of the United States on the 3'rd of last month directed me to authorise the Governor of the Western territory, or in his absence the commanding officer of the troops in certain cases to empower the lieutenants of the counties lying along the Ohio, to call forth for the protection of said counties, certain patroles, denominated scouts, at the expence of the United States—Colonel Duval lieutenant of Harrison County was charged with these orders to the Governor or Brigadier General Harmar, and from the particular interest he took in the affair, no doubt can remain but that he exerted himself to have the said orders carried into full effect.

But as it is possible that some delays may have been occasioned,*[2] and as the President of the United States is exceedingly desirous that the exposed counties may avail themselves of the provision intended in said orders, he has directed me to write to the lieutenants of the Counties of Harrison, Randolph, Ohio, Monongahala and Kenhawa in Virginia, and in case their situation required the benefit of the said provision, that they should be empowered for that purpose.

---

[2] The notation, "add—* 'by your distance or other circumstances,'" appears in the left margin of the manuscript.

Therefore Sir I do in the name of the President of the United States, hereby authorize and empower you, if in your judgment the appearances of danger are such as to require the measure, to call forth the scouts herein mentioned and under the regulations described.[3]

[For these regulations see the preceding letter of the 3rd. of March, to Govr. St. Clair or Genl. Harmar.]

To Harry Innes Esqr. District Judge of Kentucky

War-Office, 13th. April 1790

Sir,

By some recent information from the Ohio it appears, that the indians still continue their depredations on the frontiers.

A general arrangement relative to the frontiers has been contemplated, but not having been finally concluded upon by Congress, and the season of activity approaching, the President of the United States was induced from the particular situation of the Counties lying along the Ohio, to direct on the 3rd. of last march, that the Governor of the Western territory, or in his absence Brigadier General Harmar should be invested with a conditional authority; of which the enclosed is a copy.

These orders were tranmitted by Colonel Duval lieutenant of Harrison County, who would undoubtedly as he was much interested in the business, convey expeditiously the same to the commanding officer.

But as it is possible, notwithstanding that some delays may have taken place, and as the President of the United States is exceedingly desirous that the inhabitants of the frontier counties should experience the benefits of the provision contained in the said orders to the commanding officer, he has directed me to make this communication to you, and he has further directed me to empower you that in case any of the Counties of Kentucky should not have already availed themselves of said provision, and should in your judgment stand in need thereof, that you should under your hand and seal authorize the lieutenants of such counties to call forth the scouts precisely as to the numbers and under the regulations directed in the instructions to the Governor of the Western territory or in his absence the commanding officer of the troops.

The information of the wages paid for the scouts, was given by Colonel Duval—It exceeds greatly all calculations of pay to be given persons for performing military service, and were it carried to a considerable extent, no government on earth could support it.

But as this measure is regarded merely as a temporary expedient until

---

[3] This letter is from Henry Knox.

further measures are taken, the President of the United States consents to the usual sums being given which hitherto have been given by Virginia for the same services; at the same time he reposes entire confidence in your character that you will (if arrangements should not have been made by the commanding officer) guard in this respect the interests of the United States.

It is the opinion of some gentlemen well acquainted with Kentucky, that four scouts, or men, to each county would be satisfactory. If this should also be your judgment you will limit the arrangement to that number, or at least to the usual number heretofore employed. But as the information was different from that whereon the instructions to the Governor and Commanding officer of the 3d. of March was founded, it has been concluded best to make no alteration in that discretionary arrangement.

H. K.[4]

No. 3

Copy of a letter written by the secretary of War to the Lieutenants of the Counties of Washington in Pennsylvania; Harrison, Randolph, Ohio, Monongahalia & Kenhawa in Virginia; Mason, Bourbon, Woodford, Madison, Lincoln, Mercer, Nelson & Jefferson in Kentuckey.

War Office, 17th. July 1790

Sir,

I had the honor on the 13th day of April last, to address you on the subject of the incursions of small parties of Indians on the western frontiers. In that letter I authorized you in the name of the President of the United States, in certain cases of imminent danger, to call out for the protection of the county certain species of patroles denominated scouts, at the expence of the United States.

I have now the honor by the direction of the President of the United States to inform you that the authority contained in said letter relative to said scouts is to be considered as having ceased and terminated upon your receiving this letter, duplicates of which I have written and transmitted to you.

The representations of the then deplorable situation of the frontier counties, and the high estimation the said scouts were held in by the inhabitants, were the inducements of the President of the United States to consent to calling forth that expensive species of militia as a temporary measure for the protection of the exposed counties.

But as experience has demonstrated the inefficacy of defensive measures for an extensive frontier, against straggling parties of Indians, and as conditional

---

4. "H.K." is Henry Knox.

orders have been transmitted to the governor of the western territory, and the commanding officer of the troops of the United States, to act offensively against the Shawanese and outcast Cherokees joined with them, inhabiting northwest of the Ohio, who are probably the banditti, which has for some time past committed depredations on the counties lying along the Ohio, And as the militia or rangers hereafter described will in cases of necessity be permitted at the expence of the Union in lieu of the Scouts; it is presumed that no injury will be sustained by revoking the authority for calling into service so expensive a species of troops as the said scouts.

The President of the United States is anxiously desirous of effectually protecting the frontiers, and he will take all such reasonable measures, as in his judgement the case may require, and for which he shall be by the constitution, or by the laws authorized.

He has therefore directed me to inform you, that in addition to the general measures aforesaid which have been ordered he has empowered the governor of the western territory and brigadier general Harmar, or either of them to make the arrangement here after described for the internal security of the exposed counties.

The said governor & commanding officer, or either of them will under their hands & seals, empower the lieutenants such counties, lying along the Ohio, as they shall judge necessary, to call forth, the number of militia, or rangers hereafter mentioned, and under the regulations prescribed.

1st. The said militia, or rangers shall not exceed for the internal defence of any county, One subaltern, one serjeant, one corporal & twelve privates. But such less number may be ordered as the said governor & commanding officer, or county lieutenant may judge requisite.

2d. The said militia or rangers shall during the time of their actual service, receive the following rates of pay, which are the same as is by law established for the regular troops of the United States and the militia, vizt.

> Lieutenant, twenty two dollars,
> Ensign, eighteen dollars,
> Serjeant, five dollars,
> Corporal, four dollars,
> Privates, three dollars,

⅌ month.

3d. The said rangers shall be furnished with rations, in such manner as the lieutenants of the county shall think proper. The United States will allow for each ration, six pence Virginia currency, or eight & one third hundredth parts of a dollar. The subaltern to have two, and the non commissioned & privates one ration each.

4th. The lieutenant of each county will be responsible on oath, that the said rangers shall be called into service only in cases of imminent danger, and that they be discharged as soon as the danger shall cease.

That when any service shall have been performed by said rangers the following evidence thereof will be required.

1st. A return of the names, rank, ages, residence and times of service of each of the said rangers.

2d. A pay abstract, or account of the number of said rangers, agreably to the aforesaid return.

3d. An abstract of the rations agreably to the aforesaid return.

4th. These papers to be signed & verified upon oath by the Lieutenant of the county or commanding officer of the militia—who will transmit the same to brigadier general Harmar, or the commanding officer of the troops of the United States on the Ohio.

5th. Brigadier general Harmar or the commanding officer of the troops, will certify on the said return, that the said rangers were ordered into service, in pursuance of his authority, or the authority of the governor of the western territory.

6th. The paymaster of the regiment of regular troops will receive the amount of the said abstracts from the Treasury or Pay office of the United States, and pay the same to the county lieutenants, and the said county lieutenants will pay each of the rangers respectively taking triplicate receipts for the payments—two of which he must transmit to the paymaster aforesaid—within two months from the time he shall have received the money from the said paymaster—and until these said receipts shall be transmitted to the said paymaster, the lieutenants of the counties will be held responsible for the sums they may have received, or such proportions thereof for which they shall not have produced receipts & from the individual rangers (or their attornies) who performed the service.

And whereas some of the counties may be involved in such immediate danger, as not to permit the county lieutenants sufficient time to obtain the authority herein mentioned from the said governor or commanding officer; in which case the county lieutenants may order out the Rangers herein mentioned under the regulations prescribed, on condition, that as soon as may be, the said lieutenants of the county & two magistrates, make a statement to the said governor & commanding officer of the reasons which induced them to order out the said rangers.

This statement will be considered as essential, in order that general Harmar or the commanding officer may ground thereon his certificate on the pay abstracts, without which payments will not be made.

It may perhaps be considered as unnecessary, after stating the vouchers before mentioned, to add any further precautions against unnecessarily calling out the rangers before described. But as the said service is at best only to be viewed as an expedient rather temporary & desultory than permanent and regular, it is the earnest desire of the President of the United States, that it should be conducted with the highest oeconomy. He therefore has desired that the county lieutenants may be strongly impressed with this idea, as well from a personal regard to themselves, as to the common welfare of the western country and the United States.

If the permission now given be used with great discretion, and only in cases of real necessity, every consideration will in future justify a more extensive & perfect protection, should the situation of the frontiers require the same.

I shall beg that immediately upon your receiving this letter, that you will inform me thereof.

I have the honor to be
Sir
Your most obedient,
humble servant,
(signed) H. KNOX
secy. for the Department
of War

An ESTIMATE of the Expences of Scouts and Rangers, for the protection of the frontiers lying along the Ohio, the cumberland Settlements and the Settlements upon and between the forks of Holstein and french broad Rivers for the Year 1791

5 Men or Scouts to be averaged for each County and the number of Counties or divisions being estimated at 22

110 Men to be employed as Scouts from the first of March to the 30th. of
November being 9 Months at the Rate of 12 Dollars pr. month   D.   11,880.
One Ration pr. day is for the above period for 110 Men
29,700 Rations @ $\frac{8^1/_2}{100}$ pr. Rations   2,524.50

                                                                                                    Doll.   14,404.50

RANGERS

One Lieutenant one Serjeant one Corporal & 12 Men to act as Rangers for each of 21 of the above Counties
                        at the same rate of pay as the Regular Troops
21 Lieutenants at Doll. 22 pr. month is for 9 Months   D.   4,158.

21 Serjeants	"	"	5	"	"	"	945.
21 Corporals	"	"	4	"	"	"	756.
252 Privates	"	"	3	"	"	"	6,804.

three Lieutenants Six Serjeants Six Corporals & 48 Privates for the Same period for Russel County

3 Lieutenants	at Doll. 22 pr. Month is for 9 Months						594.
6 Serjeants	"	"	5	"	"	"	270.
6 Corporals	"	"	4	"	"	"	216.
48 privates	"	"	3	"	"		1,296.
					Dollars		15,039.

24 Lieutenants at 2 Rations pr. day is for 9 Months	12,960 Rations
354 non commissioned & Privates at 1 Ration	95,580 "
	108,540 Rations

at 8¹/₂/Cts. pr. Ration   9,225.90

24,264.90
38,669.40

Dollars

War department 5th of January 1791

H. KNOX secy. of War

1405

Report of the Secretary of War
with enclosures

The Secretary of War to whom the President of the United States, was pleased to refer a Letter from His Excellency the Governor of Virginia of the 4th. instant, transmitting certain papers stating the measures which the Legislature and Executive of Virginia have adopted for the temporary defence of the western frontier of that State,

REPORTS,

That it appears from the said papers, that upon the 20th. day of December last, the Legislature of Virginia authorised the Executive of said State to direct such temporary defensive operations in the frontier counties of said State, as would secure the Citizens thereof from the hostile invasions of the Indian enemy.

That at the same time the said Legislature also requested the Executive to transmit to the President of the United States the Memorial from the representatives of the frontier counties, and communicate to him such defensive measures as they may think proper to direct in consequence of the authority vested in them for the sole purpose of affording defence to the frontier citizens until the general government can enter into full and effectual measures to accomplish the said object.

That the memorial of the representatives of the frontier counties alluded to by the said Legislature was transmitted by the said Governor to the President of the United States the 10th. day of December last, and the same was reported upon by the Secretary of War, the fifth instant.

That the measures directed by the Executive of Virginia in consequence of the before recited power vested in them by the Legislature are detailed in No. 2, and amount to ten Lieutenants, ten ensigns and five hundred and eighteen non commissioned and privates at the same rate of pay allowed by the law of the United States, besides a brigadier general who shall be allowed the pay and rations of Lieutenant Colonel when in actual service.

That it does not appear that any denomination of troops termed Scouts at an higher rate of pay than the Militia have been ordered out by the Executive of Virginia.

That the expence of the said defensive system for nine months would, if the same should be necessary for so long a term, amount to thirty six thousand, seven hundred and forty seven dollars, and sixty Cents, as per estimate herewith submitted; No. 5.

That the total of the estimate submitted on the 5th. instant amounted to thirty eight thousand, six hundred and sixty nine dollars and forty Cents— But, about four twenty second parts are to be deducted from the said estimate for the County of Washington in Pennsylvania, and the districts, amounting to about three Counties for the settlements upon Cumberland and between the forks of Holstein and Frenchbroad—This would leave about eighteen parts of the said estimate for the expence of the Counties of Virginia and the District of Kentucky amounting to thirty one thousands, six hundred and thirty eight dollars and sixty Cents—Comparing therefore the expence of the plan suggested in the report of the 5th. instant with the system directed by the Executive of Virginia, the difference will be five thousand and one hundred and nine dollars, greater for the latter than the former plan.

But, in the plan suggested in the said report of the 5th. instant, only the number of three hundred and fifty four non commissioned officers and privates were stated to be employed, besides commissioned officers. The number directed by Virginia amount to five hundred and eighteen non commissioned officers and privates, besides the Commissioned officers. The reason that the difference of expence is not proportioned to the difference of numbers is that the species of militia termed Scouts are not ordered in the system directed by Virginia.

From this statement the following questions arise.

First, Is the exposed situation of the frontier Counties of Virginia such as to require that they should be protected at the expence of the United States? Secondly, If so, is the system directed by the Executive of Virginia, of such a nature as to be confirmed by the general government, and ordered into execution at the expence of the United States? Thirdly, If not, shall a regular and efficient plan be devised for the same object and put into execution at the expence of the United States?

On the first question, the secretary of War is of opinion, that the existing circumstances relative to the indian hostilities, are such as to cause just apprehensions for the safety of the frontier settlers during the approaching season. That principles of sound policy therefore, as well as of justice, require, that the said settlers should be afforded all reasonable protection at the expence of the United States.

On the second question; the Secretary of War is of opinion, that however proper the system of defence directed by the executive of Virginia may have been considering the circumstances under which it was ordered yet there are several well founded objections against its being confirmed by the general government and ordered into execution at the expence of the United States. First, Because it is too uncertain as to any material effect to be produced thereby.

Secondly, Because it is destitute of those principles of Unity and responsibility essentially necessary to guard the public from abuse.

Thirdly, Because the detachments ordered out for the other Counties besides Kentucky are evidently designed for local service only, and not to be drawn into one body, however necessary the measure may be.

Fourthly, Because it is evident the Legislature of Virginia considered the arrangement which should be made by the executive of the said State as a temporary measure of affording defence to the frontiers, until the general government could enter into full and effectual measures to accomplish the said object.

On the third question, the Secretary of War is of opinion, that the following plan for defence of the frontiers in addition to the regular troops would be the most proper for the ensuing season.

For the defence of the exposed counties of Virginia and Kentuckey, and the Cumberland and Holstein settlements, one Regiment of Rangers, to consist of one Lieutenant Colonel commandant, two majors, ten Captains and fourteen subalterns, and seven hundred and thirty eight non-commissioned and privates.

That these rangers be inlisted on the Continental establishment of pay rations and clothing; to serve from the first day of March next; until the 30th. of November, unless sooner discharged.

That a proportion of clothing equal to the annual allowance to the federal troops be issued to the said Rangers.

That if an expedition be formed against the indian towns; that the Rangers raised for the Counties of Virginia and Kentuckey, should be assembled for that purpose; that in other cases, they should be employed in ranging the frontiers most liable to inroads.

That the expence of the said corps for nine Months would amount to forty nine thousand, four hundred and fifty four dollars, as per estimate herewith submitted—But the Secretary of War conceives the efficacy and service of said corps would amply compensate for the difference of expence between the same, and the system directed by Virginia.

That the expence of defending the frontiers for the ensuing year seems to be inevitable—But there is a choice in the manner of defence. The regular troops are inadequate to afford that extensive protection required from the County of Washington in Pennsylvania down the Ohio to the settlements on the Cumberland river, and the other settlements in the southwestern territory of the United States: They must be assisted by auxiliaries, in order to defend the frontiers effectually.

The question seems to be reduced to one point; whether the defence shall be afforded in a regular efficient manner, with full proof of the service having been rendered, or whether it shall be performed in a manner less efficient, and neither regular or certain?

The Secretary of War submits the idea, that the whole Business of the defensive protection afforded the frontiers during the last year, by the general government, the System directed by the Executive of Virginia, and the plan herein proposed, should be laid before the Congress of the United States for their information and decision.

The Secretary of War will, in another report, which he will shortly submit to the President of the United States take the liberty of suggesting some observations respecting the issue of the late expedition against the Miami towns; and of the circumstances which may require another and more effectual expedition against the Wabash indians. But in case of another expedition it is conceived that the defensive provision should be made. For although, while the expedition will be in operation the Indians will not probably make incursions, yet, their predatory parties may be expected on the frontiers both before and after the expedition.

All which is humbly submitted to the President of the United States.

War Office,   H. KNOX
15th. Jany. 1791.   Secretary of War

No. 1
Beverley Randolph to the President of the United States

Council chamber Jany. 4th. 1791

Sir,

In conformity to a Resolution of the General Assembly of this State, herewith inclosed, I do myself the honour to transmit a Memorial from the Representatives of the Frontier Counties, & the Proceedings of the Executive respecting a temporary System of defence for the Western Frontier. I beg leave also to lay before you copies of two other Resolutions of the General Assembly together with the Petition of sundry Officers of the Virginia Line on Continental Establishment on the subject of the Bounty Lands allotted to them on the Northwest side of the Ohio.

I have the Honour to be
with the highest respect
Your obedt. Servant
BEVERLEY RANDOLPH

The President of the
United States

No. 2
[Extract from Journal of Virginia Executive Council]

In Council Decr. 29th. 1790

The board resumed the consideration of a Resolution of the General Assembly, authorizing the Executive to direct such temporary defensive Operations in the frontier Counties of this State as will secure the Citizens from the hostile Invasions of the Indian Enemy.

Whereupon the Board are of Opinion, that the best system of defence, which can be established under the present Circumstances, will be to order into service in the different Western Counties a small number of men proportioned to the degree in which they are respectively exposed.

That the officers commanding these parties be instructed constantly to range the Frontiers most open to invasion and either to alarm the Inhabitants upon the approach of a large body of the enemy or repel the incursions of predatory parties.

It is therefore advised, that a Lieutenant, two Serjeants and forty rank & file be allowed to the county of Harrison; an Ensign, two Serjeants and thirty rank & file to Monongalia; a Lieutenant, an Ensign, three Serjeants and fifty rank & file to Ohio; a Lieutenant, an Ensign, three Serjeants and fifty rank & file to Kanawha; an Ensign two Serjeants and twenty rank & file to Randolph; an Ensign, three Serjeants and thirty two rank & file to Wythe; and a Lieutenant, an Ensign, three Serjeants and fifty rank & file to Russel. The rangers to be ready for service by the first day of March next, to be stationed at such places as in the Opinion of the Commanding officer of each county respectively shall be most convenient to enable them by ranging the frontiers to give effectual protection.

That the Commanding officers of the several Counties be directed to procure by Voluntary engagements the Compliment of men allowed for the defence of their Counties respectively; but should they be unable to obtain the required number by this means that they detach them with the necessary officers by detail and rotation of duty agreeable to the Act to amend and reduce into one Act the several laws for regulating and disciplining the militia and guarding against invasions & Insurrections.

That for the defence of Kentucky, it is advised, that a Brigadier General be appointed to command the whole militia of the District, who shall be allowed the pay and rations of a Lieutenant Colonel when in actual service.

That the said Brigadier General do immediately endeavor to procure by Voluntary engagements two hundred and twenty six men to range the most exposed parts of the Frontiers of the District to be so stationed as will in his Judgment afford the best protection to the Inhabitants; but should he be unable to obtain the required number by Voluntary engagements, that he direct the commanding officer of the respective counties composing the District to detach their just proportion with the necessary officers by detail and rotation of duty agreeable to the militia law, to be ready for service by the first day of March next.

That in the execution of this business he be not considered as in actual service nor have authority to appoint the Staff and other officers allowed by law, but shall be reimbursed all such reasonable expences as he may necessarily incur.

That the said Rangers be furnished with rations in such manner as the Brigadier General of Kentucky and the officers commanding the several Counties without that district shall think proper—six pence to be allowed for each ration—A subaltern to be allowed two and the noncommissioned and privates one ration each. The pay and rations of both officers and privates to be the same as is allowed by law to the Continental troops.

That the following evidence of the service of the rangers be required.

1st. A return of the names, rank & time of service of each of the said Rangers.

2d. A Pay Abstract or Account for the number of said Rangers agreeable to the aforesaid Return; these papers to be verified by the Oath of the officers commanding the several Detachments and by the Signature of the Brigadier General in Kentucky, or by that of the Commanding Officers of the several counties without that District.

3d. An abstract of the rations agreeably to the aforesaid return, to be signed by the officer receiving them and countersigned by the Brigadier General in Kentucky or by the Commanding officers of the several counties without that District.

And it is further advised, that Charles Scott Esquire be appointed Brigadier General of Kentucky.

All which matters so advised, the Governor orders Accordingly.

Extract from the Journal
Attest
SAM. COLEMAN A.C.C.

No. 3
Resolutions of the Commonwealth of Virginia

VIRGINIA

IN THE HOUSE OF DELEGATES,
Monday the 20th of December 1790

RESOLVED that the Executive be authorized to direct such temporary defensive operations in the frontier Counties of this State, as will secure the Citizens thereof, from the Hostile invasions of the Indian Enemy.

RESOLVED that the Executive be requested, to transmit to the President of the United States, the memorial from the Representatives of the frontier Counties, and communicate to him such defensive measures as they may think proper to direct, in consequence of the authority vested in them for the sole purpose of affording defence to our frontier Citizens, until the General

Government can enter into full and effectual measures to accomplish the said object.

1790 December

Agreed to by the Senate   Teste
H. BROOKE C. S.   CHARLES HAY, C. H. D.

                                           A Copy
                                           Teste
                                           CHARLES HAY C. H. D.

No. 4

To His Excellency Beverley Randolph Esquire Governor of Virginia

The joint memorial of the Delegates of Ohio, Monongalia, Harrison, Randolph, Kanawha, Greenbriar, Montgomery & Russel Counties humbly represents,

That the defenceless condition of those counties forming a line of nearly four hundred miles along the Ohio river exposed to the hostile invasions of their Indian Enemies, destitute of every kind of support, is truly alarming, for not withstanding all the regulations of the General Government in that Country, we have reason to lament, that they have been hitherto ineffectual for our protection, nor indeed could it happen otherwise, for the Garrison's kept by the Continental troops on the Ohio river, if they are of any use it must be to the Kentucky Settlements, as they immediately cover that Country, to us they can be of no service being from two to four hundred miles below our frontier Settlements.

We further beg leave to represent, that agreeably to the last arrangement for our defence, as declared by the Secretary at War, a Subaltern officer, a Serjeant, a Corporal and twelve privates were allotted to some of the above mentioned Counties for their defence, and them only to be continued in service when the Continental Commanding Officer in the Western Country may approve of it, they at the same time to be under such regulations as it is impossible for the Inhabitants of our Country to comply with, the Communication betwixt him and us being cut off by a distance of two to four hundred miles, and that through an uninhabited Country exposed to the Indians, having intirely exploded our old experienced mode of defending our frontiers by keeping out Scouts and Rangers for their information and protection, owing as we are informed, that it is supposed that the new plan is less expensive, but surely if our operations must be on the defensive, a small saving (for a small saving it must be) ought not to be deemed a good reason to alter from a known measure to one that is only supposed to be as good, when the lives of so many of your Citizens are exposed to the enemy. We further beg leave to observe that we have reason to fear that the Consequences of the defeat of our Army by the Indians on the late expedition will be severely felt on our frontiers, as there is no doubt but that the Indians Will in their turn (being flushed with Victory) invade our Settlements and exercise all their horrid murder upon the Inhabitants thereof, whenever the state of the Weather will permit them to travel, then is it not better to support us where we are be the expence what it may, than to oblige such a number of your brave Citizens who have so long supported and still continues to support a dangerous frontier, (although thousands of their relatives in the Flesh have in the prosecution thereof fallen a sacrifice to savage inventions) to quit the Country after all they have done and suffered when you know that a frontier must be supported somewhere.

Permit us therefore to assure you that we think the only measure that will establish the Confidence of your frontier People in the Government and also be the means of bringing about the end proposed to Wit, their safety and protection, will be to empower the County Lieutenants in each of those Counties to send out a few Scouts to watch the passes of the Enemy and when the Winter breaks up to place some Rangers on the outside of the settlements, this we mean only as a temporary matter to continue until more effectual measures are adopted for the protection of that Country, the expence of which scouts and Rangers to be settled with your Auditor, and paid by Virginia, and the General Government to be debited with the amount thereof for which the state of Virginia ought to be credited in her Accounts with that Government. And we hope and trust that Congress will comply therewith until they extend to us that protection, that we as Citizens of Virginia have a right to expect. And we further trust and hope that the state of Virginia will never quietly rest inactive until peace is restored to all her Citizens be their situation ever so remote, under those impressions we have taken the liberty to address you upon this subject, praying that should not the Executive Council of Virginia possess Power sufficient to extend to us that relief which our necessities require, that you will in that case lay our complaints before the proper Tribunal where we may be redressed. We have the honor to be with great respect &c.

} Russel

BENJAMIN BIGGS } Ohio
JOHN HENDERSON }

JOHN EVANS jr.   } Monongalia
WM. MCCLEERY   }

GEO. JACKSON   } HARRISON
JOHN PRUNTY

CORNELIUS BOGARD   } RANDOLPH
ABRAHAM CLAYPOOL

ANDREW DONNALLY   } KANAWHA
GEO. CLENDINEN

THOS. EDGAR   } GREENBRIAR
W. H. CAVENDISH

H. MGOMRY.   } MONTGOMERY
R. SAWYERS

A Copy
Attest
SAM COLEMAN A.C.C.

No. 5

AN ESTIMATE of Pay Subsistence & forage for 9 months from the first day of march to the 30th. of November 1790 according to the arrangement of Virginia[5]

1 Brigadier General with the pay Subsistence
& Forage of a Lt. Colonel estimated to be
in Service 4 months Pay at 60 Doll. pr.
month is for 4 months   D.   240.
Subsistence 6 Rations pr. day is 4 Mo. 720
Rs. @ 12 cts.   86.40
Forage 12 dollars pr. month   36.
                    Doll.   362.40

10 Lieutenants for 9 months
Pay at 22 Doll. pr. month is for 9 mths.
                    D.   1,980.
Subsistence 2 Rations pr. day. 5,400 Rs.
@ 12/Cts.   648.
                             2,628.

10 Ensigns for 9 months
Pay at 18 Doll. pr. month is for 9 months
                    D.   1,620.
Subsistence 2 Rats. pr. day. 5,400 Rs. @
12/Cts.   648.
                             2,268.

---

[5] The phrase "according to the arrangement of Virginia" was inserted by Henry Knox.

40 Serjeants at	5 Dolls. pr. month is for 9 months	D.	1,800.
478 Privates "	3 " " " " " "		12,906.
		Doll.	14,706.

Subsistence for 518 non commissioned & Privates at one Ration pr. day is for 9 months 139,860 Rations @ 12/Cts.   16,783.20

31,489.20

Dollars   36,747.60

War office 15th January 1791

H. KNOX secy. of War

The report and the two reports that are part of C No. 1 are in A Record of Reports of the Secretary of War, Vol. I, HR, DNA. Enclosures Nos. 2–4 to the first report of the secretary under C No. 1 are mistakenly filed with the secretary of war's letter of December 8, 1790, in Reports and Communications from the Secretary of War, SR, DNA. Enclosures Nos. 2 and 3 in A, Nos. 1 through 4 in B, No. 1 to the first report in C No. 1, and Nos. 1–6 to the second report in C No. 1 are in President's Messages, transmitting reports of the secretary of war, SR, DNA. Enclosure A No. 1 has not been located. Enclosure No. 6 to the second report in C No. 1 follows on pages 1416 and 1417.

AN ESTIMATE for Pay, Subsistence, forage & clothing for 9 Months for one Regiment of Rangers formed as follows

PAY

one Lieutenant Colonel Commandant at D. 60 pr. month is for 9 months	"	D. 540.
2 Majors " " 40 " " " " " "	"	" 720.
10 Captains " " 30 " " " " " "	"	" 2,700.
10 Lieutenants " " 22 " " " " " "	"	" 1,980.
10 Ensigns " " 18 " " " " " "	"	" 1,620.
1 Paymaster additional " " 5 " " " " " "	"	" 45.
1 Quartermaster do. " " 5 " " " " " "	"	" 45.
1 Adjutant do. " " 10 " " " " " "	"	" 90.
		D. 7,740.

40 Serjeants " " 5 " " " " " "		D. 1,800.
40 Corporals " " 4 " " " " " "		" 1,440.
40 Drummers }		
40 fifers } " " 3 " " " " " "		" 17,766.
578 Privates }		
	Doll.	21,006.

DEDUCTIONS FOR CLOTHING

40 Serjeants at D. 1 40/100 pr. Month is for 9 Months D.		504.
40 Corporals " " 1 15/100 " " " " " "		414.
658 Music. & Privates " " 90/100 " " " " " "		5,329.80
		6,247.80

Amount of Pay   D.   22,498.20

14,758.20

SUBSISTENCE

1 Lieut. Col. Commt.	6 Rations pr. day is for 9 Months		1,620 Rations
2 Majors	4 " " " " " "		2,160 "
10 Captains	3 " " " " " "		8,100 "
10 Lieutenants	2 " " " " " "		5,400 "
10 Ensigns	2 " " " " " "		5,400 "
738 Non commissd. & Privates	1 " " " " " "		199,260 "

221,940 Rations at 7/100

Amount of Subsistence   15,535.80

FORAGE

1 Lieut. Col. Commt.	12 Dollars pr. Month is for 9 Months	D.	108.
2 Majors	10 " " " " " "		180.
Paymaster, Quarter Master & Adjutant each	6 " " " " " "		162.

Amount of Forage   450.

CLOTHING

738 Non Commissioned and Privates at 15 Dollars   11,070.

Dollars   49,454.

War office January 15th. 1791

H. Knox secy. of War

Information on Depredations by Indians
January 27, 1791

Rufus Putnam to the President of the United States

Marietta, Januy. 8th. 1791

Sir:

The mischief which I feared, has overtaken us much sooner than I expected. On the evening of the 2d. instant, between sunset and daylight-in; the indians surprised a new settlement of our people at a place on the Muskingum called the Big-bottom, near forty miles up the river, in which disaster eleven men, one woman, and two children, were killed: three men are missing—and four others made their escape. Thus sir, the war which was partial, before the campaign of last year is in all probability become general: For I think there is no reason to suppose, that we are the only people on whom the savages will wreak their vengeance, or that the number of hostile indians have not encreased since the late expedition. Our situation is truly critical: The governor and secretary both being absent; no assistance from Virginia or Pennsylvania can be had. The garrison at Fort Harmar, consisting at this time of little more than twenty men, can afford no protection to our settlements. And the whole number of men, in all our settlements capable of bearing arms, including all civil and military officers, do not exceed two hundred and eighty seven, and these, many of them badly armed. We are in the utmost danger of being swallowed up should the enemy push the war with vigor during the winter; this I believe will fully appear, by taking a short view of our several settlements, and I hope justify the extraordinary measures we have adopted for want of a legal authority in the territory to apply to for aid in the business. The situation of our people is nearly as follows:

At Marietta are about eighty houses in the distance of one mile, with scattering houses about three miles up the Ohio. A set of mills at Duck creek, four miles distant, and another mill, two miles up the Muskingum. Twenty two miles up this river is a settlement consisting of about twenty family; about two miles from them on Wolf Creek are five families and a set of mills. Down the Ohio and opposite the Little Kenahawa commences the settlement called Belle Prairie, which extends down the river with little interruption about twelve miles and contains between thirty and forty houses. Before the late disaster we had several other settlements, which are already broken up. I have taken the liberty to enclose the proceedings of the Ohio company and Justices of the sessions on this occasion; and beg leave with the greatest deference to observe, that unless government speedily send a body of troops for our protection we are a ruined people. The removal of the women and children, &c. will reduce many of the poorer sort to the greatest straits; but if we add to this the destruction of their corn, forage and cattle by the enemy, which is very probable to ensue. I know of no way, they can be supported, but if this should not happen. where these people are to raise bread another year, is not easy to conjecture, and most of them have nothing left to buy with—But my fears do not stop here we are a people so far detached, from all others in point of situation, that we can hope for no timely relief, in case of emergency from any of our neighbours; and among the number that compose our present military strength, almost one half are young men hired into the country, intending to settle by and by, these under present circumstances will probably leave us soon, unless prospect should brighten; and as to new settlers, we can expect none in our present situation; so that instead of encreasing in strength we are like to diminish daily, & if we do not fall a prey to the savages, we shall be so reduced and discouraged as to give up the settlement unless government shall give us timely protection. it has been a mystery with some why the troops have been withdrawn from this quarter, and collected at the Miami; that settlement, is I believe, within in three or four days march of a very populous part of Kentuckey from whence in a few days, they might be reinforced with several thousand men: Whereas we are not, within two hundred miles of any settlement, that can probably more than protect themselves.

But I forbear suggestions of this sort, and will only observe further, that our present situation, is truly distressing; and I do therefore most earnestly implore the protection of government, for myself and friends inhabiting these wilds of America. To this we conceive our-selves justly entitled, and so far as you Sir have the means in your power we rest assured that we shall receive it in due time.

I have the honor to be,
with the highest possible respect,
Sir,
Your most obedient
and most humble servant,
(signed)   RUFUS PUTNAM

To the President of the United States of America

Rufus Putnam to the Secretary of War

Marietta, January 8th. 1791

Dear sir,

I snatch a moment's time, to tell you that on the 2d instant the Indians surprized a Block-House of ours about 40 miles up the Muskingum, killed 14 Persons & carried off three others, these last lodged in a hutt about 50 Rod from the Block house—4 others who also lodged a distance from the Block-house made their escape. This event clearly proves that the expedition against the Shawanese will not produce peace, but on the contrary a more general & outrageous War; in which case there is with us but one alternative, Government must either give us some troops, or we must eventually be obliged to quit the Country, our numbers are too small to make head against an host of Savages without aid from the General Government; being confident that we deserve, we endeavour to believe that we shall obtain, their protection—and in the mean time we are taking all possible measures in our power for our own preservation, and shall endeavour not only to defend the Town of Marietta, but the most considerable out-settlements that remain, till such time as Congress shall take their measures respecting the War which has been blown into a flame, by the expedition against the Shawanese—I hope Government will not be long in deciding what part to take, for if we are not to be protected, the sooner we know it the better—better for us & better for Government—better that we withdraw ourselves at once than remain to be destroyed by piece-meal, and better that Government disband their troops now in the Country and give it up altogether than be wasting the public money in supporting a few troops altogether inadequate to the purpose of giving peace to the territory.

> I have the honor to be
> With very great Respect
> Sir, Your very hume. servt.
> (sign'd)   RUFUS PUTNAM

Honble. H. Knox Esq.

[Copy of a letter from Capt. David Zeigler to Governor St. Clair]

Sir.

I have the mortification to inform your Excellency that on the 2'nd instant in the evening the settlements called Big Bottom, consisting of 16 men, one woman and two children were destroyed by the savages, and only two men escaped and three supposed taken prisoner as the body was not found—As soon as I got acquainted, assisted Colonel Sprout to make a detachment with as many men as I possible could share towards that settlement—the indians were gone before the party arrived.

Since your departure, no indians has made their appearance here, and they are to a great number at the Great Rock and White Woman's Creek, and do not seem to be inclined to come in. The 4th. instant was the day I had appointed for George White-eyes, the old, which is amongst us, to go as far as said place, but now he is apprehensive of danger not only from them but also from own people, which obliged me to save him from trouble—Polly, the Wyandot woman is also here, and informed me the 1st instant in a crying manner that she apprehended all the savages were hostile inclined; when being in their town, numbers of the Chippewas and Otawas have passed to join those *banditti,* with their usual mode of singing, by giving farewell to their nation, for some time—To give credit to all that, I let your Excellency judge.

Since this unhappy affair happened the Ohio company voted troops to be raised for their defence and for such time, until more troops will be sent on to this post—They also voted three block-houses to be erected—the troops so raised, to have the same pay and rations (but no clothing) as the troops got last war in the service of the United States—This I am afraid will hurt the establishment.

Upon application from the directors of the Ohio in giving them assistance, shall order Ensign Morgan with fifteen men on his return to guard one of those block-houses, and any other aid possible on my part, they shall have.

All our settlements must become more careful, otherwise they may meet with the same fate.

The french families I expect will take shelter in this garrison so quartered at Campus Martius, as by their law made—The women and children in the different settlement will repair to said place.

No new Commissary has made his appearance as yet, and of course no provision.

I have the honor to be, with the highest esteem,

Your Excellency's

Most obedt. & most humble servt.

(signed)   DAVID ZEIGLER Capt.

1st. United States regt.

Fort Harmar   ⎱
Jany. 8th. 1791 ⎰
His Excellency—
Arthur St. Clair—Governor—
Western territory

N.B. It is to be observed that Capt. Zeigler is a German—A letter from Capt. Zeigler to the Secretary of War dated Jany. 8th. 1791—to the same purpose as the foregoing.

President's messages: Transmitting reports from the Secretary of War, SR, DNA.

House Committee Report
February 1, 1791

REPORT on a confidential message from the President of the United States, respecting the situation of the South Western Frontiers, received the 24th. of January, 1791, and referred on the 26th. of the same month, with the papers accompanying the same.

The Committee report, as their opinion, the following resolutions:

1. RESOLVED, that immediate and effectual provision ought to be made for the defence of the frontiers, and for the establishment of posts for their protection.

2. RESOLVED, that the President be authorized to raise an additional regiment to consist of nine hundred and twelve non-commissioned officers and privates to serve for a term not exceeding three years.

And to encourage the recruiting service,

3. RESOLVED, that a bounty, not exceeding six dollars be allowed to each recruit: a like allowance to be made to them who enlisted since the   of

4. RESOLVED, that the sum of one hundred and twenty thousand, two hundred and seventy six dollars, and twenty cents, ought to be appropriated to defray the expence arising from the said augmentation of the troops.

5. RESOLVED, that to enable the President, in virtue of the powers vested in him by law, to call into the service of the United States, such number of the militia, as he shall deem necessary for the public service (leaving it to his discretion to direct whether they shall serve on horse back, or on foot) there be appropriated a sum not exceeding one hundred and ninety two thousand, four hundred and ten dollars, as well to defray the expense of the said militia, as of such military operations as he may direct; and also, of such posts as he may think it expedient to establish.

6. PROVIDED NEVERTHELESS, AND BE IT FURTHER RESOLVED, that if the President should be of opinion, that it will be more conducive to the public service to employ troops enlisted under the denomination of levies than Militia, it shall be lawful for him to raise, for a term not exceeding four months, three regiments to consist of two thousand non-commissioned Officers and privates, allowing to each recruit, a bounty not exceeding three dollars.

7. RESOLVED, that the principles of justice and good faith, as well as the dignity of the United States, require a faithful performance of the treaties made with the Cherokee and Chickasaw nations of Indians; therefore this

House does highly approve of the measures adopted by the President of the United States to make known the Articles of the aforesaid treaties; and to warn all persons against committing any infraction thereof, on pain of being prosecuted, according to law.

8. RESOLVED, that this House will chearfully concur in any measures which may be necessary to enable the President to carry into effect, the Stipulations of the aforesaid treaties, agreeably to the principles of justice and good faith.

9th. February, 1791. Committed to a committee of the whole House, immediately—the first, second, third, fourth, fifth and sixth resolutions agreed to, and a bill or bills ordered, pursuant thereto—Seventh and eighth resolutions ordered to lie on the table.

A Record of the Reports of Select Committees, HR, DNA.

Report of the Secretary of War
February 1, 1791

A GENERAL estimate of the Expences which would be incurred by an expedition against the Wabash Indians calculated upon a Scale of 1,200 Regulars & 2,000 Levies. The period of the Expedition four Months. And also the amount of the expences for one Year of the proposed augmentation of the Regular Troops

The expence of 2,000 Levies as pr. estimate B No. 2	D.	74,770.
Bounties for 2,000 Levies at 5 Doll. pr. man	"	10,000.[1]
The difference between 3,200 Rations pr. day on the Ohio, and the proposed places of operation, the one being stated in the contract at 6 3/4 Cts. and the other 15 $^1/_4$ Cts. calculated at 120 days 384,000 Rations at 8$^1/_2$ Cts. difference	"	32,640.

[1] The following notation, which is in the hand of Ames and refers to this figure, appears in the left margin of the Manuscript: "Deduct 4,000 as the Comme. propose only 3 Dollars."

Camp equipage of all sorts,
    Boats, horses, Tents &c., and
    the transportation of the hospi-
    tal Stores, baggage for the
    army, The cannon & Stores of
    all sorts, to establish a post at
    the miami estimated in gross   "   50,000.

Medicines & Hospital Stores   "   4,000.

Contingencies   "   25,000.

                                   D.   196,410.

The amount of the annual ex-
    pences for the additional Reg-
    iment of Regulars as pr.
    particular estimate A amount
    to   D.   101,446.40

And if the bounty of 8 Doll.
for 2,128 non commissioned &
privates should be added for the
whole regular establishment
augmentation included, the
following extraordinary expences
would be incurred   "   17,024.[2]

    The establishment of a Major
General for one Year as pr.
estimate B. 2 amounts to   "   2,937.

                                 D.   121,407.40

1 Aid de Camp with the Rank of
    a Captain, and pay & emolu-
    ments of a Major, as during
    the late war

    Pay   40 doll. pr. mth.   D. 480.

    Subsistence 4 Rats. pr. day
         at 12/100   "   175.20

    Forage   10 Doll.   "   120.   "   775.20

2 Inspectors (omitted in the
General estimate of the war
department for the year 1791.
formed the 7th. december 1790)

---

[2] The following notation, which is in the hand of Ames and refers to this figure,
appears in the left margin of the manuscript: "Deduct 4,256 as the Commee. propose
only 6 Doll. Bounty."

one of whom to act as Brigade
Major.

2 Inspectors

Pay	30 doll. pr. mth.	D. 720.		
Subsistence 3 Rats. pr.				
day 12/100		" 262.80		
Forage	10 doll. pr. month	" 240. "	1,222.80	
The establishment of a Quarter				
master as pr. estimate B			1,126.80	
				124,532.20

Total to be provided for   D. 320,942.20

War department February 1, 1791

H. KNOX

secretary of War

Mr. Ames
  Chairman of
    The honorable
      Committee of the house of
        Representatives[3]

Reports and Communications from the Secretary of War, SR, DNA.

---

[3] From "to be provided for" through "Representatives" is in the hand of Henry Knox.

Military Establishment Bill [HR-126A]
February 12, 1791

An ACT for raising and adding another regiment to the military establishment of the United States, and for making further provision for the protection of the Frontiers

Sect. I. BE it enacted by the Senate and House of Representatives of the United States of America in Congress assembled, That there shall be raised an additional regiment of infantry, which, exclusive of the commissioned officers, shall consist of nine hundred and twelve[1] non-commissioned officers, privates and musicians.[2]

---

[1] On February 21, by a recorded vote of 18–8, the Senate disagreed to a motion to substitute "six hundred and eight" for "nine hundred and twelve."

[2] On February 19, the Senate agreed to the first section by a recorded vote of 15–7.

Sect. II. And be it further enacted, That the said regiment shall be organized in the same manner, as the regiment of infantry described in the Act, entitled, "An Act for regulating the military establishment of the United States."

Sect. III. And be it further enacted, That the troops aforesaid by this Act to be raised, including the officers, shall receive the same pay and allowances, be subject to the same rules and regulations, and be engaged[3] upon the same conditions, in all respects, excepting the bounty herein-after mentioned, as are stipulated for the troops of the United States, in the before-mentioned act.

Sect. IV. And be it further enacted, That all non-commissioned officers, privates and musicians, who have inlisted or shall inlist upon the terms prescribed in the aforesaid act, shall[4] be entitled to receive six dollars as a bounty.

Sect. V. And be it further enacted, That for defraying the expense of the aforesaid additional troops by this act to be raised for the term of one year, there be appropriated a sum not exceeding one hundred and twenty thousand two hundred and seventy-six dollars and twenty cents, to be paid out of the monies which, prior to the first of January next, shall arise from the duties imposed by the act passed during the present session of Congress, entitled, "An Act repealing, after the last day of June next, the duties heretofore laid upon distilled spirits imported from abroad, and laying others in their stead, and also upon spirits distilled within the United States, and for appropriating the same."[5]

Sect. VI. And be it further enacted, That in case the President of the United States should deem the employment of a Major-General, Brigadier-General, a Quarter-Master and Chaplain, or either of them, essential to the public interest, that he be, and he hereby is empowered, by and with the advice and consent of the Senate, to appoint the same accordingly. And a Major-General so appointed may chuse his Aid-de-Camp, and a Brigadier-General his Brigade-Major from the Captains or Subalterns of the line.[6]

Sect. VII. And be it further enacted, That in case a Major-General, Brigadier-General, Quarter-Master, Aid-de-Camp, Brigade-Major and Chaplain should be appointed, their pay and allowances shall be, respectively, as herein

---

[3] The Senate inserted "for the like term and" at this point.

[4] The Senate struck out "That all" through "act, shall" and inserted "each non-commissioned officer, private and musician who has inlisted or shall inlist pursuant to the Act aforesaid, or who shall inlist pursuant to this Act."

[5] The Senate struck out this section.

[6] The Senate added the following proviso at this point:
Provided always, That the Major-General and Brigadier-General, so to be appointed, shall respectively continue in pay during such term only as the President of the United States, in his discretion shall deem it requisite for the public service.

mentioned. The Major-General shall be entitled to one hundred and twenty-five dollars monthly pay, twenty dollars allowance for forage, monthly, and for daily subsistence fifteen rations, or money in lieu thereof, at the contract price. The Brigadier-General shall be entitled to ninety-four dollars monthly pay, with sixteen dollars allowance for forage, monthly, and for daily subsistence twelve rations, or money in lieu thereof at the contract price. That the Quarter-Master shall be entitled to the same pay, rations and forage, as the Lieutenant-Colonel-Commandant of a regiment. That the Aid-de-Camp be entitled, including all allowances, to the same pay, rations and forage, as a Major of a regiment. That the Brigade-Major be entitled, including all allowances, to the same pay, rations and forage as a Major of a regiment. That the Chaplain be entitled to fifty dollars per month.[7]

Sect. VIII. And be it further enacted, That if, in the opinion of the President, it will be conducive to the good of the service, to engage a body of militia to serve as cavalry, they furnishing their own horses, arms and provisions, it shall be lawful for him to offer such allowances to encourage their engaging in the service for such time, and on such terms, as he shall deem it expedient to prescribe. Provided that such allowances shall not exceed the sum herein-after appropriated.[8]

Sect. IX. And be it further enacted, That to enable the President, in virtue of the powers vested in him by law, to call into the service of the United States, such number of the militia as he shall deem necessary for the public service, there be appropriated a sum not exceeding one hundred and ninety-two thousand four hundred and ten dollars, as well to defray the expence of such militia, whether cavalry or infantry, or of such military operations as he may direct, and also of such posts as he may think it expedient to establish, to be paid out of the monies which, prior to the first day of January next, shall arise from the duties imposed by the aforesaid act of the present session of Congress.[9]

Sect. X. Provided nevertheless,[10] and be it further enacted, That if the President should be of opinion, that it would be more conducive to the public service to employ troops inlisted under the denomination of levies than[11] militia,[12] it shall be lawful for him to raise, for a term not exceeding four

---

[7] The Senate inserted "including pay, rations and forage" at this point.

[8] The Senate struck out this proviso.

[9] The Senate struck out this section.

[10] The Senate struck out "Provided nevertheless."

[11] The House amended this section by substituting "will" for "would," striking out the word "more" before "conducive," and striking out "than" and inserting "in addition to or in place of the" in its place. The Senate agreed to these amendments.

[12] The Senate struck out the remainder of this section and inserted the following at this point:

which in virtue of the powers vested in him by law, he is authorised to call into the service of the United States, it shall be lawful for him to raise, for a term months, a corps of two thousand non-commissioned officers, privates, and musicians, with a suitable number of commissioned officers. Provided, That the expences thereof shall not exceed the sum heretofore appropriated in the ninth section of this act.[13]

Sect. XI. And be it further enacted, That the President be, and he hereby is empowered to organize the said levies, and alone to appoint the commissioned officers thereof, in the manner he may judge proper.

Sect. XII. And be it further enacted, That the commissioned and non-commissioned officers, privates, and musicians of the militia, or said corps of levies, shall, during the time of their service, be subject to the rules and articles of war; and they shall be entitled to the same pay, rations, and forage, and in cases[14] of wounds and[15] disability in the line of their duty, to the same compensation as the troops of the United States.

Sect. XIII. And be it further enacted, that the non-commissioned officers, privates and musicians of the said corps of levies, shall be entitled to receive such proportional quantity of clothing, as their time of service shall bear to the annual allowance of clothing to the troops of the United States, subject, however, to a proportional deduction from their pay.

Sect. XIV. And be it further enacted, That[16] the non-commissioned of-

---

> not exceeding six months, (to be discharged sooner if the public service will permit) a corps of two thousand non-commissioned officers, privates and musicians, with a suitable number of commissioned officers. And in case it shall appear probable to the President that the regiment directed to be raised by the aforesaid Act, and by this Act, will not be compleated in time to prosecute such military operations as exigencies may require, it shall be lawful for the President to make a substitute for the deficiency, by raising such further number of levies, or by calling into the service of the United States, such a body of militia as shall be equal thereto.

In the printing inserted into the rough journal, the last phrase reads, "by calling into the service of the United States a body of militia equal thereto." The committee report was annotated by Otis to reflect the wording as agreed to by the Senate. The Senate agreed to a House amendment striking out "of" following "a corps" and inserting "not exeeding."

[13] On February 19, the Senate disagreed to a motion by Butler to add the following section at this point:

> And be it further Enacted ~~by the~~ that if the President should be of opinion that the Service for which the aforesaid Regiment is intended, can be performed by the Militia or Troops under the Denomination of levies He is fully Authorised Any thing heretofore to the Contrary notwithstanding to substitute Levies or Militia accordingly; to Continue in pay during such term only as the President of the United States in His discretion shall deem it requisite for the public Service or till the next Session of Congress. (Senate Simple Resolutions, SR, DNA, hand of Butler)

[14] The Senate agreed to a House amendment striking out the "s" in "cases."
[15] The Senate agreed to a House amendment substituting "or" for "and."
[16] The Senate inserted "each of" at this point.

ficers, privates and musicians of the said levies shall be entitled to receive three dollars as a bounty.[17]

1791, February the 12th.

Passed the House of Representatives.

Printed by JOHN FENNO.

House Bills, SR, DNA. The amendments are from the *SLJ*, pp. 623–25 and 658. The Senate amendments were recommended in the committee report unless otherwise noted. A printed copy of the bill, apparently not discovered by bibliographers, was inserted by Otis between pp. 123–24 of the Senate rough journal. With one exception, which we have pointed out in the footnotes, the printing incorporates the Senate's amendments to the House bill. It was annotated by Otis for the direction of the clerk who copied the amendments into the journal.

[17] The Senate added the following sections at this point:

SECT. _____ *And be it further enacted,* That in case the nature of the service upon which the troops of the United States may be employed, should require a greater number of Surgeons-mates than are provided for in the before mentioned Act, the President of the United States may engage from time to time such additional number of Surgeons-mates as he shall judge necessary.

SECT. _____ *And be it further enacted,* That the commissioned officers who shall be employed to recruit men for the said regiments, shall be entitled to receive for every recruit who shall be duly enlisted and mustered, the sum of two dollars.

SECT. _____ *And be it further enacted,* That for defraying the expense of one year of the additional regiment to be raised by virtue of this Act: for defraying the expense for a like term, of the officers mentioned in the sixth section of this Act: for defraying the expense of the said militia horse, militia foot, and levies, which may be called into or engaged for the service of the United States, pursuant to this Act: for defraying the expense of such Surgeon's-mates as may be appointed pursuant to the thirteenth section of this Act: for defraying the expense of recruiting the said two regiments: and for defraying the expense of any military posts which the President shall judge expedient and proper to establish, there be and hereby is appropriated a sum not exceeding three hundred and twelve thousand six hundred and eighty-six dollars, and twenty cents. to be paid out of the monies which prior to the first day of January next, shall arise from the duties imposed upon spirits distilled within the United States, and from stills, by the Act, entitled, "An Act repealing after the last day of June next, the duties heretofore laid upon distilled spirits imported from abroad, and laying others in their stead; and also upon spirits distilled within the United States, and for appropriating the same;" together with the excess of duties which may arise from the duties imposed by the said Act, on imported spirits, beyond those which would have arisen by the Act, entitled, "An Act making further provision for the payment of the debts of the United States."

SECT. _____ And to the end that the public service may not be impeded for want of necessary means—

Be it further enacted, That it shall be lawful for the President to take on loan the whole sum by this Act appropriated, or so much thereof as he may judge requisite, at an interest not exceeding six per centum per annum; and the fund established for the above mentioned appropriation, is hereby pledged for the re-payment of the principal and interest of any loan to be obtained in manner

aforesaid; and in case of any deficiency in the said fund, the faith of the United
States is hereby also pledged to make good such deficiency.
The first two additional sections and the words "for defraying the expense of such
Surgeon's-mates" through "two regiments" are not included in the committee report
and probably were added on the floor of the Senate. The House amended the last
additional section by inserting "or to apply any monies which he may have borrowed
by virtue of any law of the United States, to the purposes of this Act" after "annum"
and "for replacing the monies which may be so applied" after the word "aforesaid."
Both of these amendments were disagreed to by the Senate, and the House receded
from them.

Senate Committee Report
February 17, 1791

Amendments proposed to the Bill entitled "An Act for
raising and adding another regiment to the military
establishment of the united states, and for making
further provision for the protection of the frontiers"

Sect. 3d line 4th. after the word "engaged" insert for the like term and,

Sect. 4th. line 1st.[1] Expunge from the word "That" to the word "shall" in
the 3d/2d line and Substitute, each non-commissioned officer private
and musician who has inlisted or shall inlist pursuant to the Act
aforesaid, or[2] who shall inlist pursuant to this Act.

Sect. 5th. Expunge the whole Section.

Sect. 6th at the end add Provided always that the Major General and Brigadier General so to be appointed shall respectively continue in pay
during such term only as the President of the united states in his
discretion shall deem‸requisite for the public service.
                                It

Sect. 7th. At the end add including pay rations and forrage.

Sect. 8th. Expunge the proviso.

Sect. 9th. Expunge the whole Section.

Sect. 10th. line 1st Expunge the words "Provided Nevertheless."
line 4th./3 Expunge ~~"Militia" and Substitute~~ from the word "than"
to the end of the Section and Substitute, ~~than~~ the militia which in
virtue of the powers vested in him by law he is authorised to call into
the service of the united states It shall be lawful for him to raise for a
term not exceeding Six months, (to be discharged sooner if the public
service will permit,) a corps of two thousand non-commissioned Officers privates and musicians with a suitable number of commissioned
officers, and in case it shall appear probable to the President that the

---

[1] The number "2" was written above "1st."
[2] The word "or" was written over another word, which is illegible.

regiments directed to be raised by the aforesaid Act, and by this Act, will not be compleated in time to prosecute such military operations as exigencies may require, It shall be lawful for the President to make a substitute for the deficiency by raising ~~a~~ such further number of ~~such thereto~~ levies ~~as shall be equal to the deficiency,~~ or by calling into the service of the united states a such body of militia as shall be[3] equal therto.[4]

Sect. 14th. line 1 after the word "That" Insert *each of,* also after Sect. 14th add Sect.   And Be It further enacted That for defraying the expence for one year of the additional regiment to be raised by virtue of this Act; For defraying the expence for the like term of the officers mentioned in the   Section of this Act; For defraying the expence of the said militia horse, militia foot and Levies, which may be called into, or engaged for the Service of the united states, pursuant to this Act; And for defraying the expence of any military posts which the President shall judge expedient and proper to Establish, there be and hereby is appropriated a sum not exceeding three hundred and twelve thousand six hundred and Eighty six dollars and twenty cents, to be paid out of the monies which prior to the first day of January next shall arise from the duties imposed upon spirits distilled within the united states, and from stills, by the Act entitled "An Act repealing after the last day of June next the duties heretofore laid upon distilled spirits imported from abroad and laying others in their stead, and also upon spirits distilled within the united states and for appropriating the same" together with the excess of duties which may arise from the duties ~~on spirits foreign spirits imported spirits beyond those imposed by the on~~ by the said Act imposed by the said Act on imported spirits, beyond those, which would have arisen by the Act~~s repealed~~ entitled an Act making further Provision for the Payment of the Debts of the U.S. ~~in the aforesaid Act, If the same had not~~ And to the end that the public service may not be impeded for want of necessary means, Be It further enacted that It shall be lawful for the President to take on loan the whole sum by this act appropriated, or so much thereof, as he may Judge requisite, at an Interest not exceeding Six per Centum per Annum and the fund hereby established for the above mentioned appropriation is ~~herby~~ hereby pledged for the repay-

---

[3] The words "as shall be" were inserted by Otis.
[4] The words "equal therto" were lined out and rewritten.

ment of the principal and interest of any loan to be obtained in manner aforesaid, and in case of any deficiency in the said fund, the faith of the united states is hereby[5] also pledged to[6] make good such deficiency.

The report, in the hand of Schuyler and with annotations by Otis, is in House Bills, SR, DNA.

[5] The word "hereby" was inserted in the margin by Schuyler.
[6] The word "to" was written over another word, which is illegible.

Senate Amendments
February 19, 1791

And be it further enacted, that in case the nature of the service upon which the troops of the United States may be employed should require a greater number of Surgeons mates, than are provided for in the before mentioned act, the President of the United States, may engage from time to time such additional number of Surgeons mates as he shall judge necessary.

And be it further enacted, that the commissioned officers who shall be
　　　　to recruit men for the said Regiments[1]
employed ∧ upon the recruiting service, shall be entitled to receive for every recruit who shall be duly enlisted and mustered, the sum of two dollars.

House Bills, SR, DNA.

[1] The words "to recruit men for the said Regiments" were inserted by Schuyler.

Militia Bill [HR-81]

Calendar

Date	House	Senate
1789		
Aug. 7	President's message,[1] mentioning the need for a uniform militia, received and read.	
Aug. 8	Message debated in COWH; *resolution* agreed to by House and committed to Sumter, Hiester, and Mathews.	
Aug. 11	P. Muhlenberg and Wadsworth added to committee.	
1790		
Jan. 15	COWH considered State of the Union message in which president requested "a provision for the national defence"; on a motion by Smith (S.C.?),[2] committee to prepare a bill appointed (Gilman, Muhlenberg, Hiester, Mathews, and Floyd).	
Jan. 21	President's message[3] received, with a letter from	

---

[1] The message and enclosures are printed with the Indian Treaties Act [HR-20].
[2] *NYDG*, Jan. 16.
[3] The message is printed in the *HJ*, p. 269.

Date	House	Senate
1790		
	the secretary of war enclosing a plan for the militia; message and enclosures referred to COWH, and, on a motion by Boudinot,[4] ordered printed.	
Mar. 17	Petition of John F. Amelung, "proprietor of a glass manufactory at New-Bremen, in the state of Maryland, praying that the workmen and laborers employed in the said manufactory, may be exempted from militia duty," referred to committee on militia.	
Apr. 26	On a motion by Fitzsimons, seconded by Burke,[5] COWH discharged from consideration of plan for militia; plan referred to committee on national defense.	
Apr. 27	On Gilman's motion,[6] Wadsworth, Sumter, Thatcher, Benson, Boudinot, Seney, and Parker added to committee.	
July 1	Boudinot presented "a bill to provide more effectually for the national defence," which was read twice, committed to the	

---

[4] *NYDG,* Jan. 22.
[5] *NYDA,* Apr. 27. The *NYDG,* Apr. 27, states that Burke made the motion with an amendment by Fitzsimons.
[6] *NYDA, GUS,* Apr. 28.

Date	House	Senate
1790		
	COWH, and ordered printed.[7]	

---

[7] This bill is textually the same as the first Militia Bill [HR-102] introduced in the third session. The bill was ordered printed with the understanding that it would be laid over until the next session of Congress in order to solicit public opinion. (*NYDA*, July 2, 6) Because many amendments to the bill were offered during the third session debates, we are printing the document with the legislative history of [HR-102].

House Resolution
August 8, 1789

RESOLVED, That it is the opinion of this committee, that an act ought to pass, providing a proper system of regulations for the militia of the United States.

HJ, p. 140.

Secretary of War to the President of the United States
Enclosing A Plan for the Militia of the United States
January 21, 1790

War Office January 18th. 1790

Sir,

Having submitted to your consideration a plan for the arrangement of the Militia of the United States which I had presented to the late Congress, and you having approved the general principles thereof with certain exceptions, I now respectfully lay the same before you modified according to the alterations you were pleased to suggest.

It has been my anxious desire to devise a national system of defence adequate to the probable exigencies of the United States, whether arising from internal or external causes—and at the same time to erect a standard of republican magnanimity independent of, and superior to, the powerful influences of Wealth.

The convulsive events generated by the inordinate pursuit of riches or ambition require that the Government should possess a strong corrective arm.

The idea is therefore submitted, whether an efficient military branch of the

Government can be invented, with safety to the great principles of liberty, unless the same shall be formed of the people themselves, and supported by their habits and manners.

> I have the honor to be
> Sir, with the most perfect
> respect, your obedient servant,
> H. KNOX
> secretary for the department
> of War

The President
  of the United States

A PLAN for the GENERAL ARRANGEMENT
of the MILITIA of the UNITED STATES

THE INTRODUCTION

That a well constituted Republic is more favorable to the liberties of society, and that its principles give an higher elevation to the human mind than any other form of Government, has generally been acknowledged by the unprejudiced and enlightened part of mankind.

But it is at the same time acknowledged, that unless a Republic prepares itself by proper arrangements to meet those exigencies to which all States are in a degree liable, that its peace and existence are more precarious than the forms of Government in which the will of one directs the conduct of the whole for the defence of the nation.

A Government whose measures must be the result of multiplied deliberations, is seldom in a situation to produce instantly those exertions which the occasion may demand; therefore it ought to possess such energetic establishments as should enable it by the vigor of its own citizens, to controul events as they arise instead of being convulsed or subverted by them.

It is the misfortune of modern ages that Governments have been formed by chance and events instead of system—that without fixed principles they are braced or relaxed from time to time according to the predominating power of the rulers, or the ruled—The rulers possessing seperate interests from the people excepting in some of the high toned Monarchies, in which all opposition to the will of the princes seems annihilated.

Hence we look round Europe in vain for an extensive Government rising on the power inherent in the people, and performing its operations entirely for their benefit—But we find artificial force governing every where, and the people generally made subservient to the elevation and caprice of the few—Almost every nation appearing to be busily employed in conducting some external War—grappling with internal commotion—or endevoring to extricate itself from impending debts which threaten to overwhelm it with ruin—Princes and Ministers seem neither to have leisure nor inclination to bring forward institutions for diffusing general strength, knowledge, and happiness—But they seem to understand well the Machivalian maxim of politics, divide and govern.

May the United States avoid the errors and crimes of other Governments, and possess the wisdom to embrace the present invaluable opportunity of establishing such institutions as shall invigorate, exalt, and perpetuate, the great principles of freedom—an opportunity pregnant with the fate of millions, but rapidly borne on the wings of time, and may never again return.

The public mind unbiased by superstition or prejudice seems happily prepared to receive the impressions of wisdom—The latent springs of human action ascertained by the standard of experience, may be regulated and made subservient to the noble purpose of forming a dignified national character.

The causes by which nations, have ascended and declined through the various ages of the world, may be calmly and accurately determined; and the United States may be placed in the singularly fortunate condition of commencing their career of Empire with the accumulated knowledge of all the known societies and Governments of the Globe.

The strength of the Government like the strength of any other vast and complicated machine will depend on a due adjustment of its several parts—Its agriculture, its commerce, its laws, its finance, its system of defence, and its manners and habits all require consideration, and the highest exercise of political wisdom.

It is the intention of the present attempt to suggest the most efficient system of defence which may be compatible with the interests of a free people; a system which shall not only produce the expected effect, but in its operations shall also produce those habits and manners which will impart strength and durability to the whole Government.

The modern practice of Europe with respect to the employment of standing Armies has created such a mass of opinion in their favor that even Philosophers, and the advocates for liberty have frequently confessed their use and necessity in certain cases.

But whoever seriously and candidly estimates the power of discipline and the tendency of military habits will be constrained to confess, that whatever may be the efficacy of a standing Army in War, it cannot in peace be considered as friendly to the rights of human nature—The recent instance in France cannot with propriety be brought to overturn the general principle built upon the uniform experience of mankind—It may be found on examining the causes that appear to have influenced the Military of France, that while the springs of power were wound up in the nation to the highest pitch, that the discipline of the army was proportionably relaxed—But any argument on this head may be considered as unnecessary to the enlightened citizens of the United States.

A small Corps of well disciplined and well informed Artillerists and Engineers—and a Legion for the protection of the frontiers, and the Magazines and Arsenals are all the Military establishment which may be required for the present use of the United States—The privates of the Corps to be enlisted for a certain period and after the expiration of which to return to the mass of the Citizens.

An energetic National Militia is to be regarded as the *capital security* of a free republic, and not a standing Army forming a distinct class in the community.

It is the introduction and diffusion of vice and corruption of manners into the mass of the people that render a standing army necessary—It is when public spirit is despised, and avarice, indolence, and effeminacy of manners, predominate and prevent the establishment of institutions, which would elevate the minds of the youth in the paths of virtue and honor, that a standing Army is formed and rivetted forever.

While the human character remains unchanged, and societies and Governments of considerable extent are formed—a principle ever ready to execute the laws and defend the State must constantly exist—Without this vital principle, the Government would be invaded or overturned and trampled upon by the bold and ambitious—no community can be long held together unless its arrangements are adequate to its probable exigencies.

If it should be decided to reject a standing Army for the military branch of the Government of the United States as possessing too feirce an aspect, and being hostile to the principles of liberty it will follow that a well constituted Militia ought to be established.

A consideration of the subject will show the impracticability of disciplining at once the mass of the people—All discussions on the subject of a powerful Militia will result in one or the other of the following principles.

First   Either efficient institutions must be established for the military education of the youth, and that the knowledge acquired therein shall be diffused throughout the community by the mean of rotation.

Or Secondly   That the Militia must be formed of substitutes, after the manner of the Militia of Great Britain.

If the United States possess the vigor of mind to establish the first institution, it may reasonably be expected to produce the most unequivocal advantages—A glorious national spirit will be introduced with its extensive train of political consequences—the youth will imbibe a love of their country—reverence and obedience to its laws—courage and elevation of mind—openness and liberality of character—accompanied by a just spirit of honor—In addition to which their bodies will acquire a robustness—greatly conducive to their personal happiness as well as the defence of their country—While habit with its silent but efficacious operations will durably cement the system.

Habit that powerful and universal law, incessantly acting on the human race, well deserves the attention of legislatures—Formed at first in individuals by seperate and almost imperceptible impulses until at length it acquires a force which controuls with irresistible sway—The effects of salutary or pernicious habits operating on a whole nation are immense and decides its rank and character in the world.

Hence the science of legislation teaches to scrutinize every national institution, as it may introduce proper or improper habits—To adopt with religious zeal the former and reject with horror the latter.

A Republic constructed on the principles herein stated would be uninjured by events, sufficient to overturn a Government supported solely by the uncertain power of a standing Army.

The well informed members of the community, actuated by the highest motives of self love, would form the real defence of the country—Rebellions would be prevented or suppressed with ease—Invasions of such a Government would be undertaken only by madmen—and the virtues and knowledge of the people would effectually oppose the introduction of Tyranny.

But the second principle—a Militia of substitutes—is pregnant in a degree with the mischeifs of a standing Army—As it is highly probable the substitutes from time to time will be nearly the same men, and the most idle and worthless part of the community—Wealthy families proud of distinctions which riches may confer will prevent their sons from serving in the Militia of substitutes—the plan will degenerate into habitual contempt—a standing Army will be introduced, and the liberties of the people subjected to all the contingencies of events.

The expence attending an energetic establishment of militia may be strongly urged as an objection to the institution, but it is to be remembered that this objection is levelled at both systems, whether by rotation, or by substitutes—For if the numbers are equal the expence will also be equal—The estimate of the expence will show its unimportance when compared with the magnitude, and beneficial effects of the institution.

But the people of the United States will cheerfully consent to the expences of a measure calculated to serve as a perpetual barrier to their liberties—especially as they well know that the disbursements will be made among the members of the same community, and therefore cannot be injurious.

Every intelligent mind would rejoice in the establishment of an institution, under whose auspices, the youth and vigor of the Constitution, would be renewed with each successive generation, and which would appear to secure the great principles of freedom and happiness, against the injuries of time and events.

The following plan is formed on these general principles.

1st. That it is the indispensible duty of every nation to establish all necessary institutions for its own perfection and defence.

2'ndly, That it is a capital security to a free State for the great body of the people to possess a competent knowledge of the military art.

3'dly, That this knowledge cannot be attained in the present state of society but by establishing adequate institutions for the military education of youth—And that the knowledge acquired therein should be diffused throughout the community by the principles of rotation.

4'thly That every man of the proper age, and ability of body is firmly bound by the social compact to perform personally his proportion of military duty for the defence of the State.

5'thly; That all men of the legal military age should be armed, enrolled and held responsible for different degrees of military service.

And 6'thly, That agreably to the Constitution the United States are to provide for organizing, arming and disciplining the Militia, and for governing such part of them as may be employed in the service of the United States, reserving to the States respectively the appointment of the officers, and the authority of training the Militia according to the discipline prescribed by Congress.

THE PLAN

The period of life in which military service shall be required of the citizens of the United States to commence at eighteen and terminate at the age of sixty years.

The men comprehended by this description, exclusive of such exceptions as the legislatures of the different States may think proper to make, and all *actual mariners* shall be enrolled for different degrees of military duty, and divided into three distinct classes.

The first class shall comprehend the youth of eighteen, nineteen, and twenty years of age, to be denominated the ADVANCED CORPS.

The second Class shall include the men from twenty-one to forty-five years of age; to be denominated the MAIN CORPS.

The third class shall comprehend inclusively, the men from forty-six to sixty years of age to be denominated, the RESERVED CORPS.

All the militia of the United States shall assume the form of a legion, which shall be the permanent establishment thereof.

A legion shall consist of one hundred and fifty-three commissioned Officers, and two thousand eight hundred and eighty non-commissioned officers and privates formed in the following manner.

1st. THE LEGIONARY STAFF

One Legionary or major general

Two aids-de-camp, of the rank of major one of whom to be the legionary quarter master.

One inspector and deputy adjutant general, of the rank of lieutenant colonel.

One Chaplain.

2'nd. THE BRIGADE STAFF

One brigadier general,

One brigade inspector, to serve as an aid-de-camp.

3'd THE REGIMENTAL STAFF

One lieutenant colonel commandant,

Two majors,

One adjutant,

One paymaster, or agent

One quarter master,

4'th TWO BRIGADES OF INFANTRY

Each brigade of two regiments, each regiment of eight companies, forming two battalions, each company of a captain, lieutenant, ensign, six serjeants one drum, one fife, and sixty four rank and file.

5'th. TWO COMPANIES OF RIFLEMEN

Each company to have a captain, lieutenant, ensign, six serjeants, a bugle-horn, one drum, and sixty four rank and file.

6'th. A BATTALION OF ARTILLERY

Consisting of four companies, each to have a captain, captain-lieutenants, one lieutenant, six serjeants, twelve artificers, and fifty two rank and file.

7'th. A SQUADRON OF CAVALRY

Consisting of two troops, each troop to have a Captain, two lieutenants, a cornet, six serjeants one farrier, one saddler, one trumpeter, and sixty-four dragoons.

In case the whole number of the advanced corps in any state should be insufficient to form a legion of this extent, yet the component parts must be preserved, and the reduction proportioned, as nearly as may be to each part.

The companies of all the corps shall be divided into SECTIONS of twelve each. It is proposed by this division, to establish one uniform vital principle, which in peace and war shall pervade the militia of the United States.

All requisitions for men to *form an army*, either for state or federal purposes, shall be furnished by the advanced and main corps, by means of the sections.

The executive government, or commander in chief of the militia of each state, will assess the numbers required, on the respective legions of these corps.

The legionary general will direct the proportions to be furnished by each part of his command; should the demand be so great, as to require one man from each section, then the operation hereby directed shall be performed by single sections. But if a less number should be required, they will be furnished by an association of sections or companies according to the demand. In any case, it is probable that mutual convenience may dictate an agreement with an individual, to perform the service required. If however no agreement can be made, one must be detached by an indiscriminate draught, and the others shall pay him a sum of money, equal to the averaged sum, which shall be paid in the same legion, for the voluntary performance of the service required.

In case any sections, or companies of a legion, after having furnished its own quota, should have more men willing to engage for the service required, other companies of the same legion, shall have permission to engage them. The same rule to extend to the different legions in the State.

The legionary general must be responsible to the commander in cheif of the militia of the state, that the men furnished are according to the description, and that they are equipped in the manner, and marched to the rendezvous conformably to the orders for that purpose.

The men who may be drafted shall not serve more than three years at one time.

The reserved corps being destined for the domestic defence of the state shall not be obliged to furnish men, excepting in cases of actual invasion, or rebellion, and then the men required shall be furnished by means of the sections.

The actual commissioned officers of the respective corps, shall not be included in the sections, nor in any of the operations thereof.

The respective states shall be divided into portions or districts, each of which to contain, as nearly as may be, some complete part of a legion.

Every citizen of the United States who, shall serve his country in the field, for the space of one year, either as an officer or soldier, shall if under the age of twenty-one years be exempted from the service required in the advanced corps. If he shall be above the age of twenty-one years, then every year he shall so serve in the field, shall be estimated as equal to six years service in the main or reserved corps, and shall accordingly exempt him from every service therein for the said term of six years, except in cases of actual invasion of the state in which he resides. And it shall also be a permanent establishment, that six years actual service in the field, shall entirely free every citizen from any further demands of service, either in the militia, or in the field, unless in cases of invasion or rebellion.

All actual mariners or seamen, in the respective states, shall be registered in districts, and divided into two classes. The first class to consist of all the seamen, from the age of sixteen to thirty years inclusively. The second class to consist of all those of the age of thirty-one to forty-five, inclusively.

The first class shall be responsible to serve three years on board of some public armed vessel, or ship of war, as a commissioned officer, warrant officer, or private mariner, for which service they shall receive the customary wages and emoluments.

But should the state not demand the said three years service during the above period, from the age of sixteen to thirty years, then the party to be exempted entirely therefrom.

The person so serving shall receive a certificate of his service, on parchment, according to the form which shall be directed, which shall exempt him from any other than voluntary service, unless in such exigencies as may require the services of all the members of the community.

The second class shall be responsible for a proportion of service in those cases, to which the first class shall be unequal. The numbers required shall be furnished by sections, in the same manner as is prescribed for the sections of the militia.

OF THE ADVANCED CORPS

The advanced corps are designed not only as a school in which the youth of the United States are to be instructed in the art of war, but they are in all cases of exigence, to serve as an actual defence to the community.

The whole of the ~~armed~~ advanced corps shall be clothed according to the manner hereafter directed, armed and subsisted at the expence of the United States, and all the youth of the said corps, in each state, shall be encamped together, if practicable, or by legions, which encampments shall be denominated *the annual camps of discipline.*

The youth of *eighteen* and *nineteen* years, shall be displined for *thirty* days successively in each year; and those of twenty years shall be disciplined only for ten days in each year, which shall be the last ten days of the annual encampments.

The non-commissioned officers and privates are not to receive any pay during this said time; but the commissioned officers will receive the pay of their relative ranks, agreeably to the federal establishment for the time being.

In order that the plan shall effectually answer the end proposed, the first day of January shall be the fixed period, for all who attain the age of eighteen years, in any part, or during the course of each year, to be enrolled in the advanced corps, and to take the necessary oaths, to perform personally such legal military service as may be directed, for the full and complete term of three years, to be estimated from the time of entrance into the said corps, and also to take an oath of allegiance to the state, and to the United States.

The commanding officer, or general of the advanced legions of the district, shall regulate the manner of the service of the youth respectively, whether it shall be in the infantry, artillery, or cavalry; but after having entered into either of them, no change should be allowed.

Each individual at his first joining the annual camps of discipline will receive complete arms and accoutrements, all of which, previously to his being discharged from the said camps he must return to the regimental quarter master, on the penalty of   dollars, or   months imprisonment.

The said arms and accoutrements, shall be marked in some conspicuous place with the letters M. U. S. and all sales or purchases of any of said arms or accoutrements shall be severely punished according to law.

And each individual will also on his first entrance into the advanced corps receive the following articles of uniform clothing, one hat, one uniform short coat, one waistcoat, and one pair of overalls, which he shall retain in his own possession, and for which he shall be held accountable, and be compelled to replace all deficiencies during his service in the annual camps of discipline.

Those who shall serve in the cavalry shall be at the expence of their own horses, helmets, and horse-furniture; but they shall receive forage for their horses, swords, pistols and clothing equal in value to the infantry.

At the age of twenty-one years every individual having served in the manner and for the time prescribed, shall receive an honorary certificate thereof on parchment, and signed by legionary general and inspector.

The names of all persons to whom such certificates shall be given, shall be fairly registered in books to be provided for that purpose.

And the said certificate, or an attested copy of the register aforesaid, shall be required as an indispensible qualification for exercising any of the rights of a free citizen, until after the age of   years.

The advanced legions, in all cases of invasion, or rebellion, shall on requisition of lawful authority, be obliged to march to any place within the United States to remain embodied for such time as shall be directed, not to exceed one year, to be computed from the time of marching from the regimental parades; during the period of their being on such service, to be placed on the continental establishment, of pay, subsistence, clothing, forage, tents, camp equipage, and all such other allowances, as are made to the federal troops at the same time, and under the same circumstances.

If the military service so required, should be for such a short period, as to render an actual issue of clothing unnecessary, then an allowance should be made in proportion to the annual cost of clothing, for the federal soldier, according to estimates to be furnished for that purpose from the war-office of the United States.

In case the legions of the advanced corps should march to any place, in consequence of a requisition of the general government, all legal and proper expences of such march shall be paid by the United States. But should they be embodied, and march in consequence of an order, derived from the authority of the state to which they belong, and for state purposes, then the expences will be borne by the state.

The advanced corps shall be constituted on such principles, that when completed, it will receive one third part, and discharge one third part of its numbers annually—By this arrangement two thirds of the corps will at all times be considerably disciplined; but as it will only receive those of eighteen years of age, it will not be completed until the third year after its institution. Those who have already attained the ages of nineteen and twenty years, will in the first instance be enrolled in the main corps.

But one half of the legionary officers to be appointed the first, and the other the second year of the establishment.

The officers of each grade in the states respectively shall be divided into three classes, which shall, by lot be numbered one, two, and three, and one of the said classes, according to their numbers, shall be deranged every third year. In the first period of nine years, one third part will have to serve three, one third part six, and one third part, nine years—But, after the said first period, the several classes will serve nine years, which shall be the limitation of service by virtue of the same appointment, and in such cases, where there may not be three officers of the same grade, the limitation of nine years service shall be observed. All vacancies occasioned by the aforesaid derangements, or any casualties shall be immediately filled by new appointments.

The captains and subalterns of the advanced corps, shall not be less than twenty-one, nor more than thirty-five, and the field officers shall not exceed forty-five years of age.

Each company, battalion, and regiment, shall have a fixed parade, or place at which to assemble. The companies shall assemble at their own parade, and march to the parade of the battalion, and the battalions, to the regimental parade, and when thus embodied, the regiment will march to the rendevous of the legion. Every commanding officer of a company, battalion, and regiment, will be accountable to his superior officer, that his command is in the most perfect order.

The officers to receive subsistence money, in lieu of provisions, in proportion to their respective grades, and those whose duties require them to be on horseback, will receive forage in the same proportion.

Every legion must have a Chaplain, of respectable talents and character, who, besides his religious functions, should impress on the minds of the youth, at stated periods, in concise discourses, the eminent advantages of free governments to the happiness of society, and that such governments can only be supported by the knowledge, spirit, and virtuous conduct of the youth. To be illustrated by the most conspicuous examples of history.

No amusements should be admitted in camp, but those which correspond with war. The swimming of men and horses, running, wrestling, and such other exercises, as should render the body flexible and vigorous.

The camps should, if possible, be formed near a river, and remote from large cities—The first is necessary for the practice of the manoeuvres, the second to avoid the vices of populous places.

The time of the annual encampments shall be divided into six parts or periods of five days each. The first of which shall be occupied in acquiring the air, attitudes, and first principles of a soldier—the second in learning the manual exercise and to march individually and in small squads. The third and fourth, in exercising and manoeuvring in detail, and by battalions, and regiments. In the fifth, the youth of twenty, having been disciplined during the two preceeding annual encampments are to be included. This period is to be employed in the exercise and tactics of the legion; or if more than one, in executing the grand manouvres of the whole body—marching, attacking and defending in various forms, different grounds and positions; in fine, in representing all the real images of war, excepting the effusion of blood.

The guards, and every other circumstance of the camp, to be perfectly regulated.

Each state will determine on the season, in which its respective annual encampments shall be formed, so as best to suit the health of the men, and the general interests of the society.

The United States to make an adequate provision, to supply the arms, clothing, rations, artillery, ammunition, forage, straw, tents, camp-equipage, including every requisite for the annual camps of discipline: And also for the pay and subsistence of the legionary officers, and for the following general staff. One inspector-general, one adjutant-general, one quarter master-general, with a deputy for each state.

These officers will be essential to the uniformity, oeconomy and efficacy of the system, to be appointed in the manner prescribed by the constitution of the United States.

The quarter master general shall be responsible to the United States for the public property of every species requisite for the annual camps of discipline; and his deputy in each state shall be responsible to him.

At the commencement of the annual camps of discipline, the deputy quarter master will make regular issues to the legionary or regimental quarter masters, as the case may be, of all the articles of *every species,* provided by the United States.

The returns for the said articles, to be examined, and certified by the highest legionary or regimental officer, as the case may be, who shall be responsible for the accuracy thereof.

At the expiration of the annual camps of discipline, every species of public property, (clothing excepted) shall be returned to the deputy quarter master of the state, who shall hold the legionary quarter master accountable for all deficiencies. All the apparatus and property so returned, shall be carefully examined, repaired, and deposited in a magazine to be provided in each state for that purpose, under the charge of the said deputy quarter master, until the ensuing annual encampment, or any occasion which may render a new issue necessary.

Corporal punishments shall never be inflicted in the annual camps of discipline, but a system of fines and imprisonment, shall be formed for the regular government of said camps.

Of the Main Corps

As the main and reserved corps are to be replenished by the principle of rotation, from the advanced corps, and ultimately to consist of men who have received their military education therein, it is proper that one uniform arrangement should pervade the several classes.

It is for this reason the legion is established, as the common form of all the corps of the militia.

The main legions, consisting of the great majority of the men of the military age, will form the principal defence of the country.

They are to be responsible for their proportion of men, to form an army whenever necessity shall dictate the measure; and on every sudden occasion to which the advanced corps shall be incompetent, an adequate number of non-commissioned officers and privates shall be added thereto, from the main corps, by means of the sections.

The main corps will be perfectly armed in the first instance, and will practice the exercise and manoeuvres, four days in each year, and will assemble in their respective districts, by companies, battalions, regiments, or legions, as shall be directed by each state; but it must be a fixed rule, that in the populous parts of the states, the regiments must assemble once annually, and the legions once in three years.

Although the main corps cannot acquire a great degree of military knowledge in the few days prescribed for its annual exercise, yet by the constant accession of the youth from the advanced corps, it will soon command respect for its discipline, as well as its numbers.

When the youth are transferred from the advanced corps, they shall invariably join the flank-companies, the cavalry, or artillery of the main corps, according to the nature of their former services.

OF THE RESERVED CORPS

The reserved corps will assemble only twice annually, for the inspection of arms, by companies, battalions, or regiments, as shall be directed by each state. It will assemble by legions, whenever the defence of the state may render the measure necessary.

Such are the propositions of the plan, to which, it may be necessary to add some explications.

Although the substantial political maxim, which requires personal service of all the members of the community for the defence of the state, is obligatory under all forms of society, and is the main pillar of a free government, yet the degrees thereof may vary at the different periods of life, consistently with the general welfare. The public convenience may also dictate a relaxation of the general obligation, as it respects the principal magistrates and the ministers of justice, and of religion, and perhaps some religious sects. But it ought to be remembered, that measures of national importance, never should be frustrated by the accommodation of individuals.

The military age has generally commenced at sixteen, and terminated at the age of sixty years; but the youth of sixteen do not commonly attain such a degree of robust strength, as to enable them to sustain, without injury, the hardships incident to the field; therefore the commencement of military service, is herein fixed at eighteen, and the termination, as usual, at sixty years of age.

As the plan proposes, that the militia shall be divided into three capital classes, and that each class shall be formed into legions, the reasons for which shall be given in succession.

The advanced corps, and annual camps of discipline, are instituted in order to introduce an operative military spirit in the community. To establish a course of honorable military service, which will at the same time, mould the minds of the young men, to a due obedience of the laws; instruct them in the art of war, and by the manly exercises of the field, form a race of hardy citizens, equal to the dignified task of defending their country.

An examination into the employments, and obligations of the individuals composing the society, will evince the impossibility of diffusing an adequate knowledge of the art of war, by any other means than a course of discipline, during the period of nonage. The time necessary to acquire this important knowledge, cannot be afforded at any other period of life, with so little injury to the public or private interests.

Without descending to minute distinctions, the body of the people of the United States, may be divided into two parts. The yeomanry of the country, and the men of various employments, resident in towns and cities. In both parts, it is usual for the male-children, from the age of fourteen to twenty one years, to learn some trade or employment, under the direction of a parent or master. In general, the labour or service of the youth during this period, besides amply repaying the trouble of tuition, leaves a large profit to the tutor. This circumstance is stated to show that no great hardships will arise in the first operations of the proposed plan; a little practice will render the measure perfectly equal, and remove every difficulty.

Youth is the time for the state to avail itself of those services which it has a right to demand, and by which it is to be invigorated and preserved; in this season the passions and affections are strongly influenced by the splendor of military parade. The impressions the mind receives will be retained through life. The young man will repair with pride and pleasure to the field of exercise while the head of a family, anxious for its general welfare, and perhaps its immediate subsistence, will reluctantly quit his domestic duties for any length of time.

The habits of industry will be rather strengthened than relaxed by the establishment of the annual camps of discipline, as all the time will be occupied by the various military duties. Idleness and dissipation will be regarded as disgraceful, and punished accordingly. As soon as the youth attain the age of manhood, a natural solicitude to establish themselves in the society, will occur in its full force. The public claims for military service, will be too inconsiderable to injure their industry. It will be sufficiently stimulated to proper exertions, by the prospects of opulence, attending on the cultivation of a fertile soil, or the pursuits of a productive commerce.

It is presumed that thirty days annually during the eighteenth and nineteenth, and ten days during the twentieth year, is the least time that ought to be appropriated by the youth to the acquisition of the military art. The same number of days might be added during the twentieth, as during the two preceeding years, were not the expence an objection.

Every means will be provided by the public to facilitate their military education, which it is proposed shall be an indispensable qualification of a free citizen, therefore they will not be entitled to any pay. But the officers being of the main corps, are in a different predicament. They are supposed to have passed through the course of discipline required by the laws, and to be competent to instruct others in the military art. As the public will have but small claims for personal services on them, and as they must incur considerable expences to prepare themselves to execute properly their respective offices they ought to be paid while on actual duty.

As soon as the service of the youth expires in the advanced corps, they are to be enrolled in the main corps. On this occasion, the republic receives disciplined and free citizens, who understand their public rights and are prepared to defend them.

The main corps is instituted, to preserve and circulate throughout the community, the military discipline, acquired in the advanced corps; to arm the people, and fix firmly by practice and habit, those forms and maxims, which are essential to the life, and energy of a free government.

The reserved corps is instituted to prevent men being sent to the field, whose strength is unequal to sustain the severities of an active campaign. But by organizing and rendering them eligible for domestic service, a greater proportion of the younger and robust part of the community, may be enabled in cases of necessity, to encounter the more urgent duties of war.

It would be difficult previously to the actual formation of the annual camps of discipline, to ascertain the number in each State of which it would be composed. The frontier counties of several states are thinly inhabited and require all their internal force for their immediate defence—There are other infant settlements from which it might be injurious to draw away their youth annually for the purpose of discipline.

No evil would result, if the establishment of the advanced corps, should be omitted in such districts for a few years. Besides the forbearance in this respect would lessen the expence, and render the institution more compatible with the public finances.

The several state Legislatures therefore, as best understanding their local interests, might be invested with a discretionary power to omit the enrollments for the advanced corps in such of their frontier, and thinly inhabited counties, as they may Judge proper.

If the number of three millions may be assumed as the total number of the Inhabitants within the United States, half a million may be deducted therefrom for blacks, and pursuant to the foregoing ideas, another half million may be deducted on account of the thinly settled parts of the country.

The proportion of men of the military age from eighteen to sixty years inclusively, of two millions of people of all ages and sexes may be estimated at four hundred thousand. There may be deducted from this number as actual mariners, about fifty thousand, and a further number of twenty five thousand to include exempts of religious sects, and of every other sort which the respective states may think proper to make.

Three hundred and twenty five thousand, therefore may be assumed as the number of operative fencible men, to compose the militia. The proportion of the several classes of which, would be nearly as follows—

Firstly— The advanced corps one tenth, composed of the }
           youth of the ages of 18, 19, and 20 years.   }   32,500

Secondly—The main corps, six tenths and one twentieth.   211,250

Thirdly— The reserved corps two tenths and one   }
           twentieth.   }   81,250
                                                             _____
                                                             325,000

The following estimate is formed for the purpose of exhibiting the annual expence of the institution of the advance corps, Stating the same at Thirty thousand men.

ESTIMATE of the expence of the Annual camps of discipline as proposed in the foregoing plan—arising on each of the first three years, and after that period—of the annual expence of the institution.

THE FIRST YEAR

10,000 Suits of uniform clothing Stated at 8 }
dollars—each suit of which shall serve for   }   80,000.
the three years discipline.   }

10,000 Rations per day for 30 days, each   }
ration Stated at 10 Cents.   }   30,000.

The expence of four complete corps of   }
Legionary officers of all descriptions, for 30 } 27,870.
days, including pay, subsistence, & forage   }

Forage for the Cavalry.   4,800.

Straw—Camp kettles—bowls—axes—   }
Canteens—and fuel.   }   20,000.

    Annual proportion of the expence for   }
tents, for Officers and Soldiers which may   }   3,000.
Serve for Eight annual encampments.   }

    4 Legionary Standards.   2,000.
    Regimental Colours.   1,000.

Consumption of powder and ball—Shot and   }
Shells—damage to arms, and accoutrements,   }
and artillery, and transportation of the same, } 25,000.
stated at.   }

Hospital department.   5,000.

Contingencies of the Quarter masters and   }
other departments.   }   15,000.

General Staff, Adjutant General, Quartermaster General, Inspector General and their Deputies.	} 12,000.	
		225,670
Entire expences of the 1st. year Dollars		225,670

ADDITIONAL EXPENCES
ON THE SECOND YEAR

10,000 Rations per day, for 30 days, is 300,000 Rations @ 10 Cents.	} 30,000.	
The expence of 4 Complete corps of Legionary officers of all descriptions for 30 days including pay, Subsistence & forage.	} 27,870.	
4 Legionary Standards.	2,000.	
Regimental Colours.	1,000.	
Forage for the Cavalry.	4,800.	
Tents—Straw—Camp kettles—bowls— axes—Canteens—and fuel.	} 20,000.	
Hospital Department.	5,000.	
Contingencies, and other disbursements in Quartermasters departments.	} 15,000.	
Ammunition, damage to arms and accoutrements.	} 15,000.	
		120,670.
Combined expences of the 1st. and 2d. year carried forward.	} Dollars	346,340.

THE ADDITIONAL EXPENCES ON THE THIRD YEAR

The expences of 10,000 Rations for 10 days is 100,000 Rations @ 10 Cents.	} 10,000.	
Forage.	1,600.	
For the camp equipage.	10,000.	
Tents.	1,500.	
Hospital Stores	1,000.	
Ammunition, damage to arms, and accoutrements.	} 10,000.	
Contingencies in the Quartermasters department.	} 10,000.	
		44,100.
The total expence of the first three years. Dollars		390,440.

    It is to be observed, that the officers for four legions will be adequate to command the youth of 18. who

Commence their discipline the 1st. year, and that the
same number of Officers will be required for the second
year—the youth of the third year, may be incorporated by
sections in the existing corps, so that no additional
officers will be required on their account.

		Dollars
Hence it appears that the expence		
of 10,000 men for one year, amounts to		225,670.
20,000 for the 2nd year	to	346,340.
30,000 for the 3d year	to	390,440.

If the youth of the three ages of 18, 19,
and 20 be disciplined at once—the last
mentioned sum will be about the fixed
annual expence of the camps of discipline—
from which, however is to be deducted
6,000 dollars being the expence of the
standards and colours. the former of which
will be of a durable nature, and the Latter
will not require to be replaced oftener than

once in 20 years.		6,000.
The annual expence of the advanced corps.	Dolls.	384,440

Thus for a sum less than four hundred thousand Dollars annually, which
apportioned on three millions of people would be little more than one eighth
of a dollar for each, AN ENERGETIC republican militia may be durably
established—The invaluable principles of liberty secured and perpetuated,
and a dignified national fabric erected on the solid foundation of public
Virtue.

The main and reserved corps, must be perfectly organized in the first
instance; but the advanced corps will not be completed until the third year of
its institutions.

The combination of troops of various descriptions into one body, so as to
invest it with the highest and greatest number of powers, in every possible
situation, has long been a subject of discussion, and difference of Opinion.
But no other form appears so well to have sustained the criterion of time and
severe examination, as the ROMAN LEGION. This formidable organization,
accomodates to the purposes of modern war, still retains its original energy
and superiority. Of the ancients Polybius and Vegetius have described and
given the highest encomiums of the Legion. The former particularly, in his
comparitive view of the advantages and disadvantages of the macedonian and
roman arms, and their respective orders of battle, has left to mankind an
instructive and important legacy. Of the moderns the illustrious Marechal

Saxe, has modelled the legion for the use of fire arms, and Strenuously urges its adoption, in preferrence to any other form. And the respectable and intelligent veteran, late inspector general of the armies of the United States, recommends the adoption of the legion* "Upon a review" says he "of all the military of Europe, there does not appear to be a single form which could be safely adopted by the United States; they are unexceptionally different from each other, and like all other human institutions, seem to have started as much out of accident, as design. The Local situation of the country, the spirit of the government, the character of the nation, and in many instances the character of the Prince, have all had their influence in settling the foundation and discipline of their respective troops, and render it impossible that we should take either as a model. The Legion alone has not been adopted by any, and yet I am confident in asserting that whether it be examined as applicable to all Countries, or as it may immediately apply to the existing or probable necessity of this, it will be found Strikingly superior to any other.

1st. Being a complete and little army of itself, it is ready to begin its operations, on the shortest notice or slightest alarm 2ndly. Having all the component parts of the largest army of any possible description, it is prepared to meet every species of war that may present itself. And 3dly. as in every case of detachment the first constitutional principle will be preserved, and the embarrassments of draughting, and detail, which in armies differently framed too often distract the commanding Officer, will be avoided.

It may easily suggest itself from this Sketch, that in forming a legion, the most difficult task is to determine the necessary proportion of each species of soldiers which is to compose it; this must obviously depend upon what will be the Theatre, and what is the stile of the war. On the plains of Poland, whole Brigades of Cavalry would be necessary against every enemy, but in the forest and among the hills of America, a single Regiment would be more than sufficient against any, and as there are but two kinds of war to which we are much exposed, viz. an attack from the seaside by an European power, aided by our sworn enemies, settled on our extreme left, and an invasion of our back settlements by an indian enemy, it follows of course, that musqueteers, and light-Infantry should make the greatest part of your army."

The institution of the section is intended to interest the patriotism and pride of every individual in the militia, to support the legal measures of a free Government. To render every man active in the public cause, by introducing the spirit of emulation and a degree of personal responsibility.

The common mode of recruiting is attended with too great destruction of morals to be tolerated, and is too uncertain to be the principal resource of a

---

* Vide—letter addressed to the inhabitants of the United States on the subject of an established militia.

wise nation in time of danger. The public faith is frequently wounded by unworthy individuals, who hold out delusive promises which can never be realized—By such means, an unprincipled banditti are often collected for the purpose of defending every thing that should be dear to freemen. The consequences are natural, such men either desert in time of danger, or are ever ready on the slightest disgust to turn their arms against their country.

By the establishment of the sections an ample and permanent source is opened, whence the state in every exigence may be supplied with men whose all depends upon the prosperity of their country.

In cases of necessity, an army may be formed of Citizens, whose previous knowledge of discipline will enable it to proceed to an immediate accomplishment of the designs of the state, instead of exhausting the public resources, by wasting whole years in preparing to face the enemy.

The previous arrangements necessary to form and maintain the annual encampments, as well as the discipline acquired therein, will be an excellent preparation for war. The artillery and its numerous appendages, arms and accoutrements of every kind, and all species of ammunition, ought to be manufactured within the United States. It is of high importance that the present period Should be embraced to establish adequate institutions to produce the necessary apparatus of war.

It is unworthy the dignity of a rising and free empire, to depend on foreign and fortuitous supplies of the essential means of defence.

The clothing for the troops could with ease be manufactured within the United States, and the establishment in that respect would tend to the encouragement of important manufactures.

The disbursements made in each State for the rations, forage, and other necessary articles, for the annual camps of discipline, would most beneficially circulate the money arising from the public revenue.

The local circumstances of the United States, their numerous seaports, and the protection of their commerce, require a naval arrangement. Hence the necessity of the proposed plan, embracing the idea of the states, obtaining men on republican principles, for the marine as well as the land service. But one may be accomplished with much greater facility than the other, as the preparation of a Soldier for the field, requires a degree of discipline which cannot be learned without much time and labor; whereas the common course of Sea service off on board of merchant vessels, differs but little from the service required on board of armed Ships, therefore the education for war in this respect, will be obtained without any expence to the state. all that seem to be requisite on the head of marine service is, that an efficient regulation should be established in the respective states, to register all actual seamen, and to render those of a certain age amenable to the public for personal service, if demanded within a given period.

The constitution of the respective states and of the United States, having directed the modes in which the officers of the militia shall be appointed, no alteration can be made therein. Although it may be supposed that some modes of appointment, are better calculated than others to inspire the highest propriety of Conduct, yet there are none so defective, to serve as a sufficient reason for rejecting an efficient system for the militia. It is certain that the choice of Officers, is the point on which the reputation and importance of a corps, must depend. Therefore every person who may be concerned in the appointment, should consider himself as responsible to his country for a proper choice.

The wisdom of the states will be manifested by inducing those citizens of whom the late american army was composed, to accept of appointments in the militia. The high Degree of military knowledge which they possess, was acquired at too great a price and is too precious to be buried in oblivion, it ought to be cherished, and rendered permanently beneficial to the community.

The vigor and importance of the proposed plan, will entirely depend on the laws relative thereto. Unless the laws shall be equal to the object, and rigidly enforced, no energetic national militia can be established.

If wealth be admitted as a principle of exemption, the plan cannot be executed. It is the wisdom of political establishments to make the wealth of individuals subservient to the general good, and not suffer it to corrupt or attain undue indulgence.

It is conceded, that people, solicitous to be exonerated from their proportion of public duty, may exclaim against the proposed arrangement as an intolerable hardship—But it ought to be Strongly impressed, that while society has its charms, it also has its indispensible obligations—That to attempt such a degree of refinement, as to exonerate the members of the community from all personal service, is to render them incapable of the exercise and unworthy of the characters of freemen.

Every State possesses, not only the right of personal service from its members, but the right to regulate the service on principles of equality, for the general defence. All being bound, none can Complain of injustice, on being obliged to perform his equal proportion. Therefore it ought to be a permanent rule, that those who in youth, decline or refuse to subject themselves to the course of military education, established by the laws, should be considered as unworthy of public trust, or public honors, and be excluded therefrom accordingly.

If the majesty of the laws should be preserved inviolate in this respect, the operations of the proposed plan would foster a glorious public Spirit, infuse the principles of energy and Stability into the body politic, and give an high degree of political splendor to the national character.

THE END

Reports and Communications from Executive Departments, 1789–1814, Records of the Secretary, SR, DNA, letter signed by Knox.

Militia Bill [HR-102]

Calendar

Date	House	Senate
1790		
Dec. 9	Letter received from secretary of war, enclosing statement of information on expedition against Indians northwest of the Ohio, instructions to the governor of the northwest territory and the commanding officer, and an estimate of expenses of the expedition.[1]	
Dec. 10	Secretary's statement read on a motion by Laurance; on a motion by Sherman,[2] committee appointed to prepare a bill (Boudinot, P. Muhlenberg, Gilman, Floyd, Grout, Wadsworth, Smith [Md.], Bloodworth, Giles, Smith [S.C.], and Mathews).[3]	
Dec. 14	Boudinot presented *a bill more effectually to provide for*	

---

[1] The letter and statement are printed with the Military Establishment Act [HR-126A].

[2] *GUS, PaP, GA*, Dec. 11.

[3] The *PaP* and *GA*, Dec. 13, state that Jackson was originally appointed to this committee and Mathews replaced him on December 11.

Date	House	Senate
1790		
	the national defence, by es- *tablishing a uniform militia* *throughout the United States,* which was read twice.	
Dec. 16	Sections 1–2 debated and *amended* in COWH.[4]	
Dec. 17	*Address and memorial of the* *Quakers of Pennsylvania,* *New Jersey, Delaware, and* *the eastern parts of Mary-* *land* presented by F. A. Muhlenberg;[5] on a motion by Madison, sections 2–3 debated and *amended* in COWH.[6]	
Dec. 20	Sections 4–8 debated and *amended* in COWH.[7]	
Dec. 21	Sections 9–17 debated and *amended* in COWH; amendments reported to House.[8]	
Dec. 22	COWH amendments de- bated in House; further *amendments* debated.	
Dec. 23	Address of Quakers of New York and western New England, "represent- ing their objections to certain provisions" of the Militia Bill, presented by Laurance; on a motion by Sherman,[9] *amendments* debated.	

---

[4] *GA*, Dec. 17.
[5] *FG*, Dec. 17.
[6] *GA*, Dec. 18.
[7] *GA*, Dec. 21.
[8] *GA*, Dec. 23.
[9] *FG*, Dec. 23.

Date	House	Senate
1790		
Dec. 24	Memorial of Quakers of the western shore of Maryland and the adjacent parts of Pennsylvania and Virginia, "stating their objections to certain provisions" of the Militia Bill, presented by Smith (Md.);[10] *amendments* debated; amended bill recommitted to Wadsworth, Giles, and Tucker.	
Dec. 28	Motion by Tucker to instruct committee to add a clause, "that the militia of the several states of the union, consisting of such persons as are or may be enrolled by them respectively, shall be organized, armed and disciplined in manner following."[11]	
Dec. 29	Tucker motion disagreed to by a recorded vote of 43–8.	

[10] *FG,* Dec. 24.
[11] *FG,* Dec. 28. The *HJ* for this date records no action on this subject.

Militia Bill [HR-102]
December 14, 1790

A BILL *more effectually to provide for the national Defence, by establishing a uniform Militia throughout the United States*

Sec. 1. BE *it enacted by the* SENATE *and* HOUSE *of* REPRESENTATIVES *of the United States of America in Congress assembled,* That the militia of the United

States shall consist of each and every free, able-bodied male citizen of the respective States, resident therein, who are or shall be of the age of eighteen years, and under the age of fifty[1] years (except as is hereinafter excepted)[2] who shall severally and respectively be enrolled by the captain or commanding officer of the company within whose bounds such citizen shall reside, and that within   months after passing of this act: And it shall at all times hereafter be the duty of every such captain or commanding officer of a company, to enrol every such citizen as aforesaid, and also those who shall from time to time arrive at the age of eighteen years, or being of the age of eighteen years and under the age of fifty years (except as before excepted) shall come to reside within his bounds; and shall without delay notify such citizen of the said enrolment by a proper non-commissioned officer of the company, by whom such notice may be proved—That every citizen so enrolled and notified, shall within   month   thereafter, provide himself[3] with a good musket or firelock of a bore not smaller than seventeen[4] balls to the pound, a sufficient bayonet and belt,[5] a pouch with a box therein to contain not less than twenty-four cartridges suited to the bore of his musket or firelock, each cartridge to contain a proper quantity of powder and ball, two spare flints, and a knapsack; and shall appear so armed, accoutred and pro-

---

[1] On December 16, the COWH agreed to a motion by Gilman to strike out "fifty" and insert "forty-five" at this point and probably also later in the section. The House agreed to this amendment on December 22. (FG, Dec. 17, 18; PaP, Dec. 24)

[2] On December 22, Bloodworth moved to strike out "(except as herein after excepted)" and insert "except such as shall be exempted by the legislatures of the particular states." (PaP, Dec. 27) The GUS, Dec. 29, states that this proposal amended the second section and was for the purpose of "exempting all persons exempted by state law." The debates in both papers indicate the PaP's version to be the correct one. Sherman proposed substituting "and who are not exempted from militia duty by the respective states" for Bloodworth's insertion. Madison proposed adding "judges of federal courts" to the list of people exempted and agreed to Sherman's request that he include "all the proper officers of the general government, executive, legislative, and judicial." Bloodworth agreed to these alterations. (GA, Dec. 24; PaP, Dec. 27; GUS, Dec. 28, 29) A motion by Madison, to add "and persons conscientiously scrupulous of bearing arms" to the end of Bloodworth's amendment was withdrawn the next day after debate. (GUS, Dec. 29) On the same day, Hiester's motion that the amendment include "the laws of the states, that now are, or may hereafter be enacted" was disagreed to, 26–25. (DADA, Jan. 4) On December 23, Bloodworth's motion as amended on December 22 was divided on a motion by Stone. That part striking out "(except as hereinafter excepted)" was disagreed to, 34–17, and so the entire motion was lost. (GUS, Dec. 29)

[3] On December 16, the COWH disagreed to a motion by Fitzsimons to substitute "shall be provided" for "provide himself." (PaP, Dec. 18)

[4] On December 16, the COWH agreed to a motion by Boudinot to strike "seventeen" and leave a blank at this point. The House agreed to this amendment on December 22. (PaP, Dec. 17, 24)

[5] On December 16, the COWH agreed to a motion by Giles to move the words "two spare flints, and a knapsack," which appear later in the section, to this point. The House agreed to this amendment on December 22. (PaP, Dec. 17, 24)

vided, when called out to exercise or into service as is herein after directed, except that when called out on company days to exercise only, he may appear with a knapsack—That the commissioned officers shall severally be armed with a sword or hanger, and espontoon.[6]

Sec. 2. *And be it further enacted,* That the Vice-President of the United States, the members of Congress, with their several officers and servants attending either House;[7] the officers, judicial and executive, of the general government; the Lieutenant-Governor and executive council of the respective States; the members of the legislatures of the respective States, with their officers and servants attending their several houses; all judicial and executive officers of each State;[8] all persons conscientiously scrupulous of bearing arms;[9] all ministers of religion, actually having the charge of a church or

---

[6] On December 23, the House agreed to a motion by Moore to add "or with a good rifle, a shot bag &c." at some point in the first section. (*GUS*, Dec. 29)

On December 16, in the COWH, Parker moved to add the following proviso to this section:

> Provided that if any one called upon to perform the duties of a militia man, shall prove to the satisfaction of his commanding officer, that he is unable to provide the arms and accoutrements by law required, he shall be furnished with them by said officer, at the expence of the United States.

Parker agreed to a request by Huntington to allow the expense to be borne by the states. Vining moved to add the following to the proviso:

> which said arms and accoutrements shall be solely appropriated to their use while on militia duty and on exercise days, and shall be liable to be returned to the commanding officer at any time when he shall demand the same.

Consideration of Vining's resolution was waived and the COWH disagreed to the motion by Parker. (*GA*, Dec. 17; *PaP*, Dec. 18) Also on December 16, Hiester moved to add the following proviso:

> That every citizen so enrolled, and providing himself with the arms and accoutrements required as aforesaid, shall hold the same exempt from all executions, or suits for debt or for the payment of taxes.

This was agreed to by the COWH by a vote of 21−17. On December 22, by a vote of 25−16, the House agreed to a motion by Boudinot to add a sentence "which provided against civil processes being served on any person of the militia, when called out on days of rendezvous." The House then agreed to Hiester's proviso as amended. (*PaP*, Dec. 18, 24, 27)

[7] On December 16, Madison moved to strike out "members of Congress" through "either House" and insert "members of the House of Representatives, whilst travelling to, attending at, or returning from the session of Congress, and the members of the Senate in similar circumstances, or in case of a separate session of the Senate." After debate, Madison withdrew this motion and substituted one to strike out "the members of Congress." The COWH disagreed to the substitute by a vote of 24−18. (*PaP*, Dec. 18, 20) The *GA*, Dec. 17, reported that Madison's original motion included the vice president.

[8] On December 16, Ames moved to exempt generally "all legislative and executive officers of each state." (*PaP*, Dec. 20)

[9] On December 23, the House agreed to a motion by Williamson to strike out the clauses relating to state officers and persons religiously scrupulous of bearing arms. (*DADA*, Jan. 4) Madison, seconded by Boudinot, then moved to exempt:

> all persons conscientiously scrupulous of bearing arms, who should make a

congregation; all principals, professors, and other teachers of, together with the students in, universities, colleges and academies; every school-master actually having the charge of a school; all post-officers and stage-drivers, who are employed in the care and conveyance of the mail of the post-office of the United States; one miller to every grist-mill; all commissioned officers who heretofore served in the continental army, and all mariners actually engaged in the sea service of any citizen or merchant within the United States, together with such other persons who may be excepted by any law hereafter to be passed by the legislature of any particular State, [10] shall be, and are hereby excepted out of this act, and exempted from militia duty, notwithstanding their being above the age of eighteen, and under the age of fifty years. [11]

Sec. 3. *And be it further enacted,* That the Governor, or commander in chief of the militia of the respective States for the time being, [12] shall within one

---

declaration thereof before a magistrate, or who should produce a certificate of their belonging to a religious society, who profess such tenets: that for this exemption, they should pay an equivalent in money, to be collected as hereafter provided, and appropriated to the purposes, to which the revenue, arising from the post office, was appropriated.

On December 24, the House disagreed to a substitute motion by Clymer,
That any person in known membership with a religious community, professing to be conscientiously scrupulous of bearing arms, or any person making a declaration, that he is so conscientiously scrupulous, shall be exempted from being enrolled in the militia,
by a vote of 29–20, and to Madison's motion, 39–10. (*GUS,* Dec. 29, Jan. 1; *DADA,* Jan. 4, 7)

[10] On December 17, Laurance moved to strike out from "together with" through "particular state." Fitzsimons moved to amend this "to exempt the members of the legislatures of the states, with the officers attached thereto, and such of the executive and judicial officers of each state, as may be excepted by the laws thereof." After debate, Fitzsimons withdrew his motion and the COWH agreed to that of Laurance. (*PaP,* Dec. 21)

[11] On December 17, Jackson moved to insert a clause requiring "that all persons exempted pay the sum of   dollars" and a proviso that "those who were conscientiously scrupulous of bearing arms pay an equivalent of   dollars per annum." After debate, Jackson withdrew his motion. He renewed the first part of it at the conclusion of debate on section 2 and again withdrew it. (*GA,* Dec. 18; *PaP,* Dec. 21) Tucker's motion to exempt "physicians, practicing surgeons and apothecaries" was not seconded. The COWH agreed to a motion by Seney to exempt "persons authorized and received to preach and teach the gospel, by the societies of which they are respectively members." Jackson moved to exempt "public printers and pilots." After debate and division of the question, pilots were exempted but not printers. Boudinot moved to exempt "all such as now do, or may hereafter bear a commission in the militia." This motion was agreed to. Giles moved to exempt inspectors of tobacco and agreed to Vining's request to add inspectors of flour. The COWH then agreed to a motion to exempt all ferrymen on post roads. (*GA,* Dec. 18; *PaP,* Dec. 21; *GUS,* Dec. 22)

[12] On December 17, the COWH agreed to a motion by Fitzsimons to strike out "Governor" through "time being" and insert "President of the United States." (*GA,* Dec. 18)

year from the passing of this act, by general orders, arrange the whole militia under his command into divisions as nearly equal as conveniently may be, and those divisions into brigades, regiments, battalions and companies—That each division, brigade and regiment in the State, shall be numbered at the formation thereof, and a record made of such numbers in the adjutant-general's office in the State; and when in the field or in service in the State, each division, brigade and regiment shall respectively take rank according to their numbers, reckoning the first or lowest number highest in rank—That each brigade, if practicable, shall consist of at least four regiments; each regiment of at least two battalions; each battalion of five companies if practicable; and each company of sixty-four men—That the said militia shall be officered by the respective States as follows: To each division, one major-general, and two aids de-camp with the rank of majors;[13] to each brigade, one brigadier-general, with one brigade inspector, to serve also as brigade major, with the rank of major; to each regiment one lieutenant-colonel commandant, and to each battalion one major; to each company, one captain, one lieutenant, one ensign, four serjeants, four corporals, one drummer, and one fifer or bugle horn; that to each regiment there shall be a regimental staff, to consist of one adjutant, and one quarter-master, to rank as lieutenants, one paymaster, one surgeon and one surgeon's mate, one serjeant-major, one drum-major and one fife-major.

Sec. 4. *And be it further enacted,* That in order to promote military knowledge among the citizens of the United States in their youth, and for the purpose of furnishing the means of immediate defence in case of invasion or insurrection, the citizens of the United States forming the militia thereof as aforesaid, and who shall be of the age of eighteen years, and under the age of twenty-five years, shall be separately enrolled by the captain or other commanding officer of the company, and officered by the State, and formed into distinct companies by themselves in like manner as is herein before directed,[14] which companies shall form the light infantry or riflemen of each battalion or regiment—That to each brigade there shall be at least one company of artillery, and one troop of horse. The officers of each company of artillery shall consist of one captain, two lieutenants, four serjeants, four corporals, six gunners, six bombardiers, one drummer and one fifer. The

---

[13] On December 17, the COWH agreed to a motion by Wadsworth to strike out "with the rank of Majors" and insert "to be taken from the line." (*GA,* Dec. 18)

[14] On December 20, Fitzsimons moved to strike out "That in order to promote" through "as is herein before directed" and insert the following:

> That from the militia, enrolled as herein directed, there shall be formed distinct companies, which shall form the light infantry and riflemen of each battalion or regiment.

This motion was agreed to by a vote of 25–22. (*PaP,* Dec. 24, 25)

officers to be armed with a sword or hanger, a fusee, bayonet and belt, with a cartridge box to contain twelve cartridges; and each private or matross shall furnish himself at his own expence with all the equipments of a private in the infantry, until proper ordnance and field artillery is provided. The officers of each troop of horse shall consist of one captain, two lieutenants, one cornet, four serjeants, four corporals, one saddler, one farrier and one trumpeter. The commissioned officers to furnish themselves, at their own expence, with good horses, of at least fourteen[15] hands high, and to be armed with a sword and pair of pistols, the holsters of which to be covered with bear skin caps. Each dragoon to furnish himself, at his own expence, with a serviceable horse, at least fourteen hands high, a good saddle, bridle, housing, holsters, and a breast plate and crupper, a pair of boots and spurs, a pair of pistols, a sabre, and a cartouch box to contain twelve cartridges for pistols. That each company of artillery and troop of horse shall be formed of volunteers from the brigade, at the discretion of the commander in chief of the state, not exceeding one company of each to a regiment, nor more in number than one eleventh part of the infantry, and shall be uniformly cloathed in regimentals to be furnished at their own expence, the colour and fashion of which to be determined by the brigadier commanding the brigade to which they belong.[16]

Sec. 5. *And be it further enacted,* That each battalion and regiment shall be provided with state and regimental colours, at the expence of the field officers, and each company with a drum and fife at the expence of the commissioned officers of the company, until they can be reimbursed by the fines and forfeitures herein after mentioned.

Sec. 6. *And be it further enacted,* That each company of the militia of the United States, who shall form the light infantry or rifle companies, the artillery and troops of horse as aforesaid, shall rendezvous four times in every year, in companies, for the purpose of training, disciplining and improving in martial exercises; and twice in every year in regiment or battalion,[17] as the commanding officer of the brigade shall direct: And all other companies of said militia shall rendezvous twice in every year, in companies, and twice in

---

[15] On December 20, the COWH agreed to a motion to insert "and a half" at this point and later in the section. (*GA,* Dec. 21)

[16] On December 20, the COWH disagreed to a motion by Smith (S.C.), "that companies in the respective States, incorporated by the Legislatures, should not be disbanded or included in the militia, but retain their former station." Seney proposed an amendment to strike out "incorporated by the Legislatures." (*GUS,* Dec. 25)

[17] On December 20, a motion by Hartley, to oblige both companies and battalions to turn out once a year, was disagreed to by the COWH. Gilman moved that companies should turn out three times a year and battalions only once. The COWH agreed to a motion by Sherman that regiments turn out once a year. (*GUS,* Dec. 25)

every year in regiment or battalion, as aforesaid. The times and places of rendezvous to be appointed by the laws of each State, or the commander in chief[18] thereof, in such manner that the field and staff officers may have an opportunity of attending the several companies exercising in detail, in order to introduce uniformity in the manoeuvres and discipline of the regiment.

Sec. 7. *And be it further enacted,* That in order to prevent any injury arising from drawing off the workmen at certain works and manufactories hereafter named, to attend the several days of rendezvous as aforesaid, it shall and may be lawful for the commander in chief of[19] each State to appoint proper officers at all furnaces for manufacturing of iron, and all works for manufacturing of glass, if any such shall be within the State, whose duty it shall be to form the workmen, manufacturers and laborers belonging thereto, into a company or companies, in manner aforesaid, or as nearly thereto as circumstances will admit, and to train, exercise and discipline them in manner directed by law, excepting as to the place, which shall always be at the works or manufactories, and excepting the meetings in regiment or battalion, in lieu of which they shall meet in companies at the said works and manufactories, in manner aforesaid. And the said workmen, manufacturers and laborers, shall be excused from all other militia duty, except in times of invasion or insurrection.

Sec. 8. *And be it further enacted,* That there shall be an adjutant-general appointed for each State, whose duty it shall be to distribute all orders from the commander in chief of the State to the several corps—to attend all public reviews, when the commander in chief of the State shall review the militia, or any part thereof—to obey all orders from him relative to carrying into execution and perfecting the system of military discipline established by this act—to furnish blank forms of different returns that may be required, and to explain the principles on which they should be made—to receive from the several officers of the different corps throughout the State, returns of the militia under their command, reporting the actual situation of their arms, accoutrements and ammunition, their delinquencies, and every other thing which relates to the general advancement of good order and discipline—all which the several officers of the divisions, brigades, regiments and battalions, are hereby required to make in the usual manner, so that the said adjutant-general may be duly furnished therewith: From all which returns he shall

---

[18] On December 20, the COWH agreed to Wadsworth's motion that the times of rendezvous in regiments and companies should be regulated by the officer commanding the brigade. (*GA,* Dec. 21)

[19] On December 20, the COWH agreed to a motion by Ames to strike out "commander in chief of." (*PaP,* Dec. 25)

make proper abstracts, and lay the same annually before the commander in chief of the State: And the said adjutant-general shall have the rank of a lieutenant-colonel[20] in the militia. And there shall also be appointed in each State a commissary of military stores, who shall have the rank of a major in the militia, with as many deputies as the State shall by law direct, whose duty it shall be to take the charge and keeping of all the ordnance and military stores of the State, subject to such orders and instructions, in the execution of his and their duty, as he or they shall from time to time receive from the commander in chief of the State, or other superior officer.[21]

Sec. 9. *And be it further enacted,* That all officers who shall be appointed and commissioned to any of the offices as aforesaid, shall within ten days after notice of such appointment or commission, report their acceptance of such office to the commanding officer of the regiment or brigade; on failure whereof, such neglect shall be considered as a refusal; and the said commanding officer shall within ten days thereafter report the same to the commanding officer of the division or brigade, who shall from time to time report the same, with all vacancies that may happen, to the adjutant-general, for the information of the commander in chief of the State.[22]

Sec. 10. *And be it further enacted,* That every commissioned officer who shall be convicted by a general court-martial, of having refused or neglected to perform, or of having acted contrary to any of the duties of his office, shall be punished according to the nature and degree of his offence, at the discretion of the court, either by fine or removal from his office: *Provided,* That no fine for the first offence, shall exceed   dollars; and for any subsequent offence   dollars; which fines shall be levied and collected by warrant, under the hand and seal of the commanding officer of the regiment or battalion, directed to any serjeant of the regiment or battalion to which the offender may belong, in like manner as the fines hereafter mentioned to be recovered of non-commissioned officers and privates, for neglect or refusal of duty, are directed to be levied and collected. That the commanding officer of divisions and brigades may order courts-martial for the trial of offences within his division or brigade, the members of which shall be warned for that duty by the brigade-major, who shall keep a roster for that purpose. That the proceedings and sentence of every court marshal, by which any officer shall be removed from office, shall be in writing, signed by the president thereof; and

---

[20] On December 20, the COWH agreed to a motion by Wadsworth to change "lieutenant-colonel" to "brigadier." (*GA,* Dec. 21)

[21] On December 20, Parker's motion to strike out the last sentence of this section was agreed to. (*GA,* Dec. 21)

[22] On December 24, the House agreed to a motion by Livermore to strike out this section. (*GUS,* Jan. 1)

shall by the president be delivered to the commanding officer of the brigade, to be by him transmitted to the commander in chief of the State, who shall approve or disapprove of the same in orders: And that all other proceedings and sentences of brigade courts-martial, shall be delivered by the president thereof to the commanding officer of the brigade, who shall approve or disapprove of the same in orders. That all courts-martial for the trial of general officers, shall be ordered by the commander in chief of the State, and composed of general and field officers, who shall be warned to that duty by the adjutant-general of the State, from a roster to be by him kept for that purpose. That the proceedings and sentences of such courts shall be transmitted by the presidents thereof to the commander in chief, who shall approve or disapprove of the same in orders: *Provided,* That no sentence of a court-martial on a general officer, shall extend further than a removal from office. That all general courts-martial shall consist of at least nine commissioned officers, who shall appoint their judge-advocate, who is hereby authorized and required to administer an oath to each member of the court, which they are hereby enjoined severally to take before they proceed on business, to the following effect: "You   do swear that you will well and truly try and determine according to evidence, the matter depending between the state of   and the prisoner or prisoners now to be tried—That you will not divulge the sentence of the court, until the same shall be approved or disapproved pursuant to law; neither will you, upon any account at any time whatsoever, disclose or discover the vote or opinion of any particular member of the court-martial, unless required by a due course of law." And the president of the said court-martial is hereby authorized and required thereupon to administer an oath to the judge advocate, which he is hereby enjoined to take before he proceeds farther on business, to the following effect: "You   do swear that you will not on any account, at any time whatsoever, disclose or discover the vote or opinion of any particular member of the court-martial, unless required in a due course of law; and that you will not divulge the sentence of this court, until the same shall be approved or disapproved according to law; and that you will well and truly do the duty of a judge-advocate in this court, impartially and uprightly, according to the best of your abilities."[23]

Sec. 11. *And be it further enacted,* That every non-commissioned officer or private, not necessarily absent from the county or town, who shall neglect to appear, when warned pursuant to law, at a company meeting or rendezvous, not having a sufficient excuse, shall forfeit and pay the sum of fifty cents; and for appearing at such meeting or rendezvous without his arms, ammunition

---

[23] On December 24, the House disagreed to a motion by Livermore to strike out this section. (*GUS,* Jan. 1)

or accoutrements, as directed by this act, shall pay the sum of twenty-five cents; and for the like offences at a regimental or battalion meeting or rendezvous, for the first offence aforesaid he shall forfeit and pay the sum of one hundred cents, and for the last offence the sum of fifty cents: And in case of any disobedience of orders or neglect of duty while under arms or in actual service, he shall forfeit and pay such sum as shall be directed by the major voice of the officers of the company, battalion or regiment, provided the same shall not in any case amount to more than   and that all fines arising from offences in company only shall be adjudged of and imposed by the commissioned officers of the company, or the major part of them, and all fines to arise from offences in battalion or regiment with respect to the noncommissioned officers and privates, shall be adjudged and imposed by the field officers of the battalion or regiment, all which fines shall be levied with costs, not exceeding   cents, by warrant from the colonel or commanding officer of the regiment, battalion or company, as the case may be, directed to one or more serjeants, by distress and sale of the offender's goods and chattels: And in case any defaulter shall be under age, and live with his father or mother, or shall be an apprentice or hired servant, the father or mother, master or mistress, as the case may be, shall be liable to pay the said fines with costs, and in default of payment when demanded, the said serjeant or serjeants, shall levy the same upon the goods and chattels of such father or mother, master or mistress—such fines when recovered to be paid over by the serjeant or serjeants to the officer granting such warrant.[24]

Sec. 12. *And be it further enacted,* That all fines herein before mentioned, shall be paid by the officer issuing said warrant to and for the purpose, in the first instance of providing colours and music to and for the use of the companies of light infantry, rifle men, artillery and troops of horse; and the surplus that may remain, to be applied to the like use for the residue of the militia aforesaid; and when the said fines shall arise to a larger sum than is necessary for the said uses, the remainder shall be applied to the purchasing of arms and accoutrements for the light infantry and rifle companies.

Sec. 13. *And be it further enacted,* That all commissioned officers shall take rank according to the date of their commissions; and when two of the same grade, bear an equal date, then their rank shall be determined by lots, to be drawn by them before the commanding officer of the brigade, regiment, battalion, company or detachment.

---

[24] On December 21, Bloodworth's motion to strike out this section was not seconded. (*PaP,* Dec. 25) On December 24, the House disagreed to a similar motion by Livermore. (*GUS,* Jan. 1)

Sec. 14. *And be it further enacted,* That the commander in chief of the State, shall on the requisition of the President of the United States, authorized thereto by the express acts of Congress, order out any proportion of the militia of the State so required as aforesaid, to march to any part of the United States for the protection or defence of the same, provided that they be not compelled to continue on duty out of the State without their consent, for a longer time than   months at any one time. That while in actual service, in consequence of being so called out, they shall receive the same pay and rations, and be subject to the same rules and regulations as the troops of the United States of America.[25]

Sect. 15. *And be it further enacted,* That if any person belonging to the militia of any state, and called out into service as aforesaid, be wounded or disabled while in actual service in opposing or suppressing any invasion or insurrection, or in fighting against any of the enemies of the United States, he shall be taken care of and provided for at the public expence, without having regard to the rank such person may hold.

Sec. 16. *And be it further enacted,* That every person of the age of eighteen years and under fifty years, who are exempted from personal service in the militia as aforesaid, by the second section of this act, (except all ministers of religion actually having the charge of a church or congregation; all principals, professors and other teachers of, together with the students in, universities, colleges and academies; all school-masters actually having the charge of a school, and all mariners employed in the sea service of any citizen or merchant within the United States as aforesaid) shall pay an annual tax of two dollars into the public treasury of the United States, to be applied towards the support of the civil government thereof, and to be collected in the following manner: The commissioner of the treasury in each state, shall appoint a responsible person in every county or township in the state, as collector of the said tax, to whom the commanding officer of each battalion shall cause returns to be made of the names of all the exempts by virtue of the said second section of this act, within the bounds of his battalion, except as before excepted. That thereupon each of the said exempts being notified thereof by the said collector, shall on the month of May in every year, pay to the said collector the said two dollars; and in case of failure therein, the collector shall, within two weeks thereafter, return the names of the defaulters to the commanding officer of the battalion, who shall thereupon cause them to be enrolled, and they shall thereafter be liable to do militia duty in like manner as other citizens not exempted by this act, until the full arrears of the said tax

---

[25] On December 21, the House agreed to a motion to strike out this section. (*GA,* Dec. 23)

shall be paid into the treasury of the United States. And the said collector shall, within one month after the receipt of the said tax, pay the same to the said commissioner, who shall account therefore with the treasury of the United States in like manner and under the same penalties and forfeitures as he accounts for other public monies by him received; for all which services the said collector shall be entitled to retain the compensation of two and an half per centum on all the monies collected by him as aforesaid. And in case the said collector should neglect or refuse to pay over the said monies received by him as aforesaid, or any part thereof, to the said commissioner, within the time limited as aforesaid, the said collector shall forfeit and pay to the use of the United States, a sum of money equal to double the amount of the said taxes, or so much of them as shall remain unpaid; to be recovered by the said collector in his own name, with costs of suit, by action of debt or otherwise, in any court wherein the same shall be cognizable. And the secretary of the treasury shall cause an annual return of all these monies received on the said tax, to be laid before Congress, at their first session in every year.[26]

Sec. 17. *And be it further enacted,* That each state shall be formed into a district or districts in such manner as the legislature thereof shall by law direct. And that there shall be appointed by the President of the United States,[27] an inspector for each district, who shall be a citizen of the state to which such district belongs; provided their number shall not exceed—one for New-Hampshire, two for Massachusetts, one for Rhode-Island, one for Connecticut, one for New-York, one for New-Jersey, two for Pennsylvania, one for Delaware, one[28] for Maryland, three for Virginia, two for North-Carolina, one for South-Carolina, and one for Georgia. And the duty of such inspector shall be to attend the regimental or battalion meetings of the militia on their several parades, during the time of their being under arms pursuant to this act, at least once in every year, to inspect their arms, ammunition and accoutrements; superintend their exercise and manoeuvres, and introduce a system of military discipline throughout the district, agreeably to law and such orders as he shall from time to time receive from the commander in chief of the state; to furnish the forms of the returns that may be required, and explain the principles on which they shall be made; to make returns to the President of the United States, at least once in every year, of the militia of the

---

[26] On December 21, by a vote of 28–20, the COWH agreed to a motion by Burke, seconded by Sherman, to strike out this section. (*PaP,* Dec. 25) The *GA,* Dec. 23, reported that the motion was Sherman's.

[27] On December 21, the COWH agreed to a motion by Smith (S.C.?) to strike out "by the President of the United States." (*GA,* Dec. 23)

[28] On December 21, the COWH agreed to Seney's motion to strike out "one" and insert "two, one to reside on the eastern, the other on the western shore." (*GA,* Dec. 23)

state, reporting therein the actual situation of the arms, accoutrements and ammunition of the several corps, and every other thing which in his judgment may relate to their government and the general advancement of good order and military discipline; a duplicate of such return and report he shall also transmit to the commander in chief of the state. And the said inspectors shall have the rank of lieutenant colonel,[29] and shall respectively receive from the treasury of the United States, as a full compensation for all their services, the sum of   [30] dollars per annum.[31]

Printed by Francis Childs *and* John Swaine

Militia Bill [HR-81] as printed in July, 1790, Broadside Collection, RBkRm, DLC. This bill was printed in the *NYDA,* July 6, 7, with a heading indicating that the bill would be held over for consideration in the next session and in the meantime it was being printed for public comment. All the available evidence points to this as the same bill which was reintroduced in the third session. We are printing the document at this point, rather than with the calendar of the second session legislation, because of the many amendments to the bill offered during the third session debate.

---

[29] On December 21, Stone made and withdrew a motion to strike out the phrase giving inspectors the rank of lieutenant colonel. Bloodworth's motion to strike out "lieutenant colonel" and insert "brigadier" was agreed to by the COWH. (*GA,* Dec. 23)

[30] On December 21, the COWH agreed to a motion by Laurance to specify different salaries for the inspectors of the different states, and it left blanks to be filled by the House. (*GA,* Dec. 23)

[31] On December 21, Benson made and withdrew a motion to add a clause "for granting to the President of the United States, the power of calling out the militia into the service of the United States, &c. to repel invasions or suppress insurrection." (*GA,* Dec. 23) On December 24, Smith (S.C.) moved to add the following clause to the bill:

Whereas certain independent corps of artillery, infantry and dragoons, now exist in the several states—it is hereby enacted, that nothing in this act shall be construed to the disbanding or incorporating said companies in the militia; they at the same time being liable to the performance of the military duties herein required.

This motion was referred with the bill to a select committee. (*GUS,* Jan. 1)

Address and Memorial of Quakers of Pennsylvania, New Jersey, Delaware, and the Eastern Parts of Maryland
December 17, 1790

Philadelphia 18th 12th Mo. 1790

Yesterday a deputation of the religious society called Quakers, attended the house of Representatives of the United States with the following address and memorial asserting the rights of conscience and the reasons of their restraint from complying with military requisitions.

TO THE PRESIDENT, SENATE, AND HOUSE OF REPRESENTATIVES
OF THE UNITED STATES, IN CONGRESS ASSEMBLED

THE ADDRESS AND MEMORIAL OF THE PEOPLE CALLED QUAKERS, CON-VENED AT THEIR YEARLY-MEETING FOR PENNSYLVANIA, NEW-JERSEY, DELAWARE, AND THE EASTERN PARTS OF MARYLAND AND VIRGINIA, HELD IN PHILADELPHIA, BY ADJOURNMENTS, FROM THE 27th DAY OF THE 9th Mo. TO THE 2d OF THE 10th Mo. 1790, INCLUSIVE.

THROUGH the continued favour of Divine Providence, being once more permitted to assemble for the purpose of preserving circumspection of like, and decent order throughout our religious society, and as far as infinite wisdom may be pleased to qualify us to promote an increase of gospel right-eousness and peace in the earth. In the course of our weighty deliberations we have been informed, that a bill is published by direction of the house of representatives, that the public sentiment may be obtained on the subject, entituled, "A bill more effectually to provide for the national defence, by establishing an uniform militia throughout the United States;" in which, although we perceive that some parts thereof appear intended for the relief of such who are conscientiously scrupulous of taking any part in war, yet we apprehend it our duty to remark, that if enacted into a law, will materially affect us, and our fellow members in general, in the free exercise of con-science, as in section the sixteenth, where it enacts, that every person of the age of eighteen years, and under fifty years, who are exempted from personal service in the militia, by the second section of the said act (except all minis-ters of religion actually having charge of a church or congregation, all prin-cipals, professors, and other teachers of, together with the students in, uni-versities, colleges, and academies, all schoolmasters actually having the charge of a school, and all mariners employed in the sea service of any citizen or merchant within the United States as aforesaid) shall pay an annual tax of two dollars into the public treasury of the United States, to be applied towards the support of the civil government thereof, &c.

Although we cannot but gratefully acknowledge our obligation to the divine author and source of every mercy and blessing, that he hath so illuminated the understandings of men, and disposed the minds of the rulers of this land, as to allow that degree of freedom in matters of conscience which is already enjoyed, yet duty to Almighty God, revealed in the consciences of men, and confirmed by the Scriptures of the Old and New Testament, is an invariable rule which should govern their judgments and actions, he being the only Lord and sovereign of conscience, as by him all men are finally to be judged.

By conscience we mean, that apprehension and persuasion a man has of his duty to God, and the liberty of conscience we plead for, is a free and open profession, and unmolested exercise of that duty; "Such a conscience as keeps within the bounds of morality in all the affairs of human life, and requires us to live soberly, righteously, and godly in the world," on which depend the peace, safety, and happiness of religious and civil society; and it must be allowed on serious reflection, that every deviation from such religious duty, essentially disqualifies for that adoration and worship, which is incumbent on all men to perform, to the Supreme Being from whose bounty all our blessings are derived, and every restraint imposed or attempted by human laws on the free exercise thereof, is not only an infringement on the just rights of men, but also an invasion of the prerogative of Almighty God.

Under these considerations we apprehend, that we may reasonably solicit an exemption from being subjected to sufferings on account of our conscientious scruples; but at the same time, we may assure you that many of us are more solicitous to promote the prevalence of the dominion and government of the Prince of Peace, than to escape the sufferings we may undergo by the operation of such a law, firmly believing that all revenge, animosity, strife, and contention are utterly forbidden by Christ our Lord, as appears by his own declaration, Mat. v. 38. viz. "Ye have heard that it hath been said, An eye for an eye and a tooth for a tooth; but I say unto you that ye resist not evil," &c. And Mat. v. 43, 44, 45. "Ye have heard that it hath been said, Thou shalt love thy neighbour and hate thine enemy; but I say unto you love your enemies, bless them that curse you, do good to them that hate you, and pray for them which despitefully use you, and persecute you, that ye may be the children of your father which is in heaven, for he maketh his sun to rise on the evil and on the good, and sendeth rain on the just, and on the unjust."

Convinced of the necessity of a strict adherence to these, and numerous other divine precepts to the same effect, as well as to the peaceful spirit of the gospel; our religious society have not only uniformly declined joining personally in war, but have also considered themselves conscientiously bound to refuse the payment of any sum required in lieu of such personal service, or in consideration of an exemption from military employment, however laudable the purposes are, to which the money is intended to be applied, as it manifestly infringes on the rights of conscience.

With fervent desires that you may be favoured to discern the true interests of the people, and be qualified to judge with a righteous precision, in what relates to the important concerns of conscience, that the advancement of the glorious gospel day, prophetically declared, may not be retarded, when mankind shall no longer view each other with an indignant eye of malevolence, but cordially embrace as brethren, and nation shall not lift up sword against nation neither learn war any more.

We are, respectfully,

Your sincere friends.

Signed in and on behalf of the said

Yearly-meeting, by

Nicholas Waln,

Clerk to the meeting this year

Broadside Collection, RBkRm, DLC.

Militia Bill [HR-112]

Calendar

Date	House	Senate
1791		
Jan. 4	Wadsworth, for the committee to which the Militia Bill [HR-102] was recommitted, presented "an amendatory bill more effectually to provide for the national defence, by establishing a uniform militia throughout the United States," which was read.	
Jan. 5	Read and committed to COWH; 100 copies ordered printed. [1]	
Jan. 27	Petition of the Quakers of New England, "stating their objections to certain provisions" of the Militia Bill, presented by Bourn[2] and read.	

[1] *FG*, Jan. 5.
[2] *FG*, Jan. 27.